BODY CRITICISM

The MIT Press   Cambridge, Massachusetts   London, England

BODY CRITICISM

Imaging the Unseen in Enlightenment Art and Medicine

Barbara Maria Stafford

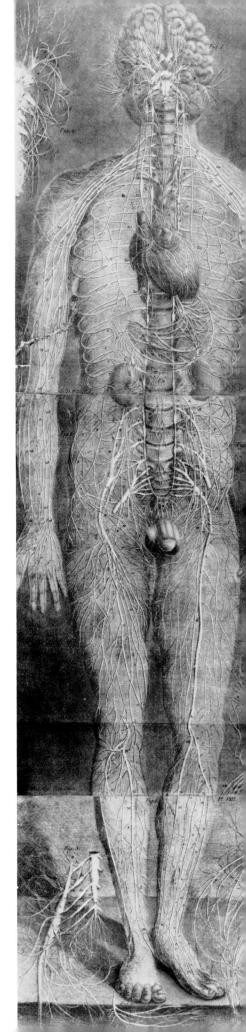

Fifth printing, 1997

First MIT Press paperback edition, 1993

© 1991 Massachusetts Institute of Technology

This book was set in Janson and Univers 67 Condensed by DEKR Corporation and printed and bound in the United States of America.

Library of Congress Cataloging-in-Publication Data

Stafford, Barbara Maria, 1941–
    Body criticism : imaging the unseen in Enlightenment art and
medicine / Barbara Maria Stafford.
        p.   cm.
    Includes bibliographical references (p.   ) and index.
    ISBN 0-262-19304-3 (HB), 0-262-69165-5 (PB)
    1. Body image—History—18th century. 2. Anatomy, Artistic—
History—18th century. 3. Medicine and art—History—18th century.
    4. Enlightenment. I. Title.
BF697.5.B63S73   1992
    306.4′2—dc20   90-21974
                                                                         CIP

For my parents: Ingeborg Anna and Col. Kelton Seymour Davis, U.S. Army, ret.

CONTENTS

List of Illustrations   *viii*

PREFACE   *xvii*

INTRODUCTION:

The Visualization of Knowledge

Somatic Metaphors   *1*

Antinomies   *24*

Hunting for Method   *34*

Surface or Depth   *38*

Picture and Text   *40*

1   DISSECTING

Searching Operations   *47*

*Physiognomics,
or Corporeal Connoisseurship*   *84*

The Calculation of Incongruity   *103*

*Pathognomics,
or the Pursuit of Looks*   *120*

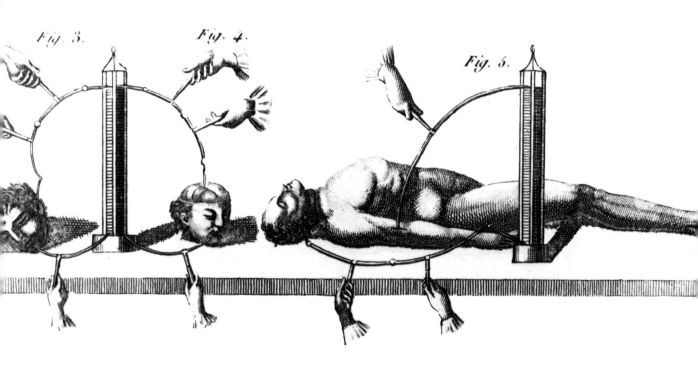

2 ABSTRACTING

Systems of Epitomization	131
Wounds of Experience	158
Distracting Styles of Pain	178
Patterns of Interiority	199

3 CONCEIVING

Barbarisms, or Strangeness Incarnate	211
"Brain-Born Images"	233
Breeding for Difference	254
Grotesques, or Ars Combinatoria	266

4 MARKING

Contagious Pointillism	281
Stains of Desire	306
"Like a Shadow on the Skin"	319
Romantic Misfits	329

5 MAGNIFYING

Microscopic Seers	341
Visual Quackery	362
Dream Projections	378
Free to Be False	392

6 SENSING

A Finer Touch	401
Mental Meteorology	417
Fluid Phantoms	437
Communicable Feelings	450

CONCLUSION:

The Aesthetics of Almost	465

NOTES	480
SELECTED BIBLIOGRAPHY	534
INDEX	574

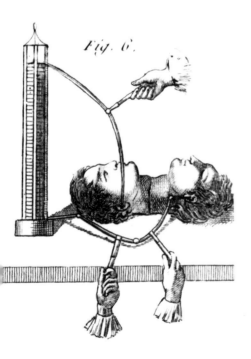

List of Illustrations

1. T. McLean, *The Body Politic or the March of the Intellect*, 1836. 13

2. Jacques-Louis David, *The Death of Socrates*, Salon of 1787. 14

3. Denis Diderot and Jean Le Rond D'Alembert, *Ecorché*, 1762–1772. 19

4. John Harris, *Mr. Wilson's Microscope and Microscopic Magnifications*, 1704. 20

5. Martin Frobène Ledermüller, *Reproduction and Multiplication of Fresh Water Polyps*, 1768. 20

6. Albrecht von Haller, *Vivisection*, 1756. 22

7. Edward Jenner, *Cowpox Pustules on the Hand of Sarah Nelmes*, 1798. 22

8. Jean-Louis Alibert, *Freckles*, 1833. 23

9. Francisco de Goya, *Correction*, 1799. 25

10. Tony Johannot, *Introduction*, 1843. 27

11. Jean-Jacques Scheuchzer, *Physicians Embalming*, 1732–1737. 30

12. Jean-Marc Nattier, *Joseph Bonnier de La Mosson*, 18th c. 31

13. Alexander Cozens, *Simple Beauty*, 1778. 32

14. Johann Caspar Lavater, *Calculating Facial Disproportion*, 1792. 32

15. La Chau and Le Blond, *Hermaphrodite*, 1780. 33

16. Martin Frobène Ledermüller, *Magnifying Glasses*, 1768. 36

17. Francisco de Goya, *The Sleep of Reason Produces Monsters*, 1799. 37

18. Anne-Claude Philippe, Comte de Caylus, *Body Fragments Resulting from Surgery (?)*, 1752–1767. 48

19. Jacques Gondouin, *Amphitheater*, 1780. 50

20. Jacques Gamelin, *Anatomy Theater*, 1779. 51

21. Laurent Natter, *Head of Jupiter Serapis*, 1754. 57

22. Laurent Natter, *Athlete*, 1754. 57

23. Giovanni Battista Piranesi, *Tempio della Tosse near Tivoli*, 1764 (?). 58

24. Giovanni Battista Piranesi, *So-Called Temple of Minerva Medica*, 1778. 59

25. William Cowper, *External Muscles and Diverse Parts of the Human Body*, 1750. 60

26. Giovanni Battista Piranesi, *Temple of Cybele (Vesta)*, 1778. 61

27. Giovanni Battista Piranesi, *Temple of the Sybil, Tivoli*, ca. 1762. 62

28. Leopoldo Marco Antonio Caldani, *Venous and Arterial Systems*, 1813. 62

29. Giovanni Battista Piranesi, *The Baths of Caracalla*, 1769. 63

30. Leopoldo Marco Antonio Caldani, *Venous and Arterial Systems*, 1813. 64

31. Giovanni Battista Piranesi, *Temple of Vespasian*, 1769. 65

32. Giovanni Battista Piranesi, *Hadrian's Villa, Tivoli, the Smaller Palace*, 1748. 65

33. Felice Fontana (?), *Anatomical Wax Figure*, 18th c. 65

34. Jacques Gautier Dagoty, *Assemblage of Legs and Feet*, 1745. 66

35. Giovanni Battista Piranesi, *The Baths of Caracalla*, 1748/1778. 67

36. William Cowper, *Skeleton Stepping into Tomb*, 1750. 68

37. Giovanni Battista Piranesi, *Campo Vaccino (Forum Romanum)*, ca. 1751. 69

38. Giovanni Battista Piranesi, *Piazza di S. Pietro*, ca. 1748. 70

39. Jacques Gamelin, *Death Holding Sheet of Drawings*, 1779. 71

40. Jacques Gamelin, *Skeleton*, 1779. 71

41. Jacques Gamelin, *Triumph of Death*, 1779. 72

42. Jacques Gamelin, *The Rape of Death*, 1779. 73

43. Jacques Gamelin, *The Entrance of Death*, 1779. 73

44. Jacques Gamelin, *Artists Studying Anatomy*, 1779. 74

45. Jacques Gamelin, *Study of Male Musculature*, 1779. 74

46. Théodore Géricault, *The Madwoman: Monomania of Gambling*, 1822–1823. 75

47. Jacques Gautier Dagoty, *Two Dissected Male Heads*, 1748. 76

48. Jacques Gautier Dagoty, *The Vessels of the Skin*, 1748. 77

49. Jacques Gautier Dagoty, *Back Muscles*, 1748. 77

50. Jean-Baptiste-Siméon Chardin, *The Ray*, 1727–1728. 79

51. Jean-Jacques Scheuchzer, *The Wrathful and Jealous Cain (Physiognomics)*, 1732–1737. 90

52. Johann Caspar Lavater, *Seeing Darkly*, 1792. 91

53. Johann Caspar Lavater, *Silhouettes of Christ*, 1792. 92

54. Johann Caspar Lavater, *Head of Christ* (after Andrea Verrocchio), 1792. 93

55. Johann Caspar Lavater, *Silhouettes of Clerics*, 1792. 94

56. Johann Caspar Lavater, *Silhouettes of Mendelssohn, Spalding, Rochow, and Nicolai*, 1792. 95

57. Johann Caspar Lavater, *Machine for Drawing Silhouettes*, 1792. 97

58. August Johann Rösel von Rosenhof, *Pinned Frog*, 1758. 98

59. Martin Frobène Ledermüller, *Dissected Frog*, 1768. 98

60. Joseph Wright of Derby, *The Corinthian Maid*, 1783–1784. 99

61. Johann Caspar Lavater, *Frederick II*, 1792. 100

62. Johann Caspar Lavater, *Voltaire* (after Pigalle), 1792. 100

63. Johann Caspar Lavater, *Lips*, 1792. 101

64. D. P. G. Humbert de Superville, *Platonic Solids*, 19th c. 105

65. D. P. G. Humbert de Superville, *Colossus of Memnon*, 1827–1832. 106

66. Johann Caspar Lavater, *The Georgian and the Bashkir*, 1792. 107

67. Félix Vicq d'Azyr, *Transverse View of the Brain*, 1786. 108

68. Félix Vicq d'Azyr, *Dissection of the Meninges*, 1786. 108

69. Jean-Fabien Gautier Dagoty, *Quartzose and Cellular "Sports,"* 1783. 109

70. David N. Levin, *Facial and Cortical 3D Models Derived from MR Images*. 109

71. Robert Fludd, *The Mystery of the Human Mind*, 1617–1621. 110

72. Pierre Camper, *From Ape to Apollo Belvedere*, 1791. 111

73. Pierre Camper, *Various Measurements of Facial Angles*, 1791.   111

74. Pierre Camper, *Youth to Age*, 1791.   113

75. Johann Caspar Lavater, *Wrinkled Countenance*, 1792.   113

76. David Hess, *Cranioscopic Examinations*, 1795.   116

77. George Cruikshank, *Bumpology*, 1826.   117

78. Johann Caspar Lavater, *Rage*, 1792.   124

79. James Parsons, *Sneering Woman*, 1745.   125

80. Johann Caspar Lavater, *Human Variety*, 1792.   127

81. R. M. Pariset, *Allegory of Painting*, 18th c.   139

82. Georges Stubbs, *Formal Studies*, 19th c.   141

83. Georges Stubbs, *Landscape Studies*, 19th c.   141

84. *Optics*, from *Encyclopaedia Britannica*, 1773.   143

85. John Harris, *John Marshall's Double Microscope*, 1704.   145

86. Thomas Corneille, *The Arts and Sciences*, 1694.   145

87. John Harris, *Arteries and Veins*, 1704.   146

88. Ephraim Chambers, *The Organization of Knowledge*, 1738.   147

89. Ephraim Chambers, *Anatomy*, 1738.   149

90. Francis Grose, *Profile Heads*, 1796.   151

91. Alexander Cozens, *The Artful*, 1778.   151

92. Pierre Camper, *Comparative Morphology*, 1792.   152

93. Johann Caspar Lavater, *Cipher of Madness*, 1803.   153

94. Johann Caspar Lavater, *Hair Growing from a Mole*, 1803.   153

95. Matthaus Greuter, *Physician Curing Fantasy*, 17th c.   154

96. James Gillray, *The Dissolution*, 1796.   155

97. William Heath, *Monster Soup*, ca. 1822   157

98. Fortunius Licetus, *Nature and Her Monsters*, 1655.   159

99. Denis Diderot and Jean Le Rond D'Alembert, *Bandages and Surgical Instruments*, 1762–1772.   160

100. George Moutard Woodward, *A Doctor in Purgatory*, 1792.   161

101. Anonymous, *Sick France Being Diagnosed*, 1789–1790.   163

102. Pierre Bayle, *Alexander ab Alexandro*, 1696.   165

103. Ephraim Chambers, *Miscellany*, 1738.   167

104. Anne-Claude-Philippe, Comte de Caylus, *A Collection of Antiquities*, 1752–1767.   169

105. Ephraim Chambers, *A Visual Summa*, 1738.   171

106. Giovanni Battista Piranesi, *Lapides Capitolini*, 1761.   173

107. Giovanni Battista Piranesi, *Roman Fragments*, 1761.   174–175

108. Laurent Natter, *Diverse Symbols*, 1754.   177

109. Laurent Natter, *Chimera*, 1754.   177

110. Anne-Claude-Philippe, Comte de Caylus, *Gryllus*, 1752–1767. 177

111. William Blake, *With Dreams upon My Bed*, 1825. 182

112. Francisco de Goya, *Until Death*, 1799. 183

113. Fortunius Licetus, *Medusa Head Found in an Egg*, 1665. 184

114. Anne-Claude-Philippe, Comte de Caylus, *Satire or "Critique": A "Bear"-Headed Roman Senator*, 1752–1767. 185

115. James Gillray, *French Generals Retiring on Account of Their Health*, 1799. 187

116. James Gillray, *The Gout*, 1799, republished 1835. 189

117. Henry William Bunbury, *Origin of the Gout*, 1785, republished 1815. 189

118. Jean-Baptiste Oudry, *Gout and the Spider*, 1755–1760. 190

119. George Cruikshank, *Indigestion*, 1825. 191

120. George Cruikshank, *The Cholic*, 1835. 191

121. Honoré Daumier, *Colic*, 1833. 192

122. Thomas Rowlandson, *The Hypochondriac*, 1788. 193

123. George Cruikshank, *The Blue Devils*, 1835. 194

124. George Cruikshank, *Hallucinations*, 1819. 194

125. Robert Burton, *Types of Melancholy*, 1632. 196

126. Francisco de Goya, *They Spruce Themselves Up*, 1799. 197

127. Honoré Daumier, *Misanthropy*, 1833. 198

128. *Spanish Marbled Paper*, ca. 1790. 200

129. *Overprinted Text on Marbled Book Wrappers*, 1786. 203

130. Nicolas-Denis Derôme, Le Jeune (style of), *"Stone" Marbled Papers*, ca. 1788. 205

131. Macé-Ruette (style of), *Fine-Combed Paper*, 1610–1643. 206

132. Bouquet (style of), *Comb Marbled Paper (Peacock Type)*, 18th c. 207

133. Anne-Claude-Philippe, Comte de Caylus, *Roman Ithyphallic Grotesque*, 18th c. 217

134. Fortunius Licetus, *Amorphous Monster (Misbirth)*, 1665. 218

135. William Dent, *The Cutter Cut Up*, 1790. 218

136. Fortunius Licetus, *Amorphous Monster (Misbirth)*, 1665. 218

137. Francis Glisson, *Rickets*, 1671. 219

138. Jean-Baptiste Boudard, *Imagination*, 1766. 221

139. Francisco de Goya, *Will No One Unbind Us?*, 1799. 224

140. Francisco de Goya, *To Rise and to Fall*, 1799. 225

141. Jean-Jacques Scheuchzer, *First Day of Creation*, 1732–1737. 227

142. Jean-Baptiste Boudard, *Obscurity*, 1766. 228

143. Jean-Jacques Scheuchzer, *Creation of the Universe*, 1732–1737. 237

144. Jean-Jacques Scheuchzer, *Second Day of Creation*, 1732–1737. 238

145. Jean-Jacques Scheuchzer, *Third Day of Creation*, 1732–1737. 238

146. Jean-Jacques Scheuchzer, *Human Generation*, 1732–1737. 239

147. William Cowper, *Fetal Development*, 1750. 241

148. Jacques Gautier Dagoty, *Human Embryo*, 1781. 241

149. August Johann Rösel von Rosenhof, *Copulating Frogs and the Laying of Eggs*, 1758. 242

150. August Johann Rösel von Rosenhof, *Larval Development*, 1758. 243

151. Jean-Jacques Scheuchzer, *Development of the Chicken Embryo*, 1732–1737. 244

152. William Harvey, *Zeus Opening the Cosmic Egg*, 1651. 245

153. Leopoldo Marco Antonio Caldani, *Gravid Uterus*, 1810. 247

154. Leopoldo Marco Antonio Caldani, *Fetus in Utero*, 1810. 247

155. G. F. Rivati, *Bacteria*, 1750. 255

156. Nicolas-François Regnault, *Monstrous Man (with "Parasite")*, 1808. 255

157. Edmé Guyot, *Anamorphoses*, 1772. 256

158. Fortunius Licetus, *Faceless and Limbless Monsters*, 1665. 257

159. Jean Riolan, *Cyclops*, 1605. 257

160. Grandville, *The Pursuit*, 1844. 258

161. Nicolas-François Regnault, *Double Child*, 1808. 260

162. Nicolas-François Regnault, *Monstrous Child with Multiple Sensory Organs*, 1808. 260

163. Nicolas-François Regnault, *Cyclops Cat*, 1808. 261

164. Nicolas-François Regnault, *Dog with Three Posteriors*, 1808. 261

165. T. M. Baynes, *The Siamese Brothers*, 19th c. 262

166. James Gillray, *Doublûres of Characters*, 1798. 263

167. Anne-Claude-Philippe, Comte de Caylus, *Grylli*, 1752–1767. 268

168. Grandville, *Misery, Hypocrisy, Covetousness*, 1828–1830. 268

169. La Chau and Le Blond, *Assemblage of Eight Heads*, 1780. 269

170. Thomas Rowlandson, *Napoleon*, 1813. 270

171. Francisco de Goya, *All Will Fall*, 1799. 271

172. Francisco de Goya, *Here Comes the Bogey-Man*, 1799. 272

173. Francisco de Goya, *Those Specks of Dust*, 1799. 273

174. Thomas Rowlandson, *A Magic Lantern*, 1799. 275

175. Thomas Rowlandson, *The Bum Shop*, 1785. 275

176. Francisco de Goya, *When Day Breaks We Will Be Off*, 1799. 277

177. Anonymous, *Cholera Prevention*, 19th c. 278

178. Jules-Pierre-François Baretta, et al., *Wax and Resin Casts of Cutaneous Diseases*, 19th c. 282

179. Chérubim D'Orléans, *Lunar Spots*, 1671. 286

180. William Cowper, *Various Portions of the Cuticula*, 1750. 287

181. James Gillray, *The Cow-Pock*, 1802. 294

182. Jean-Louis Alibert, *Pustulant Smallpox*, 1833. 296

183. Tessier (?), *Bust of Mirabeau*, 1791.
296

184. William Hogarth, *Visit to the Quack Doctor*, 1743–1745.
298

185. Jean-Louis Alibert, *Tumor*, 1833.
300

186. Antoine-Jean Gros, *The Pesthouse at Jaffa*, Salon of 1804.
301

187. Ferdinand Hebra, *Leucoderma*, 1876.
303

188. Jean-Louis Alibert, *Tree of Dermatological Diseases*, 1833.
303

189. Pigal, *Neoplasms*, 1823.
305

190. Jean-Louis Alibert, *Lepra Nigricans*, 1833.
305

191. Pigal, *The Desires of Pregnant Women*, 1823.
307

192. George Stubbs, *Brown and White Norfolk or Water Spaniel*, 1778.
309

193. Anonymous, *The Wonderful Spotted Indian John Boby*, 1803.
310

194. Ambroise Paré, *Pygmy, Hairy Woman, and Man-Calf*, 1614.
312

195. Johann Caspar Lavater, *Girl with Birthmarks*, 1792.
317

196. Georges Buffon, *A Black Albino Child*, 1749.
320

197. Fortunius Licetus, *Hirsute Man and Parti-Colored Man and Woman*, 1655.
320

198. Jean-Louis Alibert, *Vitiligo*, 1833.
321

199. Jean Dubreuil, *Cast Shadows in Artificial Light*, 1726.
324

200. William Hogarth, *The Country Dance*, 1753.
325

201. Tony Johannot, *What Courageous and Bold Travelers*, 1843.
337

202. Martin Frobène Ledermüller, *Fresh Water Polyp and Magnifying Glass*, 1768.
342

203. Martin Frobène Ledermüller, *Coral Salt "Aureole,"* 1768.
342

204. Anonymous, *Sightings of Jupiter and Saturn*, 1666.
343

205. Jean-Jacques Scheuchzer, *The Human Eye as the Work of God*, 1732–1737.
344

206. Martin Frobène Ledermüller, *Flint Sparks*, 1768.
345

207. Martin Frobène Ledermüller, *Wilson Hand Microscope and Slides*, 1768.
346

208. Jean-Jacques Scheuchzer, *Magnified Louse*, 1732–1737.
347

209. Martin Frobène Ledermüller, *"Eels" in Vinegar*, 1768.
349

210. Robert Hooke, *"Diamants" or Sparks in Flints*, 1667.
353

211. Robert Hooke, *The Point of a Sharp Needle*, 1667.
353

212. Martin Frobène Ledermüller, *Lace and Spider's Web*, 1768.
354

213. Athanasius Kircher, *Natural Impressions; Anamorphic Landscape; Camera Obscura*, 1646.
355

214. Grandville, *The Great and the Small*, 1844.
357

215. Martin Frobène Ledermüller, *Solar Microscope and Optical Cabinet*, 1768.
358

216. Edward Orme, *Specimens of Windows, Lamps, Screens*, 1807.
359

217. Martin Frobène Ledermüller, *Solar Microscope and Prismatic Projections*, 1768.
361

218. Laurent Bordelon, *Diabolic Visions*, 1710.
367

219. Edmé Guyot, *Conical Mirror and "Misshapen" Reflections*, 1772. 368

220. Athanasius Kircher, *Kaleidoscope*, 1646. 370

221. Athanasius Kircher, *Catoptric Theater*, 1646. 374

222. Edward Orme, *Philosopher in His Study*, 1807. 376

223. Jean-Honoré Fragonard, *Coresus and Callirhoe*, Salon of 1765. 386

224. David N. Levin, *Facial and Cortical 3D Models Derived from MR Images*. 391

225. Jacques Gautier Dagoty, *Nervous System*, 1775. 402

226. Albrecht von Haller, *Demonstrations of Physiology*, 1757–1766. 408

227. Giovanni Aldini, *Galvanic Experiments*, 1834. 410

228. Jean-Baptiste Greuze, *The Dead Bird*, 1792. 412

229. Bernard Picart, *Different Agitations of Convulsionaries*, 1728–1743. 412

230. Théophile Laennec, *Stethoscopes*, 1819–1826. 414

231. Jean-Jacques Scheuchzer, *Respiration*, 1732–1737. 419

232. Ebenezer Sibly, *Electrical Stars*, 1804. 422

233. Ephraim Chambers, *Pneumaticks*, 1738. 425

234. James Gillray, *Scientific Researches! New Discoveries in Pneumaticks!*, 1802. 427

235. George Cruikshank, *Organ of Ideality*, 1826. 429

236. Charles Aubry, *Madness*, 1823. 435

237. Jean-Etienne-Dominique Esquirol, *Maniac during Attack*, 1838. 436

238. Jean-Etienne-Dominique Esquirol, *Maniac after Cure*, 1838. 436

239. Pierre Camper, *Grotesques from Frieze of Golden House of Nero*, 1792. 441

240. Colin, *The Nightmare*, 1823. 444

241. Grandville, *Metamorphosis of a Dream*, 1844. 447

242. Anonymous, *Caricature of Magnetism, Somnambulism, and Clairvoyancy*, 19th c. 448

243. Ebenezer Sibly, *Mesmerism: The Operator Inducing a Hypnotic Trance*, 1794. 451

244. Jean-Jacques Paulet, *Satire on Animal Magnetism*, 1784. 452

245. Anonymous, *Crisis Rooms at Mesmer's Hôtel Bullion* (?), 1780s. 455

246. Ebenezer Sibly, *System of the Interior, or Empyrean Heaven, Shewing the Fall of Lucifer*, 1804. 457

247. Abbé Sans, *Electrical Cure of Paralysis*, 1772. 460

PREFACE

My aim in writing this book is to identify and interpret the visual strategies and theories put forward during the course of the eighteenth century for imaging the unseen. As a cross-disciplinary examination of the sensory problem of visibilizing the invisible, it seeks to assess the significance and illuminate the persisting value of a cluster of leading body metaphors derived from aesthetic and medical practices. These were the images that possessed power within their own time and to which other images and ideas clung. The significance of this undertaking, to my mind, is that it aims for the first time to analyze and historically situate a major modern epistemological, artistic, and scientific quest. That quest continues in our contemporary technological search to reveal nonapparent physical and mental experience.

During the Enlightenment, the problem of imaging what was "out of sight" became critical in the fine arts and the natural sciences. The latter are here understood in their widest sense to comprise all "field" investigations of unexplained phenomena (including those of the body) requiring of their practitioners remarkable powers of observation and manual dexterity. Thus, for the present purpose, the fine arts and the medical arts are grouped with natural history insofar as all involve sensory detection and a tactile craft. That is, all involve a practical, nonquantifiable and nondiscursive knowledge of nature and a skilled operation performed upon, and with, its materials. All must invent metaphors to conjecture about, or embody, the unknown. To that end, I have tried to cast as wide a net as possible, not limiting myself to the examination of their construction and function within a single country. My presupposition is that, to do justice to these complex tropes and images, they must be interpreted not only from the perspective of art, medical, theological, and philosophical history and criticism but equally, and much more broadly, from the vantage of cultural history. My aspiration, then, is that this metaphorology will make a contribution to the intellectual history of the early modern period as well as chart new ways for thinking about the interrelationships specifically obtaining between art and medicine in the Enlightenment.

Finally, I must confess a somewhat missionary purpose. I also argue for the need to recognize, and act upon, the occurrence of a profound and comprehensive intellectual revolution. This overturning affects all branches of daily life and even the more arcane reaches of humanistic and scientific research and practice. Simply put, it is the radical shift under way since the eighteenth century from a text-based to a visually dependent culture. We need to reflect positively on the momentous historical shift toward visualization now taking place in all fields, and to take stock of its implications. I believe this is essential for everyone working within the humanities, the social sciences, and the physical and biological sciences. Nonetheless, it seems to me that those of us who make, exhibit, study, and teach the visual arts have a special responsibility and a glorious opportunity. We possess unique skills and have indispensable insights to contribute to society on precisely this issue. Working with our colleagues in cognate areas, we need to anticipate a future in which the chief certainty is technological change. These historic alterations are embodied optically in computer simulations, artificial realities, and, of course, video and the ubiquitous television. Paradoxically, the pedagogical, social, and economic changes resulting from this transformation and, specifically, our continuing role within this new world as instructors in visual techniques and strategies, have yet to be seriously examined by members of our profession. No area of life remains untouched. Think of the miraculous new medical imaging technologies (CT, PET, and MRI scanners) that noninvasively open windows into secret depths of the body and the brain. Think, too, of electronic imagery that inverts the very notion of substantial labor. In today's workplace, computer monitors "disembody" information into ghostly green or amber apparitions that float before the eyes. Think of our legal system in which courtroom exhibits, anatomical models, and even films of the day in the life of an accident victim have metamorphosed the concept of "eyewitness account." This major and inescapable universalization of vision suggests that visual aptitude and sophisticated visual learning should no longer be considered a mere aesthetic luxury. Rather, they must assume their rightful place as an essential and serious component of modern existence and present-day education. Images must finally make their exit from Plato's Cave.

In the long process of working on this project, I have incurred many debts. I should like to express my gratitude to the John Simon Guggenheim Memorial Foundation and to the Alexander von Humboldt Stiftung, which made it possible for me to complete this book. It was begun during a happy year (1984–1985) spent as a Fellow at the Woodrow Wilson Center in Washington, D.C. Profound appreciation is especially due to Professor Dr. Georg Kauffmann, former Director and my host and sponsor at the Institut für Kunstgeschichte at the Westfälische Wilhelms-Universität Münster. He and his wonderful colleagues provided me with a stimulating intellectual home during the first stage of my Humboldt Prize sojurn in Germany. While at Münster, I also benefited from the hospitality of Professor Dr. Richard Toellner, Director of the Institut für Theorie und Geschichte der Medizin. I feel privileged to have been invited to participate in its rich programs and seminars. In London, Roy Porter and the staff of the Wellcome Institute for the History of Medicine were unfailingly helpful. Michel Lemire, at the Paris Jardin des Plantes, patiently brought out of storage rare examples of Italian and French anatomical waxes. Dr. Gérard Tilles, of the Société Française d'Histoire de la Dermatologie, was my guide at the Library and Museum of the Hôpital Saint-Louis. Marie-Véronique Clin, Curator of the Musée d'Histoire de la Médecine, Université René Descartes, Paris, graciously assisted with photographs and was unfailingly supportive. Dr. K. S. Grooss, Curator at the newly renovated Museum Boerhaave, Leiden, kindly walked me through its treasure-laden rooms of scientific and medical instruments before that collection's official opening to the public. Nowhere else can you see seven of the world's nine extant Leeuwenhoek microscopes! H. J. F. M. Leechburch Auwers, the Museum's head librarian, happily dug out material on Albinus and Camper. Lucinda H. Keister, Curator, Prints and Photographs Collection, History of Medicine Division, National Library of Medicine, Bethesda, Maryland, and her lovely staff helped me to navigate among its peerless holdings. Her unfailing enthusiasm and help with this project dates back to its inception. Marsha Reed, of the Getty Center for the History of Art and the Humanities of Santa Monica, kept unearthing tomes of ancient and forgotten lore. Anselmo Carini, Associate Curator at the Art Institute of Chicago's Department of Prints and Drawings, made it a joy to work in that superb collection.

At the University of Chicago, I have profited from the generosity of Robert N. Beck, Director, Center for Imaging Science, and Mark Siegler, M.D., Director, Center for Clinical Medical Ethics. In a true spirit of interdisciplinarity, they accepted this strange art historian into their thought-provoking programs and provided open forums for discussing contemporary medical issues and the multifaceted ramifications of the new machines. William Kruskal introduced me to the wonders of statistics. Most importantly, he taught me that two is a dangerous number. I recall with great warmth the vivaciousness and humaneness of Robert Rosenthal, who died tragically during the course of this writing. Beautiful rare books with pictures, and the Special Collections of Regenstein Library, will never be the same. In the Art Department, my dear colleague, Harrie Vanderstappen, helped me to look at vexing problems from the perspective of non-Western cultures. Frank Dowley, too, was always willing to share his expertise on all matters French. Thanks, too, to my terrific graduate students past and present for their creative insights and their sustaining enthusiasm for the eighteenth century. Pride knows no bounds for the frontier investigations of Christopher Johns, Paul Schweizer and Mary D. Sheriff. Of late, especially helpful were the participants in two interdisciplinary seminars that I gave. The first, on "Ruling Metaphors in Eighteenth-Century Art and Medical Theory," took place at the Folger Library, Washington, D.C., in the spring of 1987. The second, "Encyclopedias and Encyclopedism: Style and Method," was cotaught with Paolo Cherchi, a colleague from the Department of Romance Languages, and held at the Newberry Library, Chicago, in the spring of 1989. The fruit of that lively collaboration was an exhibition, "Encyclopedism from Pliny to Borges," held in the Joseph Regenstein Library, the University of Chicago, May 2 to September 5, 1990. Anna Sigridur Arnar, one of my doctoral students, selected the material and wrote the splendid catalogue. On this and on the present project as well, Katherine Haskins made perceptive suggestions. Elizabeth Kent Haveles shared my unnatural passion for reading dictionaries. Benjamin Powell took splendid photographs of material difficult to shoot. Tamara Faulkner toiled over the typing, the bibliography, and, just generally, kept the world at bay. Virginia Boyce cast a keen eye over the proofs. Friends, too, were understanding. Being with Denne Simon make unclear things clear. Hildette Rubenstein and Ann Seeler were sisters and muses. Where would I be without Albert's irreverent wit and Ernst's serene patience?

My greatest debt of gratitude, as always, is to my husband Fred for his unstinting encouragement and truly amiable support. When despair set in, as it so often did, concerning the low status of images, the inequitable position of their students, and the inadequate art historical study of the eighteenth century, he urged me to look to the future. Comes the revolution, this chemist will be named both an honorary imagist and a *dixhuitièmiste*.

All translations, unless otherwise indicated, are my own.

BODY CRITICISM

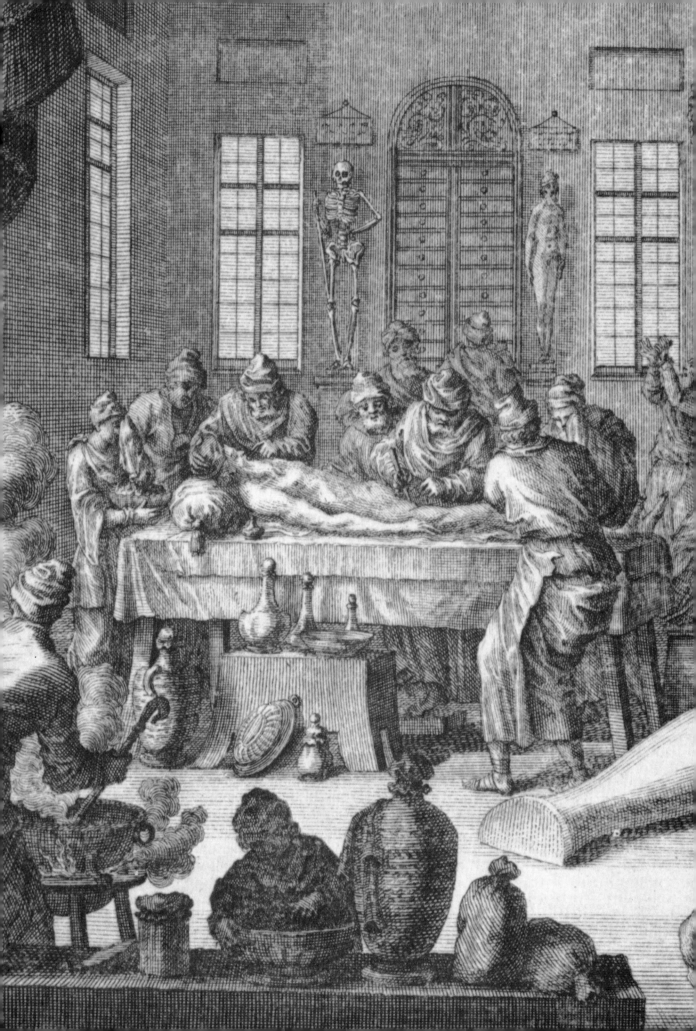

INTRODUCTION:

The Visualization of Knowledge

Somatic Metaphors

Is certainty possible in life? Can one gain firm insight into the inside of bodies
and minds? Does truth lie above or below the phenomenal tide? What is the
connection between visible surface and invisible depth? These metaphor-
laden questions are fundamental to an understanding of the yearning characterizing much of the eighteenth-century mentality. The wish to know
intimately the unseizable other is inseparable from a genetic phenomenology.
Otherwise stated, it entailed a hunt for the definitive origins or documentable
beginnings of aesthetic, ethical, biological, cognitive, and social experience.
The profound desire to get close to things that had either recently become
distant or, naggingly, had always been intellectually and spiritually remote,
or merely seemed foreign and problematic, is evident in all disciplines. We
shall examine the various ways in which the Enlightenment expressed this
aspiration to a pure and pristine experience and for a direct and uncontaminated access to the historical and suprahistorical condition of mankind. Most
typically, it took the form of a search for salvation through a reckoning
method.[1] Reinforcing the sense of abysmal loss, or of a yawning gulf stretching between absence and presence, was the dualistic construction of the
physical and corporeal cosmos inherited by the eighteenth century from the
seventeenth. What was new to the Enlightenment, however, was the dissemination and penetration of reforming systems into greater and wider fields of
inquiry. For philosopher-academicians, rigorous education was to compensate

for an imperfect understanding and a congenital sensory frailty. The uneducated masses—perpetually seduced by deceptive visual appearances—needed to be led by *Logos*, logic, and the unmistakable word. Here is the nub of another major issue with which we will be wrestling. Optical demonstration and visualization were central to the processes of enlightening. Yet from a conceptual standpoint, images, paradoxically, were reduced to misleading illusions without the guidance of discourse.

The problem, then, is to uncover the complex individual drives and broader cultural forces fueling the compulsion to find an immaterial or supernatural clarity within material or ambiguous phenomena. To that end, I focus on the diverse, relentless, and unexamined attempts to break into the obscure secrets of the somatic. The sophisticated investigations conducted by eighteenth-century students of the visual and medical arts were mutually interdependent. They relied upon the same keen observational skills. Their imaginative powers ingeniously led to the forging of common metaphors for the construction of artificial and natural compositions. Early modern aesthetics and biology shared a relational praxis and a detecting theory that focused on the puzzle of the feeling and thinking person. Most significantly for this study, these manual, perceptual, and mental operations were centrally involved with revealing, structuring, and interpreting signs and symptoms that inherently could not be written. As diagnostic disciplines, their purpose was to discover and exhibit the inarticulable relationship of interior to exterior, idea to form, private pathos to public pattern. In these perceptual fields, then, physical images and organic bodies necessarily expressed themselves differently from sequential texts. They were not naturally constructed from dependent clauses and serial sentences since their nature was precisely to make manifest that which could not be said. Contrary to a powerful, entrenched, and now institutionalized epistemocracy, I argue that this difference in form and function implies neither inferiority nor deception. Among my several aims is to expose how the visual arts, and bodily-kinesthetic intelligence in general, were damned to the bottom of the Cave of the humanities. In today's text-based curricula, sensory and affective phenomena continue to be treated as second-rate simulations of second-class reflections.

The strength and reality-quotient of metaphors is evident negatively in the capacity that certain tropes had and have in subjugating whole classes of physical experience. Coercive and authoritarian analogies such as the book of the world, clear and distinct truth, dissecting reason, and pure spirit became objective standards against which confused, or nongeometric, shapes and colored, or mutable, semblances were judged. We will see, on one hand, how dangerous it is when metaphors are taken for actuality. Think of the following common, or matter-of-fact, statements that are by no means self-evident, although they present themselves as such. Paintings *are* illusions. Pictures *are* another form of writing and, therefore, ought to be distinct and legible. Straight lines, circles, and squares *are* the ideal forms and thus should be imposed on disorderly biota. It follows from such specious but persuasive logic that, if these predetermined conditions are not met, then the rebellious expressions in question remain not only meaningless but valueless. Such ontologized, transcendentalized, and verbalized metaphors were invented to fill an epistemological vacuum. They were thrust into the *tabula rasa* of the physiological and psychological unknown about which they appeared to conjecture with certainty. In any radical dualism without an intervening milieu, tempering atmosphere, or anthropological, that is human, middle term, the act of comparison became a metaphysics. We shall see that a polarizing system or ahistorical logic of management was central both to Neoclassical abstraction and Romantic symbolism. These fundamentally negative methods, based on the establishment of insurmountable antitheses, were two sides of the same coin.

On the positive side, it is also through metaphors that unclear emotions and mixed experiences—disdained by a rationalist philosophy—can be configured in a way unattainable through bodiless concepts. Unlike the abstractions of divisive language that isolate objects and fields of inquiry, constitutive metaphors function in the imaginative manner of artistic and clinical diagnosis. Rhetorical, or dialogically communicative and unifying, they call on the beholder to combine and synthesize experiences that analysis has fragmented or dissected. This book, therefore, is a metaphorology. It aims to reveal unexpected and eye-opening similarities between two areas that heretofore were believed to be distant and irreconcilably different. This procedure, unlike imperialistic methods, is not intended to erase a sense of special identity but to open up horizons for new, significant, and egalitarian connections. Consequently, readers are invited to observe, compare, and further combine. My hope is that these findings will prompt the discovery of metaphorical ties among other and now still far apart fields. With the aid of metaphors I attempt to break out of late-twentieth-century cognitive structures in order to see those of another time. In turn, with them, I believe we can also come to see better the roots of many of our most pressing current dilemmas. From an artist's, physician's, or author's analogies, we gain access to a concealed

and otherwise unseen conceptual organization whereby she or he is uncon-
sciously or consciously guided. Moreover, "foreground" metaphors alert us
to the resemblances and discontinuities existing between an individual's personal or idiosyncratic fashioning of information and the "background" or
common metaphors governing a culture at a specific moment.[2] Simultaneously biographical and historical, singular and plural, they help to make
the otherwise elusive and submerged thought processes of a period vivid,
visible, and concrete.

Hans Blumenberg has argued long and convincingly that a metaphorology is
a powerful means for understanding the rationally ungraspable or the indes-
cribable.[3] To this category of human experience that cannot be discursively
explained, I wish to add the interpretation of figured expressions, or the
activity of visibilizing the invisible. In a wonderfully evocative analogy,
Blumenberg terms metaphors fossil clues. Poking out here and there from an
archaic substratum of cognition, these broken tracks and fragmentary traces
indicate the growth and development of an intellectual curiosity.[4] Since they
do not fit or conform to uniform layers of received opinion, these hybrids
offer insights into the evolution of a phenomenological sense of being in the
world. By metaphor I intend far more than the oratorical sense of ornaments
of speech. This noble Ciceronian connotation eventually became perverted
and trivialized to imply distracting accessories. For a rigorist age, "poetic"
embellishments, whorish coloring, or unnatural cosmetics called for surgical
excision or ritual washing. Rather, our interest lies with metaphors as both
a mode for persuasion and as an impetus for epistemological revolution. I
will show that, historically, they functioned as weighty catalysts or causal
agents for real change. Their imagistic and corporeal action created a conspicuous physical disturbance within the common run of customary signifi-
cation. They intruded a heterogeneous, problematic, and even destructive
element, belonging to a different context or relationship, into a seemingly
straightforward and transparent flow of ideas. It was precisely the normalcy
of narrative that was disrupted by the brusque and abnormal insertion of a
spatial picture, or palpable foreign body, into the temporal stream of the text.
Hence the opprobrium attached to this Rococo and showy procedure by a
rationalist school of criticism. For the geometrical spirit, metaphors were a
sort of alien "misfit" or grotesque monster of difference. Equalizing and
obtrusive figures thus embodied a threat to any homogeneous and stratified
theory of imitation predicated on congruity or the comfortable similarity of
like to like.

4

In my view, the theoretical marginalization of imagery that developed during the course of the eighteenth century occurred precisely because of its pervasiveness. Furthermore, perceptual peripheralization depended upon, included, and implied a correspondingly low status for corporeality in general. Material, affective, or "fleshy" experiences were to be placed under the hierarchical tutelage of theoretical models. This deflation, subjugation, and reconstruction of the sensory along the lines of the logical was itself brought about through ruling metaphors. The Cartesian and Newtonian valorization of immaterial reason was coupled to the severing of an absolute space, or extension, from an infinite time. The division between the unworldly and the worldly was promulgated in the printed and standardized look of a burgeoning technical literature. The abstraction, epitomization, and regularization of information presented in eighteenth-century dictionaries and pedagogical treatises personified, while authenticating, the norm of legibility. By contrast, the dark and tangled forest of data patiently gathered by the dimly seeing experimentalist seemed barbaric. The task of the enlightened critic was like that of the mathematician. He was to prune this thicket into an orderly, objective, and mechanical nature conceived according to eternal principles. The complex transformation of the physical into the conceptual, or of the probable into the formulaic, required a century to accomplish. In an increasingly specialized, professionalized, and discipline-oriented world, prismatic and indistinct effects ran athwart monochromatic and exact readings. Fleeting sensuous awareness, like the hollow carcass bereft of a soul, was judged to be an inferior type of knowledge or an empty "aesthetic."[5] I shall argue that once imagery, like the material body, became systematically drawn into a negative analogy with fraudulent apparitions, confounding dreams, and irrational delusions, there was only one, downward direction in which the process could, and indeed did, unfold. The phenomenal, the manual, the somatic were irrevocably divided from the noumenal, the theoretical, the intellectual. These menials in servitude landed in the dead end of the noncognitive where they remain today.

Consumable and manipulable images, like salable and reusable portions of the anatomy, continue to carry the weight of debasing propaganda cynically conferred by those who despise them. Burdened by shameless huckstering, they are treated without respect, as though they were worthless and possessed no glorious past. In the thoroughly politicized and one-sided talk over the contemporary plight of the humanities, no one has mentioned or mourned this monumental trivialization of nonverbal expression. In academe, the study of images is typically shunted to the edges of what "really matters," or is taken over from the outside. Improvement of a supposedly poor quality of mind is frequently carried out in the name of an interdisciplinarity that is so uncoordinated and unsynchronized as to be useless. Its other, and to my mind far more insidious, form is that of an architectonic. That is, this mock-intellectual coordination seeks to create a grand unified theory in relation to other disciplines that is grounded in the assumption of the unchallengeable superiority of one of them. What is most pernicious about this covert or overt system of ranking is that it reinforces an ancient anti-intellectual stereotype. Once again, the "unknowing" visual arts bow before the "knowing" hermeneutics of the semantic. This lazy acquiescence to antiquated power structures precludes original visual thinking and effective action in addressing ongoing visual problems. Thus imagery and imagists remain textually dominated and caught in a web of inappropriate metaphors even while appearing to engage jointly in democratic pursuits.

Explicitly or implicitly, nondiscursive articulations suffer from the fact that they do not say or read. If they wish to appear legitimate, then they must conform and perform linguistically. This fact no doubt accounts for the sameness of tone, lack of bold personal voice, and constant citation of a repetitive cast of critics in so much contemporary writing on aesthetic matters. Yet this contortion to match the identity and function of another can only be a masquerade. In a classic example of the double-bind, the sensuous image, like the body, is by definition already theoretically severed from the noble language paradigm whose duty it is to emulate. The regnant hierarchy thus remains safely intact. I shall return at the end of this book to the ironies of such an outdated cognitive model and to the void this has left in our present system of education. For the moment, let me suggest that we imagists cease approaching our colleagues in text-based disciplines, hat in hand, waiting to be methodized. Let us abandon the nonproductive and falsely self-deprecating metaphor of being prisoners, manacled to Plato's Cave and only good for gaping ignorantly at phantoms. Whatever else it may be, this demeaning position is also socially irresponsible. My overarching conviction is that we bring, and must continue to bring, something special and distinctive to the humanities and the sciences. The image world of the twenty-first century requires its informed and trained architects. As a broadly based profession of artists, builders, designers, and historians of every facet of the visual, we must awaken to our civic role and duty. We must respond to the dire need our civilization has for intelligent thought concerning nondiscursive expression. Here lies an opportunity for hope and an incentive for performance. We must rouse universities to their task in preparing students for an environment in which electronically assisted telecommunication plays an ever greater part.

Metaphorology, then, opens up a wider and truly cross-disciplinary horizon onto the past and the future. It permits us to rethink, reformulate, and perhaps even constructively reshape the abiding yet changing problem of the relation of image to text, imagination to reason, and body to soul. It recognizes the existence of multiple intelligences, not just the specious communism of a single intellectual competence. It allows us to look at cognitive abilities through many lenses. A contemporary instantiation of the age-old and universal question of what to do with sundered fields is the heroic struggle to achieve the unification of Germany. Beyond practical or economical difficulties lies the complex historical dimension of a development requiring the merger without condescension, not resentful and derogatory blending, of two separately evolved and distinctive states. Freed from the false homogeneity of a totalitarian ideology, regional and national identities have been reaffirmed. In Central Europe at large, numerous smaller actors or assertive personalities are now engaged in the agonizing process of being integrated into a recently unified and transformed Europe which, in turn, must relate to a larger international scene. Social harmony depends upon avoiding the dichotomy of first- and second-class status. Legal independence from past forcible annexations allows for future and freely chosen affiliations. It strikes me that the substantive challenge posed by this coordinative task is no different from that of reconstituting innovative and meaningful disciplinary confederations. To succeed, neither the political nor the academic ties can be construed as the wedding of rich with poor relations.

During the course of this book, I will take what has been looked upon as an unrelated string of phenomena and show that they constitute a comity of interdependent constructs. These inseparable figures, incomprehensible as tidy blocs or neat pacts, image the substructure of the eighteenth-century mentality. They were the "lived concepts" and embodied or concrete ideas invented to make the unseen seen and expressible.[6] We shall be asking how, why, and what did it mean to dissect in search of a deeply lodged, dark or luminous, truth? To what end this compulsion to abstract and geometrize in order to purify, refine, or distill imperfect organisms? How did the diverse tropes for conception or creation variously articulate the relationship between the known and the unknown? What do they tell us about the Enlightenment's outlooks concerning the mystery of how physical or mental children came to be? Against what spotted and stained actuality did the biological and aesthetic model of a flawless *beau idéal* develop? How did the geographical *terra incognita* of the subcutaneous become identified with magnified optical projections? What contributed to the conviction that only the finer intellectual "touch" of the mind could effectively bypass the decoys and traps of the senses, especially those of sight?

These somatic metaphors continue to shape and organize our deepest and most intractable existential problems. We need to replace the pervasive strategies of reductive calculation, rigid criticism, and hierarchical dichotomization with integrating and democratic images. In short, we need to forge new metaphors. Such revolutionary embodiments or incarnated thoughts would demonstrate the independence and individuality of different types of expression. At the same time, they would evoke and provoke unusual and unthought-of connections and reveal possible points of conjunction. Only when "insubstantial" images and "unthinking" bodies are remetaphorized— that is, removed from the paradigm of the logical, the lexical, and the geometrical—will they attain a substantial and serious status. My aim is to make a good start toward the reclamation of their proper significance and worth. Undeniably, our field could and should have a say in assessing the profound global impact of the new visual dimension of social exchange. Museums have increasingly taken on an activist role as educators, teaching people to become vitally engaged in understanding a complex range of visual objects. It is no small irony that curators of education are doing what their colleagues in art history departments are turning their backs upon. As academics, we must also take the trouble to make a meaningful connection with a nonacademic public. Moreover, in teaching students, or the future public, how to grapple with past imagery, we can inspire interest, prompt discussion, and reintroduce a sense of wonder for its continuing power and impact.

I offer only one possible example among many for the promotion of improved relationships among disciplines that would also lead to a better society and to a more dignified role for images within it. Because of our expertise, we are able to assist the emerging biological imaging sciences not only to interpret intricate optical information but to reflect historically on the intertwined aesthetic and ethical issues surrounding the new instrumentation. Instead of incessant argument over what intellectual paradigm deserves to be reproduced in pedagogy and research programs, the mind boggles at what the "mere practice" of our craft might accomplish. Conversely, contributing to, and being in informed touch with, the weighty modern medical issues of life, death, and disease would necessarily strengthen and deepen our understanding of the fine arts. To date, we have internalized in a paralyzing critique the venerable contempt and mistrust of phantasmagoric pictures. Why should anyone respect what we ourselves do not? I think that when we discover that our studies can make a *real* and *visible* difference, there will be no more talk about shadowy and sham appearances. From that hard-won self-confidence, we will be able to interact collaboratively with other disciplines as equals.

At the outset, I wish to place before the reader certain themes to be taken up in detail during the course of my exposition. They are linked because they hinge on the dialectic of invisible and visible that is the foundation of all dichotomies. The problem of how to get from where you are to where you are not, or cannot reach, entailed the invention of *Logos*. This selective and separating faculty and function corresponded to the logician's instrument, or the analyzing word. The surgical task of the philosopher was to take apart, or to mount a critique against, any mixture of fiction with actuality, untruth with truth. This attack on *mimesis*, launched by Plato, was exacerbated by the Enlightenment's extreme sensitivity to the multiple ways in which one's impression of reality might become corrupted.[7] A central concern for the eighteenth century was the danger lurking in a barbaric darkening of the luminous processes of conception. The dedication to pedagogy, to the production of training manuals and corrected compendia outlining the proper procedures for the developing professions, did not derive simply from the ancient notion that practice should be a slave to theory. The uneducated masses, in a favorite Enlightenment simile, were like the proverbial man born blind who later learned to see. These sudden gainers of vision had to be programmatically weaned away from the disguised manipulations of superstitious priests, the beguilements of oriental despots, and the technical wizardry of optical tricksters.[8] Ever-watchful method and overseeing reason or *Logos* constituted the healing therapy for a spoiled and rotted grasp of reality.[9] Neoclassical art theory—whose examination looms large in this book—was itself a form of pedagogical methodism erected on this reforming principle. It follows that analytical physiognomics, or the "universal science" of the eighteenth century, was inseparable from the anatomizing project of Neoclassicism. The educative purpose of this depth psychology was to ferret out imitations, that is, to uncover faces pretending to be sincere or like the original but which, at bottom, were false. Detecting pervasive human forgeries was comparable to the cognate activity of unmasking phony antiquities. Such artificial persons, who carefully constructed their social appearance, were judged to be all optical effect, magic lantern projection without solid foundation. Crafty but worthless reproductions, they resembled those duplicitous dreams invented by Descartes's *Dieu trompeur.* Feigning—whether in art or physiology—posed the danger of letting contrived images and alluring self-advertisements slip into the unaware and unwary consciousness.

Specialists in the invisible, or rescuers from such delusion, were authorities about everything opposite to manufactured seeming. The philosophical instructor possessed the right rules to ward off sophistic enticements. It is no accident that academies played a significant role in the institutionalization of eighteenth-century cultural life. Education was essential to the Neoplatonic way of Ideas subscribed to by the high enlighteners. It was in the very nature of improving Ideas to be known only secondarily, or through transmission. The academician-teacher, rather than mere subjects of sensory experience or the gullible public, was empowered by the state to transmit reality accurately. In charge of the official channels of communication, these guides to truth opposed those pleasure-seeking and producing artisans who set up individual shops and taught for money. Like the fantastic simulations they fabricated, the technician's or craftsman's specious science was only an inferior pseudo-science. The eighteenth-century popularity of polychrome wax sculpture epitomized this unintellectual delight in the aesthetics of almost, that is, in skillful and total *trompe l'oeil* replication. For the astounded and uncritical spectator, the pathos-laden anatomy *seemed* to be minutely incarnated as a living and vivid presence. Such colorful effigies appeared identical to the absent person. They were not translated or otherwise symbolized and allegorized. In these animated casts, nothing mediated between the diseased or suffering fact of the human condition and its marred, individual embodiment.

Hans Blumenberg has shown how the Platonic theory of Ideas contributed to the establishment and maintenance of philosophy as the sole teaching power within the ancient Greek polis. He has also noted the undemonstrated premise upon which this promotion rests.[10] The authority of the universe of Forms was to be mirrored in the actual fabric of the well-run republic. Just as dark appearances were subservient to radiant Ideas, the unlettered multitude was to be led by a few, select lawgivers. From the vantage of later eighteenth-century Hellenism it is significant to note that, within this epistemocratic framework, the concept of *Logos* was specifically tied both to touch and to the word. Just as the Forms immaterially directed the Demiurgus in the making of the material cosmos, stable logic governed unstable sensory media.[11] The skewing of this basic Neoplatonic tenet by the late Neoplatonists was taken up in the central Enlightenment problem of the dream. Invisible Ideas or noumenal reality—which could be touched or grazed by the disembodied understanding—resided on the far side of appearances. By contrast, apparitional phenomena or visionary unreality were merely available to sight. The haptic, like the linguistic, was thus connected to a fleshless reason. Conversely, the visual increasingly became identified with falsification, fiction, and bodily induced hallucination. For the empiricists, the world had no preoptical meaning but was a prismatic and abstract arrangement of light and colors. For Cartesian and Newtonian rationalists, it was consubstantial with deceitful phantasmagoria. For the materialists, it was impossible to separate with certainty sleep from wakefulness. My argument concerning the logocentrism inherent in the puristic, geometric, and calculating aesthetic theories of the second half of the century depends upon this point.

Throughout the ages deductive philosophers of a Platonic stamp, believing in innate ideas, were hostile to inductive and manipulating sophists. These practical instructors for hire, like Prometheus, taught humanity not to remember and imitate the Forms but to fend for themselves through creation or craft. Making or art was work, an empirical toil, not a theoretical *agon* or combat.[12] This manual business of handling, or the laborious copying of what merely is, however, was continually challenged by the intellectual guardians of a prenatal and a postmortal memory. For rational philosophers, there was only one invisible reality and one group visibly in charge of it. The rigorist or purist position involved being constantly in the posture of attack. Earthly things, like divine conceptions, should emanate immaterially. That is, they should not appear as if they had been forced to be born into substance. The abstemious diagram and the emaciated outline testified to the eschatological worthlessness of the material and corporeal cosmos. As the visible signs of intellect, they implacably battled and battered worldliness. Consequently, exaggeratedly economical contours and geometrical shapes were intrinsic to that negative Gnostic and Manichean method of reduction stretching from late antiquity down through the Enlightenment and well beyond. Inner life was associated with a perceptual and organic minimalism or refining ascetic abstraction. Eternal vigilance in the guise of hard and cold cerebration was the only sure remedy against lax producers of soft illusions. During the eighteenth century, in particular, the triumph of Newtonian mathematical and axiomatic science gave a new impetus to the Neoplatonic desire for exactness in the knowledge of inexact things. I believe that what is conventionally termed Neoclassicism was fundamentally an enactment of this Neoplatonic draining of substance through schematization. The invention of statistics further shored up the ancient numerological paradigm. The measurement of uncertainty contributed an additional and novel external pressure urging conformity to visual simplicity.[13] The wholesale, and often inappropriate, application of rigid and calculable norms encouraged the regularization of irregular, shadowy, and complex bodies in the name of an authoritative and corrective theory.

For the age of encyclopedism, the human body represented the ultimate visual compendium, the comprehensive method of methods, the organizing structure of structures. As a visible natural whole made up of invisible dissimilar parts, it was the organic paradigm or architectonic standard for all complex unions. Whether ideal or caricatured, perfect or monstrous, it formed the model for proper or improper man-made assemblies and artificial compositions.[14] Impersonation generated a wide range of tropes. These intersected with the biology, psychology, religion, and philosophy of living, historical agents. The metaphor of the body politic, for example, was embedded in the additive and subtractive scatological methods of political satire. Visual and verbal constructions permitted a host of puns fragmenting an all too corporeal state. They literally incarnated features that were out of joint, illassorted, crippled, and otherwise malformed (fig. 1).

1. T. McLean, *The Body Politic or the March of the Intellect.* 1836. Colored lithograph. (Photo: Courtesy National Library of Medicine, Bethesda, Md.)

Traditionally, Western civilization grounded many of its dualistic theological, legal, medical, and aesthetic notions on the supposition of the body's integrity and rectitude.[15] Thus, much of the visual effect of Jacques-Louis David's (1748–1825) metric *Death of Socrates* was dependent upon its ostentatiously embodied moral geometry. Socrates, stiff and naked in his Stoic uprightness, was pointedly contrasted to the pliant arcs and disheveled curves weighing down his lesser, suffering followers (fig. 2). Significantly, many intertwined aesthetic and medical issues of the eighteenth century revolved around the empathetic responses or repulsing reactions to pain. The question of the propriety of responding to, and representing, sharp and deep sensations formed a leitmotif of Enlightenment thought. The search for the seat and certain signs of acute or nuanced emotion also underlay the debate concerning the importance or unimportance of affect to cognition. Uncontrollable plea-

12

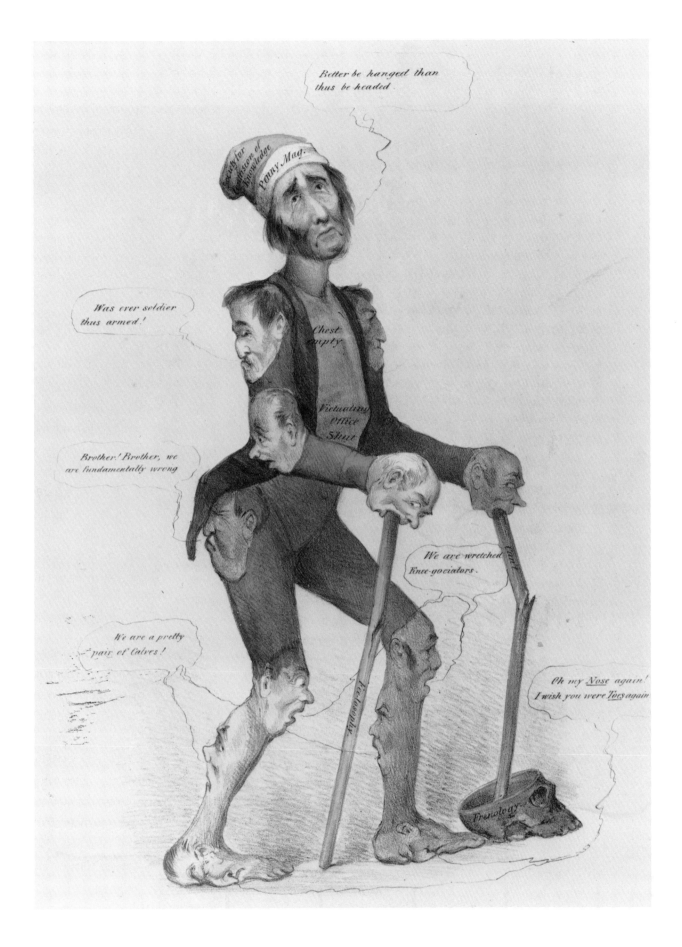

2. Jacques Louis David, *The Death of Socrates*. Salon of 1787. Oil on canvas, 129.5 × 196.2 cm. Catherine Lorillard Wolfe Collection, The Metropolitan Museum of Art, New York. (Photo: Courtesy Metropolitan Museum of Art.)

sure and distracting misery focused the problem of the oppositional relationship of an appetite-ridden and sickness-prone physiology to a rational and
unbendable intellect. In a popular Enlightenment metaphor, the mind was
incarcerated in the tenebrous cavern or prison of the afflicted body and thus
could not see or comprehend clearly. Consequently, I believe that the deeper
message of David's painting conveyed the dichotomous burial of the brain in
the misperceiving flesh. Lithic immurement personified the ancient philosopher's legendary revulsion toward sensory experience and his fearlessness in
the face of death. The depiction of his passage to an altered state was part
of that Neoplatonic fascination with the drama of the descent of Ideas into
time. Most relevant to this epiphanic revelation or genesis of Forms was not
their dissolution and decay within the world but the eventual return to their
atemporal and preconceptual origins.[16] Socrates' inflexible, unflinching, and
admonitory posture signified the moment of purification when, unlike his
emotive and still shackled followers, he rose above the vagaries and pangs of
history to speak with eternal things.

This painting, then, reinvested the rationalist philosophy with which the
name of Socrates was synonymous with the continued moral authority to
lead the unenlightened and still entrapped. More important, however, it
empowered a Neoclassical pictorial logic as well. Reality was geometrical. It
did not consist in the fakery of the visual or in the nothingness of the carnal
body. Unidirectional straight lines and curves indicated that what was true
could not be anamorphically turned to suit the perspective of different beholders. The picture addressed the atomistic many, the mixed *parterre* of the
Salon, so often misled by their desires. This public was legibly admonished
to follow the way of the enlightened one. The artist with *esprit* was not just
a conventionalized *main*. Like the philosopher-statesman, this creative genius
bestowed his wisdom freely, through an unpurchasable touch that was not
merely a crafty touch. As David later told his students, unteachable invention
separated the high calling of the painter from the *métier* of the cobbler.[17]
Emulating Socrates, the conceptual artist did not dwell on material execution.
Nor did he practice aesthetic simony, or the retailing of spiritual goods. Thus
David's taut and hard-muscled moral athlete—immune to sophistic blandish-
ments and to the agonies of an unregenerated flesh—pointed unswervingly
to that which he would have his motley audience seize by design. The
invisible immortality he was convinced he would soon grasp was congruent
with the haptic solidity of the painting's *style*. The achievement of certitude,
or the noetic attainment of Ideas by the mind, corresponded to the abrupt
outlining and unmechanical drawing of the figures. These, in turn, were to

be read rather than merely gaped at. The French painter made a conspicuous and revolutionary effort to sort out and parcelize for the untrained spectator the confusion and error inherent in sensory perception. The contours that so obviously compartmentalize the actors bear witness to the nonmanual nature of this metaphysical and theoretical activity. Rough parataxis, or tactile juxtaposition of bodies, further symbolized the uneasy dialectical tension between that which is and that which is not yet.

Appositely, for David as well as for much late-eighteenth-century aesthetic and biological theory, weak, physical bodies born to multiply endured the same fate as feeble, trumped-up reproductive images. They lacked the identical degree of substantiality vis-à-vis the firm or truth-saying intellect. Consequently, Socrates was not dressed in a flaccid, flawed, or aging body. Rather, he was already vested in the rehabilitated skin of his imminent posttemporal condition. The prenatal anatomy of the soul, not yet born into matter, was marmoreal, that is, as invincible and complete as the perfect understanding. Nor was he a slave to his automatic responses. He had not fallen prey to the chromatics of involuntary reactions nor given way to the fluid shapes of physical passion. In addition, the major eighteenth-century discovery of the nervous system would have reminded the knowledgeable viewer that physiology had increasingly become dissolved into the widened perspective of a thin network of subcutaneous fibers. A foundationless skein of hollow threads constituted a new, transitory, and stimulus-driven underworld that was as unreliable as it was incoherent. It, too, required a regimen.

Thus the body was intimately tied to the establishment and upholding of ethical norms for ugliness or beauty. It could be minimized or magnified, reduced or aggrandized, cleansed or cosmeticized. It provided a surface for the play of invisible yearnings and visible emotions. It was a site for the display of purity and pollution. As a complexly bordered zone, it was amalgamated from a nexus of physiological and psychological processes. As in the case of the *Death of Socrates*, it could signify physical nothingness in contrast to spiritual wealth.[18] The somatic, then, provides a point of entry into a larger physical and moral universe. Master metaphors were invented to grasp the body's overt forms and covert functions, to denote its intermediate status between heaven and hell. These images and figures of speech offer fascinating glimpses into the rational and the nonrational sides of the Enlightenment. Unless we understand these dominant constructs, we remain in the dark concerning that marvelous period's leading assumptions, instinctive responses, and primal obsessions. Body metaphors can disclose veiled human experience. The comparisons and relations themselves will be shown to repose upon a greater and still unexamined desire. Beneath them lay the profound need to visibilize all aspects of the invisible. In addition, they constituted an experimental protocol for penetrating a shifting and blurred social reality. Stained and patched, this reality seemed increasingly opaque and equivocal. Not unlike contemporary media critics, many of the thinkers we shall encounter treated the cinematic flow of sensory life as a sheer fabrication, a manipulable illusion of constructed appearances or simulations.

Prescriptive chiaroscural and perspectival similes constituted an Enlightenment aesthetics of longing.[19] Upon legitimate or illegitimate usage depended whether things were light or dark, present or absent, close or distant. Most important, on metaphorized procedures hinged the access to an all-important unseen realm. There were proper and improper rituals for scanning, touching, cutting, deforming, abstracting, generating, conceiving, marking, staining, enlarging, reducing, imagining, and sensing. Constituting visual styles or manners of behavior, these procedures provided right or wrong sensory and intellectual strategies for "opening" recalcitrant materials and otherwise impenetrable substances. Normal or abnormal processes and modes for proceeding could assure one, or not, of getting a glimpse into secretive physiognomies. Body tropes thus provided critical clues for how insight might be gained into the interior of any concealed territory. This held equally for the realm of the fine arts or that of the natural sciences.

The representational problem of embodiment or personification dated back to ancient rhetoric.[20] But the activity of visibilizing, or incarnating, the invisible became endowed with a special urgency in early modern art and medical experimentation.[21] The illustrative drive to turn elusive information into riveting spectacle, or into palpable demonstration, was one of the chief educational tools for attaining enlightenment. Witness the graphic "surgery" performed upon ancients and moderns alike by Anton Raphael Mengs (1728–1779) or, again, by David. In their paintings chaotic physiological experience was dissected, dismembered, decomposed. Multiple or compound events, as in the latter's *Brutus* (Paris, Musée du Louvre, 1789), were metrically divided, separated, and violently broken into their component numerical parts. Male and female actors seemed fleshed numerals ostentatiously isolated in a compartmentalized arrangement. Sectioning forced the viewer's eye to lurch across the canvas. This violent destruction of an organic composition also entailed a thwarting of expectation among his high-brow spectators. There was no well-knit corporation, no natural *tout-ensemble*, no blended *corpus*.

These traditional unities had been achieved and maintained only through the harmonious ordering of *clair-obscur* and the linking of figures in a smooth *enchaînement*.[22] Even the distinctly low-brow contingent of the Parisian Salon audience recognized David's drastic, almost caricatural disruption of venerable principles of order.[23] The creation of brusquely polarized individual oppositions (male/female, father/son, mother/sister, reason/emotion, control/dishevelment, stone/wood, undress/dress, light/dark, near/far) further served as the foundation for a radically dichotomized total construction. Most importantly, however, the fabrication of precisely demarcated and artificial boundaries was itself grounded in a vertical system of nonvisual values.[24] Methodizing painters increasingly hammered out clear and distinct but unsensuous corporeal *tableaux*. A form of painted instruction, these works were meant to unearth the invisible. They exposed a recessed skeletal bedrock or buried monochromatic core of fixed personal identity or historical certitude. The rational imposition of an abstract analytical method on the human frame and the concomitant laying aside of physiological intricacy was not surprising in an era that witnessed social upheaval and political uncertitude. Probing portraits of single figures, such as Mengs's *Winckelmann* (New York, Metropolitan Museum of Art, 1761–1762) or David's *Dead Marat* (Brussels, Musée Royaux des Beaux-Arts, 1793), and of moral gladiators gathered together in the *Oath of the Horatii* (Paris, Musée du Louvre, 1784), operated on the same stripping principle evident in the anatomical plates of the *Encylopédie* (fig. 3). Forms were flayed and divested of superfluous ornament. Individuals were pared to *écorchés* by a ruthless peeling. Thus pithed and cored, they were made congruent to an undeceptive ideal nakedness, or to a profound sincerity.[25]

This perpendicular inquisition was challenged by the pleasures of horizontal pursuit. Witness the sensationalistic and surface-bound pantomimes of a Jean-Baptiste Greuze (1725–1805), such as *The Village Betrothal* (Paris, Musée du Louvre, 1761), or of an Angelica Kauffmann (1741–1807), such as *Cleopatra Mourning at Mark Antony's Tomb* (England, private collection, 1769). These artists hunted laterally after fleeting emotions and nervous sensibilities registered upon tender fibers and swiftly communicated to the repercussive exterior.[26] As modern Epicureans and sophists, they pursued the myriad and often nameless shifting expressions that wandered predominantly across the feminine epidermis.[27] Their interest in recording superficial and distracting appearances stood in marked opposition to the grave delving for a single, immutable masculine character, or ahistorical and isolated Lebrunian generic passion. Women, even during the Age of Reason, were still identified with

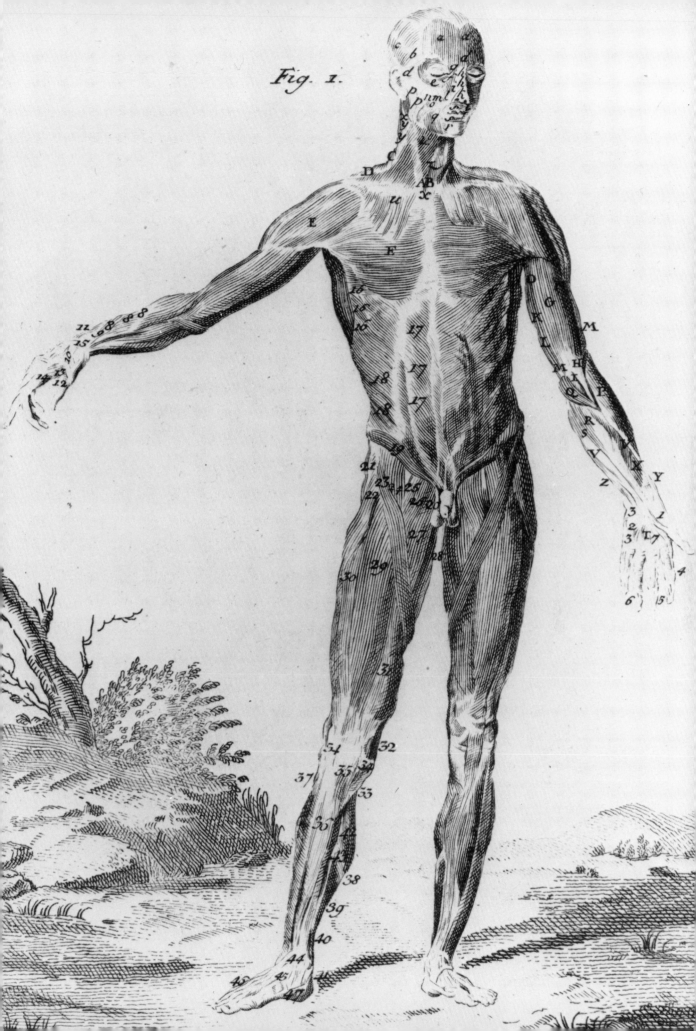

Fig. 1.

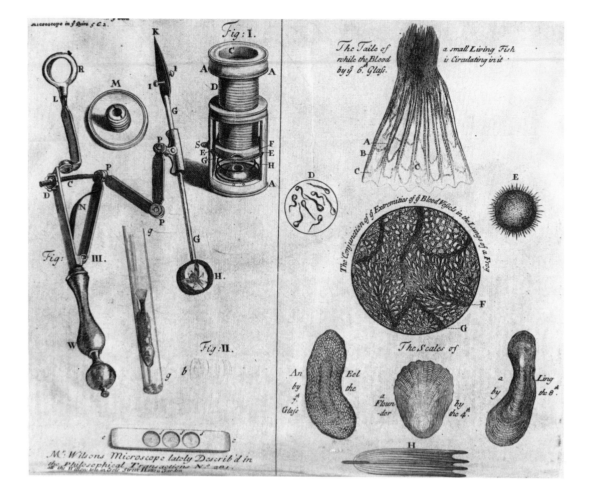

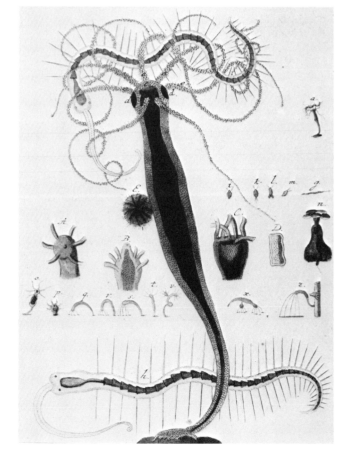

4. John Harris, *Mr. Wilson's Microscope and Microscopic Magnifications,* from *Lexicon Technicum,* 1704. Engraving. (Photo: author.)

5. Martin Frobène Ledermüller, *Reproduction and Multiplication of Fresh Water Polyps,* from *Amusemens microscopiques,* 1768, pl. 82. Colored etching. (Photo: Courtesy National Library of Medicine, Bethesda, Md.)

the Virgilian tag "various and changeable," as inconstant as the wind, as malleable as wax, as dancing as water.[28] The esteem for the level was evident, too, in the serial unfolding in space of Lady Hamilton's posturing "attitudes." In this planar ballet of forms one shape melted and gave way to another. George Romney (1734–1802),[29] in numerous portraits painted after 1782, interpreted Emma's body as a projective screen radiating a filmic succession of classical allusions. Her nonverbal performances were staged before admiring cognoscenti who had come to Naples from throughout Europe. Audience comprehension of antiquity thus became an act of optical, not textual, decipherment. Understanding the past was a matter of time spent watching in the unrolling present.

The impulse to make public the inarticulable and the concealed extended perception dimensionally not only in the artistic sphere but in the scientific as well. Indeed, I wish to argue that the latter set the example and provided the technical images and tropes for the former. The plumb-line prolongation of vision was typified by Felice Fontana's (1730–1805) production of deeply layered—and thus "excavatable"—polychromed anatomical waxes. These lifelike and manipulable simulacra of women and men and their nesting biological parts were exhibited in 1775, and again in 1786. Prepared under Fontana's supervision and in an expressly developed workshop open to visitors, they were intended for private instruction and public display. The first set was shown to great acclaim at Florence's Museum of Physics and Natural History. A second group was subsequently installed at Vienna's medical-surgical military academy, the Josephinium.[30] Nowhere, however, was the penetrating gaze of the natural historian more mesmerically in evidence than in the discovery and copying of the miniature visions hovering beneath the microscope's lens. Anton van Leeuwenhoek's (1632–1723) construction of his first simple microscope or magnifying glass in 1671 enabled him, and countless eighteenth-century biologists, to investigate the "motile" behavior of strange animalcules. He clamped a minute lens ground by hand between two small perforated plates and attached a specimen holder to the apparatus. Thus he, and other experimentalists and instrument makers, were able to observe the silent drama of asexual reproduction occurring "down under" (fig. 4).[31] Similarly, Abraham Trembley's (1710–1784) decapitation of hundreds of fresh water polyps during the 1740s revealed, seemingly across great stretches, an alien submerged world. Through the miracle of enhanced orthogonal vision, strange organisms could be witnessed disporting themselves or, disconcertingly, regenerating whole members from lopped fragments (fig. 5).[32]

6. Albrecht von Haller, *Vivisection*, from *Mémoires*, 1756, frontispiece. Engraving. (Photo: Courtesy National Library of Medicine, Bethesda, Md.)

7. Edward Jenner, *Cowpox Pustules on the Hand of Sarah Nelmes*, from *Inquiry into the Causes and Effects of the Variolae Vaccinae*, 1798, pl. 1. Colored stipple engraving by William Skelton after Edward Pearce. (Photo: Courtesy National Library of Medicine, Bethesda, Md.)

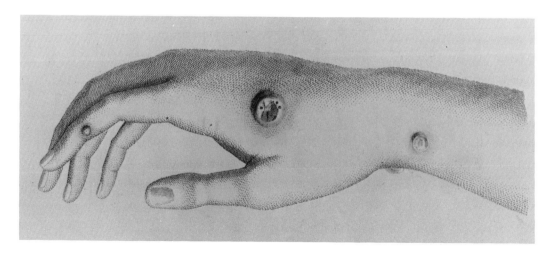

Horizontal observation was also markedly extended in this period. Albrecht von Haller's (1708–1777) cruel vivisectionist researches during the 1750s were performed without anesthesia on living dogs and other animals (fig. 6).[33] Yet, ironically, his exposure of the irritability and sensitivity of muscle fibers was used by vitalist physicians and artists to vindicate human empathy and the existence of delicate feelings. Subtle traces of an underlying tangle of nerves were deposited upon a responsive cushion of flesh.[34] On another front, the physicians Jean-Louis Alibert (1768–1837), Jean Astruc (1684–1766), and Edward Jenner (1749–1823) studied the divisionist ravages wreaked upon a smooth complexion by smallpox, syphilis, and numerous other city or country blights. These grotesque assemblages of unnatural and defiling marks— many unknown to antiquity—poked discolored holes or raised dotted pustules (like the dairymaid's cowpox) in the healthy body's smooth and blended flatland (fig. 7).[35] The systematic classification of spotted diseases in the early nineteenth century identified a host of maculated signs, variegated blisters, blotches, eruptions, and tumors. These pits and pocks constituted a loathesome compendium of the evil or comic disfigurements punctuating the modern stigmatized skin (fig. 8).

8.   Jean-Louis Alibert, *Freckles,* from *Clinique de l'Hôpital Saint-Louis,* 1833, pl. 59. Colored stipple engraving by Tresca after Moreau and Valvile. (Photo: Courtesy National Library of Medicine, Bethesda, Md.)

Antinomies

The eighteenth century, that second "age of discovery," might well be termed the "era of uncovering." That germinal period forecast our current information-rich and collaborative computer epoch. It impelled us in the direction of a minimization of distance and the collapse of space. Its visualization technologies pointed toward the present-day explosion of electronic and laser imagery and the concomitant software to produce and control it.[36] Just as supercomputers enable us to see global structures, many dimensions simultaneously, and the dynamics of hidden functions,[37] the novel scientific instruments and optical devices of the eighteenth century opened windows onto a vast other world.[38] The Enlightenment visualization of knowledge through the invention of innovative visual paradigms—evident in prints and illustrated books more even than in painting and sculpture—similarly invited interactive participation from a broad spectrum of viewers.[39]

Graphical excellence and the creation of sophisticated designs for the display of information were intrinsic to both the understanding and the dissemination of complex data, ranging from cartography to mineralogy.[40] A communications revolution resulted from the enabling reproductive technologies of color printing and aquatint. As we shall see, the latter's expressive potential for punning on the invisible and the visible, the absent and the present, was only first fully realized by Francisco de Goya (1746–1828) (fig. 9).[41] Transformative, too, were the advances achieved in older intaglio methods, such as etching, by innovators like Giovanni Battista Piranesi (1720–1778).[42] The end result of such deeply bitten copper plates and their multiple and varied impressions can be seen, paradoxically, in today's personal computer. The individual user, like the single viewer of a complexly inscribed sheet, may pull up any "window" of data at a given moment. The new technology, based on the permutability and reproducibility of the old, permits the beholder to combine at will decontextualized bits and pieces from worldwide computer networks without ever leaving a private workstation. This supremely Romantic and solitary machine, functioning according to a combinatorial logic, stretches backward to Leibniz and forward to the symbolic and parodic literary compositions of Huysmans and Borges.[43] Visually, however, it had been anticipated by Goya and Piranesi with their creation of a deliberately seamed or patched-together style. This intarsia, or inlay method, was abetted by a pattern-book production that encouraged the manipulation and borrowing of disparate images. The wide circulation of print compendia—models and manuals for the trades and professions—and the uncontrol-

Correccion

9. Francisco de Goya, *Correction,* from
Los Caprichos, 1799, pl. 46. Etching and
aquatint. National Gallery of Art,
Washington, D.C., Rosenwald Collection.
(Photo: Courtesy National Gallery of Art.)

lability of their use initiated a historical revolution resulting in our contemporary cut and paste mentality.[44]

Prophetically, the eighteenth-century viewer's struggle to pierce to the bottom of all blurred visual signals—whether emanating from eroding ancient ruins or the confusing masquerade of fashionably covered modern bodies—seems to be fulfilled in twentieth-century transparent medical visualizations. Computed tomography x-ray imaging (CT), positron emission tomography (PET), magnetic resonance imaging (MRI), and ultrasound now probe noninvasively, but publicly, formerly private regions and occluded and secluded recesses. It remains to be determined, however, just what are the social or political dimensions and the ethical implications of this generalized somatic visibilization of the invisible. Nor should it go unnoticed and undiscussed that prenatal screening for the prints and misprints of inherited health or illness continues into the era of DNA an earlier age's "physiognomic" form of analytical scrutiny. Talk of "codes," "alphabets," "letters," "sequences," "blueprints," and "spelling errors" inscribes venerable metaphors of text and reading into the contemporary screening for genetic diseases and into the testing accompanying reproductive technology.[45] Gene therapy, as a source of hope in the cure of cystic fibrosis and Huntington's disease, or as a tool for prognosis, as in Down's syndrome and Duchenne muscular dystrophy, is not without problems and controversy. The diagnosis and transplantation of "good," "normal" genes into patients in order to carry out the functions of "flawed," "abnormal" genes goes beyond biochemistry to raise the fundamental question of what exactly is a sickness, disorder, or unacceptable deviation from health.[46] I wish, then, also to look beyond the Enlightenment. I want to suggest how an understanding of eighteenth-century mechanisms for the nonverbal communication of "unspeakable" biological events might prove relevant for tackling late-twentieth-century aesthetic, medical, and indeed humanistic issues. Our Postmodern times are preeminently visual times. Ours is now chiefly a postindustrial "service" economy televising and videoing constructed, antisensual, and intangible somatic experiences rather than manufacturing actual tangible objects.[47] Increasingly we contend with disembodied information. We communicate with images of people, with "artificial persons," existing as bites, bytes, and bits of optical and aural messages. Flesh and blood, or tactility, recede in the presence of mediated encounters.

Speeding along this process of desubstantialization is the rapid development of hyperbolic simulation systems. These are currently being perfected by the

VOYAGE OÙ IL VOUS PLAIRA

computer industry to produce "virtual realities" or "virtual environments."[48] Wearing special helmets and gloves, lone visual travelers are immersed in pleasing and compelling simulations or ride around effortlessly in comprehensive three-dimensional illusions.[49] Unlike Captain Cook or La Pérouse—ploughing the resisting waves of the palpable Pacific—their computer-generated helm is controlled by a joystick. Significantly—and beyond the dreams of even the most extravagant eighteenth- or nineteenth-century imaginary voyager—such simulations need not be limited to what can occur in real life (fig. 10). A modern scientific Gulliver could experience existence as a molecule, mingling with other molecules and behaving chemically as they do.[50] Such invented ambients represent the apotheosis of the apparitional and the reification of a fictionalizing *fantasia.* They actualize what I term the eighteenth century's aesthetics of almost. Because of advances in fiber optics technology, the modern excursionist finally has the opportunity to enter without travail, journey through, and exert dominion over an electronically generated pictorial world.[51]

Consequently, we may conclude that Alberti's hallowed metaphor of painting, and of visual representation in general, as a "window" onto nature has definitively disappeared. With it, too, has gone the notion of perspective as distance from that which has been feigned. Telling instances of this metaphor's demise are the contemporary manipulated photographs of Barbara Kruger, Sherrie Levine, and Cindy Sherman.[52] Inspired by the flux and infinite variability of computer-generated graphics, these artists use the camera not in its traditional documentary role as an instrument of truth but as a cerebral tool for the manufacture of deceit. Their scavenged and hybrid illusions make no pretense at relating to some intact aspect of the world or of humanity beyond that fabricated by the media. Ambiguity rules in the new conceptual photography. The compositional principles of merger and takeover reign when no borders or thresholds exist to demarcate the inside from the outside, the phantasmagoric from the "real," the projection from the body.

Much can be gained for the present, then, by the historical investigation of the tendency to collapse all sensory experience into the visual and the human body, specifically, into an assemblage of its projected optical effects. What had been one of the chief forces for enlightenment—making visually accessible inaccessible domains—has turned into the creation of, and demand for, ghostly simulations. The history of this far-ranging *aesthetic* trend toward automated spectralization and the automatic consumption of illusions has yet to be recognized or analyzed in a systematic way.

Behind current methodological and disciplinary debates stretches the shadow of a long tradition composed of different but related contraries. This deeper conflict wears many faces throughout history. In the early modern period, as we shall see, it hardens into a system of antithetical absolutes that I am characterizing as the still unresolved tension obtaining between the visible and the invisible.[53] Physiological insights into "profound" or "obscure" bodily hollows were gained by means of the same relational or comparative system of ruling metaphors that governed eighteenth-century geographical and anthropological discussions concerning distant "foreign" countries and remote "alien" customs. These farfetched analogies depended upon establishing a movement from inferior to superior, appearance to essence, public to private, surface to depth, visual to verbal, known to unknown. Fundamentally, such hierarchical correspondences between the outer and inner of anything devolve upon the fact that the content of one (the ontologically "higher") of the paired terms is invisible, uncertain, or unclear with respect to the other (the ontologically "lower"). Some, but certainly not all, of the myriad incarnations of this fundamental antagonism include that between the mathematical sciences and the technical arts, or between the rational (*episteme*) and the perceptual (*aisthesis*), the noumenal and the phenomenal, the mental and the manual, the theoretical and the practical, the general and the particular, the abstract and the concrete, the geometrical and the experimental, the simple and the complex, the analytic and the synthetic, the normal and the deviant, the well and the sick, physiognomy and pathognomy, soul and body, dissection and combination, sequence and simultaneity, certitude and ambiguity, stasis and mutability, cause and effect, rule and instantiation.

Nowhere is the danger lurking in such stark dualisms more apparent than in the impasse reached by major Romantic artists and writers.[54] The perceived distance between historically conditioned human beings and the ahistorical, transcendent object of their desire—whether situated vertically beyond the stars, sunk within the body, or stretching horizontally into primitive and remote cultures—was so great as to become unbridgeable.[55] Think of the Neoplatonic chasm stretching between the real and the ideal, the unrefined and the refined, illusion and truth, ugliness and beauty, in the works of Caspar David Friedrich (1774–1840), Jean-Auguste-Dominique Ingres (1780–1867), Samuel Taylor Coleridge, and Charles Baudelaire.[56]

The eighteenth century was the first period to systematize these irrevocable antinomies. Opposing ways of looking at the world colored the virulent hostility of "rigorist" and "philosophic" Neoclassical critics toward "laxist" and "sophistic" Rococo artisans.[57] Lord Shaftesbury, the Abbé Batteux, Winckelmann, and Lessing excoriated conspicuously artificial and extravagant manufacture. They termed "deformed" and "unnatural" any egalitarian or truly interdisciplinary hybrids. These dissonant decorative mixtures graced the heteroclite *cabinet de curiosité* (fig. 11). According to unsympathetic critics, the equivocal ornamental grotesque embodied everything that was excessive, contaminated, and "monstrous" about the uncontrolled imagination.[58] Rococo taste produced an epidemic of illicit fanciful joinings. This catching perceptual promiscuity—encouraged by the artist and permissively encouraging to the spectator—licentiously mingled the unlike, heterogeneous "matter" of the arts and sciences in the roving activity of sight. Such optical wandering

TAB. CXIV.

GENESIS Cap. L. v. 2.3.

Iacobus aromate conditus.

I. Buch Mosis Cap. L. v. 2.3.

Der balsamirte Jacob.

G. D. Heuman sculp.

strayed amid minutiae, or things not worth much from a top-down perspective. The function of a free-wheeling vision, roaming among aristocratic toys, can be seen in Jean-Marc Nattier's (1685–1766) portrait of the amateur *physicien* Joseph Bonnier de La Mosson seated in his *cabinet* (fig. 12). The eye flits effortlessly from glinting jars of pickled monsters and eels to mechanical instruments, tasseled swag, closed volume, open sketchbook, and shell of sculpted table leg. The resulting unstable or confusing elision dangerously tied together unrelated objects from different realms conventionally kept isolated. Subversive optical associations flew in the face of that intellectual clarity and distinctness sought by a puristic strain of Neoclassical thought. The monochromatic paradigm of ideal harmony can be pictured as an unequal marriage in which the spiritual and intelligent male partner was superior to the dull and appetite-driven female. In such a union, the superficial envelope or colored "body" of the work of art, like other merely physical bodies, had to deny itself, to become "tasteless." Here is the nub of the rhetoric of

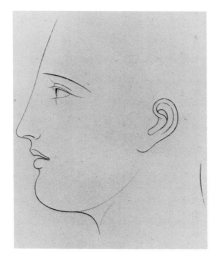

13. Alexander Cozens, *Simple Beauty,*
from *Principles of Beauty,* 1778, pl. 1.
Engraving. (Photo: Courtesy National
Library of Medicine, Bethesda, Md.)

14. Johann Caspar Lavater, *Calculating
Facial Disproportion,* from *Essays on
Physiognomy,* 1792, III, part II, pl. facing p.
271. Engraving by Thomas Holloway et al.
(Photo: Courtesy National Library of
Medicine, Bethesda, Md.)

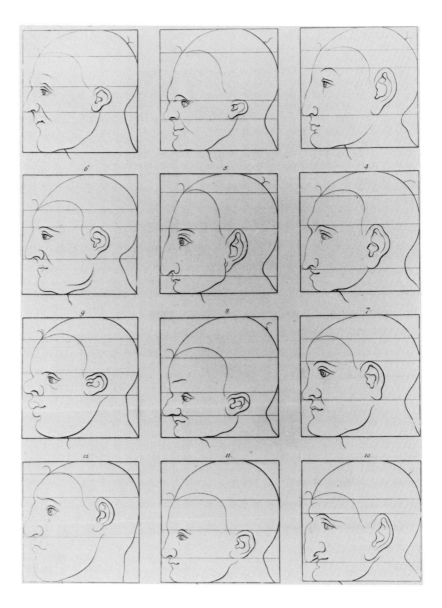

improvement, of the constant summons to earthy matter and pigmented materials to become unobtrusive, to imitate a sanitized and mentalized Nature. In this aesthetic immaterialism, the work of art's unimportant or artful casing was worn lightly, transparently, in the manner of Winckelmann's pure and watery contour. Significantly, the latter became ubiquitous in the shorthand graphism of late-eighteenth-century drawing manuals (fig. 13). Even more desirable was the extinguishing of corporeality after the fashion of Johann Caspar Lavater's dematerializing geometric grid (fig. 14).[59] Like the hermaphrodite, well known to eighteenth-century collectors of ancient coins and gems, modern artifacts were obliged either to blend their material segments or to subjugate their atomistic divisiveness to the partless Idea (fig. 15). Artistic compositions should imitate decorous human behavior. They should act and look either like a seamless androgynous blend of different but coexisting parts or function like a monogamous relationship. The latter was a hierarchical or textual arrangement that sequentially linked opposites according to a vertical scale of values.[60] Both means of bonding antitheses were predicated on the longstanding sociocultural conviction of the supremacy of the rational, the linear, the geometric, the male.[61] Both in the constructed and in the natural sphere, unruly "animal" elements, shapeless feminine "chromatic" appetites, or "passionate" particulars had to be fused into a general equilibrium.[62] The resulting perceptual union was subservient to the dominion of an underlying or overarching "bodiless" cerebral architectonic.[63]

15. La Chau and Le Blond, *Hermaphrodite,* from *Descriptions des principales pierres gravées,* 1780, I, pl. 25. Engraving. (Photo: author.)

An additional pernicious dualism—veristic, congruent words versus fantastic, incongruent images—undergirds this aesthetic debate. Baldly characterized, the schism obtains between lying "paint" and "unvarnished" logic.[64] The latter must "manage" the former by negation or control. This persisting struggle between legible methodology and illegible empirica remains inscribed in the current fate of the nonmeasurable, and thus only probable, fine arts. Despite their public ubiquity in museums, television advertisements, and on the street, images fail to "read" with any certainty. The image/word clash, moreover, reverberates in the current "deconstruction" of art history. In the ferocious process of undoing or subverting supposedly traditional values and concepts, the image is kept subservient to the model of an almighty writing that exceeds and comprehends all other forms of expression.[65] My intention is neither to defend some "conservative" past form of art history, to which I was never attached, nor to praise the demystifying debunking of the "avant-garde." Rather, I question the continuing and unthinking "privileging" of language. This is what I mean by logocentrism. Significantly, it is an attitude inscribed into the very eighteenth-century origins of the activity of *criticism*. For the founding fathers of our discipline—from Alexander Gottlieb Baumgarten (1714–1769) to Immanuel Kant (1724–1804)—it was deemed essential that a corpus of precise, theoretical, "guiding" constructs be developed that were untainted by the inferior sensuous objects under scrutiny. The liberated critic was thus freed from the tyranny of the artist, and himself became a producer and controller of meanings. With the rise in the Renaissance and reinforcement in the late seventeenth century of art as a profession fostered by academies, execution had to be regularized into rules for teaching purposes. The reification of informal precepts into formulaic dicta was coupled to the pedagogical shift from an apprentice relying on the individual demonstration of his master to the student imbibing generally applicable laws.[66] The impact of the increasing sway—from the mid-eighteenth century forward—held by "superior" interpreters of rational systems continues today in the linguistic battles over correct "method" polarizing the humanities and the social sciences. The privileging of such an absolutist and inflexible meta-discourse—despite its espousal of "plurisignifications"—has resulted in rendering invisible the unsystematic, irreducible characteristics of the specific phenomena under study. A relentless spirit of leveling has had staggering effects on current disciplinary arguments ranging from broad canon debates and Great Books advocacy to the specific unyoking of "academic" or "theoretical" art historians from "workaday" museum curators and from practicing artists.

Doubtless, every scientific and humanistic area of study can provide telling examples of the ideological struggle between top-down theorists, propounding universal methods, and bottom-up experimentalists arguing on behalf of the ways, means, and procedures believed dictated by the subject matter itself. The present "methodization" of the humanities by the quantitative social sciences, or their disorienting "pluralization" into solipsistic blur by literary "criticism," is a distant mirroring of a past "geometrization." Desensualization of indistinct phenomena was part of the intellectual anatomization of the flux. The disease of System, or entrenched power, against which the French encyclopedists railed, forced disparate things to combine into a false unity. Reacting to the seemingly mindless, sixteenth-century *Wunderkammer* amassing of multiple fragments, both the René Descartes (1596–1650) of the *Rules* (1637) and the *Meditations* (1640), and the John Locke (1632–1704) of the *Essay concerning Human Understanding* (1690) maintained that general knowledge could be obtained only through an analytical process of separation or abstraction. Responding to the desire for a stabilization of knowledge, they argued for the systematic elaboration and critical analysis of complex experience and compound ideas.[67] Importantly, despite their rationalist or empiricist differences, these seventeenth-century philosophers who contributed so significantly to the Enlightenment and, indeed, to the modern regularization of learning shared the belief in a single method. This universal path was identified with the model provided by the mathematical sciences. So, they reasoned, it must be applied to the subject matter of any discipline whatsoever if we hope to gain cognitive mastery over that discipline.[68] The hegemony of theory in contemporary thought continues to follow their "true way of definition." It favors, even in denial,[69] preexisting rules, laws, and other "systematic" or a priori generalizations in fields where such exactitude is inappropriate.

This book, then, is a history of perception. It focuses on an early constitutive moment in the communications revolution. But it is also a summons to create a new visual discipline or hybrid imaging art-science for the future. It is written in the larger hope of helping to rejoin the specialized and nonspecialized aspects of a humanistic education with the multiple practical realities of a responsible public policy. It aims to reincarnate intellection in sensory

16. **Martin Frobène Ledermüller,**
Magnifying Glasses, from *Amusemens*
microscopiques, 1768, pl. 70. Colored
engraving. (Photo: Courtesy National
Library of Medicine, Bethesda, Md.)

experience. It argues that, on all fronts, there is a pressing need today for an aesthetic and, indeed, an ethic of "embodied" diversity or complexity. Thus, it is dedicated to the revalorization of the "physical," "lesser," or "experimental" halves of those prevailing contraries cited above. It asserts that, whether we realize it or not, the late twentieth century is already in the midst of a paradigm shift of Copernican proportions in which the optical continues to unseat the "solidly" textual from its former position of intellectual, social, and political hegemony. In the video age of depersonalized phantasmagoria, disembodied simulacra, and coolly multiplying computer displays, the problematization of the body may be seen to stand for all formerly tangible— even manual—experiences that have been transformed into weightless apparitions.[70] The invisible generation of luminous streams of discontinuous or continuous 3D arrays by means of an intervening instrumentation means that the body, and indeed all bodies, lose their former indestructible organic spatial and temporal unity. Once-palpable objects have been deprived of their "substance" or "flesh."

When the paradigm of totality itself becomes phantasmal, as I believe it does in the eighteenth century, then all compositions or forms of organization become labile. They function "superficially," like a Leibnizian *ars combinatoria* fashioned from permutable floating fragments.[71] These uprooted and errant aspects possess only a delusory semblance, or provisional appearance, of unity. Let me put it another way. For the Leon Battista Alberti (1404–1474) of the *Della pittura* (1435), representation was a physical, tangible act of illusionistically taking empirica into one's arms (*abbracciare*). Corporeal embracing, seizing, and clasping gathered together the *membra disjecta* of the three-dimensional world.[72] Painting through perspective, line, and contour stabilized, and haptically fixed, the momentary. Consequently, the transitory was made more concrete in art than in external reality. For the George Berkeley (1685–1752) of *An Essay towards a New Theory of Vision* (1709), on the other hand, the activity of sight and its mimetic analogues had become touchless. Vision was the encompassing but divested sweep by the subjective gaze alone of a dreamlike and etherealized field.[73] This profound shift in viewing and recreating the environment owes, I believe, to the proliferation of optical instrumentation. The Enlightenment was the key epoch in the development of its systematic use, both in the fine arts and in technology. Magnifying lenses (fig. 16) of all sorts produced close-up, vivid, incorporeal hyperrealizations more lifelike and intense than full-blooded, but now distant, outer bodies (fig. 17). With the popularization of microscopy in particular, touch dropped out of our visive experience of the world.

36

17.   Francisco de Goya, *The Sleep of Reason Produces Monsters,* from *Los Caprichos,* 1799, pl. 43. Etching and aquatint. National Gallery of Art, Washington, D.C., Rosenwald Collection. (Photo: Courtesy National Gallery of Art.)

A word about my method. This book is organized into six chapters. Although each is headed by a gerund, my approach is not abstract but practical and particular. I continually search for the direct evidence of the relationship between art and medicine. As in an Enlightenment encyclopedia, each section is centered around a constitutive metaphor with its variants and antitheses. Basic to my classificatory scheme is a stratigraphy of increasingly complex relationships that are revealed, however, through lateral cross-references. The foundation of this study rests upon the metaphor of dissection and its anatomical, surgical, and physiognomical cognates. The analytical model of knowing by "tearing apart" fullness or "separating out" discrete physical objects from a plenum leads to a consideration of the metaphor of purification from matter. The second chapter explores the immaterializing emptiness of a bare or "naked" procedure of abstraction, reduction, and refinement. It also takes account of an opposite manner. The material activity of marbling reveled in the production and consumption of luxuriance and superfluity. These "lean" images of deprivation and want, or "fat" images of multiplicity and deviant excess, are predicated on theologically, socially, and culturally constituted conceptions of the normal and the abnormal. Thus the third chapter addresses the problem of the riotous or barbaric grotesque. We see how central the issue of unlawful and confused mixtures was to the Enlightenment in the fascination exerted by monsters, hybrids, hermaphrodites, and caricatures. The question of what produces deformity and defect depended upon one's view of generation. Both in the biological and the aesthetic sphere, the metaphorized polemic over reproduction pitted proper imitation versus improper creation. The debate embraced mental concepts and physical conceptions of all sorts. The part played by the wandering imagination in giving birth to peculiar or idiosyncratic surface marks informs chapter four's dermatological focus on the epidermal metaphor. Chapter five grows out of the eighteenth century's adventurous explorations into subcutaneous developmental processes. It investigates the complex imagery of aggrandizement or diminution arising from microscopic magnifications, reductions, and projections. Finally, the ghostly *pneuma*, "meteorological" or ethereal soul, and misty consciousness will be shown to coalesce in the epiphanic metaphor of apparitional identity. The volatile nervous system—governed by an impressionable *sensibilité* responsive to environmental effluvia—created a new medium or "atmospheric" third world of fleeting emotions and fluid instincts coursing beneath the skin.

These materializations or substantial thoughts will, I hope, configure themselves before the viewer's eyes—as they did at the time of their formation—in their full empirical and theoretical complexity. I assess how, by what means, and for whom they were produced. Through these tropes I elucidate powerful kinds of imagery that have been neglected. In the habitual art historical leap made from the seventeenth to the nineteenth centuries, the very underpinnings of modernism and of contemporary critical debates have been ignored. While I realize the possibilities for a wide margin of error and the perils of omission besetting anyone attempting to do justice to more than one field or country and looking at a broad time frame, I have deliberately chosen breadth without, I think, sacrificing depth. I believe that the sheer size and duration of the problems require such a scale and range. Moreover, I have tried to show—despite the largeness of the task and its uncharted perimeters—that coherence can be found in this abundant and unfamiliar material. Indeed, a new eighteenth century is revealed. Since I have roamed widely into theology, philosophy, biology, and art, this, too, no doubt, leaves me open to criticism. Nonetheless, I think it important to try to draw these variegated phenomena together with the same rich means that were available to the period itself. Since the formation of the *Annales* school of historical studies, it has become fashionable to do specialized and exhaustive studies of every conceivable aspect of social life. These single inquiries have yet to be pulled together. Here, too, the way of metaphorology goes against the tide. This book not only reminds the reader of the intricate formation and surprising prolongation of certain metaphors into the present, but examines the resistances and conflicts between them that reveal their interdependence. Each chapter thus builds on the preceding one and engages issues that were previously sketched but left undeveloped. The fundamental problems remain the same, but they are refracted differently so we constantly gain multiple angles and deeper perspectives.

In sum, my argument moves from a consideration of the substantial, the static, and the tactile to the growing importance, if not value, of the insubstantial, the fluid, and the visual. This push and counterpull between the exponents of depth or surface was evinced in those two profoundly related *practical* professions, the fine arts and medicine. Both were devoted to a discriminating observation of signs and symptoms, to a contextualized pattern recognition, to an informed and refined sensory judgment of appearances or looks. The experimental artist and the clinical physician, unlike the rigid logician and the measuring calculator, shared an eye for gauging the flux of passing effects. Both were obliged to judge particular embodiments in a nonnumerical and nonlinguistic manner. Individual execution or handling precluded being exclusively wedded to abstract or general principles. This deeply shared awareness of operating within an empirical field of experience—increasingly dominated by, and subtly attuned to, the evidence of individual sight—was demonstrated through a performative interaction between viewer and viewed. The well-wrought responsible performance in art as well as in medicine was simultaneously an aesthetic and an ethical enterprise. It depended, and might depend once more, upon the craftsman's supreme skill, or upon handling practiced conscientiously.

This topic is both timely and urgent. It resonates with several recent books that, I believe, address related issues in various fields. One thinks of Wesley Trimpi's study of the mathematization of literary theory since the Renaissance.[74] Stephen Toulmin's illumination of the progressive abandonment of casuistry (or of specific "questions," "cases," "issues") in ethics since the seventeenth century is also apt.[75] Allan Franklin has noted the neglect of experiment in contemporary physics,[76] just as Stephen Jay Gould has pinpointed a growing division in the sciences between what ideally should be complementary endeavors. Gould cited the unnatural separation between a "high" "Athenian" quest, searching for timeless, general, universal laws of nature, and a "low" "Mancunian" experimental puttering, charged with describing and explaining unruly and heterogenous particulars.[77] Howard Margolis, analogously, has countered the opinion that learning functions like propositional logic to suggest, instead, that cognition is about visual pattern recognition, affect, and intention.[78] Bryan G. Norton has lamented, from an environmental standpoint, the demise of natural varieties throughout the West and the dangerous trend toward biological and horticultural simplicity.[79] David Summers has remarked upon the long and oppressive shadow cast by the Renaissance demotion of the mechanical arts. The "mechanical" estimation of particulars was based on judging "merely" with the eyes. This lowly technical and manual ability was compared unfavorably by leading neoplatonizing Humanists to the high ratiocination required for the mental conduct of the precise mathematical sciences occupied with ratios and proportions.[80]

Picture and Text

Finally, it seems appropriate to note the place of this study within my own work. It emerges from two long-standing intellectual preoccupations. The first is my concern to expose the "originary," essentialist, and linguistic metaphors that propelled many major eighteenth-century theoretical endeavors. The urge to return to "the beginning" characterized universal language schemes, grammars of expression, Neoclassical and Neoplatonically derived aesthetic theories, syncretic religious and mythological investigations, and the emerging disciplines of comparative archaeology, anatomy, and anthropology. These diverse attempts at decipherment shared the physiognomic quest to return to the root characters and legible signs fundamental to all modern cultural or social institutions and aesthetic practices.

As demonstrated in *Symbol and Myth*, David Pierre Giottin Humbert de Superville's (1770–1849) pioneering semiotics represented a systematic attempt to arrive at the unconditional. Like many of the artist-theorists of his generation, he desired to image the unimageable, whether located in the distant past or in the intangible present.[81] To that end, he developed a universal hermeneutics of root lines, colors, and vectors. This scheme still remains fundamental to any understanding of the visionary and geometric strain of Romantic abstraction and of *fin-de-siècle* Symbolism. A nonverbal sign system, it claimed that certain concrete symbols such as landscape features, plants, animals, facial traits, gestural traces, tattoos, geometrical diagrams, banners, heraldic blazons, insignia, clothing, architecture, sculpture, and painting unmistakably "say something." Thus Humbert's system was also in advance of the general theory of semiotics devised in the mid-nineteenth century by Charles Saunders Peirce. It further adumbrated early-twentieth-century emblematic totemism, developed by Emile Durkheim.[82] Like these later thinkers, Humbert maintained that a schematic linear and coloristic graphism constituted a repertory of easily recognizable signs charged with potential emotions. Humbert also anticipated the French Structuralist anthropologist Claude Lévi-Strauss's method of abstracting from individuals. Their purpose was identical: to get at perennial (i.e., "unconditional"), not particular, artistic representations, political institutions, and religious situations. Thus aesthetics, ethics, cosmology, ontology, and epistemology were part of a single, figured and configuring, sign system. Its aim was to uncover the corporate or permanent character of human thought and feeling. Not unlike Coleridge or Blake, Humbert heroically, and in the face of a rampant British associationism, attempted to expose the enduring elements of cultural and social life. His daunting enterprise spanned from the mythic beginnings of history to the present.

Eighteenth-century artists and writers realized irrevocably that, as creators, they could never be new again. Literal primacy of invention belonged to the ancients. Absent periods could be *made* present, could be forced to return—witness the century's many revivals and deliberate archaisms—but the moderns could never again be radically original or naturally naive. Their ready-made atomic or "eclectic" art, as Leibniz realized, was generated by the coupling of already existing, mutable parts and was overtly combinatorial. Thus inner nature, the invisible nether psyche, like the unknowable upper realm of pure forms and blank archetypes, could be approached only by means of a negative method. The imperceptible had to be captured upside down, through an antithetical analogy or reverse correspondence. The unseen One or higher No-thing was necessarily opposite to the tangle of scenic material life. Therefore, it was like the disembodied sign, the esoteric zero, and the algebraic symbol. Romanticism's seemingly natural and diffuse organicism disguised the true object of its quest: the crystalline, inorganic, or noumenal "prototype." This singularity was either sunk fathoms "below" chaotic surface flux or riveted whitely and silently "above" the phantasmal chromatic blur. The analytical and "anatomical" procedures of an ancient rationalism were thus remapped onto seventeenth-century quests for method. And, ironically, these logics contributed, in turn, to the formation of a theurgic and irrational Romanticism. Significantly, Porphyry, Iamblichus, Synesius, and, above all, Proclus were the rhapsodic philosophers upon whose work Shaftesbury, Winckelmann, Lessing, Diderot, Blake, Coleridge, Novalis, and Friedrich Schlegel established, or counterestablished, their aesthetics.

Symbol and Myth also prefigures this book in another important way. It contains an interpretation of the body as a system of abstractable signs absolutely inscribed, and thus clearly legible, in a vast *corpus* of ancient and modern monuments. I also pinpointed a massive communications shift occurring in the late eighteenth century. Schemata, diagrams, outlines—as linguistic procedures for pictorial clarification—were increasingly called upon to bring a degree of exactitude to "shapeless" or nongeometrical phenomena. Humbert classified invariable and unambiguous artificial signs, reduced from confusing visual data. During the heyday of Picturesque subjectivism, he argued that this limited graphic vocabulary both signified and aroused specific psychological states. The claim held whether the signs were imprinted on human beings, artifacts, or natural objects. This minimalist and fleshless system of disembodied signs thus represented a decisive turn away from

Lebrunian muscular taxonomy and a stride toward a universal "science" of expression. In his symbolic physiognomics, carefully calibrated linear, directional, and coloristic analogies were interpreted as intrinsic structures or Kantian categories of perception. Grounded in common sensory codes, they could genuinely claim to be unconditional. Humbert's investigation of synesthetic or compound expressions made him the founder of a new science of uncovering surfaces. His brilliant and comprehensive visual semiotics showed that we intuitively understand the physical signs inscribed in faces, bodies, and topographies because they are already intimately ours. Noetics is the internalization of somatics.

The second impetus behind the present study was to look at an alternative model. What was the contemporaneous history and impact of a performative, participatory, and prelinguistic tradition of experiencing the world? One of my goals in *Voyage into Substance* was to look at nature from within, from its own animated internal perspective as an autonomous creating agency.[83] This vitalist view stood in opposition to the anthropocentric rational examination of nature from without, analyzed as a mechanical or dead machine. The growth of experimental science during the Enlightenment emphasized visual evidence, demonstration of function, and actual trials or practice. Thus it provided a salutary physical countermodel to the hegemony of the mental and the conceptual in all spheres of existence. This corporeal or physiological form of knowing was grounded in handling, in the frank manipulation of materials, and in the pleasures and discoveries of sight. Natural history, before its quantification in the 1780s, embodied a lively and engaging method of observation. It recorded topographical encounters with heterogeneous experiences, concrete details, and fragmentary episodes of life. A major intention of *Voyage into Substance* was to show that a Baconian empirical tradition offered different outlooks upon, and possible solutions to, both ancient and modern dilemmas. Neither experimentalism's observational epistemology nor its phenomenological methodology was mired in a pyrrhonic immobilizing skepticism or in a solipsistic relativism. Instead of writing the evolutionary history of modern nature perception from the external and atemporal standpoint of a Platonic-Cartesian geometrical model, I returned to the internal dynamics and fluidity of an Epicurean and sophistic model. This meteorological world view valued the realistic experience one gains over time through active and visceral penetration of a lively, changeable, and organic milieu. Scientific travelers and expedition artists revealed not only a revolutionary geology undergoing violent change, but a disorderly ruined topography. The earth was visibly characterized by barbaric excess, uncivilized superfluity, and grotesque disarray. The discovery, reconstruction, and exhibition of an ungovernable universe contributed to a normative change. An idiosyncratic, eccentric, or peculiar nature became the complex and protean standard for individualistic Romantic forms. It symbolized those metamorphic social, scientific, and aesthetic experiences that deviated from an unearthly ideal.

Voyage into Substance further anticipates the concerns of this book. It exposed the eighteenth-century desire to capture the imperceptible. After 1740, and spurred by meteorological investigations, landscape artists recorded transient, faint, and delicate phenomena. This physical but subtle reality seemed to lie beyond the reach of ordinary perception. Penetrating the thick and turbulent atmosphere, plumbing the sulfurous fumes of mines, piercing the obdurate sides of mountains, represented visual methods for probing the hard and resisting "other." In the process, a soft and malleable world of protean forms was made available to, and for, art. The traveling artist's kinesthesia demanded and elicited a new and complexly fluid state of mind. Locomotion was consonant with the experience of mobile and mutable aspects or shifting effects. Mind and body, consciousness and world seemed, at last, to be on the brink of merging into one another in a phenomenology of flux and reflux. Formerly clear and distinct hard outlines were vaporized into an apparitional succession of borderless appearances without substrate.

The visual encyclopedism of natural historians and experimentalists involved a synthetic *style* of cross-referencing material bits of distant reality. This on-the-spot putting together of unrelated substantial particulars also challenged a Cartesian aesthetics of separation, purity, and ascesis. The distracting fullness and misleading ambiguity of life was not available, or even visible, in a symbolic system valuing compression, attenuation, and noble simplicity. The reductive and static schematization of mathematics, appropriate to the sphere of the hard sciences, seemed misapplied when imposed upon unstable and fluctuating appearances.

Yet the continuing difficulty of unseating the mathematical model from the geophysical domain (and, as we shall see, from the biological sphere) helps to explain why an environmental aesthetic arose so tardily in the West. In the late twentieth century, we continue to find it difficult to esteem the wild, the atypical, the anomalous, the ungeometrical, the unclear, and the indistinct. Further, this unresolved struggle between the particular and the general helps us to comprehend why we continue to live with a sense of profound rupture. We still experience a separation between hidden "superior" stimuli and visible "inferior" effects, between controlling, high-tech media and manipulating, trivial and disembodied messages. At some level, then, it seems that we need to rediscover the eighteenth century's struggles. As in that complex period, we need to revisualize and cognitively reexperience contact with discrete, physical data. But we also have to get in touch with universal networks and systems that have become invisible or unreal.

In sum, the present study emerges from, synthesizes, and broadly extends twenty years of continuous work and thought on the interanimations between art and science from the Enlightenment to the present. Significantly, this work was begun in what was then a nameless area for research. Now, no longer invisible or even odd, that former *terra incognita* has become the study of the eighteenth-century *mentalité* through the pages of the illustrated book. Just as *Symbol and Myth* recuperated the visible, "unconditional" sign language of ancient monuments, and *Voyage into Substance* traced the emergence of self-picturing natural hieroglyphics, so *Body Criticism* focuses on key pictorial strategies for externalizing the internal. The difficulties of imaging the body illuminate that supreme representational problem: how does one seize the liquid inner and outer of things? How do we gain visual knowledge and come to imaginatively possess all that cannot be consumed, or subsumed, by words? This latest volume, therefore, should be seen as rounding out a trilogy, one whose dominant theme has been the increasing visualization of knowledge in the modern period.

1 DISSECTING

Searching Operations

The Galenic conception of anatomy as an "opening up in order to see deeper or hidden parts" drives to the heart of a master problem for the Enlightenment.[1] How does one attain the interior of things? Anatomy and its inseparable practice of dissection were the eighteenth-century paradigms for any forced, artful, contrived, and violent study of depths. Metaphors of decoding, dividing, separating, analyzing, fathoming permeated ways of thinking about, and representing, all branches of knowledge from religion to philosophy, antiquarianism to criticism, physiognomics to linguistics, archaeology to surgery (fig. 18). Analogies of dissection, specifically, functioned on two interrelated levels. The literal, corporeal sense derived from the tactile cuts inflicted by actual instruments. Digging knives, invading scissors, sharp scalpels mercilessly probed to pry apart and distinguish muscle from bone. The figurative sense played upon the allusion to violent and adversarial jabbing. Such excavation stood for an investigative intellectual *method* that uncovered the duplicity of the world. Discursive thought called upon powers of baring abstraction whereby the lowly particular was mentally separated from the elevated generality. The trivial predicate was severed from the significant subject, the unimportant individual was subtracted from the important universal.[2] Both meanings shared the connotation of a searching operation performed on a recalcitrant substance. One involved manual probing, the other cerebral grasping. Each suggested the stripping away of excess by decomposition and fragmentation for the purpose of control.[3] The messiness of the

Tangible _____

adj., Perceptible by the touch. Tangibility, *the quality of being perceived by touch.*
Dr. Johnson, *Dictionary*

Tactile _____

adj., Said sometimes of what might fall under the sense of feeling or touch.
Diderot and D'Alembert, *Encyclopédie*

18. Anne-Claude Philippe, Comte de Caylus, *Body Fragments Resulting from Surgery (?)*, from *Recueil d'antiquités*, 1752–1767, II, p1. 51. Engraving. (Photo: author.)

body, as well as the unruliness of everyday life, were thus managed by the use of either a reducing tool or an analytical system. The immobilized specimen under scrutiny could neither hide nor escape.

Paradoxically, what I am terming the anatomical "method" continues to live on in the twentieth-century informed environment and the nontactile age of the electronic machine. The computer-mediated milieu renders the body nakedly public. Pervasive monitors fulfill the promise for a transparent workplace latent in Jeremy Bentham's panopticon (1787).[4] Similarly, one result of the new noninvasive imaging technologies in the area of medicine is the capability of turning a person inside out. If the late nineteenth century developed the photographic sounding of the living interior through endoscopy, gastroscopy, cystoscopy, and, most dramatically, X rays,[5] the late twentieth century revealed its dark core three-dimensionally through MRI projections. Using radio waves and magnetic fields, this technique for painlessly exploring morphology nonetheless raises the specter of universal diaphaneity. It conjures up foreboding visions of an all-powerful observer who has instant visual access to the anatomy, biochemistry, and physiology of a patient. Will this open-ended trend toward complete exposure give rise to the same sense of vulnerability, shame, and powerlessness that the eighteenth century associated with anatomization?

It is with an eye to such current implications that this chapter proceeds. The tension between the manual and the mental sides of the anatomical metaphor, between handling and cognition, will be seen as fundamentally connected to the rise of physiognomics as the "universal science" of the Enlightenment. An analytical and dichotomous way of knowing the mind through the body, physiognomics functioned like an annihilating lexical "criticism." Critical inquiry dismantled and deconstructed the somatic "text." Further, and not unlike the detecting eighteenth-century connoisseur, physiognomists from Cureau de La Chambre to Lavater attempted to distinguish specious human copies, illusory appearances, painted fakes and frauds, from true character and unvarnished being. Lavater's and especially Camper's stress on mathematical accuracy and technical "expertise" linked them to the metric revolution. We shall take note of the increasing role played by measurement, quantification, norms, and standards in late-eighteenth-century moral and aesthetic matters. Lichtenberg's hermeneutics of variegated surfaces was a lonely counter to the new formal and social calculus for cutting through confusing experiences. Pathognomics distinguished between a forcible delving

inside corpses and the subtle attainment of an animated and moving inwardness acquired over the course of time. Lichtenberg experientially pursued not
geometrical abstractions, but real urban characters displaying the body in
context and in mutation.

At the beginning of the eighteenth century, anatomy became the basic science
for surgeons. And, as William Chambers noted in the *Cyclopaedia*, *surgery*
consisted "in operations perform'd by the hand for the cure of wounds and
other disorders." As a profession, it was divided into speculative and practical
branches. The latter did in effect what the former only taught. If dissection
in anatomy involved the "operation of cutting and dividing the parts of an
animal body with a knife and scissors, etc. in order to see and consider each
of them a-part,"[6] practical surgery was similarly dominated by the activity
of the hand. It rejoined what had been separated (synthesis). It divided with
discernment those parts whose union was prejudicial to health (diaresis).
Finally, it extracted with art foreign bodies (exeresis) and added and applied
what was wanting (prosthesis).[7]

Significantly, it was not medicine but surgery that was progressive during
the eighteenth century. Surgeons, not physicians, taught anatomy in special
schools through dissections carried out by titular and adjunct demonstrators.[8]
This pride in their autonomous power to instruct was commemorated by the
bloodless scene represented taking place in Jacques Gondouin's (1737–1818)
twelve-hundred-seat anatomy theater in the Paris Ecole de Chirurgie. The
college was designed in 1765 by the personal architect to Louis XV and
erected between 1769 and 1775. In 1780, Gondouin's edifice was engraved
after his drawings by Poulleau for a handsome publication (fig. 19)[9] Doctors
were limited to looking at the face, tongue, excrement, taking the pulse,
assessing the heat and moisture of the skin. But, as the scene in Gondouin's
amphitheater celebrated, surgeons were akin to painters, sculptors, and architects. Their dedication to the education of the eye in order to capture fleeting
signs and symptoms was similarly coupled to the training of an acute sense
of touch.

The simile likening the excellent medical practitioner to the hand of God
runs from Hierophilus to Ambroise Paré.[10] It was visually embodied in
Rembrandt's *Anatomy Lesson of Dr. Tulp* (The Hague, Mauritshuis, 1632),[11]
and persisted in the pointing Rembrandtesque *ostensor*-magus of Jacques

Gamelin's *Anatomy Theater* (fig. 20). The subtle varieties and refined manip-
ulations of the surgeon included the application of different finger pressures,
types of pinching, stroking, deep and superficial palpations. These orches-
trated movements were first codified during the 1720s by René Croissant de
Garengeot (1688–1759). This masterful Master of Arts and Surgery, Royal
Demonstrator at the Académie de Chirurgie in Paris, and Fellow of the Royal
Society of London, trained a generation of French and English dissectors.
He showed his students how to use their hands, and initiated them into the
advantages and disadvantages of different styles of operating.[12]

This innovative methodization of handling, based on actual experience, was
propagated in numerous pedagogical treatises published in France and England. The *Traité des opérations de chirurgie* (1720), or *Treatise of Chirurgical
Operations* (in the 1723 London edition), offered a theory and a praxis for the

proper conduct of an operation. Nor did it neglect the minute description of kinds of bandages, plasters, and types of sutures promoting postoperative healing.[13] But it was the *Splanchnologie, ou l'anatomie des viscères* (1728), with its appended dissertation on the origins of surgery, that is important for our purposes. In this insightful and passionate defense of his art, Garengeot distinguished surgery from medicine. He attributed to the former the latter's supposed primacy and upstart nobility. The French surgeon located its venerable origins in the Egyptian custom of embalming (fig. 11),[14] and in the Greek proficiency at healing the wounds of epic heroes. A leitmotif of this apology was the dignity of manual dexterity and informed labor. "Capable hands," "the activity of the hand," "the work of the hand," or sensitive and intelligent manipulations, were stipulated to be the basis not only of surgery but of medicine in general.[15]

Significantly, the *Splanchnologie* was also a lament over the rupture between the two disciplines. First introduced by Hippocrates, the division widened because of the rise of specialization. Eventually, the victory of specialists over general practitioners completely severed the exercise of the hand, accurate observation, and the knowledge deriving from the direct experience of the body, from dietetics and the pharmacological making and dispensing of drugs. Garengeot blamed "the public" for forcing these *artistes* to abandon all segments of the profession not distinctively their own, and to focus solely on one malady and its remedies.[16] This disintegration of an original disciplinary unity occurred not only because of consumer demand, or because diseases and learning proliferated beyond any one doctor's competency, but because of institutional factors. When Louis VII founded the University of Paris in 1140, medical surgeons were not admitted. These "clinicians," who visited the sick in their homes because they could not, like physicians, receive patients in their quarters, remained attached to their humble craft College of St. Cosmas. "Theoretical" physicians, on the other hand, were incorporated into the University's Faculty of Arts. Subsequently, they created their own organization modeled after the autonomous Law Faculty. For Garengeot, the formation of a distinct Faculté de Médecine guaranteed an irrevocable divorce. Physicians could now give themselves up to lofty speculations propounded disembodiedly in universities. Menial surgeons, conversely, were relegated to "lowly" handwork, the treatment of "external" diseases, and the care of the impoverished sick. Since physician-academics were no longer obliged to practice surgery, *they could not know its beauties & subtleties, which ordinarily do not manifest themselves except in those who exercise it with talent, & consequently [they] could generate in their art only a multitude of systems* [foule de sistêmes] *that were successively destroyed as a new one appeared.*[17]

Garengeot made plain that this separatist contagion was not limited to France. Indeed, we shall see it was not even limited to the art of medicine. According to his survey, foreign doctors also neglected the actual exercise of surgery in order to preserve the honorific title of theorist-physician. Ironically, while doctors ceased the practice of their art, they retained the right to teach it![18] Only in Paris did surgeons maintain both their craft and the brevet to demonstrate and publicly instruct. This happy exception led not only to the establishment in 1731 of the Académie Royale de Chirurgie and, in 1750, to the Ecole Pratique de la Dissection,[19] but to the emergence of Paris as the pan-European center for advanced surgical studies.

Garengeot's perceptive history of the progressive disjunction between theory and practice, intellect and knack in medicine had no single artistic counterpart. Nonetheless, the trajectory he traced was strikingly similar to the Neoclassical division between managing brain and tricking craft. One could argue, as I shall in different ways throughout this book, that the longstanding tension between the "practical" visual and the "theoretical" textual became, during the course of the eighteenth century, an untraversable abyss. We are still attempting to bridge it. The anatomical *method* increasingly asserts its superiority over the merely sensuous.

Like surgery, the manual fine arts comprised useful human skills. In the Platonic and especially the Neoplatonic tradition, however, this mechanical adroitness was associated with subrational and opinionative faculties. Its deceptive domain was that of blurring sensory judgment and vagrant corporeal imagination. Nor did such sleights of hand require the high probing intellection demanded of any *episteme* or science.[20] This is not to deny that antiquity occasionally valued the maker of pots or the fabricator of verses. Dio Chrysostom praised the workman's competence capable of transforming material substances by his skillful touch.[21] Pagan mystery cults relied on ritual gesture, magic benediction, and the embodiment of holy forces in an *apotropaion*, signifying incarnated divine speech, such as the Sabazios hand.[22] The tactile analogy between surgery and the visual arts most pertinent for the eighteenth century, however, was not that of divine powers visible in accomplished skillfulness, but the moral activity of dissecting and cutting. Think of the dread anatomical table for the punitive dismemberment of criminals.[23] Remember, too, the allegorized surgeon's theater displayed in Gamelin's frontispiece (fig. 20) to the *Ostéologie* (1779). These lugubrious settings visually exhorted spectators to know themselves through the charnel-house sight of skeletons or decomposing cadavers.[24] As zones of morbidity, they corresponded to a new function of the studio as an admonitory museum of mortality, and to a new erudite critic curious to the point of cruelty. These philosophical investigators hunted for the unfathomable with uninhibited mental fingers. They ignored Augustine's authoritative dictum that the human body was an aesthetic unity.[25] Anatomy, as "the science of subcutaneous parts," of external forms and underlying structures, of the precise composition of the human frame, became the platonizing method for dispelling illusion from Richardson to Camper. According to the surgeon P. N. Gerdy's *Anatomie des formes extérieures* (1829)—grounded in Camper's theories—anatomy functioned like an enlarging glass. It magnified the smallest detail, rendering distinct hidden morphologies "in spite of the skin which veiled them." It permitted the artist to observe more than he could conventionally see. He was thus able to represent forms concealed beneath an occluding matter more faithfully because they were now "clear to his mind."[26]

This expository premise similarly undergirded the elder Jonathan Richardson's *Art of Criticism* (1719).

Nature must be the foundation that must be seen at the bottom; *but nature must be raised, and improved, not only from what is commonly seen, to what is but rarely, but even yet higher, from a judicious, to a beautiful idea in the painter's mind, so that greatness and grace may shine through.*[27]

We will return to this notion of art criticism as metaphoric dissection. But first we must understand how this way of thinking about forms *in profundis* was shaped by the overriding importance of graphic means of reproduction. Intaglio printing, especially, was central to the eighteenth-century habit of looking at the top and bottom of things. Moreover, graphic operations were resolutely manual in their reliance on gouging burins and scapers, puncturing needles and corrosive acids, burnished surfaces and varnished depths. Tunneling printmaking techniques embodied the surgical, indeed the instrumental capacities of the visual arts to exhibit and display mercilessly. Even the etymology, so important to a primitivist century interested in the pursuit of cultural roots, was apt. Thus the French wood engraver Jean-Martin Papillon (1698–1776), in his history of *Gravure en bois* (1766), connected *graphein* to Celtic runes and Egyptian hieroglyphics engraved on stones, metal tablets, or bark. This term denoted the physical activity of burying or digging into resisting surfaces. Encaustic painting was also mined for its excavatory techniques. Antiquarians, such as the Comte de Caylus and the anglicized painter Fuseli, passionately sought its secret recipes. Papillon surmised that the ancients burned trenches into a wooden panel. "The hollow of this type of engraving" was then inlaid with wax or colored enamels.[28]

On another front, the master engraver William Hogarth (1697–1764), in the introduction to the *Analysis of Beauty* (1753), and with the acknowledged assistance of his physician friend, Dr. Benjamin Hoadly, developed an ingenious scheme for getting inside forms. Practicing a kind of mental dissection appropriate to a satirist, he conceived opaque and solid bodies as made up of thin shells or removable peels. Once imaginatively projected inside or below the surface, he gained a panoramic view. From the center, he could scan any object's underside, probe its vacancies or densities. Certainly, Hogarth's admiration for intricacy and complexity went against the Italianate taste of the Richardsonian connoisseur and the simplifying anatomical method. Yet his conceptualization of a tangible entry into material forms owed to the anatomist. Transparency was achieved by the mind's traveling downward and "scooping" out interiors.[29] Hogarth adored hollow shapes: bodies, bones, horns. Consequently he invented a design tool, the serpentine line, for bringing their muscular twistings and winding concavities and convexities to light.[30] The engraved trace itself was nothing more than an empty vein or tubular fiber. Waiting to be filled with ink, it was literally synonymous, for William Blake (1757–1827), with art as energetic execution. It symbolized the artist's ability to realize, or imbue with life, whatever he conceived. Blake proudly declared: "I defy any Man to cut cleaner strokes than I do, or rougher where I please."[31]

This expert concern with the physical mechanics of design, paradoxically, linked the illuminator-poet's tangible visions to the down-to-earth dissections and animal paintings of his older contemporary, George Stubbs (1724–1806). Stubbs's deliberately passionless and empirical likenesses of thoroughbred dogs and horses reeked neither of taxidermy, tanning, nor of decaying anatomical preparations. Yet he, too, in searching "portraits" like the *Whistlejacket* and *Frieze of Mares and Foals* (Collection Earl Fitzwilliam, 1762), practiced an "infernal method." He exposed on the exterior of the canvas the stilled *écorché* normally hidden beneath the pelt.[32]

No graphic works, however, better served to disseminate the habit of seeing above and below ground than the many publications devoted to the reproduction of antique cameos and struck coins.[33] Not only did the eighteenth century largely derive its formal and iconographical knowledge of Greek and Roman antiquity from the study of small, often exquisitely wrought gems, but it also learned from them the glyptic techniques of the past. Collectors and antiquarians were fascinated by the question of how ancient craftsmen performed their lithic dissections. How did they contrive those tiny figures miraculously emerging from the stone? Johann Lorenz or Laurent Natter (1705–1763), in his *Traité de la méthode antique de graver en pierres fines* (1754), provided an important demonstration of the surgical implications associated with the intaglio method. Taking a well-known head of *Jupiter Serapis* (fig. 21) found, as Natter said, in almost every famous collector's cabinet, he provided instructions for its manufacture according to modern methods. The face was schematically reduced into geometric regions allowing the buried features to be systematically excavated. Using a bow drill rather than a diamond point, the modern artisan first "digs gradually into the stone until reaching the requisite depth for the eyes." Continuing the visibilization of the concealed anatomical topography, he dug hollows for hair and beard. Smaller tools were needed for the forehead, narrower gravers for the nostrils and eyebrows. The problem of precision burrowing and the fear of gouging too deeply also preoccuppied Natter in his description of a beautiful, vermilion-colored *Athlete* carved on a jacinth or beryl (fig. 22). It had graced the collections of Clement V and Baron Stosch and now belonged to Viscount Duncannon. For Natter, this gem had no equal in size or perfection or—because of its almost flat surface—in difficulty of execution. The profile view of the standing nude indicated that the artist took advantage of adversity. The stone was probably too thin to be carved convexly. He was obliged to create the necessary depth for the head by tilting the figure forward, thus literally allowing a hidden aspect of the body to be brought to light.[34]

Natter's treatise was doubly about the art of reproduction. It was a duplicable compendium or encyclopedia (one of many, as we shall see) indebted to the technology of the printmaker. Simultaneously, in its subject matter, it was both an embodiment of the activity of engraving and a means for conveying technical information. It was also part of a larger movement beginning in the sixteenth and seventeenth centuries that employed engravings as lowly graphic carriers, or mere illustrations, of scientific and technical information. Such prints of translation had serious rivals in original prints of invention, or etchings, eagerly sought by collectors.[35] This development led during the course of the eighteenth century to an increasing disjunction. There was a

II.

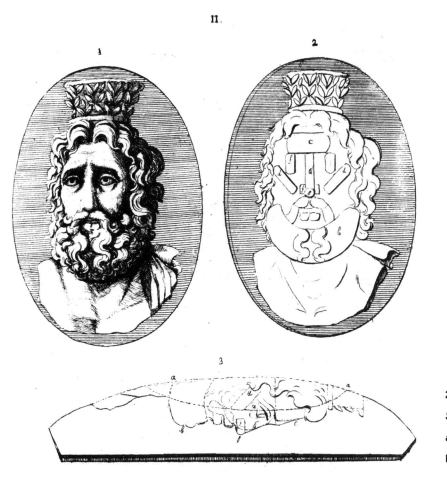

21.   Laurent Natter, *Head of Jupiter Serapis,* from *Traité de la méthode antique,* 1754, p1. 2. Engraving by Hemerich. (Photo: author.)

22.   Laurent Natter, *Athlete,* from *Traité de la méthode antique,* 1754, p1. 25. Engraving by J. Fougeron. (Photo: author.)

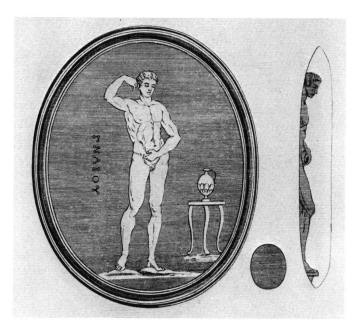

23. Giovanni Battista Piranesi, *Tempio della Tosse near Tivoli*, from *Vedute di Roma*, 1764 (?), pl. 69. Etching. (Photo: author.)

public medium, devoted to unimaginative copying and transmitting of secondary imagery for an educational or "reference" purpose. And then there was a seemingly "irresponsible" private medium, free to register the capricious motions of an individual artist's *fantasia*. One of the major and I believe still unrecognized contributions of that tireless Venetian etcher, Giovanni Battista Piranesi (1720–1778), was his use of the etching needle as a creative surgical tool to uncover information about an otherwise irretrievable past. In short, he shouldered and transformed the menial expository tasks formerly assigned to engraving. Thus he defied the general cultural trend toward separating the informative from the imaginative. More importantly, for our purposes, his discarding of the harmonizing evenness of tone and stiff linear web characteristic of earlier engraved architectural and archaeological publications owed to the visual strategies of retrieval intrinsic to anatomical publications.

Piranesi's radical experimentation with etching, a corrosive chemical process for biting a copperplate, permitted him to perform perceptual rescue work. He artistically unearthed the mutilated corpus of Italian antiquity. Note, too, that William Blake later termed his own acid stereotype process the "infernal"

method. It required printing, or exposing to light, the drawing which literally had been buried beneath an impervious ground.[36] Unlike modern archaeological restorations, Piranesi's paper excavations in black and white did not despoil eroding monuments of their pathos. They continued to be marred by "suffering" surfaces, stuccos, ornament, and even aging dirt (fig. 23). From the countless walls, temples, baths, amphitheaters of the *Antichità Romane* (1756), to the Augustan and Baroque monuments of the *Delle Magnificenza ed Archittetura de' Romani* (1760), to the subterranean chambers, cisterns, and corridors of the *Descrizione e disegno dell'emissario del Lago Albano* (1762), Piranesi uncovered and retrieved the decaying body of the ancient and modern city. Wielding the etcher's needle like a scalpel, he applied surgical procedures taken, I believe, from medical illustrations, to turn the still-living fabric of architecture inside out (fig. 24). Significantly, Vesalius's pathos-laden nudes had been recently reengraved and reinterpreted. This occurred, first, with Gerard de Lairesse for Govert Bidloo. Second, William Cowper (1660–1709) "borrowed" the originals, as did Jean Wandelaer for Bernard Albinus's (1697–1770) Leiden edition of the *De Humani Corporis Fabrica* (1725).[37] Together, these volumes constituted the most beautiful anatomical atlases of the eighteenth century. It was perhaps from Cowper's revision of Vesalius that

24. Giovanni Battista Piranesi, *So-Called Temple of Minerva Medica,* from *Vedute di Roma,* 1778, p1. 74. Etching. (Photo: author.)

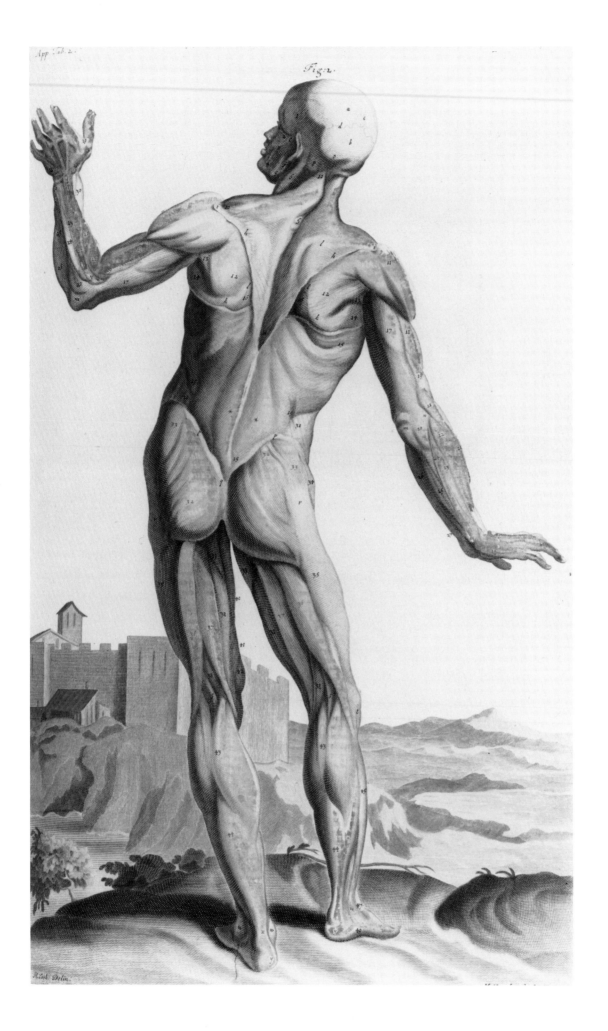

Piranesi learned to mobilize the muscled architectural dead as *écorchés* (fig. 25).[38] Flayed bodies became analogues for temples peeled of their marble. Once the rind was removed, they exhibited the fissures and channels of underlying rubblework (fig. 26).

In an important way, Piranesi resembled Vesalius, who was the first anatomist to unite the separate functions of lecturer, dissector, and practical demonstrator. Similarly, the etcher was the foremost defender, delineator, and archaeologist of Rome. As patient *ostensor*, he, too, invited participation from his spectators. The architect felt out structure through pointing "fingers" of light and shade, sharp and faint focus. In this visual and manual process of fleshed-out, not diagrammatic, showing, Piranesi emulated the Renaissance anatomist and his masterful eighteenth-century successors.[39]

Further, the intaglio process of etching permitted him to take "physiological" soundings. These probes registered superficially the deep reaction of various architectural "tissues" to longer or shorter exposure to acid, to more or less delicate or rough stimulation by the etching needle. Thus the vaulted sub-

25. William Cowper, *External Muscles and Diverse Parts of the Human Body*, from *Anatomia Corporum Humanorum*, 1750, appendix, p1. 2. Engraving by Van der Grecht after H. Cock. (Photo: Courtesy National Library of Medicine, Bethesda, Md.)

26. Giovanni Battista Piranesi, *Temple of Cybele (Vesta)*, from *Vedute di Roma*, 1778, p1. 50. Etching. (Photo: author.)

27. Giovanni Battista Piranesi, *Temple of the Sybil, Tivoli,* from *Vedute di Roma,* ca. 1762, p1. 63. Etching. (Photo: author.)

28. Leopoldo Marco Antonio Caldani, *Venous and Arterial Systems,* from *Icones Anatomicae,* 1813, III, part II, p1. 207. Engraving by Felix Zuliani. (Photo: Courtesy National Library of Medicine, Bethesda, Md.)

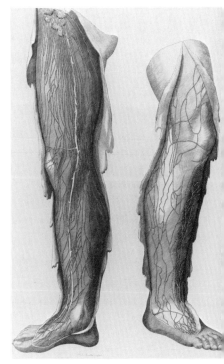

structure of the *Temple of the Sibyl* at Tivoli was plunged into shadow in contrast to the textured common stonework minutely searched out by the raking light (fig. 27). Piranesi's experimental method for visibilizing the "irritability" of the ancient fibers on metal plates was identical to the inductive procedures of his Hallerian contemporaries. One thinks, specifically, of Felice Gaspar Ferdinand Fontana (1730–1805) and of Leopoldo Marco Antonio Caldani (1725–1813) (fig. 28).[40] Like Caldani, Piranesi captured immaterial motion, or impalpable transience, by resorting to palpable pokes tearing the epidermal veneer. His view of the shreds and tatters of the *Baths of Caracalla* (fig. 29) unzipped the dark interior. Similarly, the technique was used by Caldani to pare away the sculptural stocking of the dermis in order to exhibit the stringy arterial and venous systems. But the plates to Caldani's monumental nine-volume *Icones Anatomicae* were published by Picotti in Venice only between 1801 and 1814. They were thus too late to have influenced the etcher, but not to have been influenced by him. The anatomical imagery conveyed an architectural sense of fractured blocks, not wounded flesh, of stony herms wearing flanged capes of skin (fig. 30). The lithic iconography suggested a reliance on Piranesi's innovative pictorial metaphors of archaeological ruin. One finds the same elegiac and metonymic deployment of inter-

29. Giovanni Battista Piranesi, *The Baths of Caracalla*, from *Vedute di Roma*, 1769, pl. 77. Etching. (Photo: author.)

30. **Leopoldo Marco Antonio Caldani,** *Venous and Arterial Systems,* from *Icones Anatomicae,* 1813, III, part II, p1. 226. Engraving by Felix Zuliani. (Photo: Courtesy National Library of Medicine, Bethesda, Md.)

rupted fissured friezes and partially subsided truncated columns. Both invoked the invisible integrity of an absent corporeality and grandeur (fig. 31).[41]

Piranesi presented the actual arduous and lengthy process of physical exploration that stood behind the preparation of these large and informative plates. The visual difficulty of making one's way was consonant with the artistic difficulty of graphically recreating past forms. The piecemeal and motley nature of the act of retrieval was experienced corporeally by the beholder, who was encouraged to spend time looking and wandering among the *membra disjecta* of miscellaneous fragments. The aesthetic and pedagogical power of these hieroglyphic images, then, lay in the printmaker's ability to compact, abbreviate, and synthesize complex temporal and spatial events without blurring differences. He was aided in this task by the example of medical imagery.

Piranesi, I believe, transplanted three "surgical" strategies into the domain of archaeological publication. First, he made use of accidental holes or "wounds" gaping in the sides of deteriorating masonry to allow glimpses of their internal structure, an otherwise concealed aspect of the building (fig. 32). This temporal method for revealing minute components of the fabric, and for highlighting the area of special interest by leaving it nakedly exposed, may well derive from a tradition of anatomical wax sculpture. In the eighteenth century, it was practiced most notably by Fontana. In 1775, this collaborator of Caldani's was called by the Grand Duke of Tuscany to create a Cabinet of Physics and Natural History in the Pitti Palace. The museum constituted a gigantic encyclopedia of organic facsimiles. The famous figures were elegantly dressed and coifed and displayed in blue taffeta-lined rosewood cases. Fabricated by Clemente Susini (1754–1814) under Fontana's direction, they were intended for the teaching of anatomy. The fame of these lifelike models, not decayed by the customary preservation in alcohol, transcended the frontiers of Florence and Bologna. Examples found their way into collections in Vienna, Montpellier, Pavia, Paris, and London (fig. 33).

Although too late in date for Piranesi to have been directly influenced by this set, the Italian origins of ceroplastics went back to the late seventeenth century. Their popularity during the Enlightenment was specifically related, I believe, to the eighteenth-century phenomenon of color printing. Count Francesco Algarotti (1712–1764), world traveler, art patron, antiquarian, student of natural history and mathematics, offered important evidence for the existence of such simulacra in Piranesi's day. The *Essai sur la peinture* (1769)

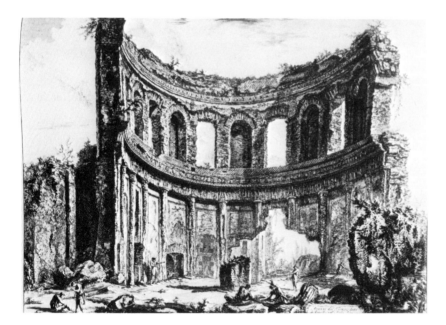

31. Giovanni Battista Piranesi, *Temple of Vespasian,* from *Vedute di Roma,* 1769, pl. 49. Etching. (Photo: author.)

32. Giovanni Battista Piranesi, *Hadrian's Villa, Tivoli, the Smaller Palace,* from *Vedute di Roma,* 1748, pl. 85. Etching. (Photo: author.)

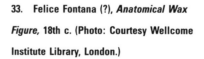

33. Felice Fontana (?), *Anatomical Wax Figure,* 18th c. (Photo: Courtesy Wellcome Institute Library, London.)

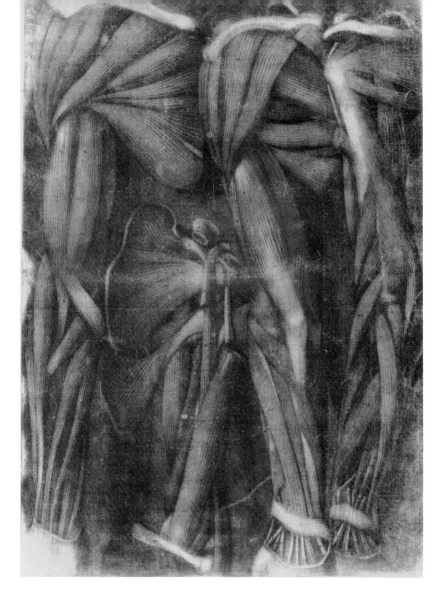

34. Jacques Gautier Dagoty, *Assemblage of Legs and Feet,* from *Essai d'anatomie,* 1745, pl. 50. Multiple-plate mezzotint. (Photo: Courtesy Resource Collections of the Getty Center for the History of Art and the Humanities.)

advocated the dyeing of different muscles to prevent the artist from becoming confused in his study of the body. A familiarity with polychrome waxes seemed to underly his proposal that "one could color anatomical figures the way one illuminated maps to mark the borders and provinces which compose a state, & the countries subject to the rule of each sovereign."[42] If not through Algarotti, then simply by renown, Piranesi must have been aware of the well-known specimens of Gaetano Zumbo (1656–1701), Cosimo III's artist in wax. Zumbo's famous Baroque scenes of plague devastation and allegorical putrefaction, however, were transformed by Fontana into a scientific exhibition of automata. The human system was viewed narrowly and in depth. Not only the cadaver in its entirety, but bones, muscles, nerves, and veins were laid out in Fontana's dark and secular sanctuary. His studio of the biologically damned epitomized the scientific laboratory well before Mary Shelley's factory for genetic engineering, described in *Frankenstein or the*

35. Giovanni Battista Piranesi, *The Baths of Caracalla*, from *Vedute di Roma*, 1748/ 1778, p1. 76. Etching. (Photo: author.)

Modern Prometheus (1817).[43] Neither amusement *cabinet de figures de cire*, like that of Philippe-Guillaume Mathé Curtius (1737–1794) opened at the Palais-Royal in 1783, nor a Madame Tussaud London gallery of crime, Fontana's museum displayed a calm corporeal purity susceptible to corruption, a fragile beauty in ruins.[44] Consequently, in their shared educational, not theological, attitude toward bodily or architectural parts, Fontana and Piranesi were kindred spirits of the Enlightenment. The models' sequentially removable nesting organs, the constant dialectic between somatic interior and exterior, the doubling overlay of immediate and remote structure, and the contrived cavities, all operated like Piranesi's masonry apertures.

Piranesi's second "dissective" strategy was to exhibit multiple images limblike on the same plate. The method was characteristic of certain views of temples (fig. 27). Different stages of building, types of construction, ground elevations,

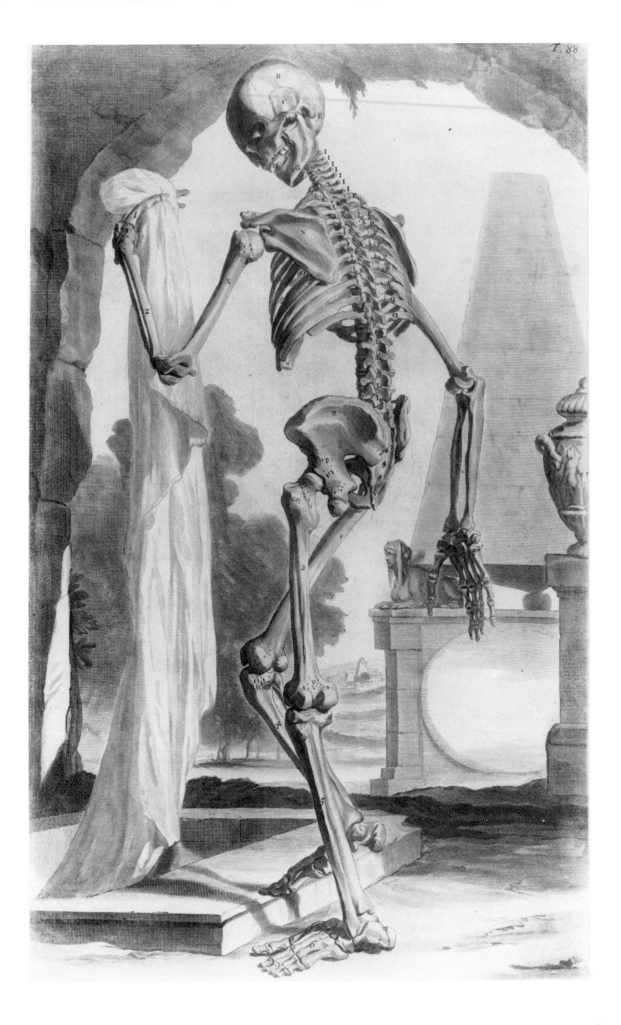

and variable conditions of erosion necessitated a dual device. The edifice was dismembered piece by piece and paratactically recomposed. The parts, thus juxtaposed or inlaid, formed an assemblage (fig. 34). Third and finally, Piranesi invented hypothetical or "scarred" solutions. This frequently occurred when a substructure was unknown, as in the famous case of his divination of the buried buttresses of the Castel Sant'Angelo. Or it might happen when building components were partly concealed under accumulated debris, as in the silted-over columns of the Temple of Vespasian (fig. 31). Like a surgeon, Piranesi responsibly sutured the certain to the conjectural, thereby allowing the seamed nature of his vision of the whole to show. He did not obfuscate individual, and even divergent, elements to cook up a generalizing *capriccio* blend. The intricate chambers of the carcass-like Baths of Caracalla were articulated with a precision characteristic of the analysis of a skeleton (figs. 35, 36). In anatomical fashion, he taught the viewer to estimate the unknown by knowledgeably judging a maze of isolated and scattered remains. Signifi-

36. William Cowper, *Skeleton Stepping into Tomb*, from *Anatomia Corporum Humanorum*, 1750, pl. 88. Drawing and engraving by Gerard de Lairesse. (Photo: National Library of Medicine, Bethesda, Md.)

37. Giovanni Battista Piranesi, *Campo Vaccino (Forum Romanum)*, from *Vedute di Roma*, ca. 1751, pl. 100. Etching. (Photo: author.)

38. Giovanni Battista Piranesi, *Piazza di S. Pietro,* from *Vedute di Roma,* ca. 1748, pl. 101. Etching. (Photo: author.)

cantly, however, anatomization, or the visual separation of segments, was only the means to a larger end, the totality of the graphic ensemble. His ultimate aim was synthesis. The pried-apart limbs and members had to be reintegrated into a heroic span of views. Piranesi thus helped his contemporaries to recontextualize the ruins of the past (fig. 37) into the living organism of modern urban Rome (fig. 38).

There was an intimate connection, then, between the etching process and the exploration of hidden physical or material topographies. Important, too, was the entire panoply of probing instruments, chemicals, heat and smoke, revealing and concealing grounds. There was also a metaphoric aptness in the medium that made it an unusual, but effective, vehicle for anatomical publications. The *Nouveau recueil d'ostéologie et de myologie* (1779), by the Toulouse printmaker Jacques Gamelin (1738–1803), was intended for use both

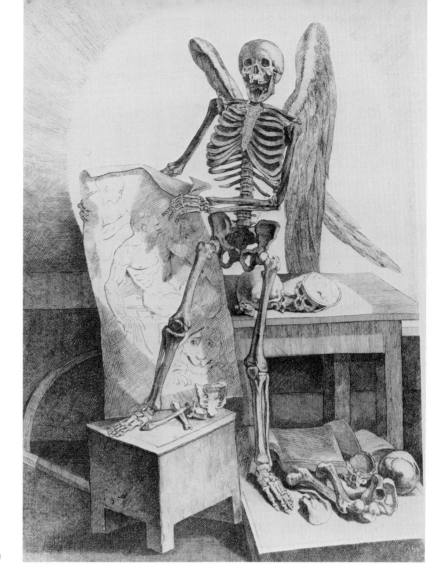

39. Jacques Gamelin, *Death Holding Sheet of Drawings,* from *Nouveau recueil d'ostéologie et de myologie,* 1779, I. Etching. (Photo: Courtesy National Library of Medicine, Bethesda, Md.)

40. Jacques Gamelin, *Skeleton,* from *Nouveau recueil d'ostéologie et de myologie,* 1779, I. Etching. (Photo: Courtesy National Library of Medicine, Bethesda, Md.)

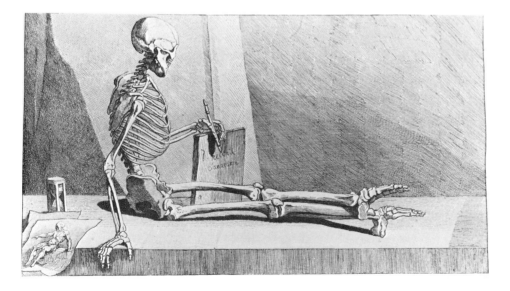

41.   Jacques Gamelin, *Triumph of Death,*
from *Nouveau recueil d'ostéologie et de
myologie,* 1779, I, title page. Etching.
(Photo: Courtesy National Library of
Medicine, Bethesda, Md.)

by anatomists and artists. The author assured the former of the accuracy of the images, and the latter of the reliability of the pictured muscular effects.[45] Like Piranesi's firsthand experience as a dirt archaeologist, Gamelin attended hospital dissections and prepared his drawings "from life." If Piranesi transformed the Venetian *vedute* tradition by deepening and darkening it, Gamelin exaggerated to hyperbole the lurid or grisly allegorizing tendencies of Baroque anatomical illustration (fig. 36). The fleshless line etchings characteristic of the osteology portion of the *Nouveau recueil* metamorphosed the dry study of bones into dramatic moments. An unnaturally active, and triumphant, skeleton indicates ironically the vanity of the art that brought him into being (fig. 39). The dessicated but finely articulated gridwork of the background deliberately mimics the rib pattern of another decomposed skeleton caught in the futile act of composition (fig. 40). These singular, full-plate figures were expanded into orthopedic epics recording the military conquest and universal rape of death. But, paradoxically, instead of being magnified on a grand scale, scenes of mortal combat were compressed into small vignettes (figs. 41, 42).

Gamelin remarked on the technical virtuosity and conceptual novelty of his work. He easily switched from outline etching to the more difficult and expensive crayon manner employed in the myology section.

72

42. Jacques Gamelin, *The Rape of Death,*
from *Nouveau recueil d'ostéologie et de
myologie,* 1779, I. Etching. (Photo: Courtesy
National Library of Medicine, Bethesda, Md.)

43. Jacques Gamelin, *The Entrance of
Death,* from *Nouveau recueil d'ostéologie
et de myologie,* 1779, I, frontispiece.
Etching. (Photo: Courtesy National Library
of Medicine, Bethesda, Md.)

44. Jacques Gamelin, *Artists Studying Anatomy,* from *Nouveau recueil d'ostéologie et de myologie,* 1779, II, title page. Mezzotint and crayon manner. (Photo: Courtesy National Library of Medicine, Bethesda, Md.)

45. Jacques Gamelin, *Study of Male Musculature,* from *Nouveau recueil d'ostéologie et de myologie,* 1779, II. Crayon manner. (Photo: Courtesy National Library of Medicine, Bethesda, Md.)

46. Théodore Géricault, *The Madwoman: Monomania of Gambling*, 1822–1823. Oil on canvas, 77.0 × 64.5 cm. Musée du Louvre (Photo: Réunion des Musées Nationaux.)

To be useful I had to become original, to vary my figures, to contrast them, & to seek in occasional bizarre postures, effects unknown until now of the play of muscles always dependent on the attitude of the model.[46]

A genre atmosphere sometimes crept into the osteology volume. The vignette-frontispiece showed a roistering Dutch gambling and carousing scene rudely interrupted by the apparition of a *danse macabre* (fig. 43). Nothing, however, quite prepares one for the stark, straightforward realism of the *académies*. Heroic nudes stand or sit under the sputtering and glaring artificial light of the eighteenth-century studio (fig. 44). In their sculptural tactility and dispassionate investigation of the swellings and hollows of the live body (fig. 45), they adumbrated Géricault's strongly muscled male figure studies. They also anticipated the searching sensitivity to mood characteristic of the great French Realist's physiognomic portraits of the insane. In both the anatomical and the psychiatric instance, the models were treated diagnostically as a substitute for the actual sufferer. They were, literally, clinical case materials or vivid simulacra, replacing the actual presence of the patient in the lecture room (fig. 46).[47]

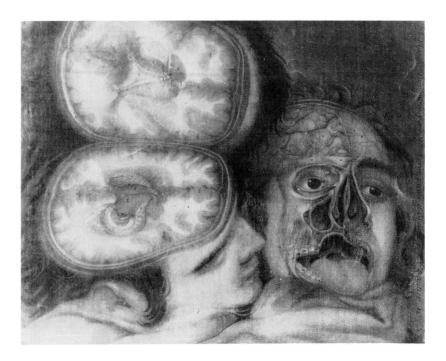

Gamelin's use of black and white etching for anatomical illustrations remained anomalous. Innovative multiple-plate color mezzotints, or "printed paintings," were touted as bringing new precision and exactitude into medical and scientific texts. They reproduced objects in their natural color without relying on hand tinting.[48] The peripatetic Jacques-Christophe Le Blon (1667–1741) studied painting in Rome with Carlo Maratta and developed, in 1741, a three-color process of printing based on Newton's primaries. Algarotti praised the scientific up-to-dateness of his invention and its ability to reproduce the nuances of oil painting.[49] But it was his Parisian student and eventual rival, the virulent anti-Newtonian Jacques Gautier Dagoty (1717–1785), who systematically applied the modified procedure to scientific and medical works.[50] Dagoty's secret recipes involved the addition of black to Le Blon's triad of red, yellow, blue. There was also the mysterious concoction of a varnish intended to render the print surface lustrous. These efforts formed part of a lifelong search for a graphic equivalent to the brilliancy of pigment on canvas. His associates included the surgeon at the Jardin du Roi and famous student of hearing disorders, Joseph Guichard Duverney (1648–1730), who made the anatomical preparations.[51] But the experimental artist performed the dissections himself, declaring: "I am the demonstrator, the painter, & the engraver rolled into one." Significantly, the *Essai d'anatomie* (1745) was dedicated to La Peyronie, the President of the Paris Academy of Surgery, and was intended for use by medical students, artists, "and all those interested in the health and investigation of the human body."

48. Jacques Gautier Dagoty, *The Vessels of the Skin,* from *Anatomie de la tête,* 1748, p1. 1. Multiple-plate mezzotint. (Photo: Courtesy National Library of Medicine, Bethesda, Md.)

49. Jacques Gautier Dagoty, *Back Muscles,* from *Anatomie de la tête,* 1748, p1. 14. Multiple-plate mezzotint. (Photo: Courtesy National Library of Medicine, Bethesda, Md.)

Both Duverney and Dagoty underscored the importance of "this new art of printing in natural color" representing "nature itself." They promised that the *Essai* was only the beginning of a much larger and comprehensive anatomical inquiry not possible before this technological breakthrough.[52] Dagoty's monumental plates (15 inches high by 12 inches wide) possessed neither the sharp clarity nor the transparent tinctures he desired. The use of varnish imparted, instead, a wonderfully dreamy and aqueous quality to the heroically scaled figures floating in the muted olive sea of the background. Cracked male skulls and disconcertingly decayed faces (fig. 47) formed strange contrasts to evocative and disembodied heads (fig. 48). Wearing their nerves on the skin, alert and ethereal children drifted within a glaucous plasma. The French printmaker also poetically transformed the muscles of a female cadaver, seen from the back, into great fluted dorsal wings. These flapped around the ribcage—an embroidered, high-necked, tight-fitting corselet worthy of Bronzino's (1503–1572) *Eleanor of Toledo* (London, Wallace Collection) (fig. 49). The equivocal effect of dressed, undressed, of decorative bony stays juxtaposed to "naked" buttocks, and of dead carcass to living revery has no equivalent except in Fontana's later anatomical waxes.

The analogy is apt because Dagoty specifically stated that he also modeled his dissected figures in wax and painted them.[53] Thus he may well have been an as yet unrecognized intermediary between Zumbo and French ceroplasts. He stood somewhere in between the enigmatic early-eighteenth-century surgeon Guillaume Desnoues and the *fin-de-siècle* surgeon to the Cent-Suisses, Pinson (1746–1828). After all, the engraver's four-color system, as he repeatedly insisted, aimed at the fabrication of the ultimate anatomical simulacrum.[54] His expressive fragments, with their polished and varnished look, evoke a later host of waxy painted figures. Paradoxically, and in spite of their dreaminess, they recall Baron François-Pascal Gérard's (1770–1830) *Cupid and Psyche* (Paris, Musée du Louvre, 1798). Both reveled in the same unnatural smoothness and erotic slipperiness of body surface, teasingly promising tangibility while witholding it. Jean-Dominique Ingres's (1780–1867) *Madame Rivière* (1806), *Bather of Valpinçon* (1808), and the *Grande Odalisque* (1814) possessed the identical, slightly yellowish translucent porelessness evocative of an irradiated artificial substance rather than flawed flesh.

This aspiration of the inventors of color printing to replicate, to produce as it were a two-dimensional automaton, aroused the critics' wrath. Michel Huber praised nonsimulating prints in black and white. He castigated the French and British for their abject catering to the gaudy tastes of "know-

nothings" (*Nichtkennern*).[55] On a more positive note, Dagoty's filmy polychrome prints evoke an earlier era. In their "ragoûtante" tactile and painterly
veilings, they prompt one to look backward to that other artist-artisan, Jean-
Siméon Chardin (1699–1779). Initiating Diderot into his scrupulous craft, he
argued that the painter's long and arduous technical preparation was
unmatched even by the professional training of the physician, lawyer, or
academic.[56] Further, I believe that the French master's canvas of a splayed
and gutted ray should be considered a genre *anatomie* (fig. 50). The anthropomorphism of the eviscerated fish suggests that it was an ironic replacement
for the noble subject matter he could not render. The artist's *morceau de
reception* vicariously offered a suffering animal substitute for the epic nudes
his lowly academic ranking would preclude him from officially exhibiting.
Thus Chardin deliberately transposed the high human art of thinking in
depth and patient probing for truth to a marine still life and to the back wall
of a kitchen.

50. Jean-Baptiste-Siméon Chardin, *The
Ray,* 1727–1728. Oil on canvas, 114.5 ×
146.0 cm. Musée du Louvre (Photo:
Réunion des Musées Nationaux.)

In his *Lettres sur l'Italie* (1786), the French traveler Jean-Baptiste Dupaty
(1744–1788) reflected upon the fragrant effigies on display in Fontana's dim
studio: "You see the most secret parts of this complicated mechanism. . . .

Philosophy has been mistaken not to dig deeper into physical man; it is here that mortal man is hidden. The exterior man is only the projection of the internal man."[57] Dupaty's double-edged allusion to "digging deeper" as both a menial, physical, and a lofty, philosophical task allows us to pick up a temporarily abandoned thread. We return to the theme of dissection used as a metaphor for an intellectual "taking to pieces."[58] In France, the academic codification and rationalization of manual guild practices into rules—in progress since 1648[59]—gave birth to the modern analytical critic. The type spread throughout Europe with the founding of academies. Two interconnected factors contributed in his rise: first, the importance given to rules to which the work of art was judged to conform or not; and, second, the increasing sense of impotence surrounding manual execution. The modern artist "could not reach with his hand what his mind conceived."

The mindlessly gathering *curieux* or the unsystematically amassing virtuoso was, in Sulzer's deprecatory words, "destitute of thought." Seated in his messy cabinet, this relic of a less demanding age stood little chance of survival before the onslaught of the serious "scientific" connoisseur and the classifying *philosophe*. Drawing primers, for example, drew medical analogies to sane or right thinking. The critical desideratum was to judge "healthily," i.e., to determine the *correct* size of a body, its *true* beauty. This could be accomplished only by following infallible rules. Analogously, it was impossible for the physician "to judge diseases, or deformed limbs if he did not possess a correct idea of health, & of a body born in all its perfection." Dominique Bouhours (1628–1702) had equated natural, reasonable good taste with the rhetorical notion of proper ideas as healthy and true. Mengs similarly drew upon the Ciceronian dictum that only a healthy reason could rightly gauge bodily beauty.[60] André Félibien (1667–1727), in the *Entretiens* (1725), noted how the architect's sound judgment required the guidance of simple preexisting ideas to purify matter.[61] Algarotti similarly asserted that practice must be led by theory so that the painter could stride without fear of making *faux pas*. He concluded that those who proceeded without rules or the direction of science walked with trembling and hesitation, "searching their way with the brush the way the blind tap, with their canes, the places they do not know."[62]

No *technai* or treasure trove of helpful rules, however, could make up for congenital inadequacy. The human condition was never to be without fault, in the words of Algarotti. The eighteenth century was still an age that divided the natural from the supernatural world, handling from content, mastery from desire. A leitmotif of the period was that perfection in art could never be attained by the merely artisanal. A host of rationalist critics harped upon the disjunction between matter and spirit. Or, as Daniel Webb (1719?–1798) succinctly put it, in the imitative arts the critic must distinguish the "mechan-ick" parts from "the Ideal." For Webb, the current scarcity of good pictures arose from the modern painter's poverty of invention, not from any difficulty inherent in execution.[63] Lord Shaftesbury (1671–1713), with Neoplatonic disdain, had, even earlier, connected the unseemly physical yen for making to the alchemist. This barbarous relic, still flourishing in the "age of philos-ophy," required more labor of hands than brain for his recipes. "We have a strange Fancy to be Creators, a violent desire to know the knack or secret by which Nature does all."[64] The alchemical laboratory epitomized the dishon-orable methods of extraction, separation, and fusion. It was identified with wrongful aspirations to transmutation. Worse, its decomposing metals and palpable bangs and stinks[65] were not unlike the printmaker's foul workshop or the anatomist's putrescent theater. The Abbé Dubos's (1670–1742) other-wise broadmindedly empirical outlook did not embrace those "vile workers [*ouvriers*], & [their] maneuvers," i.e., artisans and their operations bereft of genius, or divine enthusiasm.[66]

But it was the elder Jonathan Richardson (1665?–1745) in the *Theory of Painting* (1715) and the *Science of a Connoisseur* (1719) who continually reiterated the shortfall between idea and execution. He marveled that things neverthe-less so considerable could be "produced out of materials so inconsiderable, of a value next to nothing." His disquisitions concerning the difference between originals and copies were similarly predicated on an analysis of adulterated compounds. The connoisseur was like the assayer and unlike the alchemist. He dissected false from true, measured the ratio of base metal to pure gold. This cult of optical detection or assessment was not merely an avocation but a symbol of authority embodying hierarchical values concerning standards. For Richardson, the connoisseur's practice of leveling or striking was associated with the high moral purpose of separating the authentic hand, dividing the valuable inclusion of the individual artist from any corrupting material dross. Further, he had to compare and weigh the differing powers of various hands to form what the mind conceived.[67] One has the impression that, for both Shaftesbury and Richardson, the ideal work of art was like those wonder-working *acheiropoieta*, i.e., supernatural images that were *non-manufactum*, wholly brain-born, or unwrought.[68] Divine artistic ideas should be stamped directly, automatically on the canvas. Their active power and authenticity depended on a denial of the physical. Shaftesbury's and Richardson's model, surely, was the faint trace of Christ's bodily features deposited on Veronica's veil. For such critics, the mechanical implied the drab trades and slavish toil, not rational, liberal, and heavenly invention free of soiling matter. Winckelmann—steeped in their writings—concurred on the relative unimportance of execution. If it were the highest or first aim, he joked, then those Tirolean artists who carved God the Father on a cherry pit would be deemed paragons![69]

The critical mind was closely associated with the Enlightenment. Intelligence and reason, the *philosophes* argued, ought to be able to cut through superstition and error. It was also endemic to a self-conscious age that saw itself as being poorer in the production of great works but richer in the possession of better powers of judgment. The eighteenth century, then, was the source of that modern malaise expressed by Mallarmé and Duchamp: there are no ideas in the world, only criticism.[70] The contemporary notion of critical inquiry as an inquisitorial metadiscourse that ceaselessly deconstructs or de-defines the work of art was already inscribed in the eighteenth-century conception of criticism. It was dubbed the rational science for the destruction or dissection of putative wholes. The task of the critic, intoned that organ of the Scottish Enlightenment, the *Encyclopaedia Britannica* (1773), was to "pierce still deeper: he must clearly perceive what objects are lofty, what low, what are proper or improper, what are manly, and what are mean or trivial. . . . Thus the fine arts, like morals, become a rational science." John Oldmixon (1673–1742), in his *Essay on Criticism* (1728), had noted that the good critic should not bother with hunting after little superficial technical slips and practical negligences. "A wen or a mole in the face is sooner perceiv'd than the harmony of features." This fine proportion or beauty "must be sought below the surface." Richardson claimed, "it was little to the honor of painting or of the masters of whom the stories are told that the birds have been cheated by a painted bunch of grapes; or men by a fly; or a curtain, and such like; these are little things in comparison of what we are to expect from the art." This privileging of philosophical and textual content over the material manner of expression also undergirded J. G. Sulzer's (1720–1779) essay on the word "thought" (1774). Thought, in the fine arts, he declared was what persisted "of a performance when stripped of its embellishments," i.e., its form or "dress." Thus a poet's thoughts were what remained of his poems when pared of their versification.[71]

If artistic status depended principally not on any visible physical properties of the work but on invisible concepts, it followed that empirical or artisanal artists were poor judges compared to more theoretical authorities. The problem with untheoretical artist-critics, according to Webb, was that they seldom rose like gentlemen and scholars "to an unprejudiced and liberal contemplation of true beauty." They were so tied down to the "mechanick and self-love and vanity." For Richardson, the perspicuous commentator or connoisseur observed method and order in his way of thinking. He would not dream of engaging in an undisciplined mixing and jumbling of different kinds of observation. In his attempt to overcome the uncertainties of art criticism, Richardson even advanced the adoption of Roger de Piles's notorious scale. Numerical values were to be assigned to qualitative experiences, rating composition, drawing, color, expression. Ultimately, this transformation of art by criticism took two forms. It could concoct a metrically dissociated assemblage of assessable parts. Or it could mold an inferior and specious philosophical object demanding special powers of penetration. Both possibilities were evident in Marc-Antoine Laugier's (1711–1769) rationalist *Manière de bien juger* (1771). The architectural theorist bestowed on the critic that rarest of talents, a *finesse d'esprit*, not *des yeux*. Employing a medical trope that owed to Junius and Hobbes, Laugier stressed how the critic's penetrating judgment isolated and dissected. Like the microscopist, he saw more than others and better. But, unlike the naturalist, "the inquisition of his gaze" should not extend to the smallest details and the most imperceptible particularities. Such fine-grained investigation would merely stamp his cognitive activity as a trade. The profound critic, then, like the physician was a theorist of depth. He discovered secret, hidden distempers, spied and searched "into many things that do now shew themselves at first view."

The conceptual approach to criticism that, like Laugier, reified either solid, "scientific" reasoning or irrational, intuitive sensibility managed on both counts to denigrate the role of practice. Hence Dubos's castigation of critics. He spoke bitingly of persons "who make a profession of art from which a new work arises." Hence, too, this *érudit*'s praise of "the public" and its ability to judge fairly.[72] The *Réflexions critiques* (1719), however, was a fairly solitary document. Dubos's notion that feelings and vision teach us better how to perceive the merits of the work of art than the calculation of its strong or weak points was a critique of geometric reasoning well in advance of Romanticism. The idea that art was intelligible only in terms of its excavatable concepts was intrinsic to the logocentric aspects of eighteenth-century culture. But the separation between the "theoretical" and the "practical," as Garengeot's history of surgery showed, transcended the aesthetic.

Physiognomics was body criticism. As corporeal connoisseurship, it diagnosed unseen spiritual qualities by scrutinizing visible traits. Since its adherents claimed privileged powers of detection, it was a somewhat sinister capability. This "science" supposedly divined what untrained eyes could never see about a person's character. The activity of searching inquiry linked medical diagnostics to textual criticism and cerebral expertise. Symptoms, or marks visible to ordinary laymen, were converted into esoteric graphic signs. These physical enigmas were indicative of hidden causes legible only to specialized interpreters. Whether analyzing a body, a text, or an image, the pattern of reasoning moved from effect to cause, from evident to nonevident, made accessible with the "right" detector. The master eighteenth-century physiognomist, Lavater, noted that men form conjectures "by reasoning from the exterior to the interior." He continued: "What is universal nature but physiognomy. Is not everything surface and contents? Body and soul? External effect and internal faculty? Invisible principle and visible end?" But not everyone possessed the ability to extract the intrinsic value of things from their superficial manifestations. Lavater could say with Richardson that "thus nicely to distinguish things nearly resembling one another, whether visible or immaterial, is the business of a connoisseur." Or, again, "put a wise man and a fool side by side, dressed or disguised as you please, one will not be mistaken for the other, but distinguished with the first glance of the eye." The good connoisseur of art, as of men, detected copies from originals. He absorbed, retained, and managed clear and distinct ideas independent of the sensory trivia spread before his eyes. Most importantly, he was in possession of a rational method. With its help he could discern "wherein the differences consist when two notions very nearly resemble each other, but are not the same or to see the just weight of an argument and that through all its artificial disguises . . . in a manner that few of all those multitudes that pretend to reasoning have accustomed themselves to."[73]

The anatomical metaphor and the actual practice of comparative anatomy were also operative in the physiognomic probing of the soul. Character, as Sulzer reminded the readers of his dictionary, was "personal or distinctive to a thing, by which it separated itself from others of its kind."[74] The imitative or mirroring notion that the outer body reflected the inner spirit invited the dissection of the exterior to get at the interior. Cutting through density was, literally and metaphorically, a way of piercing any opaque morphology, of achieving transparent self-knowledge and the knowledge of others.

The systematization of the ancient practice of physiognomics, however, did not begin with Lavater. The Cartesian physician to Louis XIV, Marin Cureau de La Chambre (1594–1669), prefaced his *Art de connoistre les hommes* (1660) with an allusion to the outmoded Roman metaphor of the Glass of Momus. With the help of Descartes's method, there was no longer the need to complain "that nature did not place a window in front of the heart to see the thoughts & designs of men." Cureau rejoiced in the demise of the barbaric desire for such a strange aperture. Diving into the heart's recesses would not make the invisible available to the senses. Moreover, a surer way of achieving legibility had been discovered. No cardiac surgery was required in this case, since the soul extended speakingly over the entire face. Its motions, habits, inclinations were clearly and distinctly "written in characters so visible & so manifest." Undergirding Cureau's rationalist analysis of body language was the mathematical principle of the mean or center. Both the somatic and the spiritual *milieu* occupied the calculable middle between two opposites: order and disorder, shapeliness and unshapeliness, beauty and ugliness, truth and falsehood, good and evil. Cureau's praise of indifferent *médiocrité*, or centricality, as knowing neither additive excess nor subtractive lack owed to a Neoplatonic construct. Reinforced by Descartes and Pascal, it maintained that geometrical spheres of being radiated from the center of a circular figure. Forms located at the extremities of this homogeneous, bodiless, and divine point of emanation were more characterized or determined than those nearer the middle. Echoing Descartes's radical anthropomorphism, Cureau located man alone "in the middle [*milieu*] of everything, & thus it must be that he is equally susceptible [to vice or virtue], because he is indifferent and indeterminate by nature." Idiosyncratic temperament and particularized anatomy or physiology shaped natural inclinations. Together, they provided the heterogeneous human soul with equal opportunities for uncentering. Equal slopes led "toward one & the other of their [the inclinations'] extremities."[75]

But the moral and aesthetic problem was not merely that of self-sufficiently holding to the center, as slippery a concept as that might be. Nor was it simply a question of not inclining toward one side or the other. Rather, attempts to improve behavior called attention to the vice of public dissimulation and to the sins of interpersonal communication. Physiognomics was included in the sweep of Descartes's New Method through Cureau's efforts. Thus it was to be the rehabilitated science of the well-regulated emotions and constitute a purged social logic (*lexis, habitus*).[76] Cureau indicated that it was an infallible means for exposing feigning, so difficult to uncover since its *raison d'être* was the veiling of true intentions under various pretexts: "And among actions, exteriors can hide themselves beneath contrary appearances, & interiors, which are thoughts and passions, can easily be dissembled." Bowing to Descartes, Cureau proposed an optical model for a general theory of detection. An acute observer was to interrogate the body to determine whether the mind was truly or falsely united to it. There were twelve essential steps to this connoisseurship of insincerity. The classificatory scheme unintentionally and comically revealed a minute taxonomy of increasing desperation haunting the science of knowing. First, the analyst must examine the feint in isolation and inquire whether any verisimilitude existed between speech and looks, and if the effects accorded with one another. Second, the deceiver must be constrained to reveal himself by means of persuasion; third, through force; fourth, through recompense either, fifth, now, or sixth, in the future. If still recalcitrant, the pretender could, seventh, be pleaded with; eighth, plied with wine; ninth, treated either as timid or bold depending upon his reputation or status as an inferior or superior; tenth, feared because of his rank as prince or master; eleventh, have his deception recognized by an immediate outburst either of anger, or twelfth, of joy.[77] The procedure was predicated on a Cartesian mechanical model of the face, likened to a dial plate with wheels and springs activating the muscles. The animal spirits were set in motion by the sight of external objects. Habit, which unalterably set the countenance, was, in this system, nothing but the result of their continual furrowing impression, or engraving of the pliant facial tissues.

Cureau's language—steeped in the seventeenth-century atmosphere of masking etiquette—lived on in the age of the Enlightenment. The expressive issue, however, was no longer courtly ritual but the mechanical observation of rules codified in manuals of deportment for learning civility. The identical gesture, look, or stance could, as Cureau's taxonomy indicated, take on different meanings depending on the station of the person. What was new to the eighteenth-century experience—as codes of polite behavior spread to broader and lower strata of society—was the frightening possibility that nothing stood behind decorum. No gold standard guaranteed inflated or deflated currency; no original preexisted the copy; no durable skeleton shored up the frail anatomy. Fashion, masquerade, theater, cross-dressing emphasized the total disagreement between seeming and being, the deliberately fabricated incongruity between exterior and interior. Nowhere does one get a keener sense that fakes, counterfeits, tricksters, liars were the rule of the day than in Antoine-Joseph Pernety's *Discours sur la physiognomie* (1769). World traveler, librarian to Frederick the Great, member of the Berlin Academy of Sciences, and Swedenborgian, the defrocked Benedictine Dom Pernety (1716–1801) was obsessed with denuding and mortifying illusory social appearances. As the author also of an important dictionary of alchemy, he applied the purifying processes of "good" chemistry to specious corporeal mixtures. He reduced corrupt compounds to uncompoundable prime matter. Metaphors of dissolution and sublimation, ablution and separation, were transposed from the annihilation of base earthly substances to the purification and clarification of the precious soul, dirtied by a succession of putrifying somatic appearances. The task of physiognomics, then, was to uncover false transmutations. Ruthlessly, it was to disclose that ungenuine social alchemy destructive both of metals and of health, which turned even gold into obfuscating smoke and vile black ashes.[78]

Like Cureau, he too, but for different reasons, disparaged the Glass of Momus. Even if nature had contrived a window onto the heart and our gaze could penetrate its depths, would we then be able to interpret "the craftiest of eyes?" Or would we witness only a beating organ and nothing else? Citing Cicero's opinion that the human soul was veiled in deceit, Pernety concluded that merely tearing into its anatomy was insufficient. Only deductive reasoning and consummate visual study of the misleading ways of the world could unravel this "chaos" of seeming. In that sense physiognomics was, for Pernety, a kind of political observational history, where politics was "the art of knowing the state." It was "the study of the world," just as history was "the physiognomics of times past." He maintained that all arts and sciences were fundamentally physiognomic insofar as they externally bore "a distinctive sign, a hieroglyphic sign, by means of which an observer knew very well how to recognize secret virtues & properties."[79]

The *Discours* offered a disturbing picture otherwise unavailable of uncontrolled chatter circulating about town. We are catapulted into an intellectual and social milieu rent by small coteries abuzz with tittle-tattle and flying *canards*. Gossip was characterized by intrigue, scandal, hearsay, rumor, making it all the more pressing to read between the lines. In its wide-ranging critique of a libertine society run amok, the treatise provided insight into the larger Enlightenment epistemology of *clair-obscur*. With Pernety's work, physiognomics became comparable to Diderot's great art of experimentation described in the *Interprétation de la nature* (1753). The task of experimental, not mathematical, science was to distinguish a new phenomenon from "a travestied phenomenon," a "central phenomenon" from one simply presenting "a different face."[80] Given the duplicity of modern culture, physiognomics was an empirical skill necessary to survival. Significantly, Pernety—relying on the sympathy of his general reader—addressed him as "you, who have so often been the victim of this deceitful mask." As a chaplain to Bougainville, his indictment was not limited to a bourgeois court in a small German state. He lamented that people in all contemporary societies played games. Men and women attempted to blindfold one another and worked at not being found out. Pernety's mundane *commedia dell'arte* was stocked with the same Rococo degenerates that paraded through Diderot's critical *Salons*. These eavesdroppers and yarn-spinners floated about garbed in "false graces, affectation, mincing preciosity, ignobleness, false dignity, false pain, false piety, grimace, manner." Pernety could have been describing Boucher's unnatural pastorals when he mourned: "What perplexity, what difficulty to succeed in divining precisely the person under the tone of the affected voice, under the grotesque posture, & under the borrowed dress with which he presents himself." Ordinary human beings were everywhere accustomed to being duped by a face "painted [*fardé*] with hypocrisy or a deceiver cloaked in the mantle of friendship." Such obscuring tactics required the enlightened connoisseur to pierce the disguise.

To the eyes of the naive observer, it [the mask] is a light cloud; but for a man born physiognomist, this mask is only a subtle vapor that dissipates at the approach of the luminous rays of the torch of nature. In vanishing, it reveals the truth in all its brilliance. It is the shadow in a painting that imparts value to the lights.[81]

In the *Maladies de l'âme* (1777), Pernety unmistakably identified his target as the eighteenth-century narcissist suffering from *amour-propre*. This perturbing mania or exaggerated egoism was the Stoic source of all illnesses of the soul. It developed when "man considered himself an isolated being, independent & to whom others must relate." From this excessive valuing of self sprang lies, and with them "ruse, disguise, dissimulation, deception, fraud, imposture, calumny, falseness, cheating, hypocrisy." For those who cherished truth, and with it "uprightness, good faith, frankness, candor, naiveté, & fidelity," physiognomics was the only salvation. No matter how the countenance was masked, it helped the observer "to know [*connoître*] the true & the false." Narcissism, or the diseased root of the passions, spread like a pernicious contagion because of the infectiousness of social imitation. Imitators, or worldly copyists, possessed no fixed character of their own. They displayed a "smallness of soul akin to slavery" and were mere "translators," incapable of producing but always repeating what others made, thus disfiguring "the originals." Moreover, they did not emulate worthy traits, but preferred flaws and even the ridiculous. For Pernety, then, the physiognomy of this libertine age was marked by inconstancy, and, unlike Cureau, he despaired of ever seizing the mean or holding to the center. The false wit was the grotesque portrait of the modern sophist as *arriviste*. He "allied things most opposite: all contraries found themselves reunited in him, modest & proud, gentle & innocent, chaste & lubricious, loquacious & taciturn, . . . liar, truthsayer. The inconstant [person] is all that, depending on the circumstances in which he finds himself; because he has no tenacity, his soul is fickle, malleable, & always disposed to bend to the impulses of circumstances."[82]

Physiognomics, as diagnostics of the wandering passions and as preventative medicine against the traps of cheating appearances, was also necessary to the spiritual health of those engaged in the commerce of the world. Pernety drew upon the Neoplatonic and Stoic traditions that there was an evil of the soul, or disease, and a malignity of the body, or ugliness. He postulated—like the later French Idéologues who tapped the same ancient sources—that only the anatomizing physician could properly understand the connection between moral and physical vice. Only he could bring dark symptoms into daylight, distinguish voluntary from involuntary motions, and separate the signs of manufactured manner from those of natural composure.[83] He claimed that external physiognomic indicators were not the "form" of the soul and did not "constitute" it. Nonetheless, they were a sort of "image" of it, because the form of the soul imparted "the form which they [the signs] have."

Pernety's system, consequently, was an important prolegomenon to Lavater's semiotic, with its Neoplatonic emphasis on the earthborn soul's potential for sickness, sin, distortion, disproportion, and unfitness. Both clerics shared the belief that individual likenesses were a kind of "flowing, an emanation, a development" of a constant but distant God. The remote Deity was known physiognomically only through His opposites, or the many changeable modes of material being. This new brand of enlightened inquisition, then, was also a scientific theology. It appeared as such in Johann Jacob Scheuchzer's (1672–1733) natural historical emblematic Bible, the *Physique sacrée* (1732–1737). The differing reception accorded to Cain's and Abel's sacrifice to Jehovah became the pretext for a prophetic medical physiognomics (fig. 51). The developmental stages of Cain's vicious rage and jealousy, in contradistinction to Abel's virtuous serenity, were visualized physiologically. The emotive heads framing the central scene mirrored a succession of psychic states: sadness, devotion, piety, joy, despair, and, finally, hate and anger. Cain's feverish condition was

TAB. XXXIII.

GENESIS Cap. IV. v. 4.5.

Cain Irâ fervens, Invidia pallens.

I. Buch Mosis Cap. IV. v. 4.5.

Der zornig und neidige Cain.

H. Sperling sculp.

explained medically as a loss of equilibrium in the nervous fluid and blood, permitting the animal spirits to course impetuously from the brain to the heart. It was also interpreted spiritually as a Senecan loss of tranquility, akin to a boiling or drunkenness of the soul. This mad chase of the blood revealed his sinful and sick condition. It caused the murderer's "face to inflame, the eyes to glitter, the mouth to foam, the lips to tremble; & all the limbs of the body, agitated by deranged movements, to dispose themselves for battle."[84] But Pernety's and Lavater's divination was a more visionary, and less applied, prognostication. Its purpose was to see "what we do not naturally see," to know what we do not humanly know. It wished to comprehend the indeterminate determinately, and the unstable stably and firmly.[85]

The initial set of Johann Caspar Lavater's (1741–1801) *Physiognomische Fragmente* was published in Germany in 1775. The expanded French version appeared in The Hague in 1781, 1783, and 1786. Henry Hunter's English translation of the French edition—supervised and furnished with drawings for contracted engravings by the Anglo-Swiss painter Johann Heinrich Fuseli (1741–1825)—expanded it into five sumptuous quarto volumes "completed" in 1792. By 1810, there were fifty-five editions. England headed the list with twenty, priced to accommodate every purse.

Lavater's earliest thoughts on physiognomics evolved in collaboration with Fuseli. They were friends and literary associates in Zurich where, in 1761, or just at the time that the system was in gestation, both became ordained as Zwinglian ministers.[86] Not unlike the mystic, Proclusian negative theology espoused by the Catholic Pernety, Lavater's "Nestorian" Protestantism was strongly laced with a sense of the gulf stretching between creator and creation. It, too, was replete with visionary yearnings for the manifestation of another, invisible world on this side of eternity. Citing Cureau, Lavater also dismissed the dream of an artificial device for opening the profundities of the heart. Instead, he relied upon an anatomical optics with which we are now familiar. Lavater's physiognomist was obliged to examine a complexly and deliberately disguised humanity "to the bottom."[87] The no longer transparent face was a table of brass on which thoughts were engraved in cryptic characters. Yet Lavater admitted that his decoding encyclopedia, or massive compendium of isolated decipherable features, was necessarily fragmentary. The pessimism and despair Lavater derived from the St. Paul of 1 Corinthians 13:12 pervaded the entire semantic enterprise (fig. 52). Or, echoing Origen (185–250/254 AD), seeing with the unredeemed senses meant one dwelled outside "the well of vision." It was like "looking through nets," blurring "snares" of fraud, and "the carefully crafted gins of the devil."[88]

51. Jean-Jacques Scheuchzer, *The Wrathful and Jealous Cain (Physiognomics)*, from *Physique sacrée*, 1732–1737, I, pl. 33. Engraving by H. Sperling. (Photo: Courtesy Resource Collections of the Getty Center for the History of Art and the Humanities.)

52. Johann Caspar Lavater, *Seeing Darkly*, from *Essays on Physiognomy*, 1792, I, part I, p. 68. Engraving by Hall after J. H. Fuseli. (Photo: Courtesy National Library of Medicine, Bethesda, Md.)

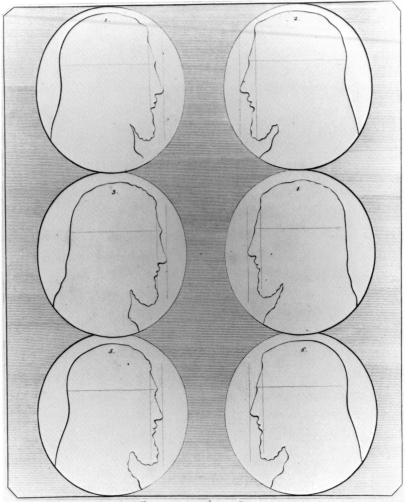

SILHOUETTES OF CHRIST.

53.   Johann Caspar Lavater, *Silhouettes of Christ*, from *Essays on Physiognomy*, 1792, II, part I, p. 212. Engraving by Thomas Holloway et al. after J. H. Fuseli. (Photo: Courtesy National Library of Medicine, Bethesda, Md.)

Now we know but in part, and our explanations and our commentaries are nothing but fragments; but when perfection is come, these feeble essays shall be abolished. For they are hitherto only the ill-articulated language of a child, and these same ideas, these efforts shall appear childish to me when I arrive at maturity. Now we see the glory of man darkly as through a veil; we shall ere long behold face to face. Now we know but imperfectly, but I shall soon know, as I myself have been known.[89]

This absolute connoisseurship, or knowing in Pauline fullness, was equated by Lavater with the central figure of his work. Christ was the perfectly intelligible Word, the supreme incarnation of a transfigured and readable humanity. Significantly, no artistic representation was adequate to the Savior of legibility. Neither empty profile silhouettes (fig. 53) nor Fuseli's labored transcriptions of Italian "primitives" (fig. 54) satisfied Lavater's quest for the accurate physiognomy of the eternal Logos. There were no unerroneous visual signs congruent with such an elevated subject. There were no images incapable of being misunderstood. Finding an adequate icon of Christ would have provided Lavater with a perceptual paradigm for the divine in man.

92

This initial corporeal perfection was defiled and distorted through the Fall. Without this model, we are soiled idols, false and corrupted likenesses, contrary to the transparent body of the radiant prototype.[90] And physiognomics itself could not attain clairvoyancy, but remained a dim partial knowledge, a broken revelation.

Temporal portraiture, recording the distorted marks of an unregenerated humanity, stood in caricatural opposition to the unique and beautiful Christological symbol. Its unfit and multitudinous subjects were everywhere only too much in evidence. Needless to say, this monstrous and devilish crowd of characters posed no difficulty to Lavater in his search for graphic equivalences. A motley throng of wayward souls was clad in variegated corporeal garments. They strayed into deviancy during their descent to earth. Mutilated and deformed, these existential specimens became the physiognomist's staple. He wished to determine their "every passion, the seat of its residence, the source from which it flows, its root, the fund which supplies it." He probed

54. Johann Caspar Lavater, *Head of Christ* (after Andrea Verrocchio), from *Essays on Physiognomy,* 1792, II, part II, p. 293. Engraving by Thomas Holloway et al. after J. H. Fuseli. (Photo: Courtesy National Library of Medicine, Bethesda, Md.)

55. Johann Caspar Lavater, *Silhouettes of Clerics,* from *Essays on Physiognomy,* 1792, II, part I, p. 24. Engraving by Thomas Holloway et al. (Photo: Courtesy of the National Library of Medicine, Bethesda, Md.)

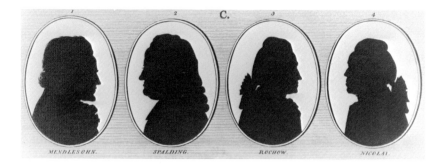

56. Johann Caspar Lavater, *Silhouettes of Mendelssohn, Spalding, Rochow, and Nicolai,* from *Essays on Physiognomy,* 1792, II, part I, p. 187. Engraving by Thomas Holloway et al. (Photo: Courtesy National Library of Medicine, Bethesda, Md.)

the myriad modifications veiling mankind: "rank, condition, habit, estate, dress." "To pierce through all these coverings into his real character, to discover in these foreign and contingent determinations, solid and fixed principles by which to settle what the Man really is," was "difficult, but not impossible."[91]

Two techniques assisted in the exposure. The geometrical layout of the page consisted of divisions into rectangles, circles, ovals. The diagrammatic reduction of individuals to ascetic outline profiles isolated them within a silent and vacant space. Both strategies fostered an etymological approach to the face. Six unrelated portraits of clerics, for example, were paratactically juxtaposed like verbless nouns (fig. 55). Scavenged from countless, often unidentified sources and then reengraved, these examples were representative of Lavater's schematic and airless combinatorial art of reused images. All pictorial elements in the *Essays*, as in a logic, were equal. This nominal attitude toward the deep grammar of the soul was evident in the accompanying descriptions. Thus figure four was judged to stop not at "calculation, abstraction, classification." He loved more than the other five, and it was probable that he would "become stationary about the point which is equally distant from these two extremes [spirituality, sensuality]." Figure five, then, was the optically established mean or geometrical "mediocrity" whose social, or human, fate had been sealed. Lavater prophesied he would "remain in a medium sphere of activity," would "sink from prudence to timidity, but never rise to heroism."

Compartmentalization and antithesis were essential to the black and white silhouette technique. Extracting root meanings was contingent neither upon interpersonal relationships nor upon the impact of surroundings (fig. 56). These visual devices exposed Lavater's deep religious fatalism and social determinism. Each person according to his distinctive form and features was "placed apart" in a particular zone. Here, he might "exercise a certain measure of liberty and force outside of which he was capable of executing nothing of importance." Or again: "Man is free as the bird in a cage. He has a circle of activity and sensibility whose bounds he cannot pass. As the human body has lines which bound it, every mind has its peculiar sphere in which to range; but that sphere is invariably determined." And yet again: "A man can only do what he is capable of doing; or be what he is. He can rise to a certain degree; but farther he cannot go. Every man ought to be measured according to his own powers." Lavater was shocked by the skeptical and libertine notion that "the order established from eternity" was nothing but a dexterous imposture; and he was offended by "the effrontery to commonsense of affirming that joy and sorrow, pleasure and pain, love and hatred" were designated by the same signs. This assertion was tantamount to affirming that human beings were not marked at all. "To ascribe every thing to arbitrary causes is the death of science, the philosophy of madmen."[92]

Physiognomics was human connoisseurship (representing "the whole man to an experienced eye").[93] But it was also a graphology of character ("the wonderful analogy between language, gait, and handwriting").[94] The connection was based on an underlying anatomical method. The leitmotif of the *Essays* was the need to examine "to the bottom a characteristic face." Physiognomics meant "taking apart a man and then putting him back together again." Since every figure left tactile impressions that a dissimilar one would not have produced, the physiognomist must "study every part and every member of the human body separately, the connections, relations, and proportions which they have to one another." The grand secret of the science was "to simplify, to abstract, and to separate the principal and fundamental features with which it is of importance to be acquainted." Its chief virtues consisted in discovering "what does not immediately strike the senses," discerning in every external feature, attitude, and position of the human body what man internally "really is."[95]

The physiognomist's chief tool, drawing, was itself anatomical in nature. Lavater extolled it as "the only medium of fixing with certainty, of portraying, of rendering sensible an infinite number of signs, of expressions, of shades, which it is impossible to describe in words." This cadaverous ideal of art as riveting a dusky outline was propagated by the *Essays* (fig. 57). Shadow painting was invented by Etienne de Silhouette (1709–1769), and first became fashionable in aristocratic circles during the 1760s. The popularity of the technique, however, rose after the publication of the *Essays* and lasted until the middle of the nineteenth century. Fuseli and Lavater relied heavily on

A SURE AND CONVENIENT MACHINE FOR DRAWING SILHOUETTES.

This is the Character I would assign to the silhouette of this Young person. I find in a Goodness without much Ingenuity; Clearness of Idea, & a ready Conception, a mind very industrious, but, little governed by a lively Imagination, & not attached to a rigid punctuality; We do not discern in the Copy, the Character of Gaiety which is conspicuous in the Original, but the Nose is improved in the silhouette, it expresses more Ingenuity

57. Johann Caspar Lavater, *Machine for Drawing Silhouettes,* from *Essays on Physiognomy,* 1792, II, part I, p. 179. Engraving by Thomas Holloway et al. (Photo: Courtesy National Library of Medicine, Bethesda, Md.)

58.   August Johann Rösel von Rosenhof, *Pinned Frog,* from *Historia Naturalis,* 1758, pl. 11. Colored engraving (Photo: author.)

59.   Martin Frobène Ledermüller, *Dissected Frog,* from *Amusemens microspiques,* 1768, pl. 1. Colored engraving. (Photo: Courtesy National Library of Medicine, Bethesda, Md.)

this simple method for arresting gesture and suspending time. Helplessly immobilized in a *camera obscura*—like a pinned live (fig. 58) or a clamped dissected (fig. 59) frog—the sitter was turned into a victim. The young woman under study was converted into a natural history specimen destined for narrow and searching scrutiny by a concealed viewer. Free of cruel hooks that tore the flesh, and of the peering microscopist with his mercilessly magnifying lens, the physiognomist's confined subject nevertheless was equally stripped.[96] What a striking contrast in relationship between observer and observed existed in Joseph Wright of Derby's *Corinthian Maid.* Lover faced sleeping beloved and tenderly recorded his cast shade (fig. 60).

Taking silhouettes, and the desire to stop fleeting reflections, corresponded to Lavater's vision of physiognomics as a science of essentials. A sort of *frottage* or *acheiropoietic* body print, the silhouette was "the immediate impress of nature." It bore "a character of originality which the most dexterous artist could not hit, to the same degree of perfection, in a drawing from the hand." Although freely admitting that silhouettes were the feeblest and least finished

60.   Joseph Wright of Derby, *The Corinthian Maid,* 1783–1784. Oil on canvas, 106.3 × 130.8 cm. National Gallery of Art, Washington, D.C., Paul Mellon Collection. (Photo: Courtesy National Gallery of Art.)

61. Johann Caspar Lavater, *Frederick II,*
from *Essays on Physiognomy,* 1792, II, part
I, p. 227. Engraving by Thomas Holloway et
al. (Photo: Courtesy National Library of
Medicine, Bethesda, Md.)

62. Johann Caspar Lavater, *Voltaire* (after
Pigalle), from *Essays on Physiognomy,*
1792, II, part I, p. 90. Engraving by Thomas
Holloway. (Photo: Courtesy National
Library of Medicine, Bethesda, Md.)

of portraits, Lavater maintained they were also "the justest and most faithful."
They represented only a single contour of the figure in which we behold
"neither motion, nor light, nor volume, nor features." Indeed, the corpse
most nearly satisfied the physiognomist's desire for a reliable facsimile.

*The Dead furnish a new subject for study. Their features acquire a precision and an
expression which they had not when either asleep or awake. Death puts an end to the
agitations to which the body is a perpetual prey. . . . It stops and fixes what was
before vague and undecided. Everything rises or sinks to its level; all the features return
to their true relation.*[97]

Thus a silhouette of the "variable," "irritable," "wild, prodigiously eccentric,
imaginative" Frederick the Great metamorphosed the enlightened ruler into
a pathological study of the "animal at rest." Or, as in the case of the witty
and urbane Voltaire, the *philosophe* was transubstantiated into an inanimate
and colorless plaster cast (figs. 61, 62).[98]

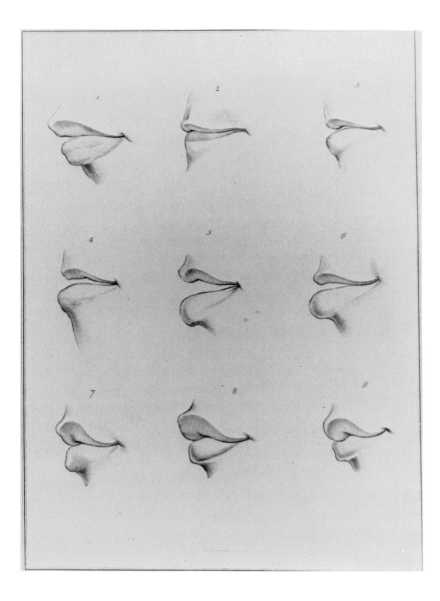

63. Johann Caspar Lavater, *Lips,* from *Essays on Physiognomy,* 1792, III, part II, p. 404. Engraving by Thomas Holloway et al. (Photo: Courtesy National Library of Medicine, Bethesda, Md.)

The emphasis on the inflexible bony topography assumed that the body was all skull or skeleton with no temperament or motion. Nor was this the only indication of Lavater's anatomical preoccupation with the paralyzed, stiff, and cold signs of death.[99] With Fuseli's assistance, he also reduced the organism to pithy ruins and detachable members. Fragments of lips (fig. 63), remains of eyes, noses, foreheads were seemingly surgically excised from their contexts. They functioned like cleaned-up bits of archaeological debris mysteriously anchored in a sea of blankness (fig. 18). Somatic morsels, like the nine mouths, were "read" from left to right. Their aura of universal legibility depended upon an evenness of vertical and horizontal progression. Calibrated steps methodically indicated the regular spacing of the figures. Biological parcels moved sequentially across and up and down the page as if they were infinite texts or endless lists without copulas. The favorite tripartite or syllogistic composition comprised a sort of corporeal cartouche or framed hieroglyphic. This tidy grouping encouraged the viewer to "average" extremes and to "discover" the mean between high and low, ideal and unideal features. Concise arrangement also prompted an aphoristic reading of the amputated segments. Thus the sixth pair of lips would "not win the prize"; the seventh had "the greatest affinity to genius"; the upper lip of the third possessed "qualities denied to the lower"; and the fourth belonged "to the same degenerate race."[100] Free-floating miniature pieces of discourse, much like slogans or dicta, were similarly abstracted from any total narrative. Both the mosaic image and the fragmented text, then, collaborated in producing nuggets of impersonal information. Speculative bits of wisdom were dished out independent of any practical existential situation. The reader/viewer as would-be physiognomist was allowed to ponder at leisure a dissonant pictorial and linguistic parade of ever more finely divided private parts.

The motley crew itself, however, owed less to any firsthand knowledge of deformed and monstrous individuals and more to artistic representations. The awareness of deviancy "from the general parallelism of the human figure" was always filtered through an image. Analogously, the recognition of perfect conformity was screened through a painted or sculpted ideal. The neglect of empirical evidence proved especially detrimental when Lavater extended his researches into the domain of physiology and neurology in order to determine "the face of health."[101] Karl Heinrich Baumgärtner (1798–1886), professor at the Freiburger Medizinischer Klinik, criticized Lavater's habit of ignoring the aspect of the patient and diagnosing from the work of art. Like his great French contemporary Jean-Louis Alibert, the founder of modern clinical dermatology, Baumgärtner stressed the importance of the accurate illustration of actual diseases. A true *Krankenphysiognomik* would catalogue "the infinity of diseased forms." Thus it differed doubly from Lavater's enterprise. First, it would be based on the close examination of the myriad faces of illness in order to establish a semiotics of identifiable signs. The patient's "interior would be spread open and he would lie before us as if on the anatomical table." Second, it would be grounded in the investigation of physical muta-tions occurring during the living of a life. Lavater, on the contrary, was interested only in supernatural characteristics imprinted on human beings "from the beginning." Although Baumgärtner believed there was a corre-spondence between the soul, or rather "spiritual powers" (*die geistigen Kräfte*), and the external morphology, he denied Lavater's premise that every trait invariably carried the inscription of an internal quality. Baumgärtner's pedagogics belonged to the positivistic nineteenth century. The scientism of his self-proclaimed "reliable" method of observation was coupled to a disparagement of outmoded occult attempts to decipher things hidden from view. Departures from normalcy, the physician declared, were measurably expressed through tangible, material manifestations.[102]

The Calculation of Incongruity

Lavater's *Essays* disseminated a reductive image of the body inexorably trapped or imprisoned in a geometrical grid (figs. 14, 53). His work was part of the larger drive toward biological epitomization, best personified as a whole divided into an assemblage of inorganic parts ("sculptural" lips). Simplification was representative of a broader cultural reform movement on the rise in the second half of the eighteenth century. Neoclassicism was characterized by a mentality that promoted not thick description but summarization, codification, schematization. My intention now is to show that optical meagerness was anatomy pushed to geometrical anorexia. "Thinness" was impelled both by a Neoplatonic mathematical symbolism and by the increasing quantification of all branches of knowledge. Metric revolutions and the rise of statistics during the Enlightenment as an independent discipline went hand in hand with a geometrized aesthetics. No complexity existed that could not be measured, numbered, or exemplified by rudimentary figures. Lavater had freely admitted to his critics that he made use of "abstractions" and "classifications." Otherwise, if he had been obliged to invent a specific sign "for every individual situation, every gradation of shade, for every variation, every breath, every motion, this were to aim at being God!"[103] Only categorization, systematization, and standardization saved the "scientific" physiognomist from being overwhelmed by the mob, i.e., by the Romantic intricacy and multiplicity of his miscellaneous subjects.

But it was specifically the intellectual descendants of Lavater—Camper, Gall, Spurzheim, Sue, Baumgärtner, Freud—who metamorphosed the uncertain study of empirical phenomena. In their analytical hands, changeable things were transformed into a certain "science" of the contingent. Physiognomics, medicine, ethics, the natural sciences, literature, and the visual arts, were progressively removed from the realm of the senses. These studies were "elevated" from the sphere of likely explanation, or "opinion," and turned into abstract "objects of science" subject to definitive judgments concerning their truth or falsehood.[104] Rigorous calculation or geometric exposition was

Assemblage

noun, *A collection, a number of individuals brought together. It differs from* assembly, *by being applied only, or chiefly, to things;* assembly *being used only, or generally, of persons.*

Dr. Johnson, *Dictionary*

Epitome

noun, *Abridgment or reduction of the principal materials of a large work, contracted into a much narrower volume.*

Diderot and D'Alembert, *Encyclopédie*

thought to overcome the laxness of libertine skepticism and the unchecked proliferation of conflicting interpretations of experience. The prevalence of the anatomical metaphor in biology, archaeology, printmaking, physiognomics, criticism, and connoisseurship signified the inability to tolerate ambiguity. It exposed the need to attain exactitude, not just degrees or shades of knowing.

Counting, reckoning, weighing, measuring were intellectual and metaphysical skills essential to a new breed of body critic. As we have seen, the multiplication of professions and their institutionalization during the eighteenth century required theorists whose special knowledge would carry deliberations beyond the confusion of ordinary manual practice. It took great analytical ability—far beyond Lavater's aphoristic intuitiveness—to forge architectonic compendia out of disparate elements. Even more difficult was the task of codifying fragments into teachable systems governed by rules, axioms, and invariable laws. In short, secular exegetes evolved to control the expanding data and to provide the "right" interpretation.

This overestimation of Logos and of reasoned calculation, making incommensurable things commensurable, went back to Plato.[105] But it was the Neoplatonists who spread the conviction that the key to the cosmos was hidden in a mathematical and diagrammatic symbolism requiring an elite cadre of decoders. We have observed Pernety and Lavater employing metric metaphors to designate somatic and spiritual norms or deviations. Geometrical concepts of congruence or incongruence, evenness or oddness, rectitude or deviation, were transposed from the clear and distinct realm of equations to the maze of the body. The unchanging nature of mathematics or geometry was likened to the eternal soul. So, following a theory of universal analogy, what was proved for the one held for the other. This isomorphism, or correspondence, between distant and unrelated things was predicated on a model of participation found especially in Proclus (b. 412 AD). Significantly, it was his brand of Neoplatonism that became so influential in the eighteenth century and beyond. Before this book is completed, we shall see that it left a traceable wake in aesthetic theories from Shaftesbury to Coleridge, Crousaz to Winckelmann, Diderot to Baudelaire.

Proclus operated with a model of the relationship between downward-proceeding parts and a stationary One, or whole. The former "participated" more or less in the latter proportional to their higher or lower position in the descent.[106] The *Commentary on Euclid* was the key text for the eighteenth century to make the case that the degree of participation of generated or

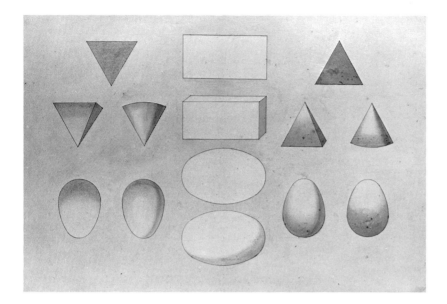

64.   **D. P. G. Humbert de Superville,**
Platonic Solids, 19th c. Watercolor. (Photo:
Courtesy Printroom, Rijksuniversiteit,
Leiden.)

"becoming" appearances in unmoved Being, or *Nous*, was a *quantitative* matter.
Mathematics was explicitly made the norm for a measured, orderly moral
and philosophical life. Citing Plato's *Gorgias* (508a) and *Republic* (587d), Proclus
approvingly quoted Socrates' rebuke of the dissolute Callicles: "You are
neglecting geometry and geometrical equality." But it was not just ethics that
was brought under numerological dominion. Mathematics conferred on the
other sciences and arts "completeness and orderliness." It stood—as it increasingly did in the second half of the eighteenth century—as a paradigm for the
poetical arts, and as the standard from which to gauge any deviation. "All
the arts require the aid of counting, measuring, weighing, and all are included
in mathematical reasonings and are made definite by them."[107] The *Commentary on Euclid* transformed the down-to-earth practical geometer into a Pythagorean mystic. Moreover, it disseminated a universal theurgy of mathematics
embodied in visual symbols. The arithmetical imagination was divine, all-
powerful. It functioned like Kant's and Coleridge's primary imagination.
Unifying and collecting the manifold, the mind divided the simple into the
diverse, the more general into the particular, "and the primary ideas into
secondary and remoter consequences of the principles." It alone could move
the soul upward to attain unitary and immaterial insights. It alone turned it
away from darkness to aspire "to bodiless and partless being." Appositely,
for an entire generation of proselytizing Neoclassical theorists, the beauty of
mathematics was visible in almost invisible figures: in tenuous straight lines,
immaterial circles, denuded squares, or the Platonic solids (fig. 64). "For the
objects of mathematical knowledge do not appear now in one guise and now

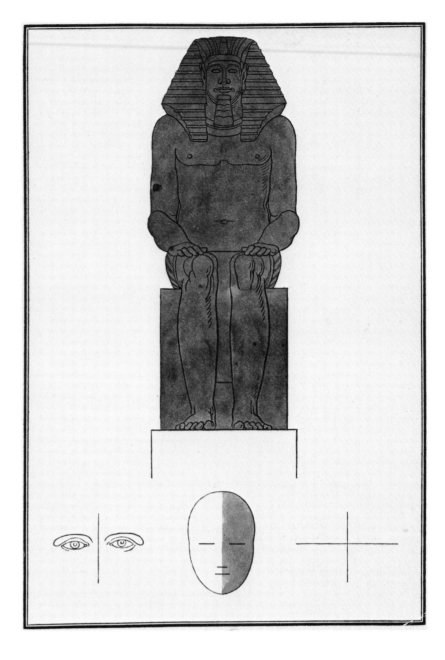

in another, like the objects of perception or opinion, but always present themselves as the same, made definite by intelligible forms." The shape of the unseen soul or countenance of everything psychical—passionately sought by the physiognomist—was imaged in "immaculate" right angles, in the undeviating uprightness that was uninclined toward evil. "Rightness" preserved "the identity of being" and was like "the essence in things themselves." The perpendicular was also "a symbol of directness, purity, undefiled unswerving force" (fig. 65). Good and beautiful virtue resembled "rightness," whereas vice was constituted "after the fashion of the indeterminate obtuse and acute, possessing both excess and deficiencies and showing by this more-and-less its own lack of measure." Vice, then, resembled heterogeneous matter. Formless, that is, nongeometrical, it was a ruleless, orderless, disproportionate multiplicity. And, as such, was deemed both evil and ugly.[108]

Many factors coincided and contributed to the popularization of a mathematical style of reasoning. Neoplatonism tied together mathematics as a metaphysical theology with ethics and aesthetics. On a more worldly plane, statistics appeared to offer an equally unsuperficial and pervasive application of quantified expressions to social data. This social science of numbers was developed between 1755 and 1770 by the mathematicians Johann Heinrich Lambert in Berlin, Pierre-Antoine de Laplace in Paris, Daniel Bernoulli in Basel, and George William Stimpson and Thomas Bayes in England. Statistics calculated mathematical probability to assess uncertainty and to turn inferences into coherent wholes. Although it was increasingly used in the interpretation of demographic phenomena, its initial area of application had been astronomy.[109] I wish to suggest that, together with Neoplatonism, the misuse of statistics fostered an oversimplification of such concepts as norm, type, ideal, perfection, deviation, defect. Further, it promoted a formulaic approach to the body, as if it were a calculable assemblage. The graphic layout of the illustrations to the *Essays* may now be seen as Fuseli's and Lavater's stumbling attempt to select the mean between measurably discordant features and figures. The latter were grouped together as homogeneous visual data taken from various sources but reengraved to look standardized. The efforts to derive representative types, deduced from many different observations, should be seen as the desire to appear "statistical." Indeed, the whole project could be characterized as one of assessing with certainty what was uncertain or undefined. The "science" of physiognomics was predicated on the ability to draw inferences from "known" surfaces to unknown depths, and from parts to wholes.[110] Even the multivolume encyclopedic format seemed to suggest that the greater the accumulation of evidence about the unknown, the closer we were to certain knowledge. It epitomized the belief that uncertainty was decreased as the number of observations was increased.

Physiognomics after Lavater became an overt "calculus" of observations based on the pseudo-comparison of measurements and the supposed consideration of equally likely cases. A source of this slide toward mathematical reductivism was the ambiguity inherent in the term "normal." Equivocal also were the diverse connotations of "typicalness" or of the "representative." These concepts could be interpreted as signifying the average, the mean, or the ideal. One sense of "normal" was that of a fact capable of description by statistical measurements taken of a large population. The other sense was that of the

66. **Johann Caspar Lavater, *The Georgian and the Bashkir,* from *Essays on Physiognomy,* 1792, III, part I, p. 263. Engraving by Thomas Holloway et al. (Photo: Courtesy National Library of Medicine, Bethesda, Md.)**

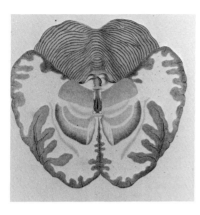

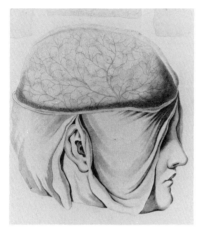

67. Félix Vicq d'Azyr, *Transverse View of the Brain,* from *Traité d'anatomie et de physiologie,* 1786, I. Colored engraving by Claude Briceau. (Photo: Courtesy National Library of Medicine, Bethesda, Md.)

68. Félix Vicq d'Azyr, *Dissection of the Meninges,* from *Traité d'anatomie et de physiologie,* 1786, I. Colored Engraving by Claude Briceau. (Photo: Courtesy National Library of Medicine, Bethesda, Md.)

normative or the ideal. By this term was intended an aesthetic, religious, and moral principle of approbation for a prototype or perfect form, and of disapprobation for anything that strayed or deviated from it.[111] Lavater conflated both connotations. Beyond that, however, the *Essays* also marked the merger of a biological demand for the actually normal, or typical, with an aesthetic and ethical demand for the perfect. The latter was synonymous with a fictional or uncommon beauty (fig. 66).[112]

The idea of "normative" anatomy had existed since Vesalius. It was customary to urge that the cadaver used for public dissections ought to be as "normal" as possible (a "middle" or "general" form). Thus other bodies might be compared to it with an eye to assessing nonnatural deviations from that norm.[113] Implicit in this admonition was the attendant notion that beauty resided in a sculptural canon. The purpose of this corporeal law was to establish a perfect commensurability among the various limbs and members. Abstract symmetries and proportions received renewed emphasis because of deep changes occurring in the late-eighteenth-century study of natural history. The anatomical figure was increasingly divorced from any sense of the fleshed "natural" body and turned into a lithic, even a mineralogical, specimen.[114] Félix Vicq d'Azyr (1748–1794) was in the vanguard of those reformers, like Philippe Pinel (1745–1826) and Camper, who wished to introduce the rigorous precision of the exact sciences into the study of comparative anatomy. As a celebrated physician, perpetual secretary of a rival society to the Faculté de Médecine, and a strong proponent of public health policies after the Revolution, Vicq was an important spokesman for the need to confer certainty on the discipline. Author, with Hippolyte Cloquet, of the *Anatomy* volumes in that compendium of the newly specialized professions, the *Encyclopédie méthodique* (1792–1819), he argued at length that each organ should be treated as a geometrical solid (fig. 67). Inspired by the abstract geometries characterizing contemporary French crystallographic research, he urged anatomists to analyze animal morphology in the regular and systematic way their colleagues probed crystals.[115] "First the exterior planes should be examined, then the edges and angles. The same methods and divisions apply for the study of the interior" (figs. 68, 69). But Vicq's ideal of a calibrated, sequential stripping away of tissue structure to obtain a simultaneous exterior rendering of the face and the underlying cortical surface would not be fully realized until the advent of MR images (fig. 70).

The introductory *Discours sur l'anatomie simple et comparée* was both encomium and summons. No science touched man as closely or had been more

69. Jean-Fabien Gautier Dagoty,
Quartzose and Cellular "Sports," from *Le*
règne minéral, 1783, pl. 30. Colored
engraving. (Photo: Courtesy the British
Library.)

70. David N. Levin, *Facial and Cortical 3D*
Models Derived from MR Images. (Photo:
Courtesy Maurice Goldblatt Magnetic
Resonance Imaging Center, Department of
Radiology, University of Chicago.)

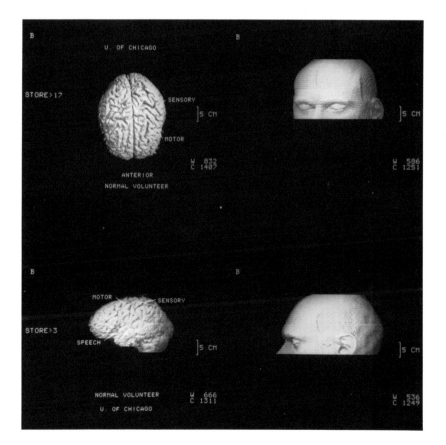

neglected. Vicq lamented that it was not a field like botany or chemistry, underwritten by rich *amateurs*. The wealthy no doubt found repugnant the sight of man's nothingness at close range. This ignorance of self was especially intolerable, however, while practical anatomy still awaited proper cultivation. He praised the contributions of his predecessors: Garengeot, Duverney, Glisson, Bidloo. But he was forced to conclude that, although men and animals had long been dissected separately, their methodical comparison had only slightly advanced. Much had been gathered, little compared. Never "has work been conducted on a common plan. Each [anatomist] described accord-

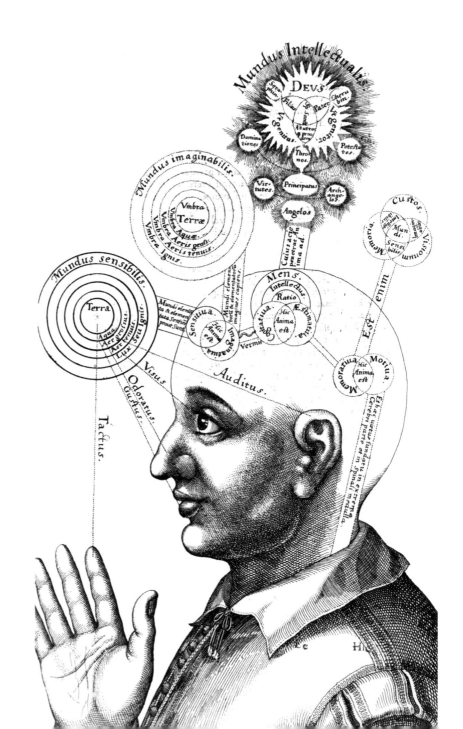

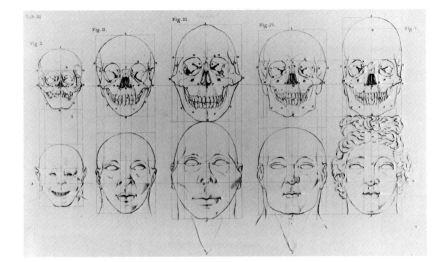

72. Pierre Camper, *From Ape to Apollo Belvedere,* from *Dissertation physique,* 1791, p1. 3. Engraving. (Photo: Courtesy National Library of Medicine, Bethesda, Md.)

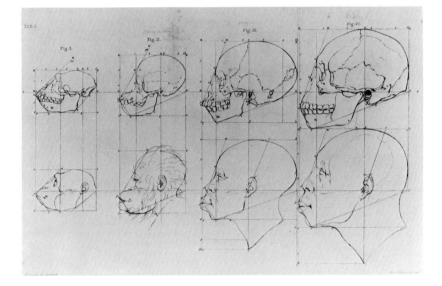

73. Pierre Camper, *Various Measurements of Facial Angles,* from *Dissertation physique,* 1791, p1. 1. Engraving. (Photo: Courtesy National Library of Medicine, Bethesda, Md.)

ing to his manner, & in the sequence he conceived best according to his system or his habits; & sometimes even without any determined order." Only now had nomenclature moved toward standardization, creating a new language of the body. Useless verbs, overloaded or confusing descriptions, and equivocal terms were excised (fig. 71).[116]

Petrus or Pierre Camper (1722–1789), Dutch surgeon, virtuoso executant of anatomical drawings, university professor, friend to Buffon, Vicq d'Azyr, Hemsterhuis, and John Hunter, was the linchpin in the development and dissemination of a body calculus.[117] Ironically, this effect was inadvertent and occurred in an illustrated reference book destined for art students. Nonetheless, his pyrrhonic search for a criterion of truth in the projection of the body provided the susceptible reader with the opportunity to imbue precisely measured skulls with a Neoplatonic value system of normative straight lines and deviant angles.[118] The standardized line engravings, with their flawlessly "technical" appearance, spoke volumes in spite of the contradictory text (figs. 72, 73). The drawings were made according to a geometrical method in which the subject was viewed from a wandering visual point. This meant that the optical axis was always at right angles to the object being rendered. The resulting designs constituted a seemingly incontrovertible optical demonstration that measurements do not lie. From his teacher, rival, and eventual antagonist, the Leiden anatomist Bernard Albinus's *Annotationes Academicae* (1754–1768), he learned to draw the skeleton not freehand, but from measurements taken from three polarized points. Thus Camper became adept at constructing composite models. Already in the 1720s—with the help of the *peintre-graveur* Jan Wandelaar—Albinus had hoped to capture more than the idiosyncrasies of any particular system of bone or musculature. He sought to establish a universally representative, or average, type free from abnormalities. This artificial, or codified, *homo perfectus* was deduced from a heterogeneous collection of specimens taken from different bodies.[119]

Architecture, the most abstract language of design, also provided an important model for the technique of drawing in parallel projection. Like contemporary French theorists such as Etienne-Louis Boullée (1728–1799) and Claude-Nicolas Ledoux (1736–1806) and comparative anatomists such as Vicq d'Azyr, Camper considered the art of body building as a form of rational writing. Both types of construction were to generate a progression of fundamental, symmetrical, or "perfect" characters. Circles, spheres, rectangles, squares were not only geometrical figures but skeletal symbols of an underlying and permanent cosmic order. Thus, in creating a diagrammatic and abstract structure that spoke precisely to the eyes, the "science" of architecture was intrinsically physiognomic.[120] Camper—following its example, and unlike earlier anatomists (figs. 25, 36, 39, 40, 45, 49)—did not set the figure within a localizing, "aesthetic," or vanishing-point perspective.[121] Imitating the orthogonal rendering of the elevations, profiles, and sections of an inorganic building—presented as they invariably *are*—he situated fragmented limbs and members within an illusion-free vacuum. Morphology was to be looked at from an "objective" or indeterminate distance, thus avoiding the sensory distortions accompanying subjective vision.[122] Detached body parts subsisted, as it were, in a Newtonian ether, mysteriously pinned to the void.

Two years after his father's death, Adriaan Gilles Camper published the *Dissertation physique* (1791), which shortly thereafter was translated into

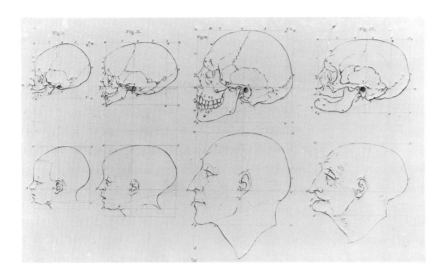

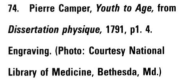

74. Pierre Camper, *Youth to Age,* from *Dissertation physique,* 1791, p1. 4. Engraving. (Photo: Courtesy National Library of Medicine, Bethesda, Md.)

English by a physician. The illustrations provided incontrovertible proof for how deeply systematics dominated Enlightenment zoology. As we have seen, the time was ripe for the reception of a "scientific" classification of bone structure, including the cranium, ranging from the fetus to the adult. Moreover, in an age of museum founding, the visual display of the progression from superior to inferior classes of animals constituted a veritable microcosm of the descent of man. The *Museum Camperianum,* and the lectures compiled by his scientist son, together spread before the late-eighteenth-century viewer or auditor a formal architectonic. A confusing multiplicity of phenomena, including extinct races, ancient inhabitants of the earth, and exotic peoples, seemed to demand a grand and orderly theory of the human body that summarized all its varieties and relations.[123] But it was specifically this posthumous compendium of the elder Camper's ideas on the facial angle that publicized the underlying geometry of nature's works and made of the broadminded anatomist a seemingly bigoted epistemologist. Anticipating the theories of L. Adolphe Quetelet (1796–1874) concerning the "common man," Camper's equivocal imagery further served to confuse the reigning ambiguity between normality interpreted as a measurable average and as an ideal. The latter connotation was tied up with the goal of ethical and physical uniformity, health, and beauty.[124] The subject was initially broached by Camper in 1764. That year, the topic of one of his annual anatomical lessons at Groningen University was on "The Origin and Color of the Blacks." His dissections were intended to refute the specious notions about the inferiority of the Negro promulgated by the German anatomist Meckel.[125] Subsequently, the

75. Johann Caspar Lavater, *Wrinkled Countenance,* from *Essays on Physiognomy,* 1792, II, part II, p. 254. Engraving by Thomas Holloway, et al. (Photo: Courtesy National Library of Medicine, Bethesda, Md.)

topic of standard parameters in the physical description of mankind was broadened in a series of lectures delivered, in 1768, before the Academy of Design in Amsterdam. Their avowed purpose was to show "that national differences may be reduced to rules" concerning the directions of the facial line or angle. Constituting a basic norm or canon again, derived not from human beings but, in this case, from classical sculpture, it was intended to prevent the artist from indiscriminately "blending the features of different nations in the same individual." Like Lavater, Camper was obsessed with the need "to distinguish between accidental forms [caused by disease, age, youth, etc.] and national marks" (figs. 74, 75). This proper, legible distribution, and avoidance of improper, illegible blending, were to be achieved by imposing schemata on the body. Superimposed ovals, circles, and squares—the very design principles fundamental to every eighteenth-century manual on the elements of drawing—became the corporeal ideal (fig. 64).[126]

Camper laid out a visual progression comparing the proportions of parts of the head of an orangutan, Negro, Calmuck, ancient Roman, and the *Apollo Belvedere* (fig. 72). He asserted that the ideal facial angle of 100 degrees was not to be found in nature but existed in Greek art alone. The utmost ideality permitted to any European was 10 degrees behind or before the perpendicular line HI. Lines exceeding in either direction lost their beauty and even became misshapen. But Negroes also had their maximum and minimum of comeliness (fig. 73). If they sank below 65 degrees, they approached the ape, the snipe, the dog. It must be underlined again, however, that Camper did not attach a taxonomic significance to quantifiable differences in facial angles. Like Buffon and Maupertuis, he was a monogeneticist believing in the fundamental unity of mankind.

Camper's *text* emphasized that his system was an *aide-mémoire* for the artist, and its primary purpose to assist in creating pleasing optical effects. The "New Method" for delineating heads (first forming the skull, then marking the facial line, then arranging the parts) was not inflexible. It was better "to deviate a little" from the strict rules of proportion in order to increase the beauty of a piece than to render it less pleasing "by a servile conformity." Moreover, he explicitly stated that his intention—unlike previous writers on the passions from Leonardo to Le Brun—was "not to speculate concerning the workings of the soul, but to enquire what changes take place in the body, in consequence of its operations." In every emotion, particular nerves were affected; thus artists ought to be familiar with anatomy.[127] His concern, then, was to demonstrate incontrovertibly, and unlike other writers on aesthetics, in what precisely beauty visually consisted. Reverting to the language of body connoisseurship, Camper lamented how difficult it was to distinguish loveliness in works of art. "The more they are complicated, the less are their beauties discernible by the vulgar." Yet anyone with a claim to taste must be able to discriminate the excellent "from every mixture of imperfection." Art academies, therefore, had the obligation to instruct in "the manner of correcting any defects that may be conspicuous." Accuracy was a pedagogical concern because beauty did not depend on external circumstances but on some teachable "relation and proportion between different parts." The fashionable silhouette was useful to the artist in helping him ascertain "the precise situation" of actual eyes, nose, mouth, and chin. The "nicest proportions," however, did not stem from reality but, in quasi-statistical fashion, from a selective sampling taken from a great variety of artificial or fictive persons.[128]

As was true of anatomical treatises and drawing manuals in general (and Camper's reference book was both), the illustrations were of greater importance than the text. They conveyed more, and different kinds of, information than the printed page. The engravings constituted an international, technical "imagistic" universally comprehensible without translation. Camper's optical theories for determining a "fine" countenance in *works of art* could be interpreted from the plates as positing useful standards for *human* comparison. Further, they could be understood as constituting an infallible anthropological method for visibilizing psychic perfection and imperfection in different ethnic groups.

Camper unintentionally, through the persuasiveness of his abstract heads, advanced the search in progress for some measurement whereby anatomy and intelligence could be correlated.[129] Take the case of the physiologist and professor of anatomy at the Ecole des Beaux Arts. Jean-Joseph Sue (1760–1830), in the *Essai sur la physionomie* (1797), praised Camper for his proof that men, animals, and plants possessed national forms "striking" in their differences. Significantly, this diversity was to be sought deep in the anatomy. The critical artist "must bring the scalpel" to the human machine. He must "traverse, visit, interrogate all its paths . . . disjoin and rejoin its articulations; to finally know [*connoître*] the entire internal mechanism in order better to seize the changes that can occur on the exterior." Sue transformed the painter's abbreviated means of diagramming the body into a caricatural end: "the methodical epitome of anatomy." A quick sketching device or pedagogical technique for acquiring the rudiments of design was metamorphosed into

a semiotics. Geometrized corporeal signs were indicative of inward perfection: upright stance, oval head, square and planar forehead, round eyes, arcuated brows, convex cheeks, obtuse and convex chin, almost straight-line lips, parallel teeth.[130] Sue could, and did, say with Proclus that everything just is equal, and everything equal is fair. "The unequal is ugly and without proportion because it is out of accord." His goal was statistical quantification with "measurements taken specifically from a large number of subjects" in order to fix the mathematical point at which beautiful nature came into existence. But we are no longer merely in the realm of art. Sue literally constructed the soul out of mathematical forms, divided it according to numbers, bound it together with proportions and ratios, and deposited in it the primal principles of all figures: straight line, circle, square, triangle. Thus the Frenchman and the Circassian possessed the appropriate beauty, "whereas the Greenlander and the Calmuck preferred a face of deformed size, with tiny eyes and two holes instead of nostrils." Bedouins and African women painted their chins and lips blue and tattooed a multitude of "bizarre shapes on various portions of their bodies." Mongols cut their skin into flower forms and painted them, while the Siamese stained their teeth black. Most of these "savages" were lazy, superstitious, ignorant, and "strangers to the idea of the good as well as the beautiful."[131]

The "anatomical" tendency to simplify, abstract, isolate, and detach segments of the body in order to calculate incongruity continued in the popular phrenological exercises of Franz Josef Gall (1758–1828) and Johann Georg Spurzheim (1776–1832). Their pioneering work in the localization of cerebral

77. George Cruikshank, *Bumpology*, 1826. Aquatint and etching. (Photo: Courtesy National Library of Medicine, Bethesda, Md.)

function, published between 1810 and 1819, immured the most impalpable functions of the psyche within the material cortex. They exceeded even Thomas Willis's (1621—1675) physiognomics of the brain. According to the British physician, the "best figure" was "globous" so that the spirits could pour forth equally from its middle part to bathe the whole body. "Flat," "sharp," or otherwise "improportionate" heads further indicated "some noted fault of the Animal Function." But phrenology deduced normal or abnormal intellectual capacities from healthy or aberrant skulls.[132]

The craze for cranial criticism—a comic inversion of Garengeot's knowledgeable surgical touch—released a flood of satire on its "feeling" adepts obscenely palpating protruding knobs and sprouting excrescences (fig. 76). George Cruikshank's (1792–1878) "bumpologist" Deville "pores o'er the cranial map with learned eyes/ Each rising hill and bumpy knoll descries,/ Here secret fires, and their deep mines of sense/ His touch detects beneath each prominence" (fig. 77). The fashionable phrenologist systematically classified numbered "organs" or partitioned regions according to the dual categories of sentiment and understanding. Similarly, Cruikshank's mental reader elucidated unseen morals ("excellent character") and intellectual faculties ("very large wit") from the unprepossessing appearance of his client's lumpy head.[133] John Varley (1778–1842), a member of the Blake circle and a successful watercolorist, was perhaps a more serious but no less ardent believer in phrenology. In his *Zodiacal Physiognomy* (1828), Varley praised its astrological ability to unlock a person's quality of mind, temper, and disposition. He believed such analyses tended to confirm synecdochically that a part of nature disclosed, or at least indicated, the whole. Thus "naturalists often discover by seeing only a fragment of a bone, to what animal it belonged." It was for Varley that Blake prepared his "Visionary Heads," or "portraits" of famous personages, "appearing" during the course of their seances together. Thus phrenology became yet another attempt to capture the invisible. Like ghosts, it was the material manifestation of the world beyond the immediate senses.[134] For the less enthusiastic, however, like the physician Baumgärtner, it denoted the misguided striving to measure spiritual energy from bony outcrops. It seemed symptomatic of the woeful lack of correspondence between impalpable powers and volumetric organs.[135]

But phrenology was merely the logical extension of a quantified physiognomics or calculating "science" of the unseen. It continues to thrive in the late twentieth century in any "technicism" or interpretation of the world viewed myopically through one interpretive strategy. As we have seen, physiognomic theory represented an idolatrous fixation on a single unified method for arriving at universal truth. In ignoring the need to pay attention to discontinuities, and in the radical simplification of empirical complexity, it was not unlike contemporary systems analysis. Promulgated by cyberneticians, the latter's goal is the establishment of a new "generalist" basis of intellectual inquiry.[136] Physiognomics also anticipated the original psychiatric tactic, replete with the assumption of linguistic and analytical superiority over a patient supine and immobilized on a couch. Sigmund Freud (1856–1939) extended the vertical language of body criticism to the all-knowing connoisseurship of the concealed and deviant properties of the mind.[137] In this mental archaeology, hidden motives and shapeless desires were laid bare in the systematic process of excavation. More recently, prenatal screening and genetic testing for Huntington's disease should prompt us to ask whether physiognomics has not disappeared but merely become further interiorized. Alcoholics and violent psychopaths have been discovered by a new age of psychiatrists to possess brains that look different. Will social and correctional judgments, as well as medical decisions, be deduced from internal lesions?

Present-day connoisseurs of art analogously make use of old and new scientific techniques (autoradiographs, infrared reflectography, thread counts) to peer below the painted and illusory surface of their object of study. These state-of-the-art methods of detection—like DNA fingerprinting in biology—are intended to objectify and quantify elusive spiritual qualities. They seek to identify the artist's indisputable yet phantom hand in the physical traces of his work.[138] Think, too, of the modern connoisseurs' Neoclassical ancestors seeking semantic clarity below the empirical rubble. Winckelmann and Mengs had objected to the lack of clarity and legibility in Baroque art. Appositely, aesthetic properties today are still assumed to consist solely of codifiable, observable attributes or of decipherable systems of lines, vectors, geometric shapes, and colors.[139]

Getting unruly phenomena under control also informed the "engineering ideal" operating in biology laboratories from the late nineteenth century onward. In this hothouse milieu, natural objects declined as artificial constructions expanded.[140] The move toward artifice is most evident, perhaps, in the "laboratory" of the elective plastic surgery clinic. Lavater's prayer for physiognomic predictability and the erasure of a welter of irregular facial details has been answered in the disembodied manipulations possible to the computer monitor. Malleable and unmoored spare body parts have attained—because of video imaging—the infinitely reproducible status of Duchamp's manufactured "readymades." No doubt, it is in the field of cosmetic surgery that induced conformity to normative and culturally defined standards of conventionally understood, or "average," good looks will reach its apogee. The new "facial architect" or "psychosurgeon" has color imaging systems at his fingertips. Dr. Mark Kaplan, a notable advocate of "facial harmony," claims to be responding to our society's belief that "prettier people are more intelligent. Prettier people advance more in the workplace. Prettier people have more satisfying interpersonal relationships. And it's all true."[141] In the summary of a recent symposium on the topic, participants ranging from sculptors to directors of model agencies were reputed to have talked "about how you could make the eyes more important, how you could eliminate some of the accidents, the disorder of the face. . . . There is so much chaos in the outside world." Art was called upon to assist in the general process of beautification by providing more interesting ideals, transcending all those "cute, bland faces." According to one plastic surgeon present, his was the only area of medicine where the possibility existed of being creative. One is, in fact, "doing a form of sculpture on flesh and bone . . . I take the art I see in museums into the operating room and translate that into actuality."[142] No matter that negative reactions to successful type-changing operations also included loss of identity, a sense of "not looking like myself."[143] Concern over the surgically created ideal face and body, however, was not new. Lavater's corporeal cartoon expunged marks of individuality and pruned to the limits of graphic economy. Its uninteresting reductivism had worried earlier defendants of a cluttered and unsymmetrical biological and aesthetic complexity.

Pathognomics, or the Pursuit of Looks

Indirect _____

adj., Not straight; not rectilinear. Not tending otherwise than obliquely or consequentially to a purpose.

Dr. Johnson, *Dictionary*

Randonnée _____

noun, Hunting term, it is the name of the course that hunters take in pursuit of the beast they are chasing.

Diderot and D'Alembert, *Encyclopédie*

The sequential knife of anatomy or reason, dividing the world or the body into assessable parts, cut the universe in two. What lay motionless underneath sensuous appearances acquired timeless importance. A contrary, empirical method posited reality as a dynamic flux. Inherently unknowable in depth, actuality was pursuable across variegated surfaces. Change was not accessible through linear, straight-as-an-arrow directedness. Its graduated fine adjustments, in the words of Hogarth, led "the eye a wanton kind of chace."

Pursuing is the business of our lives; and even abstracted from any other view, gives pleasure. Every arising difficulty, that for a while attends and interrupts the pursuit, gives a sort of spring to the mind, enhances the pleasure, and makes what would else be toil and labour, become sport and recreation.[144]

Hunting, with its "frequent turns and difficulties," its random and idiosyncratic animal movements, its diverging multiple paths, stood for everything resistant to quantification, logic, and immutability.

Lichtenberg's hermeneutics of uneven surfaces, or pathognomics, adumbrated Gibson's twentieth-century environmental psychology of "ambulatory vision." For both thinkers, visual awareness was panoramic and persisted during a lifetime of locomotion. Unlike the physiognomist or phrenologist, they posited our need to see not vertically but kinetically, continually, and all around a body. It was the essence of active human perception to take different points of observation, not to freeze dichotomized views. An "ecological" mutuality existed between milieu and human being. Both were heterogeneous flatlands separated by a medium, not by a homogeneous ether or "space." Their encounter was reciprocally marking.[145] This topographical notion of surface, not interior, as the place where the action was, carried over to the geography of the body. Corporeal landmarks invited not penetrating dissection but visual journeying. According to one of Lichtenberg's aphorisms, physiology was an explorable terrain. "The most entertaining plane [*Fläche*] on the earth is that of the human countenance."[146] Physiognomics considered the face grammatically, "abstracted from all the fleeting signs which paint the actual situation of the soul." Pathognomics, on the other hand, hunted after symptomatic behavioral and gestural meaning in the layout of an exterior. Like the tracking of ambiguous traces and vanishing spoor, it was an unfolding art of pattern recognition.[147] The body was no longer merely a wayward figural language requiring surgical management by correcting words. With pathognomics, it became the subject of sport. Puzzling, subtle, elusive expressions eluded language but not perception.

The metaphor of the hunt for knowledge stretched from Plato to the nineteenth-century *flâneur*, stalking fleeting sensations. When our mind does not have a clear contact or sight of objects, it must make elaborate excursions. It "advances on them step by step and endeavors to capture them by their consequences."[148] Unlike the mathematical method based on arithmetic and geometric order, however, hunting signified tangible ways and myriad paths of pursuit. It was an experimental quest, a practical Baconian voyage, encouraging each person to conduct his own research on nature. Representing a distrust of system, it was consonant with an open-ended impressionistic format. The haphazard and fragmentary arrangement of visual data mimicked the incoherent and simultaneous manner in which experiences actually presented themselves to a mobile observer.[149] It discouraged memorization and ritualized reading. It frowned on a trained moving back and forth from perplexing image to explanatory text.[150] Attention, instead, was directed to shifting optical properties.

Hunting was inseparable from human evolution. Under the veil of civilization, we are still imprinted with the raw drive to pursue. The architecture and function of the modern brain remain crisscrossed with ancient neural pathways along which our ancestors groped.[151] Paleolithic hunt magic became transformed into pleasurable bodily diversion associated increasingly, after the fall of the Roman Empire, with aristocratic power and freedom of movement. The right to hunt—in spite of occasional enlightened protests—was intrinsic to feudal society as a privilege of the court. The nomadic existence of early hunters was also progressively internalized during a more sedentary age. As roving intellectual curiosity, it stalked and trapped elusive conceptual game. Both activities came together in the aristocratic hunt that attained its high point in the eighteenth century. Hunting with hounds, or coursing, mounted hunts after bear and boar, or chases, runs after stag, or venery, the hunt on foot, with blunderbuss and flintlock, or stalking, and beating out game: all provided images rich in metaphorical connotations of purposeful pursuit.[152] Thus I wish to argue that the hunter is the model of the pathognomist chasing after mutable appearances.

Hunting enjoyed popularity both as an intellectual and as a physical exercise. But it is to the mental aspect of the chase that we now turn. In general, it had three principal components: the practical reason or cunning of the hunter, the instinct of the wild animal, and the trap. Thus the *Encyclopédie* noted, it "is necessary for the successful maintenance of traps to know well the instinct and habits of the animals one seeks to catch." The adroit hunter must know the tendencies of the animal he is hunting. "The important point is to be well acquainted with the animal's ruses, and to lack neither care nor vigilance."[153] Using this sensory understanding, the hunter attempted to lure the beast into his trap. As described in the *Encyclopédie*, hunting dealt strictly with the intellectual maneuvers employed to outwit a constantly shifting and wily prey. Thus the experiential knowledge of the kinds of enticing bait (*appâts*) needed to attract different species was essential. Further, the hunter had to understand precisely how to set various types of snares tailored to the specific animal pursued.

In sum, the "superficial" sport of hunting was like the charms of love, the game of knowledge, and the play of life. The "maladroit or negligent hunter" was "frequently deceived by the animal in front of him."[154] "Deception" was a key term in this game of wit and knowledge (*connoissance*). When the hunter lacked appropriate subtlety, he was outsmarted by the beast. Another major concept was that of the "path." It was directly tied to the choice of location for the trap and, consequently, to firsthand sensory awareness of the animal's bent and disposition. Traps "must be disposed in such a manner that the animal, in following its natural gait, passes over them to reach the proffered bait." The term *trace* (spoor, track, footprint) was directly related to the notion of path, since the successful hunter required a working experience of habitual trails. The article on "venery" explained how dogs must be permitted to feel out or sniff (*goûter*) any routes with which they were unfamiliar. By using their keen sense of smell, they traced the most recent byways taken by the hunted prey.[155] But the beast itself represented evasive instinct and the metamorphic life of the senses. Different animals habitually had different

122

means of trying "to escape pursuit." The successful hunter thus needed to be aware of the looks of all these "distinctive inclinations." Nonetheless, even when girded with appropriate and individualized types of knowledge, success was not assured.

It is not sufficient for the hunter to be instructed in information relative to the animals he wishes to seize, he must be armed with a good bloodhound who has an acute and well-trained nose, who does not abandon the old paths, and who is not carried away to the extent of barking up those which are fresh. On the sureness of the dog often depends the success of the hunter's quest.[156]

The pathognomist's oblique pursuit of ephemeral looks was not an anatomical war waged against changing sensory data, nor a perpendicular conquest, but a kind of physiological angling. Like the sophist, he fished not for essence or character but for the myriad "airs" of animate things.[157] James Parsons (1705–1770), antiquarian, famous physician, and friend to Hogarth, was an important proponent of the elusive expressiveness of the total organism. Praising the "great Addison," he cited his motto to the eighty-sixth *Spectator* paper:

Every passion gives a particular Cast to the Countenance, and is apt to discover itself in some Feature or another. . . . The Air of the whole Face is much more expressive than the Lines of it [fig. 78]: *The Truth of it is the Air and is generally nothing else but the inward Disposition of the mind made visible.*

Not the skeleton but the muscles were the most suitable medium for capturing the mutable patterns of bodily energy. The "Bent or Disposition of the Mind" shaped habitual appearance. In the Crounian Lectures on muscular motion, read before the Royal Society in 1746 and published in 1747 as *Human Physiognomy Explain'd*, Parsons rejected prior systems. In this first wide-ranging English medical study of the passions, he mocked the ancients' focus on the bones of the head as the seat "of a good or bad turn of mind." Preferring the more modest term "metoposcopy" ("arising from a view of the face alone"), Parsons's project—which, like Camper's later *Dissertation physique*, was intended to be helpful to artists—was physiognomic in title alone. Anatomy was used not as an ethical metaphor. Its sole function was to prove which muscles determined the expression of particular passions. Further, it was to demonstrate their specific role in the formation of general symmetry (composure) or dissymmetry (joy, grief, fury, ill-nature). Musculature provided a nuanced and responsive differential support for the sliding skin of the face.[158] For the metoposcopist, then, the countenance was "the *Nuncio* of the mind." He hunted its fleeting messages in the motions regularly crossing it. Unlike the physiognomist, Parsons recognized the sane person's chameleon power to change his opinion and, even in the manner of the actor, for a short

time voluntarily or artfully to "put on the grimace." Much like Pernety, he was occupied with facial fraud. But he was also convinced that the muscles found one out in the end by revealing incongruous motions. Reminiscent of Oliver Sacks's aphasiacs, he was preternaturally sensitive to any falsity or impropriety in bodily appearance. The physician possessed a keen sensory understanding beyond words of what constituted authentic or inauthenic expression. Thus a cheerful mien could be distinguished from "a fictitious mirth put on." Although the mouth assumed a smile, it seemed forced—like that of a player in a comedy—"for want of the mind's influence." Similarly, the muscles of the eyes and mouth were not in accord in a feigning look that tried to disguise contempt while the lips sneered (fig. 79).[159]

DISSECTING

79.   James Parsons, *Sneering Woman,*
from *Crounian Lectures on Muscular
Motion,* 1745, p1. 4. Engraving by J.
Mynde. (Photo: Courtesy National Library
of Medicine, Bethesda, Md.)

Parsons's medical awareness of the suppleness of physiology and his psychological insight into the complexity of voluntary and involuntary compound
expressions were pathognomic. His heir in the knowing chase after mobile
appearances was the anglophilic essayist, astute interpreter of Hogarth, and
professor of natural sciences and philosophy at the University of Göttingen,
Georg Christoph Lichtenberg (1742–1799). In his sustained attack on the first
edition of Lavater's *Physiognomische Fragmente,* wittily entitled *Über Physiognomik, wider die Physiognomen* (1778), Lichtenberg advanced a passionate apology for existence on the level. In contrast to physiognomics, with its deep
soundings of the body's inflexible and solid structure, pathognomics was "the
entire semiotic of the emotions, or the knowledge of the natural signs of the

passions' movements, according to all their gradations and mixtures." Reverting to the imagery of the chase, Lichtenberg tackled the key expressive problem of inwardness, or the relationship of visible spoor to invisible propensity. Human animals "do not walk on all fours, but they move with all fours." That is, not the head as in physiognomics or phrenology, but all members were energetic and "spoke." On the corporeal plane, the discerning hunter encountered "signs and traces of thoughts, inclinations, and capabilities." For the physiognomist, this shifting "life on the surface [was] the source of all error." Conversely, for the pathognomist the senses "exhibit only superficies, and all else [are but] conclusions drawn from them."[160] Individuals were refracting, not reflecting corrugated surfaces, no different from their opaque surroundings or the Gibsonian rough and speckled textures of the world. Like that milieu, then, they were equally difficult to see through.[161] Their astonishing formal variety (fig. 80) was misunderstood by Lavater as exhibiting moral and voluntary causes.[162] Diversity, instead, was affected by the impact of the involuntary lashes of fate, toil, climate, disease, food. Shortsightedness, tooth loss, pock marks, even singing or intense listening, could transform the play of features without touching the character. Conversely, not everyone was imprinted identically by the same circumstances. Wrinkles, for example, arising from the thousand-fold repetition of a single motion were less perceptible in certain people (fig. 75). It was only Lavater's antiquarian pedantry that permitted him to suppose Winckelmann meant by beauty the absolute congruity between perfect soul and typical body. If this were the case, Lichtenberg quipped, then the speediest way to transform Germans into Greeks would be to imitate English breeding practices. Hybridization aimed to convert homely domestic sheep and horses into Spanish and Arabian thoroughbreds![163]

Lichtenberg disparaged physiognomics as an art of prophecy. It was no more reliable than weather forecasts in spite of a century's worth of meteorological measurements gathered by scientific academies. He wanted to halt such prognostication of behavior. Divining would be accurate if individuals were not free agents and if their bodies had developed "in the purest ether." Then, indeed, they would have been modified only by the motions of their own souls, undiverted by any external force. Yet like a crystal, whose pure geometrical planes were never perfect when encountered in nature, human beings developed eccentrically. They turned into anomalies through social interaction, or adaptation, carried out within an atmosphere. Other people, and physical events beyond control—not just moral actions—eroded our edges

and distorted our contours. "Thus our body stands between soul and ambient world, in the middle, mirror of the effect of both," and causing even the most practiced observer to err in its interpretation.[164] Character was principally expressed by the succession of changes in the same face that no portrait, much less the abstract silhouette, could represent (figs. 56, 57, 60, 61). The pathognomic alterations occurring in a living countenance were "a language for the eyes," uttering forth an entire being. For Lichtenberg, then, corporeal "tone" was embedded in a total material expressiveness that transcended the verbal. Dress, bearing, demeanor, the shape of a hat and the public manner of wearing it told reams about the sense of self. It superseded long hours of physiognomic deduction made from the immobile portions of the body.[165]

Lichtenberg possessed a Rococo and Epicurean sensibility. Like Antoine Watteau (1684–1721) or Gabriel-Jacques de Saint-Aubin (1724–1780), he was attuned to arabesqued gestures, balletic attitudes, and a whole *pittoresque* of spirited airs.[166] These painters of modern life frequently drew their fashionable figures from the back, avoiding the naked crudeness of physiognomic frontality. Similarly, the pathognomist was fascinated by the oblique adventures and misadventures of the clothed body caught up in the social chase. Physiognomics was "Neoclassical" and male in its linguistic and single-minded will to impose sequence and logic on experiential confusion. Path-

80.   Johann Caspar Lavater, *Human Variety*, from *Essays on Physiognomy*, 1792, II, part I, p. 43. Engraving by Thomas Holloway et al. (Photo: Courtesy National Library of Medicine, Bethesda, Md.)

ognomics, however, was "Rococo" and female in its tolerance of optical indirection and refusal to subjugate baffling inconsistencies. Lichtenberg's sympathetic sense for corporeal decrepitude and the uncontrollable power of decay found a counterpart in the sculpture of Jean-Baptiste Pigalle (1714–1785). The terracotta sketch for the *Naked Voltaire* (Orléans, Musée des Beaux-Arts, 1776) was pathognomic in its disregard of decorous atemporal beauty. The sculptor bravely exposed the *philosophe*'s aging body in flux with its flabby torso, veined arms, sunken cheeks, and pursed mouth.[167]

Lichtenberg was also an embodiment of the often-unrecognized latitudinarian strain of eighteenth-century culture. He defended both the supposed ugliness of the Malicolan natives Cook encountered during his first voyage to the Pacific and the unconventional looks of the African black. No wonder the latter's profile was taken to signify the ideal of stupidity and recalcitrance. No wonder he was branded as incarnating the asymptote of the European facial line designating dumbness and meanness. Lichtenberg derided the false anthropology that routinely juxtaposed Negro slaves and sailors "with a candidate in *belles-lettres*" (fig. 72). Falling back on an architectural analogy, he declared one must first understand the country in which a building stood before judging its construction. Yet, unheedingly, the physiognomist jumped from similar noses to analogous states of mind, and from measured deviations of external forms to deformations of the soul.[168]

This sympathy for a broad range of human types and experience was joined to the generous belief that most people possessed something inward, distinctly their own, and thus valuable. Pluralism made Lichtenberg an astute observer of urban life. He remains the still unsurpassed interpreter of Hogarth's city satires. As a dwarfish hunchback, he resembled those "remarkable" perambulating characters populating the *Harlot's* (1732) and *Rake's Progress* (1735) and the *Marriage à la Mode* (1743–1745). These engravings comprised a compendium of London paupers, vagabonds, imposters, and performers, displaying their deformities, or moral "backsides," in "common-street exhibitions."[169]

The *Commentaries on Hogarth* were first published in installments between 1794 and 1799 and further fueled the immense popularity of the English artist among the German middle and lower classes.[170] Lichtenberg engaged in the same fine-grained hermeneutics, initially evolved in the pathognomical studies, when he trained his eye on the prints of contemporary high and low life. In this area, too, he differed from the anatomizing art critic or physiog-

nomical connoisseur. These specialists in negation expunged evidence of
deviant handling and banished unconventional departures from an "authentic"
canon. Freely admitting the difficulties inherent in interpretation, Lichtenberg acknowledged the complexity of the work of art. Resembling an intricate
human being, it was "not just casually flashed onto the canvas by a single
coup de main." Furthermore, since Hogarth, or "the sole pair of eyes who saw
this work with total clarity," was dead, the interpreter must compensate for
the weakness inherent in any single point of view. This dense and rich graphic
production demanded a plurality of observers and a multiplicity of observations. Summing up an interpretive credo equally applicable to art or life,
Lichtenberg inquired, what did it matter that he might have added thoughts
to the work of a great artist? This augmentation was unimportant, "so long
as I have not subtracted or explained away such as are patently present."[171]

2 ABSTRACTING

Systems of Epitomization

The extraordinary regard with which simplicity was held throughout the eighteenth century developed, by its close, into a full-blown theory of abstraction. Camper and Lichtenberg represented its "bare" and "dressed" antitheta, its dual formal tendencies toward either a radical linear emptiness or an extravagant chromatic complexity. From the Neoplatonists—whose resurgence we witnessed—to the nineteenth-century French idealists, the making of art increasingly involved the mathematical denaturalization of matter. This cerebral process of detachment was evident both in a general and unconditional grammar of fundamental geometrical shapes and vectors and in a prismatic science of heterogeneous colored parts.[1] Whether naked diagram or mosaic assemblage, the two types of abstraction shared the Neoclassical drive toward systematization and the Romantic compulsion to locate the prototype below the manifold of appearances. Dictionaries, technical tracts, model books, penmanship and drawing manuals promoted a logic, or universal characteristic, of essential, teachable elements. These were both an alphabet of design rudiments and a metaphysics of invariant ciphers. Art could thus simultaneously inform and reform the world.

Since the eighteenth century, one trend of Modernism has been to eliminate touch and other signs of manual construction. Painting, sculpture, and architecture have been diverted away from their roots in body performance toward critical mental activity. Art as visible language, moving toward ever more

Abstract _____
adj., Separated from something else; generally used with relation to mental perceptions; as abstract mathematics, abstract terms, in opposition to concrete *. . . refined, pure.*
Dr. Johnson, *Dictionary*

Abstrait _____
adj., It is said of persons and things. An abstract mind [esprit] *is an inattentive mind, uniquely occupied with its own thoughts . . .*
Diderot and D'Alembert, *Encyclopédie*

abbreviated and dematerialized expressions, characterized concrete poetry, De Stijl, Suprematism, Conceptualism, and now computer graphics. Mondrian's "New Painting" reduced the world to pure essences invoked through the calculation of intangible relations on a plane. Mies van der Rohe's highly abstract architecture, or the art of building as "almost nothing," was indicative of a Proclusian minimalism. The better a construction, the less it was. Think, too, of Malevich's turn toward silence, black and white, the spaceless and formal zero, in the attempt to have painting declare its theory directly without linguistic intervention.[2] Paradoxically, however, this desire to escape language was itself logocentric. Rarefied schemata, fleshless diagrams, and epitomizing symbols were semantic strategies for deflating visual intricacy and for perpetuating an anesthetized optical nihilism. The mental operation behind the starvation of a fat reality into elegantly thin formulas was congruent with anatomizing criticism. It employed the identical negative procedures for dissecting, amputating, and thus removing the contradiction, ambiguity, and superfluity of experience. This calligraphy of absence, circumscribing the blank absolute, was part of a decontaminating tradition inherited from antiquity and seeking eternal, immutable principles. Its practical application was to result in artistic compositions cleansed of the dung of life. They looked like what they were aiming to diagram, like nothingness, like an ideal inner vacancy contrary to the collage of external confusion. Thus the rigor of geometry was the prototype of all theoretical, atemporal reckoning, or apodictic dogma, transmitted in a priori linear and monochromatic stereotypes. As half of a long-standing anthropological dualism, it was in deep conflict with a practical and sophistic way of straying among specific details, temporal circumstances, and individual instances.[3] This rhetorical or indicative approach—devised from the empathetic standpoint of Lichtenberg's experiencing psyche—did not regard the world as a prison or the body as living in exile at a site of contamination. Compositions resulting from this view aimed at visibilizing not pure and compressed thought but the welter prior to thought. This social mode of communication was neither cathartic nor a solitary ritual act of purification. Rather, it welcomed pathognomic digressions, feeling flourishes, and emotive detours into multiple effects. These distracting "caricatural" compositions looked like what they were aiming to capture. They resembled the real, not sterile, home of internal sensations papered over with pleasure and pain. In this scheme, an individual was not a reducible cipher but a complex rejoicing and suffering person incapable of further subdivision.[4]

A disproportionate emphasis on philosophical content and analytical procedure was reintroduced into Christian theology, ethics, and epistemology during the seventeenth century. Its main purpose was to separate offending heretical propositions from true beliefs. Geometry was deeply rooted in a new Protestant critical attitude—which spilled over into aesthetics—attempting to reform lax, wayward, and perverse sectarian doctrines and to forge an unmuddied natural theology dependent upon the unchanging mathematical content of nature. Mathematics as the single unsullied method of knowing was the standard of rational learning, the sole path to wisdom free of controversy. And *Logos*, or the power to enumerate, was the means by which the more technical aspects of mathematics were proved and presented through geometrical figures. From Isaac Newton's (1642–1727) *Principia* (1687) until the challenge posed by Joseph-Louis Lagrange's (1736–1813) *Mécanique analytique* (1788), the Euclidean assumption held that geometrical symbolism was adequate to the expression of mathematical relations. In the mechanistic philosophy, God possessed absolute power over the created world, and human beings were powerless. Similarly, nature possessed no vital energy of its own since matter was inert and passive, incapable of moving or forming anything by itself. Yet, simultaneously, a Platonizing ontology emphasized that the divine mathematical symbols *underlying* phenomena were the key to its unblurred understanding.[5]

Descartes embodied this new, northern *esprit critique* and did more than any other thinker to establish the need for correctness and punctilious analysis in metaphysics, physics, medicine, and aesthetics. Through the writings of Locke, this same abstracting methodology—intended to bring about certain knowledge of material things—was applied to the eighteenth-century study of morals (i.e., political theory) and to religion. *Methodos*—a way or path— became, because of Cartesian and Lockean philosophy, the general conduct of reason, the epitome of mental and social comportment both within the republic of letters and in civic life. It was "the art, or rule of disposing things in such a manner, as they may be easily comprehended; either in order to discover truth . . . or to shew and demonstrate it to others."[6] Method was part of a greater obsession, the desire systematically to order and control almost every aspect of intellectual and practical activity. It gave priority to rational axioms over unaided sight and to simple or general ideas decomposed or abstracted from complex experience. Abstraction was the linchpin of the process. Formal condensation represented the will to resolve every maximal thought or figure into its physical and optical minimum. In the words of Chambers's *Cyclopaedia*, abstraction was that "operation of the mind whereby we separate things naturally conjunct, or existing together and form and consider Ideas of things thus separated." Although the reality of the existence of abstract ideas had lately been called into question (chiefly by Berkeley), the term was customarily extended to connote "purity, simplicity, subtlety." Thomas Corneille, in the *Dictionnaire*, contrasted the abstract to the concrete. "It is a quality, an accident, a world that one detached through thought from a subject to which they [these qualities and accidents] were really attached."[7]

The modern theory of abstraction as a sign of superabundant cerebral power—whether expressed in textual criticism, the reduction of ambiguity to scientific exactitude, or the calculating simplicity of Minimalist art guided by the sharpness of edges and the orthogonal rule—was indebted to the persistence of Neoplatonism. Proclus, in the *Commentary on the Timaeus* (heavily influencing the English Romantics through Thomas Taylor's translation), identified this quasi-divine force with the philosophical mind remaining among the higher unitary causes and refusing to descend and consider mixed particulars.[8] Boethius (480–521/5 AD), in the *Isagogen Porphyrii Commenta* and the *De Trinitate*, offered, however, what would become the definitive treatment of the technique of abstraction. His discussion was important because it was couched in the context of an argument that was both theological (the Trinity consisted of a diversity of persons unified in the simplicity of their substance), and epistemological (there were many things that might be separated by a mental process, although they could not be separated in fact). Appositely, he also connected this activity to the aesthetic notion of "the altogether beautiful." Each mortal thing had its being from the components of which it was made. Mundane objects, then, were a concatenation of "this and that," i.e., the totality of their parts in conjunction. When severed, "this and that" referred to form separated from matter. No earthly thing had form without accidental, material qualities. God alone, or the Supreme Good, the Divine Substance, and "The Altogether Beautiful," was form without matter, and thus unabstractable. Significantly, in order to claim that compound man was also good, Boethius mentally detached or excised the predicates dividing humanity from divinity. By abstracting superficial obfuscations, he arrived at an underlying essential core or character resembling the heavenly substance.[9] This antinomian language of admixture/oneness, plurality/simplicity, particularity/generality, composition/unity was fundamental to the mystical theology of the Thomist school with its opposition between abstract comprehension (*ratio*), on one hand, and immediate sense perception and feeling

134

(*aisthesis*), on the other. We cannot follow the Medieval and Renaissance stages of what was to become the philosophy of aesthetics. Nonetheless, it is still possible to recognize the language of Boethius and Aquinas in Descartes's profane will to differentiate an intellectual *ens* from everything corporeal, to divide form unerringly from matter.

The procedure was also operative in Locke's "way of ideas," intent upon separating the simple from the complex, whereby the mind had the power to abstract general representations from particulars. It was further evident in Gottfried Wilhelm Leibniz's (1646–1716) subtle discussion of abstract entities, or essences of things, detached from every particular existence other than that subsisting in the mind. Refining upon the ancient language of included and excluded predicates, of reality and irreality, he proposed two types of complex ideas: those that were possible, i.e., whose ingredients were compossible, representative of substances such as really existed; and those that were chimerical, artificial aggregates or collections that had never been found in any substance. He gave the example of a centaur.[10] As we shall see in chapter 3, Leibniz's fertile suggestion that ideas were chimerical only when we attached to them the notion of effective existence became the Romantic theory of the grotesque. It was the source of the view of abstraction as a fantastic combination fabricated, or made, to exist.

These rarefied speculations concerning mental composition and decomposition were vulgarized in pedagogical manuals and dictionaries meant to be accessible not just to the intelligentsia but to the upwardly mobile middle class. George Campbell (1719–1796), in the *Philosophy of Rhetoric* (1776) or analysis of different forms of speech and writing, included a long section on abstract terms and their role within the structure of language. "The more general any name is, the more individuals it comprehends under it and therefore requires more extensive knowledge in the mind that would rightly apprehend it." Criticizing Locke's undue and unprecedented use of the term *idea* in his *Essay concerning Human Understanding* (1690) to signify traces of things retained in the memory and images formed in the fancy, this correspondent of Hume similarly maintained that general abstractions were "the inventions and creatures of the understanding."[11] That is, they were the result of a deliberate and methodical intellectual effort to remove ideal qualities from the unideal substrate to which they adhered. Carl Friedrich Flögels's *Erfindungskunst* (1760), or logic of invention, linked abstraction to the art of discovery whereby obscure things bound together in thought were artificially pried apart in order to clarify them. Not surprising from an author who also composed a monumental history of comic literature, he insisted that the technique for enlightenment was always negative. This was true whether similar concepts were divided from those that were dissimilar, or unlike qualities and characteristics were isolated within a single concept. Abstraction, then, was an artificial system of wit for discovering incorporeal universals not of this world, for inventing pure and complete thoughts invisible to sensuous perception. It was a surgical method for subtracting material surplus and for creating mathematical order visualized in the optical minimum of the point, line, plane. Flögels compared his vision of a unified theory of arts and sciences—in which diversity was suppressed in the aesthetic perfection of *brevitas*—to a short poem shorn of verbosity and to a concise picture erased of amplification.[12]

The paradigm of intellectual pruning can be firmly identified, then, with the trend toward systematic abstraction in eighteenth-century aesthetics and poetics. William Wotton (1667–1727), in *Ancient and Modern Learning* (1694), reflected upon the importance of system to "modern methods of philosophizing"—in contrast to the unsystematic ancients—and upon its pivotal role in instructing the young. Beginners "must have a general notion of the whole work before they can sufficiently comprehend any part of it and . . . must be taught to reason by the solutions of other men before giving rational solutions of their own." Shaftesbury, in *The Moralists*, connected the vision of rising degrees and orders of beauty, and the power of the aspiring soul to combine them as it ascended, to the coalition of a utopian society. A general harmony of ideas, like the "Common-Weal," was based on the existence of "a healing Cause" or "Universal Mind" to oversee this "distracted Universe." Abstraction, then, was a mental and social medicine purging restless individualism for the health of a larger, stable community. Before entering society, man resembled "some solitary insect" that itself mirrored the primitive chaos of an atomistic and polytheistic wilderness. This desert was at the antipodes from "the admirable simplicity from whence the One infinite perfect principle" derived.[13] The Deistic language of the mathematical, monotheistic, and matterless polity also infused John Dennis's (1657–1734) *Grounds of Criticism* (1704). Poetry could be either an art or a "whimsie and fanaticism." If an art, it must abstract its forms from the vulgar crowd of divergent sensations. Only with law could the arts instruct and reform the world and "bring Mankind from Irregularity, Extravagance and Confusion, to Rule and Order." Further, the professor of mathematics and philosophy at the Académie de Lausanne, Jean-Pierre de Crousaz (1663–1750), in the *Traité du beau* (1715), specifically established physics, or the "system of truth," and mathematics—from whence physics largely derived—as the foundation of aesthetic beauty. He defined the latter as the contemplation of form without matter. The "hard" sciences were summoned to aid the unrigorous fine arts in establishing an a priori congruency between the different parts of their compositions. Thus signs of conflicting elements and dissonant passions were to vanish from the final work. Crousaz's ideal was the "infinitely small," that Leibnizian other world verging on nothingness. Matter, like the work of art, was divisible to infinity. It was important in both cases to arrive at the minimum. This smallness without boundary was invisible even under the most exquisite microscope.[14]

Abstraction was a social and aesthetic purgative. As a sobering philosophical cathartic, it watered the opulence and equivocation of Baroque and Rococo art into denominated, distinguishable, and abstemious prose. Severed from poetry's fanciful pirouettes and cabrioles, from coloring tropes, false figures, dark allegories and enigmas, corrected painting resembled, in the words of Richardson, "a sort of writing." More specifically, his ideal was "plain writing" that made objects "easily legible." No "supernumerary figures or ornaments, ought to be brought into a picture. A painter's language is his pencil, he should say neither too little, nor too much, but go directly to his point, and tell his story with all possible simplicity." He praised Polygnotus's murals for the Temple at Delphi because the Greek artist identified by name those he represented. The early Italian and German masters were also singled out for having invented labeled "speaking figures," with "that written on them which they were intended to say." Even Raphael and Annibale Carracci condescended to write "rather than to leave any ambiguity, or obscurity in their work." The ability to create a communicable digest or unmistakable abstract was essential both to the portraitist and to the history painter. The visual historian composed not the chronicle of a few years, an age, or a country, but of all times and nations. He that painted history well must be able "to write it with his brush." He "must conceive it clearly and nobly in his mind, or he can never express it upon the canvas."[15]

A major thrust of Neoclassical criticism was to reestablish the primordial link between painting and writing. Fuseli was only one of many to remind the young artist of the similarity obtaining between graphic tools and methods. Letters originally were lines, and the first paintings were skiagrams or "simple outlines of a shade, similar to . . . Silhouettes" (fig. 60). Then followed the monogram, or cut-out, without light or shadow but with some addition of the parts inside the contour. In the subsequent evolution from primitive monochrome to full-blown polychrome, the use of a stylus and the concept of a stained drawing remained constant.[16] There was a striking mutuality and reinforcement between the high conceptual abstraction of Neoclassical pedagogics—with its Neoplatonic precepts of subtraction, withdrawal, and removal from the tangle of the world—and the diagrammatic techniques evident in the most mundane drawing and penmanship manuals. In both high theory and low practice, the net of rationality was equally and coldly standardized in a trellis of austere and wiry lexical and graphical characters. R. M. Pariset's *Nouveau livre des principes de dessein* stressed the affinity between drawing and writing since, in both instances, the eye must become accustomed to correctness and the hand must acquire fluency guided by good taste. Citing Michelangelo, he stated that the draftsman must have a compass in his eyes so as scrupulously to render horizontals and verticals (fig. 81). As was true for the writer, the artist must begin with the grand scheme before entering into details. Gérard Hoet's *Principaux du dessein* (1723) allied measurement—originally deduced from actual corporeal parts: foot, thumb, palm, elbow, hand—to the artificial partition of the body. The compass of the intellect sectioned it into an alphabet of calculable proportions detached from any individual incarnation. William Austin's *Specimen of Sketching* compared that summarizing activity to shorthand "which collects the sense, and even preserves the words." He also noted that manner in writing or drawing was "a certain style or peculiarity discernible in the execution." Flaws in one area of graphic handling constituted deformities in the other.[17] Thus James Beattie (1735–1803) disparaged "fashionable hands" replete with "flourishes, that either require time, or mix with any other part of the writing; all those heads and tails of letters, which are so long as to interfere with one another; and all those hair-strokes (as they are called) which are so fine as to be hardly visible, or which require too great nicety in cutting the pen." Children ought to be taught "durable and distinct" characters. Nor should letters be like social gadflies "which are known from their situation [in relation], but would not be known if they stood alone." This Scottish poet, essayist, and moral philosopher established a metric analogy, based on codes of etiquette, between the geometrical "body" of letters and the formality of the painter's elemental shapes. Thus letters, like cultivated members of society, ought "to be erect and of a square shape." They should be evenly spaced so that the heads and tails of one row would not impinge upon those of another.

Compartmentalization reigned, in short, as in Lavater's *Essays*. Emulating the lapidary clarity and rectilinearity of Roman epigraphy and regularized Roman

81. R. M. Pariset, *Allegory of Painting,* from *Nouveau livre des principes,* 18th c., frontispiece. Engraving by P. Bodart. (Photo: Courtesy of the Trustees of the British Museum.)

P. Bodart fec:

typeface, written lines also needed to be perfectly straight and of uniform breadth. Words ought to be distinctly separated with points or stops punctiliously observed. George Bickham's *British Youth's Instructor* (1754)—training the new commercial and merchant classes—provided an abstract of the theory of writing couched in the metaphor of detachable somatic parts. Letters must be even at the head, just as the feet must always tend exactly in one direction and be equally spaced. The fluency of "fast and fair" was the ideal: "the more you join in running hand, the better." Bickham's *Universal Penman* emphasized the Neoclassical ideals of proportion, calibrated spacing, but above all legibility. Proper writing was hailed as painting "unbody'd thought." In a kind of graphological physiognomics, Bickham adjusted the overt hand to the covert sentiment. Large, clear, and simple strokes betokened honor. An upright court and a chancery hand, without finical "spriggings" or ostentatious "thrown" strokes, were *"not designed for a Gawdy Shew* among Knots and Flourishes but to be useful for instruction by their Plainness and Number." Just as the teaching of art followed an anatomizing and abstracting method dissecting wholes into elements (fig. 82), so, too, the instruction of penmanship depended upon "cutting them [letters] asunder" in order to lay them before the learner "one piece only at a time."[18] Handwriting, like drawing, was a public art useful for commerce, for communication among members of a state able to employ common, or abstract, terms rising above the specialized jargon of their trades. Beattie noted that while soldiers could talk with soldiers, farmers with farmers, scholars with scholars to please and instruct one another, there was a higher aim to social intercourse. Whenever people from different walks of life gathered together, "conversation ought to be general" so that all could understand and relish it.[19]

The art of portraying character in "masterstrokes" was likened to an "abstract" or epitome divested of extraneous clothing. It was a pictorial abbreviation—like a contraction in writing—compressing a person into his naked and durable history stripped of caricatural accretions. Whether painted, written, or spoken, the formal presentation was politely succinct, taking up as little room as possible. This textbook method of diagrammatic characterization led to the dismantling of the body into detachable heads, feet, arms, and legs collected from different sources, pieced together, and reduced into a composite figure (fig. 82).[20] Graphic amputation and retrenchment into combinable segments was not limited, however, to the humble domain of penmanship and drawing manuals (fig. 83) but entered the burgeoning Neoclassical literature on the theoretical nature of art. For Reynolds, not unlike Richardson,

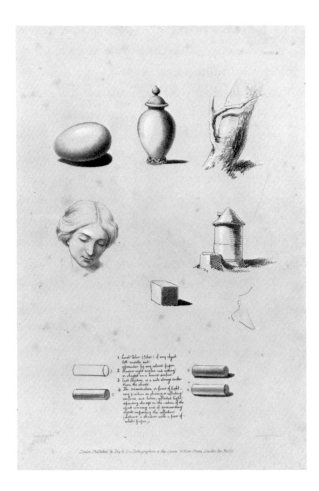 

82. Georges Stubbs, *Formal Studies,* from
An Illustrated Lecture on Sketching, 19th
c., pl. 9. Chromolithograph. (Photo:
Courtesy of the Trustees of the British
Museum.)

83. Georges Stubbs, *Landscape Studies,*
from *An Illustrated Lecture on Sketching,*
19th c., pl. 4. Chromolithograph. (Photo:
Courtesy of the Trustees of the British
Museum.)

the ideal or "central form" "was itself an empirical abstract of the various individual forms belonging to that class," and remote from all peculiarities. In the ninth *Discourse*, he lamented that painting, like the other arts, drew upon and addressed a lower, sensuous faculty. Therefore it must methodically grope its way toward reason, must purify itself from everything gross through examples, principles, and precepts in order to produce "publick benefits" and to bestow "refinement of taste" on entire nations. Anton Raphael Mengs (1728–1779), too, maintained that the general conception on which hinged the real excellence of a painting was an abstract construct. This idea coalesced scattered and divided parts, bringing them together into an artificial unity. As in rhetoric, *idea* meant style (*stylus*) or a linear standard. Mengs thought of the painter, like the writer, as expressing one unchanging truth—close to the religious conception of an eternal verity or to the mathematical notion of the indivisible point. This ability to create supernatural harmony out of disparate limbs was akin to the rational control of matter.[21] Most profoundly, it was a critical gesture of correction aimed at distinguishing the genuine from the spurious. Intellect was a weapon directed at defective and imperfect life. The reflective mind, according to Gerard de Lairesse (1640–1711), did not imitate existence as it ordinarily appeared but "as it ought to be, in its greatest perfection." This distinction between visible vice and invisible virtue was, for Laugier, the distinction between manual copy and spirited original. It was at the root of Neoclassical academicism with its constraining system of a priori rules and public censure. Goya's etched satires on restrictive art education openly opposed the Mengsian principles of clear and distinct corrections punitively applied to a fluctuating and dark nature (fig. 9). Similarly, Robert Adam (1728–1792) mocked the learned laws of architecture dear to Laugier as "frequently minute and frivolous." The great masters of antiquity "were not so rigidly scrupulous."[22]

Of all eighteenth-century pedagogical manuals, official and unofficial compendia transmitting technical know-how, none was more important in the dissemination of graphic information with a uniform and abstract "look" than dictionaries (fig. 84). Digests were accessible to almost any reader as a sort of universal and abbreviated reference book. They could be consulted in the new libraries, public reading rooms, and cafés of Europe. Moreover, in a society that was still primarily oral, they formed part of a graphic ensemble. Like playing cards and caricatures, their illustrations gained an active role in creating new forms of expression, in stimulating revolutionary intellectual and physical activity. They did not merely transmit and circulate the more

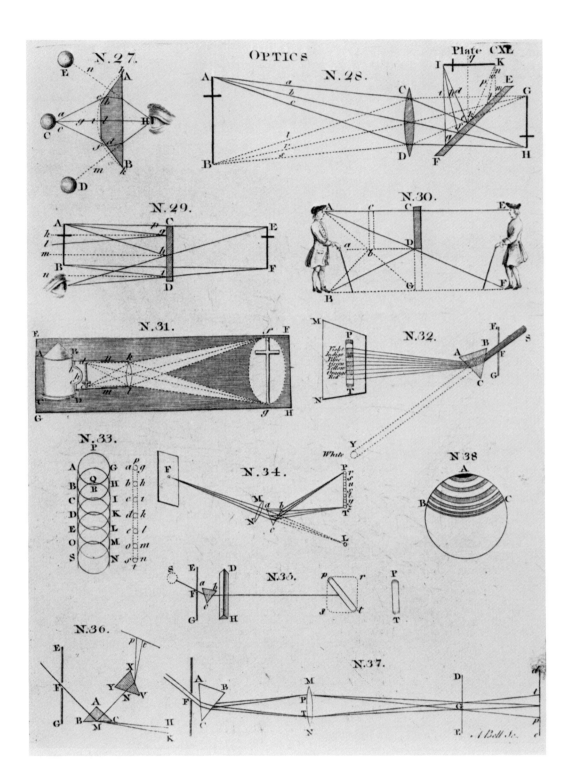

84. *Optics,* from *Encyclopaedia*
Britannica, 1773, III, pl. 140. Engraving.
(Photo: author.)

limited contents of print culture. A subgenre of the scientific illustrated treatise—so characteristic of, and important to, the Enlightenment—the epitome used geometrical figures or other easily apprehended linear modes to convey information "cleanly." Easily legible diagrams seemed to guarantee propriety, stability, and objectivity. Simultaneously, they served as a neutral method for stimulating even the minimally educated user to discover for himself steady and solid facts within a precariously shifting and expanding intellectual universe (fig. 85).[23] They were an extension of the Protestant educational system that aimed to cut through the enigmas and wrangling of the casuists—always arguing on both sides of a case and thus never escaping the labyrinth. The English Baconian and empirical tradition, not French rationalism, was responsible for the development of the modern lexicon. It took the form of an abundantly engraved, large-format volume chiefly occupied, at its inception, with the observational sciences and new commercial technologies. Unlike the mosaic appearance of Elizabethan polyglot dictionaries—with entries juxtaposed in a verbal intarsia and spelling marred by irregularities and blots—the new standardized thesaurus was doubly logical.[24] First, modern dictionaries were visibly abstracts of shared meaning, or "commonsense," not of difficult and esoteric "nonsense." Second, they embodied both a "short and plain" geometric system or single method, and a dispassionately bare or noncontentious style of presentation. As an intellectual synopsis and an optical shorthand, the unambiguous printed dictionary reinforced the two connotations of "abstract." Unlike seventeenth-century hermetic polymathy—mounding up esoterica and seeking to establish a *summa* of strange data—the scientific lexicon systematically culled, ordered, and classified.[25] It did not merely amass but encouraged the making of connections. In that sense, these modest and even portable rational codifications adumbrated the multivolume and gargantuan *Encyclopédie* or *Dictionnaire raisonné* of Diderot and D'Alembert. Following the principle of analogy, they also succinctly pulled fields together according to abstractions held in common. These overarching schemata could be visualized in outlines, plans, trees, or maps.

John Harris devised the earliest compendium in which illustrations were integral to diagramming the relationships obtaining in a system of knowledge. The *Lexicon Technicum* (1704), with its double columns, pithy and lucid paragraphs, and large fold-out plates often adjoining the pertinent text, embodied an industrial "plain style" or elegant technical minimalism achieved through projective geometry. The preface explicitly declared its departure from Fure-

tière's and Moreri's *Grand Dictionnaire* of the French Academy. These had "no cuts or figures at all" and were, like Thomas Corneille's *Dictionnaire* (fig. 86), mostly a bare explication of terms of art. These definitions were designed more "to improve, and propagate the French language than to inform and instruct the human mind." Unlike the borrowings endemic to earlier productions, Harris—as Diderot was later to do—emphasized that he culled from the best original authors. He did not copy from other dictionaries. Nor was he limited to the arbitrary ordering imposed by an alphabetical sequence. Mathematics was the central discipline of the collection (entire treatises were devoted to its various aspects under the rubrics of "trigonometry," "geometry," "surveying"). But it was also the paradigm of the *"New Methods, or universal ways of investigation"* he followed when gathering information of "vast use and benefit to mankind." The *Lexicon*, then, functioned like a concise overview or universal textbook of modern learning ("a Book useful to be *read*

85. John Harris, *John Marshall's Double Microscope*, from *Lexicon Technicum*, 1704. Engraving by J. Sturt after B. Lens. (Photo: author.)

86. Thomas Corneille, *The Arts and Sciences*, from *Dictionnaire des arts et des sciences*, 1694, I. Engraving by Pierre-Jean Mariette. (Photo: author.)

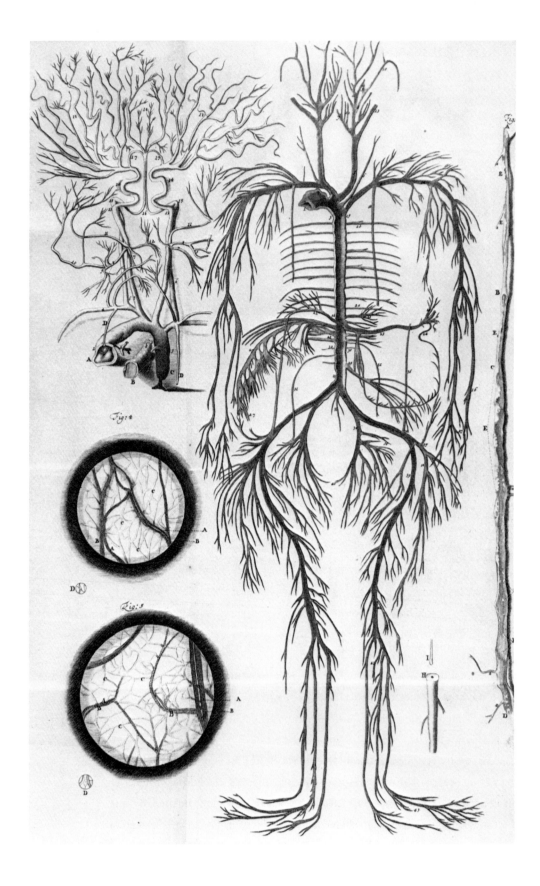

KNOWLEDGE, is either

Natural, and Scientifical, which is either

Sensible; consisting in the perception of phænomena, or external objects — called PHYSIOLOGY, or NATURAL HISTORY; and which, according to the different kinds of such objects, divides into { METEOROLOGY 1. HYDROLOGY 2. MINEROLOGY 3. PHYTOLOGY 4. ZOOLOGY 5.

Rational; consisting in the perception of the intrinsic characters or habitudes of sensible objects — either their

Powers, and properties — called PHYSICS, and NATURAL PHILOSOPHY 6.

Abstract — called METAPHYSICS 7, which subdivides into { ONTOLOGY. PNEUMATOLOGY.

Quantities — called PURE MATHEMATICS — which divides, according to the subject of the quantity, into { ARITHMETIC 8 — whence { ANALYTICS 9. ALGEBRA 10. GEOMETRY 11 — whence { TRIGONOMETRY. CONICS. SPHERICS. STATICS 12.

Relation; to our happiness — called ETHICS 13, or NATURAL RELIGION, or the doctrine of Offices, which subdivides into { POLITICS 14. RELIGION — whence { LAW 15. THEOLOGY 16, or REVELATION.

Or, Internal; employed in discovering their agreement and disagreement; or their relations in respect of truth — called LOGICS 17.

Artificial and Technical, (consisting in the application of natural notices to further purposes) which is either

Real, employed in discovering, and applying the

Latent powers and properties of bodies — called CHYMISTRY 18 — whence { ALCHYMY. NATURAL MAGIC, &c.

Quantities of bodies — called MIXED MATHEMATICS; which, according to the different subjects, resolves into

OPTICS 19, CATOPTRICS, DIOPTRICS, { PERSPECTIVE 20. — whence { PAINTING 21.

PHONICS — whence MUSIC 22.

HYDROSTATICS 23, HYDRAULICS.

PNEUMATICS 24.

MECHANICS 25 — whence { ARCHITECTURE 26. SCULPTURE 27. TRADES 28, and MANUFACTURES.

PYROTECHNIA 29 — whence { The Military Art 30. FORTIFICATION 31.

ASTRONOMY 32 — whence { CHRONOLOGY 33. DIALING 34.

GEOGRAPHY 35, HYDROGRAPHY, { NAVIGATION 36. — whence { COMMERCE 37.

External, which is either

Structure and œconomy of organical bodies — called ANATOMY 38.

Relations thereof to the preservation and improvement — either of

Animals — called { MEDICINE 39. PHARMACY 40.

Vegetables — called { AGRICULTURE 41. GARDENING 42.

Brutes — called { FARRYING 43. MANAGE — whence { HUNTING, FALCONRY. FISHING, &c.

Symbolical, employed in framing and applying { Words, or articulate signs of ideas — called GRAMMAR 44. Armories — called HERALDRY 45. Tropes and Figures — called RHETORIC 46. Fables — called POETRY 47.

carefully over"). And it also operated as a series of specialized studies replete with registers, lists, and ephemerides (to be consulted occasionally).[26] Harris's thesaurus promulgated standardized images of scientific equipment manufactured by Britain's entrepreneurs.[27] Merchants were avidly interested in learning about, and producing goods for, the expanding world. Globes, quadrants, telescopes, barometers, hygroscopes, air pumps, and John Marshall's heroically scaled microscope (fig. 85) spilled off the pages, along with representations of the hidden functions they observed (fig. 87). A premium was placed on the inviting aspect of the neat and tidy imagery, encouraging user participation. Specimens were turned, drawers opened, the venous system helpfully enlarged, difficult junctures extracted, profiled, and sectioned, and numbered parts coded to explanatory texts. The fact that figures were "mathematized" within an abstract, not a pictorial perspective made their appeal more general.

Ephraim Chambers's *Cyclopaedia* (1728), unlike Harris's tomes, provided the consumer with a table of its overall structure (fig. 88). Combining the cartographic and hunt metaphors, this introductory itinerary, devised by the former London globemaker, chased data from one art to another, referring from one province to an adjoining one, until the "whole land of knowledge"

87. John Harris, *Arteries and Veins,* from *Lexicon Technicum,* 1704. Engraving. (Photo: author.)

88. Ephraim Chambers, *The Organization of Knowledge,* from *Cyclopaedia,* 1738, I. (Photo: author.)

lay open. Although the totality, at first, might appear to resemble a wilderness, "t's a wilderness thro' which the reader may pursue his journey as securely, tho' not so expeditiously and easily as thro' a regular parterre." The table relied upon Locke's theory of abstraction. Chambers (ca. 1680–1740) noted that since ideas were "singulars" or "individuals," it was natural to consider complex knowledge in its proper parts, anatomized into separate articles, rather than as a pansophic assemblage. This "Division of Knowledge" was like "a precise Partition of the Body," both in logic and in medicine, demonstrating the origin and derivation of the members and their relation to a common stock and to each other (fig. 89). Thus Chambers declared his effort differed significantly from the grotesque patchwork of his predecessors "as a System [does] from a *Cento*." Dissection, as an intellectual taking to pieces, operated in the isolated tracts as well as in the images: wholes (for example, *écorchés*) were considered absolutely in themselves, but also relatively (as organs). Their ties to the totality were pointed out through cross-references. These were bound together by the linear web or uniform pattern of engraving and moved from generals to particulars to premises to conclusions to causes to effects, and vice versa.[28]

I wish to suggest a homology of method between the new lexical systems for the idealized reduction of complex information and the demolition of the body by the abstract diagram (figs. 13, 88). Both involved the violent intellectual simplification of mixed empirica or compounded biota. These were then reconstituted incorporeally without flaws. The lexicographer and the minimalist artist shared identical instruments. They bored, polished, and made an alien matter pliant. "All which operations," according to Proclus, "do not insert form, but take away the inaptitude of the recipient form." The bodiless diagram, since Plato's *Meno*, was the perfect tool for proving that learning was recollection. Thus since its Greek beginnings, it was an educational device for prompting the mind to remember originary simple ideas lost amid confusing sense perceptions.[29]

We can now fully comprehend the fundamental link between geometry and pedagogy, and the exaggerated intellectualization of images as rarefied schemata in Enlightenment manuals of all sorts. By its virulent purity, the absoluteness of its divisions into black and white, the detached and unentangled diagram performed a mental and optical disinfection. Taut and unsuperfluous lines visibly dispelled obscurity by strictly defining and limiting meaning.

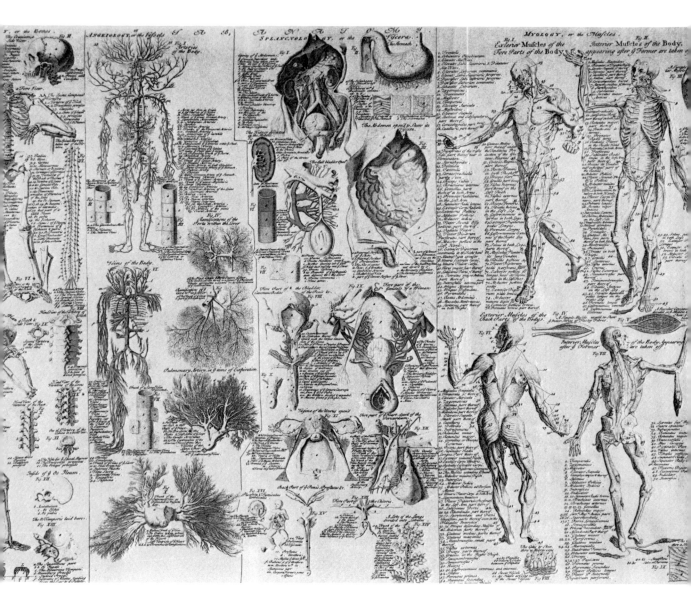

89. Ephraim Chambers, *Anatomy,* from *Cyclopaedia,* 1738, I. Engraving. (Photo: author.)

The analytical composition was the equivalent of decontaminating criticism. Both systematically annihilated sensory digression by hitting the mark with precision and clarity.

Diagrams were also elementary in the sense of being first. They were the graphic rudiments of an undefiled alphabet from which all images might be constructed. In this they resembled the primary theorems of geometry that served as starting points for the demonstrations that followed. That is, they were logically prior to, and physically under or above, variegated experience in the same way as the plan or plot of a drama preceded and transcended its colorful characters.[30] The diagrammatic also implied a code of behavior: earnestness, restraint, silence, cleanliness. It involved certain social ideals: an isolated and superior distancing from the disorderly and cacophonous crowd, the avoidance of pointless activity or evident signs of toil, and the valuing of monochromatic reason and intelligence over the emotions.[31] It even fostered a somatic ideal of ascetic leanness whereby inner spiritual forces exerted control over fleshly corpulency.

Alexander Cozens's *Principles of Beauty* (1778) promoted a teachable aesthetics of the "insipid" and the "tasteless," captured in hairline engravings without shading, in order "to approach something like mathematical precision." It was one of three pedagogical "systems" Cozens (1717–1786) developed during the 1770s.[32] The *Principles*—unlike the chiaroscural splash method of "blotting" for inventing landscapes by stimulating the imagination of amateur, student, and mature artist—was a treatise on mapping the face. It provided a chart for graphic wayfinding among too lengthy or garbled expressions. Abstraction was both the visual ideal and the technical means for organizing spatial information. It was also an indispensable critical tool for summarily picking out and symbolizing character. *Simple Beauty* (fig. 13), or the statistical mean of the system, was discoverable only in the mind. He established it as the norm or standard for future epochs, comparable to the uncompounded zero of "pure, elemental water." As void of any predominant mental characteristic, the "vacant mind"—indicated by an extreme simplicity of countenance—was one and the same at all times and places. Cozens's graphic science was codified in outlines systematically removing visual distractions or "noise." Distillation involved first collecting human features, then obliterating and redrawing them as life-sized profiles stripped of sensuous peculiarities. Finally, as in Chambers, outline tracings could be compared to the table or plan of the dictionary. They formed the groundwork or baseline for any new combinations of features (fig. 88). The reader/user was encouraged to

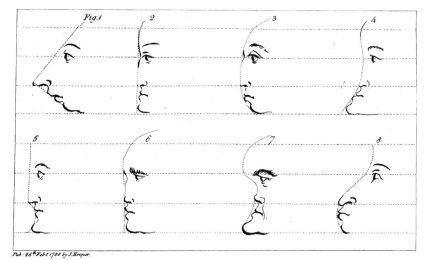

Pub. 26.th Feb.y 1788 by S. Hooper.

Rules for drawing Caricaturas Pl.I

manipulate movable tracings of diverse headdresses, thus engaging in a kind of cross-referencing. From unmixed simple beauty various "charactered" or "superinduced" beauties could be systematically derived. The process was one of carefully calibrated optical mixtures. As in musical variations—or, one might add, as in formulaic caricature—the artist moved from an unimpassioned arrangement to others deviating from but not incompatible with it (fig. 90). *Artful Beauty* thus departed incrementally from the simple straight nose and perpendicular alignment of the nostril with the nasal ridge (fig. 91). These almost imperceptible degrees of linear variation were measurably correlated to nuanced psychic qualities.[33]

Cozens's skeletal drawings obeyed a linguistic paradigm. Simple beauty was, in a sense, punctuationless. It displayed "some faint appearance of all the mental characters," just as white light contained the prismatic colors. The chromatic addition of temperament and personality by tiny doses may be likened to the cosmetic application of distinguishing marks to a text or to the presence of scars on a face. These supplements characterized or deformed any blank plane.[34] Cozens, like many of his contemporaries, also adhered to the Neoplatonic thesis that, in Junius's words, perfect beauty "of necessity must be but one," a nature cleared of accident, defect, excrescence. The unpaintable—or a world cleansed of a medley of shreds and bits—required an extreme tenuousness, an almost invisible delicacy of trace "drawn so lightly, so swiftly." Surely Cozens remembered the esoteric tradition of diagrams and Pliny's account of the contest between Apelles and Protogenes. Fuseli still reminded Royal Academy students in 1830 about those fabled concise designs. Reputedly, they had been sketched "with nearly miraculous subtlety in different colours, one upon the other or rather within each other." The British academician drew the lesson that it was "the little 'more or less'

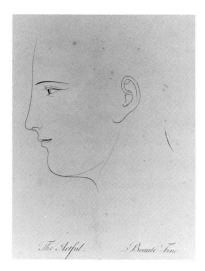

The Artful. *S.Beauté Fine*

imperceptible to vulgar eyes which constitutes grace and established the superiority of one artist over another." Camper's comparative study of superimposed human and animal anatomies similarly diagrammed thinner over thicker contours evident to the judicious and trained eye (fig. 92). The graphic rarefaction of irregularities into schematized lines of beauty also connoted silence. The obliteration of idle talk meant a soaring above narrative to self-evident geometrical demonstration.[35]

Cozens's pictorial abstemiousness participated in the same logocentric illusion of the dictionary, i.e., that the image possessed the transparency and homogeneity of the word declaring itself unproblematically on paper. But it was the abridged Lavater, or the epitomized *Régles physiognomiques* (1803), that was closest to the British artist's clean penmanship and dematerialized ideograms. In this compilation of cryptic body language, morphological complexity was condensed into a primitive shorthand. Three-dimensional objects were known only by their projections on a flat surface. Thus they seemed to be on the verge of volatilization. The *Cipher of Madness* was diagrammed as a rigid vertical, wiping out by its optical diminution any sense of surface clutter (fig. 93). The serpentine twistings of a hair sprouting from a mole on the suppressed neck or chin was extrapolated and read as a sign of libertine voluptuousness (fig. 94).[36]

The diagram, then, as Gibson might have argued, hovered perpetually between being a projected and an unprojected plane. It existed somewhere between visualization and obliteration, proximity and distance, revelation and concealment, up and down.[37] Moreover, attenuation had the potential for becoming a monster of subtlety, identified with excessive refinement and extreme evaporation. Reynolds warned his students that when simplicity, instead of being a corrector, "sets up for herself" and makes an ostentatious display, then it was as "disagreeable and nauseous as any other kind of affectation." As in painting, so in morals. "Simplicity, when so very artful as to seem to evade the difficulties of art, is a very suspicious virtue." He contrasted such overly cultivated subtlety with "barbarous simplicity"—proceeding from mere want. He identified this visual meagerness with the too inartificial penury of naive and awkward Italian and German primitives with their dry, hard style. Richardson, earlier, had castigated this absence of civilized ornament, this lack of sumptuary distinction and inobservance of the qualities of office. He likened such optical poverty to wild animals inhabiting the bare walls of caves, and to "savages" wearing nothing but functional coverings to protect themselves from the weather.[38]

67.

Quiconque fourit fans fujet, avec une lèvre de travers; quiconque se tient fouvent ifolé, fans aucune direction, fans aucune tendance déterminée; quiconque falue, le corps roide, n'inclinant que la tête en avant, eft un fou.

CHIFFRE DE LA FOLIE.

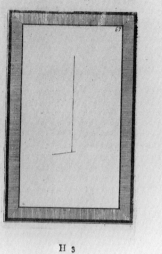

H 3   Un

87.

Un cheveu long, faillant en pointe d'aiguille, ou fortement crépu, rude & fauvage, planté fur un tache brune, foit au cou foit au menton, eft l'indice le plus décifif d'un penchant extrême à la volupté; penchant qu'accompagne presque toujours une extrême légéreté.

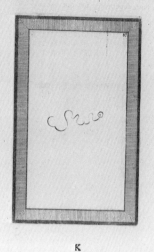

K   CA.

93. Johann Caspar Lavater, *Cipher of Madness*, from *Règles physiognomiques,* 1803, p. 61. Engraving. (Photo: Courtesy National Library of Medicine, Bethesda, Md.)

94. Johann Caspar Lavater, *Hair Growing from a Mole,* from *Règles physiognomiques,* 1803, p. 73. Engraving. (Photo: Courtesy National Library of Medicine, Bethesda, Md.)

If the excessive stiffness and unadorned naturalness of the childlike Pre-Raphaelites were reprehensible, academic censure of them was nothing compared to that directed against the sophistic maker of "fine thoughts." Bouhours declared, in the *Manière de bien penser*, that an excess of *délicatesse* was vicious. In going beyond the tenuously perceptible, the thinker was no longer in the realm of *finesse* but of affected *raffinement*. Bouhours distinguished between improper and proper ingenuity. The latter, or the *je ne sais quoi*, was associated with valuable miniature experiences. Their "matter was almost imperceptible" and demanded, as it were, that the perspicuous *esprit* make use of a microscope. One might argue that the distinction between right and wrong delicacy was itself overly subtle! Like the vanishing hairlines of Cozens's *Simple Beauty*, it was so little marked that one could barely glimpse it. For Bouhours, however, only enlightened minds could divine this precious "tiny mystery" *in minimis*. Bernard Le Bovier de Fontenelle (1657–1757), in turn, distinguished worthy, aristocratic *délicatesse* from the undiscriminating judgment of "the people." *Le peuple* always remained arrested at the surface. But he also detached it from the overly sophisticated "sybaritic" or luxuriant fantasies of the *esprits raffinez*. The latter, by dint of so much subtlety, dissolved themselves into vain and chimerical imaginings (fig. 95).[39] This alchemical or pneumatic evaporation (fig. 96) yielded ethereal abstractions. Removed from solid thought, these unseizable mists—represented in broadsheets from Matthaus Greuter (1554–1638) to James Gillray (1757–1815)—designated insane liquidity, the loss of reason in uncontrollable effluvia.[40]

Abstraction, then, was also the mental disease of pathological single-mindedness. It surfaced as such in Antoine Le Camus's (1722–1772) compendium

95. Matthaus Greuter, *Physician Curing Fantasy*, 17th c. Engraving. Philadelphia Museum of Art, SmithKline Beckman Corporation Fund. (Photo: Courtesy Philadelphia Museum of Art.)

The DISSOLUTION, ——or——The Alchymist producing an Ætherial Representation

96. James Gillray, *The Dissolution,* 1796. Etching. (Photo: Courtesy National Library of Medicine, Bethesda, Md.)

of maladies associated with professional and nonprofessional intellectuals. In the *Médecine de l'esprit* (1753), the Regent of the Faculté de Médecine in Paris connected abstraction to the overly studious savant. Bristling with Greek and Latin learning, the obsessed scholar was "carried away" by enthusiasm. The natural historian and investigator of clouds Jérôme Richard, in the *Théorie des songes* (1766), similarly diagnosed this atmospheric illness as a diagrammatic obsession. The "abstraction of ecstasy" was stronger than any other because the outside world was totally excised. In such artificially induced transports— here identified with the mathematician—sensory deprivation and mental concentration resulted in self-generated and vaporous idealizations. The hyper-abstracted person, then, was the portrait of the radical idealist, deliberately withdrawn from the noise of the mundane crowd. The famous archaeologist and historian Lodovigo Antonio Muratori, in the *Forza della fantasia* (1745), connected the alienated visionary with the willful and unswerving fabricator of airy chimeras. Significantly, for Muratori (1672–1750)—as for Le Camus and Richard—it was difficult to register in practice the difference between these aberrant perversions of subtlety and correct "intellectual ideas." As Bouhours's and Fontenelle's analysis indicated, the latter were equally deliberate and remote from sensuous experience.[41]

The phrase an "absent man" implied habitual inattention owing, according to Beattie, to his singular taste for "ruminating upon a few things and overlooking others." Sticotti claimed that the inward-looking *esprit abstrait*—usually an author or a geometer—was "uniquely occupied with his own thoughts." His mirror opposite was the *esprit distrait*, perpetually distracted "at every occasion by some new external object detouring his attention."[42] Distraction opened itself to the reception of piquant effects. Abstraction, on the other hand, removed all seasoning or idiosyncratic accent from the "infinite ragoût" of art and life. Tasteless water was central to the metaphor of physical diminishment. It washed away spicy flavors and insistent traces. Cozens noted that simple beauty escaped the coarse attention of most of mankind. Their deforming passions did not dispose them to discern its "insipidity," just as those inured to "stronger liquors" could not relish "elemental" water. The hygienic abstractionist, then, was the logician of imperceptible feeling, the specialist in subtle savoring, whose ultimate sensory test was the perception of a decorporealized fluidity. Like the connoisseur, he always discovered something spiritual "that the painting did not denote."[43]

Submerged beneath defiling matter and materials was ineffable grace or *charis*, that supernatural power available only to heightened sensing.[44] Johann Joachim Winckelmann's *On the Imitation of the Painting and Sculpture of the Greeks* (1755) was the paradigm of a theory of aesthetic abstraction formulated in terms of a spiritual force or mana dwelling within the aqueous. He thus departed notably from an aesthetic tradition that favored the addition of sprinkles of "salt" to compositions to prevent their tasting flat. Even the discriminating Bouhours had objected to the insipidity of certain epigrammatists and to the cooking of a poetic gruel "that tasted only of water," i.e., "a soup *à la grecque*." Winckelmann (1717–1768), however, turned a vice into a virtue. "Noble simplicity and quiet grandeur" of expression was compared to the bottom of the sea lying peaceful beneath a foaming surface. He spurned Roman Baroque "sauces" and Rococo piquant seasonings, championed by French theorists such as Claude-Henri Watelet (1718–1786) and Michel-François Dandré-Bardon (1700–1783), for a radically naïve beauty without cosmetic or artifice. Like an undulating garden stream or the fresh complexion

MICROCOSM dedicated to the London Water Companies

MONSTER SOUP commonly called THAMES WATER, being a correct representation of that precious stuff doled out to us!

97. William Heath, *Monster Soup,* ca. 1822. Etching. (Photo: Courtesy National Library of Medicine, Bethesda, Md.)

of a young girl free of makeup or blemishes, the ideal was a gently moving whiteness. The emotional tranquility residing in ancient sculpture was the antithesis of Bernini's caricatural or drunken statues. Winckelmann described the great Baroque artist's carving as if it were lithic satire. Frothing passions and dropsical proportions contorted decorous serenity and equipoise.[45] In contradistinction to such inappropriate agitation, Winckelmann established a spiritual congruency. The delicate inner sense of the observer, able to detect the almost tasteless subtleties of Greek art, was correlated to the intellectual ability to abstract thin filaments of thought from hydrophilic matter.

A prime mover in the establishment of a refined and sensuous physiology of perception, Winckelmann likened the rare ability to feel the beautiful to a "still-liquid plaster mold." This gently flowing and touching fluid cast subtly insinuated itself into the rising and sinking contours of the *Apollo Belvedere.* Such hypersensitivity to barely visible private parts, needless to say, was difficult to teach. Winckelmann registered his disinterest in instructing those young people forced to earn their daily bread. He preferred to focus, instead, on almost divine youths who possessed the leisure, means, occasion, and genius for the free contemplation of works of art.[46] By their unencumbered and untroubled vision, these noble water drinkers diluted opaque and resistant matter. Ironically, however, such disinterested connoisseurs were literally bathed in the infected air of modern Rome. These purists, like their poor city counterparts, were inescapably immersed in the lethal miasmas issuing from Piranesian ruined drains. They drank from, and swam in, polluted wells and fetid cisterns. Paradoxically, Winckelmann would have his initiates erect a rarefied aesthetic system on a probably nonexistent environmental purity.

Bernini's grotesquely overcharged sculpture and the contaminated urban atmosphere shared, for Winckelmann, a similar monstrous or foul materiality. Waste water was identical to artistic sewage (fig. 97).[47]

His aesthetics, then, was also a hygienics. Nakedness as dietetics—a sort of visual liposuction—optically removed amplifying flesh. The body of the *Apollo Belvedere* was sublimated into a weightless, lightly swelling veil of skin. The *Apollo*'s simple nudity, like the ideal, stood prior to, and above, the sartorial mutilations of civilization (fig. 22). The god's sexual ambiguity, circumscribed by an undulating outline, resembled the duplicity of the legendary hermaphrodite. Conceived from the union of Hermes and Aphrodite, he was loved unrequitedly by the nymph of the spring Salamacis (fig. 15). When the youth bathed in her softly rippling waves, the two blended into a neutral or tasteless harmony. The indeterminate androgyne—born from water—was, for Winckelmann, the graceful opposite of mechanical men fashioned from earth.[48] He was the supreme abstraction, the sublime intelligible without interval, the absolute fiction or immaterial invention emanating from the artist's mind. This Greek poetic creation was a compound of the perfections of both sexes. Winckelmann insisted that the lovely mythic being had nothing in common with repugnant, unnatural monsters. He meant freaks—composing a living caricature—assembled from deformed male and female traits (fig. 98). Nor did that deity resemble the erotically sensual castrato—so conspicuous in fashionable Roman society—with his layers of subcutaneous fat, abundant hair, and densely physical femininity.[49]

Wounds of Experience

To sin _____

verb, *To neglect the laws of religion; to violate the laws of religion . . . to invert the laws of order.*

Dr. Johnson, *Dictionary*

Péché _____

noun, Peccatum, *is in general all infraction of the rules of natural equity and of positive laws, of whatever type they may be . . .*

Diderot and D'Alembert, *Encyclopédie*

Incisions of experience were the inverse of diagrams. The geometrical method attempted to chart an ideal straight line among the twistings and marblings of practical life. Yet it faltered in the imposition of simplicity on empirical messiness. Right thinking and mathematical logic could seem absurd in the face of the daily muddle. Abstraction—visualized in seamless contours, silhouettes without sutures, and intact profiles without bandages—was a totalizing system giving the illusion of homogeneity and health amid flux and change (fig. 99). The reality of a conspicuous and deep existential wound stood in opposition to the fable of the androgynous blend. Garengeot defined this tangible breach as "a division of the soft portions of our body recent & still bleeding, made by an external cause capable of cutting, bruising, tearing, puncturing, & changing by whatever disunion, their natural disposition."[50] Surgery was the art of restoring and binding disjointed parts, reminiscent of

F. LICETVS
DE
MONSTRIS.

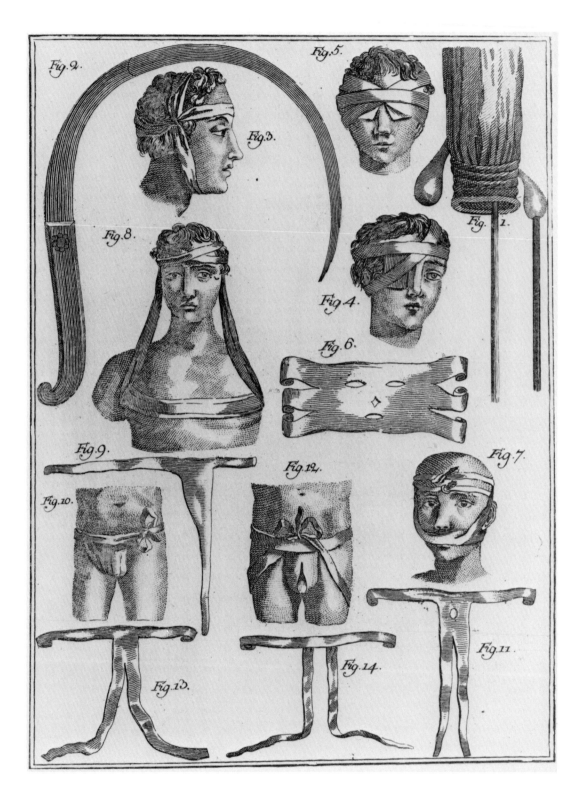

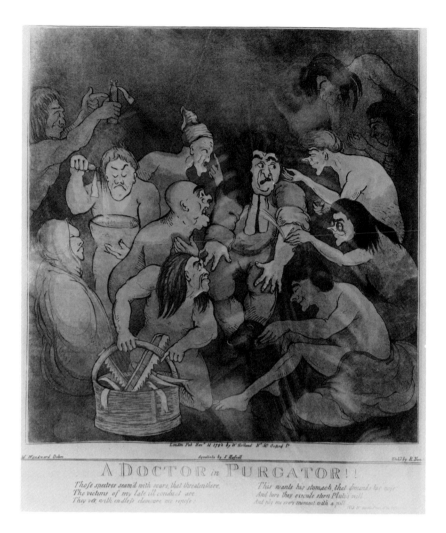

A DOCTOR in PURGATOR!!

Those spectres seam'd with scars, that threaten here,   This wants his stomach, that demands his nose
The victims of my Late ill conduct are   And here they excite stern Pluto's well
They vex with endless clamours my repose   And ply me ev'ry moment with a pill

99. **Denis Diderot and Jean Le Rond D'Alembert,** *Bandages and Surgical Instruments,* **from** *Planches de l'Encyclopédie,* **1762–1772, II, pl. 27. Engraving by Prevost et al. after Louis-Jacques Goussier. (Photo: Courtesy National Library of Medicine, Bethesda, Md.)**

100. **George Moutard Woodward,** *A Doctor in Purgatory,* **1792. Aquatint and etching by R. Newton. (Photo: Courtesy Library of Medicine, Bethesda, Md.)**

the humble craft of masonry with its evident mortaring of bricks. Chambers described the suture as that "seam made to close the lips of a wound" in order to promote its healing. The *Cyclopaedia* managed to paint a gallery of medical tortures merely by the sober classification of types of junctures. Incarnatives, for example, might be interrupted, intertwisted, penned, or feathered and clasped. (Chambers noted that the latter method was obsolete, being too cruel and barbarous.) Restrictives stopped the flow of blood when numerous vessels were cut. Conservatives closed large openings to prevent further receding from the loss of substance. Intertwisted sutures left needles sticking in the wounds—in the manner of tailors—with thread wrapped around them. Dry closures, used for the face in order to prevent scarring, employed leather and cloth indented or overlaid like the teeth of a saw.[51]

Being "seam'd with scars," then, was both a fact of eighteenth-century life (fig. 100) and a metaphor for dissonant interferences ruining any finely adjusted composition. Thus inoculation was the incision of the skin to introduce the venom of small pox into a channel of flesh. For its opponents, the insertion of this contagion was like permitting the enemy to penetrate the walls of a town during a siege. Lichtenberg compared all visible diseases to structural "breaks" in the sufferer's corporeal facade. The architectural analogy between gaping stones and somatic apertures colored Shaftesbury's description of a mind weakened by the assault of improper ideas, boring a hole "for all to enter and take possession." Joseph Trapp (1679–1747), in the *Lectures on Poetry* (1742), compared disjointed scenes in a drama to disagreeable cracks within the fabric of a building. Mengs cautioned against the imitation in a painting of violent passions that "wound" the sensibility through their rupturing and ugly lines.[52] Surely David remembered, and deliberately disobeyed, this injunction when he purified the decaying features and ennobled the putrefying body of the cadaverous *Marat* (Brussels, Musée Royaux des Beaux-Arts, 1793), but accurately represented the gaping slash gouged by Charlotte Corday's knife. The hideous stigmata, incised in the waxlike integrity of the corpse, was thus emblematic both of the puncturing of the *ancien régime* and, in turn, of the subsequent treacherous assassination of its over-throwers. During the eighteenth century, the view also took hold that scientific change and political affairs were characterized by unhealable rifts and strident discontinuities.[53] The rhetoric of cataclysmic disruption in all facets of human events—intensified by the terminal "illness" of the French state (fig. 101) and the purgative of the Revolution—spoke not only of radical breaks with the past. All modern studies could be interpreted as a kind of wounded knowledge, wrenchingly divided from the integral "plainness" and security of ancient geometrical certitude.

Even in a secular age, as we saw with Lavater, original sin remained the model of that incurable and irreparable breach from which imperfections ramified. Since Adam, our unitary nature has been broken. Inherited concupiscence was the sickness of the flesh riddled with gullies from which moral infirmities and physical defects sprang. To be conscious of living in a fallen world, whether one was religious or not, was to be aware of a severed totality.[54] Rational philosophy expended its efforts on remembering and eclectically recreating the fullness of the ahistorical moment when humanity was still one with God. Conversely, the empirical approach picked up the pieces the moment after, i.e., when humanity entered the chaos of history and wandered distractedly among the ill-sorted syncretic clutter. Diderot—no friend of organized religion—in the *Interprétation de la nature*, launched a critique against the seamless geometrical method and spoke on behalf of the collecting experimentalist. Unlike the proud architects of luminous systems, the patient gatherer groped in the dark. Conscious of yawning gaps, he seized

everything coming his way and only met with meaning, if at all, at the end
of his journey. The rational philosopher and metaphysician began, instead,
with "great abstractions" that shed only a dim light. For "the act of gener-
alization tends to strip concepts of everything sensuous. As this process
advances, corporeal phantoms recede; notions gradually pull away from the
imagination toward the understanding & ideas become purely intellectual."
Diderot likened this cerebral remoteness, identified with Newton, to the
mathematician looking at a plain from a mountain summit. From the top, he
could observe solipsistically merely his own thoughts. No one else could
follow him to those transcendent heights or breathe in the thin air. Wittily,
and no doubt alluding to Pierre Bayle's unfinished dictionary project, Diderot
commented on the need for a volume entitled *"The Application of Experience to
Geometry, or Treatise on the Aberration of Measurements."* The art of experimentation recognized the limits of quantification when dealing with nature. The
galant *philosophe* personified nature as a woman, not stripped of her individual

**101. Anonymous, *Sick France Being
Diagnosed*, 1789–1790. Colored engraving.
(Photo: Courtesy National Library of
Medicine, Bethesda, Md.)**

properties, but "fond of travesty" and wearing different disguises. The experimentalist's pleasure in physical and manual operations, his habit of maneuvering, often resulted in inspired premonitions. Diderot obviously admired this tactile scientific skill in the same way as he marveled at Chardin's knowing manipulation of pigments (fig. 50). He could say both of the searching naturalist and the exploring artist that they possessed the "spirit of divination." This coupling genius stitched together "conjectures, founded on oppositions or analogies so distant, so imperceptible, that the dreams of a sick person appeared no more bizarre, no more disconnected."[55]

Empeiria—like chemistry, cooking, medicine, rhetoric, art, antiquarianism, the compiling of encyclopedias—was the knack for sewing together the disparate and the random. As an ongoing routine, it did not force data to harmonize or fit prematurely into a preconceived whole. The experimentalist continued to resemble the Francis Bacon (1561–1626) of the *Sylva Sylvarum* (1627), content to hunt unsystematically in the forest. He did not disdain the chase after mutable patterns or the collection of material fragments that might eventually build a picture of life.[56] In the important article on the *empiric*, Chambers remarked that the term was bestowed in antiquity on physicians who formed rules and methods based on their own practice and experience. Hippocrates, as Garengeot similarly recorded, was the first to introduce reason into medicine. This development gave rise to a sect of *theoretici* who deduced their diagnoses rather than remaining open to the reception of corporeal impressions. Conversely, *experience* connoted a kind of knowledge acquired by long use and without the example of authorities. *Experiment* was a trial or essay based on the comparison of observables. Chambers approvingly declared that the making of experiments of late had grown into a kind of "formal art." He saw his epoch abounding in ways of experimentation and in courses of experimental philosophy.[57]

The incompleteness of riven experience was visualized as a wound, patched, bandaged, or otherwise conspicuously tied together. This existential realization necessitated the devising of an equally discordant prose and painting style. Error and mistake were endemic to earthly life. This theological, aesthetic, and natural historical posture received expression not within the clean pages of the diagrammatic and technical lexicon, but within the old-fashioned intricacies of the seventeenth-century Dutch *variorum*. Pierre Bayle's *Dictionnaire historique et critique* (1697) bristled with polyphonic digressions and fugal commentaries. Thus it was everything that the orderly and

ALEXANDER AB ALEXANDRO (*A*), Jurisconsulte Napolitain, qui avoit beaucoup d'érudition, a fleuri vers la fin du XV siecle, & au commencement du XVI (*B*). Il s'attacha au Barreau avec ardeur, prémiérement à Naples, & puis à Rome (*a*) ; mais, tout le tems qu'il pouvoit dérober aux embarras des procès , il le consacroit à l'étude des belles Lettres : & enfin, il abandonna entiérement le Barreau , afin de mener avec les Muses une vie plus tranquille & plus agréable. Voici la raison qu'il allegue pourquoi il renonça à la profession d'Avocat (*C*) : il dit que ce fut à cause de l'ignorance ou de la méchanceté de ceux qui rendoient la justice , & qu'il aima mieux vivre en repos , que prendre beaucoup de peine à bien étudier la Jurisprudence, puis que cette peine ne servoit de rien contre la témérité d'un mauvais Juge (*b*). Il avoit vu à Rome bien des exemples de ce desordre , lesquels il cita à Raphaël Volaterran, qui lui avoit demandé la cause de sa retraite. Il est un peu étrange, que de ce grand nombre d'hommes doctes, qui vécurent de son tems, ou qui ont fait l'éloge des Savans de son tems-là, il n'y en ait presque aucun qui fasse mention de lui (*D*). Nous saurions très peu de chose de sa Vie, s'il n'en avoit touché lui-même quelques particularitez dans son Ouvrage (*c*). C'est là que nous aprenons qu'il a été logé à Rome dans une maison où il revenoit des esprits (*d*) : & ainsi, voilà un témoin à citer à nos incrédules ; un témoin, dis-je, qui se vante d'avoir vu, & qui raconte des singularitez étonnantes du spectre qui tourmentoit cette maison. Il dit aussi, qu'étant fort jeune, il alloit aux Leçons de Philelphe, qui expliquoit à Rome les Questions Tusculanes de Ciceron (*e*). On peut recueillir du chapitre XII du IV livre, qu'il étoit à Rome, lors que Nicolas Perot, & Domitius Calderinus , y faisoient les Leçons publiques sur Martial (*E*). Je ne sache point qu'il ait parlé de la charge de Protonotaire du Roiaume de Naples , qu'on prétend qu'il a glorieusement exercée (*f*). Je ne sai point quand il mourut ; mais, je sai qu'on l'enterra dans le Monastere des Olivets (*g*). Tout le monde l'a blâmé de l'affectation qu'il a témoignée de ne point citer les Auteurs qui lui fournissoient ce qu'il débite (*h*). Tiraqueau a remédié à ce desordre par un docte Commentaire, qui fut imprimé à Lion, en 1587 (*i*). On l'a réimprimé à Leide, en 2 volumes in 8, l'an 1673, avec les Notes de Denis Godefroi, de Christophle Colerus, & de Nicolas Mercerus, sur le même texte. J'aprens de la Bibliotheque de Gesner, que l'Edition qu'on fit à Paris de cet Ouvrage d'*Alexander ab Alexandro*, l'an 1532, étoit plus exacte que les autres, & que Gerard Morrhius de Campen, qui la corrigea, avoit collationné aux Originaux les endroits que l'Auteur avoit pris d'autrui. Il avoit donc collationné bien des choses ; car, les six livres des *Jours géniaux* ne sont presque que des pieces de raport. C'est un mélange d'une infinité de recueils concernant l'Histoire & les Coutumes des anciens Grecs & Romains : on y trouve aussi plusieurs questions de Grammaire. L'exactitude n'y est point dans sa perfection (*F*). Je ne crois pas que

(*a*) Alex. ab Alex. Gen. Dier. Libr. II, Cap. I.

(*b*) Ibid. Libr. VI, Cap. VII.

(*c*) Initulé Genialium Dierum Libri VI.

(*d*) Alex. ab Alex. Dier. Gen. Libr. V, Cap. XXIII.

(*e*) Eum ego adolescentulus senem inter exteros coevos meos colui & observavi. Ibid. Libr. I, Cap. XXIII.

(*f*) Panzir. de claris Leg. Interp. Libr. II, Cap. CXXII.

(*A*) *Alexander ab Alexandro.*] ☞ [Je lui donne son nom Latin , comme l'ordonnent nos Grammairiens.] Ceux, qui traduisent *Alexandre d'Alexandrie* (1), s'abusent. Notre Auteur étoit d'une famille Napolitaine , dont le nom étoit Alexandre. On prétend qu'elle avoit déja produit des gens illustres, comme Mr. Moreri le raporte , après Lorenzo Crasso. Chacun fait la plaisanterie de Balzac : *N'y a-t-il pas eu, dit-il* (2), *au Roiaume de Naples un Grammairien Jurisconsulte , qui s'est fait apeller* ALEXANDER AB ALEXANDRO? *Et se peut-il rien imaginer de plus magnifique que de plus superbe , que d'être deux fois Alexandre, que d'avoir Alexandre pour son nom, & de l'avoir encore pour sa Seigneurie* (3)?

(*B*) *Il a fleuri vers la fin du XV Siecle, & au commencement du XVI.*] Ce qui me fait parler ainsi , est que notre Auteur , ☞ [en parlant des calamitez du Roiaume de Naples, les a conduites jusques à la mort de Frederic, fils de Ferdinand I (4), c'est-à-dire , jusques à l'an 1504; outre qu'il] parle de Jovien Pontan , comme d'une personne qui n'est plus (5). Or, Jovien Pontan n'est mort qu'en l'année 1505. C'est à quoi n'ont pas pris garde ceux qui ont placé la mort de notre Alexander à l'an 1494, en quoi Mr. Moreri leur donne beaucoup plus de témoignages de son aprobation , que de son incertitude.

(*C*) *Voici la raison qu'il allegue pourquoi il renonça à la profession d'Avocat.*] Je crois que pour en montrer toute la force , je suis obligé de la raporter dans les propres termes de l'Auteur. *Qua cum viderem, dit-il* (6) *, patronisque contra vim potentiorum & gratiam nihil presidii esse , nihil opis ; frustra nos in legum controversiis & ediscendis tot casuum varietatibus tam perliculate editis , tantum laboris & vigilantiam suscipere , tantoque nos studio fatigari dicebam , cum ad ignavissimi impuritissimique cujusque temeritatem juri dicendo imsidere quem leges cirum bonum esse volunt , non aquo jure sed ad gratiam & libidinem judicia ferri , decretaque legum tanto causio edita convelli & labesactari viderem.* Il fit beaucoup mieux d'abandonner le Barreau , que d'imiter quelques autres Avocats , qui , aiant perdu plusieurs bonnes causes , prennent le parti de se charger des plus mauvaises. Je lisois l'un de ces jours , qu'un Avocat des plus fameux de ce siecle , à qui ses conséres demandoient pourquoi il se chargeoit de méchantes causes, leur répondit en riant, que c'étoit qu'il en avoit perdu quantité de bonnes. C'est une mauvaise excuse, poursuit l'Auteur : *un Avocat , qui , après avoir examiné une cause, la trouve insoutenable , est obligé de l'abandonner* (7). J'ai trouvé un autre endroit dans le Livre d'*Alexander ab Alexandre*, qui marque la droiture de son cœur (8). Un de ses amis, voiant qu'il ne poussoit point sa fortune , lui conseilla de se servir des expédiens qui avoient si bien réussi à tels & à tels qu'il lui nommoit : c'étoient toutes personnes, que la faveur avoit élevées aux honneurs & aux prelatures , malgré le mérite de leurs personnes , & qui etoient parvenus à la faveur par des voies illégitimes. Notre Auteur n'ignoroit pas ces exemples, & il en favoit de pires. Il avoit vu , dans sa jeunesse, un fort honnête homme, favant & en Latin & en Grec , qui n'aiant fait que luter contre une extrême pauvreté pendant qu'il se fioit à

(1) Simon Goulart l'a fait dans la Version de Philip. Camerarius.

(2) Balzac, Préface du Socrate Chretien.

☞ (3) Pour parler exactement, il est faux dire, qu'Alexandre étoit son Nom de bateme & son Nom de Famille. Une pareille chose s'est vue en d'autres Personnes : voiez Molierus au Traité De Scriptoribus Homonymis.

(4) Alex. ab Alex. Genial. Dier. Libr. III, Cap. XV, sub fin. pag. 738.

(5) Id. ibid. Libr. I, Cap. I.

(6) Id. ibid. Libr. VI, Cap. VII.

(7) Journal des Savans, 1690. pag. 301 d'Edit. de Hollande.

(8) Alex. ab Alex. Gen. Dier. Libr. I, Cap. XVI.

sa vertu & à sa science, se résolut de tenter une autre voie: il se jetta dans un si vilain métier, qu'on n'oseroit le nommer ; &, peu après, le voilà riche & puissant, & pourvu de bons Bénéfices. *Eo vesanie processit , ut coactus inopia obscenis & libero homine indignis artibus vacaret , quibus verò artibus non libet dicere : ita fœda & pudenda sunt , constabatque sibi res ex sententia , namque haud multo post & saceldotio & opibus auctus , affluens & beatus tranquillissimè vitam egit* (9). Mais , ces exemples n'ébranlerent point notre Avocat : il aima mieux se contenter de sa médiocrité , que de risquer sa conscience. *Longè igitur multumque prestat , satinusque fuit suti ingenio meo , vacuumque his molestiis modico civilique cultu contentum esse , neque in ambitionem non necessariam incurrere , quam bona animi , si qua sibi homo studio & labore paravit, ea turpi questu pessimo exemplo sœdare* (10). Le conseil , qu'on lui donnoit, ressemble fort à celui-ci:

Aude aliquid brevibus Gyaris & carcere dignum,
Si vis esse aliquis. Probitas laudatur & alget (11).

Il dédia son Livre au Duc d'Atri. Ce Duc étoit fort savant, comme nous le dirons sous AQUAVIVA.

(*D*) *Il n'y a presque aucun de son tems qui fasse mention de lui.*] Cependant , si nous en croions Mr. Moréri , tous les grans hommes de ce siecle-là , un George de Trébizonde , un Theodore de Gaze , un Domitius Calderinus , un Pontanus , &c , étoient ses amis & ses admirateurs. Tout ce que l'on peut recueillir du Livre même d'*Alexander ab Alexandro*, c'est qu'il ouït en sa jeunesse les Leçons que Philephe déja vieux faisoit à Rome (12); & qu'il mangeoit quelquefois avec plusieurs personnes des Lettres chez Jovianus Pontanus (13), chez Hermolaüs Barbarus (14), chez Sannazar (15) , chez Gabriel Altilius (16), &c. Il faut un fondement plus solide que celui-ci , pour affirmer que certaines gens admirent certaines gens. Voiez la Remarque suivante.

(*E*) *Il étoit à Rome , lors que Nicolas Perot & Domitius Calderinus y faisoient des Leçons publiques sur Martial.*] Voilà tout ce que l'on peut recueillir de ce qu'il raporte touchant Nicolas Perot & Domitius Calderinus ; car , pour cette grande familiarité , que Panzirole prétend qu'il ait avec eux (17), il la faut chercher quelque autre part : & je ne sai s'il est possible d'en trouver les preuves. Je ne doute point que Panzirole n'ait dit cela à vue de pais , & sur la foi de la mémoire , sans prendre garde que la mémoire est un moule où les objets changent de forme très aisément.

(*F*) *L'exactitude de son Ouvrage n'est pas dans sa perfection.*] J'aime mieux le dire par le témoignage de l'un des Commentateurs, que de mon chef. Voici donc ce que dit Nicolas Mercerus. *Est profectò , mi Linoceri* (18), *verum quod ajunt. Fuit Alexander vir eruditus & multa lectionis : multa ad utilitatem publicam scripsit eleganter , multa tamen , ut hominum est infirmitas , minus accurate vel memoria vitio , vel imprudentia lapsus. Quæ lectoribus indicari magni inserfuit.* Je ne suis pas le seul , qui trouve mauvais que ceux qui nous donnent des *Variorum* , retranchent les Epitres dédicatoires & les Préfaces (19). Ils devroient tous faire ce qu'on a fait

(*g*) Letmd. Albert. Descript. Ital. pag. 277.

(*h*) Barclaius, de Regno, Libr. VI, Cap. VI; Cyprian. de Sponsal. Cap. XIII, num. 81 ; Vossius, de Hist. Lat. pag. 609; Meibomius, de Vitâ Mecenatis, pag. 138.

(*i*) Sous le Titre de Semestria in Genialium Dierum Alexandri ab Alexandro Libros VI. C'est un in folio. On la réimprima à Francfort , en 1594, in folio.

(9) Alex. ab Alex. Gen. Dier. Libr. VI, Cap. XVI.

(10) Id. ibid.

(11) Juven. Sat. I, Vers. 73.

(12) Alex. ab Alex. Libr. I, Cap. XXIII.

(13) Id. ib. Libr. I, Cap. I. Cap. I. Libr. III, Cap. VIII.

(14) Ibid. Libr. III, Cap. I.

(15) Ibid. Libr. II, Cap. I.

(16) Ibid. Libr. V, Cap. I.

(17) Absurdos familiaris sunt. Panzirol. de claris Leg. Interp. Libr. II, Cap. CXXII.

(18) C'est celui à qui il dédie les Notes.

☞ (19) Voiez Mr. Crenius , au Chapitre I de la Partie des Animadversionem Philologicarum, & le Remarque (R) de l'Article MAROT à la fin.

102.   Pierre Bayle, *Alexander ab Alexandro,* from *Dictionnaire historique et critique,* 1696, I, p. 158. (Photo: author.)

systematic *Lexicon Technicum* and *Encyclopaedia Britannica* were not (figs. 84, 85). Bayle (1647–1706) studied Cartesianism in Geneva and subsequently had an active career as a professor of philosophy at the Protestant Academy of Sedan and the University of Rotterdam. As a pyrrhonian, with a bias toward Manicheanism, he practiced a negative method in his important dissections of evil. The French Calvinist leveled a punctillious criticism against the sins of ancient and modern philosophical or theological charlatanism.[58] No sect or ideology was spared. His antiquarian pedantry, however, was outmoded in an age that valued calibrated simplicity and measured clarity in historical narrative. Yet, significantly, the mosaic appearance of the text was the image of eighteenth-century experimental procedure. Bereft of anything so frivolous as illustrations, the *Dictionnaire* nonetheless had a distinctive and labored look. Ostensibly a supplement to Louis Moréri's compendium, not only was it more erudite, but its copious annotations ironically undid the seeming orthodoxy of the articles. Taking any page at random, the reader was struck by the absence of homogeneity, smoothness, and graceful fluidity. The entry for *Alexander ab Alexandro* (fig. 102), for example, even footnoted the name. The article was a dense clutter of erudite corrections, recondite annotations, and detouring quotations. Bayle formally communicated his deconstructing strategy through disturbing and clumsy divisions of the page. The primary entry, located at the top, was simultaneously being dismantled by the massive commentary welling up uncontrollably from the bottom. There were no signs of French lexicological lucidity, no helpful gestures toward the user (fig. 86). Margins were overrun with tiny citations. There were no short and tidy paragraphic divisions, no typographical magnifications or minimizations to orient the hunter in this forest of unpunctuated minutiae. No narrative flow invited easy pursuit. Rather, this demanding juxtapositive, or *Wunderkammer*, style was a textual collage. As a heterogeneous grotesque, it did not disguise under courtly nonchalance the difficulty of finding one's way.

Bayle's original and never fully realized project was to publish a "Dictionary of Mistakes" (*fautes*). In the prospectus of 1692, he announced that in order to be comprehensive all shortcomings, large or small, would be included. Needless to say, this lugubrious catalogue of human frailties was not to the sophisticated taste of his subscribers! Bayle consequently altered the initial conception, dividing the work into two segments. First, and no doubt more pleasing both to his Protestant and Catholic readership, there was to be a succinct account of the facts. Second, and clearly the residue of the reluctantly abandoned litany of faults, there was to be "a great commentary." The latter

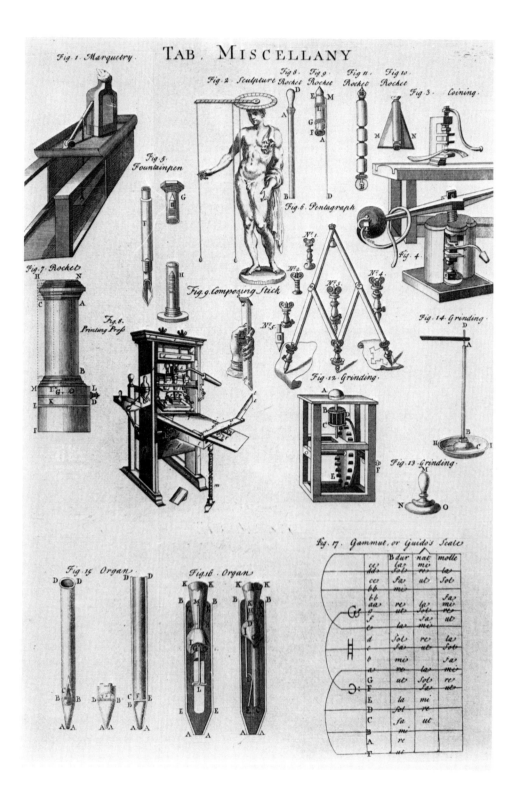

103. **Ephraim Chambers,** *Miscellany,* from

Cyclopaedia, 1738, II. Engraving. (Photo: author.)

comprised a "mixture [*mélange*] of proofs & of discussions, wherein I allow the censure of several defects to enter, & sometimes even a tirade of philosophical reflections."[59] This "variety," directed simultaneously at the uncritical and the critical user, accounted for the final *Dictionnaire*'s resemblance to a visual miscellany of the kind illustrated by Chambers (fig. 103). Juxtaposed on the same plate, as warring sects might be counterpointed in Bayle's tomes, Chambers ranged disparate items that defied conventional categorization. A pointing device, printing press, coining machine, fountain pen, organ pipe, and rocket disjointedly occupied the same space.

Bayle's subversive critique was thus more Epicurean criterion than Neoplatonic criticism. The former, according to Chambers, was "a rule or standard, whereby to compare propositions and opinions in order to discover their truth or falsehood." The latter was the art of judging concerning discourse and writing. Bartoli's *Dictionnaire* defined *critique* as that "wise guide obliging the traveler to halt or stop in daylight so as not to get lost in the dark." The critic's freethinking insight, his nurturing of intellectual pursuit, and his constancy in inquiry contributed to the enlightenment of a perpetual eclipse of nature. Bayle's prefaces defended—before the jury of an age increasingly accustomed to simplicity and abbreviation—the amplification of his wandering articles. His admittedly fat four folio volumes were meant to serve as a reference library. His consumers were those un-Winckelmannian, laboring truth-seekers who could not afford to purchase the books quoted, or who did not possess the leisure to consult them. Bayle thought these people would, nevertheless, prefer to find the original words and languages of the author placed before the eyes rather than having them digested or epitomized.[60] His admirable and tolerant refusal to cut and paste reminds us that epitomization was also the desecration of once entire works. Like the current practice of chopping films for television, or editing for the insertion of commercials or, worse, "colorizing" for modish updating, dictionaries comparably shortened, caricatured, and discolored a complex preexisting totality.

Bayle's skeptical and surgical critique, then, behaved and looked very differently from systematized, unified, or diagrammatic criticism. In short, he updated Baroque polymathy. Chambers disdainfully defined the latter as "frequently little more than a confused heap of useless erudition, occasionally detailed, either pertinently or impertinently, for parade." Avoiding curio-like dilettantism, Bayle endowed esoteric research with an educational purpose, while retaining its wayward trajectory and appearance of bricolage. His intricate scholarship was a liberating counterexample and antidote to the prevailing ideal of minimalist abstraction. Maligners, such as Joseph Spence (1699–1768), identified this digressive manner with those commentaries on the classics wherein "the limbs of the poet are so scattered by these inhuman manglers, as to be almost incapable of being brought into a body again." Bayle's ostentatious erudition and undisguised visual presentation of broken knowledge found its closest correspondent in the antiquarian or archaeologist. The Comte de Caylus's *Recueil d'antiquités* (1752–1767) was the *Dictionnaire critique* of the fragmentary artifact. Unlike the totalizing connoisseur, the puttering antiquarian was constantly exposed to the rubble of the past. More often than not, he remained ignorant of the ancient whole to which stray bits and pieces must once have adhered. Like Bayle and the experimentalist, he followed "the way of comparison." Error was revealed in the actual juxtaposition of discordant evidence and by the encouragement—through publication—of others to do likewise (fig. 104). Caylus (1692–1765) thought the antiquarian should adopt a modest, not an imperious tone but, above all, should "banish absolutely from his work all species of systems." He regarded them as "a mental illness," caused and maintained by *amour-propre*. This self-love forced the most disparate debris to unite, and tyranically erected a throne on the flotsam and jetsam of contradictory opinions. Caylus sought to emulate not the mathematician but the voyager. The explorer "in arriving in a foreign country sees objects, so to speak, without seeing them; he is amazed by them: far from being able to distinguish different conditions, he is equally struck by everything; consequently his ideas long remain imperfect, or rather very dim." There was also an additional drawback for the reader back home of an account or memoir. Since the same object could be viewed under multiple aspects, he was disadvantaged in fully comprehending the complexity of events. Caylus mused that, if it took such a long time for the traveler to discern customs, formulate accurate perceptions, and communicate them in writing, how much longer was required for the antiquarian. How difficult it was "to know the taste for work of a people no longer extant . . . how often must he repeat the phrase 'I do not know.'"[61]

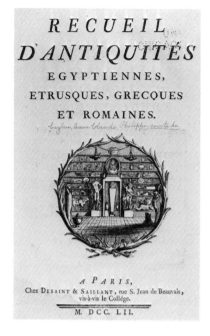

104. **Anne-Claude-Philippe, Comte de Caylus,** *A Collection of Antiquities,* **from** *Receuil d'antiquités,* **1752–1767, I, title page. Engraving. (Photo: author.)**

Paradoxically, Bayle's and Caylus's style of knowing the world was that of the modern Epicurean or libertine, that is, it was personal, partisan, and open-ended. Bayle excoriated the false "purism" of those who censured the *Dictionnaire* for using supposed obscenities and filthy language. He contrasted linguistic "purists" with Jansenists—the age's "most able moralists," who nonetheless talked crudely in a kind of barbaric plainness. Bayle spoke bitingly of an overly refined "delicate taste" that condemned expressions for their coarseness while favoring others just as capable of arousing impure thoughts. His *précieux* purists were rigorists of delicacy, arch-correctors, and hairline abstractionists. These dematerializing prudes snaked around meaning "with the subtlety of their brush," seeking to apprehend a wholly spiritual or intellectual significance.[62] Bayle opposed the blending tendencies both of a diluting and contracting purism and of an epitomizing and averaging eclecticism. The "monotheistic" eclectic refused to attach himself to any particular dogma. He selectively imitated and harmonized into a single unity what was good in each. On the contrary, Bayle's creatively composite, or polyphonic, way was that of the synthetic chemist or the ragpicker syncretist. Diderot disparagingly described the syncretist as one who seized from others scattered shreds of costume "& made from these tatters a bizarre, polymorphous, and variegated attire."[63] The "polytheistic" jumble of the *Dictionnaire* avoided giving the impression of uniformity, and thus mimicked the disheveled dress of a sinful world.

Ironically, the French Huguenot's legacy of seamed and heterogeneous knowledge evading ready classification thrived in England. The large and comprehensive frontispiece to Chambers's encyclopedia visualized what Bayles's dictionary could not. The reified and jostling experimental sciences—born of Baconian inductivism—were represented as standing uncomfortably cheek by jowl (fig. 105). Nor did Mariette's coy, sedate vignette for Corneille's *Dictionnaire* match Chambers's throng about to burst the frame. Putti, engaged in miscellaneous manual and intellectual activities, could not adequately convey the pressing sense of ongoing and uncontrollable discoveries (fig. 86). Chambers's visual encyclopedia in miniature was also a very different kind of summary than the diagrammatic *Table* outlining the plan of the work (fig. 88). Lullian lucidity was effaced in strange contiguities. Magic lanterns, cylindrical and flat anamorphoses, peep show boxes in dark rooms, heraldic blazons, geometrical demonstrations, cartographic surveys, anatomical preparations, and engineering machines of all sorts littered a Burlingtonian piazza. Here, there was no closed circle of arts and sciences, no disciplined abridgment, no scientific abstract, no "reduction of a large matter into a little compass." Instead, one discovered a paratactic florilegium of *analecta* or *excerpta*.[64] Miscellaneous small pieces, choice morsels, the finest and brightest parcels were gathered together in defiance of a rational system.

This indeterminate and crowded optical anthology mirrored Chambers's alphabetical arrangement. Textual unity was similarly shattered by the arbitrary yoking of unconnected words. The authors of the more methodical

105.   Ephraim Chambers, *A Visual Summa,*

from *Cyclopaedia,* 1738, I, frontispiece.

Engraved by J. Sturt. (Photo: author.)

Encyclopaedia Britannica reflected on these and other shortcomings prevalent among digests. How preposterous was the "method of dealing out the Sciences in fragments, according to the various technical terms belonging to each." Chambers had not yet devised "one, uninterrupted Chain" of conclusions, but allowed subjects to be "dismembered" in a "fortuitous distribution." From the vantage of the Scottish Enlightenment, such older compilations wearied the inquirer because of their "derangement and demolition." Agriculture, for example, was absurdly split and scattered through the alphabet under a multitude of words: *vegetation, root, soil, manure, tillage, plough,* etc. Both the studious and the indolent reader, ignorant of the order in which to pursue references, found themselves in a labyrinth with no clue to direct their course through the windings.[65]

The decomposing structure of Chambers's frontispiece, not of the composed table, mirrored the experiential nature of reality. The image was located somewhere in between Bayle's grotesque farrago and Diderot's and D'Alembert's crusading *Encyclopédie.* The latter's ironic cross-references, both in the text and the plate volumes, deliberately set ideas in opposition to one another (fig. 99). Contradictory connotations (such as healing and damaging, surgery and torture) were secretly meant to unsettle and overturn conventional patterns of thought. More generally, Chambers's frontispiece—like the natural historian's specimens or the archaeologist's ruins—visualized the compiler's predicament. New matter continually threatened formal containment and integrity. Consequently, as Harris declared, there could be "no such thing as a *Perfect Book of this kind.*"[66]

Certain of Piranesi's etched compendia may now be situated within this syncretic and encyclopedic tradition (figs. 106, 107). Both the broken form and subject of the *Lapides Capitolini* (1761) escaped dogmatic final definition. The heroically scaled fold-out plate, with its juxtaposed snatches of inscription, lengthy but incomplete lists, severed friezes, and detached bits of ornament, was a pictorial *Dictionnaire critique.* Ancient Rome was displayed as a miscellany of deciduous remnants. These skeletal bones and lacerated corpses from the noble past fell on the modern viewer and were left to him to flesh out. Piranesi issued an optical invitation to restore wounded monuments, just as Bayle summoned his reader to correct and fill in textual lacunae. The "bandaged style" of the etching was that of a coarse mosaic, riddled with crude tesserae and irregular incisions. It represented a synoptic, not a simplistic, form of abstraction. The ideal or unbroken thread of historical narrative was deliberately interrupted through the visual insistence upon the real

172

I · B
PIRANESII
LAPIDES
CAPITOLINI
SIVE
FASTI·CONSVLARES
TRIVMPHALESQ·ROMANORVM
AB·VRBE·CONDITA
VSQVE·AD·TIBERIVM
CAESAREM

Veneunt apud Auctorem in ædibus Comitis Thomati via Felici prope templum SS. Trinitatis in Monte Pincio.

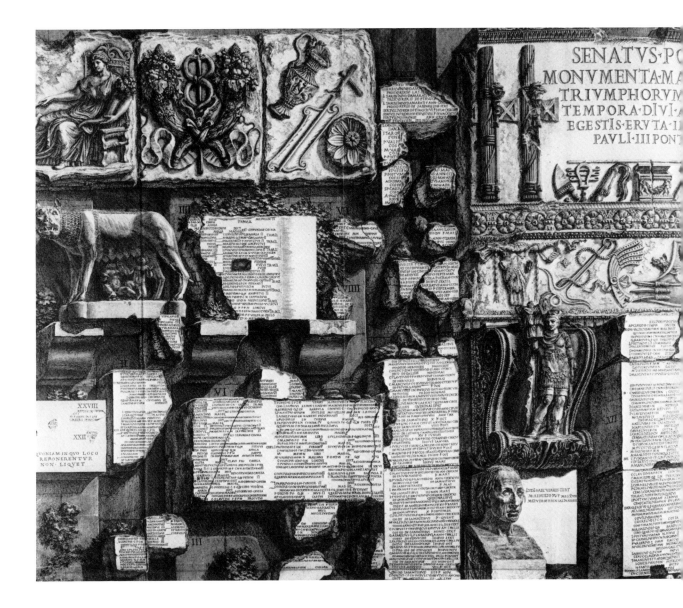

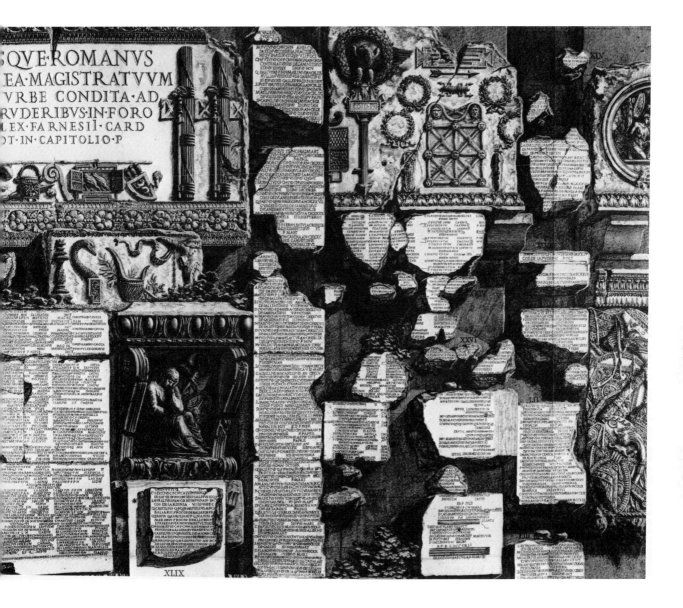

107.   Giovanni Battista Piranesi, *Roman Fragments,* from *Lapides Capitolini,* 1761. Etching. (Photo: author.)

presence of physical morsels wrenched from their context. This artificial mixture of sculptural spolia was compressed into a jigsaw puzzle of highlit excerpts interspersed with a shadowy, gaping matrix.[67]

The encyclopedic exhibition of mismatched information as textual or visual assemblage was the province of satire. Satire, Trapp declared, was "a miscellaneous Poem, full of a variety of matter." Like Bayle's or Diderot's critical dictionaries, it was dependent upon the perspicuousness of the reader to pursue a multiplicity of intersected paths and to connect various pieces of data for which there was no known order. As the archetypal mixed genre, it was unlike the linear and continuous writing of annals, or the fluidity of the uninterrupted contour. In an encyclopedic fashion, it put contrasting units of information in communication with each other while neglecting to inform the consumer what to deduce (figs. 108, 109). Piranesi's thesaurus of interior decoration, the *Diverse Manner of Ornamenting Chimneys* (1769), was, in this sense, both satiric and encyclopedic. It formed part of a large polemic deriding "lovers of simplicity," such as Sir William Chambers (1726–1796). The British architect had objected to the illegibility of the Venetian's designs, seeing them as merely digressive and overloaded with minutiae. Praising the mixed and chimerical character of hieroglyphics, Piranesi declared—in contradiction to Chambers—that ornamental complexity ought not be measured by quantity or number. Rather, it should be judged solely according to visual criteria. He defended the delightful caprices of the Egyptians, claiming these were not enigmatic philosophical symbols requiring decipherment, but attractive and combinable pictorial elements. Their value and evolving meaning were dependent—like the Capitoline fragments—on ingenious interpretations and diverse experiences accrued over time.[68]

Piranesi's "witty" method of restoration (just like his grotesque way of decoration), presented antiquity as a medley. Thus it departed from the totalizing practices of his contemporary rivals. In the *Lapides Capitolini*, segments were admired for their own beauty. Busts were not scoured or whitened, corrosion was not removed with rasp, pumice, or polishing wheel, joints were left irregular and not made to fit.[69] At his best, then, Piranesi, like Bayle or Giambattista Vico (1668–1744), distinguished the manufacture of entire pastiches and the fabrication of complete fakes, sold as genuine antiques, from the candid demonstration of partial historical remains. This etched miscellany, or perceptual riddle, appealed to the imagination and asked Socratic, open-ended questions of the viewer (fig. 110).[70]

176

108.   Laurent Natter, *Various Symbols,* from *Traité de la méthode antique,* 1754, pl. 186. Engraving by Hemerich. (Photo: author.)

109.   Laurent Natter, *Chimera,* from *Traité de la méthode antique,* 1754, pl. 178. Engraving by Hemerich. (Photo: author.)

110.   Anne-Claude-Philippe, Comte de Caylus, *Gryllus,* from *Recueil d'antiquités,* 1752–1767, VI, pl. 40, fig. 1. Engraving. (Photo: author.)

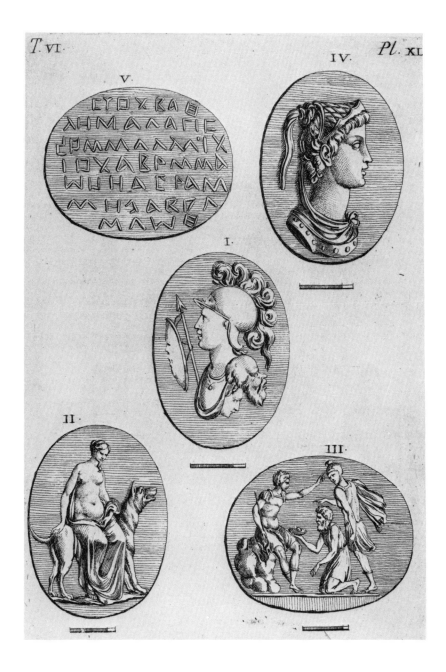

noun, The powers of the mind; the mental faculties; the intellect. . . . Imagination, quickness of fancy; sentiments produced by quickness of fancy.

Dr. Johnson, *Dictionary*

Esprit _____

noun, This word, insofar as it signifies a quality of the soul, is one of those vague terms, to which those who utter them attach things other than judgment, genius, taste, talent, penetration, expansiveness, grace, finesse; . . . One could define it, ingenious reason . . .

Diderot and D'Alembert, *Encyclopédie*

The well-bred diagram embodied an emotional Quietism, indifference to punishment, and silence. The vulgar incision flaunted pain. Pleasurable hits and hurtful cuts of experience were sharp, distinct, unfused. The Stoic, Neoplatonic, and Cartesian view of the body and sense of being in the world divided beautiful health from ugly disease. But ancient and modern sophists and Epicureans alike went beyond the narrow confines of number and measure to recognize a universe crisscrossed with entangling contours and suffering shapes. If mathematics and geometry captured one facet of existence— essence or type circumscribed by a formal system—then empirical synthesis seized organic intricacy and individuality.[71] Such are the bare and prismatic sides of modern abstraction: chaste, vaporizing symbolism and satiric, pulverizing allegory. Analysis glorified *sang-froid*, the mind's contemplative withdrawal toward the internal and celestial, thus annihilating the testimony of the senses. Distraction, on the other hand, was propelled by feeling and chased after shifting external lures and delights to be caught in the traps of sickness and passion. Yet no righteous philosophical maxims, as even Pernety remarked, could prevent the onset of mordant illnesses.[72]

To be distracted was to be out of control and dependent on sensation. It was, as Origen said, to turn away from the Lord, to pay attention to the "furthest corners" of His house, rather than being "disregarded." Turning to "Him and giving attention to this one study" meant that the earthly multitude was "disregarded." Proclus compared the soul's shaky experience in this world to intoxication. Baudelaire later memorably incorporated this image of the drunk and disorderly being, digressing and staggering in "the surrounding indeterminateness," into his Romantic poetics. The drinker lost sight of the infinite, but now muddied and blurred, ideal. Conversely, sobriety was identified with rectifying mathematics, with the watery and virginal style of Stoic and Neoplatonic philosophy. But inebriation resembled the pleasure-seeking sophists, paid professionals straying from subject to subject, collecting and arranging far-fetched metaphors the way painters juxtaposed pigments.[73]

Distraction was like intarsia, or the differential inlaying of glittering stones that pricked the eyes and jabbed the emotions. Nonillusionistic *pietra dura* work stood for the Epicurean image of life as marbled pleasure and pain chromatically contingent upon one another. Democritus originally developed the analogy between contrasting patches of color and particles of being unlike the One. Phenomena were mottled and mixed. They resembled a prismatic mosaic of individual blows and were thus dissimilar to the indivisibility of divine things. Being in the world, then, was synonymous with atomistic and detouring distractions visualized as emotional strikes or hits.[74] This tangible language, predicated on the erasure of any distinction between body and soul, marked the materialist strand of eighteenth-century thought. It led to the development of diverting but nonetheless palpable embodiments of the internal sensations of pain. Caricatural, not tragical, representations captured the fast and deep ways suffering actually felt at different moments depending on the stimulus.

As early as 1755, Lessing projected an extended critique of Winckelmann's *On the Imitation of the Painting and Sculpture of the Greeks.*[75] In dissecting the poetic from the painterly activity, the German playwright's real target was the famous passage concerning pathos-laden expression. We have examined Winckelmann's watery metaphor (the depths of the sea always remain calm no matter how much the surface is agitated) from the perspective of dematerializing abstraction. Winckelmann claimed that the Hellenistic *Laocoön Group* revealed in the central figure of the Trojan priest just such a tragic and resolute soul tranquil in the midst of great corporeal and psychic affliction. But Gotthold Ephraim Lessing (1729–1781), in his *Laocoön* treatise (1766), implied that this discussion of ideal beauty failed to take into account how the proper arena of a particular art influenced the correct choice of subject matter. I wish to offer a rereading of that famous controversy and suggest that it was fundamentally about establishing permissible parameters for the representation of pain and identifying what medium might rightfully show it. This reinterpretation should help us understand the Neoclassical premium placed on the maintenance of heroic decorum even in monumental suffering. Lessing's ban on the hideous, disgusting, and ugly in a painting effectively transferred conventionally repulsive and disfiguring experiences to the domain of caricature. It was left to false wit, poor taste, and deranged allegory to paint the likenesses of wounds and comically to seize the ridiculous, swollen, deformed, and contrary aspects of illness.

Lessing's tenacious spatial aesthetics of the beautiful and pleasing, more than Winckelmann's visionary writings, succeeded in minimizing and trivializing the visual arts' relation to, and possible impact on, life. It was Lessing who categorically severed them from the domain of responsible or irresponsible symbolic speech. Furthermore, he placed the representation of the daily struggle of the damaged beyond the legitimate imitative power of imagery. We shall return to the implications of this continuing pictorial impotence, as opposed to linguistic hegemony, in chapter 5. For the moment, it is sufficient to call attention to the prevalence of manipulated and manipulating images of bodily and mental pathos in our society. Think of the flourishing legal business of liability litigation that routinely involves the filming of "bad babies," severe mental retardation, and grim paralysis. In the era of video ache and spasm, it is common courtroom practice to show a supposedly objective tape of "a day in the life" of an accident victim or a disfigured infant. Why have we not heard the voice of the knowledgeable art historian raised against this ignorant and cynical misuse of pictures by the verbal legal profession? Where are the proactive visualists who will unmask tricking tapes, made to compel lottery-like verdicts in major disability cases, produced ostensibly with the honorable aim of documenting sickness, harm, and a lost quality of existence? Who will speak on behalf of the power of pictures to be not merely cold, calculating, and controlling, but truly demonstrative and sustaining during the hard living of a life?

But let us first examine the source of our contemporary malaise. As part of his general thesis that the painter, unlike the poet, was compelled to compress his picture into a single "pregnant moment," Lessing excluded the transitory and the accidental from the sphere of the plastic arts. This rule, of course, situated him squarely within the contracting trend I have been terming diagrammatic abstraction. The face or body distorted in pain was just such a passing moment that violated the principle of abbreviated beauty. While no right-thinking artist would voluntarily depict such an offensive instant, extending over time, the poet could describe such ugly episodes. The effect of his superior medium was consecutive, not permanent and coexistent. "Ugliness offends our eyes, contradicts the taste we have for order and harmony, and awakens aversion irrespective of the actual existence of the object in which we perceive it." Consequently, Lessing attacked Winckelmann's comparison of the sculptured Laocoön's sufferings to those of Sophocles' Philoctetes. Cries of anguish and disjointed moanings that might be appropriate to barbarians were not to be heard from Homer's masculine gods or heroes. According to Lessing even the great Greek poets, although not forbidden by their medium, nonetheless stifled human emotions and did not allow their virile characters to give way to tears and invectives. Laocoön's scream had to be softened to a sigh when depicted in stone. The reason Lessing gave was not, as Winckelmann suggested, because such an action betrayed an ignoble soul. Rather, his objection was purely physiognomic or external. He did not wish the features to be distorted "in a disgusting manner." Extreme physical pain must be smoothed and stilled to a less intense degree. Works of the painter and sculptor were given at a glance, but also intended to be repeatedly contemplated. Thus the choice of the single but elastic moment at which to silence the mobility of features could not be too carefully selected.[76]

Although absolutely severing painting from poetry (and wholly to the advantage of the latter), Lessing forced painting to emulate the clear and distinct grammatical constructions of Greek usage. He mocked the "indistinct and indeterminate picture[s]" provided by the German language. Its descriptive bent had the effect of regaling the reader with three predicates before he was even informed of the subject. The Greeks, on the other hand, as the visual arts ought to do and in conformity with the natural order of thought, painlessly and accurately wove together subject and first predicate. The reader became properly "acquainted with the thing itself, and then with its accidents." Lessing incessantly reiterated that immoderate physical suffering, such as the terrible wound of Philoctetes, was insufficient to evoke audience pity. This dogma was intrinsic to his conception of linguistic and dramaturgical propriety. Horrible, disgusting, and ridiculous emotions were like isolated, insistent, and detailed predicates falsely blurring the nominative clarity of a picture or a performance. Neither in art nor in language did they arouse compassion. Instead, they existed as "separate things"—like sharp *argutiae* or glaring points in a speech—and "did not blend closely" with the primary elements. A *cento* or patchwork in poetry was like a deformed and overwrought style violating the delicacy of mingled emotions. Neither the reader nor the viewer could pick out "a single thread and follow it through all its interlacing." Lessing, like the French Academy's Dandré-Bardon, believed that artistic compositions could be *pathétique* without the presence of disruptive sharp pathos. That is, paintings could exist merely on the level of "pure spectacle."[77] Nor did Blake, that most unacademic of artists, in the engravings for the *Book of Job*—the archetype of human suffering—violate the decorum of stylized and anesthetized pain. *With Dreams upon My Bed Thou scarest me & affightest Me with Visions* obeyed the Neoplatonic ideal of elevation from earth, even in persecution. Blake arrested the expression of torment that might realistically have accompanied the destruction of Job's flesh (fig. 111).[78]

Lessing's diatribe against the ugly and deformed in the visual arts owed to Moses Mendelsohn's (1729–1786) and, especially, to Christian Ludwig von Hagedorn's (1713–1780) analysis of disgust. Certain objects became revolting merely through the association of ideas. For example, Hesiod's Goddess of

My bones are pierced in me in the
night season & my sinews
take no rest

My skin is black upon me
& my bones are burned
with heat

The triumphing of the wicked
is short, the joy of the hypocrite is
but for a moment
Satan himself is transformed into an Angel of Light & his Ministers into Ministers of Righteousness

With Dreams upon my bed thou scarest me & affrightest me
with Visions

Why do you persecute me as God & are not satisfied with my flesh. Oh that my words
were printed in a Book that they were graven with an iron pen & lead in the rock for ever
For I know that my Redeemer liveth & that he shall stand in the latter days upon
the Earth & after my skin destroy thou This body yet in my flesh shall I see God
whom I shall see for Myself and mine eyes shall behold & not Another. tho consumed be my wrought Image

Who opposeth & exalteth himself above all that is called God or is Worshipped

WBlake invenit & sculp

London. Published as the Act directs March 8. 1825 by Will. Blake N.º 3 Fountain Court Strand

Proof

Hasta la muerte.

Sorrow was a monster of repugnance because her personal qualities reminded the reader of real offenses to sight, taste, smell, and touch. She was described as awash in tears, grinding her teeth, pale, disheveled, dessicated, knobby-kneed, with bloody cheeks, talon nails, dusty shoulders, and nostrils filled with phlegm. Hagedorn took note of the fine line separating disgust from laughter. Unlike Atreus devouring his children, or the terrible repast of Tereus, the snotty-nosed goddess did not excite horror. Excessive disagree-ableness in the fine arts produced the ridiculous. Hagedorn, like Lessing, worried about trespassing over that physiognomic boundary. A handsome old man whose wrinkles betokened a moral life (fig. 75) was quite a different matter from "a powerful and studied ugliness." Think of Goya's mocking caricature of a shriveled Maria Luisa of Parma, wounding the eyes of the beholder by her horribleness (fig. 112). The painter was further advised to soften his canvas the way the poet muted his tale and, above all, to avoid the

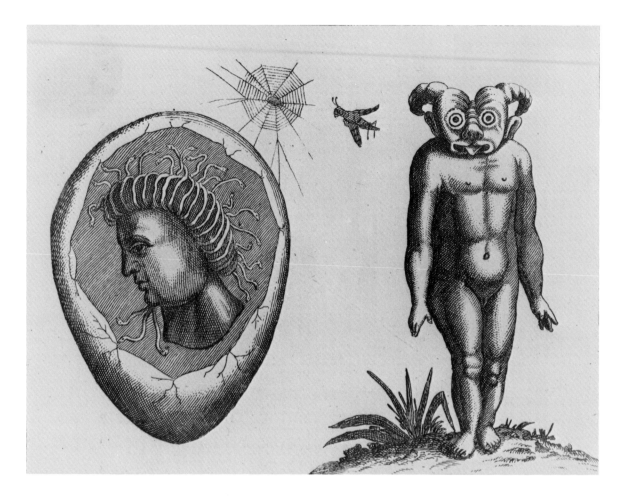

113. **Fortunius Licetus,** *Medusa Head*
Found in an Egg, **from** *De Monstris,* **1665,**
p. 238. Engraving. (Photo: Courtesy
National Library of Medicine, Bethesda, Md.)

114. **Anne-Claude-Philippe, Comte de**
Caylus, *Satire or "Critique": A "Bear"-*
Headed Roman Senator, **from** *Recueil*
d'antiquités, **1752–1767, VI, pl. 76, fig. 1.**
Engraving. (Photo: author.)

grotesque. Thus Homeric monsters such as the giants Typhon and Briarus must not be depicted. Or, when they were shown, in the case of Perseus's chimerical adversary (fig. 109) or the crippled Vulcan, it was to set Andromeda's or Venus's beauty in relief. The circumspect moderns often imparted loveliness to Medusa's face to offset her gruesome snaky locks (fig. 113). Hagedorn's nemesis, like Lessing's, was Ovid. The tirade against the grotesque was leveled at irrational fables permitting the obscene metamorphoses of human beings into monsters. Hagedorn unequivocally declared that "monsters are for natural history cabinets, & not for painting galleries." Adam Elsheimer (1574–1632) and Peter Paul Rubens (1577–1640) pandered to the *amateur*'s false taste for ingenious novelty when they represented the legend of the inhabitants of Delos, but showed them as only partially transformed into frogs. This caricatural degradation of the integrity of the human body by planting an animal head on the torso—in the ludicrous manner of Egyptian or Indian idols—created shocking hybrids, "alarming in nature, ridiculous in the arts" (fig. 114). Hagedorn concurred with the Abbé Batteux (1713–1780) and with Horace's poetics that an artist ought not to assemble in a painting serpents, birds, lambs, tigers, unless he wanted his composition to frighten birds.[79]

German Neoclassical theorists clearly wanted to frighten artists and have them steer away from a staple of Mannerist aesthetics. Scare tactics, apparently, were needed to keep them from the depiction of extreme ugliness in order to incite mirth. Paul Barolsky has suggested that the deformed characters in Leonardo's drawings and the exaggerated grimaces of discomfort contorting Giulio Romano's giants in the Palazzo del Tè (ca. 1530) were intended to amuse.[80] I wish to suggest that, for the eighteenth century, the diverting representation of the horrors of disease constituted an innovative style of pain that went beyond the laughable. Caricature vividly demonstrated the dehumanizing and grotesque disturbances occurring in body perception and body image when one was sick. Ignoring Lessing's "pregnant moment," it stitched together the patient's distracted story from typical anecdotes. It humorously opened the sufferer up, not through dissection or step-by-step reasoning, but by allowing the viewer to feel imaginatively for him. Caricature, like experimental science, combined the immediate observation of superficial and particular symptoms with a general, deep, or characteristic perspective. This humane viewpoint was gained from observing the countless modalities of illness over time. As a therapeutic genre, it appeared to anticipate Oliver Sacks's summons to the contemporary clinician to return to earlier days. In the nineteenth century, Sacks believed, there was still a visual natural history. But already in the eighteenth century, this energetic description and intimate examination of disorders was as yet unspoiled by the analytical concepts of an aseptic science (fig. 115).[81] In Gibsonian fashion, caricature was also about the awareness of self in the world, the coperception of the mutable perceiver as well as the mobile ambient.[82]

Significantly, Lessing condemned the offensive manifestation of physical imperfections past and present. He spurned—in its ancient guise—"Greek Ghezzis" or "painters of filth," such as Pauson and Pyreicus. He scorned—in its modern incarnation—those "Dutch artists" who, in their copies, exaggerated "the ugly parts of the original." He excluded from the fine arts' domain the *bambochades* of life, i.e., that marginal mob or burlesque crowd of idlers and unemployed gawkers wandering the streets seeking distractions. It was this raw, heterogeneous, and unassimilated throng whose medical body was servilely and viciously captured, according to Hagedorn, by the Netherlandish "pygmies of art." Unlike the diagrammatic "Wound Man" or "Disease Woman" of the medieval miniature, the portrait in poor taste of the unheroic and lowly sufferer was more than a peg on which to hang written diagnoses. Anticipating the mangled and suppurating bodies of Francis

115. James Gillray, *French Generals*
Retiring on Account of Their Health, 1799.
Colored etching. (Photo: Courtesy National
Library of Medicine, Bethesda, Md.)

Bacon, the patient in the early modern period was constructed out of disgusting humors. Secretions, emissions, purgings, swellings were extracted or exteriorized in an unignorable corporeal presence.[83] The pictorial strategy was that of reification, making literally or physically present an unseen sensation (fig. 116). This patched materialization of unappetizing substance—the inverse of divine hypostasis—was achieved through fragmentation and realignment. Mental or somatic states were personified in painful physical projections that led a concrete life of their own. Only after the middle of the eighteenth century, in the British satires of James Gillray, Henry William Bunbury (1750–1811), Thomas Rowlandson (1756–1817), and George Cruikshank, did allegorization and the exploration of deformed identity come together.[84]

Gillray's *Gout* (1799)—in defiance of Lessing's temporal strictures—evoked the clawlike grip and monstrous bite of the affliction as it enlarged and spread with time. The contorted graphic idiom of staccato, broken, and interrupted etched lines made tangible deep, pinching muscle pain. It demonstrated its relentless advance, how spasms were conducted along large nerve fibers to the extremities of the tumid foot. Gillray was occupied with the same images and imitative methods that concerned his empiricist contemporaries. David Hume, in the *Treatise of Human Nature* (1739/40), argued that the idea or impression of ourselves was always intimately present to us. According to Hume (1711–1776), one could feel sickness or acute pain "from the mere force of the imagination," and make a malady real by often thinking of it. Compassion, or sympathy for another's woes, was predicated on the viewer's being able to conjure up a lively idea. To "feel the passion" meant the empathetic beholder reacted in the same manner as if he were actuated by it. "Passion always turns our view to ourselves, and makes us think of our own qualities and circumstances." Hume gave the example of a fit of gout to illustrate the inseparability of body and soul. He also used it to support the fact that corporeal pleasures and pains were the source of our so-called mental passions.[85] Gillray embraced this central tenet of empiricism by showing that the spectator looked upon any infirmity with an eye to how it affected himself. Bunbury's more conventional and maladroit scene (fig. 117)—deprived of Gillray's ingenious fragmentation and magnification—was, nevertheless, equally removed from the banality of high-minded narrative (fig. 118). Bunbury played on the incongruous proximity of an emblem (a black devil) and a corpulent, tippling, and ruddy-faced musician crippled by gout. Their jarring copresence in the same composition persuasively brought to conscious-

The GOUT.

116. James Gillray, *The Gout,* 1799, republished 1835. Etching. (Photo: Courtesy National Library of Medicine, Bethesda, Md.)

117. Henry William Bunbury, *Origin of the Gout,* 1785, republished 1815. Colored etching by Thomas Rowlandson (?). (Photo: Courtesy National Library of Medicine, Bethesda, Md.)

LA GOUTE ET L'ARAIGNÉE . Fable L.

ness the startling intrusion of pain. Like the astonished recipient, the viewer was awkwardly forced to retreat from the ludicrous, but burning, apparition. George Cruikshank was an especially inspired creator of new realities or pictorial allusions.[86] *Indigestion* (1826) managed to make simultaneously present two different grotesque realms in competition with one another. Together, they produced a single, dense, and more complex mosaic of experience (fig. 119). He amputated an ordinary genre figure from his cozy domestic setting to embed him in pie-in-the-sky Lilliput. Dwarfish bewitchments and a plague of cooked enchantments wittily reminded this gourmand Gulliver of his gigantic culinary excesses.

This burlesque intarsia, or ridiculous antithesis, was, I suggest, a configured neologism. Beattie had warned against the coining of outrageous and hyperbolic new terms or letters. If permitted, language would become perplexing.

190

Indigestion.

119. George Cruikshank, *Indigestion,* 1825. Colored etching. (Photo: Courtesy National Library of Medicine, Bethesda, Md.)

The Cholic —

120. George Cruikshank, *The Cholic,* 1835. Colored etching. (Photo: Courtesy National Library of Medicine, Bethesda, Md.)

It would soon be "disfigured and altered" through the absence of *"callida junctura,"* or the right arrangement of words.[87] Caricature, as neologistic medley, was irreverently compounded from new or complex ideas not found together in empirical reality. Nonetheless, it corresponded to the contradictory "feel" of that reality (fig. 120). Of course, neither synthetic distractions nor diagrammatic abstractions, roamed the world. Yet the satiric miscellany—unlike the empty outline—resembled the sudden and shattered distresses of existence.

Honoré Daumier (1808–1879), in the manner of his British counterparts, heaped together what the ideal Neoclassical composition kept pried apart (fig. 121). Lessing had urged that the poet and painter must imitate (although differently) an orderly progression of thought. But Hume had proffered a counterphysiology of the passions. He crumbled identity into minutely elab-

orated pains and pleasures impertinently and obtrusively wandering around on their own. Disorderly ideas—personified as strangling savages and sawing demons—were violently yoked together in a novel and comic *art brut*. Hume's French follower, the materialist Baron D'Holbach (1723–1789), similarly posited that the soul was subjected to the same vicissitudes as the body. It shared the fine-grained texture of its health and the shapelessness of its disease. Like the palpable wind, the soul was continually modified and buffeted by the density of the atmosphere, the change of seasons, and even by "food entering the stomach." Thus the pain of colic or gout produced a sensuous idea, or physical modification, in the brain, transmitted as a tangible impression to the sufferer. In this scheme, sensations, perceptions, and ideas were identically material. Thus the soul was not pure or spiritual, but visibly diverted by real hits or pangs striking and irritating the nerves.[88]

122. **Thomas Rowlandson,** *The Hypochondriac,* **1788. Aquatint. (Photo: Courtesy National Library of Medicine, Bethesda, Md.)**

123. George Cruikshank, *The Blue Devils,*
1835. Etching. (Photo: Courtesy National
Library of Medicine, Bethesda, Md.)

124. George Cruikshank, *Hallucinations,*
1819. Etching. (Photo: Courtesy National
Library of Medicine, Bethesda, Md.)

The caricaturist thus managed to bridge the gulf, described by Diderot, separating the suffering "I see" from the suffering "I feel."[89] This conjoining ability was evident in the allegorical treatment of thoughts as if they were material objects of the senses (fig. 96). Rowlandson's obsessive *Hypochondriac* (1788) reified spectral snatches of suicidal fears (fig. 122). The partially decomposed phantoms or broken visions of death by runaway coach, poison, asp, knife, sword, dart, water, and rope humorously besieged a young woman obviously stuck under a dark cloud. The typicality and even conventionality of this burst of imagery in no way minimized or dispelled the reality of the individual's anxiety. Rowlandson's shamanistic allegory touched upon a preliterate and folkloric animism. The image was a visual encyclopedia of high cultural debris caught in the process of demythologization. Collective memories and private thoughts mingled and decayed. His disintegrating and depressed personality type was surrounded by a crowd of readymades, a grab bag of eighteenth-century pictorial commonplaces. Skeleton, witch, Chinamen, Cleopatra, Medusa were stock characters of art and theater. Seized at the moment of unraveling and dissolving, they were reamalgamated to form new and melodramatic structures of identity. Caricature, then, was like theurgy in late Neoplatonism, i.e., an irrational element of popular culture appearing at the end of a long rationalistic tradition. It, too, relied not on reason but on the emotional potency of fetishes. Like Jean Dubuffet's earthy and barbarous materializations, the *Topographies* or *Texturologies* (1957–1958), rough caricature was the least literary of graphic genres. It attempted to objectify, and give texture to, raw body experience lying beyond words and behind shape.[90] Rowlandson, Gillray, Cruikshank, and Daumier selected tangible signs or visible tokens possessing marvelous ornamental or singular qualities. These curious rarities and oddities reminded the humble spectator of the miraculous ability of art to visualize inner life (figs. 123, 124). Their medicinal prints were material charms credited with mysterious powers for magically exorcising real or hallucinatory miseries through laughter.

The physician Louis Poinsinet de Sivry (1733–1804), in his *Traité du rire* (1768), created a nuanced taxonomy of risibility. Long before Nietzsche, Bergson, or Freud, he concluded that all types of laughter from the smirk to the grin involved some form of release through the temporary suspension of reason and order. As a symptom of transitory irrationality, the uncontrollable peal combated folly nonintellectually. But it could also inappropriately snicker or roar at the sight of infirmities, deformities, and imperfections. Whether the outbursts were proper or improper, involuntary or voluntary, the physiological weapons were identical. Vulgar grimaces, Laocoön- or Philoctetes-

ABSTRACTING

Se repulen.

125. Robert Burton, *Types of Melancholy,* from *The Anatomy of Melancholy,* 1632, title page. Engraving. (Photo: Courtesy National Library of Medicine, Bethesda, Md.)

126. Francisco de Goya, *They Spruce Themselves Up,* from *Los Caprichos,* 1799, pl. 51. Aquatint and etching. National Gallery of Art, Washington, D.C., Rosenwald Collection. (Photo: Courtesy National Gallery of Art.)

like inarticulate sounds, mixed expressions, caprice, frivolity, and extravagance comprised its arsenal.[91] Chuckle-inducing caricature—because of its unaccustomed or foreign vernacularism—was a "barbaric" device for bringing unseen afflictions to sight. It could produce joyous, liberating, or apotropaic medical effects far beyond the reach of opiates. By their noisy expressiveness, caricatures were the antidote to vacuum and nothingness, to the nonatmosphere of calm abstraction as ideal surcease of pain and freedom from stimulus. Pernety unflatteringly had compared unnatural inertness and apathy, touted by the Stoics as a mark of perfection, to an insensible stone statue or automaton.[92]

Caricature, then, was also the optical antithesis of obliviousness. *Anaisthésie,* Le Camus declared, was the deprivation or diminishment of sensation because of too watery blood. But the sluggish *ennui* conspicuously labeling Cruik-

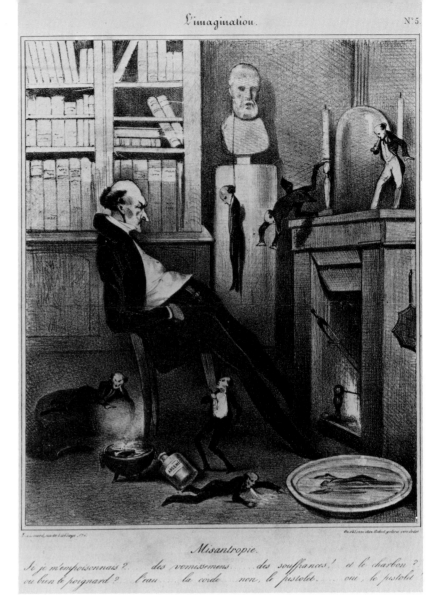

Misantropie.

127. Honoré Daumier, *Misanthropy,* from
L'Imagination, 1833, pl. 5. Lithograph.
(Photo: Courtesy National Library of
Medicine, Bethesda, Md.)

shank's image of apoplexy satirically undermined the elevated notion of Stoic
langor. By representing it as a ferocious attack, Cruikshank exhibited the
cruel stagnation of the soul (fig. 123).[93] Robert Burton's (1557–1640) lofty
black lethargy was thus turned into the onset of the prosaic blues (fig. 125).
Unlike the compartmentalized and solitary symbols of the stupefied melancholic framing the title page of Burton's treatise, Cruikshank visualized the
fitful antics of a cohort of goblins. Stirred-up fantasies speedily and energetically dished out the sharp and distracting torments of despair or revenge.
These bitter embodiments of anxiety literally troubled the mind through
itching, macerating, poking, scalding, and whispering. In contrast, the *Anatomy of Melancholy* (1632) merely listed "dull, sad, sorry and lumpish" vexa-
tions.[94] And the light-headed wits in Matthaus Greuter's contemporaneous
engraving were likewise obliged humorlessly to distill or excrete the disconnected and undigested babble of their madness (fig. 95).[95] It was eighteenth-

century caricaturists, then, who initially conveyed the convulsive eruption of loose and unexpected thoughts arising from a perturbed imagination's monstrous fits (fig. 124). Like a wandering or intermittent fever, a hectic delirium was shown to shift frenetically from place to place, painting the busy portrait of the erratic.[96]

Goya, not Courbet, first transposed the caricaturist's phantasmagoric mixture of distorted corporeality and animality to the level of modern, or "real," allegory. Bestial and somber troops of spirits replaced the giggle-provoking farcical hybrids that had once cheerfully acted out the agonies of gout, colic, ague, or hypochondria (fig. 126).[97] Goya, like Gillray or Rowlandson and, later, Cruikshank or Daumier (fig. 127), imparted a sense of objective and organic integrity to the externalized shapes of his fantasy (fig. 17). Yet such physiological and psychiatric phenomena were sardonically, not merrily, conjoined in the *Caprichos* (1799). Black humor and a derision that gripped the entrails finally decomposed the corpse of idealism. Encyclopedic and satiric assemblage was, by the close of the eighteenth century, perfectly congruent with the dark and grotesque underbelly of reality.

Patterns of Interiority

Not only the diagram was inward-bound. The comic representational collage abruptly and amusingly externalized the internal. The perceptual and the instinctual surfaced in an agitated stream of consciousness and in an explosion of unconscious associations and drives. Conversely, its nonobjective and fluid counterpart traced the chromatic patterns of pathos, the undulating decor of a normally hidden inwardness. Marbling—another class of popular, massproduced, and widely distributed printed works—stained wallpapers and other plane surfaces, in Chambers's words, "with various clouds and shades resembling in some measure the divers veins of marble." This supremely manual art consisted in the production of fleeting patterns by swimming dyes on a liquid, and then dipping blank sheets of paper or edges of a book into the vat.[98] Fluctuating and tinted waves, I suggest, were the visual and nondiscursive equivalents of mental errancy, of libertine dispersiveness sheltered behind a defensive perimeter (fig. 128). Thus Laurence Sterne (1713–1768) could use the metaphor of the motley marbled page to paint the portrait of Tristam Shandy's irregular and excursive mind.[99] This prismatic, variable, and floating psychic world—buffeted by chance or haphazard occurrences— was the sensual opposite to Winckelmann's deep pool of filtered, transparent, and silent water.

Wander

verb, To rave; to ramble here and there; to go without any certain course. It has always a sense, either evil or light, and imports either idleness, viciousness or misery. To deviate; to go astray.

Dr. Johnson, *Dictionary*

Égaré

verb, He who has lost his way; dispersed hither and yon; deceived; distracted; who has quit the path of virtue, duty, religion . . .

Diderot and D'Alembert, *Encyclopédie*

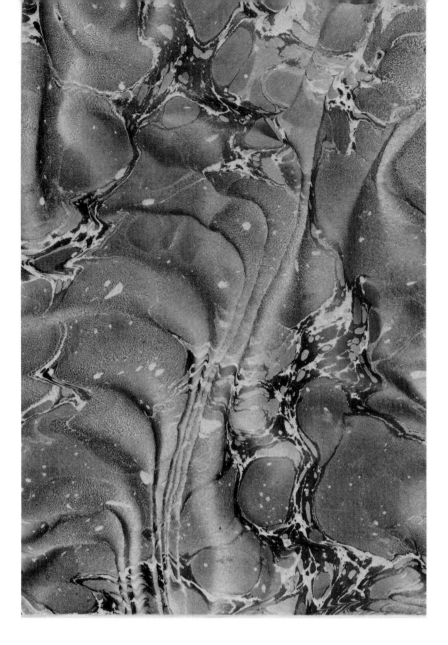

128. *Spanish Marbled Paper,* ca. 1790. British Library, Box 18, J1632. Reproduced by permission of the British Library.

The proliferation of densely decorated papers belonged to the embellishments of the home, to textiles and furnishings announcing a desire for self-presentation. Eighteenth-century domestic architecture invented rooms with specialized functions, creating separate spaces for bathing, sleeping, dining, reading, conversing, making music, and other activities conducted in privacy.[100] Yet—until late in the century—retreat, solitude, and revery were largely confined to playful withdrawal, to descents into the grottoes and *fabriques* lying at the bottom of the English garden and the *jardin anglo-chinois.*

We have seen in these first two chapters that, in the Enlightenment dialectic of exterior and interior, the uniform facade generally had priority. The private person was expected to live up to and convey, either sincerely or through a mask, the physiognomic values of the public realm. Lichtenberg, however, had dared to state that the inflexible architectural wall was false to the plasticity of the inner room. Caricature also suggested that behind the seamless front of social proprieties, ordinary people inhabited disrupted and variegated spaces papered over in a variety of grotesque styles. But caricature, as the picture of distraction, did not liquefy the distinction between inside and outside. It did not dissolve the shapes of the world and of the personality into an identical abstract flow mirroring a phenomenology of wandering.

The vindication of the self-defining person and his claim to a psychologically gratifying life stood in opposition to the public, or civic, sphere. Privacy was seen as essentially a negative condition, a vice of social isolates who sought to conceal or shelter their dubious activities from the view of the community. Prior to the twentieth century, such libertine behavior was associated with erring in a biblical sense. To stray, rove, ramble was a symbol of revolt because it inevitably led one from the straight road of collective duty, or right line of direction, into secret compartments where mistake, blunder, and sin reigned. The licentious image of fallibility was the arabesque, the deviously marbled and veined course that wounded correct thought and rational harmony by its loose orchestration. As complex and fanciful interior arrangement, it stood in opposition to the severity of corporate statement uttered and judged in the bright light of day. Shifting feelings and mobile desires— as the most intimate and hidden aspects of temperament—were also associated with feminine activities. Spinning or weaving imaged the undecidability of a wily infinity of threads.[101] In the Adamic myth, the diabolic serpent tempting Eve was the counterlikeness to God. By imitating the devil's tortuous twistings and harlequin disguises, fallen man missed the target and lost himself in anomalous detours, diverging and turning back irrationally on themselves. To err without measure meant one possessed no criterion for rectitude, and thus behaved as if intoxicated. In monstrously centering life upon oneself, the social derelict was open to multiple, dissimilar, and fugal attractions. This "Romantic" alienation, both in Helleno-Hebraic exegesis and in Neoplatonism, could be cured only by cathartic purification. The latter expunged the dominion of the sensible and the empirical. But even when rehabilitated, health was not completely restored. The soul retained the scars of its transgressions. During its journey through life, it kept the propensity to wander promiscuously in the evil lace of matter.[102]

We have witnessed in countless ways the ubiquity of this long shadow cast by Gnostic or Manichean abstraction. The abstinent view legislated that the individual must subtract himself from all that was mixed. This negative ethic and nihilistic aesthetic of emptying abnegation looked upon the world as a land of darkness incised with breaches, gulfs, abysses, ditches, dikes, and crevasses.[103] A mathematized art and a geometrized ethics were like fasting; they thinned and subtilized the defiled soul compounded with body. From this perspective, a fleshly art and a concupiscent morality were forms of addition. Unseemly passions and other "worthless and filthy things," as the Montanist Tertullian (fl. 197–222 AD) wrote, were the result of coupled and superimposed excesses. This art of occluding reveled in multiplying a surfeit of random signs in which the viewer got lost.[104]

Additive deviancy can be compared to overprinted palimpsests, a sort of "tapestry on paper." Such reused and cheap cloaking papers were used to conceal binding threads on the inside covers of a book and to line the drawers of commodes and secretaries, and the interior of jewelry boxes, letter caskets, coffers, armoires, and other domestic recesses. They belonged to, and helped define, an intimate and conventionally unimportant world of secluded places: garden retreats, private studies, perfumed closets, and rarity cabinets. Detritus and refuse were commonly employed in ornamental paper manufacture during the seventeenth and eighteenth centuries. These veneering and screening linings, made of disposable goods, were used to fit out, and even to image, a hidden, sometimes clandestine realm put between wrappers. Like Robert Adams's festive and flat architectural groteseques, decorative papers were destined exclusively for interiors (although humble, not wealthy) and for private enclosures. Ruleless and brightly colored designs were also "damasked" over banned or waste literature to obliterate suspect or unwanted documents (fig. 129).[105] One telling example has marbled patterns overprinted on an outmoded gory tale from the *Book of Martyrs*. These stratified designs, interweaving serpentine interlace with the description of barbarians hacking Christians to pieces, formed the endpapers of a fashionable treatise on the principles of politeness![106] The intricately layered and labyrinthine visual effect was similar to that of *pentimenti* bobbing up in an oil painting. In this rare example, now preserved at the British Library, an abandoned, or insufficiently buried, text surfaced seemingly spontaneously and accidentally. Analogously, Leibniz, in his critique of Locke's *tabula rasa* view of the mind as a vacancy before the inscription of experience, had compared the soul to a veined tablet of marble. As a proponent of innate ideas, he suggested that certain thoughts preexisted in the mind the way the image of Hercules emerged from the mineral's feeble markings. Similarly, what seemed to be unknown or new ideas impressed by experience were merely the emitted

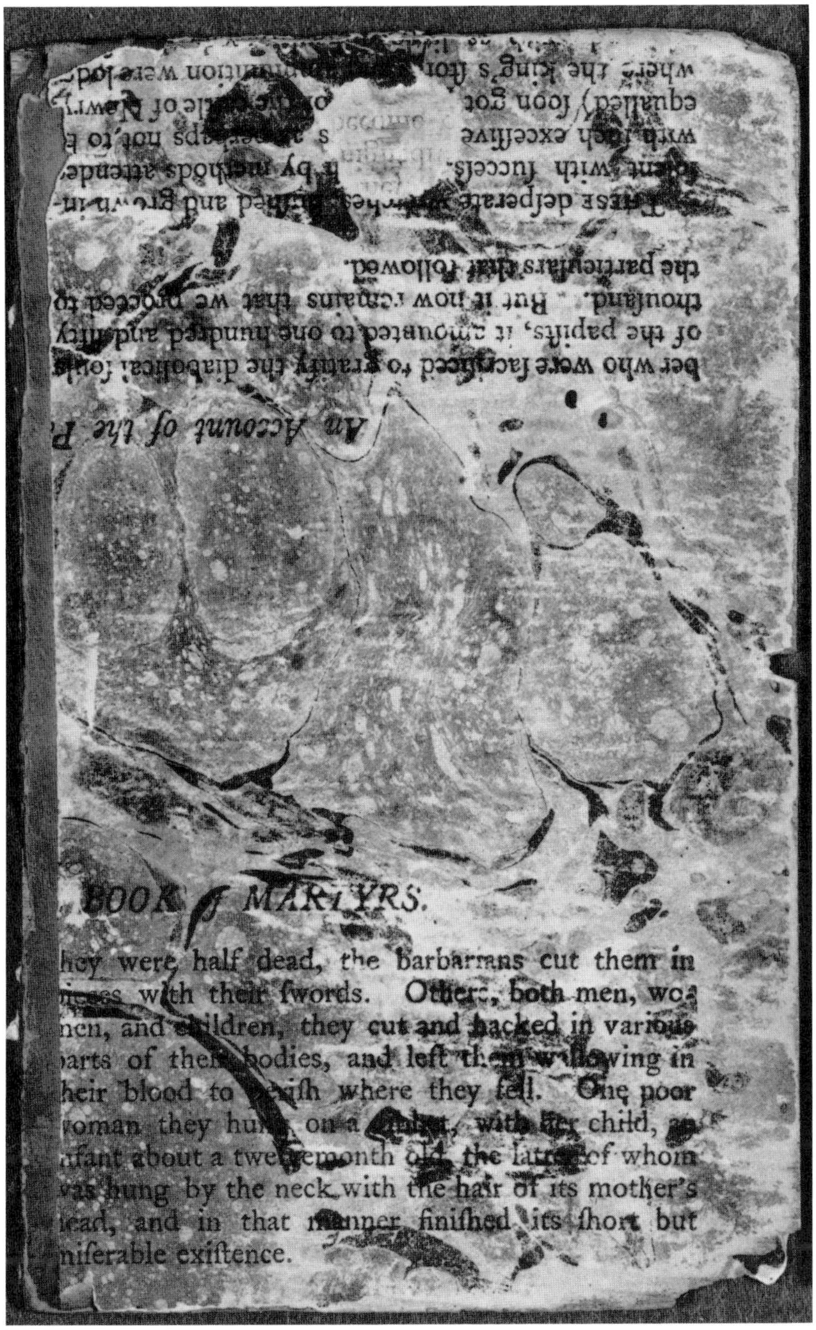

129. ***Overprinted Text on Marbled Book Wrappers,*** **1786. Reproduced by permission of the British Library.**

curls and wisps of a preformed spirit. These mental tendrils were faint signs of notions still covered by substance, or of delicate sensations of which we were as yet not completely aware.[107] Like outwardly straying *pentimenti*, or Leibniz's upwardly drifting *petites perceptions*, private musings and internal lines roamed onto the surface brocade. I want to suggest a parallel, operating within the eighteenth-century mentality, between this aqueous marbled maze and the mental tangle of floating dispositions and habits. Both errant colored patterns and permeating temperamental inclinations were betrayed by wandering into consciousness. They were like faint watermarks, produced by shaping wire into figures and placing them in the bottom of a mold. Embedded in thousands of sheets of fine- or poor-quality paper, they revealed their complex strands and, presumably, their significance, only when held to the light.[108]

The eighteenth-century aesthete, or libertine, was less concerned with stable society than with liquid psyche. He expected to define himself from within. For the Enlightenment, the portrait of the errant in social, spiritual, and intellectual matters continued to be the modern Epicurean. The major dictionaries of the period defined him as someone who abandoned conventions and laws to travel a subjective, irregular, and dissipated route. Libertinage wounded norms by endorsing unrestrained behavior that refused to follow preestablished formulas.[109] Since the sixteenth century, it was a key term for designating amoral pantheists engaged in illegitimate discourse and possessing a roving wit. These freethinking spirits uninhibitedly jumbled distinctions in a riot of rhetorical colors.[110] Calvinists and Post-Tridentine Catholics alike—think of Bayle's relentless hunt for error or Pernety's pursuit of facial fraud—sniffed out these unstable or moody wits, with their fantastic thoughts, false beliefs, and capricious demeanor (figs. 95, 96). Seventeenth- and eighteenth-century reform movements, however, specifically attacked the lax Baroque and Rococo fondness for ornamental labyrinths, "unintelligible" instrumental music, exotic spices, and even the costly bizarreness of the striped tulip.[111] The merely aesthetic was to be suppressed by the ascetic. The new Cartesian analytical method and the rigorism of an Augustinian Jansenism were also part of what became the Neoclassical drive to wash language, art, and morals of the excesses of liberty. They were to be cleansed of showy ostentation and, most fundamentally, of the cosmetic imagination.[112] This condemnation of fleshly delights was precipitated by a fear of the collapse of order. The same puritan phobic anxiety of imminent dissolution underlay the view of disease as the Adamic, or inherited, inability to control the flux of reality.[113]

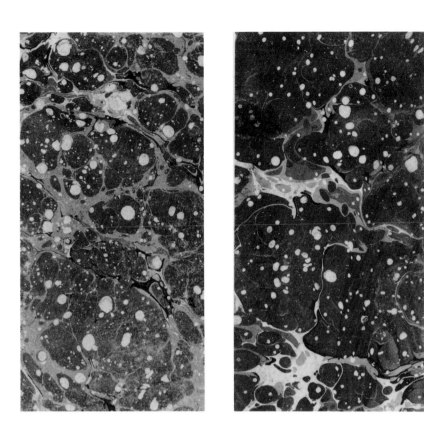

130. Nicolas-Denis Derôme, Le Jeune (style of), *"Stone" Marbled Papers,* ca. 1788. British Library, Box 17, J1541–1542. Reproduced by permission of the British Library.

Outlines and diagrams were the artistic weapons of health wielded to subjugate congenital *pathema*, the unrefined melt of vagrant affect and external happenstance. Fractional and flat monotones of cognition reduced the sick and dangerously unlimited to the limited, and cut mobile concepts off from additional entanglements. Like the foveal organization of the retina—operative in one-point spatial constructions—sensory confusion could be selectively gathered and fixed through the concentration of a resolving power in the eye (figs. 68, 72, 73, 74, 84, 85, 91).[114]

Conversely, for the rational side of the Enlightenment, the picture of unfocused "madness" or aimless pandemonium was incarnated by marbling (fig. 130). These mutable patterns, by their distracting directionlessness, evoked associations to irrational erring, idle talk, monstrous combinations, and the expression of normally unacceptable ideas nonsensically grafted together (figs. 108, 109, 110, 114).[115] Chromatic jabberwocky characterized the garrulous wit, irresponsibly suturing diverse and permutable fragments together. If loquaciousness was the disease of Logos,[116] then marbling was the insanity of the visual. From the vantage of Neoclassicism, optical copiousness constituted a Rococo plague of decorative and feminine images without thoughts. It epitomized Lessing's hatred of "mere perception," spatially

unshaped and grotesquely uncontrolled either by reason or language. Marbling was Epicurean, sophistic, Ovidian, or fundamentally "rhetorical." It visualized the flexibility needed in the face of life's unending metamorphosis. From this vantage error was not erring but errant knowledge pursuing the free-hand filigrees of life. This protean and womanly attempt to adjust to the manifold meanders and openwork of matter seemed "mad" from the rationalistic perspective.[117]

Color, traditionally, was the antagonist to fixity. It was connected to change and superficial appearances that seized the eye. In Roman wall painting of the first style, the imitation of rare and exotic marbles made no attempt to suggest projection or recession. The tints and figurations floating within porphyry, alabaster, basalt, and verd antique were copied and arranged by craftsmen into attractive panels or representationless pictures.[118] Going beyond visual delectation, heraldic blazons and Mannerist poetics contrived symbolic and flat paintings resulting from the juxtaposition of colors alone. It was the German Romantics, however—especially Novalis—who first con-

206

ceived of a systematic hieroglyphics or nonobjective algebra of art. Noncontextualized lines and colors were to be combined ingeniously into a fantastic synthetic compendium.[119] Obeying a lateral, formal or musical logic, these infinitely permutable pictographic rudiments wittily destroyed, by inversion, the upright limits set by "proper" abstraction. But it was the eighteenth-century thesaurus of decorative motives that constituted an unrecognized, yet major way station along the road to the Romantic encyclopedia of fragments. These graphic compilations interwove playful snatches of pattern sequences, fortuitous clusters of atoms, and flowing films of pigment.

Kant declared that wallpapers had no intrinsic meaning. They represented no object subordinated to a concept but were untrammeled visual beauties unbounded by narrative.[120] The Rococo period was the high point in the production of decorative papers. Marblers—many of them women—belonged to the book trade and were to be found among illuminators, stencilers, letter painters, binders, and stationers. The method of manufacture, Turkish in origin, was introduced into Europe in the seventeenth century. Both Francis

132. Bouquet (style of), *Comb Marbled Paper (Peacock Type)*, 18th c. British Library, Box 18, J1492. Reproduced by permission of the British Library.)

Bacon and Athanasius Kircher (1602–1680) described the immense range of anamorphic designs arising from a mix of colors and the controlled hand of an artisan "combing" the liquid. To obtain the marbled effect, paints were scattered one after another with a brush, then skillfully raked. Each narrow (fig. 131) or widely gapped tooth (fig. 132) traced a scintillant wake of color. Consequently, every impression was original, differing from copy to copy. Myriad "fantasy marbles" existed, classifiable—in addition to the comb patterns—according to the ripples breathed or exhaled upon the waters to evoke the agitated waves of the sea (fig. 128). There were also antique or compound stone marbles mimicking the dark or white inclusions found in agate and sardonyx (fig. 130).[121]

Papillon, in his *Gravure en bois* and again in the article commissioned by Diderot for the *Encyclopédie*, conveyed the magical and talismanic qualities originally associated with paper used as mural decoration. French *dominotiers* in the late medieval period created small utility papers bearing printed, often religious, illustrations. *Domino*, or the enveloping cape worn by a bishop as the symbol of temporal and spiritual authority, during a more secular age came to designate the concealing cloak or mask hiding the wearer's identity at a ball. Similarly, dual-purpose decorative papers evolved from crude wood engravings—"embroidery" or "black work"—used by the lower classes. By the eighteenth century, they had developed into elegantly bizarre illuminations favored by the bourgeoisie.[122] Still a mass-produced popular art, these hand-painted papers now carried stripes, dots, rosettes, garlands, and marbling. They bore the embellishments of profane inwardness instead of holy images. Production was not limited to France but was distributed throughout Europe. The proliferation of "paper staining" in England, *Buntpapier* in Germany, *dominotier* engravings in France, advertised an infinite range of multiple-use mottled, speckled, spangled, flocked, flowered, wainscotted, tapestried, and damasked coverings. Thus, in the privacy of the nonnoble household (since such inexpensive imitations were banished from the dwellings of the nobility), personal taste could be exposed on one's own four walls.

Decor, like caricature, reified the inhabitant's distracted soul, but not into a concrete object. Scintillant mazy ornament personified ambiguity, the sensual and psychic shimmer that gives way as we look at it.[123] Decoration pictured internal mirage. It was consonant with spiritual space, the *Luxe, calme et volupté* of a nonanthropocentric world, unsubmissive to hierarchical structures. The eighteenth century thus created a domestic poetics of wallpapered intimism well in advance of Pierre Bonnard's (1867–1947) and Edouard Vuillard's (1868–1940) clotted Parisian interiors.[124] In the latter's small and claustrophobic fin-de-siècle works—frequently executed on cardboard—the living person was just barely distinguishable. The viewer must strain to perceive the muted actors imprisoned in the inanimate welter of somber arabesques and broken forms that eventually coalesce into recognizable furnishings. But for the Enlightenment marbler, bodies and a distinctly human presence were excluded from a variable yet repetitive private reality in which all things joyously merged. The beholder's attention—as with ephemeral magic lantern projections—was directed not at the flesh and blood fabricator or his painted surrogate, but toward the dreamy and ineffable effect. The suggestive vacillation of colorful tendrils was like the ceaseless smoke and flux of Epicurean *eidola*.[125] What is continuous illusion but the creation of a unified decor? The pleasurable and painful emission and dissolution of appearances took place both in the vat and in a darkened room. Marbling symbolized the unspeakable openness and unpredictability of life, its essence as nondiscursive libertinage. It also provided a momentary glimpse of the kaleidoscopic fullness lying beyond the grasp of reason. The observer of art and of existence, immersed in the chromatic phenomenal tide, was ignorant the instant before, and the moment after, of what shape the final composition would take.

3 CONCEIVING

Barbarisms, or Strangeness Incarnate

If we want to know what the eighteenth century most profoundly valued or despised in all aspects of culture, then we must examine its fearful disdain of mixtures. Strange barbarisms symbolized everything ostentatiously foreign to, and lying outside, conventions, customs, and norms. They were images at their most assertively primitive, nakedly powerful, and uncontrolled by rational semantic order. Like many of the issues already addressed, understanding this iconoclastic aspect of early modern mentality highlights the past formation and development of current dilemmas. In the process of unraveling what the Enlightenment considered monstrous or grotesque, I hope to reveal older attitudes underlying contemporary debates concerning nonstandard human reproduction. Now that the beginning and the end of life have been identified as the major biological frontiers of the twenty-first century, we need the perspective of history to help us wrestle with these unclear boundaries. Venerable metaphors for correct or incorrect generation, for proper or improper origins, for right or wrong combinations, still shape present day discussions of babies "abstractly" and technologically made without sexual mingling. Ranging from artificial insemination to gestation in a host uterus (surrogacy), these creative methods challenge traditional notions about procreation and the responsibility for a private, covert act with public, or overt, consequences. Further, perhaps pro-choice advocates will find provocative Harvey's and Malebranche's logocentric analogy of ideas in the mind to the

Confusion, _____

noun, Irregular mixture; tumultuous medley; disorder; tumult; indistinct combination. . . . Jumble, to mix violently and confusedly together . . .

Dr. Johnson, *Dictionary*

Enigme, _____

noun, For the ancients it was a mysterious sentence, a proposition given one to divine, but hidden under obscure terms, and most often contradictory in appearance . . .

Diderot and D'Alembert, *Encyclopédie*

fetus in the womb. This intellectualization of a corporeal phenomenon called attention to the accidental and contingent value placed on the embryo: an abortable or abstractable product of the conceiving mind. For preformationists, conception in the world and in the intellect were immaterial, i.e., without body, acheiropoetic, or not made by hand. Pro-life advocates, in turn, by focusing exclusively on the rights of the fetus, also manage to singularize, detach, and thus verbalize experience. Like the materialists, they transform phenomena into ever more minimally visible fragments. Ironically, and in part because of the new imaging technologies, the viability of a separable organism continues to be pushed back toward conception.[1] Conversely, the folk belief in maternal impressions raises the question of who is responsible for an infant's exteriorized deformity. Not just during the Enlightenment but even today, the superstition exists that mothers have the capability of imprinting their unborn children with marks resembling their deviant thoughts and aberrant fantasies.

Undeniably, the situation is more complicated now since the body and its increasingly smaller parts have become highly commoditized. Nonetheless, the eighteenth-century legacy of encyclopedias and morphological classifications persists. The genome project is routinely, and metaphorically, described as a lexicological enterprise. The task is systematically to collect the protein and chemical bits and pieces constituting a human being and making up the "book of life." The alphabet of DNA subunits will result, it is hoped, in the ultimate genetic compendium. Paradoxically, the trope of an inanimate catalogue or dead "library" is used to talk about the original cells of existence. One of the purposes of this biological *ars combinatoria* would be to accelerate the identification of congenital defects. If the sequence of letters is out of order, the words are deranged. Consequently, reproduction has become part of the textualized and symbolized world of duplicable or disposable goods. Wanted ciphers can be kept, just as the diseased or unwanted ones can be discarded. Transposing living physiology into abstract language makes it easier, and less problematic, to justify manipulation. Like any dictionary or digest, the consumer may refer, alter, or combine decontextualized tiny elements at will.

This chapter, then, is about extremes. It looks at the edges of categories, at the outer margins of the inner brain and body. I examine those foreign or kindred filiations the early modern mentality chose to exclude or include from aesthetic, biological, and cultural discourse. Moreover, I ask by what principles it was done and why. The eighteenth century's notions of what was out or in, lacking or perfect, remain recognizable in the late twentieth century. Monsters and hybrids, exaggeratedly spiritual or material conceptions, all dwelled at the limit of light and dark, at the boundaries of natural viability and social acceptability. Aberrations in language, body, and imagery incarnated unenlightenment in the Age of Enlightenment. Consequently, a discussion of barbaric usage and grotesque composition opens and closes my argument. These complementary perspectives on the problem of mixtures bracket, and rely upon, a central section devoted to the varieties of conceiving. The preoccupation with origins reminds us of the importance of the search for roots to the eighteenth century. The antinomies under investigation, as always, remain constant. The ruling metaphor guiding each chapter, however, refracts the material differently, revealing new aspects.

Arnaldo Momigliano noted a paradox existing at the heart of the struggle between the polytheistic Roman Empire and monotheistic Christianity. The cultural standardization of the pagan state had produced a vast syncretism. Christians criticized this pictorial amalgamation of local cults and local gods from the provinces of Western Europe, Asia, and Africa with Latin and Greek gods, and used it in their vituperations against a polyglot religion and government. The irony Momigliano pinpointed was that the plural and open structure of the pagan state favored an intellectual, iconographic, and linguistic unification that absolutist—indeed fundamentalist—Christianity was unable to preserve.[2] This polemic between pagan pluralists and Jewish and Christian exclusionists takes us to the heart of the battle between improper mixture and proper simplicity that reerupted during the Enlightenment. Encyclopedias of ancient gems and artifacts served to familiarize eighteenth-century collectors and cognoscenti with the myriad guises of alien and mixed beings (figs. 21, 108, 109, 114). Joseph Spence took to task such compilers for their habit of jumbling indiscriminately Tuscan gods with Roman divinities, "old Gallic figures, with those of Syria; and the monsters of Egypt with the deities of Athens." James Beattie thought that even worse was the habit found among idolatrous nations of spawning male and female deities. Whereas beings superior to man were "spoken of as masculine in most modern European tongues," some heathens "have given even to the Supreme Being a name of feminine gender." This intolerable breach of theological decorum was not much better than the coining of imaginary or fantastic multiple beings.[3]

Today, the meaning of compound deities remains perplexing. The most widely held theory concerning their origin continues to be that they are intermediaries in a developmental process leading toward virile anthropomorphization. Dio Chrysostom, in the *Twelfth, Olympic, Discourse*, was the progenitor of the antithesis between uncultivated barbarians, who absurdly symbolized the divine by animals, and civilized Greeks who, thanks to Phidias, embodied the numinous in human likenesses.[4] This theory has been challenged both by students of the later Ice Age and by Egyptologists. Unlike Cartesian rationalists, members of ancient cultures did not seem to be bothered by the merger of two or more images. For paleolithic artists, hybrids represented not a stage in the evolution toward some best, or ideal, human form but the embodiment of an all-embracing nature not divided or separated into distinct categories.[5] Similarly, Egyptian ideograms were meant visibly to link a deity with attributes that better served to define her or his complex essence and multiple functions. As the archetypal form of writing constructed like a picture, hieroglyphics connected the subject with its myriad predicates. No matter what the current interpretation, it is significant that such composites caused an early and passionate rejection of the Egyptian religion.[6] For its opponents, the rich variety, equality among disparate elements, and infinite possibilities for combination threatened the prevailing order. Pictograms were assaulted for their aura of bestial animism and undiscriminating polytheism. "Idolatrous" or "chimerical" mixtures became the paradigm for all false, shocking, and grotesque fusions that had gotten out of hand.

Taylor's annotations to Proclus's *Commentary on the Timaeus* distinguished "composite" from "compounded." The latter denoted mingling, whereas the former signified the contiguous union of one thing with another. The distinction was appropriate for a work intended to be a medical "physiology," or survey of "wholes and parts" unfolding in nature. Thus, as was also born out by the commentaries on Euclid and Alcibiades, mixtures may come about in two ways. They are produced either properly, by fusion, or, as in the case of images of the Egyptian gods, improperly, by juxtaposition. This reprehensible paratactic style was compared to the material multitude. The mob refused to be "grouped together about one element in it that is best."[7] The only justification for this jarring, entropic, and individualistic mode lay in its symbolic, not naturalistic, use. That is, as in negative theology, polymorphic figures—standing outside a blended community—were to be taken as mystical signs signifying their opposites. As a method of contrary correspondences, conglomerations could make evident the indivisible and undivided by exposing what the true, but ineffable, divinity was not.

This Neoplatonic antagonism toward real, not symbolic, mixtures thrived within heretical Christian sects. Gnosticism and Manicheanism identified evil with actual *mélange*, or the rupture of a primitive duality of light and dark. Primordial man's luminous soul was befouled when it carnally combined with matter. Significantly, for our purposes, this sullied composition was associated with the libido and the reproductive drive. Evil had its roots in erotic desire and sexuality. Indeed, opaque darkness was pleasure (*hêdonê*), just as barbarous matter was sex.[8] The revulsion against anything mixed, confused, or animalistic led, as we have already seen, to the establishment of an ideal of simple immaculateness, to an aesthetic of reticent and translucent forms, and to the identification of beauty with purity. If the Eastern, Greek Church evinced nostalgia for a lost angelic cleanliness, then the Western Church—especially in the writings of Augustine (354–430 AD)—thought of concupiscence as a kind of dirty contagion, uncontrollable by the will and avoidable only through grace.[9] Both views inevitably led to a jaundiced perception of the procreative act that perpetuated the exile of the soul in matter. But it was St. Paul (d. ca. 60 AD) and Tertullian (fl. 197–222 AD)—remember Lavater and Winckelmann—who graphically described the war between worldly flesh and spirit. Only baptism helped the torn believer regain a primal, undifferentiated, and androgynous unity.[10] When we recall that Hellenism was a major discovery of the eighteenth century, it does not seem accidental that so much reformist aesthetic theory bears an ascetic stamp. Neoclassicism's strictures against the pornographic and gratuitous couplings of Rococo ornament must be situated against the backdrop of a vast influx of information concerning the abominable and infamous practices of the non-Greek pagan world. Heathenish Egyptians and Pythagoreans—believing in the transmigration of souls—were compared to freethinking Socinians, Deists, sophists, Epicureans, hermeticists, pantheists, and atheists. In spite of their differences, they shared the most dangerous and libertine belief of all, i.e., in those "Vicissitudes and Alterations [of matter], which turn everything into anything, as Vegetables and Animals become part of us, we become part of them."[11] This materialistic world view—characteristic of Hobbes, Spinoza, Diderot, and D'Holbach—suggested that organic beings were democratically joined in a dynamic and heterogeneous assemblage. A single spark was diffused throughout all substances. What you saw was what you got. Souls die with bodies; sin was an illusion; paradise a dream.[12] For its detractors, this heterodoxy of the multitude—permitting different social orders and kingdoms of nature perceptibly to coexist—was "sophistication." That is, it adulterated "anything with what is not good or genuine," like the compounding of bad medicines, or the polluting of vintage with cheaper wines, or the mixing of fine with coarse materials.[13]

Admirers of a theurgic plethora, on the contrary, valued configured experiences clothed in the most disparate shapes. For them, hieroglyphics were an "artistic and mystical algebra." The sober Realist critic Louis-Emile Edmond Duranty (1833–1880), in his essays on the Egyptian museum housed in the Louvre, praised the happy union of man and animal. He spoke of the Egyptian artist as gravely, and clearly and distinctly, realizing the mystical merger of diverse, incomprehensible, and overcharged contraries dwelling at the heart of divinity.[14] Earlier, as we observed, Piranesi—in his polemics against Chambers, Caylus, Winckelmann, Allan Ramsey, and Pierre-Jean Mariette—defended Egyptian "grotesks." He also praised the ornamental beauty of irrational and fabulous Greek creatures. Sirens, chimeras, and hippogriffs were compared to the complicated "testaceous" forms of fossils and shells. "Mankind is too fond of variety to be always pleased with the same decors." Confounding "high and low," and the neglect of "a certain variety of degrees," however, was offensive.[15] The tolerant Hogarth, similarly, was intolerant of confusion. Joining opposite ideas into "elegant monsters" was proper embellishment. Inelegant or awkward junctures produced only laughter. Lavater, in the same vein, criticized "burlesqued caricaturas," stating that admiration ceased "the moment we perceive in any subject incongruous parts." Homogeneousness, not heterogeneousness, was the essence of the human race.[16]

The grotesque, then, had two major connotations during the eighteenth century. Both involved the upstart power of images to disconcert by their very looks. Both were predicated on the defiance of convention by flaunting unsuitable, dissonant, and unconnected *actual* mixtures. The first sense was farcical and owed to Horace's description in the *Art of Poetry* and in the *Epistle to Pisoes*. The Augustan writer conjured up despicable images of worthless pieces of ornament. Deformed figures were maladroitly constructed out of a man's head, horse's neck, bird's wing, and fish's tail. Dryden, in the preface to the *Art of Painting* (1694)—the English translation of Charles-Antoine Dufresnoy's (1654–1724) *De Arte Graphica*—compared this irrational jumbling

216

of parts of different species "to the mad imagination of the Dawber; and the end of all this (as he [Horace] tells you afterward) is to cause Laughter. A very Monster in a Bartholomew-Fair for the mob to gape at for their two-pence."[17] Beattie—in the most penetrating analysis produced during the eighteenth century on the aesthetics of the burlesque—provided a taxonomy of humorous modes of pictorial combination. Significantly, and unlike Lessing, he claimed in "Of Laughter and Ludicrous Composition" that painting was superior to poetry in this one area. The ridiculous effect arising from "mere contiguity of the objects, may therefore be better exemplified by visible assemblages." He underscored the special efficacy of pictures—albeit in a low or comic genre—in presenting simultaneously two or more irregular and jarring coincidences. Although still arguing on behalf of the general superiority of words, Beattie admitted that images could more competently display a polyphonic or absurd medley. The sudden revelation provoked by the view of compounded things—disposing the mind to form a comparison—created, or literally conceived, something new. The beholder had a flash of insight into an unexpected similitude or relation between unlike objects.[18] Although Beattie did not say so, this visionary glimpse, was Proclus's negative symbolic method or dark allegoresis of remote correspondences transposed to a light, or witty, mode. Thus, in spite of himself, this professor of moral philosophy and logic recognized the potency of images in compelling the birth of what had not existed before, even if it was only a monster.

Francis Grose (1731–1791), in his *Rules for Drawing Caricaturas* (1789), cited Beattie on the abuses of laughter, or the incompatible and "uncommon mixture of relation and contrariety." He distinguished between that acceptable or "slight deviation" from European ideals of beauty, known as *character* (fig. 91), and out-of-bounds *caricatura*. The latter was an unacceptable and "peculiarly aggraved" departure from expressive standards associated with animate and inanimate conglomerates. The antiquarian and amateur draftsman warned the artist not to "overcharge" with oddities the peculiarities of their subjects, for, rather than producing the ridiculous, they would engender only the horrible and a sort of vulgar ugliness (fig. 90).[19] I wish to suggest that excessively distorted *caricatura*, or the formless grotesque, reduced its components to contradictions and lifeless impracticalities. We will examine this phenomenon more closely in the last section of this chapter (fig. 133). For the moment, it is important to recognize that, to eighteenth-century eyes, it posed the supreme danger of shapelessness. It was a wholly visual brutalism only possible to, and identifiable with, imagery that willfully bypassed orga-

133. Anne-Claude-Philippe, Comte de Caylus, *Roman Ithyphallic Grotesque,* from *Recueil de trois cents têtes et sujets de compositions,* 18th c., fig. 211. Engraving. (Photo: author.)

134. Fortunius Licetus, *Amorphous Monster (Misbirth),* from *De Monstris,* 1665, p. 302. Engraving. (Photo: Courtesy National Library of Medicine, Bethesda, Md.)

135. William Dent, *The Cutter Cut Up,* 1790. Colored etching. (Photo: Courtesy National Library of Medicine, Bethesda, Md.)

136. Fortunius Licetus, *Amorphous Monster (Misbirth),* from *De Monstris,* 1665, p. 303. Engraving. (Photo: Courtesy National Library of Medicine, Bethesda, Md.)

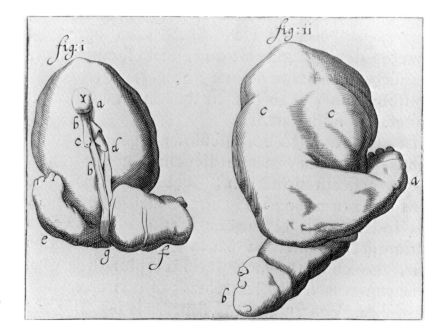

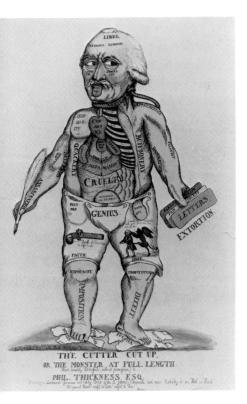

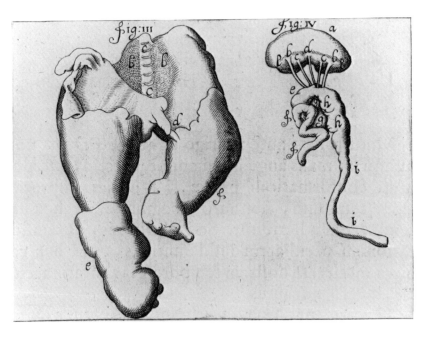

GLISSONIUS
De
RACHITIDE

LUGD.
BATAV.
}Ex Officina{
FELICIS LOPEX de HARO
et
CORNELII DRIEHUYSEN 1671

137. Francis Glisson, *Rickets,* from *De Rachitide,* 1671, title page. Engraving by G. W. (Photo: Courtesy National Library of Medicine, Bethesda, Md.)

nization. And its impact, I believe, was comparable to the terrible sight of physiological amorphousness (fig. 134). Equivocal and unviable artistic assemblages (figs. 1, 135) possessed the same extreme ambiguity as juxtaposed, abortive biological parts that had no rhyme nor reason (fig. 136). The horror, not humor, inspired by the sight of such misfits can also be deduced less dramatically from countless manuals on good posture and medical treatises (fig. 137). Their leitmotif was the social obligation to take care to have "a good bodily grace." Nicolas Andry, in *L'Orthopédie,* declared that orthopedics was found on the principle of corporeal fitness. "We are born for one another; we must avoid possessing anything shocking, & even if one were alone in the world, it would not be proper to neglect one's body to the point of allowing it to become deformed; this would be going against the very intention of the Creator."[20]

What obtained for physiological misbirths held for mental manglings. Barbarisms were the multifold idols and omniform cripples of the imagination (fig. 138). They represented the supreme linguistic grotesque: the conspicuously false or rickety idea externalized as a verbal freak. Like those other visible deviants, the monster, the grotesque, and the burlesque satire, these savage mixtures were the result of wrongful copulations. Delinquent and farfetched nouns were forcibly jointed together—without the civilized glue of verbs—to form textual caricatures. This brings us to the second and more somber connotation of the grotesque as a repellent and indistinct conceptual multiplicity. Bouhours described two-faced thoughts as if they were ruined statues of polytheistic gods. He envisaged them as maimed "in the sense that they are not complete, and possess something monstrous, like those imperfect or totally mutilated sculptures, that provide only a confused notion of what they represent" (fig. 98). Origen had compared a "double-minded man" to those unstable worshipers of demons who refused to withdraw from foreign gods to follow the Lord with complete and perfect faith. In that sense, as Campbell remarked, heathenish barbarisms were also half-formed, i.e., mixed, impure, unsteady. Their semantic sin was pictorialism. They acted as if they were pictures, confusing elements to the point of obscurity, unintelligibility, and vacuity.[21] According to Quintilian, they violated the first virtue of composition. Perspicuity, or the proper and clear arrangement of words, was contravened when the reader or auditor was assailed by a heap of bizarre ideas. Ambiguity resulted because the speaker crowded his notions and "put his words badly together."

Quintilian compared such execrable language that was "too unconnected, composed not of members but of bits" to an unshaded figure in a picture. Such glaring and interfering tesserae gave birth to enigma and obscurity because they refused to unite (fig. 135). He concluded that an excessively curt style allowed every isolated and compartmentalized thought to "make as it were a stand, as being complete in itself." For the rhetorician, this impropriety was the hallmark of vulgar, unsavory, and "mean" words, whose confusing jostling offended not only the ear but the mind, by falsifying sense.[22] This criticism of unblended and crude mixtures—like all censure of

IMAGINATION.

138. Jean-Baptiste Boudard, *Imagination,* from *Iconologie,* 1766, II, pl. 103. Engraving. (Photo: Courtesy the Resource Collections of the Getty Center for the History of Art and the Humanities.)

grotesque interminglings—revealed a fundamentally linguistic bias. That is, when, to the ambiguity in words, there was added a false notion in the matter conveyed, grammatic decorum was violated by an act of *visual* ingenuity. Punning words behaved like the contradictory mosaic parcels composing William Dent's (fl. 1787–1793) *Cutter Cut Up* (1790). Unlike correct prose, the *double entendre* bits resembled unstable images in their untranslatability, vanishing into nothing but gibberish when one tried to transplant them into another language. A simultaneous display of paratactically inlaid and warring details (faith/hope, hypocrisy/prostitution) without proper junctures yielded a synthetic and mutually negating pattern. Texts became babel. Verbal units were liberated from their proper domain within an unfolding sequence, and from an invariable sense, to flout Lessing's rule against mimicking the spatial contiguity of pictures.

The comparison between a literary composition and the fitting together of the human body from various members stemmed from ancient rhetoric. *Membrum* or "limb" also signified "clause." The reestablishment of the connection between painting and writing in Neoclassical pedagogics focused again on Quintilian's dictum that the artist must put together an integrated corpus from detachable elements, smoothly flowing from one section to another. Dandré-Bardon taught that "thoughts are the limbs of a composition and must be distributed over the canvas with a just economy." This basically phraseological skill—gliding from corporeal syllables to sentences—averted the creation of tortuous somatic monsters whose parts did not belong. Analogously, Joseph Addison (1672–1719) disparaged as the creations of false wit the use of obsolete words or barbarisms, rusticities, absurd spellings, complicated dialects, and the outlandish construction of poems made up of concrete objects. The essay on "True and False Wit" took to task "tricks in writing" and decadent signs of "Monkish" taste. These were evinced in the visual turning of one set of terms into another and resembled "the Anagram of a Man." The limbs of syntax were distorted and set in foreign places where they did not rightfully occur.[23]

Anagrams, chronograms, acrostics, figured grids and mazes were outmoded attempts to visualize or illuminate language. These decorative rebuses and labyrinths had been especially popular during the Medieval era and then again in the Baroque. To the scientific or rationalist literary critic, to Galileo Galilei (1564–1642) or to Addison, such picture-text marriages and optical poetry amalgams seemed barbaric and weird. In his *Considerazioni al Tasso*

(1593), Galileo associated the lapidary intarsia style of the *Gerusalemme Liberata* (1573) with the piecemeal arrangement of a cluttered and dusty *Wunderkammer*. The wizened antiquarian, or unenlightened collector of dessicated curios, delighted in ornamenting his dark cabinet with a jumble of strange small objects. Broken bric-a-brac was abruptly and crudely juxtaposed. Galileo contrasted Torquato Tasso's (1544–1595) "horribly worked," confused, and "mutilated" allegory with Ariosto's *Orlando Furioso* (1516). The fluid narrative of the latter resembled a lofty and well-lit art gallery, stocked with a hundred beautiful classical statues and crystal and agate vases to delight the connoisseur. Ludovico Ariosto's (1474–1533) mellifluous and dissolving style blended and shaded lines and colors in the manner of an oil painting. But Tasso's harsh style was like the unfinished sketches of Parmagianino or Baccio Bandinelli. The viewer or reader got bruised in this painterly or poetic *Variokasten*. He constantly stubbed his sensibilities by bumping into alien petrifactions: a rotten crayfish, a dried-up beetle, a despicable fly or spider caught in amber, and one of those gimcrack clay idols dug up from an Egyptian tomb (figs. 11, 104).[24]

From the civilized perspective, then, barbarisms were the impure image of a gratuitous, extravagant, and superfluous mixture of miscellaneous and distinct petty idioms. They were like the grotesque miscellany of hydras, gorgons, and chimeras polluting a magnified drop of Thames water in William Heath's (1795–1840) *Monster Soup* (1822) (fig. 97).[25] The well-known Scottish professor of divinity George Campbell—like Beattie, a native of Aberdeen—specifically addressed this overarching issue of unmixed purity or "monotheism" of construction in the *Philosophy of Rhetoric*. According to this published course of lectures, grammatical immaculateness implied three conditions. These could hold equally for the arrangements of the visual arts as well as for the biological organization of organic bodies. First, the words in a composition must be in English, i.e., ungarbled and entirely in one's native tongue. Second, the formulations must be easily comprehensible. Third, the phrases employed should be unequivocal and convey the precise meaning assigned to them by custom. Barbarisms—or foreign, obsolete, strange, technical, neologistic, and unusual terms intelligible only to antiquarians—corrupted the pristine perspicuity of regular English by their wayward anomaly and intricacy. They offended etymology by their "polytheistic" pluralism, the way sprouting solecisms—or alien constructions—violated the integrity of syntax. Beattie also noted that distracting images and occult comparisons conveyed in quaint and elaborate terms, or strewn about in unconnected words, obliged the

139. Francisco de Goya, *Will No One Unbind Us?,* from *Los Caprichos,* 1799, pl. 75. Aquatint and etching. National Gallery of Art, Washington, D.C., Rosenwald Collection. (Photo: Courtesy National Gallery of Art.)

¿No hay quien nos desate?

reader "to take time to collect all the parts of the idea." He became disgusted upon the realization that the unmeaning compound was the premeditated effect of art, "rather than the instantaneous effort of a playful imagination."[26]

As always, rationalist critics underscored the visual nature of these abuses. Spence linked the confusion of farfetched puzzles to the multiple improprieties committed by Baroque allegories and emblems. He was at a loss as to what Cesare Ripa's odd and obscure conjunctions—appropriated by Goya—meant (fig. 138). These queer and singular assemblages exceeded the tolerable capricious coupling of extremes, or what logicians called *disparates,* that is, the grouping of items ranked under no common genus (fig. 103). Instead, they studiously threw together things both dispersed and incongruous with-

CONCEIVING

Subir y bajar.

140. Francisco de Goya, *To Rise and to Fall,* from *Los Caprichos,* 1799, pl. 56. Aquatint and etching. National Gallery of Art, Washington, D.C., Rosenwald Collection. (Photo: Courtesy National Gallery of Art.)

out reconciling, or melding, opposites (figs. 139, 140). Trapp similarly warned the modern writer to avoid distant and heterogeneous metaphors "too much wrested to a foreign sense." Samuel Johnson (1709–1784), in his condemnation of the metaphysical poets, likened this analytical and synthetic strategy to Newton's unnatural prismatic dissection of the rainbow: "They broke every image into fragments."[27] Analogously, the pell-mell absurdity of Italian opera divided to conquer. It united unexpected, abstruse, and remote contiguities into a barbaric spectacle sinning against linguistic perspicuity. Richardson mocked its chaotic display and unintelligible music, "in an unknown tongue," as "mere shew and sound," beyond tragedy, beyond probability. Even Algarotti, in the *Essai sur l'opéra* (1752), lamented its decline into hyperbolic visual aberration and monstrous acoustic license. He approvingly cited

Saint-Evremond's *mot*. Opera was a "stupidity [*sottise*] charged with music, dances, machines, decorations, a magnificent stupidity, but a stupidity nonetheless." The rationalist reformer concurred, noting the lack of accord between words and music. This was not surprising since the composer was interested only in the chromatics of instrumentation, not in the contours of the plot, thus distorting it. Moreover, what could one expect "from a troop of performers where no one was content with the place assigned them; where so much chicanery was contrived against the conductor, & even more so against the poet who should be in charge of it all." Algarotti was of the same mind as Remond de Sainte-Albine (1699–1778). Caricature in the theater was identical to that in painting. Actors may go beyond nature, but not against it to create monsters.[28]

Dufresnoy cautioned artists to avoid obscene and impudent particolored "objects full of hollows, broken into little pieces" that were "barbarous and shocking to the eyes." In short, they were to steer clear of "all things which corrupt their natural Forms by a confusion of their Parts which are entangled in each other." In this matter, there was no distinction between painter and poet. Both must reject scattered contrary and foreign incidents. "They are the Wenns and other Excrescences, which belong not to the Body, but deform it." Diderot maintained that in all the arts unity of imitation was as essential as unity of action. "To confound or associate together two manners of imitating nature is a barbarous thing and of detestable taste." For Lavater, the original genius melted down his materials and, by a skillful disposition, formed of them one homogeneous whole. But the incoherent copyist collected and "pounded together" "motley assemblages," "patchwork," "checquered work," "mosaic work," and "ponderous abortions." Nature, on the contrary, composed at a single cast. "Her organizations are not inlaid work." Nor did she function "as a compositor for the printing press, picking the characters out of different cases."[29] Lessing reminded modern painters who delighted in delineating monsters faithfully that the civilized Thebans enacted a law commanding idealization in art. Digressions toward outlandishness were legally punishable.[30]

The mention of Lessing returns us to that fundamentalist fear concerning the disruptive invasion of the figurative outsider. We have witnessed the steadily mounting emigration of heteroclite images from their proper confines to flood formerly uniformly verbal enclaves. Dictionaries, encyclopedias, manuals,

TAB. II.

GENESIS cap. I. v. 2.
Opus primæ Diei.

I. Buch Mosis Cap. I. v. 2.
Erstes Tagwerk.

141. Jean-Jacques Scheuchzer, *First Day of Creation,* from *Physique sacrée,* 1732–1737, I, pl. 2. Engraving by J. G. Pinz. (Photo: Courtesy the Resource Collections of the Getty Center for the History of Art and the Humanities.)

handbooks, and treatises of all sorts had their texts swamped by multifarious illustrations often conveying a meaning counter to, and more memorable than, the words themselves (figs. 72, 73, 74, 84, 85, 87, 99, 103, 105). This exodus spawned textual bastards (figs. 89, 102, 107). The impious intermarriage of graphic symbol and letter bred teeming monsters of language, syncretic image-word composites that threatened linguistic hegemony (figs. 1, 10, 96, 97, 115, 135). Even worse, the proliferation of alien imagery engendered swarms of polyvalent and engimatic barbarisms beyond the grasp of certain interpretation (figs. 108, 109, 110). Or, conversely, low-class mobbing pictures introduced dialects. Vernacular alloys embraced polymorphic experiences—on the other side of the sheets, so speak—that correct and simplifying idiom would not touch (figs. 116, 117, 119, 120, 121, 122, 123, 124, 126, 127). Nothing seemed more reprehensible to the high enlighteners of language, however, than the bane of obscure thought. This outmoded vice was identified with unintelligible and abstract allegories, or the metaphysical monster of writing as painting.

142. Jean-Baptiste Boudard, *Obscurity,*
from *Iconologie,* 1766, III, pl. 24. Engraving.
(Photo: Courtesy the Resource Collections
of the Getty Center for the History of Art
and the Humanities.)

Such a polytheistic profusion of dim and confusing chimeras had not been witnessed since the decadence of the Roman Empire. The clash between orthodox and heterodox aesthetic creeds revived memories of the iconoclastic Reformation. Critics spoke of the foreign and idolatrous onslaught of forced and farfetched comparisons in terms of the rape and plunder of strict and sound linguistic purity. Spence connected the decline of poetry under Tiberius, Caligula, and Nero to the debility of the new post-Augustans. He contrasted contemporary Europe with antiquity. "The fall of the Roman Empire shattered every kingdom into pieces." These petty principalities were "not yet re-united into one great body." Modern allegories reflected a similar "jumble" of "broken ideas," "blemishes," and "ridiculous imaginations."[31] Winckelmann placed the erosion of oratory and the ruin of art even earlier, in the Hellenistic period when Attic rhetors and sculptors contracted some "stain" from Asiatic "foreign ways."[32] Gerard de Lairesse (1640–1711)— noting the distinction between the permanence of things ancient and the modishness and mutability of things modern—declared they could not, without contamination, be united. History painting must remain faithful to luminous "old stories, pure and uncorrupted," without current borrowings. Above all, they must not be blended promiscuously "and without distinction, as east, west, south, and north in a *chaos-manner*" (fig. 141).[33] Félibien shared Lairesse's preference for lucid ancient histories over dark modern riddles. Aptly, he compared the former to conversing with people one knew, whose language one understood, as opposed to speaking with strangers whom one could not comprehend.

Dubos made plain that what was being strenuously opposed was not just the mingling of invented with historical figures, as Rubens so famously or infamously (depending on one's perspective) did in the *Marie de Medici* cycle for the Luxembourg Palace (Paris, Musée du Louvre, 1622–1625). The opprobrium was general when it came to uncouth and obsolete "excessive" allegory. The normally laxist diplomat joined rigorists in decrying cacophonous compositions, wholly compounded of unnatural or symbolic persons, as offensive to polite eyes. Bouhours compared such mongrel grotesques to prostitutes clad in black *domino*. These outsiders walked the streets masked to conceal their identity. Whereas a little mystery in one's thoughts was considered evidence of *délicatesse*—a thin veiling crepe—obliterating the countenance of a conception courted unintelligibility (fig. 142).[34] Jean-Baptiste Boudard (d. 1778) in the *Iconologie* (1766) warned art students against the immoderate commixture of fabulous allegorical creations. Rude hodgepodges of hieroglyphic enigmas were insupportable to the enlightened spectator.[35]

Turgid violations against expressive perspicuity, then, denied that the medium was classically transparent like air, glass, or water. The problem with barbarisms, as with miscegenation, was, as Campbell noted, that the least obscurity, ambiguity, or confusion in the appearance or style instantly removed attention from the general matter to the personal and unlettered manner of creation. If any flaw adulterated the purity of the idiom, or the homogeneity of the statement, the viewer saw through it dimly to an imperfectly represented, or misrepresented, object. This intervening pattern immediately refracted his vision back to the self-assertively vulgar and unpolished surface.[36]

For the eighteenth century, this occluded perception was not simply the hallmark of conspicuously unclassical and "decadent" Mannerist or Baroque poetics. Complicated "Gothick" romances were similarly illiterate from a plain-style, or Ciceronian, vantage. Often written by "the fair sex," they were "quite out of the way of nature" and "sprung from the mere dregs of chivalry or knight errantry." Shaftesbury linked these "false, monstrous" anachronisms, or decaying odds and ends of modern gallantry, to the licentiousness of foppish courtly humor. Significantly, his denunciation of hybrid novels was situated within the larger framework of a discussion of the virtues of Deism over polytheism. The belief in a single supreme being meant the acceptance of evil and good "everywhere interwoven." The refined interfusion of pleasure and pain, beauty and deformity, resembled those "rich stuffs where the flowers and ground were oddly put together, with such irregular Work, and contrary Colours, as looked ill *in the Pattern*, but mighty natural in the *Piece*." This monotheistic shading of "dismal parts" into the "Beauty's of the Creation," however, stood at the antipodes from blatant magical combinations.[37]

It was precisely the awkward display of such "monsters, dragons, and serpents," and other strange fairytale creatures that delighted Richard Hurd (1720–1786). The *Letters on Chivalry and Romance* (1762) countered the common wisdom concerning the ruin of Western civilization by "the caprice and absurdity of barbarisms." This outspoken opponent of French Classicism dared to suggest that irrational Gothic tales might have their "own reason, even if it is not ours." Hurd emphasized as a virtue the extravagantly pictorial elements that rationalist critics found so offensive. Spenser and Tasso inlaid their poems with a minute tapestry of colorful dress, armor, heraldic blazons, and rich accoutrements (figs. 128, 130, 131, 132). They childishly and undiscriminatingly studded fanciful allegories with unfused tiny events: a legend, a tradition, a rumor, a superstition. Hurd agreed that it was this marbling, or constant intertwisting of pagan fables, adventure stories, and specious enchantments, that French and British critics found so odious. The unity observed was not the classical dramatic unity, or the seamless landscape grouping of a William Kent (1684–1748). Rather, it resembled the harsh interruptions and dispersions of medieval garden knots. The wood or grove was cut into many separate walks, each with their several destinations, but "brought together and considered under one view by the relation these various openings had, not to each other, but to their common and concurrent center."[38]

What Hurd found admirable, the defenders of simple, clear, and exact commercial or prosaic composition excoriated as cramped, dry, and stiff. Dufresnoy, for example, had no relish for "gothique ornaments." They "were so many Monsters, which barbarous ages have produced." When art first began to rise after the "terrible devastations of superstition, and barbarity," it produced "the old bad painting." For Richardson—who was of two minds about the faulty style of the German and Florentine primitives—"Gothicism," in the end, was more repugnant than pleasing in its remoteness from ancient euphony. Although not a hash of stitched-together fantasies, like the romance, panel paintings and armorial imagery were also gracelessly juxtaposed medleys, not illusionistic blends. Fuseli marveled that art revived during the fifteenth century at all, considering the heterogeneous stock on which it was grafted. Its saviors, paradoxically, were "a race inhabiting a genial climate, but itself the *foeces* of barbarity, the remnants of gothic adventurers, humanized only by the Cross, mouldering amid the ruins of the temples they had demolished, the battered fragments of the images their rage had crushed." The British academician thought that, even more astounding than the fact that modern art arose from the shambles of feudalism, was its origin in "materials so unfit and contaminated, and defective." Yet this refuse achieved the magnificent system he currently contemplated.[39]

The uncouth manner of a time that preferred arms rather than the man possessed none of the elegance and fluidity of civilized narrative history. Oldmixon compared rude and unpolished "Dealer[s] in Records" or "Library Keepers" to "raw memoir" writers. One could expect nothing from these primitives of the pen (or from illuminators and antiquarians) but the juxtaposition of "naked Facts without Form or Order, without Ornament, or even Cloathing."[40] This compressing and interlarding of isolated shapes was seen to be the distinctive hallmark of Gothic architecture. Bouhours identified irregular shambles with "solecisms in stone." They heaped up metaphors, contracted and mixed strange figures, to produce visual confusion.[41] Félibien criticized the foul multiplicity of angles and bristling deformities flourishing in French building practices prior to the advent of the classical *style Louis XIV*. He compared such barbaric atrocities to the disabled beggars of Jacques Callot (1592–1635). The French printmaker depicted "an infinity of postures, made to amuse himself, of men who had the back or shoulders higher than the head, the arms broken or twisted in diverse ways, the legs of different lengths, & the headdresses more ample than the rest of the costumes." In their capricious edifices, "as in the grotesques of this etcher, one sees that all the members are crippled, & they constitute an image of disproportion and irregularity, rather than an imitation of beautiful symmetry & of proper fitness such as might be sought in the body of a well-proportioned man."[42] Louis-Sébastien Mercier (1740–1814), in *Du Théâtre*, compared the French false worship of antiquated rhyme in verse to the extravagances of Gothic construction. Both shared the "same barbaric fathers," the enemies of simple, delicate nature, preferring "heavy and superfluous ornaments, pure works of chimerical caprice." He railed against rhyme's "tyranny" and the constraining "despotism" of an ornamental technique that refused to enter into the matter of poetry. Mercier banned this singular and halting idiom from the stage just as he excluded bizarre edifices from sight. The intricate decorativeness of both slowed and impeded the listener, or the viewer, rather than speeding his progress as "natural" prose recitation would do.[43] Similarly, Trapp railed against cluttering adventitious persons, or "figures to let" in a drama. They were like "Gothick Buildings," disfigured "with Props and Buttresses, and other superfluous Out-Works." He contrasted them to ancient architecture "where all the Columns, and several Parts of the Fabrick, mutually support each other; where there is nothing but what is necessary, nothing but what is beautiful; and the whole therefore beautiful, because everything is necessary." Robert Adam, while praising the eccentric and raw genius of the architect John Vanbrugh (1664–1726), similarly complained about his motley archaizing works. These were "so crowded with barbarisms and absurdities, and so borne down by their ponderous weight, that none but the discerning could separate their merits from their defects." *Castle Howard* (b. 1700) and *Blenheim Palace* (1705–1722) were like unpolished, unrefined "rough jewels of inestimable value."[44] These ruthless and enormous piles, by their disarrangement of forms, traduced a reasoned reading. They seemed foreign in their assertive robustness to the Augustan and post-Augustan age ruled by courtesy and propriety.

Lessing thought the aggressive bravery, characteristic of the early iron ages, was embodied in the "wild cries" of marauding Norsemen. Rather differently, the uncivilized Trojans—commanded by Priam not to weep or wail as they marched into battle—were equally the out-of-date denizens of a rusty and preterlapsed past. He contrasted their crude and senescent lack of emotional control with that mature acme of cultivated restraint, "the resolute silence of the Greek heroes." Eighteenth-century classicists wished to emulate the fresh youthfulness of Hellenism, swept of antiquarian cobwebs, dark medieval dodderings, and other arcane reminders of caducity and decrepitude. For Lessing, the present enlightened era of tender manners fostered "a passive courage of endurance."[45] It went hand in hand with an official vindication of clean and appropriate literal meanings that shut out gerontic or superannuated mysteries.

Barbaric allegories, then, bring us to the heart of the negative meanings surrounding crumbling surfaces or moth-eaten mixed conceptions. They were looked upon as visual and linguistic fossils. These extinctions, however, like diluvial debris, continued to surface disturbingly as brute farcical compendia, grotesque remnants of yore, or Gothic relics of old-fashioned and now superseded confusion. For the Romantic generation, however, they became the highest, indeed the immemorial form of symbolic unification. False or total allegories were the visible signs of creative primogeniture, the authentic and ancestral productions of Coleridge's esemplastic imagination. Their outlandish and obsolete appearance indicated, through outmoded contrarieties, a venerable truth irrecoverable by direct imitation.[46] "Mythologic, feodal, local incongruities, fleeting modes of society, and fugitive fashions," the far and the near, the spiritual and the material, the light and the dark, could be violently sutured together by the savage wit.[47]

"Brain-Born Images"

In the search for self-knowledge unfolding through the centuries, a key question has been how we come to have any knowledge at all. Further, how one knows was intimately tied to the conundrum of how one came to be. Mental and physical genetics involved the propagation and inheritance of order and its embodiment in manifest shapes. With the growing autonomy of formal systems in the eighteenth century, the origin of normative or deviant organizations, such as barbarisms, became an all-encompassing preoccupation. Indeed, we shall observe that physiology was often confounded with

Conceive

verb, *To admit into the womb; to form in the mind; to imagine; to comprehend; to understand; to think.*

Dr. Johnson, *Dictionary*

noun, Term of geometry: the formation of a line into a plane, into a solid by the movement of a point, to a line, to a surface; term of physics, an action to produce that which did not exist before; the change of one body into another; the generation of bodies in general—a mystery to which nature reserves the secrets.

Diderot and D'Alembert, *Encyclopédie*

metaphysics. Underlying the aesthetic polemic about proper and improper conceptions was the theological, epistemological, and biological debate concerning the nature of conceiving. For the Enlightenment, there were two main paths and several byways leading toward the unraveling of the enigma of cerebral and corporeal procreation. Either the body and its reproductive functions were interiorized in the soul, or the fabricating soul was absorbed into the body's physical arrangement. Generation was formulated in terms either of emanation, an immaterial becoming, or as down-to-earth reproduction, the giving birth to material multiples. This translated—most conspicuously in Winckelmann's theories—into an antithesis between art as visionary revelation and as mere making, or handiwork.

To focus the central issues, I shall concentrate on the metaphor of thought as incarnation or of the concept/conception. The exalted or transcendent notion of unfurling forms maintained that they preexisted any physical coming into being. Spiritual inventions—whether infant ideas or embryonic persons—were preformed, i.e., became perceptible through a serial unboxing from a passive and shapeless matter. We have already observed this principle at work in physiognomic theory. Recall that, for Lavater, differences of external form were believed to be the result of *preexisting* differences of internal character. Further, I suggest that this "masculine" biological preformationism should be seen as an essentially bodiless abstraction of the flow of production. Epigenetic modifications of the Aristotelean view of reproduction strove, on the contrary, to maintain an ontological balance between the roles played by matter and form. The materialists, finally, submerged the latter in the former. All elements of the psychic and physical world arose immanently from an inextricable coalescence of dynamic atoms. Think of Lichtenberg's "feminine" chase after multiple and multiplying visible phenomena. Individuals in this pathognomic scheme were the particularized or marked issue of a process of material reproduction that continued throughout life. Physical birth merely extruded them from an eternal kinetic substance into the developing social realm of other modular and recombinable ready-mades. These discussions were further complicated because they revolved around almost imperceptible minima. Microscopic "germs," "seeds," "eggs," or "animalcules" were believed to be the building blocks or fundamental particles of mental and bodily conceptions.

The first and primary theory for how things came to subsist derived from Neoplatonism. Preformationism, which I believe fundamentally shaped Neoclassical principles of artistic creation, postulated the reality of a distant, unborn, and immaterial central agent. Divine thought, and its human imitation, were at a remove from the filth of sensible phenomena. In this scheme—reintroduced by Vico and Leibniz—creation was spectral. It involved the emission of a continuous living river of light flowing vertically from the creator to bathe his perishable creations.[48] Note the metaphors of liquid kinesis. Generation was thus visualized as a procession of intangible effects streaming from their changeless and monadic cause. Speciation, or the active exfoliation of Being, was also a timeless articulation obeying a logical order. The genealogy of emanations was based on a descent from subjects to predicates, principles to details, axioms to hypotheses, ideas to organisms. And then—as Gnosticism, Manicheanism, and negative theology were to make so much ado about—they reverted to the intelligible after living in exile within a barbarically divided nature.[49] The decline and fall from intellect into multiplicity occurred through a mathematical and geometrical division of the unities into fractional deviations from the One. Deficient and incomplete existence was synonymous with mixture and radically unlike, or the reverse of, the perfect and inexhaustible Power.

As in logic, the supreme principle generated a bodiless plan for the temporal world. Intellect, which was absolutely dissimilar from matter, could not—without paradox—physically produce it. Rather, in the manner of a genetic map or a DNA library, it provided formal schemes or preformed patterns of as yet unrealized spatial configurations that might eventually be realized or conceived. Recall Leibniz's faint innate ideas and *petites perceptions* bobbing up or imprinting themselves on the consciousness. But it was Proclus's various commentaries on the Platonic theology that were, for the eighteenth century, the ultimate source of this physiological yet matterless procession of realities. Parentage, in this system, was mental "participation" in the algorithms of the gods through the theoretical "Plan of Life."[50]

The speculative plan was itself embodied (or, more accurately disembodiedly outlined) in abstract symbols. *Symbolon* denoted point or needle, dart or plumb bob, something fallen. But it also connoted a moment of motion melting together at the source. Like water, it evoked running together, falling away, leading or joining, and two entities dissolving into one.[51] For Proclus, superior symbols were diagrammatic abstractions, or nonimitative blueprints, unseizable by sense perception, yet indicating—because of their formal minimalism—the null of unity. As utmost point, tenuous straight line, or simple plane, they approached the numerical fundamentalism of divinity. Yet simultaneously, by their fractured and plural divisiveness, they departed from, and were the opposite of, that essential void.

The symbol shared with water not only the activity of silently flowing together into a central point, but the ability to mirror what lay above its still surface. This led Vico to assert that truth entered history upside down. The divine could never be encountered in its proper likeness, i.e., right side up, within the temporal continuum. In other words, imitation takes place in reverse. Whatever is present in excess in the higher realm is reflected as deficiency in lower, mixed existence.[52] Thus, beginning with Proclus, similitude and imitative mimicry were no longer the sole characteristics of symbols. On one hand, their pure and geometrical look mimicked the logical outline and mathematical structure of the cosmic plan. On the other hand, their juxtapositive, contrary, and contaminated parts puzzlingly and inversely indicated the invisible mystery they could not directly reflect. Not recognizing this Janus face of "double-minded" symbolism has wreaked havoc with the interpretation of late-eighteenth- and early-nineteenth-century art. Depending on the aspect emphasized, as we have seen, Proclusian aesthetics led either to condensed Neoclassicism or to grotesque Romanticism, to codifying abstraction or to fantastic distraction. As a system, or grammar of conception, it favored the cerebral even in the creation of irrational effects. Samuel Taylor Coleridge (1772–1834) in the *Biographia Literaria* (1817) made no bones that "the *rules* of the imagination are themselves the very powers of growth and production."

Furthermore, Neoplatonism stressed self-fashioning. It was from within, from the inner faculties, that the rehabilitated soul engendered itself, not through the sensible world or the coupling of bodies. Coleridge criticized Wordsworth specifically for his empiricist and externalist focus, for "the minute painting of local imagery."[53] Rules, logic, *schemas* were a sort of artistic birth control, or science of the imagination, preventing the insemination of, and even aborting when necessary, faulty and deceptive conceptions. They gradually refined and intellectualized messages and stimuli, stripping them of their corporeality. For the Neoclassicists, then, formal decency, beauty, and decorum corresponded directly to the inward propriety of their elevated conceptions. For the Romantics, apparent surface disorder, enigmatic deficiency, and dark disguise were metaphors for their concealed and farfetched opposite, the imparticipable and absent One.

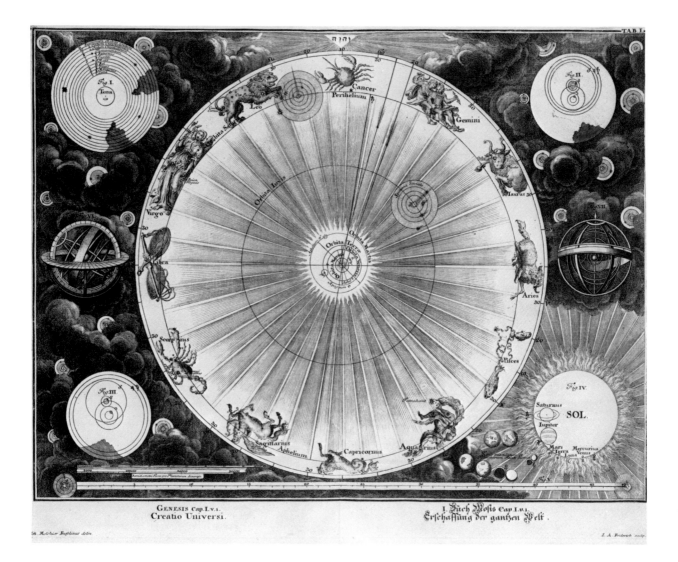

143. Jean-Jacques Scheuchzer, *Creation of the Universe,* from Physique sacrée, 1732–1737, I, pl. 1. Engraving by I. A. Fridrich. (Photo: Courtesy the Resource Collections of the Getty Center for the History of Art and the Humanities.)

But the production of ugly deformity was endemic also to the alchemical method of procession and division. While the luminous cause always maintained its original attributes, pure and unadulterated, the emitted entities necessarily became obscured, corrupted, and distorted during transmission.[54] Further, to the metaphor of fraudulent sophistication and illegal manipulation was added the trope of cloaking disguise. Matter negatively aped higher generation by reproducing a tapestry of multiplicity. It pluralized itself by giving birth to illusory appearances, to "a phantasmagoric reality and to non-being." The Panathenaic festival—or ritualized dressing, once every four years, of an archaic statue of Athena with a peplos—was, for Proclus, the epitome of the phenomenal "weaving art." The woolen robe was the symbol of intertwisted mixture, "of the *Minerval fabrication* of the universe." The clothing and veiling of the goddess embodied "the last image of the whole contrariety of things." This unholy matrimony of threads and dyes spun monstrous outcasts and estranged bastards. The tangle of weaving, like mar-

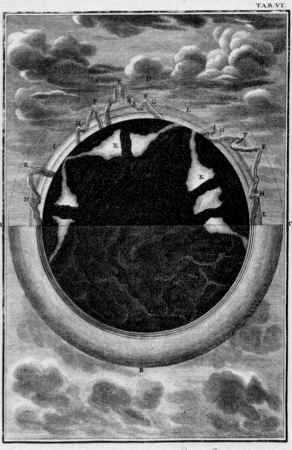

GENESIS Cap. I. v. 6 7. 8.
Opus secundæ Diei.

I. Buch Mosis Cap. I. v. 6.7.8.
Zweytes Tagwerck.

GENESIS Cap. I. v. 9.10.
Opus tertiæ Diei.

I. Buch Mosis Cap. I. v. 9.10.
Drittes Tagwerck.

144. Jean-Jacques Scheuchzer, *Second Day of Creation,* from *Physique sacrée,* 1732–1737, I, pl. 4. Engraving by J. G. Pinz. (Photo: Courtesy the Resource Collections of the Getty Center for the History of Art and the Humanities.)

145. Jean-Jacques Scheuchzer, *Third Day of Creation,* from *Physique sacrée,* 1732–1737, I, pl. 6. Engraving by J. G. Pinz. (Photo: Courtesy the Resource Collections of the Getty Center for the History of Art and the Humanities.)

bling, was the opposite of ideal and lawful wedlock. Its progeny was streaked with barbaric otherness. From it no mathematical sameness could be deduced. On the contrary, a proper genetic continuum signified that "children receive a physical similitude from their parents, and participate in a certain dignity and excellence from their begetters." Similarly, numbers, propositions, theorems, and ideas were "likenesses" going forth, yet still legitimately participating in the first cause.[55]

Christian exegesis also maintained that, at the moment of Genesis, Jehovah pulled order from the dark and shapeless abyss (fig. 143). Scheuchzer, as a good Cartesian, emphasized that this unique, eternal, perfect, and unchanging Being—a single God in three persons—formed the world by fiat, or intellectual gesture. The Lord did not spin it, like a spider, from the entrails of "the divine substance." As a purely spiritual construct, He could not be identical, as the heretical Benedict Spinoza (1632–1673) would have it, to the fabric of

146. Jean-Jacques Scheuchzer, *Human Generation*, from *Physique sacrée*, 1732–1737, I, pl. 23. Engraving by I. A. Fridrich. (Photo: Courtesy the Resource Collections of the Getty Center for the History of Art and the Humanities.)

the passive and mechanical universe. Thus the earth continued to participate in the atomistic mingling or chaos God divided in the beginning, when his spirit floated above the black waters (figs. 144, 145). "To create," Scheuchzer asserted, was "to produce something from nothing." And an infinite distance stretched between the initial nothing and the subsequent something. Even multiplied to infinity, the latter would never yield unity or, even less, beget a number.[56]

The work of the sixth day made man in the Lord's likeness (fig. 146). The Swiss natural historian claimed that the human microcosm, or abstract of the macrocosm, was also produced by the power of the fiat. Yet the soul differed as much from that of brutes as it did from the essence of God. The moralized allegory framing the illustration of the Adamic creation demonstrated that radical dissimilarity. Like the other 759 engravings in this monumental encyclopedia of sacred history, with its zoological, geological, astronomical, and biological emblems and fantastic borders, the designs were the inventions of Johann Melchior Füssli and executed by a group of Augsburg engravers. The drawing showing human creation was based specifically on the celebrated anatomical collections of Frederick Ruysch (1648–1731), which were placed on public exhibition in five rooms of his Amsterdam house and were subsequently purchased by Peter the Great. In addition to preparing organs (preserved in a mixture of white talc, wax, and cinnabar for injecting veins, and an embalming fluid made from wine and black pepper), Ruysch also concocted three-dimensional mortality symbols from his pathological specimens. Macabre sculptures, composed of once-living vessels and tissues, have been numbered, combined, and rearranged in Scheuchzer's plate around the central and illuminated figure of Adam to tell the subsequent sad story of sexual reproduction. Mortals emerged from the female egg (fig. i) and began their material trajectory, developing from grain-sized indistinct embryos (fig. ii) to ever more articulated and divided fetuses. Appositely, skeletons enacted this month-by-month existential progression in the womb that concluded with birth into material life, greeted by weeping (fig. xi). Scheuchzer's physicotheological compendium, like Cowper's treatise on human anatomy, displayed a grotesquely individuated evolution, monstrously unlike the divinity's sexless hypostasis (fig. 147).[57] This negative genetic process—disjunctively represented on the frame as a lurching from bits to pieces, from fractions to fragments, from minima to maxima—begins and ends with death.

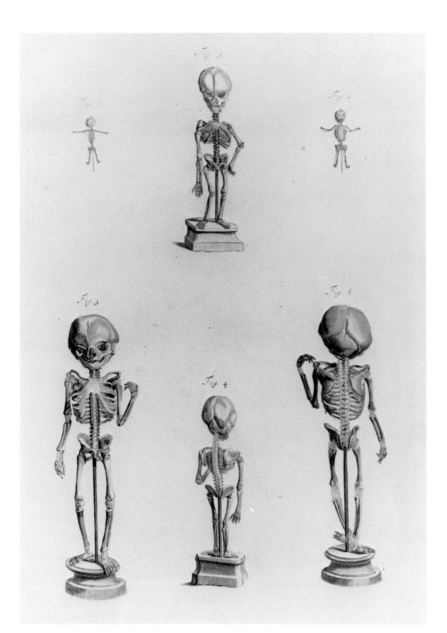

147. William Cowper, *Fetal Development,* from *Anatomia Corporum Humanorum,* 1750, pl. 100. Drawing and engraving by Gerard de Lairesse. (Photo: Courtesy National Library of Medicine, Bethesda, Md.)

148. Jacques Gautier Dagoty, *Human Embryo,* from *Historie naturelle,* 1781, I, p. 16. Multiple-plate mezzotint. (Photo: Courtesy the Resource Collections of the Getty Center for the History of Art and the Humanities.)

As an ovist, Scheuchzer adhered to one of the two major hypotheses concerning biological reproduction. Preformationists (Spallanzani, Haller, Bonnet) were in the ascendancy until the end of the eighteenth century. They believed that human beings were created by God at once, at the beginning of time. Preexisting tiny germs (the fabled homunculi) were immaterially encased in molds, or boxed—as in *emboîtement*—within the egg waiting to be actualized by the male sperm (fig. 148). Coming forth simply meant that beings were unveiled, revealed, or unfolded in successive temporal generations. Epigenesis (Fontana, Buffon, Needham, Maupertuis) focused, instead,

149. **August Johann Rösel von Rosenhof,**
Copulating Frogs and the Laying of Eggs,
from *Historia Naturalis,* 1758, pl. 17.
Colored engraving. (Photo: author.)

150. **August Johann Rösel von Rosenhof,**
Larval Development, from *Historia*
Naturalis, 1758, pl. 2. Colored engraving.
(Photo: author.)

on the physical and *ad seriatum* development of a seemingly undifferentiated mass of matter into organs and, finally, into an exquisite structure (figs. 149, 150). The observation of the healing powers of organisms boosted the doctrine of epigenesis. This theory, as well as materialism, was given a shot in the arm by Trembley's discoveries in the 1740s of the alarming ability of "polyps" to regenerate themselves from amputated cuttings (fig. 5).[58]

The importance of these scientific debates for aesthetics was their introduction of the trope likening the infant in the womb to the idea as the child of the mind. Brain-born images were the epitome of that which could not be manufactured. We shall see that the origin of embodied thought, first deriving from somatic metaphors, gradually lost its contact with immediate physical experience. By the time we get to Winckelmann, the desire to create a spiritual realm caused him to ontologize the body. In order not to get ahead of ourselves, we must pick up the discussion of concept as conception in the seventeenth century. The incubation of the egg in the hen was one of the

242

Tab. II

TAB. XIII.

151. Jean-Jacques Scheuchzer, *Development of the Chicken Embryo,* from *Physique sacrée,* 1732–1737, I, pl. 13. Engraving by I. A. Fridrich. (Photo: Courtesy the Resource Collections of the Getty Center for the History of Art and the Humanities.)

152. William Harvey, *Zeus Opening the Cosmic Egg,* from *Exercitationes Anatomicae,* 1651, title page. Engraving. (Photo: Courtesy National Library of Medicine, Bethesda, Md.)

GENESIS Cap. I. v. 20.
Opus quintæ Diei.

I. Buch Mosis Cap. I. v. 20.
Fünfftes Tagwerck.

major case studies for investigating human reproduction (fig. 151).[59] William Harvey's (1578–1657) *Anatomical Exercises* (1651) comprised a large collection of observations on embryology difficult to characterize. His emphasis on the egg led to the long search for the mammalian ovum and helped to entrench the belief that the organization, or rational plan, of the chicken embryo existed before fertilization. His conclusions were based on dissections performed on does taken from Charles I's hunting preserves. Contrary to the prevailing belief in preformation, Harvey taught that life developed epigenetically, either

Gulielmus Harveus
de
Generatione Animalium.

literally in an egg, or, somewhat ambiguously, according to the analogy of the egg. His motto "Ex Ovo Omnia," included in the frontispiece, summarized this crucial idea (fig. 152). Yet the unresolved ambiguity was apparent in a fascinating chapter entitled "Of the Conception," in which Harvey revealed his debt to Neoplatonism. In it, he developed an extended simile between the physiognomy and function of the brain and the uterus. The apprehension of ideas, or *sententiae*, in the mind was like the reception of forms in the womb. Both were "without corporeal essence," i.e., abstracted from sense impressions. Thus, the pandemonious medley of creatures unleashed by Zeus was simultaneously reality and phantasm (figs. 95, 96, 97). Carrying out dissections made Harvey aware that the substance of the uterus looked like the gray matter. It "doth so neerly resemble the constitution of the Braine [figs. 68, 153]: why may we not imagine that both their functions are also alike . . . [and] are equally called Conceptions, and both are Immaterial." Following Aristotle, he argued that the male, being the more perfect animal, contributed the superior plastic principle to the defective menstruum of the imperfect female. Once women had been impregnated by a rational idea, their eggs could become the efficient cause of generation. This spiritual implant was compared to the builder erecting a house according to his "preconceived" plan. Not only architecture but "artificial generations" or abstract "conceptions," then, mimicked this procreative activity. Harvey established a physiological aesthetics of nihility, of extinguishing imitation, or of abstraction, in which nature and artifice engendered likenesses "devoyd of all matter." Bodies were like the disappearing plaster molds, the material substance melting away without a trace, in the lost-wax process of casting sculpture. The hollow "Braine of the Artist," analogous to the fertilized egg, unfolded "by meere *Phansie*" impalpable things that were not present to palpable consciousness. It outlined the empty channels and blank traces of an absent Idea actualized as ideas voided of corporeality. Harvey concluded his observations with a grand theory of universal emulation, a purely mental genealogy founded on the transmission of spiritual conceptions. "A House erects a House, one Face limnes another, and one Image formeth another Image . . . as a Minde begets a Mind; and one Opinion another Opinion."[60] The son looked like the father, just as the painting resembled the painter, because of cerebral impregnation.

Junius spoke allegorically, and without scientific pretension, of "inward" and "uncorrupt images" of a perfect beauty seen in the "looking glass" mind. Artificers must avoid conjuring monstrous and prodigious things not known

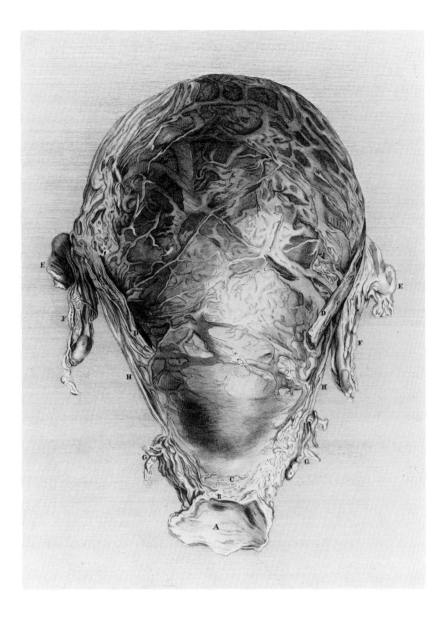

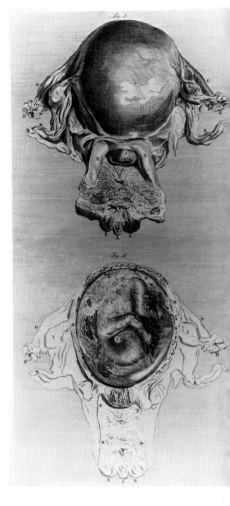

in nature. Rather, they should reflect images "even as it [the mind] receiveth them, not admitting any distorted, false-coloured, otherwise shaped figures."[61] But it was Henry More (1614–1687) and the Cambridge Platonists who transmitted the nonmechanist view of active mental principles intimately connected with the causation of a divine agency. And it was More, in particular, who asserted "the imperium of the soul's will over matter." His insistence that the higher operations of reality could not have sprung from so contemptible a principle as bare body left its mark even on Newton. Harvey's immaterial conception, then, became the "plastick virtue," or universal spiritual "force," casting the vehicle of the soul into "personal shape," like "the fetus in the womb" (fig. 154).[62] Preformationist hypotheses about the unfolding of life, and preexistence theories concerning the offspring of the mind, agreed that making was inferior to revealing.

153. Leopoldo Marco Antonio Caldani, *Gravid Uterus*, from *Icones anatomicae*, 1810, III, pl. 151. Engraving by Felix Zuliani. (Photo: Courtesy National Library of Medicine, Bethesda, Md.)

154. Leopoldo Marco Antonio Caldani, *Fetus in Utero*, from *Icones anatomicae*, 1810, III, pl. 161. Engraving by Felix Zuliani. (Photo: Courtesy National Library of Medicine, Bethesda, Md.)

Shaftesbury was deeply indebted to the Cambridge Platonists and to their view of concrete ontogenesis as the pure manifestation of preformed structures. For the British Deist, as well as for Winckelmann who avidly read him, the concept of a systematic, hierarchical succession of living beings offered a powerful philosophical alternative to the Cartesian impasse over how to bind together the thinking *res cogitans* with the unthinking *res extensa*.[63] Shaftesbury openly displayed his intellectual parentage when, as Philocles in *The Moralists*, he declared that "Conceptions," or "mental children" were innate and "like eggs in the fetus." "Pre-Conceptions" were the "anticipating Forms" of the fair and beautiful, whereas physical bodies merely came and went. Significantly, these procreative analogies occurred at the important moment in the dialogues when Philocles was epiphanically converted to Theocles' rhapsodic Neoplatonism. The denial of his former empiricist shallowness obliged him to abandon broken surfaces in order to "go far in the pursuit of *Beauty*, which lies very absconded and deep." The beautiful in art was defined totally by its ideas and conceptions and not in any way by its materials. Matter resembled the "savage" and the "idiot," i.e., the monstrously shapeless or defective mind that was "Deformity itself."[64] Shaftesbury, via Harvey and More, engendered the basic tenet of Neoclassical art theory propagated by Winckelmann. He established the physiognomic identity between lovely mental and physical children. Indeed, there was no distinction since the plastic idea generated both.

Richardson further developed the model of the "new world" in the mind from whence first forms or ideas flowed. These were elevated far above the ignoble drolls and *bambochades* of life. The exaltation of the human species to "the angelic state," disguising or hiding animal *saletés* or defects, was the grand end of poetry and painting. These "impregnate our minds with the most sublime and beautiful images of things; and thus our imaginations do raise all nature some degrees above what is commonly, or ever seen." Félibien, relying on the same trope, declared that the greatest obstacle an artist could encounter was a malformed idea. "A child born before its term . . . causes more pain to the mother that gives it birth, & rarely grows into a state of perfection." The painter must thus avoid behaving like the laborer who abortively struggled to reproduce bodies through mechanical travail. Rather than the toiling *ouvrier*, he should emulate the learned and intellectual *auteur* whose inventions stemmed "solely from the *esprit*."[65] Nicolas Malebranche (1638–1715), in France, had propagated the view of a God who intervened on every occasion. Moment by moment, He generated the conceptions of sensible things within the individual understanding. While the *Recherche de la vérité* (1674/1675) was not yet Berkeley's full-blown immaterialism, it veered toward the same thesis. Matter did not exist, and what we assumed to be objects in the world were, in fact, vivid and colorful but disembodied ideas present to the mind.[66]

This metaphor of a spiritual and biological power radiating from a single prototype, moving from interior to exterior and, in the process, generating conceptions, was taken up most memorably by Winckelmann. Before arriving in Rome from Dresden in 1755, Winckelmann was already steeped in the Neoplatonist metaphysics of Proclus, Junius, Shaftesbury, Leibniz, and Baumgarten.[67] What has not been recognized, however, is that this utopian idealization, or Deistic desire to ontologize experience, itself grew out of the polemic concerning the nature of reproduction. Neoclassical art theory and Enlightenment rationalist philosophy and physiology came together on the major question of what organized beings or, indeed, any creations. The biological basis of Winckelmann's aesthetics was already apparent in the *Thoughts on the Imitation of the Painting and Sculpture of the Greeks*—the work that was to spread his fame in European intellectual circles. Unlike the subsequent Italian writings, based on the firsthand archaeological knowledge of antiquity, this book derived largely from literary sources. Citing Proclus, Winckelmann asserted the preformationist's credo. The ideal forms of Greek art were "brain-born images." Relying on the *Commentary on the Timaeus*— itself a physiology of cosmic generation begotten by the "Demiurgus of Wholes"—Winckelmann, too, formulated "a flowing condition of being." He reified a wholly conceptual beauty without physical incarnation. The liberal observation of disease-free male nudity in the gymnasium, theater, or bath prompted the Greeks to go beyond the evidence of the senses. They elevated these handsome, yet inferior, corporeal visions of the palaestra above the reach of mortality. Distilled into purely mental models, they attained an abstract perfection not born of hands.[68] He contrasted such immaterial icons to the unnatural idols of modern *caricatura*, or manual "pictures void of thought." As "painters of the soul," the Greeks required perceptible signs that were not palpable in order to embody suprasensible ideas.[69] Hence Winckelmann's famous compendium of barely visible minima: hair-breadth contours, empty outlines, disembodied silhouettes, monadic unities, and "central" forms drained of distinguishing characteristics.

The key position assigned to watery metaphors in his aesthetics was directly related to the outflowing fecundity emanating from an eternally brimming first cause. Water, as Plutarch wrote, was requisite to the chemical trans-mutation of bodies into souls. Picking up the analogy, Winckelmann spoke of the need to change observations from nature into the painter's "essence and soul."[70] In medicine, it was the tenuous substance of the Galenic humors, those transparent and spiritual liquors that circulated through the body. The suppleness and mobility of an individual's temperament depended on such *humeur*, or psychic liquidity.[71] Winckelmann's praise of the fluid outline of fair forms, or of the subtle contour the young wrestler imprinted when he silently withdrew from the sand, was part of a new, delicate genetics of artistic generation. Drawing in the sand was like Ovid's evanescent game of love.[72] This vain and vanishing sport left lingering doubts as to the perma-nence of art as material reproduction. Upon arising from the ground, the athlete left behind only the negative, bodiless pattern of pure inwardness that could not be expressed by soiling material means. These almost imperceptible traces of an ineffable beauty resembled those Neoplatonic, hollow "interior molds," bringing conceptions down to earth.[73]

Winckelmann's discussion of workmanship in sculpture, and the ancients' supposed preference for vanishing wax over persisting clay, was based on the view that the absolute was like a well at the center of the universe. This never-depleted dynamic source was a stream of energy gradually inundating, but not physically bonding, with peripheral matter. Similarly, the delicate internal feeling, bubbling up in the sensitive beholder at the sight of beauty, was likened to a dip cast of the *Apollo Belvedere*, Winckelmann imagined the reimmersion of a gesso head of the god into still-molten plaster. Like Auguste Rodin or Medardo Rosso in the late nineteenth century, he thereby won for the reproduction a fresh or youthful softness, a gentle animation, and an edited pristine smoothness of surface. He hypothetically created for the *Apollo* a weightless second skin, a mysterious fluency, and liquefaction of materials that masked any blemishes endemic to the manufacture of copies.[74] Winck-elmann's thoughts concerning a liquid medium were further developed after reading Vasari. In his biography of Michelangelo, the Florentine painter gave an account of the great sculptor's practice of floating wax models in a vessel filled with water. The buoyant figure could be raised by degrees to the surface. Winckelmann emended the story to imagine the sculptor marking the sides of the vessel with ideal dimensions that he then transferred to the model. Like preexisting conceptions in the mind, the perfect form was already encased in the hollow vat. Prominent or elevated parts were unveiled, while the lesser or lower elements remained sunken. The gradual drawing off or removing of liquid not only literally manifested "the heights or depths" of the figure, but metaphorically revealed the contours of the artist's emergent idea. Like the faint depression stamped by the athlete in the sand, the void between the rim of the vessel and the surface of the water "was the exact measure of what might be safely subtracted from the block." When the wrestler withdrew from the floor, or the fluid drained from the vat, the artist discovered the insinuating and undulating linear signs of divine beauty that would otherwise have remained concealed.[75] Both the melting plaster cast and the swimming wax figure, then, symbolized the inverted coming forth of the supernatural. They represented not fixed, hard, tangible bodies but their purely formal or intangible apparition during a moment of grace.[76]

It was through barely perceptible motion, the diminution of water, the permeation of liquids, the suffusion of ideas, that the divine diagram for art and human beings diffused into existence. It does not seem accidental that Winckelmann subsequently sought to isolate a coherent overall pattern of development occurring within the stylistic evolution of forms. The *History of Art* (1764) was an encyclopedia of connoisseurship, a genealogical directory for the recognition of barely perceptible qualities. Moreover, it outlined a seemingly atemporal and universal *plan* of development unfolding from the archaic, to the high, to the beautiful, to the mature, to the declining periods of material production. Rational order was visualized as a mathematical trajectory sketching the contours of the Idea's descent into nature. This preformationist art history was based on the paradigm of spiritual *emboîtement*. Eras were "unpacked" and fluently succeeded one another without any serious gaps or uncertainties. They emerged from a divine Greek conception, the original artistic womb, or the primordial portmanteau.[77]

Mengs, whose house Winckelmann frequented while in Rome, shared his compatriot's Neoplatonic and antinomian outlook—expressed as the rigorist desire to escape the dregs of a Baroque modernity. He, too, wished to imbibe the atmosphere of pure inwardness the original Greeks supposedly inhabited. Like More and Shaftesbury, the German artist spoke of a numinous plastic force or nonempirical virtue residing in the soul that mysteriously shaped bodies. Natural imperfections and corporeal defects were caused when that fleeting spark mixed with matter, giving rise to distortions, passions, and disease. The presence of such misrepresentations owed to the fact that neither the world nor the body was self-caused. They were generated from above and outside, by a remote power to which they remained unequal. Significantly, Mengs employed a biological analogy with which we are now familiar. Art surpassed the poverty of nature because it had the luxury to operate freely. Guided by a vision of the suprahistorical plan, the disciplined mind of the artist selected choice parcels from among inert materials. These could offer no resistance to the imposition of rational structure. On the contrary, "nature was permitted to take the substance for the reproduction of man only from his mother: and this, morever, became the source of many accidents."[78] Art intellectually engendered the ideal lying beyond incomplete or mutilated experience.

Mengs and Winckelmann, then, adhered to the Leibnizian reformulation of Neoplatonism—drastically severing appearance from reality—that was prevalent in German intellectual circles. Pernety, at mid-century, best summarized this reception of Platonic philosophy and the tenacity of the belief in a preexisting, permanent, and simple concept pitted against incessant material instability and multiformity. Physical, or plural, births were merely physiognomic, that is, accidental deviations from the abstract type. They altered only the face of appearances without modifying the emitted underlying or overarching essence. Likening variation to the gradual transformation of a chrysalis into a butterfly, Pernety declared that "all individuals in the universe owe their existence only to a successive evolution of metamorphoses that changed nothing at bottom, but only forms & figures."[79] Lavater similarly asserted his faith in an unfathomable and humanly uncontrollable creative power (*Schöpfungskraft*) releasing momentary conceptions: "Grubs, in any event, allow themselves to be made. But animated, efficacious beings—internally and externally self-resembling—images of God—were created—generated—and not out of the concupiscence of the flesh, nor out of the desire of man—but from God."[80]

Coleridge derived from a Neoplatonically drenched German Idealism and transcendental philosophy the same liquid, hylomorphic model of mental procreation. His organic "esemplastic" power possessed the ability to communicate the Logos, or generative intellect. He shared with Blake the belief that the knowledge of ideal beauty was not to be acquired. "Innate Ideas are in every Man, Born with him; they are truly Himself." According to Coleridge, the primary imagination was unique, vital, and divine. But the overflowing eternal act could be negatively repeated, like a dark "echo," in the finite understanding. The fertile secondary imagination "dissolves, diffuses, dissipates in order to re-create; or, where this process is rendered impossible, yet still, at all events, it struggles to idealize and to unify." According to the

Romantic poet, reproductive fancy, on the contrary, merely toyed with "fixities and definities." It functioned epigenetically, so to speak. Material wit (*Witz, esprit*) mechanically and willfully combined, associated, and mixed empirica. It received minimal and trivial counters—"mental" eggs or sperm—ready-made from experience, not grand wholes from divine emanation.[81] Like memory, it traded in the decaying shreds and tatters of sense impressions. Fancy's inferior midwifery allowed a private thought or idiosyncratic notion to be born publicly from the circuitous interchange between external world and physical brain. The mind did not contain innate ideas, just as the uterus did not hold tiny germs. Rather, a special Socratic and dialogic situation had to be created to facilitate the fabrication of the psychic fragment or biological bit, not existing before. Thus essentialism, or the imitation of like by like, abstracted dissimilarity from conceptions to make them resemble their originary cause. But reproductive fancy, on the other hand, operated according to the principles of a self-organizing matter. It did not presuppose the deep structural regularity and invisible uniformity of the species. Instead, it reified Epicurean chance and the spontaneous play of superficial differences. Palpable couplings begot hybrids and monsters. In this scheme, ideas were fantasies, the plastic inventions or dreams of physical organisms.

Julien Offray de La Mettrie's materialistic *L'Homme machine* (1748) and Diderot's *Elémens de physiologie* (1778) embodied this fluid and instinctual erotic phenomenology that removed fixity from living forms and released nature from constraining molds. French materialism presented a radically physical view of reproduction at the antipodes from Winckelmann's intellectual sensualism. Libertine or disorderly organisms were free to mingle experimentally, giving birth to monstrous races and eccentric assemblages. The body and brain were one. A concept was a material like any other substance. Consequently, the more one exercised the imagination, the plumper it got, the more it expanded and became sinewy, robust, vast, and capable of thought. Borrowing a Physiocratic agrarian metaphor, La Mettrie (1709–1751) declared that, if the brain were genetically well-organized and subsequently well-educated, then it was "a fertile field, perfectly sown, that could reap a hundred-fold more than it had received." The trained intellect "gave birth to new relations [among ideas] by comparing them to the originals" and discovering a perfect resemblance. Such was, according to the *philosophe*, the distinctly nonspiritual "generation of the mind [*esprit*]." His dynamic and pansexual model of intellectual development, like Diderot's, was based on a concrete, not an insubstantial, example. He likened it to the continual circulation of atoms or "errant germs" within the ocean of matter (fig. 155). Their egalitarian and indiscriminate couplings were responsible for all mixtures. These incessantly destroying, rebuilding, and transmuting rudimentary particles proliferated to infinity. Nor was humanity exempt from this physical chemistry. The operative metaphor for this earthy group was not that of disembodied embryonic thought but of vigorously copulating elements and of fundamental, palpable particles. As Diderot wittily quipped: "the wise man is only a composite of mad molecules."[82]

Breeding for Difference

Hybridous ————————————

adj., *Begotten between animals of different species.*

Dr. Johnson, *Dictionary*

Greffe ————————————

noun, *The graft is the triumph of art over nature. By its means, nature is forced to take on different arrangements, to follow other paths, to change its forms, and to substitute the good, beautiful, great in place of the abject; finally, one can by means of the graft transmute the sex, species, and even types of trees . . .*

Diderot and D'Alembert, *Encyclopédie*

The controversy between preformationists and epigenetists was also about classification. For the eighteenth century, taxonomy, by and large, was a system linking perceptibly similar phenomena. Conception involved a notion of physiognomic frugality, or of formulaic humanity. The existence of biological monsters challenged the theory of imitation according to which classes of being might be methodically included or excluded depending on their looks. They defied a belief in the simplicity of the species, and in an invisible, innate property irrevocably stamping individuals belonging to the same category.[83] Corporeal anomalies, like aberrant mental or artistic conceptions, were the physiological counterparts to the miscellaneous encyclopedia or graphic satire. Their alien and caricatural elements could be grouped, assembled, and combined, but not made to belong to an orderly plan. Natural and artificial monsters, then, raised problems concerning declassification and unclassifiability. They could shamelessly exhibit themselves, but no linguistic categorization was adequate to, or could reduce, the complex perceptual experience (fig. 156). The monster began and ended in the incorrect image, in the indelibility of the flawed, strange, and incongruous impression. Its verbal cognates were those barbarisms we looked at earlier. Irrational and perverted image-word copulations were falsely modeled on the simultaneity of pictures, and thus denied the correct sequentiality of language. They included those hybrids that Neoclassical criticism deemed wrongful nonrepresentations: allegorical obscurities, distorted grotesques, and jumbled nonsense. The monster is central to my argument precisely because it interrupts, through glaring excess or defect, the plenitude of succession. The abrupt stoppage of the effortless flow forces the observer or reader to think. Consequently, the monster is the true face of imagery, not as verbal continuum but as thought-provoking simultaneity. (The logocentric television industry might well ponder this fact when it proffers a mindless series of images

155.   G. F. Rivati, *Bacteria,* from *Dizionario scientifico e curiosa* (?), 1750, III, pl. 17. Engraving. (Photo: Courtesy National Library of Medicine, Bethesda, Md.)

156.   Nicolas-François Regnault, *Monstrous Man (with "Parasite"),* from *Descriptions des principales monstruosités,* 1808, pl. 21. Engraving. (Photo: Courtesy National Library of Medicine, Bethesda, Md.)

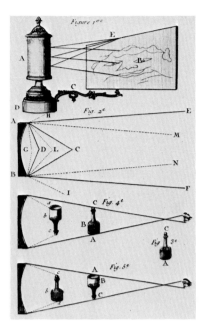

157. Edmé Guyot, *Anamorphoses*, from *Nouvelles récréations*, 1772, VI, pl. 13. Colored engraving by J. F. Leizel. (Photo: author.)

modeled not on their proper essence but on a stream of words.) Finally, the monster incarnated illegitimacy. Its anamorphic shapelessness situated it not within culture but beyond culture, beyond the imposition of geometrical norms (fig. 157).[84] It presented the distorted portrait of the primal universe as deregulated *ars combinatoria*, an immense chaos, as Pernety maintained, "without physiognomy."[85] It continually reminded the beholder of his active need and responsibility to make sense of the world.

The paradox of eighteenth-century genetic research was that it studied irregular occurrences in order to discover something about how regular organisms conceived. In the absence of viable experiments on minima, it was hoped that the evidence provided by biological failures would resolve the debate between preformationists and epigenetists.[86] Since antiquity, monstrous births posed the problem of whether they were rightly or not rightly propagated from human beings. For Enlightenment *philosophes*, however, it was no longer a question of interpreting them as portents of divine displeasure or evil signs predicting natural, religious, and political cataclysms.[87] Already by the sixteenth century, Mannerist theorists classed natural singularities among surprising and fantastic wonders, or *capricci*, that "jumped" like a stag beyond the limits of the ordinary. Giovanni Paolo Lomazzo (b. 1538), in the *Idea del tempio della pittura* (1590), praised painting's ability to teach the discernment of beauty in all things, including "deformity." Most notably, Bartolomeo Garzoni's encyclopedia, *Il Seraglio* (1613), was divided into rooms stocked with the strange beauty of aberrations fabricated by "l'Ingegnosa Natura."[88] As part of this fascination, Fortunio Liceti (1577–1657), a Paduan male midwife, collected the various notions concerning abnormality then prevalent (fig. 158). The first edition of *De Monstris* (1616) was unillustrated, but the second, in 1643, the third, in 1665, and the French edition of 1668 contained a rich iconography culled from Lycosthenes to Ambroise Paré (1510?–1590).[89] While the frontispiece (fig. 98), with its bizarre assemblage of outlandishly coupled forms, mirrored the Mannerist delight in amusing conceits, Liceti's compendium was indicative of change. Even earlier, the Parisian anatomist and apothecary Jean Riolan (1538–1605?) wrote a treatise on a "Cyclops," born in 1605. He augmented his eyewitness acount with comparative material (fig. 159). This case history was a more limited indication of the same shift toward medical incorporation. By the late seventeenth century, monsters had fully entered the discipline of embryology. These "shows" (from the verb *monstrat*) would now become the basis of a new science of teratology, eventually flourishing in the nineteenth century with the investigations of Etienne

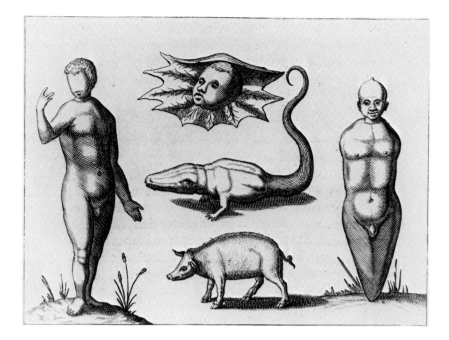

158. Fortunius Licetus, *Faceless and Limbless Monsters,* from *De Monstris,* 1665, p. 70. Engraving. (Photo: Courtesy National Library of Medicine, Bethesda, Md.)

159. Jean Riolan, *Cyclops,* from *De Monstro,* 1605, pl. 2. Engraving. (Photo: Courtesy National Library of Medicine, Bethesda, Md.)

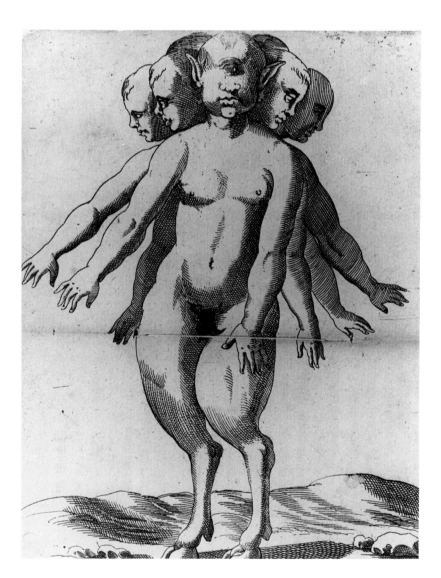

LA POURSUITE.

160. Grandville, *The Pursuit,* from *Un
autre monde,* 1844, p. 106. Wood
engraving. (Photo: Courtesy the Library of
Congress.)

(1772–1844) and Isidore (1805–1861) Geoffroy de Saint-Hilaire. Jean-Ignace Grandville (1803–1847), in his comic illustrated fantasia *Un autre monde* (1844), spoofed their much-touted teratological researches in his own "dualism of phenomena." He concocted visionary medleys showing the prodigious possibilities for combinations offered by the comparative anatomy displays on view at the Jardin des Plantes (fig. 160). Neither of the two Saint-Hilaires, father or son, were epigenetists. Since 1821, Etienne had explained that the perturbation of preexisting germs redistributed the genetic material such that an unpredictable, unknown, and truly new creation arose. This completely different and radically individual being was the monster.[90]

We shall see, however, that for the eighteenth-century mentality, such departures from the norm still retained a panoply of earlier connotations. Thus biological anomalies could serve as the paradigm for all deviant forms. In spite of the pressure applied to the enigma of monsters by an analytical philosophy, they resisted the collapse into simplicity. The demonic freak reigned not only in the high, or scientific, study of malformations, but in animal husbandry, antiquarian research into Gnostic gems, folkloric caricature, and polemical modern *grylli*. No matter whether the investigator was an ovist or animalculist, the appearance of abnormality was still described according to the hallowed Aristotelian terms of excess or defect. Chambers defined it as "a birth, a production of a living thing, degenerating from the proper and usual disposition of parts, in the species it belongs to." It possessed "too many members or too few; or some extravagantly out of proportion." The *monstrum* parodied *emboîtement*. The etymology of the word derived from *monstrado* ("shewing"), and was thus connected to "the box wherein relics were anciently kept." A sort of *Vario-* or *Zwerch-Kasten*, it encased disparate contents too small and unrelated to be stored in a cupboard filled with grander, classifiable objects.[91]

Between 1724 and 1743 a "quarrel of monsters" erupted in the Royal Academy of Prussia between two anatomists. Its notoriety helped focus the key issues for European natural historians for several decades thereafter. The polemic is important for our purposes because it provides a point of entry into the polyvalent attitude of the Enlightenment toward monstrosity. It also makes accessible an entire descriptive vocabulary of negative terms concerning the melting of boundaries between species, one that was readily transposed from biology to aesthetics. Pierre-Louis Moreau de Maupertuis (1698–1758) discussed the fracas at length in *The Earthly Venus* and again in the wide-

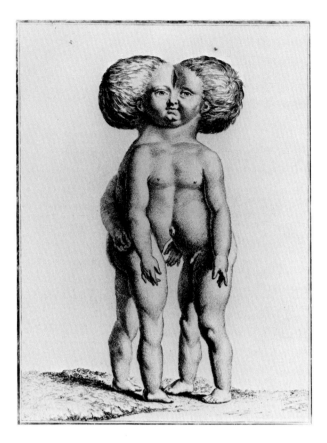

161. Nicolas-François Regnault, *Double Child,* from *Descriptions des principales monstruosités,* 1808, pl. 19. Engraving. (Photo: Courtesy National Library of Medicine, Bethesda, Md.)

162. Nicolas-François Regnault, *Monstrous Child with Multiple Sensory Organs,* from *Descriptions des principales monstruosités,* 1808, pl. 30. Engraving. (Photo: Courtesy National Library of Medicine, Bethesda, Md.)

ranging article on "Génération" he composed for the *Encyclopédie*. The French physiologist Louis Lemery (1697–1743) and the Danish anatomist Jacques-Bénigné Winslow (1669–1760) were both ovists. Although Maupertuis did not say so, at stake was not simply physiology but a venerable quandary of theology. Do multiple monsters possess more than one soul? Were both heads baptized or given the last rites? But to return to the debate. Lemery maintained that the confusion between two germs in one egg produced "monsters by excess, or individuals born with superfluous parts." He further imagined that the combining of two bodies *in utero* resulted from superficial fragments of the embryo having been torn apart and then falsely reattached. Siamese twins (figs. 161, 162) and polydactylism embodied the extremes of this disorder. Winslow's dissections of the former, however, led him to doubt that they originated in the kinds of accidental severings and recouplings envisaged by Lemery. Monsters by defect, ranging from the acephalic and unviable fetus (figs. 134, 136), to the armless herm (fig. 158), to the single-eyed Cyclops

(fig. 163), were similarly explained by Lemery as owing to the violent, externally caused disturbance of the afflicted members, preventing their proper development.[92]

The epigenetist Maupertuis was equally obsessed with the interpretation of double monsters. These were considered to be among the most grotesque of animal or human freaks. Traditionally, they lined the hunter's trophy case. Foxes with two tails, hares with eight paws, and dogs with three rumps (fig. 164) were often reproduced in technical treatises and sporting pictures. They testified both to the period's love of the chase and its fascination with specimens of irregularity. Superabundant deformities were portrayed in medical tracts, such as Nicolas Regnault's (1746–1810) *Descriptions des principales monstrosités* (1808), in sumptuous folios glorifying venery by the famous Augsburg engraver Johann Elias Riedinger (1695–1767), and in Jean-Baptiste Oudry's (1686–1755) strange *trompe l'oeil* paintings. In the 1740s, the *animalier*

163. Nicolas-François Regnault, *Cyclops Cat,* from *Descriptions des principales monstruosités,* 1808, pl. 13. Engraving. (Photo: Courtesy National Library of Medicine, Bethesda, Md.)

164. Nicolas-François Regnault, *Dog with Three Posteriors,* from *Descriptions des principales monstruosités,* 1808, pl. 9. Engraving. (Photo: Courtesy National Library of Medicine, Bethesda, Md.)

THE SIAMESE BROTHERS.
Aged 18
Drawn on Stone & Published by T. M. Baynes, 41, Burton Street, Burton Crescent. Printed by C Hullmandel

commemorated bizarrely mutilated antlers from stags killed by Louis XV in the forests of Rambouillet, Marly, and Compiègne.[93] Such abnormalities, of course, also found their way into natural history cabinets (figs. 6, 12, 115) as well as Bartholomew Fair sideshows. The multiplicity and oddity of these duplications clearly intrigued not only gapers and gawkers, but artists and philosophers. They could take the poignant form of the asymmetrical para-site—as in the famous cases of the Genoese Lazarus Colloredo and James Poro—who proudly displayed their infantile and fragmentary other selves (fig. 156). Or, as in the example of the exotic rarities, *Chang and Eng*, they could be identical and symmetrically fused (fig. 165). These attached twins were born near Bangkok, but toured Great Britain and the United States to great acclaim as late as 1829.[94] Such *doublûres* were also staple ingredients in the satires of Goya (fig. 139) and Gillray (fig. 166).

CONCEIVING

166.   James Gillray, *Doublûres of*
Characters, 1798. Colored etching. (Photo:
Courtesy National Library of Medicine,
Bethesda, Md.)

Maupertuis's investigations highlight the difference between the English and the French attitude toward misconceptions during the eighteenth century. The British tended to gape uncritically at the "monster market" on view at the Bartholomew and Southwark Fairs, while the French took the lead in seriously studying them within scientific institutions. The Newtonian Maupertuis hypothesized the existence of a cohesive attracting force in nature that caused similar particles to adhere. Contradicting the preformationists, he argued that the infant was born from atoms belonging to both parents. When tiny germs joined with those with which they were intended to be contiguous, then a perfect child resulted. But if some superfluous seeds discovered a spot available for bonding, even though it was already properly occupied, then a monster by excess was produced. Conversely, if the seeds remained too far apart, "or of unsuitable shape, or too weak" to create a close union, then a monster by defect emerged. Maupertuis presciently noted the strict observance of order in the organization of defective limbs. Notwithstanding the ballyho of carnivals, ears were not found on feet, nor fingers on the head. The rationalist *philosophe*, demonstrating his aversion to confusion, denied that he had ever witnessed human grotesques with the head of a cat, dog, or horse (figs. 113, 114). "Never have I found an individual showing signs of parts belonging indubitably to a species other than his own."[95] Maupertuis's research, then, relocated the monster within the realm of pathology. Like the *De Rachitide* (1671) of the English physician Francis Glisson (1597–1677), in which deformed children were seen to result from malnutrition (fig. 137),[96] the *Earthly Venus* derived infant abnormality from situations occurring in nature.

The hybrid posed a special problem for those who worried about purity of forms, interfertility, and unnatural mixtures. Both the plant and animal kingdoms were the site of forced breeding between species that did not amalgamate in the wild. The metaphysical and physical dangers thought to inhere in artificial grafts surfaced in threatening metaphors of infection, contamination, rape, and bastardy. Moreover, they were routinely described as "the wounds of plants." While it was accepted that vegetable growth could be improved through "copulation, innoculation, incision," it was common agricultural practice to urge the bonding of similar species. The coupling of radical differences produced either transplants, which did not take, or "monstrous, knotty, fissured trees, or those that remained weak & almost sterile." These false implants were like burrowing parasites. Botanical monsters, or models of inappropriate, unmatched marriage, weakened and drained of nourishing sap the partner to which they so tenaciously clung. Mistletoe invaded the young plant, altering and distorting its natural fibers until the limbs were obliged to grow "in a false direction and entirely contrary to nature." This "vice of organization," if allowed to persist unpruned, exploded into a multiplicity of obstacles forcing the host to assume grotesque figures.[97]

Hybridization was rampant in livestock (mules, cow-calf freemartins) and sport (horses, dogs, foxes, wolves, jackals) breeding. But what was frowned upon in plant suturing became barbarous in animal reproduction. The aesthetic claims of clarity and distinctness were more insistent as one mounted the evolutionary ladder. Elaborate theories abounded concerning the virtue of pure strains, the detection of good or bad combinations, and the presence of blazes or marks thought to denote inner constitution. All were predicated on the judgment that mixtures abstracted from normal procreation easily led to the monstrous. Prior to the era of genetic engineering, they represented an infraction of the immemorial rule concerning sexual segregation.[98] Like Pythagoreanism's metempsychosis, or materialism's metamorphosis, hybridization accepted the democratic equivalence and interchangeability of different forms of creation. Before the nineteenth century, explanations concerning genetic variations and the human intervention in mating did not stem from animal breeders but from philosophers, natural historians, and physicians.

The horror inspired by the sight of parasites in plants was outmatched by that of the hermaphrodite in animals. Here was a questionable, nonstandard, or bastard merger of sexual characteristics that smacked of laboratory decisions. John Hunter (1728–1783), the famous Scottish surgeon, in his *Account of the Free Martin* distinguished between natural and artificial hermaphrodites. The latter represented a malconformation of the genitalia from "the attempt to unite the two parts in one animal body." Occurring now and then in every tribe, these disjunctive freaks might possess to perfection secondary sexual characteristics, but they could never possess perfectly the primary procreative organ common to both.[99] His conviction stemmed from the close study of imperfect female calves, twinborn with males. The spurious synthesis of man-woman incarnate had long been connected to incest, comic parti-colored transvestism (or intersexual masquerade), and the degeneracy of twofold idols (fig. 114).[100] We have already encountered the androgyne as pure, artificial abstraction, as Winckelmann's spiritual symbol of a higher unity (fig. 15). Actualized as an equivocal bisexual compound, however, it was neither creative fiction nor novel marvel, but an extreme monstrosity. The real abnormality of generative organs (fig. 134) was the upside-down image of the perfect blend prayed for by Salamacis when she implored the gods to dissolve her body with that of the son of Hermes and Aphrodite.

The eighteenth century was well aware that the ancients cast such infants into the sea at Athens and into the Tiber at Rome.[101] Duplicity of sex, Beattie declared, was like an excessive contraction in language. It disfigured, by compression, the gender of nouns. Similarly, the neuter hermaphrodite was sterile and incapable of using either organ. Antiquarians and numismatists, in particular, were obliged to wrestle with the meaning of these and other anomalies so frequently appearing on gems and coins. La Chau's and Le Blond's *Pierres gravées* (1780) abandoned the realm of mythology for that of a dubious anthropology. There was no doubt in the authors' minds that creatures uniting both sexes really existed. They were especially prevalent in the torrid zone, or so inattentive travelers believed when they beheld women with exaggerated vaginal lips and concluded they were both male and female. This anatomical malformation inspired lurid abuses recorded by ancient writers. Lucian, Seneca, and St. Paul launched anathemas against courtesans who claimed to possess all that was needed to slake every desire. The enlightened compilers scoffed both at pornographic tales and at current sloppy observations. The latter resulted in the same hermaphrodite being declared "a man in Toulouse and a woman in Paris." While it was up to naturalists to pronounce definitively concerning such matters, "everyone" now agreed they were monsters "in the absolute sense of the term." They "strayed from the configuration of their species in the essential parts." As Montesquieu said of *castrati*: they belonged neither "to the sex we loved nor to the one we esteemed."[102]

Grotesques, or Ars Combinatoria

Deformity _____

noun, Ugliness; ill-favouredness; ridiculousness; quality of something to be laughed at; irregularity.

Dr. Johnson, *Dictionary*

The Galenic problem of less than integral mixtures of inimical substances was reintroduced with a vengeance to the eighteenth century as a byproduct of Hellenism.[103] Having looked at biological theories of normal and abnormal procreation, we can take up again, from a different angle, the conundrum of polytheistic grotesques. A multitude of Gnostic gems—reproduced in Montfaucon, Gori and Passeri, Caylus, Cochin, Natter, La Chau and Le Blond—illustrated animal-headed Archons and astral Dekans.[104] Elegant small engravings, paradoxically, presented a vast periodic table of transformable vile elements seemingly bereft of intellect. These micrographical assemblages, issuing from an unnatural pagan fancy, were the antithesis of the geometrician's or mathematician's simple brain-born ideas. They visualized, in another mode, artificial aesthetic monsters of excess and deficiency, scatological hybrids, and rebarbative hermaphrodites. Human and bestial materials—like volatile gases, evaporating liquids, and combustible powders—fornicated in a materialistic chemism. The ineluctable and otherwise concealed matrix of life was dramatically incarnated in incongruously addorsed heads of men, rams, bears, asses, horses, superimposed on cocks' and birds' legs, and adorned with dragons' tails. Thus, for example, matter's quirky atomic components were imagined as being pulled along in a triumphant procession by redoubled phalluses—like performers in a cosmic comedy (fig. 133). This theater of the optically absurd pictured the universe as manufactured out of unstable chemicals and according to a caricatural alchemy. Along the same lines, the classicist Spence sarcastically "decimated" Montfaucon's ugly and shameful gods. Recall how vexed he was "to see a deity with a dog's or a hawk's head upon its shoulders: and could never have been brought to view a Squat-Jug, with the respect that may, perhaps, be due to what was formerly the divinity of a great and learned nation" (fig. 114). He deplored gorgons, harpies, centaurs, giants, hydras, and chimeras as "these bad beings." Unlike Piranesi, he was no advocate of things Roman. Spence claimed that these and other monstrous combinations appealed to their degenerate taste, especially after Latium had been increased by the barbarous "refuse of the nations round them." The Grecophilic Spence surmised that this spurious visual twaddle was connected to now-lost "dumb shews," or to indecent "extempore farces," too contemptible to describe for "polite ears."[105]

Significantly and unintentionally, the compilers of glyptic thesauruses made available to the moderns the inexhaustible and "libertine" ancient ways of compounding mixtures out of alien differences. The perplexity, and even censure, recorded by the authors of these digests highlighted the absence of conventional structure-conferring strategies in such contradictory imagery. Unrestrained fecundity was believed to be an essential ingredient of this Manichean iconography. Some authors thought these enigmatic vignettes were talismanic amulets empowering their possessor with fertility. Symbols of the principal of water (fig. 108), the mask of Pan (fig. 109), priapic and ithyphallic motives (fig. 133) seemed to evoke the concurrence of atomic parcels in the procreation of all things.[106] The sexual act was obliquely configured in multiple burlesque associations and repetitions. These visual encyclopedias of tiny aberrations—along with reproductions of lascivious

Caricature _____

noun, This word is French, from the Italian caricatura; *and it refers to what one formerly called* charge. *It applies principally to grotesque and extremely disproportioned figures, either in the whole, or in the parts, that a painter or sculptor or engraver makes expressly to amuse himself and to cause laughter. Callot excelled in this genre. But there is a* burlesque *in painting, as in poetry: this is a type of* libertinage *of the imagination that one should not allow oneself or, at the most, only for diversion.*

Diderot and D'Alembert, *Encyclopédie*

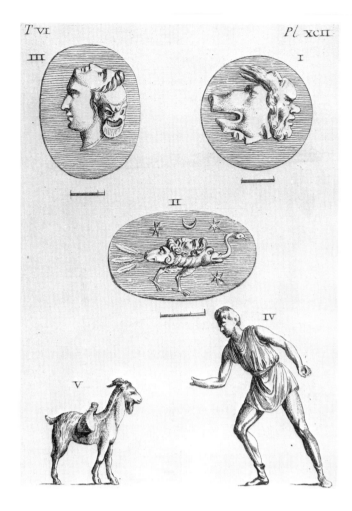

167. Anne-Claude-Philippe, Comte de Caylus, *Grylli,* from *Recueil d'antiquités,* 1752–1767, VI, pl. 92, figs. 1-3. Engraving. (Photo: author.)

168. Grandville, *Misery, Hypocrisy, Covetousness,* from *Les Métamorphoses du jour,* 1828–1830, pl. 14. Lithograph by Langlumé. (Photo: Courtesy National Library of Medicine, Bethesda, Md.)

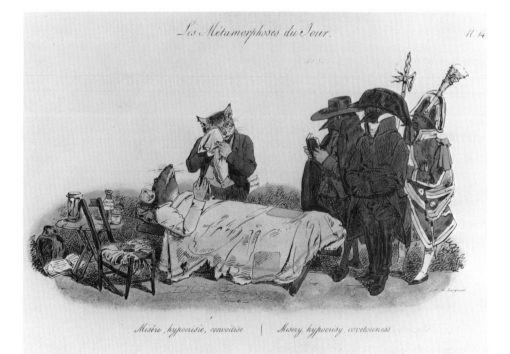

CONCEIVING

Pompeiian and Herculanean large-scale wall paintings[107]—were the eighteenth century's book of changes.

Gori connected multiform constructions of bird, lizard, ram, and eagle fragments to magic. He noted that such "grotesque copulations of imaginary bodies" were variously termed *gryllos, gryphos, aenigma.* La Chau and Le Blond spoke of such conglomerations, known from "an infinity of ancient intaglio gems," as if they were unrectified and unrectifiable floating anamorphoses (fig. 157). Masks existed "grouped & coupled in a thousand ways, sometimes carried on the feet of a bird, & sometimes so arranged that one could scarcely distinguish them except by searching for the right view point" (fig. 167, ii).[108] Like their colleagues, they were bewildered as to the possible aim of these miniature deformities. Was it ridicule? Were they moralized allegories alluding to vices, virtues, or passions? Were they merely the artist's caprices or fantasies? The commentators leaned toward satire as the most plausible interpretation of more straightforward human and animal bondings. But the singular heaping up of lifeless or unviable multiple masks entered "into the class of false witticisms."[109] We will return to the latter shortly. As to the former, Caylus had pointed the way with his publication of a bronze statuette of a toga-clad Roman senator wearing a bear's head (fig. 114). As an arch-Grecophile and one of the chief adversaries of Piranesi, it is significant that Caylus identified this as a Classical *critique,* or proper *charge*—notably taken up by Grandville in the nineteenth century in his anthropomorphized and fabulous bestiary (fig. 168). These sequential transformations, maintaining the clear identity of the two adjoined species, were bequeathed by the Greeks to the Romans, who in turn perverted them. As a classifier, Caylus noted that there were several categories of *satyriques.* This modulated deviation, or tolerable defect, was cryptic because the character of the lampooned person remained unknown. Thus it was impossible in modern times to recognize the jest or appreciate the subtlety of the banter. Another variation of the permissible "Greek *critique*" attached addorsed masks—such as those of Socrates and of a handsome youth—to a central bust (fig. 110). Caylus compared this carnelian—done in the right ornamental manner, or "nobly treated in the fantastic taste"—to extravagant and inanimate Roman and "Oriental" hodgepodge (fig. 167, i). He found it difficult to conceive a motive behind "those reversed heads, coupled & singularly grouped to form parts of different subjects," and facing pell mell in opposite directions (fig. 169). This base "*bizarrerie,* multiplied & repeated, to which the moderns have correctly given the name *chimera,* can only confuse the mind."[110]

Aßemblage de huit Têtes.

169. La Chau and Le Blond, *Assemblage of Eight Heads,* from *Description des principales pierres gravées,* 1780, II, pl. 64. Engraving. (Photo: author.)

NAPOLEON

170. Thomas Rowlandson, *Napoleon,*
1813. Aquatint and etching. National
Gallery of Art, Washington, D.C.,
Rosenwald Collection. (Photo: Courtesy
National Gallery of Art.)

Caylus's Roman hybrid farrago—interfertilizing different species by coupling three human-headed shields (two bearded and one clean-shaven) with the head of a pig—was, I suggest, the visual equivalent of Varronian or Menippean satire. It was all blatant screen, surface, facade. This nonillusionistic improbability may be looked upon as the esoteric mate to Rowlandson's jigsaw-puzzle portrait of *Napoleon* (fig. 170). Following the compositional principle of the improper *gryllus,* the British caricaturist obscenely inlaid a squirming tangle of naked bodies into the deathly still profile of the conqueror. The external organizational device of the portrait head was simultaneously undermined and distorted by the revolting internal patchwork. Rowlandson indiscriminately coupled animate with inanimate shapes and, even worse, jumbled the three kingdoms of nature. Similarly, the Greek Cynic philosopher Menippus, whose doctrine Varro followed, created "a Sort of Medley, consisting not only of all Kinds of Verse and Prose mix'd together," but of abnormal ribaldry, ridicule, and scurrilousness. It was the original chaotic plenum (*satur*), full of monstrosity. According to Trapp, whereas Horace designed jocose satires to reprove the vices and follies of mankind, and Juvenal devised serious poems for the same purpose, Menippus abandoned himself to the "wretchedly silly." He produced comic stage effects defying the laws of the organized universe and the structure of living organisms. There were "monstrous changes, as of *Progne* into a bird; *Cadmus* into a serpent; [these] are too gross to be imposed on the Senses: they are Representations therefore, not so much odious, as ridiculous."[111] These burlesque caricatures, like Rowlandson's hieroglyph of the emperor and Goya's grotesque composites (fig. 171), were patent fakes. They resembled those basilisks manufactured for the virtuoso's cabinet of curiosities, the heraldic beasts of chivalric romance, and other made-up freaks of bricolage intended to demonstrate mental fertility.[112] In that sense, they were a demonstrative and epideictic form of visual rhetoric that could be either satiric in censure or panegyric in sheer ornamental display.[113] It does not seem fortuitous that the *Capriccios* were given that title—common for graphic cycles since the sixteenth century—and that it was interchangeable with the rubrics of *grilli,* moods, and ingenious notions.[114] But Goya went far beyond the light and life-enhancing pleasures of making fantasies or, *scherzo*-like, just moving the paint around. The modern Menippean *gryllus,* nourished by numismatic collections or compendia of strange ancient symbols, constituted the basis for a new *capriccio* as dark caricature. It formed the elementary alphabet of Goya's "universal language." This subtitle for the print series suggests that it was intended to be a general

Todos Caerán.

171.   Francisco de Goya, *All Will Fall*,
from *Los Caprichos,* 1799, pl. 19. Aquatint
and etching. National Gallery of Art,
Washington, D.C., Rosenwald Collection.
(Photo: Courtesy National Gallery of Art.)

172. Francisco de Goya, *Here Comes the Bogey-Man,* from *Los Caprichos,* 1799, pl. 3. Aquatint and etching. National Gallery of Art, Washington, D.C., Rosenwald Collection. (Photo: Courtesy National Gallery of Art.)

Que viene el Coco.

critique—mounted by masquerading images—that spoke to all the world. It was not merely a negative advertisement or a distorting commercial, but was intended to enlist the viewer's participation in altering himself and thus revolutionizing his epoch. What Caylus desired to keep separated (the "natural" Horatian and Juvenalian satire from the unnatural Menippean grotesque), Goya indecently joined together (fig. 171). Moreover, as we have often had occasion to see, he embraced the entire gamut of monsters available to the Enlightenment. The eighty aquatints served up for the judgment of cultivated and uncultivated eyes alike the micromegalic abnormalities of gigantic excess and dwarfish deficiency rampant in Spanish society (figs. 172, 173). But it was specifically in those prints that relied on outrageous hybridization, or unnatural ridicule, that Goya most successfully decomposed and

CONCEIVING

Aquellos polbos.

deconstructed the unenlightened debris of his country and century. These scrurrilous bits and decorative pieces were recombined, without illusion or euphemism, into coarse aphorisms, giving evidence for proverbial superstition, injustice, and vice.

With Goya, we understand what it meant to see the world in grotesque terms. Decontextualized conglomerates, juxtaposed or crudely mixed, mirrored the modern condition of barbarism. The *Capriccios* offered a spectacle of permutable empty masks, bestial unions, and shifting viewpoints impossible to get right in this world. They no longer possessed the movable parts, fold-over techniques, or even the round volvelles used to illustrate the movement of planets common to sixteenth-century broadsheets. Yet the ready-made images, nonetheless, separated and joined both on the plate and in the viewer's consciousness.[115] Goya deliberately bred a race of disintegrating genetic mutants, divided from a simple and rational organic process. Detachable heads, limbs, and wings from diverse species were oddly resoldered and put on display as gobbets of distorted thought.

This chapter, then, has been about setting one thing against another, or allowing them imperceptibly to flow into one another, in the biological, mental, and aesthetic spheres. Barbarisms, monsters, *grylli*, and grotesques were polysemic combined pictures that sabotaged the clear and distinct monosemic good taste of intellectual, or spiritual, language. As rebuses or caricatures, they were instantaneous forms of visual and nonsequential communication. They captured the unregulated and vagrant patterns of erratic speech and freely darting thought. These trivial combinations were unlike esoteric emblems or difficult allegories and could be recognized by anyone. The latter were destined for the literate few—since they were modeled on writing—and required inscriptions in order to be "read." Grotesques, on the other hand, belonged to a continuous folk world of oral and visual usage making up a multisensory idiom.[116] They were the improper collage doubles of the high Enlightenment indoctrination by diagrammatic imagery.

For the eighteenth century, looking at monsters developed into an indoor sport. Caricatures were bought or rented, glass slides produced, and friends invited over to gape at the vulgar spectacle of the material body's grossest functions (fig. 174). Eating, drinking, fornicating, defecating needed no translation and were universally understood as aspects of daily life.[117] If lofty allegory magnified the spiritual and the conceptual (fig. 146), the grotesque twisted and minimized those same values through travesty and incongruous contiguity (fig. 133). Poinsinet de Sivry remarked that ridicule was like looking through a telescope. It diminished or exaggerated our esteem for an individual. For Sticotti, this external alteration in perception revolutionized our internal judgment through conversion or perversion. It was a constant refrain in analytical or philosophical criticism that the grotesque was a fault always manifested on the surface or exterior of a body. For the wordsmith guardians of a system of correct art, the grotesque dangerously pictured questionable or equivocal sexual acts and controversial amalgams. Ostentatious structural malformation, and provocative revolt against conventional mores, lay at the heart of its aesthetic operations. Dangerous and uncontrollable expressive freedom constituted its chief formal transgression, irrespective of the genre.[118]

174. Thomas Rowlandson, *A Magic Lantern*, 1799. Aquatint by Merke. National Gallery of Art, Washington, D.C., Rosenwald Collection. (Photo: Courtesy National Gallery of Art.)

175. Thomas Rowlandson, *The Bum Shop*, 1785. Aquatint and etching. National Gallery of Art, Washington, D.C., Rosenwald Collection. (Photo: Courtesy National Gallery of Art.)

From the rationalist and traditionalist perspective of the Enlightenment it seemed that the less civilized a people were, the more their language was figured and the greater their reliance on images. Conversely, intellectual refinement—think of Winckelmann—was congruent with the official eradication of barbaric tropes and obscene innovations. The artist should concentrate on the unproblematic generation of barely perceptible, immaterial ideas. This search for tasteful literacy, amid too much gross visualization ("bizarre chimeras," "bambochades," "grotesques"), motivated Mengs to lament that beauty was "no longer the product of genius but of the eyes." For the Neoclassicists, the filtered or censored symbol on the verge of visual extinction facilitated an escape to a pure and nonmaterial reality. But *Symbolon* also connoted an object broken into two pieces.[119] The grotesque thus pictured that disunited condition at its point of maximum separation from, and greatest distance between, radically disparate parts. This sort of symbol, denoting distraction not abstraction, configured the plight of the outsider. It indiscriminately embraced—without correcting or transforming them—a carnival of highwaymen, ventriloquists, enthusiasts, "old Raree show" exhibits, mutilated, handicapped, or diseased performers, and even eccentric painters (fig. 135).[120] The grotesque was an encyclopedia of actual but unreal *bambochades*. They appeared to be more specimens in a freak show than ordinary people (Figs. 175, 176). Yet these contradictory perceptual bundles gave aesthetic expression to experiences that otherwise would have received none. Lowly *jeux d'esprit* contravened social rules and proprieties. Consequently, they provided a framework for those bizarre, eccentric, confused, absurd, disaffected, distorted, and sick characters (fig. 177) and unamalgamated elements that lay beyond the pale of system.[121]

The fantastic hermaphroditism of the symbolic grotesque, then, imaged not only interlaced animal idols and coarse rustics, but all marginal and undigestable phenomena. Contrasting pairs were not submerged and well-chewed, but crudely entangled, as in mosaic, weaving, or metalwork. Arbitrary breaks in unity and forced links or patches exhibited the fact that these monsters were out of bounds (figs. 139, 140, 149, 156, 160, 161, 165, 170, 171). Moreover, in journalistic fashion, grotesques stitched together characters from their questionable accessories. The *Woman Warding off Cholera*, for example, was thick-sewn with multiple herbal- and patent-medicine remedies. Overloaded with extraneous pieces of physical detail, she resembled a mad *cento*, or bizarre quilt made up of scraps and rags.[122] This loss of humanity or

276

Si amanece ; nos Vamos.

176.   Francisco de Goya, *When Day
Breaks We Will Be Off,* from *Los
Caprichos,* 1799, pl. 71. Aquatint and
etching. National Gallery of Art,
Washington, D.C., Rosenwald Collection.
(Photo: Courtesy National Gallery of Art.)

PORTRAIT van een CHOLERA PRÄSERVATIVE VRAUW

Een flanel onderkleed met een koper borstlap, en weder een van gom Elasticum over dit kleed een
gordel van kleine kijsteenen, met een achteruitsliegende flip, van gewaschte taf de onderbroek aan de
voeten driedubbeld met kuiden zakken garneerd boven de schoenen warmflesschen Groote mouwen
met flanel gevoerd, hierin zijn doeken zandzakken en Borstels ingepakt, om den hals een Colier van Zout
steen en peperkorrels, in de drie haarvlechten heeft zij azijnflesjes, Chlor kalk potjes, op haar Kruin
een moletje om de lucht te reinigen, ooringen van Knoflo en vijen, waaraan noch een Kamphor fles
je hangt, een lint welk onder de kin toegebonden van Jeneverbessen met een parfumeur fles, in de
hand een mandje met een oekonomisch vuurhaard onderbuik & in de andere hand een opgeslagen
parasol met een fleertak, kleine zakjes met chlor kalk hangen aan de balijnen aan de punt een nootschel
haar schoothontje loopt achter na! met een Cholera band om het lijf votjes in sokte, draagt nog een kle
steerspuit, om den hals een kopere plaat met de inschrift niet bang.

177. Anonymous, *Cholera Prevention,*
19th c. Colored engraving. (Photo: Courtesy
National Library of Medicine, Bethesda, Md.)

CONCEIVING

viability by drowning in *parerga* was scorned by those who would turn art into an inferior form of philosophy. Lessing and Sulzer spoke on behalf of a legion of classicizing critics when they declared that secondary things (*Neben-sachen*) must never obtrude upon, or occlude, the primary actors in a composition.[123] "Inlays," "variegated spots," gapped mosaics overtly "strewn with stones," constituted a venerable, language-fueled vocabulary directed against visual sweepings. Daring to combine into parodic and misshapen unity, they became the roistering images of leveling masquerade.[124]

Chaotic mixture allowed the low to assume equal status with the high and threatened to crowd the latter out of existence. Crousaz drew a social and political analogy validating a state-approved art. It was difficult for the multitude to distinguish between licentious or tyrannical freedom and right-thinking equality. Some members of the third estate wanted honors to rotate, which was tantamount to having them depend on blind caprice. "Such an exaggerated egalitarianism offers nothing beautiful, it reverses all proportions, destroys regularity, it is only a confused union."[125] For Batteux, humped and lame contrarieties were a threat to sanctioned government because they were like "a continual barbarism," or amalgam of strange and superfluous words foreign to the ruling and dominant usage.[126] Dennis and Oldmixon found "the vulgar" and "the peasant" to be similarly given over to ruleless extravagance. They were ignorant "of all other Distinction, but that of a Jest and a Dull."[127] Even Hogarth compared the dehumanizing invasion of a profusion of unimportant shapes to Vaucanson's unthinking automaton-duck. "The more variety we pretend to give our trifling movements, the more confused and unornamental the forms become." For Lichtenberg, "the parade of worthless trinkets," of "foolish jokes and filthy things," of illogical juxtapositions, bred not only deformity but lifelessness.[128] These mannered and implausible counterfeits, ill-suited and ill put together, could not survive in the mainstream of art or life. The extreme, heaped-up grotesque was not generated but artificially reproduced. From the standpoint of proper assemblies and well-regulated organizations, it was stillborn and nonexistent.

4 MARKING

Contagious Pointillism

To walk into the museum of the Hôpital Saint-Louis in Paris is to change one's view of the world (fig. 178). The handsome building—situated on what had been the outskirts of the city and originally dedicated to the care of the poor and the contagious—houses the scholarly works of the founders of modern dermatology. Foremost among them are Lorry and Astruc, Willan and the charismatic Alibert, of whom more later.[1] But it is the cabinet of cutaneous horrors, located on the second floor, that arrests the modern beholder. The overwhelming exhibits, compressed into this large room and spilling into the adjacent corridor, remind the spectator that this, of all diagnostic disciplines, was predicated from its eighteenth-century beginnings on direct observation. Moreover, the abhorrent contents proclaim unforgettably that one age's abnormalities are another's normalities. The walls are lined with glass cases containing four thousand polychrome waxes reproducing every imaginable dermatologic affliction. The lifelike simulacra were intended for use in nosographical instruction. Some five hundred of these monstrous corporeal fragments were created between 1867 and 1914 by the Belgian specialist in startlingly realistic papier-maché fruits, Jules-Pierre-François Baretta (1834–1923).[2]

These surgical casts, although dating from the nineteenth century, open an otherwise inaccessible prospect onto the European urban street before our

Contagion _____

noun, The emission from body to body by which diseases are communicated; infection; propagation of mischief, or disease; pestilence; venemous emanations.

Dr. Johnson, *Dictionary*

Contagion _____

noun, Quality of a disease, by which it can pass from the affected subject to a healthy subject, and produce in the latter a malady of the same type. . . . Contagious illnesses are communicated, either through direct contact, or through clothing, furniture or other infected bodies, or even by the air which can transmit at a considerable distance certain miasmas or morbidic seeds [semences]. . . .

Diderot and D'Alembert, *Encyclopédie*

178.   Jules-Pierre-François Baretta, et al.,
*Wax and Resin Casts of Cutaneous
Diseases,* Musée de l'Hôpital Saint-Louis.
(Photo: Courtesy Bibliothèque Henri
Feulard, Musée de l'Hôpital Saint-Louis,
Paris.)

era. Baretta's terrifying display is a sobering witness to the fact that in days before x-ray, ultrasound, SPECT, and other imaging modalities, diseases only existed when they became manifest on the skin. Today, as with fetal abnormalities, physicians generally catch disorders when they are still hidden from sight, or subcutaneous. But in the museum, the visitor is catapulted into the past when the sufferer nakedly wore his disgusting symptoms. Like the early modern city dweller, the beholder is compelled to stare at a vast medical encyclopedia of epidermal marks. These relentlessly showed the evolution and often fatal course of infantile syphilis, scarlatina, measles, mumps, leprosy, scurvy, scrofula, lupus, smallpox, ringworm, and impetigo. In addition, there were countless and nameless running sores, ulcerated scabs, fungous infections, and disfiguring spots that would not heal. The painful severity of the toxic cures were also faithfully recorded. Caustic ravages of mercury- and iodide-treated flesh were juxtaposed with untreated variegated welts, spongy tumors, and parasitic excrescences. These surface erosions and growths dehumanized a person, transforming him into a vegetable or mineral travesty. To encounter such grotesques today one must travel in sub-Saharan African, trawl the edges of the Caribbean, brave the poorest of India's states, the most backward of Latin American countries, or simply conjure up the global nightmare of AIDS.

This medical panorama, unfurling the universal garb of rot, instantaneously clarifies the premium placed during the Enlightenment on an aesthetics of immaculateness. Given the prevalence of perceptible illnesses, the perfect eighteenth-century countenance—oval in shape, with regular features, a white, flawless complexion, and lightly carmined cheeks—was as rare and mythic as the ideal work of art. Both preexisted either as an unrealizable conception in the mind or as an abstract taken from myriad and marred incarnations. The poisonous ceruse of cosmetics, and the white-lead primer for canvases, helped blemished phenomena to put on a good face in public. As a concealing mask or smoothing ground, they attempted to obliterate existential signs. False ornaments of ruptured capillaries and ugly discolorations, or pathetic patterns of bodily decay, made mortality uniquely visible. This chapter is about the fascination with segmented skin and its uncanny powers for making seen the unseen, fragmentary self. Further, it speaks of perceptible differences and the difficulty of their integration into a confederated whole. It shows that art, like dermatology, is fundamentally about the concealment or display of stigmatization. The artist is someone who both makes a mark and is marked.

It was no accident that a preoccupation with surface-deep beauty dominated drawing manuals and treatises on the visual arts, and more generally supplied epidermal metaphors and analogies to a whole array of social, political, and religious experiences. Consequently, one reads with a new and sympathetic comprehension those perpetual injunctions to copy perfect models, or the best limbs and members, derived from figures prescreened by art.[3] Litanies of what to relinquish—such as parts "disagreeable to the Sight"—take on a different slant and become more than mere academic drill. Bickham was one of many to indicate that there was only a single way of being healthy and lovely, but an infinity of ways of being sick and wretched. This dermatological aesthetics transfigured the squamose and scurfy natural body into an icon unlike anything seen in ordinary life. In this light, too, Winckelmann's disquisitions concerning the pampered, fluvial skin of ancient sculpture reflected the distaste of "people of condition" for filthy, gross, or unimproved anatomy. We can now understand that revolting superficial concavities and convexities, or loathesome breaches and wounds, were to be avoided at all costs. Objects full of hollows were to be shunned, as well as those "broken in pieces or parcels; all those things inhuman, shocking to the eyes . . . in short, all things which corrupt their natural Forms, by a confusion of their parts which are entangled in each other: For the Eye looks down with Horrour on those Things which the Hands will not condescend to touch."[4]

Algarotti noted that it was imperative in the education of the artist that he learn "to embellish the most hideous head of a [studio] model."[5] But it was Diderot who wrote most searchingly and expansively on the gulf yawning between the real, unamended, mortified human being and the ideal type. Adumbrating the pessimism of Baudelaire, he declared in the *Eléments de physiologie*: "On the entire surface of the earth, there is not a single man perfectly constituted, perfectly sound. The human species is only a mass of individuals more or less deformed, more or less ill." The materialist *philosophe* sardonically commented that, under these circumstances, humanity was not obliged to offer a eulogy to the Creator; rather, He owed it an apology! Not just mankind but beasts, plants, even minerals evaded Leibniz's optimistic tag, "everything is good," to heed, instead, Diderot's motto, "everything is bad" relative to our idea of perfection.[6] But it was the introduction to the *Salon of 1767*—composed after he had read Richardson and Winckelmann ("our modern Plato")—that offered a protracted Neoplatonic reflection on the difference between the faultless, inalterable ideal and the servile, flawed copy.

Again, his musings were prompted by actual sights. Among the bevy of feminine heads dotting the Jardin de Luxembourg or the arcades of the Palais-Royal on a splendid day, or encountered on a promenade, or at the theater, or during a social gathering, not one was perfectly symmetrical or possessed even features. Not now or ever had an animal, or even a portion of one, existed that had not suffered and become in some way deformed. None, therefore, could serve the painter as "primary model." Lichtenberg similarly remarked that earthly bodies did not unfold within the ether. Their exposure to a miasmic atmosphere generated irregularities and defects. Whereas the pathognomist valued the environmental incursion of accidents, Diderot stressed the need for a reforming and refining vision of truth stemming from a mental emanation. The act of making something beautiful necessarily implied that the artist was making what was not, and could never be. To create a statue of a lovely woman, the sculptor was forced to undress many women, many of whom exhibited "deformed parts." Thus nature's works were tainted, shadowy and degenerate *phantasmata*. Diderot likened this activity of withdrawal from the maladies of the world to the artist's distancing himself from microscopic face-painting. He must remove himself from the "false line" to ascend to the general archetype that existed nowhere. The impaired *ligne portraitique* was consonant with the infirm and unbred appearances found in daily life.[7] Laugier, in the *Manière de bien juger*, took up Diderot's semiotics of defilement. Nature rarely produced the beautiful. Not only did it frequently present the mediocre but, worse, the shapeless and the defective. Life's supposed marvels were "rarely pure & without mixture."[8]

Lavater—who also absorbed Winckelmann's epidermal vocabulary—connected contemporary stains to the decline of a corrupted race. "We are but the refuse of past generations." Relying on a powerful symptomology of spots, scars, and warts, he contrasted the luminous soundness, elegant forms, and lustral simplicity of the ancient Greeks with his depraved contemporaries' traits, speckled by dirty vices and infectious diseases. The spiritual condition of the abscessed moderns was described in somatic and pathological terms. Lavater's dermatological constructs evoked a procession of stigmatized patients wearing the blotched mien of their distempers. Jaundice, burning fevers, squinting eyes, and, above all, the heterogeneous patches of venereal disease comprised the "unclean marks of mortality" (figs. 7, 8).[9] Lavater's theological nosology relied upon the venerable belief that only the resurrected face was fair. At the end of time, the maculate visage would become immaculate, would be "renewed according *to the Image of Him who created it*, not

179. Chérubim D'Orléans, *Lunar Spots,*
from *La Dioptrique oculaire,* 1671, p. 298.
Engraving. (Photo: Courtesy National
Library of Medicine, Bethesda, Md.)

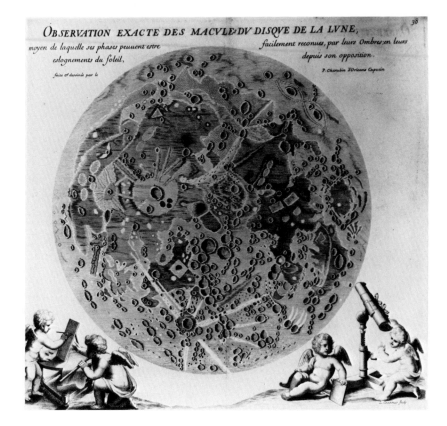

having spot or wrinkle or any such thing, but . . . holy and without blemish."
Similarly for the Deist Mengs, all corporeal phenomena were ragged,
unequal, with clefts and gaps ruining their lineaments as in a misjoined work.
Thus surrounded by scattered imperfections, the eye could not see unitary
perfection. Rather, the soul must feel what lies hidden under corroded surfaces, or remember the divine uniformity lying beyond the sensible
hodgepodge.[10]

These authors leaned on the time-honored analogy between *chroma* and *chros.*
Both Greek terms, signifying color, had as their primary meaning "the surface
of the body" or "skin."[11] That is, tints were thought to lie, or float, on the
tops of objects. They thus rendered the otherwise imperceptible material
world perceptible by their coloration or, more aptly for us, their discoloration
of planes. Further, Roman rhetoric developed the analogy by binding a
chromatic physiology together with ethics. Quintilian spoke of "figures of
complexion" (*colores*) that imparted a particular cast to a cause. *Complexio* thus
referred to the properly or improperly tinctured countenance of things. The
simile was predicated on establishing a tight link between normal or abnormal
physical appearance and the general moral makeup of a person or arrangement
of a visual argument.[12] Consequently, a disfiguring gallimaufry of mottled
scales or lesions on the body, or stubble and pits on the flatland of a painting,
violated the decorum of sight. Propriety of aspect undergirded the theory of

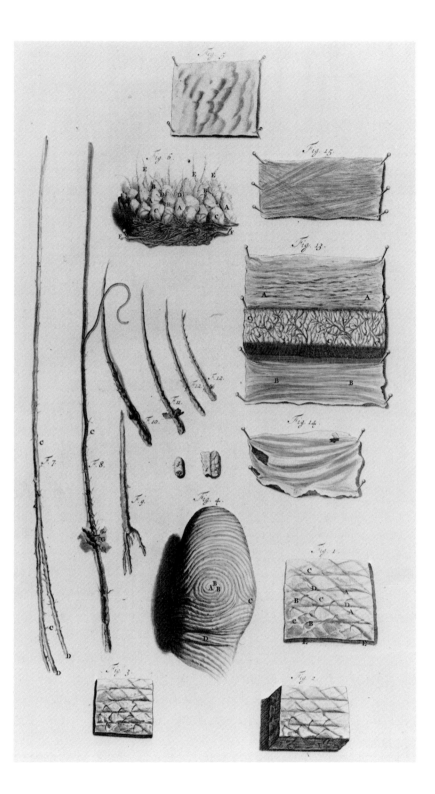

180. William Cowper, *Various Portions of the Cuticula,* from *Anatomia Corporum Humanorum,* 1750, pl. 4. Drawing and engraving by Gerard de Lairesse. (Photo: Courtesy National Library of Medicine, Bethesda, Md.)

reflective imitation. Mirrors bounced back rays at the same angle at which they struck the glass, such that the reflection suffered the "least disorder and the slightest disarrangements." Algarotti, in explaining Newtonian optics to his marquise, used the example of light emitted from her limpid face. Like the mirror, her complexion was unified, smooth, even. If, however, it had

rough spots, inequalities, i.e., if portions of the surface formed elevations or variously inclined levels, then the beams could not rebound regularly . . . ; they would follow the direction impressed upon them by the tiny depressions on which they fell; they would disperse to all sides, & this irregular reflection would prevent it [the glass] from duplicating the image facing it. [13]

Such unruffled uniformity of surface was as rare in a likeness as on the ground or in the water. The isolatable and pocked features of sublunar reality resembled Newton's redefined prismatic bundle of light (fig. 179). They were neither pure nor simple, but a separable and colored aggregate of reflectable and refractable parts. [14]

The purest or most flawless-seeming complexion was not uniform (fig. 180). The anatomist Cowper illustrated magnified "thin" (no. 1) or "thick" (no. 2) segments of the cuticula raised from the back of the hand or taken from the sole of the foot. Even in a healthy dermis, such as that found on the tip of a thumb (no. 4), the cuticle was "variously wreathed and contoured, conformable to the subjacent papillary Protuberances of the True Skin." Stripping off the former to reveal the latter, or cutis, still resulted in a microscopic vision of an irregular geology: furrows (no. 1, BB), bladderlike elevations (no. 1, CC), and "divers *Strata* or Beds of Scales." One episode in this riveting account of subcutaneous travel provided startling proof that the surface of even the most fine-grained body, when viewed with an enlarging lens, was like an assemblage. A minuscule slice of dermis (no. 6) bristled with pyramidal papillae (AA), tiny aqueous vessels or pigment capillaments (BB), sweat glands (CC), hairs (EE), nerves, and lymph ducts (FF). Cowper concluded with the same message hawked by every successful eighteenth-century seller of masking pomades, vanishing creams, and ablutionary lotions. "Hence it appears that the skin can no more be esteem'd a Similar or Simple Part, than any of those call'd Dissimilar or Compounded Parts." [15]

In the age of smallpox, itch, and scurvy, however, this declaration was no more than an ironic truism. Glazing the pores with artificial pink and white paint was not mere vanity or Boucher-glamour, but a social duty. Dexterously laying on a lunar coating of disguising powders and prophylactic unctions represented a thoughtful gesture of *politesse.* [16] It was courteous not to offend tender sensibilities by the revolting display of facial disease. Andry, in *L'Or-thopédie*, compiled a fearsome catalogue of complexional blights marshaled and ready to attack the ideal floral tint. The latter was a matte alabaster or lily, melded with a hint of rose. Departures from this budding perfection ranged from birthmarks, extreme pallor, excessive redness, to a greasy shine. Such fake radiance, characteristic of unhealthy "dolls of the palace" or street grisettes, was the result of rubbing the face morning and evening with bouillon until it glowed in the dark.[17]

Artificial colors, or cosmetics, signified the conspicuous application of method to an imperfect body. In the eighteenth century, these artful preparations were meant to improve a horrendous nature. As a logic for regulating the mutable integument, they conformed to an aesthetic ideal rarely, if ever, discovered in actual experience. Pomatum presented a unified effect through the ostentatious covering of weak points and eyesores. Like a foreign or dead language, the unnaturally encased countenance seemed fixed, eternal, and immune from decay.[18] If disease was protean in its ability to destroy linea-ments, makeup was a permanent and alien system overlying fluctuating physiology in a manner incongruent with, or remote from, damaged human nature. Like artistic style, it was a foreign remedy pasted over material poverty, whitewashing disfigurement and miraculously restoring a ravaged corporeality.[19] Charles Baudelaire (1821–1867) was following in the footsteps of those eighteenth-century irregulars, the charlatan-vendors of hygiene and grooming aids, when he founded his aesthetics on the antithesis of "the natural look." "In Praise of Make-Up," from *The Painter of Modern Life* (1863), com-plimented the heroism of women. He found especially valiant feminine attempts, from time immemorial, to consolidate and immortalize fleeting beauty. In the poet's hand, talc became a curative nostrum whose purpose "was to hide all the blemishes that nature has so outrageously scattered over the complexion, and to create an abstract unity of texture and colour in the skin, which unity, like the one produced by tights, immediately approximates the human being to a statue, in other words to a divine or superior being."[20] As for mascara and rouge, these outlandish and erotic ornaments had the opposite effect. Instead of a monochromatic art of contrivance that concealed blots, these satanic decorations exacerbated the chance disfunction or acci-dental malformation. Contouring the rims of the eyes and flagrantly accen-tuating the cheeks with daubs of red also surpassed nature in a kind of epidermal barbarism. Moreover, this divisionist punctuation interrupted the timeless powdery mask and signified "a supernatural, excessive life" experienced by a singular and temporal human being.[21] Baudelaire's Romantic pointillism sinned twiced against the decorum of classical expression. First, he spurned legitimate and blending variety by advocating the monotony of appearing "all of one complexion." The overly treated face, like the porelessly primed surface of a picture, resembled closely woven cloth or small ivories that possessed no consistency because of an exaggerated *délicatesse*. For Bouhours, this hyperbolically subtle, finespun, and "quintessenced" manner evaporated matter.[22] Furthermore, extreme uniformity flouted religious strictures. Makeup wrongfully concealed the sinful *tunicae pellicae*, or soiled and diseased body, that God gave to Adam and Eve as a sign of their muddy vices.[23] Second, Baudelaire condoned the opposite, fragmenting and particularizing fault of style within the same somatic and artistic composition. As an accompaniment to evenness, he allowed for the seemingly tautological repetition of tiny formal units (black outlines and red smudges). Georges Seurat's (1859–1891) pleonastic and prismatic dots were the logical extension of such willful redundancy. The divisionist burdened a blank canvas with a superfluity of sameness, a plague of excessively dissected minutiae, a contagion of spoiling spots.

Skin disease hit the poor especially ruthlessly. It was an affliction specifically, although certainly not exclusively, of the anonymous and otherwise faceless crowd. This throng lived in the dank filth and reek of cramped northern European cities. Eczemas, tubercules, mange, and pruritus erupted and spread within such immured institutions of the Enlightenment as the prison, the hospital, the poorhouse, the military camp, and the maritime industry. But the phenomenon was not new. The anticivic and rootless rabble jumbled within late antique Mediterranean metropolises aroused Proclus's invectives. He fulminated against the overwhelming multitude, simply defined as "people in a city." The aesthetic, political, and medical durability of the metaphor of vulgar and "mobbing" variegation, as "the most pedestrian part of us," testified to a constant within the historical landscape. Spotting scourges and irrational morbidity came and went with the unwashed flux of the counterculture. This teeming, material mass was not controllable like "the people." The latter was "united to itself," whereas the former was an indeterminate, incoherent, confused, and riotous "populace." Mob rule, or orochlocracy, thus differed from democracy, drawn up under the laws, by its conspicuous and fractious divisibility.[24] This heterogeneous manifold gave evidence of social discord, just as its unsavory *corpus* betokened infection by being riddled with alarming blurs and bruises. The healthy and wellborn few tried to maintain their distance from this fickle and slovenly swarm. As we have seen, the purificatory metaphors of cleansing bath, abstract void, and surgical amputation were meant to keep disorderly contagion at bay in all spheres. At a fundamental level, Neoclassicism was about establishing stable and negative zones of purified emptiness, or swept privacy, within an opaque groundswell.

To be sure, eighteenth-century London or Paris far exceeded the challenges to traditional authority accompanying the waning days of the Roman Empire. Sprawling urban conglomerations raised inevitable hazards of faulty sanitation. Pollution expanded with an accelerated industrial growth unknown to the ancient polis.[25] Perusing the medical treatises on rampant contamination in the early modern period, the twentieth-century reader is struck by the increasing power of disease to permeate. The ubiquitous presence of dirt and excrement, noxious vapors, vitiated atmosphere, adulterated food in markets or fairs, made it more difficult to shield an inviolable group or community from the perils of admixture. No class was immune from the vision of outsiders parading their abject penury and deteriorating flesh in the street. The city, then, was the archetypal milieu of evil and death, the site of shocking squalor and sick air. The malodorous urban setting thus became the prime locus for posing the ancient problem of the barbaric invasion of a lethal and impecunious otherness, with all its ethical, metaphysical, and artistic dimensions.[26]

The British physician Joseph Adams's (1756–1818) investigation *Epidemic Diseases* (1809) graphically outlined the dangers of infected social contact. Fatal pestilences multiplied and rapidly spread wherever "men congregated in numbers." His experience with London's smallpox and inoculation dispensaries confirmed him in the belief that crowding prevented the community from having enough of "the common air." And if an illness did arise in such a perniciously enclosed space, then a new or septic "artificial air was generated." Camp, ship, jail, or hospital fevers contaminated the healthy by inducing a similar malady in them. Adams echoed the popular belief that spotted plagues (smallpox, measles, scarlet fever) were unknown in antiquity. It was generally believed that these arose, and were mercilessly transmitted, among the volatile urban poor in recent times. To stem this uncontrollable tide drowning the already distressed, he presciently suggested an agenda of reforms. Chief among them was the preventative measure of paying larger wages so people could afford better living quarters. Adams, like contemporary epidemiologists, recognized that major outbreaks depended both on the constitution of the atmosphere and on "the state of society."[27]

This physiological, sociological, and ontological interpretation of massive and sporadic distempers held that they were transported either from another, polluted country, or from that foreign, inferior territory located within one's own nation. This uncontainable island of domestic strife and feverish torment lay outside the state's official preserve of health, sanity, and reason.[28] In his taxonomy of barbaric pestilence, Sir James Carmichael Smyth (1740–1826), physician extraordinary to George III, distinguished two major kinds. Specific incursions, such as smallpox or measles, happened only once in any given individual. But general contaminations arose from a general putrid cause seditiously fermenting in nature, to which "water as well as all vegetable and animal substances, under certain circumstances, are liable." His medical treatise on *Contagion* (1799) also harped on the fact that both types developed when masses of people were "shut up in a close place, without the greatest attention to cleanliness, and a renewal of air." He painted a repellent picture of the eighteenth-century urban compost heap. Prisoners, almshouse denizens, infirmary or asylum inmates, and sailors wallowed in perspiration, excretion, and fumes. The virulent corruption penetrated not only the body of the oppressed, but their clothing, furniture, walls, the boards of their habitations, and even the sides of their ships. Putrefaction—propagated through direct communication, through breath, touch, and sheer contiguity of effluvia—possessed a distinctive physiognomy. Its dread symptoms were those dissident "appearances of the skin," indicating the breakdown of solid flesh, the shattering of somatic integrity, the destruction of pigmentation.[29]

But it was the French, both before and after the Revolution, who took the lead in rehabilitating one major source of persistent contamination, the public hospital. Smyth, for example, cited the chemist Louis-Bernard Guyton de Morveau's (1737–1816) *Instructions* for fumigating and purifying the air in the military hospitals of the Republic.[30] Further, it could be argued that crowding fostered the emergence, after the middle of the eighteenth century, of a practical observational medicine. Specialized medical centers became epidemiological sites for teaching, research, and, above all, optical examination.[31] They advanced knowledge concerning the perceptible signs of rare and common illness springing from an enforced close proximity.

Of the forty-eight hospitals in Paris on the eve of the Revolution, none was more ruinous in its disorder than the gigantic Hôtel-Dieu, a medieval charitable institution located in the heart of the capital. Its crying need for modernization, for a rational plan in the care of the sick, improved hygiene, and financial reform in management, did not substantially differ in kind but only in scale from other *ancien régime* public health organizations. One thinks of the Infirmerie de la Charité, the Hospice de Bicêtre, and the Salpêtrière. For their unhappy occupants, little distinction existed between being impoverished and being ill. The deplorable condition of the patients—three to four were commonly obliged to share the same bed—and the noxious habit of mixing different diseases on the same ward, led to the highest death rate (25 percent) in Europe. When the sinister establishment burned in 1772, medical reformers such as Cabanis, Pinel, and Vicq d'Azyr rejoiced.[32]

I shall not trace the convoluted saga of success and failure accompanying the Hôtel-Dieu's rebuilding on the same spot. Significant is the fact that the investigatory report of 1777, issuing from the Académie des Sciences's Commission Charged to Examine the Means for Ameliorating the Diverse Hospitals of the City of Paris and ordered by Necker, led to the future specialization of Parisian infirmaries. Thus, in 1780, the Hôpital Saint-Louis opened its doors as a new parish hospice. Formerly this venerable annex of the Hôtel-Dieu, erected under Henri IV in 1607, had served the northern sector of the city's population only in periods of epidemics. The final transformation of this erstwhile sanitorium into a general center for immunology, welcoming all patients suffering from chronic diseases, took place in year III of the Revolutionary era, under the architect Nicolas-Marie Clavareau (1757–1816). Thereafter, the Hôpital Saint-Louis rapidly became the regnant model for a new and salubrious pavilion arrangement that was to dominate infirmary construction for the next century. The innovative and low-slung multiple structures, grouped around an open court, allowed for the free circulation of air. These buildings thus displaced the old and frightening monolithic block that hermetically sealed in fetid fumes. Most importantly, however, and under the brilliant direction of Alibert, this hospital was destined to become the premier clinic for the study of skin disease.[33]

Cutaneous pathology was the heart of darkness of the Enlightenment. What were these unclean invasions of macules and papules; how did they look; and what metaphors captured their poisonous sprawl? In short, what was der-

The Cow Pock _ or _ the Wonderful Effects of the New Inoculation! _ Vide. the Publications of y̆ Anti-Vaccine Society.

181. James Gillray, *The Cow-Pock,* 1802. Colored etching. (Photo: Courtesy National Library of Medicine, Bethesda, Md.)

matology before Alibert's invention of dermatology? A putrid and festering state of the skin, vermin-infested, with blotches and eruptions, was a rebuke to social and religious order. For the eighteenth century, the creeping rash of smallpox and a confusing array of foul venereal maladies largely supplanted leprosy as the prime source of external disfigurement. The latter, which could appear as unnaturally livid as talc, or as red as an unfused mosaic of pustulant boils, was frequently confounded with psoriasis, eczema, and leukoderma.[34] Leprosy's unblended palette of minute and juxtaposed particles of pigment ruptured corporeal integrity.[35] From antiquity down through the Middle Ages, a shining hue and randomly distributed blisters constituted the iconography of this unclean curse. Its divisionist splashes symbolized impurity, sin, and defilement, just as the leper's clapper and ointment jar signaled avoidance. The stigma of moral violation, sexual license, and heterodoxy clung to softened bones or cartilage and to tattered flesh, dead in life.[36] An extensive biblical and patristic literature, extolling simplicity and spotlessness, testified to the opprobrium attached to a complexion stained with many changing colors and brilliant points.[37] Cutaneous lesions besmirched mankind's originally luminous and immaculate congenital vestures. They garbed a guilty humanity in small violaceous scabs and a false or glaring whiteness. This mottled clothing was like the symbolic emblems sullying the condemned heretic's shirt of shame.[38]

But it was smallpox—first differentiated in the sixteenth century from the huge pustules of syphilis, or the great pox—that literally transfixed and transfigured the eighteenth century. As late as Charles Aubry's graphic satire on minor and major illnesses, or the *Album comique* (1823), it was the subject of bitter doggerel. "Strike the face! That is the war-whoop of smallpox: the nose, the mouth, the eyes dissolve as in a cast, and it is useless to hope for the chance of a recast, since the results are so plainly predictable." When discrete, it left behind "pleasant ditches, agreeably raking up the uniformity of the skin." When tumescent or confluent, the gray mien was "ploughed in a thousand furrows"—sinking an eye, swelling a nose—until even friends were unable to identify the sufferer.[39] Aubry mordantly proselytized on behalf of vaccination, just as Gillray militantly opposed it. The British caricaturist preyed on the worst fears of his bumpkins. He satirized the metamorphic potential of inoculation, in this case against the cowpox (fig. 7).[40] Gillray wittily suggested that exposure to the ministrations of Edward Jenner's (1749–1823) Vaccine Institute threatened the purity of the race by producing bulbous hybrids and animal-shaped eruptions (fig. 181). Underlying these visual jokes lay serious concerns. Like the current discussions about donor organs and transplants, the early debates over inoculation questioned the physician's right deliberately to introduce a harm into the system. Further, they asked what fundamental transformations might occur in the receiver when a foreign body was injected into the bloodstream.

But to return to smallpox. Contemporary historians of medicine claim that this scourge was the ancient "pestilence of fire." They identify it with the "Plague of Athens" that melted and calcined the sufferer's body into a raised relief of malignant atoms or a depressed checkerboard of craters (fig. 182). Thucydides gave a memorable account of its arrival from Ethiopia, its subsequent sweep through Egypt and Libya, and its ultimate decimation of the Greeks during the Peloponnesian War (430 BC).[41] This, however, was not the typical view of the Enlightenment. Jean-Jacques Paulet (1740–1826), in his epic *Histoire de la petite vérole* (1768), scoured chronicles stretching from Cicero to Gregory of Tours (528 AD), to Marius, Bishop of Avranches (570 AD), and to Ambroise Paré, for evidence of this assault and battery of the countenance. His analysis was etymological. The proof of a disease's newness was the

182. Jean-Louis Alibert, *Pustulant Smallpox,* from *Clinique de l'Hôpital Saint-Louis,* 1833, pl. 9. Colored stipple engraving by Tresca after Moreau and Valvile. (Photo: Courtesy National Library of Medicine, Bethesda, Md.)

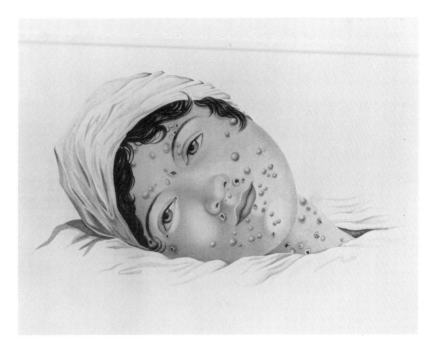

183. Tessier (?), *Bust of Mirabeau,* 1791. Plaster. Musée de Carnavalet. Copyright 1990 ARS N.Y./SPADEM.

absence of an ancient Greek or Latin designation. No such lack characterized modern European idioms. He pinpointed its initial appearance in Gaul and Italy during the sixth century, and noted that the onslaught was accompanied by an explosion of aggressive vocabulary. Gregory termed it *valetudines, variae morbine*, to denote that "bizarre and particolored assemblage of morbid maladies joined by their pustules & vesicles on the skin." Marius added the feminine suffix of *ola*—appropriate to the terminology of a postlapsarian disease—to Gregory's *varia*. This neologism "painted" the prismatic appearance of the eruption, just as the medley of measles was picturesquely seized by the words *rubeola* or *roseola*. By the thirteenth century, this plague of small red dots had stormed every corner of Europe and left its imprint on vernacular languages. The German *Pocken* and the French *picote* vividly captured its cannonade effects by alluding to the cruel beak of a bird that pecked, and to a pick, or farm tool, that poked and dug holes in smooth terrain.[42] Rare was the person who then or later turned these brutal ravages into an advantage. The Comte de Mirabeau (1749–1791), the most powerful orator of the French Revolution, member of the *Comité de Cinq*, and, in 1791, president of the Assemblé Nationale, was famous for being ugly as Satan. Deeply scarred when still a child by confluent smallpox, this turbulent and irascible friend of the physician Cabanis proudly displayed his excavated skin. It was the corporeal stigma that best symbolized his uncosmeticized and tough individuality (fig. 183).

If there were doubts about when to date the inception of smallpox, no one wondered about the existence of sexual *polluti* in antiquity. They were chased from Israel's camps and mocked by Juvenal.[43] Fallopius (1523–1562) suggested that syphilis—which had attained epidemic proportions in the sixteenth century—derived from *syn philos* ("companion in love"), or the Homeric *sys philos* ("swine-lover"). Although, along with gonorrhea, it had existed in Europe before Columbus, sailors subsequently bore the blame for introducing this peppering foulness attacking the genitals and shelling the features.[44] Paulet attributed to Rabelais the acuity of having first noted the resemblance between the pox and the clap. But he vehemently denied that the former was the offspring of the latter, as was commonly thought. Be that as it may, the raking symptoms of both comprised a repertory of false Rococo ornament, a decorator's synthetic collage of morbidity. The forehead was striped with a pimply "crown of Venus," the temples were veined with hard buds or "white flowers," the cheeks were marbled with red and horny pustules.[45] John Hunter's *Treatise on Venereal Disease* (1786) similarly reinforced the distinction

184. William Hogarth, *Visit to the Quack Doctor*, from *Marriage à la Mode*, 1743–1745, pl. 3. Engraving by C. Mottram. (Photo: Courtesy National Library of Medicine, Bethesda, Md.)

between an incursion of the *lues venera* and the inroads of scorbutic smallpox. But this tract was composed after Wallis's, Cook's, and Bougainville's voyages to the Pacific. Thus both poisons were compared to unnatural tattoos or "artificial impressions" scarring the body. Hunter predictably attributed the deadly malady to the French. Citing the account of Cook's third voyage, he lamented that the affliction—which the amorous Tahitians ascribed to intercourse with Bougainville's men—had taken its toll in the once pristine South Sea paradise. Initially entering the organs of generation, the lethal matter eventually assailed the rest of the constitution. These forays into healthy strongholds brought with them a host of attendant ailments that punched endless grapeshot into the epidermis. A rush of "blotches on the skin," canker sores, "breaches in the solids," sycosis, scabies, porrigo of the scalp, indicated how one spotted "disorder excited another."[46]

This fearsome imitation continued in a beleaguered and sapped reproduction. "Impure coition," or what Pierre Fabre (1716–1796) in the *Maladies vénériennes* (1773) termed commerce with "a spoiled person," resulted in pocky mothers giving birth to blistered children. Moreover, wet nurses could be contaminated by suckling "a foul child." Since the malady routinely went underground and could be transmitted when the symptoms were invisible, women might unwittingly continue to "breed" scabbed, "scurfy," "sallow," and discolored infants.[47] The babies they propagated were "half rotten," and covered with ulcers. The physician and Fellow of the Royal Society, John Gregory (1753–1821), marveled that one constantly witnessed sensible people anxious to "preserve or improve, the breed of their horses," yet who thought nothing of "tainting the blood of their children, and entailing on them, not only the most loathsome diseases of the body, but madness, folly."[48] John Wall's (1708–1776) *Plain Directions*, or preventative recipes against infection, stood for an entire class of popular and practical literature warning the poor rogue and the debauched libertine to be on the defensive. "The government of the passions" was the unrealistic but key ingredient for a cure. To prevent a relapse, no woman should be permitted to cross the patient's path, nor might his fancy "rove." Since the surgeon's purpose—like Hogarth's—was to take up cudgels against an irrationally copulating human nature, his technique was equally graphic. Wall painted a disagreeable prose portrait of the malady's relentless progress. "When the venereal disease is diffused through the whole habit, and taints the skin and flesh with serpiginous eruptions; when pustules and pocky warts beset the forehead, sides of the face, lips, chin, etc., when scabbs and spreading tettars, affect the arms, breast, shoulders, back, and thighs; when foul ulcers occupy the neck, limbs, and legs, attended with severe night pains, in the bones of the arms and legs, as if dogs were gnawing of them," then one might be assured "of a broken constitution."[49] In life, flat, round, and branny spots infested the moist corners of lips, the chapped sides of nostrils, the scaly edges of the hairline, just as in art. Thus, costly silk or taffeta beauty patches ironically gilded venereal sores in the scenes symbolizing moral decrepitude from *Marriage à la Mode* (fig. 184). Hogarth's Dr. Pillule was branded by "the black medical seal." Alias Dr. Misauban, this noted French charlatan had a lucrative London practice. He routinely dispensed those nibbling white spots now firmly ensconced between the rakish Lord Squanderfield's legs. Lichtenberg remarked that the useless medical transaction, depicted in the third plate of the series, aptly took place beneath the quack's heterocite curio cabinet. The patchy appearance of its variegated contents was intended to be as visually repellent as the eroding spiritual and

185. Jean-Louis Alibert, *Tumor,* from *Clinique de l'Hôpital Saint-Louis,* 1833, pl. 35. Colored stipple engraving by Tresca after Moreau and Valvile. (Photo: Courtesy National Library of Medicine, Bethesda, Md.)

physical ailment supposedly being treated. Here, too, were "monstrous magnifications of the minute." Narwhal tusk, crumbling bricks, barber's basin, urine flask, giant's bone, hydrocephalic child's head, gallows, broken combs, high hat, spear, shield, lance, slippers, drawing of an abortion, and insect, betokened the sickly dregs and "sweepings of nature and art."[50]

Into this miscellany of confusing blots entered Jean-Louis Alibert (1766–1837). His singular importance was due to the introduction of an observation-based classification of cutaneous illnesses according to a botanical method. More important, however, was the insistence—unlike his predecessors—that the changing aspect of these maladies be scrupulously illustrated. The precisionist visual arts were to raise medicine from merely a conjectural endeavor to one of the physical and natural sciences. Alibert, I believe, should be inscribed in the annals of art history as the diagnostician of blighted, or modern, looks. It is impossible to imagine nineteenth-century French Realist portraiture without this trailblazing truth-sayer (fig. 46). He momentarily undid the lie of idealism by showing a painful actuality that had long been too anxiety-provoking to represent plainly. The French dermatologist broke Neoclassicism's addiction to deception by studying the shattering, immediate, and unbearable reality circulating in the eighteenth-century street.

A student of Pinel's at the Salpêtrière, Alibert was largely the product of a post-Revolutionary educational system. This training encouraged a reformist passion for the injection of ethical values into medical studies, matched by a concern for public instruction. His open-air lectures under the lime trees were in keeping with the Stoic-laced moral teachings of the *Idéologues,* who believed "example was contagious." He, too, hoped for and worked toward the goal of the disappearance of disease in a regenerated society.[51] In 1800, Alibert was appointed director of the six-hundred-bed Hôpital Saint-Louis. This "sewer of all the countries of the world" was bursting with outsiders: lepers, scorbutics, syphilitics, and victims of scrofula. Briefly told, he launched his publication career with the *Description des maladies de la peau* (1806–1811). It cost the then enormous sum of 600 francs to produce. When the *Nosologie naturelle* appeared in 1817, in a glorious folio edition printed on vellum and accompanied by magnificent plates, the 100,000-franc expenditure exceeded his wife's dowry. Although the atlas was greatly admired, and after the Restoration he was made a baron and physician to Louis XVIII, he never recouped financially.[52] His final medical masterpiece, the revised and enlarged *Clinique de l'Hôpital Saint-Louis* (1832–1834), fully exploited the "frightening" seventy-three color engravings. These prints, retouched by hand, were

186. Antoine-Jean Gros, *The Pesthouse
at Jaffa,* Salon of 1804. Oil on canvas, 53.2
× 72.0 cm. Musée du Louvre. (Photo:
Réunion des Musées Nationaux.)

intended to assist the physician in recognizing the evolutionary stages of skin disease, not just a static instant in its development. Beyond diagnostics, however, the ordinary reader was meant to be "struck," to see what the clinician saw. The painters Moreau and Valvile—of whom nothing is known—and the Sicilian engraver Salvatore Tresca (?1750–1815?) were closely supervised by the author and instructed to make the revolting phenomena under examination spring to life (figs. 8, 182).[53] A mythic figure, Alibert's exploits contributed to the nineteenth-century model of the heroic physician. His fumigation of the sickroom—at the moment when the artists were on the verge of fainting from the stench of gangrene—was the stuff of legend.

Alibert's revolutionary method of learning, by direct and unvarnished contact with the visible, led him to invite interesting specimens encountered along the road to sit for their portraits. This microscopic concentration on pathological detail—whether in a "found" person or an indigent patient—accounted for the memorable vividness of the likenesses. These clinical studies were simultaneously dispassionate reproductions of fragmenting corporeal afflictions and moving images of individual Stoic heroism, transcending the tumor-burdened body (fig. 185). Even a detached and extended arm "spoke." The disquieting and contradictory message of perfection overlaid with morbidity was that no one was secure. The underlying porcelain faces and limbs—slurred with the most horrible smears or eaten by the most agonizing ulcers—were as serene as those painted by an Anne-Louis Girodet-Trioson (1767–1824) or a Pierre-Narcisse Guérin (1774–1833) (fig. 182). Although these powerful depictions postdate Baron Antoine-Jean Gros's (1771–1835) Napoleonic battlefield sagas, one can still wonder what would have been their impact. Perhaps the reddened and swollen bubos discreetly festooning the ennobled remnants of the *Grande Armée* quarantined in the infirmary at Jaffa would have been less euphemistic (fig. 186).

Although Robert Willan's (1753–1812) *Cutaneous Diseases* preceded Alibert's use of color engravings, the British physician still considered verbal description superior in the rendition of "the various degrees of opacity and clearness of pustules." And despite Thomas Bateman's enlarged and wider-circulating 1817 edition of Willan,[54] Alibert's volumes continued to educate "sight through sight." They reigned supreme until the Viennese Ferdinand Hebra's (1806–1880) softer, chromolithographed *Atlas der Hautkrankheiten* (1876) finally supplanted them (fig. 187).

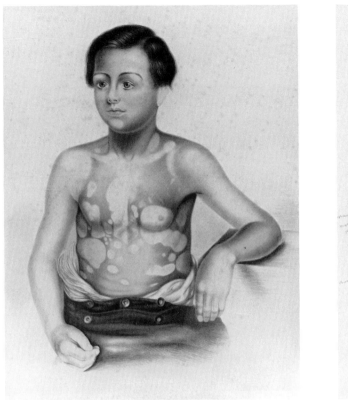

Alibert's *Clinique* was a magisterial philosophical compendium whose dermatological information was organized—like the *Encyclopédie*—by a tree (fig. 188). Its ramifications clumped maladies according to their visual similarities, following the ubiquitous principle of analogy that we have so often met. The branches sprouted neologisms, coined in the wake of Antoine-Laurent Lavoisier's (1743–1794) and Antoine-François Fourcroy's (1755–1809) attempts to standardize chemical nomenclature. Like a David painting, Alibert's schematic plan of the unholy garden of skin disease bristled with intractable, thorny, and inflammatory figures (fig. 2). Ostentatiously compounded from Greek roots—*cnidosis, pityriasis, ichthyosis, exanthema, erysipelas,* etc.—hard words imaged an anti-paradise of decay, the otherworldly *corpus* mutated into Baudelairean flowers of evil. Conscious of creating a new science, Alibert inquired how else one could express "new things without having

187. Ferdinand Hebra, *Leucoderma* (after Anton Elfinger), from *Atlas der Hautkrankheiten,* 1876, pl. 10. Chromolithograph. (Photo: Courtesy National Library of Medicine, Bethesda, Md.)

188. Jean-Louis Alibert, *Tree of Dermatological Diseases,* from *Clinique de l'Hôpital Saint-Louis,* 1833, frontispiece. Colored stipple engraving by Tresca after Moreau and Valvile. (Photo: Courtesy National Library of Medicine, Bethesda, Md.)

recourse to new terms."[55] Consequently, the blasted and parasite-ridden tree of knowledge, with its scaly serpent coiled around the trunk, was also a graphic botanical metaphor of epidermal disfigurement. Its irregular bark was invaded by pernicious grafts counter to nature until the original, healthy peel was obliterated by lesions, lichens, and burls.

The proof that mocking imitation was the sincerest form of flattery came in the form of a humorous, lithographed album of "picturesque pathologies," to which a stable of French draftsmen contributed. It satirized, while simultaneously acknowledging, Alibert's solemn vision of what occurred outside Eden. Tubercled features and lumpy skulls were divertingly located within a weedy and epidermal *Jardin des plantes*. Melon-shaped galls, or a sort of somatic "hors d'oeuvre," grew on the heads of old geezers like humps from a back (fig. 189).[56] This comic *critique* aside, Alibert was at his most eloquent when he described the slow metamorphosis of the human body into degraded wood or stone. The leper became unrecognizable rind as his surface turned into crust.[57] Discolorations resembling granite (fig. 187) or rain drops (fig. 8) mineralized and spattered the cutis. Black "spots of death" thatched the dermis with kernels of soot (fig. 190). Devouring cancers (fig. 185) parasitically attached themselves to the most sensitive portions of the anatomy as to a prey, causing "an inconceivable destruction." The murderous efflorescences of smallpox and mossy herpes, abounding in the rank and humid lower-class dwellings of Paris, barbarously altered the skin with "soiling imprints." Each consuming disease had its leguminous physiognomy. Syphilis pushed up pustules like bulbs that, in turn, resembled seeds. But, in the end, vegetative language failed Alibert in the sin-laden description of "the progress of our corruption." Like the "immortal Jenner," he believed that man deviated from the original natural state, thus becoming a prolific source of disease. How was it possible, the French dermatologist wondered, adequately to describe that scourge brought about through our contaminated social alliances, hereditary vices, and the so-called progress and refinement of civilizations? Who could do justice to "that multitude of stigmatas and hideous signs, those fungous growths and vegetation, those deep and fetid ulcers that constantly sadden the view?"[58] He invited his fellow citizens to enter, if they dared, the Hôpital Saint-Louis. Just below the comforting bourgeois illusion of a well-off world lay the intransigent reality of misery that would not go away. In the clinic, those who routinely averted their gaze from repugnant specks would behold an unbleached world. Here, nature exhibited itself "attacked and disfigured in a thousand ways, as if better to deceive us."[59]

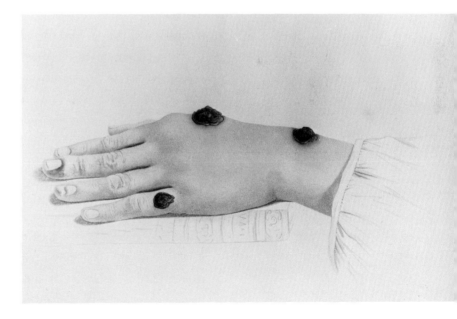

189.   Pigal, *Neoplasms,* from *Album comique de pathologie pittoresque,* 1823. Lithograph by Langlumé. (Photo: Courtesy National Library of Medicine, Bethesda, Md.)

190.   Jean-Louis Alibert, *Lepra Nigricans,* from *Clinique de l'Hôpital Saint-Louis,* 1833, pl. 33. Colored stipple engraving by Tresca after Moreau and Valvile. (Photo: Courtesy National Library of Medicine, Bethesda, Md.)

Concupiscence ———————

noun, Irregular desire; libidinous wish, lust; treachery; wandering cogitation.

Dr. Johnson, *Dictionary*

Concupiscence ———————

noun, Among theologians, it signifies appetite, or immoderate desire or covetousness of sensual things, inherent in man since the Fall. Father Malebranche defined concupiscence as a natural impulse that the traces, the impressions of the brain make on the soul to attach it to sensible things . . .

Diderot and D'Alembert, *Encyclopédie*

The lingering folk belief that mothers smeared their children with ugly birth moles or warts represented, at bottom, the terror of contamination by sight. This ancient superstition contributed an unrecognized and major component to the history of the modern surface. The same *Album comique de la pathologie pittoresque* that satirized the new dermatology poked fun at prenatal adventures. The plantlike growths endemic to the aging skin were thus jokingly connected to the disfiguring look of mutilating hereditary traits. The letterpress banter mocked "revolutions" occurring in the female stomach giving rise to "depraved tastes." Usually it was at the end of the first trimester that the avid delirium arose and "gastric oracles" began. *The Desires of Pregnant Women* (fig. 191) illustrated the ludicrous genetic physiognomics that postulated that heads, still *in utero*, might be transubstantiated into vermin or fruit. The caricaturist wittily encapsulated the details of this optic-based credulity. A wife out strolling with her husband and son chanced upon a virile young baker dressed as a Scotsman and lightly dusted with flour. This seductive spectacle aroused a ravenous craving, and she lunged to bite his shoulders! The droll text commented that the hapless mate, not unaware of the dire consequences of this anthropophagous tendency, tried unsuccessfully to restrain her. He himself was stigmatized on the forehead with the sign of the rat that scared his mother. Moreover, his eldest child was stamped with a bunch of grapes on the cheek—a constant reminder of his spouse's uncontrollable voracity.[60] Such satire underscored the pictorial nature of this biological hunger. The wandering and deviant fancy tinctured and tainted flesh with variegated pigmentation the way the irrational painter splattered unblended pigments. It is striking how the spotted symptomatology of skin disease was inscribed into artistic "malpractice." Conversely, the deliberate infractions of "mosaic" technique were intrinsic to the descriptive language of nascent dermatology.

The theory concerning the illicit powers of the maternal imagination—much debated during the eighteenth century—touched upon a number of our key themes. These include a rash and falsifying fantasy, a passive matter, and a preformationist notion of generation. Accordingly, individuating blazes, coat markings, and epidermal patterns could be inherited not at the moment of, but after, conception. Partisans of packaged embryos, or of *emboîtement*, thus freed God of any guilt of having created chaotic traits, and placed the burden instead on unrestrained passions and innate human concupiscence. Before

306

191. Pigal, *The Desires of Pregnant Women,* from *Album comique de pathologie pittoresque,* 1823. Lithograph by Langlumé. (Photo: Courtesy National Library of Medicine, Bethesda, Md.)

dismissing what, at first glance, may seem a ridiculous polemic, we should remember that it touched upon a deep and abiding anxiety. The late twentieth-century medical and aesthetic idealism of many Americans is captured in the expectation of perfect babies and perfect physician-machines who are not permitted an honest error. This perfectionism flies in the face of even our own "improved" instrumental reality. But for the eighteenth-century European urban dweller for whom monstrosity loomed large, and infectious skin afflictions abounded with no successful drug treatment, just whom could one blame for an unsightly injury or unjust deformity? There were no court decisions awarding huge sums for emotional damages incurred when mothers inflicted "wrongful life" on their severely impaired offspring. No pressure was exerted to have genetic tests and therapy during which, inevitably, both doctor and patient discovered more than they were seeking. There was no prorated compensation for defects on a sliding scale from "ghastly" to "trivial," based on an unspoken yet normative standard about what constituted the "right" looks.[61] Yet the issue of a woman's obligation to her fetus, and the nagging question of the voluntary or involuntary source of a harm or handicap preexisting birth, was already posed in the early modern period.[62] Furthermore, eugenics and the mirage of procreating more beautiful faces and bodies even crossed Malebranche's and Lavater's minds. The "contagious communication" of "false traces" or disorders of the fantasy was as catching as the imitation of regular and symmetrical traits.[63]

The concept of embryonic imprinting as a result of a mother's irrational fears or desires (*naevi materni, voglie, envies, Muttermahler*) originated with Hippocrates and was perpetuated by Pliny.[64] The feminine imagination, so the argument ran, was the mistress of errors and behaved even more capriciously than normal during pregnancy. During this altered state, it was credited with the physical ability to materialize, by simulation, objects either wishfully or fearfully perceived. These external entities were believed to exert an internal repercussive pressure on the delicate fibers of the fetus. Christian exegesis picked up this pagan idea because it confirmed the dogma of original sin. Augustine's relentless voluntarism turned already austere Pauline doctrine into stone. The bishop of Hippo maintained that all humanity was contained in Adam's loins. Consequently, sin was an "inherited guilt," a vice anterior to every personal fault and linked to the very fact of birth itself. The congenital infecting and blackening of mankind was passed along through succession, and thus resided in the multiplying impulse of sexuality.[65]

192. George Stubbs, *Brown and White Norfolk or Water Spaniel,* 1778. Oil on canvas, 80.6 × 97.2 cm. Paul Mellon Collection, Upperville, Va. (Photo: Courtesy Paul Mellon Collection.)

Animal breeders had long assumed that structural and physiological features were inherited at the moment of conception. Yet, according to Varro and Appian, farmers and hunters regularly attempted to manipulate their stock and contrive the manifestation of certain conformational or "fancy points" in herds. At the moment of coupling, they exposed to the sight of the cow or the mare the bull or the stallion adorned with the same marks as they wished to appear in the calf or foal. The author of Genesis 30:38–39 similarly recounted how Jacob placed colored rods in view of mating beasts. "And the Flocks conceived before the Rods, and brought forth Cattel ring-streaked, speckled, and spotted."[66] No eighteenth-century painter better exemplified this concern for the visibilization of distinctive or rare bloodlines and noble pedigrees than George Stubbs. His paintings of supremely well-bred Arabians, flashed with white, piebald Norfolk or water spaniels (fig. 192), and dappled Brockesby fox hounds, testified to a nonbiblical pride in showing off quality markings. The view of flecked muzzles, croups, and stockings was familiar to Stubbs's sporting patrons. The British landed gentry were accustomed to the practice of inbreeding and linebreeding, that is, fixing "the type and the prepotence to transmit it."[67] Géricault was not so fortunate. When the *Wounded Cuirassier* (Paris, Musée du Louvre, 1814) was exhibited at the

193.   Anonymous, *The Wonderful Spotted Indian John Boby,* 1803. Engraving. (Photo: Courtesy National Library of Medicine, Bethesda, Md.)

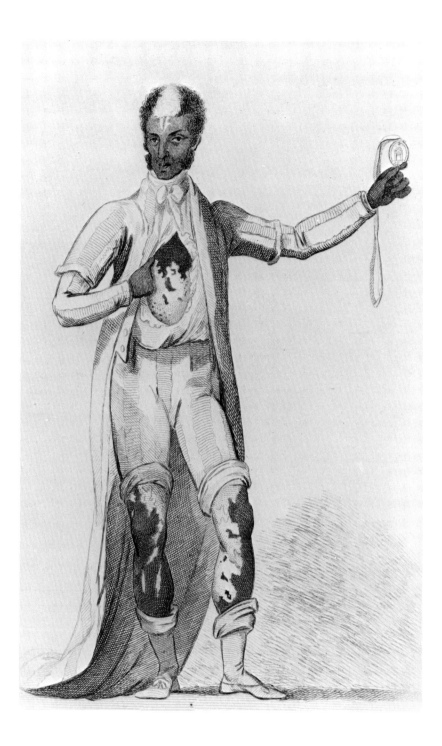

310

Salon, the French painter was criticized for turbulently spotting the horse's chest so that it looked like coarse mosaic work. What could be a desirable and even exotic sign in domestic or wild animals, however, was an ignoble aberration in man. Striped zebra, painted leopard or cheetah—studied scientifically by Stubbs in parks, Queen Charlotte's collections, and as stuffed specimens in John Hunter's museum—were quite a different matter from vitiligo-splashed human curiosities. That there was something less than human about such mottling was indicated by the case of the spotted Jamaican. John Boby exhibited himself, as if in a menagerie, throughout England and Scotland (fig. 193). While it was common to keep different orders of nature, and even races, apart, Stubbs may have been inspired to think at least about gross, cross-species analogies. Significantly, his dissections for the *Comparative Anatomical Exposition of the Structure of the Human Body with That of a Tiger and a Common Fowl* (begun 1795), and the reading of Dr. Thomas Cogan's 1791 translation of Camper's *Works*, prompted such reflections (fig. 92).[68]

We are returning, then, to a piece of unfinished business. The discussion of conception and misconception in the last chapter temporarily set aside the issue of possible external contagion, or action at a distance, impinging on the egg, sperm, or seed implanted in the womb. The preformationist emphasis on the duplicating power of the mind in all matters of generation especially seemed to offer an explanation for the existence of abnormalities. Complicating matters was the tenacious Aristotelian notion that the fetus—formed from a mixture of liquors expended by both sexes—owed its generative principle only to the male. The female substance was exclusively responsible for nutrition and growth. Who, then, imparted family or alien resemblance, and when? Paré, citing Aristotle, Hippocrates, Empedocles, and Moses, noted that a nocturnal vision experienced by the couple at the moment of conceiving impressed itself on the child. Thus a hairy girl, a black infant born to white parents, and a hideous monster with calf's head and hooves could emerge from unsuitable sights and mixed fantasies (fig. 194). Just as Jacob deceived Laban when he bred variegated goats and sheep by compelling them to look at mottled staves, hirsute or sooty human offspring might arise. Paré gave the example of mothers who gazed too intently on an image of the unkempt John the Baptist or at the portrait of a Moor.[69]

Junius, in reflecting on "the particolored spots of precious stones" and strikingly grained agates, drew a genetic comparison predicated on the identical principle of universal analogy. Such lithic "miracles of nature" might seem

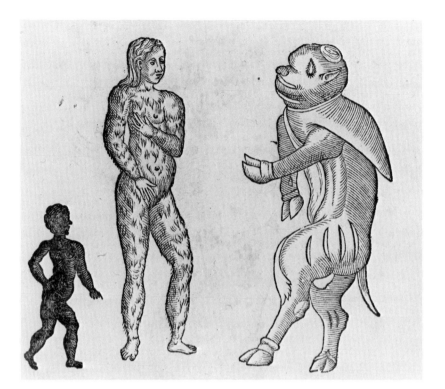

to fall out by mere chance. But they were as determined as the "many generations issuing forth out of one man who had a certaine marke." These "do constantly retain the same mark in some part of their bodies, receiving it as by the succession of a most sure and perpetuall inheritance." He approvingly recalled Plutarch's comment that warts, moles, and blemishes originated "in the eye of parents."[70] Aptly, Junius took up the issue again under the rubric of the uses of imitation and imagery. The combative Spartans knew that well-turned bodies were best suited for the conduct of war. Desirous of begetting handsome children, they showed their pregnant wives pictures of fair Apollo, Bacchus, Castor, Pollux, Narcissus, and Hyacinthus, hoping to induce corporeal emulation. Junius also relied on Pliny's belief that shapely conceptions depended on shapely thoughts, that anatomy and physiology were linked. Fantasies running through the minds of the couple at the moment of union imparted a whole or fragmentary form to the embryo. Thus one discerned greater morphological variation in man than in any other species, "seeing the nimbleness of his thoughts, the swiftness of his minde, and the varietie of his wit." Mental agility imprinted "in him images of many and several fashions: whereas all other creatures have immovable minds, and [are] in their own kinde alike."[71]

312

The ovist Harvey claimed that the evidence of succession "at a vast remove" proved Pliny's point concerning the repetition of the crest of the Daci, emblazoning every fourth birth in that family. Similarly, diseases "also produce their like in other subjects; as the Leprosie, the Gout, Syphilis, or French-Pox."[72] Likewise, it was through magnetic or sympathetic attraction, More argued, that "the stubborn matter of the Foetus" assumed the similitudes of cherries and claret-colored mulberries. Because only the "Eternall Minde" or "Spirit of Nature" could create perfect signatures, these resemblances to fruit were necessarily imperfect, since they emanated from "the fancy of the mother." More's discussion of maternal impressions in the *Saducismus Triumphatus* (1656) belonged to a larger Neoplatonic theory of fascination, whereby the imagination possessed magical powers of transformation, simulation, and dissimulation.[73]

But it was the preformationist Malebranche's *Recherche de la vérité*—going through five editions between 1721 and 1772—that brought the entire imaginationist theory of correspondences to the threshold of the eighteenth century.[74] He clarified past ambiguities. Was it the father, the mother, or both in concert who were responsible for likeness? Conversely, he left unanswered the difficult question of whether there was a difference between genetic tattoos and markers (the arms of the Daci, the smudges of venereal disease, albinism) and a pathology of the skin (prurigo, psoriasis). Malebranche made even more explicit the Neoplatonic "invisible bonds," or strong ideational connections, supposedly uniting mother and fetus.[75] Moreover, he spelled out the physiological workings of a torrent of animal spirits leaving traces of the brain in another's body. Violent emotions experienced by a pregnant woman—such as those prompted by the view of a large wound or the beating, gashing, and execution of a criminal—rained pathological and teratological horrors upon the tender fibers of the developing infant.[76] Thus it was not the parents in sexual unison, or at the instant of fertilization, but the mother alone who was susceptible to the natural or artificial environment. She was responsive to, and responsible for, the impact of frightful ulcers or beautiful works of art. Thus she conferred on the child growing in the womb emotional reactions to what she saw or felt. In a sort of pre-Freudian fetal psychology, the infant took on the literal shape of the trauma, or the experience that had left a profound negative or positive groove in her psyche. Hence offspring visibilized concealed or surrogate passions on their surfaces. Like a blank sheet of paper, the skin became marbled by pathos, mottled by an alien pattern of interiority.

Malebranche's hypothesis concerning genetic impressionism and peccant transmissions ranged from the ludicrous to the tragic. If mothers imprudently yearned for and conjured up visions of pears or grapes, then their fetuses were animated by an identical longing. The rush of spirits excited by such fantasies coursed through the tiny body and were "capable of changing the figure because of its softness; these poor babies became like the things they [mothers] too ardently desired." The coarser and less malleable humors of the host-woman, however, remained unscathed. But for the occasionalist Oratorian and mystical Cartesian, this "communication" of resemblance could have far more deleterious moral effects than the mere insertion of material changes into the otherwise fixed process of reproduction.[77] His greater purpose was to demonstrate that the corporeal imagination led astray, and that its errors arose through the influence of sensible perception. Mothers, therefore, not only marred their children with finite, occasional (i.e., not divine) inclinations transmitted through the nerves, but corrupted their hearts and reasons for life. Malebranche argued that, since there were few women who were not moved by some appetite during the term of their pregnancy, there were correspondingly few children "who did not gain a malformed spirit in some way, & who did not acquire some ruling passion."[78] Women's covetous bodies were literally the zone for the conception of waywardness, just as the mind of God was the site of immaterial ideas or truths.

The French philosopher's stance on the capability of imprinting the shape of a hankering, shock or fear was absorbed within the broader eighteenth-century "quarrel of the monsters." The *De Morbis Cutaneis. A Treatise on Diseases incident to the Skin (1712)* by Malebrache's keen defender, the British surgeon Daniel Turner (1677–1740), launched the epidermal phase of the polemic. His staunch opponent was the mysterious Frenchman, James Augustus Blondel (1665–1734). This Leiden-trained physician practiced medicine first, possibly, at Oxford and then, certainly, in London.[79] His counterattack on this "vulgar error" was also, alas, unillustrated. Yet the treatise on *The Strength of Imagination in Pregnant Women* (1727), and the expanded pamphlet of 1729, were addressed to a more general, and even a feminine, public. The latter, he believed, were often wrongfully accused of wanton mistakes actually made by sloppy *accoucheurs*, who covered their tracks with imaginationist theories. Similarly, birthmarks were merely *lusus naturae*, or sports of nature. Blondel heaped scorn on absurd occult hypotheses that metamorphosed the female fancy into "a petty Pedlar" dealing in ill-made "foolish pictures." Nor was the imagination "a Knife, a Hammer, a Pastry

Cook, a Thief, a Painter, a Jack of all Trades, a Juggler, Doctor Faustus, the Devil and all." Mother and child possessed separate circulatory systems, thus conception was necessarily independent of maternal will, just as the mind could not extend its force beyond the sphere of the body it inhabited.[80] In defense of women, he inquired further how, without their knowledge and contrary to their bent, they could obliterate lineaments preexisting conception, and "subsisting even since the creation of the world."[81] As a Cartesian and a preformationist, Blondel was unusual in establishing barriers through which thought could not permeate. Even La Mettrie and Le Camus sided with Malebranche although, paradoxically, for materialist reasons. The latter's immaterial conceptions were transformed by the atheistic *philosophes* into atomistic ideas producing a sensible impression, like a channel furrowing wax. Muratori, the pioneer of modern Italian historiographical studies, also turned his attention to the debate. The *Forza della fantasia* formed part of his series of penetrating studies devoted to the history of institutions, economics, social customs, and religion. In his fight against superstition, this Jansenist enemy of the Jesuits also surprisingly decided against Blondel. Women, with their vivid mental "geography" or "topography," could produce infantile "configurations." Nonetheless, he confessed ignorance as to how these might be transported to the skin.[82]

It was more typical of epigenetic theory to stress the distinct individuality and isolated condition of the embryo, solitarily housed within its tangled web of membranes and humors (fig. 154). Thus the mathematician, astronomer, and observational scientist Maupertuis, in the *Earthly Venus*, disdained those "countless stories" about facial transplants, whereby mothers transferred the countenance they admired or found detestable. In lieu of a doctrine of sympathy, he put forward the notion of empathy. He had no doubt that when people witnessed the suffering of others they felt their pain. Fear could thus cause a rupture within the fetus, but this tear bore no resemblance to the experience eliciting it.[83] Again relying on the painterly or pictorial practice underlying all these spotted metaphors, Maupertuis argued that observers, who read into suggestive moles the "exact drafts and similitudes" of fish or cherries, were simply completing the *non-finito*. Whether investigating mutilated abortions, freakish new species, or ugly birth marks, the *philosophe* found it scandalous to believe God created enveloped germs that were monstrous from the beginning.[84]

Maupertuis's thesis was the subject of controversy as far away as St. Petersburg and as nearby as Germany. Dr. Theodore Eller (1689–1760), Director of the Royal Academy of Prussia, published a long discussion in the *Mémoires* reviewing the entire history of ideas surrounding the maternal imagination. Like the French scientist, and against Turner, he adopted a theory of nerves. These tubes were believed to explain how external blows might logically be conducted to the uterus and cause red blotches or velvety spots to discolor the epidermis.[85] Thus by the latter part of the eighteenth century, the jury was still out on the question, and the imaginationist analogy thrived.[86]

Lessing, in the *Laocoön*, openly alluded to it when he declared that the lovely statues of the Greeks actually generated handsome men. Conversely, among the moderns, the highly susceptible "imagination of mothers seems to express itself only in producing monsters."[87] Mengs introduced a variation on the trope, significantly also within a discussion of the beautiful. Just as among gems only the diamond was perfect, and among metals only gold, so, too, among animals, man occupied the apex. But no human being was free of distorting passion. Just as painful and protracted labor harmed the infant, so a creature born to be spotless became flecked and ugly.[88] It was Lavater, however, in his "Observations on the Marks which Children bring into the World upon Them—On Monsters, Giants, and Dwarfs," who most eloquently tied together and propagated the aesthetic, medical, and metaphysical components of the belief. He spoke of a remarkable singularity, a "spotted [six- or seven-year-old] girl," who allowed herself to be taken around and exhibited (fig. 195). She was completely covered with hairy excrescences. In addition, fawn-colored fungal growths decorated her back. Lavater recounted the tale of how, supposedly during pregnancy, her mother fought with a neighbor over some venison. The preformationist physiognomist then provided an important summary of the current myth of marking at a distance.

When the imagination is powerfully agitated by desire, love, or hatred, a single instant is sufficient for it to create or annihilate, to enlarge or contract, to form giants or dwarfs, to determine beauty or ugliness: it impregnates the organic fetus, with a germ of growth or diminution, or wisdom or folly, of proportion or disproportion . . . and this germ afterwards unfolds itself only at a certain time, and in given circumstances.[89]

Lavater confessed he was standing on the brink of a hermeneutical abyss, since the young girl's stains possessed no similarity to anything even vaguely resembling a stag. Yet, for him, the distinct possibility remained that maternal desires had an impact on the physiognomy of the child. Moreover, the theory seemed to hold out the attractive eugenic promise—already envisaged by Malebranche—of reproducing better and more harmonious facial traits. But

316

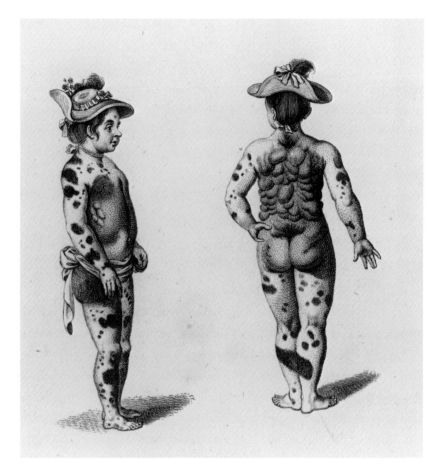

195. Johann Caspar Lavater, *Girl with Birthmarks*, from *Essays on Physiognomy*, 1792, III, part I, p. 193. Engraving by Thomas Holloway. (Photo: Courtesy National Library of Medicine, Bethesda, Md.)

like the twentieth-century genetic engineer after him, he wondered whether rules might be imposed to account both for the initial formation of the embryo and for its subsequent malformation.

Lavater was indebted also to Malebranche for the belief in a transbiological and transhistorical succession of pollution. Human beings were born with concupiscence. This enslaving original sin, associated with sexual pleasure, was "communicated" in the same fashion that straight or twisted thoughts were. From the vantage of eighteenth-century theories concerning a ruined or broken skin, we can now look back on the *Essays* as a fragmentary chronicle recording the birth and transmission of an infinity of transgressive corporeal traces. The fatalistic and Augustinian Malebranche declared that, after the Fall, when the soul was obliged to join a body in the womb, we were "infected by the corruption of our parents." Augustine had fixed the main lines of the Church's teaching concerning the "disease" of concupiscence and the "contagion" of carnal generation. He introduced pathological epidermal metaphors into the Western tradition that were ineradicable even in a secular age. In this book, we have become familiar with: "the ancient *wound* of the serpent," "sinful *flesh*," "the *stain* of this bodily flood," falling "*ill* through sin," "the *unclean* spirit," "the *blows* by which we are assailed within ourselves," and "the enticement of *visible things.*"[90] At the root of vices and passions was the "foreskin," signifying original sin. "For the origin of those who are born is through that member, and through that sin we are said to be by nature children of wrath."[91]

According to Malebranche, since that primordial moment of mating, humanity loved sensual enjoyment. This postlapsarian, and especially feminine, addiction to physical things was incarnated in the female brain divided by ineffaceable tracks. These no longer virginal, used and flawed, creatures necessarily engendered sinners perceptibly blotted with revolting disorders.[92] The serpent transmitted to Eve, "the mother of all living," a primal blemish that she passed on to her descendents. While the taint of this inherited spoiling was purged when the newborn became baptized, the weakness and vulnerability of this basic infirmity endured.[93] Original sin, then, was externalized as a real and physical spot of suffering infecting likenesses. It worked, as Blondel said of imaginationist "transanimation" or "transformation," from "a vast distance."[94] Although all "excrescences and funguses of the mind," like pock scars and "the warts or corns" of the body, were loathesome and needed to be excised, the conglomerate birthmark seemed the most odious.[95] This shadowy smudge on the empty horizon of eternity was the image of original sin's criminal and sullied substantiality. It was the somatic symbol of evil's tangible emergence into the world with Adam, the fractured blazon shamelessly announcing voluntary unclean mixing. Only at the close of the eighteenth century would Blake contradict Reynolds's dictum: "Peculiarities in the work of art, are like those in the human figure. . . . They are always so many blemishes." To which Blake angrily retorted: "Infernal Falsehood! Peculiar marks are the only merit."[96] By this outburst, the engraver-poet meant that idiosyncratic mental and artistic particularity, or ostentatious "imperfection," constituted the sign of original genius. He was thus unlike the idealistic aesthete and scientist in Nathaniel Hawthorne's (1804–1864) short story, "The Birthmark." Aylmer surgically removed his wife's inky mole at the cost of her life, whereas Blake deliberately created eccentric corporeal runes.[97] He believed that the eradication of sharply differentiating personal punctuation in art or existence led only to blurred chaos or to the blank sheet.

Typographical metaphors of print and misprint stamped a major aspect of the imaginationist debate. The case of the white negro, in particular, focused both the aesthetic and the dermatological issues. This embodiment of cutaneous scrawl challenged well-mannered chiaroscural antitheses by its scribbled cacography. Were such ethnographical and biological oddities—with their pigmentation in conspicuous disarray—the result of a mental tattoo or of a maculating morbidity of the skin? (fig. 196) This intriguing episode in the annals of medical and cultural anthropology revealed once again the modernity of the eighteenth century: its obsession with minced surface, disguised or submerged identity, flamboyant novelty, and the mass communication of bizarre spectacle (figs. 156, 157, 165). The blatantly nonstandard and nonuniform example of dashed and dotted dark nakedness, streaked with glaring highlights, served the Enlightenment as the model of impropriety. The opposite of masquerading dress or fancy pictures, it stood for any piebald epidermis, or broken skin of paint, tricked out in ripped domino (fig. 197).[98] From the perspective of Western culture, then, the white Negro was so unnaturally natural, so undressed, so uncivilized, so unmade up, as to appear wholly made up.

The theory of maternal impressions attempted to solve not only the persistent problem of heredity, but the conundrum of skin coloration. On both counts— as the epitome of *semion* or mark—discordant epidermal signs formed a major chapter in the history of the visibilization of the invisible. Vitiligo (from the Latin *vitium*, or disease) was a rare form of lupus, not dangerous but disfiguring. Alibert classified its three major manifestations: as *albus*, with whitish roughened areas "like scattered drops" (fig. 8); as *melas*, black "like a shadow on the skin" (figs. 193, 195, 196, 198); and as *leuce*, with inlaid shining splotches penetrating more deeply than in *albus* (fig. 187). The ancients held achromatism in horror (*odiosa vitiligo*), and Alibert concurred. "There indeed was something hideous and repulsive in those dull white and branding spots arising from a feebleness, or, rather, an insufficiency of vitality." Whether sodden or bright in appearance, the malady signaled a dysgenic absence of those "animating globules" and nervous "chromatic corpuscles" that quickened and invigorated the blood.[99] Proper pigmentation, then—furnished by the male, Alibert maintained—was the insignia of potency and life.

Blot _____

verb, To obliterate; to make writing invisible by covering it with ink; to efface; to erase; to make black spots on a paper; to blur; to disgrace; to disfigure; to darken.
Dr. Johnson, *Dictionary*

Tache _____

noun, A mark, a strange impression that spoils something; maculae, *dim spots observed on the sun . . .*
Diderot and D'Alembert, *Encyclopédie*

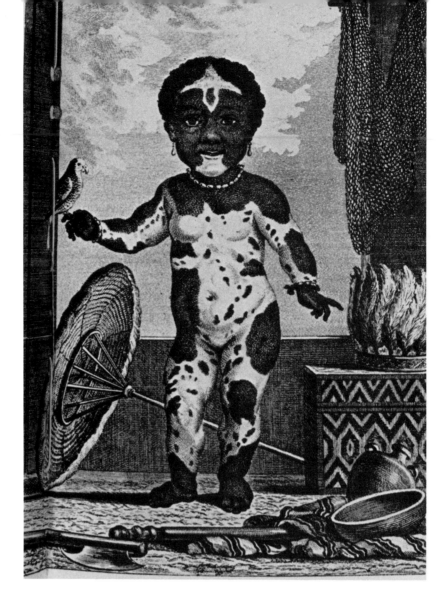

196. Georges Buffon, *A Black Albino Child,* from *L'Histoire de l'homme,* 1749, IV, p. 253. Engraving after Jacques de Sève. (Photo: Courtesy National Library of Medicine, Bethesda, Md.)

197. Fortunius Licetus, *Hirsute Man and Parti-Colored Man and Woman,* from *De Monstris,* 1655, p. 149. Engraving (Photo: Courtesy National Library of Medicine, Bethesda, Md.)

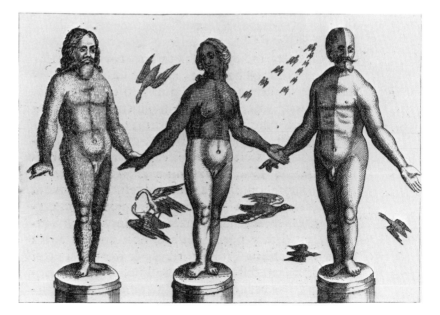

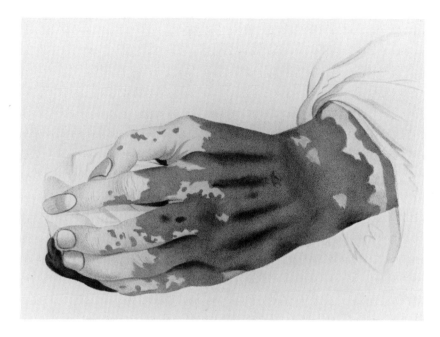

198.   Jean-Louis Alibert, *Vitiligo,* from *Clinique de l'Hôpital Saint-Louis,* 1833, pl. 61. Colored stipple engraving by Tresca after Moreau and Valvile. (Photo: Courtesy National Library of Medicine, Bethesda, Md.)

Maupertuis's *Le Nègre blanc* (1744) and the *Vénus physique* [*Earthly Venus*], published in the following year, focused on the intractable problems still plaguing an understanding of the processes of generation. The first treatise, and part two of the second, were inspired by a black albino child, born in Surinam and trotted around the Parisian *salon* circuit in the early 1740s (fig. 196). This was by no means the only well-known case of partial albinism. Buffon was enchanted by the spotted example of Marie-Sabina, born on a Jesuit plantation at Matuna and coming to his attention through a now lost portrait recovered from a British ship captured by the French in 1746. Apparently the picture was brought to him and he had it engraved for his great natural historical work.[100] We know, too, that Curtius fleshed out his wax displays at the Palais-Royal with natural curiosities and monstrous attractions. Notably, he exhibited the celebrated achromatic girl-dwarf, born in Santo Domingo of entirely black parents, and painted in life-size dimensions by the Portuguese artist Joaquim Leonardo Rocha (1727–1786) (Paris, Musée d'Histoire de la Médecine, 1786).[101] The painting, commissioned by the Brazilian princess Dona Maria Francesca Benedeta, long ornamented one of the examination rooms at the Paris Faculté de Médecine. There were also two slightly earlier but equally remarkable examples. The French artist Le Masurier, residing in Martinique, depicted the characteristic white and brown splotches disfiguring the faces and anterior portions of the bodies of a vitiligo-riddled twelve- to fifteen-month-old infant and a thirteen-year-old girl (Paris, Musée de l'Homme, 1782).[102]

In his interpretation of this obviously fascinating phenomenon, the epigenetist Maupertuis drew upon Harvey's theories, neglected in the general metaphysical rage for preformation. For Maupertuis, like the British ovist, the embryo was formed from contributions made by both parents.[103] The French scientist initially entertained Montesquieu's hypothesis concerning the role of climate and the possibility that blacks owed their swarthiness to the merciless equatorial sun. In the end, however, he became convinced of the importance of recessive and acquired traits. Maupertuis compared visibly flawed *blafards*, or violations in the standard mechanism of reproduction, to animal hybrids. White crows, white blackbirds, striped pigeons, or dappled dogs were examples of atavism. Secondary traits owed to a distant ancestor might accidentally surface or become dominant. Through art, one could even breed these fortuitous misfits and transform them into a new animal species. Human seminal and germinal fluid also contained vestiges from the past. Consequently, remote imprints of an otherwise hidden lineage could bob up suddenly in abnormal individuals.[104] Maupertuis thus set the study of heredity on firm footing by suggesting that the investigation of living beings was linked to many biological factors and to other organisms.

Although resembling the majority of his contemporaries in espousing the fixity of the species, the French Newtonian, paradoxically, was the progenitor of the Romantic taste for strange beauty. The *Earthly Venus* contained a visionary passage certainly known to Baudelaire. From the Tropic of Cancer to the Tropic of Capricorn, dusky tribes spotted and adorned the world with shadowy forms. Asia was peopled with reddish nations of countless shades. The far north and the extreme edge of the temperate zone contained the whitest inhabitants, the blonde and dazzling Danes. Musing on this "remarkable color law," Maupertuis nonetheless asked, "in those extreme lands where all are white or all are black, is there not too complete a uniformity? Would not a mixture produce new beauty? It is on the banks of the Seine that this happy variety is found."[105]

When, in 1749, the Comte de Buffon (1707–1788) published the introductory volumes of the *Histoire naturelle de l'homme*, he continued Maupertuis's efforts to unseat the stasis associated with the mechanical philosophy. The white negro provided a case showing that living matter was composed of organic molecules, and that nature possessed its own inherent vitality and activity. The notion subsequently made a profound impression on the materialist Diderot, suffusing both the *Encyclopédie* articles and the *Salons*. Checkered or streaked *blafards* were dressed in the disorderly livery of nature's initial anarchy (fig. 196). Buffon, far more than Maupertuis, believed in the need to describe each animate being in its complex peculiarity. He thus opposed the reductivism of the Linnaean system of classification.[106] The albino, then, was an important ingredient in a future "Romantic" argument for the existence of radical individuality and irreducible difference. In addition to the emblazoned child, Buffon peppered the *Histoire naturelle* with a motley assortment of Siamese twins, Cyclops, hairy girls, dwarves or giants, and obese men. Nonetheless he asserted that the unity of the species was not threatened and even flourished, in spite of such flagrant singularity.[107]

Buffon's notions about freely mixing seeds and mutually attracting molecules, darting about in the melting pot of the universe, were picked up in Berlin. They were transmitted in Eller's discussions printed in the *Mémoires*, which is where Pernety, Lavater, and Lichtenberg encountered them. Yet the success of Maupertuis's and Buffon's biological theories had to await the nineteenth century. The Malpighian layer, or deeper stratum of the epidermis (the originary site of pigmentation), long continued as the zone on which the maternal imagination was believed to make an impact. Thus the Prussian debaters could argue that this psychic influence was responsible for metamorphosing the original white color of the human race into black. Or, conversely, they could maintain from the evidence of microscopy that the depth of subcutaneous darkness present in the Negro skin infallibly proved they were "a different species of man" (fig. 73).[108]

The polemic erupting around the white Negro tells us much about the aesthetic drama of savage, ill-formed, and concocted chiaroscuro. For the eighteenth century, garish black and white blotted a blank sheet the way an overly peppered and salted stew spoiled tasteless water. Gastronomy and aesthetics alike were founded on a refined sensibility attuned to the nuanced blend.[109] The scientific, medical, and theological reflections on crude and impalatable mixtures we have so far considered exposed a pervasive artistic injunction. Raw materials required cooking. As Bouhours declared: "well-managed antitheses please infinitely, just like the lights and darks in the picture that a good painter knows how to distribute."[110] The analogy he drew was to the expression of unmixed and undigested obscure or glittering thoughts. The former, or rigmarole (*galimatias*), involved overcast sense and dimmed reason. The latter, or flashy bombast (*phébus*), took the form of a blazing rant or fustian, as tenebrous in the end as balderdash.[111] Significantly, lumpish obscurantism as well as specious sparkle was construed in terms of unsightly points and unassimilated specks of light and dark. These illegible bits tore the surface of a comely thought or composition. Blake spelled out the physicality of these obfuscating and corruscating pictorial blemishes. His criticism of Rembrandt and Rubens, launched in the *Public Address* (ca. 1810), was coupled to an attack on the lamentable foreign collecting habits of his fellow countrymen. "Most Englishmen, when they look at a picture, immediately set about searching for Points of Light & clap the Picture into a dark corner . . . A point of light is a witticism; many are destructive of all art. One is an Epigram only & no grand work can have them."[112]

But we must not leap to the end of our tale. Eighteenth-century aesthetic theory was riddled with rules alerting the artist to the urgency of fusing these extremes. Avoid the chalk, the brick, and the charcoal, admonished Richardson, since perfect black or white was disagreeable.[113] Dufresnoy described these eyesores as actual "hits," "bold strokes," and "a kind of Minced Meats in Painting." Rather than permitting the principal light in a picture to "outshine" the rest, and casting things not deserving of such care into shadow, the rude artist allowed them barbarously to jostle in an ungraduated and "unnatural mingle."[114] Lairesse defined as "mis-shapen shadows" those contrary and deformed parts that impinged "too sharply on each other." Double or multiple irrational lights and unusual shades were unnerving because they made familiar objects seem "strange and unknown." Sputtering torches, flickering candles, and glaring studio lamps (figs. 44, 45), according to Jean Dubreuil (d. 1775), caused a distension of forms producing artificial and bizarre effects totally unlike their naturalistic subjects (fig. 199).[115] On another front, Hagedorn lambasted an entire Rococo aesthetic based on the use of an untamed and reverberating *papillotage* (fig. 12). He excoriated the butterfly dance of gilt and the mirrored dazzle of bouncing silvery reflections, which busily distorted and noisily slurred what ought to be quiet and serene compositions.[116]

199. Jean Dubreuil, *Cast Shadows in Artificial Light,* from *Practice of Perspective,* 1726, p. 149. Engraving. (Photo: author.)

It was especially for the high-contrast medium of prints, however, that the strictures became most strident. Abraham Bosse (1602–1666), in *Le peintre converty* (1667), counseled the engraver to "gray" his whites lest the shadows, juxtaposed against the unmodulated metallic plate of the background, appear so harsh as to pain the eyes (figs. 172, 173, 176).[117] Le Blon, in the chapter "Of Broken Lights" from *L'Art d'imprimer,* reminded the printmaker of the

need for a dominant source of illumination radiating from the middle of a performance. This "hero of the theater," nevertheless, must not be left to declaim alone. Blacks must be blended with whites as they gradually receded from center stage.[118]

But it was Hogarth, in the *Analysis of Beauty*, who first demonstrated a clear connection between ill-disposed tinctures in an artistic arrangement and a heathenishly splotched complexion (fig. 200). The British satirist recognized the paradox inherent in illustrating the chapter "Of Coloring" with an achromatic engraving. The top border surrounding the *Country Dance* was dominated by the emblem of the painter's palette covered with neatly laid out and imperceptibly shaded pigments. Their properly ascending and descending chiaroscuro established correct artistic practice in the composing of chromatic mixtures (no. 94). The boxed pictograms and eccentric rebuses, inlaid like a rough-cut mosaic or jigsaw puzzle along the edges and down the sides of the frame, designated various departures from that central norm. Specifi-

200. William Hogarth, *The Country Dance*, from *Analysis of Beauty*, 1753, pl. 2. Engraving. (Photo: author).

cally, the artist devised the ruse of showing a "virginal" and "blooming" feminine profile in which the black hatches of the print unintentionally covered the face in carnival domino. Hogarth insisted that this strange mask or disguising tattoo was to be read inversely "as the white threads of the cutis network" (no. 95). That is, "where strokes thickest, paint blackest, you are to suppose that flesh would be whitest." The ambiguity of this transpositional strategem—exchanging healthy skin for vitiligo's shadowy patches—emerged in his description of a pristine marble bust (no. 96). Here, viewers were to understand what, in point of fact, they did not see. Observers were to behold "colors united" and "mellowed" as the result of the penetration of blots of color into the luminous and porous stone. Analogously, we were to imagine how "a drop of ink sinks in and spreads itself upon course [sic] paper, whereby each tint will graduate all around."[119] The outcome, on the contrary, resembled those outlandish and dusky patches castigated in Hogarth's chapter "Of Light and Shade" (no. 91).

Instead of a progressive rise and fall of values occurring against the backdrop of a veinless bust, rough interruptions dented, scratched, or cracked a uniform tablet or block. I wish to suggest that figure 91 of Plate II of the *Analysis* was the graphic equivalent of the *blafard* (fig. 196). Genetic and engraved misprints displayed identical inky stains and glaring gaps on a plane. Thus Hogarth's uncultivated assemblage incarnated the "disagreeable" portrait of chiaroscural *gaucherie*. Scattered "little spots," like a visual cacophony, constantly disturbed the eyes and rendered the mind uneasy. This negative image violently reversed the "breadth of shade and simplicity in the disposition of a great variety." It was the raw opposite of properly cooked "retiring shades." These went off by degrees, according to Hogarth, and were inscribed in the very tapestry of nature and art. They softly ornamented animal coats, flower petals (nos. 92, 93), foggy skies (no. 89), the painter's mounting gamut (nos. 84, 85), and the musician's sliding scale.[120]

Lichtenberg specifically remarked on Hogarth's deliberate deployment of arbitrary and fractured shadows "to suggest the presence of things which he could not put on his plates directly." More pertinent was his "false" use of the diseased and scrabbled chiaroscuro of figure 91 to indicate infractions against the moral order. Recall the moment when, in Plate V of *Marriage à la Mode*, the host and the constable burst in on the death of Lord Squanderfield. The wastrel has succumbed in a duel, after surprising his wife with the lawyer Silvertongue in the bagnio. The stable lantern's draft holes cast their rays like blots on the ceiling. The dermatological motif of the freckled canopy, gaudily overarching a scene of dissoluteness, was reiterated in Plate VI with its unrepaired window panes. Shattered glass grotesquely cracked and disfigured the elegant bay window.[121] Inharmonious patchwork, then, violated the chief rule of proper organization, namely, the duty to bring forth large masses. Dispersed and strewn tinsel or tarnish, like the constable's spangling lamp or the white Negro's showy blazes, bruised the unity of the whole. Thus, as late as the nineteenth-century Anglo-French water colorist Georges Stubbs's (fl. 1838–1848) manual on sketching the importance of clear execution in the touching in of shadows was maintained. The landscapist could not afford the composer's tolerance of the *ébauche*. Such musical sketches "may be great, however blotted his score and stiff his fingers, for others perform what he designs; but the painter must himself execute as well as compose, and that scientifically and artistically, or his conceptions, his poetry, his melody is nothing but a blurred canvas or a bit of spoiled paper" (figs. 82, 83).[122]

For many Neoclassical critics, Rembrandt van Rijn (1606–1669) epitomized the production of disgustingly squalid and "dirty" little splotched etchings. His subject matter was redolent of dingy kitchens and grimy, unsavory hovels. Appositely, along with Claude Lorrain (1600–1682) and Marco Ricci (1676–1729), he was frequently censured for his poor execution and patchy assemblages. Especially "caricatural" was the incongruous distribution of pinprick lights and smoky shades. Moreover, Rembrandt's liberal use of nonrepresentational markings and scorings obtrusively called attention to the handmade and made-up character of the prints.[123] These pits and pocks represented the cicatrization of the copper plate. They should be compared to the livid or dun maculae bestrewing the "skin" of Hogarth's marred canvas or print (no. 91). A scarred surface, no matter the substance, displayed ungentlemanly welts striking precisely because of their vulgar insistence. Filippo Baldinucci (1625–1696), in the *Cominciamento, e progresso dell'arte dell'intagliare* first published in 1686 and reedited in 1767, spoke of the Dutch artist's "bizarre style of etching which he invented, and which employed irregular scratches and hatchings."[124] The leitmotif of a heterogeneous touch coupled to a monstrously divided chiaroscuro was pervasive. Jean-Baptiste Descamps (1706–1791), in *La vie des peintres flamands, allemands, et hollandais* (1754), thought his doublings and oppositions of smudge and glitter strained credulity. To find them believable, the viewer had to imagine a gloomy studio receiving daylight only "through a hole," as in a *camera obscura*.[125] While praising Rembrandt's forceful management of light and shade in painting,

Antoine-Nicolas Dézallier d'Argenville (d. 1794), in the *Abrégé* (1745–1752), paid him a backhanded compliment concerning his etching procedure. Rembrandt's manner was not to outline contours, nor to trace external lines, nor to crosshatch within figures. Perney's *Dictionnaire portatif* lifted the critical passage pertinent to the rationalist side of the eighteenth century verbatim from Dézallier. Rembrandt, wrote Perney, pelted his plates with "an assemblage of clashing, exaggerated, discordant, scrappy blows, redoubled by [the presence] of an outspread chiaroscuro."[126]

Similarly, Fuseli termed Rembrandt and Rubens "the two meteors of art in whatever relates not to form." The "spell of chiaroscuro" impelled Rembrandt, in particular, to tinge his pencil "in the noon-day ray, in the livid flash, in evanescent twilight, and rendered darkness visible." But this friend of Blake's warned the students of the Royal Academy that cometic license was dangerous. A pyrotechnical meteorology of streaking bolts, flickering will-o'-the-wisps, and phosphorescent scintillas imperiled pictorial unity. Fuseli fully anticipated John Ruskin's (1819–1900) criticism of James McNeill Whistler's (1834–1903) *The Falling Rocket* (Detroit Institute of Arts, ca. 1875), a painting of an amusement garden on a velvet night shown studded with cascading fireworks.[127] In such mottled nocturnes, as in Rembrandt's light-shot gloom, as Fuseli had declared, the whole ran the risk of getting "lost in confusion, or crumbl[ing] into fragments."[128] Blake, on the same grounds, had opposed the Dutch painter-etcher's, and his eighteenth-century follower Sir "Sloshua" Reynolds's, smeared and smoky effects. These pastose and motley daubs inevitably led to incoherence and loss of detail. Ironically, although Blake was blind to it, Rembrandt did not "manufacture" engravings in the cosmeticized "Patches, Paint,/ Bracelets & Stays & Powder'd Hair" French mode. These smooth foreign horrors were "Niggled & Poco-Peu'd, and all the beauties pick'd out & blurr'd & blotted." The seventeenth-century master's visual barbarity lay, ironically, in those very "Spots & Blemishes, which are Beauties and not faults," that the English artist admired.[129] Rembrandt's personal and divisionist idiom—although the reverse of Blake's "minute" linear style—was similarly "peculiar," as both his critics and supporters observed.

This graphic art of untranslatable specificity was at the root of Romantic idiosyncrasy. It had emerged early in Piranesi's invention of raking beams and somber stains. These textural antitheses riddled the mysteriously umbraged second edition of the *Carceri d'invenzioni* (1761) and the soiled archaeology of the later *vedute* (figs. 26, 27, 29, 107). One's naive *idioma*, or way of speaking and doing, as Goya realized, expressed itself in sharp points and momentary flares of enlightenment punctuating great pockets of darkness. The brilliant illumination and intense deprivation of the *Caprichos* were inimitable *idiotismes* (figs. 17, 171, 172, 173, 176).[130] Similarly, the white Negro was a irreproducible *idiota*, or original, whose spots were unmistakably his own.[131] Neither Goya's shockingly ruptured aquatints nor Buffon's coarsely shredded anomaly had been softened by the patina of civilization. "As in new killed Meat, or new gathered Fruit, there is a Rawness and Sharpness, which time alone concocts and sweetens, by mortifying that which has too much life, by weakening that which is too strong, and by mixing the extremities of every colour into one another."[132]

Romantic Misfits

Francis Bacon, the twentieth-century British painter of the unpardonable and the voluptuary of an agonized flesh, recently explained his repellent imagery. "Anything that's at all accurate about life is always macabre."[133] His focus on the mundane brutality and isolation of tortured bodies belongs to an intensely physical view of existence. As he said of his triptych (Washington, D.C., Hirshhorn Museum & Sculpture Garden, 1967) inspired by T. S. Eliot's poem "Sweeney Agonistes," life is about gruesome marking, primal copulation, and violent death. Bacon's art illuminates a fundamental tension within aesthetic experience that we have been terming the difference between Neoclassicism and Romanticism. Some people are happy studying sanitized series, while others are driven to observe contaminated individuals. The obsession with a quirky and thus personalized integument and with a broken or suffering veneer belonging to a nonsqueamish Romantic outlook. Alibert's new science of dermatology and a divisionist chiaroscuro, together, reposed on the externalization of idiosyncrasy. Both dramatized a lapsed human being's internal disjunctions. They exhibited a reality besmirched by substance and experienced from a Manichean and phenomenological perspective.

There is yet another way of characterizing the difference between Neoclassicism and Romanticism, already variously refracted through the master metaphors of this book. It lies in the acknowledgment that irregular specimens are not atypical accidents but grotesques intrinsic to, and made by, living. By the late eighteenth century, the concept of the symbol had mutated from preformationist fluidity to epigenetic fracture. When two or more eggs,

Eccentrick, Eccentrical ⎯⎯⎯
adj., Deviating from the centre; Not having the same centre with another circle; . . . Not terminating in the same point; not directed by the same principle; Irregular; anomalous, deviating from stated and constant methods.
Dr. Johnson, *Dictionary*

Individu ⎯⎯⎯
noun, This is a being all of whose determinants are expressed. . . . The species only expresses things common to individuals, omitting the differences that distinguish them. Indicate therefore those differences and you depict by that the individual . . .
Diderot and D'Alembert, *Encyclopédie*

germs, or seeds coupled, the opportunity always existed that an errant misfit might occur. A physiological preoccupation with misjointed surface, or spotted and infected epidermis, rebelled against the intense intellectualization of the *idea* common among body critics. Rationalists cosmetically retouched, plastically reconstructed, and ruthlessly corrected a depraved, blotched, and sexually begotten actuality. Body epicures, on the contrary, systematically presented failed pleasures and durable pains. They highlighted the compositional and complexional deterioration accompanying the divisiveness that was one of the wages of original sin. Corporeal sophistry deliberately displayed the warts inside the mind, on the blemished body of the person, and on the mortified canvas.

A puritanical and Deistic abstraction had banished heterogeneous patches of color, barbaric gloom, and "Gothick" streaks of light, in favor of brightness and unclogged homogeneity in all aspects of moral and artistic life. The Romantic symbol, I wish to suggest, not only swerved into the empirical realm of bodily distractions, but it bifurcated. On one hand, as synthetic metaphor created by the higher imagination, it still strained toward totality. On the other hand, as differentiating allegory fabricated by the lower and patching fancy, it ironically juxtaposed life's incongruities. Fundamental to both senses was the need to make manifest signs adequate to the complexity of concupiscence and human multiplicity. This rupture of the symbol developed a possibility lying dormant within its etymology. The term embraced, as we know, a supernatural watery fluency, or confluence. But it could also designate a whoring coupling, or discrete and ugly bonding.

Modern knowledge is broken knowledge. The circle of perfection cracked by mathematical science and critical philosophy was already a Renaissance topos.[134] But in the eighteenth century the belief finally foundered that things could still be sewn up tightly, imitating nature's unity. Like the diseased skin, neither the work of art nor the life of the mind could seem naively whole again. Microscopy, as we shall see in the following chapter, had much to do with fostering a sense that small, foul, yet self-sufficient and self-generating elements crowded out and obliterated any encompassing *corpus*. The mounting criticism against the mere fitting together of pieces into a jigsaw puzzle was an indication that the one felt overwhelmed by the many. When every material particle of an organism or member of an organization was considered vital, active, and sensitive, then they eluded systematic integration. Reminiscent of Hogarth's patchwork frame enclosing the *Country Dance* (fig. 200), isolated individuals existed merely in contiguity, and without the benefit of an explanatory text. Much like an irregular mosaic, they built up an *opus sectile* out of ribcages, fingers, fluted horns, and grimacing faces placed in harsh proximity. This process of decentering (or dismantling) established structures and of localizing ipseity was evident in the emphasis given to imperfect forms. The unfinished sketch (fig. 200, no. 116), the dangling conversation, the digressive *pour et contre* of graphic satire (figs. 107, 115, 119, 120, 122, 123, 124), the incomplete *pensée*, and the fragmentary essay were a kind of process art. Monsters by defect or excess, they constituted open and dynamic assemblages incapable of completion.[135]

From the vantage of Neoclassicism, to be without the possibility of conclusion was profoundly destabilizing. It signaled atheistic *amour propre*, the egoistical refusal to detach oneself from eccentric limitations in order to rediscover the underlying character common to all. As both Neoplatonism and Augustinian theology made plain, it was the least personal qualities of women and men that made them like God and unlike their unique, diseased, and sensual natures (fig. 183).[136] Both secular and religious hermeneutics, then, stressed that there was no similarity between God and the world. Leibniz, who made a significant contribution to Romantic theory, simply stretched this awareness of radical dissimilarity to cover the fact that all things were at variance. Everything in the universe existed only in differences. Thus Blake called atoms of identity those peculiar, distinctive, and energetic characteristics allowing us to recognize the unlikenesses separating Michelangelo from Raphael and even from Blake himself. Thus, too, in his composite art, every single image and word was treated in earnest since it possessed a personality unblended with, or foreign to, any other graphic form.[137] The English illuminator-poet was fully in accord with Leibniz's Neoplatonic view that each being was a radical singularity. Individuals were preboxed as particulate and monadic unities apprehending themselves alone. The accumulation of such "singles" was prevented from being planless by the precarious intervention of God. He preestablished their harmonious confederation through a divine algebra or logic imposed from on high at the onset.

Leibniz's thought also cast its long shadow over Novalis, who declared that "romanticizing was analogous to algebraicizing." Significantly, Novalis's rough-draft encyclopedia, *Das Allgemeine Brouillon* (1798–1799), was intended to be fragmentary from its inception. The 1,151 dynamic and independent units making up this project were part of a greater and open-ended whole.[138] These charged bits and pieces, therefore, were not incomplete but themselves symbolized a new epistemological paradigm based on a mental calculus. As we noted when speaking of Coleridge, there was nothing intrinsically incompatible between an epideictic Romanticism and a structural grammar or logical schema, between a condensed sketch and an organized setting together of pieces. In the light of the eighteenth-century explosion of dictionaries and lexicons, Novalis's aim was not to put together more information about material data, but to organize critically the disorganized arts and sciences. Unlike the integrating method of geometry that undergirded Neoclassical theory and even Blakean and Coleridgean Romanticism, Novalis's witty algebra played upon irreconcilable differences. His ultimate dream was that even the most irrational disagreements in this life would produce transcendent syntheses in another. To that end, polar opposites within the disorderly historical continuum were wrenched from their customary neighbors, or rescued from predictable comparisons, and violently yoked together. The intention was to force the occasional negative epiphany.[139] His aphoristic compendium, therefore, was like the fantastic work of art. This decentralized federation of distant and farfetched tesserae was made to fit together solely through the quick fancy of the user or the *esprit* of the artist.

Novalis's morselized and still blundering (hence the title) encyclopedia was a manufactured creation. As a surgical *corpus* of stray limbs, sutured and transplantable parts, it resembled a "synthetic person." This modern artifact was ostentatiously engineered, or reunified, from several persons at once. The German author's articulated, abbreviated, and broken style itself embodied a new prosthetic art of artifice. The fragmented text incarnated the contemporary, denatured, molecularized body and mottled consciousness. As such, it captured the antinomian and incompatible side of Romantic aesthetics. "Romantic. Absolutizing-Universalizing. *Classification* of individual moments, of ind[ividual] situations, etc. is the actual essence of Romanticizing."[140] Moreover, the combination and cross-referencing of every conceivable earthly possibility was brought about through a small number of "algebraic" rules for transformation. As unconditional structural principles forming an underlying architectonic, they determined the infinite connections that might happen among superficial things.

There was a twofold danger lurking within this retooled but still anatomizing approach. One might never arrive at the cumulative scene, but only drown in the unamalgamated details. The abstract invisible laws for achieving a superior coalescence were easily submerged beneath disconnected empirica.

Incoherent and isolated impressions could lose contact with a crowning logic amid the constant buffeting of flux and change. On one hand, the diseased condition of a failed Romanticism resembled Oliver Sacks's present-day description of a desperately creative visual agnosia. Sufferers from Korsakov's amnesia paved themselves—like Baudelaire—with a cold, unfeeling, and brilliant mask signifying a self perpetually patched together to replace vanishing meaning. Like Heinrich von Kleist's (1777–1811) marionette, the patient made every move through artifice, adopting poses through a voluntary automatism. Unable to feel, he learned to operate as an assemblage, but was unaware of how to be. Further, like the deregulated and gapped grotesque, breaches in memory were incurable. Creation was a constant grafting operation that could never fill the hiatus, but brusquely inserted foreign material flagrantly hostile to, and refusing to be integrated with, any coherent design. These unplasterable scars were exteriorized as a visual anarchy, a chaotic and unalive aggregate teetering on the brink of decomposition.[141]

The peril accompanying a solipsistic fancy was the generation of an endless stream of formal chimeras, delusory fictions, and absurd confabulations that were purely capricious or unreal (fig. 17). These visionary voyages into inner space, or flights of pathological conception, as Goya realized, led not to a refined and distilled psychic state but to painful uncertainty and turbidity. There were few artists before Edouard Manet (1832–1883) who could maintain themselves in John Keats's (1795–1821) condition of "negative capability."[142] The latter, or Romantic irony, was that deliberate disequilibrium between the function or style of the citation, or borrowed particle of material, and the stylistic system into which this alien morsel was inserted. Think of Manet's "barbaric" grafting of seventeenth-century Spanish bodies, or undisguised "quotations," onto Parisian urban types from the 1860s. Both old and new pictorial "spots" simultaneously signaled their specific identity and lack of fit within an organic whole. These painterly "points" and nugatory double arguments set out opposing positions on public issues with the seeming implication that either, or no, side could be held with equal confidence. Hence Manet's baffling ambiguity![143] In hindsight, too, Goya's *Sleep of Reason* seemed to offer a proleptic satire on the difficulty of keeping oneself passive and receptive to incongruity, of remaining open to the two contrary idioms of reality and irreality. His tormented dreamer fabricated monstrous mental blots unlike himself (because man-made) and improperly exhibited (because offering no resolution).

On the other hand, as a purified form of a priori philosophy, sublimated thought was volatilized out of its own autonomy. It, too, resulted in sensory bereftness and in a disfigurement of another kind. Fearing that a piecemeal marquetry of irreducibly individual shapes would lead only to Goya's state of muddled confusion and to Novalis's "blundering," idealism returned with a vengeance to seamless and bodiless universals. Eighteenth-century empiricism had emphasized blotched, wrinkled, and unretouched particularity. Coleridge, like Novalis, yearned to vault above this array of trivial and aberrant specimens, but he meant to achieve a fusive unity in multeity. He wished to get beyond the quirk, the specific, the anomalous, the contradictory, all representative of the associating and conglomerating function of a splintering fancy. The secondary imagination was to be the noble agency for soldering antinomian ideas and images. The soaring "esemplastic power" took on the aura of Leibniz's soul. It was to shape, join, and otherwise unify a sundered and obdurate existence into something "one & indivisible." Coleridge's poetics admittedly built upon the mannered writings of the late Latin "Silver and Brazen Age" (Lucretius, Catullus, Terence) and the English Metaphysical poets (especially John Donne). For him, their works demonstrated that even the wildest conceit had "a logic of its own, as severe as that of science; and more difficult, because more subtle, more complex, and dependent on more, and more fugitive causes."[144]

This profound stylistic connection between Mannerism and Romanticism, previously hinted at, needs explicit elucidation. *Maniera* can be identified with those deforming expressive or rhetorical features that give rise to aesthetic objections over the centuries.[145] In this specific sense of cabinet or studio malpractice, chimerical Gothick romance, obtuse Baroque allegory, licentious Rococo floridness, and juxtapositive caricature, all betrayed a classical decorum by their insistence on difference. Classicism was grounded on the precept that the painter or author must achieve a general and seemingly effortless likeness. In violation of this stricture, pointed figures were densely inlaid in a straitened or compressed space for the sheer delight in creating a combinatorial filigree. The Neoclassical critics discussed in the preceding two chapters variously censured the artistic casuistry that reveled in convoluted exceptions to simple norms and standard meanings. Thus Winckelmann, in the *Versuch einer Allegorie* (1766), defined allegory as signifying something other than what the statement appeared to be saying.[146] The "mannered" Baroque and Rococo laxism that permitted the torturing of "objective" facts to suit a bizarre "subjective" situation could be likened to the idiosyncratic and perverse twinings of grotesques and arabesques. This casuistic forest of discrete, deviant, and contradictory shapes existed only in the visual occasion, from probable case to case, from anomalous example to example.[147]

Similarly, and not unlike Neoclassicists, Romantic critics such as Coleridge worried about the labyrinth of a myopic descriptive empiricism. In this tangle, both the ego and the object lost themselves in minute and infinitely nuanced differentiations. Romanticism, therefore, could express itself dualistically. Like Novalis's artificial person, compositions could be seemingly, and inorganically, thrown together into speckled and circumstantial "misfits." Romantic *allegory*, thus, refracted an already extravagant particularity. As the organic superimposition of the absolute onto a temporal and historical entity, the Romantic *symbol* integrated the One with the Many. Thereby it tried to overcome the double pitfalls of an easy appearance of naturalness and the ruleless heaping up of internal and external things. These two formal systems, or styles, were in stark contrast: juxtaposition versus synthesis. Nonetheless, they responded to the same existential condition of suffering in the face of chaos, carnality, and illness.

It was specifically allegorical, or ironic, Romanticism that was indebted to Mannerism's contrived discoveries. Both fabricated an intensely individualistic world from unnaturally arrested obstacles and through a mobile ingenuity, wit, or fantasy.[148] This free-roaming capacity for hunting out and bringing together abruptly the distant and the close-up without eliding their differences, went beyond aesthetics into sociology and ontology. A Romantic art and literature, conscious of their own autonomy, crafted their own rhetoric and theory within the expressive fabric of the work itself.[149] The artist and author no longer relied on manuals written by "experts," but produced their own aesthetics and poetics embodied in the technical process and structure of creation. Hence change, of all kinds and at all levels, could be made directly by having ideas and people become something different, but not by being converted or translated into something else. The social character of such self-constituting assemblages was part of a post-Revolutionary society. Neologistic images and words identified an actively shaping subject laboring to form a particular ambient. Intrinsic to this sensibility, then, was the awareness that no two persons occupied identical milieus, since each was forced to stitch together his or her surroundings.[150] Think of how Géricault's patched and spliced portraits of cavalrymen seem to address simultaneously the loss of conviction and the departure of atmosphere from ambiguous historical events.[151] Equivocal times demand that one scratch together the pieces of a persona. The space of a figure was thus the result of its own configuration, the manufacturing of its own internal and external dimension.

The open and discontinuous structure of allegory actualized a warped anamorphosis or puzzle of ungeometrical pieces (fig. 157). The closed dialectic of the symbol pictured the spherical motion of going out from, and returning into, a shapely unity (fig. 143).[152] Each activity corresponded to a tension within Romanticism. As crystalline analysis, the former was skeptical of the distracted mind's propensity to blend antitheta. As undemolishable synthesis, the latter asserted a boundless confidence in the imagination's priority. Fractured by doubts or obsessed with seamlessness, this polarity was inscribed in the substantive *symbolon*. Its complex etymology denoted two parts that fit together like a cube, or two elements flowing into a single circumference. The sense of a liquid dissolving two moments into one was, however, subtly undermined. Ligneous and lapidary connotations of sawn pieces of wood, meshed like teeth, or of rough and scabrous stones, painfully set together, clashed with the image of fluid plenitude.[153] Coleridge alluded to the sympathetic bonding inherent in the primary meaning. The poet "diffuses a tone and spirit of unity that blends, and, (as it were) *fuses*, each into each, by that synthetic and magical power, to which we have exclusively appropriated the name of imagination."[154]

Such saturated language, suggestive of the watery reconciliation of opposites or of discordant parts, and of the gliding merger of sameness with difference, was overturned when the juxtapositive half of this special knowledge became reified. Allegory, as mutilated symbolism, signaled amorphous strangeness and the malformed other. It drew the ordinary and the extraordinary, the real and the unreal, tortuously into proximity. As a contorted tableau, discontinuous vignette (fig. 201), or truncated excerpt, it interrupted the iconic wholeness of the symbol and wrecked narrative fluency.[155] Furthermore, it refused to conceal its spotty artifice and marquetry-like pattern or scheme. This heuristic process yielded a thought awkwardly made before the eyes, with its digressive jumps and heteroclite components nakedly exposed. Thus Winckelmann ascribed to the Egyptians the invention of enigmatic spoors, traces, prints, or reticulated pictograms. This sacred hieroglyphic presented a riddling and riddled surface in which the arbitrary, exoteric image bore no relation or similarity to the esoteric concept.[156] The dominance of form— indeed its personification—was highlighted precisely because of the darkness

Que courageux et hardis piétons qui traversent
les sables brulants des déserts, et qui gravissent les pics escarpés
des Alpes et des Cordillières!...

201. Tony Johannot, *What Courageous and Bold Travelers,* from *Voyage où il vous plaira,* 1843. Wood engraving. National Gallery of Art, Washington, D.C., Gift of Lucien Goldschmidt. (Photo: Courtesy National Gallery of Art.)

and discontinuity of form. Its insistent demonstration of shadowy absence and disjunction challenged the viewer to question a sequential story line. Negative allegory, unlike the positive symbol, therefore, was a specifically visual and educational genre. Emblems, allegory's artistic counterpart, did not merely illustrate the content of a conceit, but exhibited the means whereby the observer could discover relations among disparate particulars (figs. 138, 139, 140, 141, 142). Their thrown-together look, or built-up character, embodied the teratological disfigurements of a sinful and equivocal world through which we were compelled to hunt and pick (figs. 98, 159).[157] Again, Winckelmann's remarks prove apt. As the proselytizer for an inobscure modern allegory forged along Greek, not Baroque, lines, he conceived of it as a general language of imagery comprehensible without a text. Yet he saw no merit in a "doubtful," "unfounded," or "forced" pictorial idiom creating uncommon thoughts and particolored fantasies.[158]

Winckelmann, of course, like grave Neoclassic, or spiritual Romantic, theorists, was repelled by the sight of another, comic world intertwisted with our daily, stunted and mangled lives (figs. 10, 160, 168). Wit conquered transcendence by detaching singularity from a normative foundation. A walking incongruity was a joke, a misfit out of step with himself and false to his social role (figs. 1, 135, 177). Neither one with the crowd nor common—in the sense of having its pecularities effaced—this naive construct departed from the population mean. The arch-Romantic deviant stood in lowly opposition to that creature of a positivistic social physics, the "average man." This cipher was numerically confected from large, unhomogeneous aggregates by smoothing away random variations.[159] As a nonimitating emblematic portrait, on the other hand, the garbled misfit was both actual and ideal, compiled and chimerical, epigrammatic and exemplary, funny and sad (figs. 123, 124, 126, 127, 146).

Burlesque humor used ridicule to pry apart cultural and aesthetic orthodoxies. It uncemented exclusive coteries and ideological cohesiveness, grounded in conditional reflexes and protected by official sanctions. The eccentric person or the nonconforming work of art, by his or its naiveté, broke the beholder's automatic responses. Significantly, the visual pun like the verbal was predicated on the impossibility of depicting a negative experience except paradoxically.[160] Recall that Hogarth's perfectly modulated chiaroscuro, embodied in a porcelain- and rose-complected woman, could be depicted only by an incongruously stained visage (fig. 200, no. 95). Remember, too, Rowlandson's anatomically deficient harridans, who literally made something out of nothing (fig. 175)! This lowly eighteenth-century jest or polysemous rebus[161] was raised by the Romantics to the status of high art. It became the composite emblem of a mismatched otherness worn at the pigment level. It was the incoherent image of a docked and lopped reality, the living opposite to divine harmony. Thus a multitudinously marked or morbid epidermis escaped being merely caricatural or derisory. Dotted or dented, it inversely pictured a healthy and immaculate truth turned upside down (figs. 182, 185, 190, 198).

Postmodern aesthetics and poststructural literary criticism proudly stand under the sign of difference. The allegorical technique of exposing fissures and voids, unbreachable partitions and irreconcilable omissions, is very much with us.[162] For the Romantics, and those second-generation Romantics the *fin de siècle* Symbolists, tour de force assemblages of bits of everything were ultimately intended to arrive at a plenary art. Gustave Moreau's (1826–1898) painted mosaics from the 1880s, for example, dovetailed jewel-encrusted histories with the lacy debris of myths. These filigrees of bygone odds and ends asserted the copresence of the painterly and the linear, the sensual and the cerebral, amalgamated within the universal ornamental grotesque.[163] Twentieth-century collage techniques, conversely, surgically sundered and caulked together chips and chunks of everyday detritus severed from their situational context. Yet even the most singular scraps, crumbs, and particles constitute only an aesthetic moiety. And now, in the age of electronic imagery, endless streams of lopped and laminated pictures are further falsely allegorized. Surreptitiously manipulated, excised, patched in or out of a specific time or place, they coldly molecularize experience without seeming to do so.[164] Television, in particular, doses us with a computerized and crazed dermatology of "spots," "snippets," and "bites."[165] An epidemic of divided and then seamlessly rejoined pointillist photo opportunities are forced to rush by, to behave pervertedly, like a series of atomistic words. Denatured by a hectic pace and severed from a thought-provoking simultaneity, images lose their difference. They are transformed into linguistic monstrosities. Obliged to abandon their nature, their pecularity, by those who despise them, they no longer behave characteristically. They have been stripped of their glorious history and mission as the signs and interpreters of experiential complexity. Consequently, we are still awaiting a new sensory style, or truly micromegalic mode, capable of doing mutual justice to the sweeping symbolic panorama and to the subdivided allegorical plot.[166] We are still searching for graphic methods congruent with the intricacy and detail of artificial information and with a highly dimensional world. Finally, we are still anticipating the resurrection of the perceptual from its disintegrated and data-thin status vis-à-vis the verbal. I speak of that glad day when imagery and an imagistic intelligence assumes its rightful and constitutive role as the maker of both particular and general meaning in an increasingly visual environment.

5 MAGNIFYING

Microscopic Seers

By the late eighteenth century, the model of the body as an integral whole finally fell apart (figs. 59, 87). The repeated incursions of smallpox and syphilis did much to hasten its demise (figs. 182, 184). But it was microscopy that drastically transformed how people perceived coherent organisms. The epidermis suddenly seemed to recede by several levels. Like modern imaging technologies, magnification turned the underside of the skin out. The body was decorporealized into a wraith, into an electrified substance. Today, when certain illnesses leave the corpus intact and ravage the mind (Alzheimer's disease) or demolish the physiology and leave the intellect sharp (Lou Gehrig's disease), the issue of how the psychic is valued in relation to the somatic, and to what *kind* of a soma, remains of central importance. It makes us think about what constitutes personhood then or now. Under the remorseless lens, a well-behaved anthropomorphic unity was pulverized into tiny and teeming minima. Not only were individuals overwhelmed by their corpuscles, but animals seemed to dissolve into the strangeness and indescribability of irregular polyps and multitentacled hydras (figs. 4, 202). Nor was it accidental that Renaissance formalism simultaneously reached an impasse. The theory of imitation, predicated on gathering severed human beauties and blending them into a decorous totality, left no room for the metamorphic imagination and the disruptive or dissident fancy. Like these inward-bound faculties, the microscope exposed the thickness of experience, the depth of the level.

Anamorphosis _____

noun, Deformation; a perspective projection of anything, so that to the eye, at one point of view, it shall appear deformed, in another, an exact and regular representation. Sometimes it is made to appear confused to the naked eye, and regular, when viewed in a mirror of a certain form.

Dr. Johnson, *Dictionary*

Anamorphose _____

noun, In perspective and in painting, said of a monstrous projection, or of a disfigured representation of some image, that is produced on a plane or on a curved surface which nevertheless, at a certain point of view, appears regular and properly proportioned. This word is Greek.

Diderot and D'Alembert, *Encyclopédie*

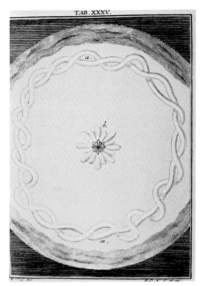

202. Martin Frobène Ledermüller, *Fresh Water Polyp and Magnifying Glass,* from *Amusemens microscopiques,* 1768, pl. 67. Colored engraving. (Photo: Courtesy National Library of Medicine, Bethesda, Md.)

203. Martin Frobène Ledermüller, *Coral Salt "Aureole,"* from *Amusemens microscopiques,* 1768, pl. 35. Colored engraving. (Photo: Courtesy National Library of Medicine, Bethesda, Md.)

Microscopy also ushered in another world, the wondrous phantasmagoria of the subvisible and the micromechanical (figs. 150, 155).[1] Today, it is common to speak of the corruption of visual information, its distortions and impostures, or the crookedness of its tinkered re-creations. This logocentric prudery, railing against the spectral, makes it difficult to convey the excitement over moving pictures experienced in a bygone era. Once upon a time, microscopic discoveries were both news and entertainment. Convinced that the perceptual was not a shortcut to nor an evasion of thought, the Epicurean strain of the Enlightenment mentality delighted in sophistic simulations, *trompe l'oeil* make-believe, larger-than-life projections and miniature spectacles. These novel and enticing sights were intended not only to evoke amazement but to provoke intelligent comment and passionate discussion among the assembled viewers. Moreover, as an aesthetic experience, they resembled ornament or play in being a therapeutic cure for *ennui*. Visions soothed the tired businessman and amused the fashionably bored woman. They thus helped to shape the nineteenth-century bourgeois attitude that separated the useless enjoyment of natural and artificial creations from serious and purposeful preoccupations.[2] Miniature phenomena were inseparable from the privatization and interiorization of art as diversion.

Optical instrumentation was developed, along with a home entertainment industry, for the pleasing and informative goal of making intangible things seem actual. Lenses and cylinders, originally manufactured in order to understand the universe, supplied the initial impetus for our current spate of mass-produced images. They are the ancestors of that digital technology beckoning us to enter into and to live the illusion. A democracy of phantoms, available to everyone, did not need to await the invention of HBO, cable service, and music videos. Empiricism was the environment in which solid and material things became converted into impalpabilities, and a "genuine" reality became cosmeticized into fantastic and "tricking" apparitions. This chapter examines that system of substitution. Impersonation and replication resulted in meaning becoming glassy or turning into a succession of synthetic dreams. Fabricated and prefabricated, decomposed and juxtaposed, the world increasingly swayed like a vision on an animated and ghostly screen.

The eighteenth century was convinced that many of life's secrets resided in the subvisible. The debates over generation occurred in large part because of the marvelous but confusing sight of small entities: seeds, germs, animalcules

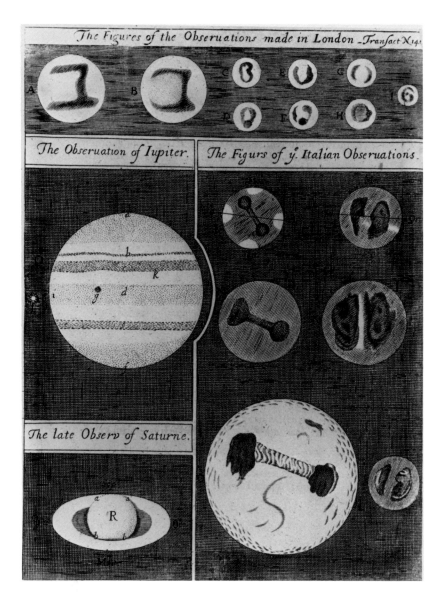

204. Anonymous, *Sightings of Jupiter and Saturn,* from *Philosophical Transactions,* 1666, I, no. 14, p. 231. Engraving. (Photo: Courtesy National Library of Medicine, Bethesda, Md.)

(figs. 148, 152). We have seen that Enlightenment biologists puzzled over the developmental plan allowing a fertilized egg to mature into an adult (figs. 146, 147, 151). Detailed images conveyed information and brought to the surface, as it were, the mysterious structures of life floating somewhere below the skin. Instruments sent a flood of lightning-swift nonverbal and graphic messages from an unknown and beautiful dimension. The extension of vision permitted a new form of travel. Opaque depths were opened up, becoming transparent without the infliction of violence (fig. 28). The veil of the invisible was gently and noninvasively lifted (fig. 203). The eye could easily voyage through and beyond the densities of a plane, or silently journey beneath the stratified level.[3] The intangibility accompanying such radical instrumentation allied microscopy most closely with the illusionizing devices and the prismatic coloring of painting.

TAB. DLXI.

Fig. I. Fig. II. Fig. III. Fig. IV. Fig. V. Fig. VI. Fig. VII. Fig. VIII. Fig. IX. Fig. X. Fig. XI.

PSAL. XCIV. v. 9.
Deus ὀφθαλμοτέχνης.

Psal. XCIV. v. 9.
Das Auge ein Werck Gottes.

I. A. Fridrich sculps.

Getting beyond the superficial was like going to an alien planet. The behavior of its peculiar denizens fell outside custom and commonsense (fig. 5). Johannes Kepler's (1571–1630) astronomical telescope, in use during the 1630s and 1640s, had directed the gaze on the heavens, only to reveal them upside down and maculated (fig. 179). John Marshall's (1664–1732) microscope, employed in the mid to late seventeenth century and early eighteenth century, relied on the same small telescopic aperture to let light enter the cylinder, and the same small mounting (fig. 85). This time, however, vision was trained on the terrestrial spectacle. Indeed, microscopes were often compared to telescopes (fig. 204), and suffered from the same chromatic and spherical aberrations resulting either from bubbles trapped in blown glass or from the shape of the lens.

Flaws aside, they were responsible for altering the way in which the eighteenth-century beholder construed the perceptible and imperceptible aspects of his ordinary existence. Algarotti spoke of the age's "happy talent for observation." With telescopes, the immensity of the sky was being explored. But microscopes permitted the penetration of sight "into the interior of even the most hidden of bodies."[4] He believed that only through such perceptual probes would medicine, chemistry, and physics attain perfection. Le Camus coupled his praise of instrumentation to an empiricist eulogy of vision. The eye was truly the noblest sense, the divine conduit whereby the mind obtained all knowledge (fig. 205). Distance glasses, managing to take a bead on the stars, and magnifying lenses, monitoring little curiosities (fig. 16), allowed the observer to perceive clearly what otherwise would remain shadowy. Through enhanced or artificial optics, investigators "discovered thousands of phenomena in this universe, of which they otherwise would have remained ignorant; they have been enriched with a new world, infinitely smaller than that which they inhabit."[5] More importantly, the Cassinis, the Bernoullis, Kepler, Leeuwenhoek, Malpighi, and Newton were responsible for the creation of "a piercing vision" that advanced cognitive operations on all fronts. Looking through tubes seemed to actualize Leibniz's metaphysics of possible worlds.[6] The German philosopher's conception of imaginary, multiple and discrete *cosmoi* was realized in the experimentalist's freedom of visual maneuvering among distant and detailed eccentricities (fig. 206).

The microscopic seer was the secular priest of the Enlightenment. Through scientific rites he brought the faraway and foreign close in luminous epiphanies. Swarming empirica were not merely data, but mantic signs and

205. Jean-Jacques Scheuchzer, *The Human Eye as the Work of God,* from *Physique sacrée,* 1732–1737, VI, pl. 561. Engraving by I. A. Fridrich. (Photo: Courtesy Resource Collections of the Getty Center for the History of Art and the Humanities.)

206. Martin Frobène Ledermüller, *Flint Sparks,* from *Amusemens microscopiques,* 1768, pl. 62. Colored engraving. (Photo: Courtesy National Library of Medicine, Bethesda, Md.)

207. Martin Frobène Ledermüller, *Wilson
Hand Microscope and Slides,* from
Amusemens microscopiques, 1768, pl. 6.
Colored engraving. (Photo: Courtesy
National Library of Medicine, Bethesda, Md.)

208. Jean-Jacques Scheuchzer,
Magnified Louse, from *Physique sacrée,*
1732–1737, II, pl. 128. Engraving by I. A.
Fridrich. (Photo: Courtesy Resource
Collections of the Getty Center for the
History of Art and the Humanities.)

nongeometrical emblems indicating a fantastic realm. Hieratic researchers into the atomic communicated the cold "feel" of otherness accompanying monadic and bright visions detached from their three-dimensional objects. Through vivid illustrations and energetic descriptions, they conveyed a paradox intrinsic to all allegory. Clarity of visual information oddly amplified and objectified characters. Thus, in the process of making certain subjects unforgettably present, they rendered them impenetrable, or cut off from normal experience.

Magnification became associated with the positive male virtue of seeing problems intensely and analytically. Negatively, as myopia, it signified the overweaning importance assigned to irrational and atrophied vision.[7] The uncritical and coquettish eye was easily duped by petty illusions and maggoty marvels. Both a masculine and a feminine optics depended upon the antinomies of enlargement and reduction, on the constant vacillation between seeing more or less. The diminutive was routinely aggrandized either by means of a simple (fig. 207) or a compound microscope (fig. 85). The former made do with one lens while the latter employed two. Strangely, the compound microscope was invented first.[8] It derived both from telescopes and from simple Dutch "flea glasses," commonly used to increase the size of ants, bees, mites, midges, and marsh infusoria. These and other puny vermin were responsible for inflicting the gargantuan tortures of the rashy itch (fig. 208). Scheuchzer's heroically scaled and distended blood-sucking louse, like those other tormenting insects, could already be seen with the naked eye.[9] Understandably, however, the eighteenth century was obsessed with examining at close range that plague of grotesquely armored, pincered, and antennaed small fry. Only as big as the point of a pin, this microfilth nonetheless wreaked havoc with the skin when burrowing into soft flesh.

The simple microscope produced better images for scientific work than did the compound microscope, with the exception of Robert Hooke's (1635–1703) experiments. Consequently it became the dominant apparatus for instruction, demonstration, and recreation for the better part of the eighteenth century. Its main drawback—evident in the popular Wilson hand microscope (fig. 207)—was that the magnifying power of a single lens increased as the curvature of its surface became greater. This meant, as lenses evolved, that they also became progressively smaller and harder to use. The projection of glass slides was one effort among many to augment that restricted vision. Specifically, their attachment to the solar microscope (to be discussed later) represented a major attempt to remedy a narrowed and shrunken prospect.

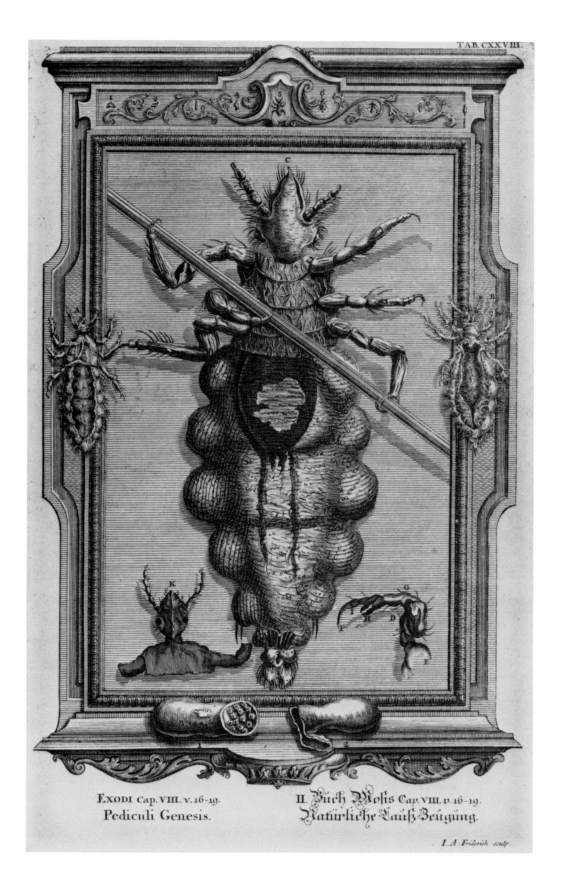

TAB. CXXVIII.

EXODI Cap. VIII. v. 16-19.
Pediculi Genesis.

II. Buch Mosis Cap. VIII. v. 16-19.
Natürliche Laus-Zeugung.

I. A. Friderich sculp.

To capture the initial magic of condensed, yet widened, powers of observation, we need to revisit the seventeenth century. Robert Hooke—distinguished natural historian, founding member of the Royal Society, Cartesian opponent of Newton—established modern microscopical studies. Although there were earlier and other important investigators, he cogently identified the key representational problems and intellectual issues inherited by the Age of Reason. The preface to the *Micrographia* (1665) triumphantly sounded the Royal Society's ambitious program of exploration. Artificially improving the sense of sight meant that the scientist could better survey this world. Indeed, he could even procure "Terra-Incognitas" for our admiration.[10] Henry Power's *Experimental Philosophy* (1664) antedated Hooke's work by a year, and by at least two years in actual performance. It clearly spelled out the Baconian empiricism fueling Royal Society–sponsored research into atomy grubs and grains.

The knowledge of man (saith the learn'd Verulam) hath hitherto been determin'd by the view or sight, so that whatsoever is invisible, either in respect of the fineness of the body itself, or the smallness of the parts, or of the subtilty of its motion, is little enquired; and yet these be the things that govern Nature principally: How much therefore are we oblig'd to modern industry, that of late hath discover'd this advantageous Artifice of Glasses, and furnish'd our necessities with such Artificial Eyes, that now neither the fineness of the Body, nor the smallness of the parts, nor the subtilty of its motion can secure them from our discovery?

The physician Power (1623–1668) envisaged no stopping "this darling art." With the rapid developments occurring in dioptrics, "we might hope, ere long, to see the magnetical effluvium of the Loadstone, the Solary Atoms of Light (or globuli *aetheri* of the renowned Des-Cartes) the springy particles of Air, the constant and tumultuary motions of the Atoms of all fluid Bodies, those infinite, insensible Corpuscles." He also demonstrated how this new science succeeded in pushing minutiae downward along the scale of magnitude and visibility to ever slimmer "parvitudes" and vanishing microbes. The "artificial advantages" of inflating and deflating glasses exposed a paradoxical truth. The least bodies visible to the unassisted eyes "are but middle proportionals (as it were) 'twixt the greatest and smallest Bodies in nature, which two Extremes lye equally beyond the reach of human sensation."[11]

Significantly, microscopes and telescopes also revealed that there could be no rest in nature. There was no such thing as absolute quiescence. Bits and pieces of organic particles disconcertingly hopped about on slides. Stellar bodies swam in the ethereal fluid. Microscopic and macroscopic substance, bacteria and planets, were in perpetual motion. The new optics, therefore, captured the complex activity and multiple order of existence, resistant to geometrical explanation. Addison popularized this vitalism propagated by microscopist-travelers. Like deep sea divers, they plummeted to the bottom of a liquid and lively topography. In the *Pleasures of the Imagination* (1721), he enthusiastically praised "the discoveries they have made by glasses." The perambulating naturalist could discern, with such tools, "a green leaf swarm[ing] with millions of animals." Addison believed microorganisms proved that the imagination was working its way both upward, to the vastness of the firmament and, downward, to the "minute inexhausted fund of matter."[12]

This lengthening vertical perspective threatened the mechanical philosophy by seeming to allow for creation *de novo*. Thus George Adams's (1720–1773) *Micrographia* (1747) colorfully described those idiosyncratic fingerlings anarchically abounding in fermenting fluids. "Inexpressible Numbers of minute living creatures peculiar to themselves, but of various forms and sizes," darted about in coagulating pastes and steeping broths brewed from rotting hay, straw, grass, or oats. Eels, serpents, "or little worm-like animalcules" were seemingly spawned when vinegar was exposed to the air (fig. 209).[13] Microscopy, then, also played a decisive role in the polemics over the nature of procreation. Spontaneous generation, or random and chance proliferation, was by no means a dead hypothesis. Buffon's notion that animate beings were composed of multitudinous moving molecules suggested that all animal and plant structures were the result of self-induced material actions and entropic forces. Since vitality existed in each mote "of these wee particular lives," organisms could reproduce merely by joining into an autonomous assemblage.[14] John Tuberville Needham (1713–1781), the British microscopist who settled in Brussels in 1768 as director of what would become the Royal Academy of Belgium, was also a key player in propagating the theory that life originated by means of a generative power. He endeavored to prove through a mass of microscopic observations of plant and animal substances that a force existed within nature capable, under proper conditions, of giving rise to new, organized beings. Like other dedicated natural philosophers of the eighteenth century, chief among them the Lombard Lazzaro Spallanzani (1729–1799) and the Genevan Charles Bonnet (1720–1793), he was fascinated by the regrowth of bodily parts. Abraham Trembley's (1710–1784) notorious experiments with the fresh water polyp during the 1740s had set the biological world agog. In defiance of reason, he demonstrated that an organic chit or speck could regenerate into a whole and healthy organism (fig. 5).[15] Scientists

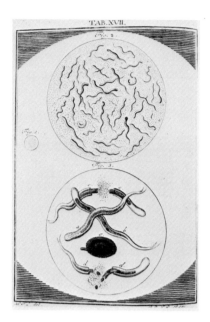

209. Martin Frobène Ledermüller, *"Eels" in Vinegar,* from *Amusemens microscopiques,* 1768, pl. 17. Colored engraving. (Photo: Courtesy National Library of Medicine, Bethesda, Md.)

subsequently engaged in a frenzy of amputation: segmented earthworms, horned slugs, footed snails, limbed toads and frogs were variously lopped to test their regenerative capacities. Their stumps were then carefully observed under a microscope. The Nuremberg painter and naturalist August Johann Rössel von Rosenhof (1705–1759) concentrated on amphibians and reptiles. His beautiful and famous *Historia Naturalis Ranarum* (1758) even elicited a preface from Albrecht von Haller. Amid sumptuous and graphic illustrations of copulating frogs, shown in their marshy habitat, were scenes of larval development that suggested an autonomous power lodged within dashing motes (fig. 150).[16] Was it possible, then, that insects originated from the process of decay, that beings sprang from matter, that order arose from disorder? The hypothesis was in defiance both of preformationism and epigenesis. As the *Encyclopaedia Britannica* gravely observed, this zoomorphic curiosity seemed at variance with the modern system of reproduction that supposed animals to be entirely formed within the egg. Yet there was no doubt that "the polypus, a species of the hydra . . . , although cut in a thousand pieces, and in every direction, still exists, and each section becomes a compleat animal.[17] These unruly and colorful fragments were thus responsible for making a new aspect of the invisible visible. Such crazy configurations and madcap creations were not serene mathematical intelligibles or Platonic solids, but comic cavorters. They seemed to vindicate the antimechanistic view that matter was alive, grotesquely populated with tailed vermiculi, aquatic salamanders, and jaunty self-patterning cells.

This "unlawful" *ars combinatoria* returns us to Hooke's reflections concerning the inner workings of things. He outlined an agenda for attentive inspection that was to guide experimentalists in the century to come. The plumbing of nature at first hand was to yield a Baconian catalogue of ordinary, yet extraordinary, particulars. No barbarous and obscene midgety antiquities (figs. 167, 169), no gnatty Bayle-like citations (fig. 102), but a sound and honest natural history was his aim. Specious scholarship was to be exorcised through the laborious gathering of exact and "useful informations" about "Common Things." Hence the *Micrographia* fit within the Royal Society's reformist enterprise of improving the manual arts. This founding document demonstrated that supposedly inexplicable functions were performed by "small machines." Such Tom Thumb "looms" were no more perplexing than those on which "Tapestry or flowred Stuffs are woven."[18]

Baconian, too, was Hooke's assessment of the infirmities of the senses. Erroneous information arose either because of the disproportion of the object to the organ, or else from mistaken perception. Alas, many things that came within sensory reach were not received "in a right manner." Memory, too, was duplicitous, frequently storing up the "frivolous or false" and obliterating the "good and substantial." To avoid the drowning of nature's truths under "frothy notions," the mind should occupy itself not with misleading or deviant conceptions, but with a scrupulous and strict examination of reality. Hooke recommended perpetual vigilance in determining which particulars might enter into and be retained by the brain. Admitting all impressions indiscriminately, whether extravagant or sober, led only to "darkness and confusion." Most importantly, the idolatrous bent of impaired vision, its congenital propensity to stray, needed to be compensated for. "Artificial organs" were the salvation of a fallen humanity, the cure for a contaminating and irregular fantasy. Optical instrumentation permitted nothing to escape human inquiry or to evade comprehension.[19]

Yet this brave optimism faltered when Hooke confessed the difficulty of seeing through a microscope. Before him stretched a mine field of incomprehensible chiaroscuro. "For it is exceedingly difficult in some objects, to distinguish between a prominence, and a depression, between a shadow and a black stain, or a reflection and a whiteness in the colour." Although he informed his readers that the engraver explicitly obeyed directions, glaring and distorting refractions hampered finding "the true appearance" and militated against drawing a "plain" representation. Reflections, too, when viewed through convex glasses, made certain portions of the object so bright that they annihilated the whole in a dazzle of "radiant spots." Of course, there was also the nightmare of multiple and conflicting perspectives. The transparency of many specimens subjected them to atmospheric changes. Thus, "in the Sunshine, they look like a Surface cover'd with golden Nails." But in another posture they resembled "pyramids," and in yet another aspect or light, "cones" (fig. 210).[20]

The question of angle, of what was proper to expect from a human, not a divine, point of view will concern us in many ways throughout this chapter. For the moment, we must take note that Hooke, and indeed a succession of empiricists, were torn by an unresolvable dichotomy. They nourished the ungodly aspiration to see more than was humanly appropriate, or even possible. Simultaneously, they recognized an antithetical verity, namely, that misperception was a necessary accompaniment to incarnation in a material body. The microscopist embodied the Symbolist's desire to erase the discrepancy between unearthly and earthly powers. In short, he confused epistemology with perception. The scientific seer believed he would come to *know* things stably and eternally by *seeing* them proximately and minutely.[21] Thus Hooke spoke a double language. He maintained that the new instruments helped to expose defective senses so that they might be repaired. Nothing seemed impossible to the assisted eye: neither the discovery of living creatures in the moon nor "the figures of the compounding Particles of Matter, and the particular Schematisms and Textures of Bodies." At the same time, in Pauline fashion, he mourned our "lame and imperfect sensations." These caused us to "take the Shadow of Things for the Substance, *small* Appearances for good Similitudes, Similitudes for Definitions; and even Many of those, which we think to be the most solid Definitions, are rather Expressions of our own misguided Apprehensions than of the true nature of the Things themselves."[22] The universal panacea for the "fine Dreams of Opinions" was "solid Histories, Experiments, and Works" to be constantly tested and retested by future generations of researchers. Thus all conclusions remained open to overthrow, and all observations remained subject to skepticism.

Hooke's attack against spurious imaginings was launched, I believe, against the Cambridge Neoplatonists. Henry More, in particular, dabbled in speculations and ran mad with "many hot scalding fancies and words." Perpetually enamored of useless Latinisms, taken with immaterial "parvitudes," spiritual "indiscerpibles," and exiguous "virtues," he was the hermetic opposite to the sincere and no-nonsense natural historian.[23] Hooke's emphasis "on material and obvious things" must be understood in light of such false wits who fabricated verbose quibbles, obscure neologisms, and brilliant thoughts.[24] "Why should we endeavor to discover Mysteries in that which has no such Thing in it? And like the *Rabbins* find out *Caballisms*, and Enigmas in the Figure, and placing of Letters, where no such Thing lies hid."[25]

Further, Hooke's examination of little odious vermin was the deliberate, and iconoclastic, counterpart to Neoplatonic charlatanism. He pitted Thomas Sprat's (1635–1713) "plain style" against mystifying Signatures and the "hard words" of high matter, dark art.[26] In Hooke's hands, the microscope became a leveling tool for belittling literary artifice and amplifying nature. Human ingenuity, which seemed colossal to More, was contracted into the runty dimensions of a pygmy. Significantly, many of the great seventeenth-century

microscopists were Dutch. Leeuwenhoek, notably, belonged to that Netherlandish tribe lambasted for baseness and lowness throughout a classicizing Europe.[27] The inhabitant of a flooded land built on a quagmire of silt, he trained his gaze on foul and swampy microorganisms growing in muddy waters. It was precisely these "paltry fragments," tiring the eye, that were conventionally associated with the Dutch landscape painter. This mere copyist magnified chunks of decaying wood, slimy pebbles, and clods of earth.[28] Such unclean smatterings or dirty trivia—ranging from blue mold bedecking the red sheepskin covers of a small book, to a bit of frothy cork, to metallic flitterings (fig. 210)—composed the heroic subject matter of Hooke's treatise.[29] The monstrous and deceitful enemy of painted and patched artifice constituted its ignoble antithesis. Observation I, "*Of the Point of a Sharp Small Needle*," initiated the demolition of sophistic creations by demonstrating, at the outset, the "rudeness and bungling of Art" (fig. 211). Microscopic examination of this man-made tip (no. 1, D) completely destroyed its superficial appearance of smoothness to the unenhanced eye. A searching lens showed

210. Robert Hooke, *Flint Sparks,* from *Micrographia,* 1667. Engraving. (Photo: author.)

211. Robert Hooke, *The Point of a Sharp Needle,* from *Micrographia,* 1667. Engraving. (Photo: author.)

212. Martin Frobène Ledermüller, *Lace
and Spider's Web,* from *Amusemens
microscopiques,* 1768, pl. 54. Colored
engraving. (Photo: Courtesy National
Library of Medicine, Bethesda, Md.)

213. Athanasius Kircher, *Natural
Impressions; Anamorphic Landscape;
Camera Obscura,* from *Ars Magna Lucis et
Umbrae,* 1646, p. 810. Engraving. (Photo:
author.)

it, in fact, to be broad, blunt, uneven, and "very irregular." Under close
scrutiny, then, this manufactured pin could no longer hide "a multitude of
holes and scratches and ruggedness."

Hooke, however, reserved his greatest scorn for printed and written full stops
or periods. Reproducing the roundest and most perfect of the lot (no. 2), he
nonetheless exposed it as being "abundantly disfigur'd" and "misshapen."
Magnification verified that it was quite immaterial whether such specks were
made by pen, copperplate and roll press, or type setting. Without exception,
they were all "bungling scribbles and scrawls," with "the most curious and
smothly [sic] *engraven Strokes* and *Points,* looking as so many Furrows and
Holes, and their printed Impressions, but like smutty Daubings on a matt
or uneven Floor." Hooke expressed an almost pathological hatred of artistic
marks. Seemingly black and no bigger than the dot inscribed in the middle
of the circle A, the period's domino mask was torn off by the microscope.
Expanded, this gray spot resembled nothing more than "a great Splatch of
London Dirt."[30] His obscene language of fecal virulence extended to the
scatalogical blots of ink marring a coarse piece of "shag'd cloth" or staining a
corrugated sheet of paper.

Hooke set in motion what would become a dominant antinomy in subsequent
micrographical publications. Even earlier, Henry Power had commented that
dioptrical glasses both heighten the works of nature "and disparage and
depretiate those of Art." When increased to the point of truth, a printed line
was discontinuous, indented, and filled with the "rugosities and seeming
protuberances" of the paper. This speciously uniform plane was itself mottled
by "whole clouds as it were of ragges." The most diaphanous Brussels lace
was a chaotic tangle compared to the airy and elegant symmetries of a spider's
web (fig. 212). Paradoxically, art was "inartificial," given this "pinched and
streitened" workmanship.[31] Nature, on the other hand, was the supreme
artificer whose execution was flawless.

Hooke and his successors, I suggest, reversed the normal practices of anamorphic perspective. Those witty optical games, so dear to Neoplatonic
mathematicians, required a familiarity with cylindrical and curved mirrors
in order to correct contrived surface distortions. Microscopists, as masters of
catoptrics and dioptrics, turned the tables on that ingenious race. For them,
no adjustment could set right caricatural scrap and scrabble. "For the Productions of Art are such rude mis-shapen Things, that when view'd with a
Microscope, there is little else observable, but their Deformity. The most

curious Carvings appearing no better than those rude Russian Images we find in Purchas, where three Notches at the End of a Stick stood for a Face. And the most smooth and burnish'd Surfaces appear most rough and unpolish'd."[32] The playful and momentarily perplexing *Vexier-* or *Verkehr-Bilder* of Hooke's contemporary, the German polymath Athanasius Kircher (1602–1680), were predicated on the capability of being reversed (fig. 213, L). Professor of Mathematics at the Roman College, hub of the Jesuit order, he amassed a museum of artifacts, singularities of natural history (D), and scientific apparatus renowned throughout Europe.[33] In that magisterial compendium of Baroque optical tricks, the *Ars Magna Lucis et Umbrae* (1646), Kircher devised double-speak landscapes. Two contrary and farfetched messages—a rocky, vegetation-strewn hillock and a bearded head—were simultaneously encoded in a single image.[34] The eye was distracted or diverted from one metaphoric meaning to another, depending on whether the picture was stationed horizontally or vertically. On the contrary, for Hooke, there was no casuistic wavering between two equivocal optical signals, no possible choice between real and unreal. Observation XIII, *"Of the Small Diamants or Sparks in Flint"* (fig. 210), described a cavity crusted over "with a very pretty candied Substance," visible when the stone was broken open. "Changing the Posture" of this miniature cave in relation to the incidence of light exhibited many small and brilliant reflections.[35] These adamantine bodies manifested, without confusion, the thoroughgoing beauty of even the lowliest phenomena. Artificial constructs were always grotesque with respect to nature's profound perfection.

The probing microscope, therefore, was an epistemological and educational tool for revolution. By changing our level of perception, it was meant to turn our values, to convert our interest from the molehill of material surfaces to the mountain of immaterial depths. Thus the *Micrographia* was fundamentally intended to deconstruct the false, muddled, and reversible appearances of art. Hooke's aim was to demolish admiration for shifty semblances and malformed blotches. By decomposing devious lines and dots, he recomposed our esteem for a straightforward nature whose overt physiognomy did not differ fraudulently from its covert parts.

Hooke's high-minded deposing of mannered artfulness continued in the Neoclassical missionary zeal to unmask Rococo illusion. It does not seem accidental that it was precisely during the early eighteenth century that the

LES GRANDS ET LES PETITS.

214. Grandville, *The Great and the Small*, from *Un autre monde*, 1844, p. 55. Wood engraving. (Photo: Courtesy the Library of Congress.)

microscope evolved from being an instrument of truth-saying in the clear light of day into an apparatus for glowing home entertainment watched in the dark.[36] Ironically, its viewing potential was increasingly shifted from accurate account to show, from boring history to fun docudrama. Recall that Hooke, however, had warned the unwary observer about the variability of scratched ground glasses, their tendency to refract, not to reflect, the invisible realm. Along with details of the wonders of enhanced instrumentation (fig. 84), such cautions were also transmitted in lexicons.[37] Moreover, the artificial creation of unlikely size, whether gigantic or dwarfish, teetered dangerously on the brink of monstrosity (fig. 214). The menace of excess or defect, of enormity or puniness, of Brobdignag or Lilliput, was that it escaped the boundaries of normalcy to enter the amusing sphere of the grotesque and the fantastic (fig. 97).

215. Martin Frobène Ledermüller, *Solar Microscope and Optical Cabinet,* from *Amusemens microscopiques,* 1768, pl. 1. Colored engraving. (Photo: Courtesy National Library of Medicine, Bethesda, Md.)

The simple microscope—the eighteenth century's equipment of choice—was commonly employed for studying the circulation of the blood. Trimmed with an elaborately shaped plate, it was garnished with adjustable hooks over which a frog or fish might be stretched and then examined through a small convex lens. The latter was surrounded by a concave mirror, or *Lieberkühn*, named after its inventor, the German microscopist Johann Lieberkühn (1719–1769).[38] Light was thus reflected on the side of the specimen facing the observer (fig. 59). Unlike the limited field accessible with the double microscope, the eye could see the object distinctly, and in an erect position. It was magnified in the ratio of the distance of the focus to the distance of the specimen. Consequently, a dizzying diversity of simple microscopes best lent themselves to the successive application of improving modifications.

Already by the 1730s, "optical cabinets" were being fitted with specialized devices. When a scioptic ball (to rectify the inverted image) was added to a Wilson screw-barrel microscope (fig. 207) and the tube was inserted into a window shutter, the solar microscope was born. First developed by Gabriel Fahrenheit (1686–1736), it was introduced into England by Lieberkühn in 1740, using mirrors supplied by the famous London optician John Cuff (ca. 1708–1772). Soon it was being manufactured by leading English, Dutch, and French instrument makers.[39] This widely disseminated optical system, popular in teaching, group demonstrations, and domestic diversions, was related to the camera obscura (fig. 213, M) and the magic lantern (fig. 174). Unlike those toys, however, its abiding charm consisted in the projection of "perfectly clear and distinct" images produced when bright sunlight was reflected from a concave mirror, passed through a lens, and fell into a room from which all other illumination was excluded (fig. 215). Its one drawback was that it could be used only in the daytime. This obviously restricted its educational uses. Itinerant lecturers in natural philosophy—like those demonstrators of the principles of pneumatics and phosphorescence painted by Wright of Derby—could not employ it in their evening courses. Consequently by the late eighteenth century, solar microscopes had become part of the fashion, not the profession, of science.

George Adams's *Micrographia Illustrata* (1747) dubbed that most "curious and entertaining instrument" the "*camera obscura* microscope." Amalgamating it with his invention, the universal microscope, he threw transparent views on the largest available "elephant paper strained on a frame which slides up and down on a round mahogany pillar, in the manner of some Fire-Screens" (fig. 216). These vividly colored scenes were originally of "extream minute-

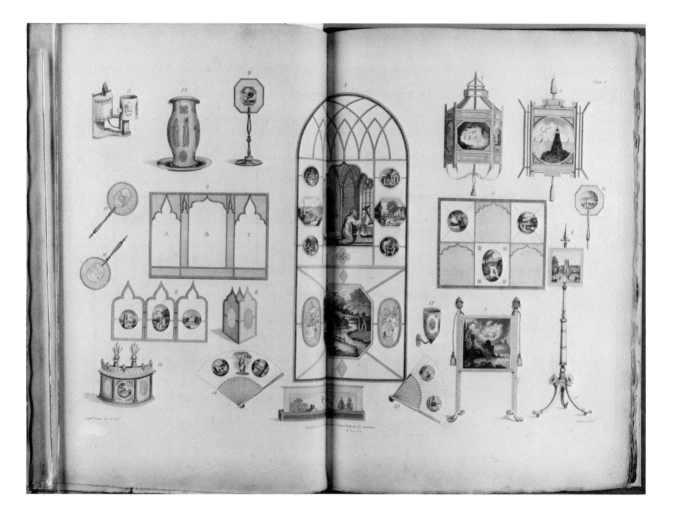

216. Edward Orme, *Specimens of Windows, Lamps, Screens,* from *An Essay on Transparent Prints,* 1807, pl. 4. Engraving by Swaine. Copyright 1990 The Art Institute of Chicago. All rights reserved.

ness." Yet they could be sharply "magnified to a degree that cannot be conceived by those who have never seen the experiment." Noting the many conveniences of this sort of display, Adams remarked that it showed items from microbes to maggots without fatiguing the eyes, and larger than in any other type of projection. It was the ideal communications medium, engaging a diversified audience in a vivacious and nonpompous manner. "Numbers of people may view an object at the same time, and may point to the different parts thereof, and by discoursing on what they see, may understand each other better, and more probably find out the truth, than when they are obliged to look one after another."[40]

Adams marvelously pinpointed a simple fact that we seem to have forgotten. Unlike television, which continues to borrow its strategies from serially printed words and solitary readers, the solar microscope was initially meant to stimulate discussion by the simultaneous viewing of imagery. He believed, along with other enlighteners, that demonstration, showing, making evident was essential to the persuasive imparting of knowledge. In a still largely illiterate society, experimentation exhorted, encouraged, and moved the beholder to learn through shining visions.[41] On the verge of illiteracy again—not just in verbal communication, but in the dominant visual media of our culture—we can perhaps learn from his lesson. Adams realized that an exciting packaging was part of the allure of information. Modish and stylish graphic enticements incited the beholder to become actively involved, passionately interested in further pursuit.

These attractive machines were part of an inviting range of instruments crafted for the gentleman dilettante's *cabinet de physique* (fig. 12), the optical complement to the tome-lined library. They energetically enacted the dry and diagrammatic natural philosophy buried in manuals and dictionaries, metamorphosing them into theatrical productions. Jean-Antoine Nollet (1700–1770), "electrician" to Louis XV, popularized the new technology. His *Leçons de physique* (1749) sang the praises of the solar microscope for the receptive ears of the French. First introduced into Paris in 1743, by way of London, the device was judged far superior to magic lanterns by Nollet. "Prodigiously amplifying" moving pictures cast on a white cloth, it was capable of transforming fleas into sheep.[42]

But it was Martin Frobenius (or Frobène) Ledermüller (1719–1769), curator of the Margrave of Brandenburg's cabinet of curiosities, who created the most seductive and complete encyclopedia of magnified "recreations." Part of an important and largely unstudied vogue for literature popularizing science through imagery, it was published in German (1761), French (1768), and Dutch (1776) editions. These ongoing and serially issued "microscopic amusements" unfurled an endless stream of edifying pleasures lodged in the scarcely visible or subvisible world. Significantly, Ledermüller emphasized that there were multiple perspectives possible to the assembled viewers vis-à-vis the simulation. Spectators were encouraged to arrange the chairs "according to their fancy" (fig. 215). Yet he also seemed to suggest that delightful illusions could become an end in themselves, a twenty-four-hour fiction, a torrent of blown-up emissions. Once the spectator was in the possession of a dark room, myriad "optical representations" could be contrived (fig. 217). In this nocturnal theater of irreality, "an infinity of other beautiful experiments" might be performed.[43]

Newton's famous trials with the prism (1704) allowed a luminous beam to penetrate by means of a small aperture into a blackened chamber.[44] That performance became the image-laden paradigm for getting in contact with the invisible and the impalpable. The resulting weightless and flamelike apparition made English science *à la mode* in France. Algarotti laughingly reported that fine ladies "visit the Abbé Nollet to watch him refract light the way they go to see the staging of Voltaire's *La Zaïre*"[45] Decomposing the rainbow and throwing the image abroad, however, created a new object. This artificial *spectrum*, or bundle of heterogeneous colors, was more vivid and memorable than its homogeneous natural source. The danger inherent in the "chameleon" and "Proteus of optics" was identified by the anti-Newtonian Louis Bertrand Castel (1688–1757). According to the inventor of the color clavichord, prisms were impostors because they flexibly adjusted themselves to all perceivers seated within "the playhouse of magical dreams." Newton created not science but enchantments, "a pure phenomenon, a fantastic object that was connected to nothing, to no objective body. It bore more on the nothingness of things than on their being, their substance, their extension."[46] The Jesuit and Cartesian presciently foresaw that the great mathematician and his optician successors erected secondary effects into primary causes, and established "the spectral as reality." He took "the plaything [*joujou*] of pretty colors," the disembodied prismatic phantasm, for the faithful mirror of nature. Newton forgot that the phenomenal glass reposed only on the undeceptive bedrock of black and white.[47]

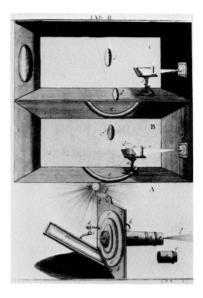

217. Martin Frobène Ledermüller, *Solar Microscope and Prismatic Projections*, from *Amusemens microscopiques*, 1768, pl. 2. Colored engraving. (Photo: Courtesy National Library of Medicine, Bethesda, Md.)

Reality ——————————

noun, Truth; verity; what is, not what merely seems (Addison, Beattie); something intrinsically important; not merely matters of show (Milton).

Dr. Johnson, *Dictionary*

Réalité ——————————

noun, Often taken as the opposite of appearance. One says, for example, of a truly pious man and of a hypocrite that one possesses the reality or the thing itself; and that the other only has the appearance. It is the opposite of specter, phantom, image; here is the thing, this is the reality; there is only the shadow.

Diderot and D'Alembert, *Encyclopédie*

The electrifying and bewildering image world of the eighteenth century scandalized logocentric critics. An inescapable presence of optical media fueled the debates between a grammatical physiognomics and a perceptual pathognomics, an absenting cerebral abstraction and a consenting empiricist distraction. As we have seen, the power and the pervasiveness of imagery permeated discussions of conception—imagery flowing like a river of words—and misconception—imagery patched together like a showy monster. Even the concern for compositional spotlessness was a reaction to the unavoidable sight of blemishes on parade. Mighty media events of flashing videos, walls of blinking televisions, and pulsing strobe lights ultimately derive from a seductive aesthetics of mesmerizing mobile apparitions and simulcast patterns drawn in space. The Enlightenment was the first and key period to see the systematic use of optical instrumentation. The mirror, as machine, tool, paradigm, and toy, was at the center of all apparatus magnifying a reduced reality into a concentrated and enhanced picture.[48] Newton's *speculum*, Castel feared, rendered meaning slippery and sophistically bypassed the viewer's analytical processes. Instead of the hallowed tranquility of text-oriented exposition, it accelerated the pace toward ubiquitous visual quackery. Castel predicted that what would come to count was the unmoored effect, the preternatural impression, or the pleasing design image of events, personalities, and products, rather than their substance.

The ancient prejudice against graphics was redoubled in an environment saturated with "false" appearances. Counterfeiting shows, extravagant exhibitions, eye-catching performances, diverting or strange masquerades, dominated the marketplace, the theater, and the public garden.[49] In European cities, the strolling quack, dressed in bizarre garb, was accompanied by harlequins, clowns, and zanies. Supremely image-conscious, he or she was surrounded by advertising props. Like walking gibberish or senseless cant, this fictitious physician was artificially constructed from the dubious nostrums and potions being peddled (fig. 177).[50] The essence of showmanship was visual persuasion. The rhetoric of salesmanship depended upon the broadcasting of bogus abilities and superhuman powers through dumbfounding pyrotechnics.

Dictionaries revealed the tight system of interconnections linking quacks, empirics, mountebanks, enthusiasts, and theurgics in the eighteenth-century mind. This troop of exorbitant barkers, illegal healers, and paid pretenders, however, was subsumed under a greater category of illusionists, that of the fraudulent sophist. A common thread running through the negative criticism targeting such fabricators was that they ostentatiously drew attention to themselves, shamelessly hawking their personalities while selling their wares. Thus Chambers remarked that the term *empiric* was now "more odious than ever." It described those untheoretical charlatans who practiced "physic at random without a proper education, or understanding anything of the principles of the art." In addition, he defined the *charlatan* as a quack "who retails his medicine on a publick stage, and draws the people about him with his buffooneries, feats of activity, etc."[51] The lying *ciarlatano*, or nimble circulator, sold foolish spectacles to the uncritical and ignorant masses at fairs.[52] He catered to the lower order, to those illiterate gapers rendered idiotically happy by mere gazing. Remember that this was a society where half of the adult male population and three-quarters of the adult female population could not read, and a large proportion of the remainder could not read well. Official guardians of linguistic authority were thus keenly aware of the power of whoring imagery to adulterate the uncultivated senses.[53] The riotous multitude valued picture over text, entertaining curiosities over hard fact. Daniel Webb echoed Quintilian when he declared that the learned know the principles of an art, while the illiterate were content with its sham effects and wanton show.[54]

Since Plato, the archetypal charlatan was the sophist. We have already met, on various occasions, this diabolical magus-manipulator, filled with outrageous *amour-propre*. His realm was that of the *trompe-l'oeil* artisan, not of the intellectual philosopher. His area of expertise was apparent truth, the casuistic and constant making of perspectival adjustments. This simulator corrected illusions relative to humanity so that it would not perceive the infirmity of the senses, so that it took the mask for the real thing.[55] He stood for everything Hooke despised. As anamorphist, he disguised the disproportion obtaining between God and his creatures by claiming proudly to create himself. The sophist was thus the focus of that primal fear against coercing manufacturers of spectacle who turned their audience into animals, or into mere spectators. He was the entrapping huntsman, resembling the changeable prey he pursued. His bait and decoys were as variable and multiple as shifting phenomena.[56]

Believing that delight stemmed from the eyes, the undisciplined crowd readily abandoned itself to an aesthetics of almost. It worshiped the shadow, the imaginary, or the quasi-nothing. Thus the mathematician Jacques Ozanam, in his *Récréations mathématiques* (1693), commented that in the time of the emperors Diocletian and Constantine, mathematics was suspect. Its instructors were condemned under the law, along with sorcerers, for possessing criminal knowledge injurious to civil society. Ozanam (1640–1717), whose enlightening aim was "to teach the entire world to perform such witchcraft," believed the problem anciently lay not with his noble discipline, but with a throng of mumbojumbo charlatans. These number-crunching fakes improperly used their gulling skills "to impose & to deceive the credulousness of the ignorant."[57]

Moréri, in the *Grand Dictionnaire*, indicated that *sophiste* was a name first honorably bestowed on philosophers and then dishonorably transposed onto rhetors and orators. These traveling persuaders, wandering from city to city, "made a profession of eloquence, with some semblance of philosophy." Subsequently, the term became derogatorily attached to anyone who excelled in an art or science, whether physician, jurist, or theologian, and who practiced it for financial gain. Moréri underscored the fact that the title had a negative connotation, even among the Greeks. From Protagoras to Gorgias, it denoted those handlers and traders who "engaged in a sordid traffic with their students, putting a price on wisdom and eloquence." Thenceforth, they were derided by an honest and virtuous public for coupling the "exhibition" of learning with "a vain ostentation of words," and all for the love of money.[58] The craft of these avaricious dialecticians consisted entirely of frivolous disputes and "the pure chicanery" of showy, useless, and captious babble. Thomas Corneille's *Dictionnaire* reinforced this sense of the con artist, able to produce everything but whose simulations, unlike philosophical truth, were not worth much. The costly *Eidos* or *Logos* was not accessible to the greedy imitator who, unlike the sage, deceived by "false reasonings those whom he tried to convince."[59] *Criticism*, and the analytical linguistic *critique*, were thus intended to expose such mendacity. Recall how we have observed that it was the Neoclassical critic's self-appointed task to cut lying out of the liberal and the fine arts.[60] But more of this later.

The sophist was intimately related to the magician. Chambers's *Cyclopaedia* noted that Zoroaster, the acclaimed father of magic, discovered "a science" teaching "wonderful and surprizing effects." This originally innocent study of wisdom, or *gnosis*, became corrupted when the Persian magi started to dabble in astrology, divination, and necromancy.[61] Like sophistry, magic came to signify any unlawful and diabolical pursuit dependent upon conjuring tricks and mass fascination. The sophist, as mechanician or technician, was also a fantast. His mesmerizing artistry polluted praiseworthy imitation. Physical routines and alluring execution gratified the senses but numbed the mind. Sophistry like rhetoric and witchcraft, then, was an ingenious, untheoretical, and pseudo-scientific art, blameworthy in its invention of clever wonders.

In the eighteenth century, sophistical and sacrilegious prestidigitation was invariably connected to hypnotic optical and light effects. We may now fully comprehend Coleridge's excoriation of Hartleian vibrations and other empiricist attempts "to render that an object of the sight which has no relation to sight." The aniconic poet scorned "that despotism of the eye (the emancipation from which Pythagoras by his numerals, and Plato by his musical symbols, and both by geometric disciplines, aimed at)."[62] His Romantic symbolism assailed not only the universality of images but an optical fetishism that forced numinous verities to coincide with luminous effects. Trapped within a "delirium" of cheating appearances, the cognitive "I" was reduced to "causeless, effectless beholding." Consciousness became "a something-nothing, a quick-silver plating behind the looking glass."[63] Hence Coleridge's and indeed all geometrical abstractionists' vindication of displacing signs. As barely perceptible vestiges or disembodied traces, lifted above the visible surface of matter, they indicated something invisible, lying beyond the incantatory sensory impression.

The theurgic fetish, or material idol, was the opposite of the symbol, always mounting above the mirage.[64] When this unnatural fabrication or forgery ironically displayed the misrepresentation inherent to any process of manufacture, it was termed allegory. Artificial bodies, or assembled *factici corporis*, were none other than caricatural Romantic grotesques. They did not require Hooke's detecting magnification to expose their conspicuous malformation. As flickering external hoaxes, they lacked the inner spirituality and coherence expected of symbols. The conjuring theurgist or cunning allegorist operated with similitudes, improbably trying to make living gods out of inanimate substances.[65] Instead of generating heavenly beings, his machinations only juggled with feathers and beads, with painted gewgaws and mock effects.

Vision, therefore, was synonymous with swindle. It epitomized the entire ruse of misconception associated with the bastardy of phenomenal life. In Neoplatonic symbolism, it meant ecstatically thinking the *Nous*, touching it mentally, not physically or invidiously beholding it. In heretical gnosticism, or syncretic allegory, it incarnated *curiositas*, the Christian vice of misleading seeing, the wasteful labor expended on patching misfitting misinformation together. This specious science of the bizarre and the fabulous misrepresentation combined "all sorts of filth and dirt" to seduce the faithful.[66] Earthly vision was identical to the thousandfold shapes of the Antichrist. It was consonant with Simon Magus's feigned miracles, meretricious spells, and diabolical charms. Sophistic Satan, in the guise of dissimulating entertainers, encouraged those colorful vanities and sensual pleasures of bath, tavern, stage, brothel, cosmetics, and sumptuous dress that duped the majority of mankind.[67] Master of transformations, the devil was the creator of stupefying prodigies. His monstrous and manifold incarnations appealed to vulgar visionaries or simple and mindless fools who took the imaginary for real (fig. 218). The horns, trumpets, purple eyes, pincers, and hairy legs of *incubi* and *succubi* were superstitious obscenities. Demons, who fascinated the eyes, could be said to describe any trumped-up specter or barbarous phantom still lingering within the dark pockets of the Enlightenment.[68]

Vehement disapproval of sensory ambush, fiction, and untruth could thrive only in a world littered with optical toys. Until the middle of the nineteenth century, traveling exhibitionists (figs. 156, 165, 193) set up raree shows stocked with monsters, magic lanterns, and peep boxes. Perspective games such as concertina-folded views, anamorphoses (fig. 157), mirror metamorphoses (fig. 214), and polyoptic pictures (figs. 84, no. 27; 219) were both playful and scientific amusements. Visual knickknacks flourished equally in the magical demonstrations of the drawing room or *salon* and on the shelf of the artful showcase (fig. 12).[69] Already by the late seventeenth century, ingenious slides were produced. The German natural historian Johannes Zahn mounted pieces of clockwork for animation, and the Dutch microscopist Petrus van Musschenbroek (1692–1761) created small mobile plaques painted with the sails of a windmill or the waving arms of a man. By the early eighteenth century, this occasional and odd entertainment had been transformed into a projection mania, magnifying all sorts of subject matter of diverting, educational, and religious interest (fig. 207). French *bibeloterie*, German *Guckkasten*, and Italian *specchi* were "monolingual" or perceptual forms of communication. The pan-European marketing of scientific baubles and luminous effects indicated that engaging indoor sports migrated well. Appar-

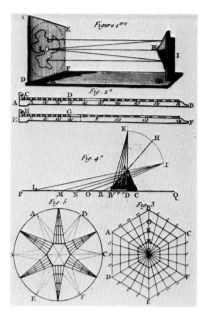

219. Edmé Guyot, *Conical Mirror and "Misshapen" Reflections,* from *Nouvelles récréations,* 1772, II, pl. 10. Colored engraving by J. F. Leizel. (Photo: author.)

ently, then as now, there was an insatiable need to fill screens. Illusionistic scenes ranging from tempests to odd geometrical figures were accepted and understood without translation. A new form of comic theater, projections needed to be experienced rather than read. Distance was collapsed between substantial spectator and airy and insubstantial *tableaux*. Magnifications, on one level at least, supported the old saw that truth on the stage lay in "the concurrence of appearances aiming to deceive the audience."[70]

Yet eighteenth-century scientific popularization was often synonymous with adult education made palatable to the nonprofessional. The spread of history (fig. 104) and natural history (fig. 184) cabinets encouraged the publication of easy-to-use manuals accompanying the objects on display.[71] In addition to sober catalogues listing botanical and zoological specimens (fig. 6), there were compendia of "amusements," "physical recreations," and "mathematical games." These mostly pictorial compilations illustrated how to make and perform optical, electrical, and magnetic experiments before a *parterre* of bewitched *amateurs*. An unrecognized legacy of the Rococo era was the realization that education should be entertaining. Edmé Guyot's *Nouvelles récréations* (1772)—existing in both French and German editions—was typical of this new class of literature demonstrating that physics and mathematics were not only worthwhile in themselves but entrancing. An astute behavioral psychologist, Guyot (1706–1786) realized that humanity needed distraction in order for the abstract intellect to become engaged. To help matters along, he envisaged publishing four new volumes each year, attractively filled with nonsupernatural diversions. He argued that an overly long preoccupation with serious matters fatigued in the end. Fascinating amusements refreshed and perked up strained or weary minds and helped students of all ages and from all walks of life to think geometrically. The mathematician-educator subtly argued that understanding something elicited its own peculiar and personal gratification. The brain relished lifting difficult obstacles to comprehension, or discovering a secret others were as yet incapable of grasping.[72]

Guyot's inspired defense of the clandestine enjoyments attendant upon visual learning was based on a Mannerist aesthetics of the unexpected.[73] Initially perplexed by startling phenomena, the spectator subsequently found it satisfying to work at unraveling their hidden causes. Nothing was deemed too frivolous or too insignificant in furthering Guyot's pedagogical aim. He wished to instill zest for the hard sciences, or for those disciplines whose subject matter was conventionally without figure, color, or human contact.

368

Card games, optical tricks, chemical frolics, phosphorescent jokes, merry enchantments fabricated from air, water, electricity, and magnetism were intended to generate wonder and to produce gusto in others while simultaneously instructing them. Yet the danger inherent in manipulating vanishing quantities, or playing with rigorous analyses, was that the mathematical imagination would become as free to disport itself as speculative metaphysics.

These winning enticements were grounded invariably on optics, explaining the illusory appearances presented by objects placed at a distance, or on catoptrics, dealing with the myriad ways in which light could be reflected (figs. 199, 220). The latter, especially, was also closely allied to *skenographia*. Scene painting attractively showed how figures might be represented by images that did not appear shapeless or disproportioned when beheld from afar (fig. 219). The camera obscura, invented by Giovanni Battista della Porta (1535–1615) and brought to general notice by Kircher during the seventeenth century, continued as the foundation for much eighteenth-century optical technology. It was adopted, adapted, and produced in a staggering variety of shapes and sizes. These ranged from full-scale rooms to tabletop machines to microdevices insertable on the top of a building, in the knob of a sedan chair, in a pocketbook, or in the tip of a cane (fig. 84, no. 28).[74] Its lasting hold owed not only to ease of use and convertibility to diverse purposes, but to its literal and metaphoric associations with the mechanism of vision. Allowing light entering a circular aperture to pierce a black interior and to cast an inverted image onto the opposite wall gave birth to "a small world in another world." The structure of the eye, said Scheuchzer, resembled "a camera obscura of an infinite kind, & without which all the beauties of the world would be nothing" (fig. 205). In both the miniature natural, and the large artificial, dark room, "external objects, buildings, trees, men, & the perspective of an entire countryside are represented" (fig. 213, M).[75]

Kircher developed this visual machine into a spectacular toy that, like sight, permitted light and colors instantaneously to enter an enclosed space without touching it. Both the nontactile retinal image and the intangible projection were optical effects existing disembodiedly either within the human brain or inside a constructed box. In the *Ars Magna Lucis et Umbrae*, Kircher unleashed a weightless *ars chromocritica* and a ghostly Epicurean *photosophia*. He was thus in part responsible for the upsurge in eighteenth-century allusions to slender films and shimmering species released by material substances.[76] As diaphanous apparitions, tints and rays exerted a subtle visual and immaterial pressure

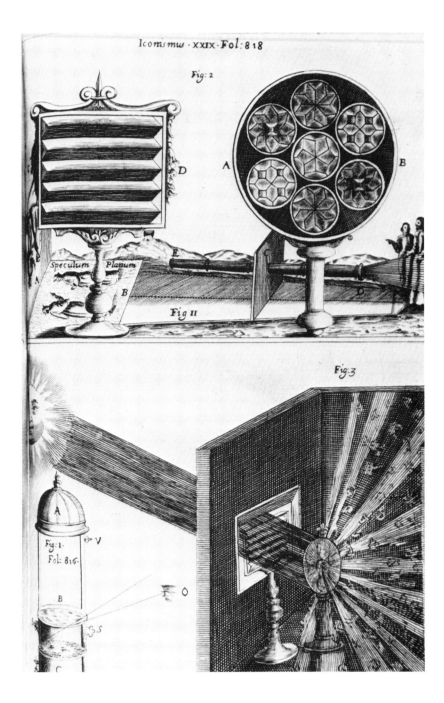

on their receptors. The Newtonian Algarotti, popularizer of the new science, continued to tout the use of this phantasmic device in art. Painters should rely on the camera obscura "the way astronomers employ glasses, & physicists the microscope: all these instruments equally contribute to the better knowledge of nature & to capturing her with greater accuracy." Algarotti regaled the artist with the witchery of "this artificial eye." Lenses and mirrors transported distant vistas onto a suspended linen cloth. These views were procured with an extraordinary "clarity and inexpressible energy" compared to the originals. Vivid and rich colors, or redoubled reflections, permitted the observer to see things that would otherwise remain unseen. This instrument was epiphanic in enabling him also to concentrate on a single object without being distracted by the rest of the environment. Multiple and confusing light beams, weakening the intense vision of a solitary phenomenon, were excluded.[77]

French and English optical boxes, German *Kulissenbilder*, and the Italian *mondo nuovo*—popularized in the paintings of Pietro Longhi (1702–1785), Alessandro Magnasco (1667–1749), and Giandomenico Tiepolo (1727–1804)—were extensions of the camera obscura. These pantoscopic devices made *imaginary* prospects seem three-dimensional or real. The diffusion of simulations, of "news" from "novel other realms," occurred within the dim privacy of homes rather than in the glare and tumult of the marketplace or fair.[78] The success of peep shows, *vues d'optiques*, and cutout perspectives depended on the agility and the experience of the operator. Manual dexterity was required to beguile an audience seated at close range rather than milling about in the dusty chaos and bright light of the public square. The heyday of optical boxes, such as those heaped in the left foreground of Chambers's frontispiece (fig. 105), spanned from the second quarter of the eighteenth century to its close. Usually they were either horizontal, and viewed directly, or pillar-shaped, and viewed through a lens and an inclined mirror placed at the top (fig. 84, no. 31). Their sides were often papered with engravings, many of which were manufactured in Augsburg. As one of the major centers for book illustration, this city served as the hub for distributing visual pleasures over much of Europe. Instructions for their assembly could also be found in the optics section of every major dictionary and encyclopedia.

Rather than just documenting the layout of great European cities, the plans of noteworthy palaces and churches, and the sites of famous battles, these illusions introduced a make-believe dimension. Idealized *vedute*, rural sports, *fêtes champêtres*, hunts, equitation, music making, picturesque peasantry, scenes of gaming and smoking, piquant Freemasonry rituals were presented in a theatrical way.[79] Cataclysmic subjects, eliciting the same shudders of delight that would later accompany Philippe Jacques de Loutherbourg's (1740–1812) lurid *Eidophusikon* landscapes of the mid-1770s, could also be had. Simulated earthquakes, torrents, shipwrecks, and volcanic eruptions aroused a *frisson* in the face of the safe sublime. There were also less sensational but quietly intriguing catoptric games ingeniously playing with the different ways in which light bounced from a polished and curved plane. Common to all reflecting and refracting mirror emanations was the deliberate stimulation of doubt as to where an object was really located. Bewilderment was also increased through the contrivance of irregular images differing dramatically from the regular objects emitting them (figs. 157, 219). Guyot filled volumes with instructions for voyeuristic and sophistic spectacles. The clever manipulator could make it seem he was looking straight ahead while actually gazing in the opposite direction, perusing an opaque print while really examining a transparency. He could make the viewer believe he was looking into an empty mirror in which "a sort of phantom" suddenly and mystifyingly floated. These perspective curiosities reached their apogee in *polémoscopes* or prying glasses that let the beholder survey a spot without being seen.[80]

Portability was at the root of this vast diffusion. If the would-be entertainer did not wish to construct his own apparitions, they could be readily purchased from the peddler's pack.[81] A great variety of transparencies for magic lanterns, or thickly aquatinted and varnished "fancy prints," could also be bought at booksellers like Ackermann's. Rowlandson's waxy impression of two *commedia dell'arte* characters was fabricated for that popular trade (fig. 174). The rowdies in this tenebrous drama could be cast in chalky enlargements onto a wall or sheet. They were magnified by moving the projector slowly away from the screen, and reduced by pushing it forward. It took considerable skill to prevent the scenes from wobbling and to smooth out variations in light intensity as the apparatus receded or approached.[82]

Ozanam's *Récréations mathématiques* was the learned inspiration behind Guyot's vulgarizing and more broadly accessible enterprise. Yet this grave professor of mathematics also felt obliged to provide instructions for "megalographic" magnifications. "Hideous specters"—in this case painted in distemper on small panes of glass and mounted in wooden holders—could be rendered enormous. Prodigies, attaining "a gigantic & monstrous size," were agreeable to those in the know and filled them with admiration. But the credulous could easily be persuaded that frightening grimaces and terrifying ghosts were the result of "magic & of necromancy."[83] Long before Louis—Jacques-Mandé Daguerre (1789–1851) opened his Paris diorama in 1822, then, there were a host of figures freely floating in the air surrounded by the telltale halo of light signaling the magic lantern's presence. Robert Barker's (1739–1806) 360-degree paintings or panoramas, invented in 1789, inaugurated an illusion that was to be both total and seamless. Sir David Brewster's (1781–1868) kaleidoscope was equally intended to engross the eye. This animating tube, invented in 1817, presented geometric transfigurations combined from mobile pieces of colored and faceted glass. The British scientist developed an idea already found in Kircher (fig. 220) and reiterated by Ozanam, namely, that multiform tesserae and luminous mosaics could be decomposed and recomposed at will into prismatic abstractions.[84]

During the Baroque period, such technological conceits formed the basis of witty metaphor machines. These devices generated extravagant metamorphoses occurring within sealed and shadowy chambers. Kircher prefigured and actualized Emmanuele Tesauro's (1591–1675) rhetoric of chromatics. Looking at the world through the "Aristotelian telescope" of human ingenuity, or fantasy, was likened to looking through a magic mirror. All sights were compressed into, and moved inside, its frame. Across its reflecting and refracting surface flitted the identical, but always different, objectless colored patterns.[85] The Jesuit's machine for provoking *stupore* required that a spectator enter a hermetic box to undergo symbolic transformations. A hidden rotating wheel was emblazoned with emblems cast surreptitiously upon a mirror. As the observer gazed into the looking glass he glimpsed not himself but a succession of novel and chimerical identities imprinted upon his labile features (fig. 221).

These esoteric and mannered games, intended for the aristocratic few, should be contrasted with the eighteenth century's attempts to popularize and widen the impact of specialized information. An enlightened science was to be purged of any smatterings of the occult. Furthermore, in their semantic equivocation, pictorial cryptograms and anamorphoses stood in sharp opposition to the industrialization of flickering imagery meant to enliven the middle class home. By the close of the century, optical cabinets had increasingly altered arcane formal and theoretical experiments into usable marvels. It was now big business to manufacture reveries for the average household. Edward

221. Athanasius Kircher, Catoptric Theater, from *Ars Magna Lucis et Umbrae,* 1646, p. 901. Engraving. (Photo: author.)

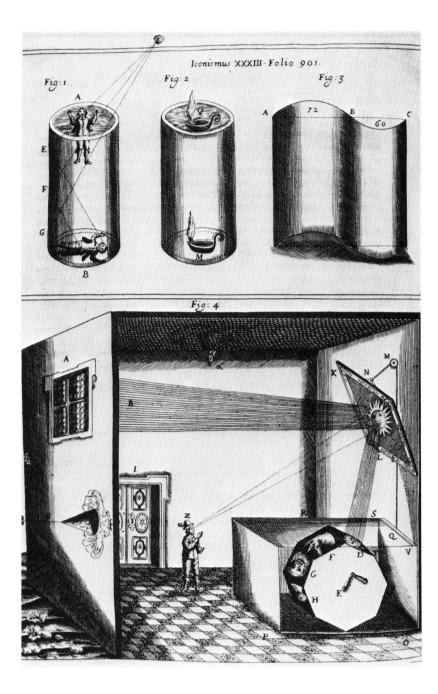

Orme's *An Essay on Transparent Prints, and on Transparencies in General* (1807) wrenches us from the domain of distorting ciphers and monstrous *imprese* to speak, instead, of practical delights. This London-based landscapist and portraitist (fl. 1801–1807) compiled a compendium of specially prepared color aquatints. Chemically treated so that certain portions of the design would appear translucent when held to the light, they were meant inexpensively and eclectically to outfit the domestic interior with bliss-inducing furnishings. Glowing medieval shutters, Venetian windows, chimneypiece ornaments, firescreens, ladies' fans, and Chinese candle or lamp shades conjured up affordable effects "without the dust, dirt, or expense of coals and wood" (fig. 216). Orme even envisaged a transparent panorama, since "they were so much in fashion."[86]

The British artist claimed to have been the first to develop transparent prints in 1800. The purpose of his essay—significantly published simultaneously in French and English—was to give minute instructions for carrying out "this pleasing, simple, and delightful art." Light-shot simulacra were intended as an inexpensive imitation of glass painting. Instead of the privileged audience capable of appreciating curious perspectives, virtuoso puzzles, and the abuses of illusion, this work was destined "for the public at large, including those totally unacquainted with the use of the pencil."[87] He admitted that East and South Asians have known, since time immemorial, how to paint on linen, silk, or gauze. But these were costly and fragile materials, Orme explained, and consequently of limited appeal. In experimenting with varnish used in oil painting, he accidentally spilled some drops on an engraving. Serendipitously, this chance happening suggested the idea of producing in a relatively cheap and mass medium, and by the same means, "a strong transparent light in prints previously prepared for effect." Both the Romantic subject matter and the exaggerated chiaroscuro were fueled by the rage for Gothic novels, for *Castle Spectre*, for William Beckford's *Revelation Chamber*, and for the Prince of Wales's fairy pavilion at Brighton.[88] Colored and dipped papers were illuminated with sparking fires, haunted abodes, and beturbaned sages meditating in cozy cave alcoves (fig. 222). This new form of tracery functioned as a kind of sensory substitution for the real and tangible thing. Two-dimensional changelings, rather than three-dimensional goods, were vicariously to warm humble and dank cottages on cold, wet nights. Orme remarked that the themes best suited to this diaphanous and somnambular medium were those involving the greatest contrast of shade and light, of "the gloomy with the lively." Thus the varnished and tinted engraving of the *Philosopher*

in His Study—reminiscent of certain of Wright of Derby's necromantic and chemical scenes—opposed the reddish flames of the hanging lamp to a lunar silver glow. More generally, the bright and snug interior was the antithesis of the cool evening air and the blackened stones framing the entrance.[89]

The vogue for prints lit from behind and watched in the dark domesticated credulity, while reifying phantoms. They accustomed the viewer to visual replacements. Magnifying hyperbole and lucid *enargeia* were lavished on simulations that appeared truer and more desirable than life.[90] Hyperreal reconstructions or forceful reenactments induced intense feelings exceeding the emotions aroused by the pale sight of the objects they impersonated. Think of how this rage for specters and the apparitional invaded late eighteenth-century painting. Thomas Gainsborough (1727–1788) not only specialized in phantasmic portraits but, according to Ozias Humphrey, kept his studio even by day in "a Kind of darkened Twilight." This friend of de Loutherbourg's also constructed a peepshow box (ca. 1781–1782) for which he made small landscape transparencies.[91] Fuseli propagated a tenebrist tribe of Eddic and Miltonic ghosts. Girodet, in thrall to the singular effects produced by artificial light, specialized in showing the charged lambency of marble turned into glittering flesh. The phosphorescent *Sleep of Endymion* (Paris, Musée du Louvre, 1793) seized the vaporizing impact of a nightly *insolatio*.[92] Ingres's shadowless *Napoleon* (Paris, Musée de la Grande Armée, 1806) was criticized for apparently having been painted by moonlight. Most dramatically, perhaps, Goya's flying imaginings, colossal *Caprichos*, or "black paintings," were designed to be seen from below. With the aid of Robertson's "fantoscope," they materialized above the heads of the astonished beholders seated or standing in the darkened dining room of the Quinta.[93] The Belgian balloonist and scientific entrepreneur Etienne-Gaspard Robert, or Robertson, had delighted Parisians at the Palais-Royal during the 1790s with his *Fantasmagories*, or "great art of light and shadow."[94] A horde of his successors similarly tried through a nocturnal prestidigitation to abolish time, to make the absent present, and to animate the inanimate.

There seemed to be little difference between the experience of heightened internal visions while awake and the living of life as a series of augmented pictures, or as a dream. Both were the result of images, or of the indicative power of light to make things appear. As Jérôme Richard noted in the *Théorie des songes*, strange shapes and other sports of the fancy could be set in motion given the slightest impetus: by a sight, a sound, or a sensation. These external stimuli prompted the unfurling of condensed and bizarre *tableaux*. The real stage "is in our mind, & it is on its condition that depends the length, duration, or variety of the spectacle that the imagination performs there."[95]

Dream Projections

Fiction _____

noun, The act of feigning or inventing; the thing feigned or invented; a falsehood; a lie.
Dr. Johnson, *Dictionary*

Fiction _____

noun, A product of the arts which has no complete model in nature. There are four categories of fiction: perfect, exaggerated, monstrous, fantastic. . . . The fantastic is the disordering of the imagination or the debauch of genius. . . . It is that assemblage of the most distant genres and of the most disparate forms, without progression, without proportion, without nuance. . . . It is everything that the delirium of a sick person makes him see that is most bizarre. . . .
Diderot and D'Alembert, *Encyclopédie*

Information became disembodied, that is, predominantly visual, during the eighteenth century. Paradoxically, a hedonistic withdrawal from reality into make-believe was promoted by two antithetical schools of philosophy. Empiricism, as a form of skeptical iconoclasm, continually harped on the difficulty of distinguishing the fictional from the factual. Cartesian rationalism, equally implacable toward the lie, the feint, the trick, de-realized the world into a dream metaphysics. This double-barreled assault left the visual arts in the precarious position in which they find themselves today. Long associated with the pleasure principle, with the creation of self-indulgent fancies, with the intangible idols of desire, they fell outside any serious production that "counted." Even their market value was used to deflate them into the playthings of consumer demand. Sophistic artists were considered inventors of new and useless wants. Advertisers of ornamental needs, they seemed to cater to human avarice, acquisitiveness, stupidity, and venality. This demotion to entertaining clown or to material fetish posed a singular problem for painting, which could correct false images only by the fabrication of more images. Among major empiricist and rationalist critics, painting became increasingly reduced to the frivolous art of the simulacrum, unhooked from public life. Its shams were connected to the untouchable semblances produced by optical gadgetry. Flat projections and fake flimflam further delusionized solid objects. Phoniness tainted the very activity of beholding the world. Technological gimmickry thus advanced an abstract knowledge steadily supplanting the belief in a cohesive, shared, and fully rounded social experience.

Thomas Hobbes's (1588–1679) and John Locke's empiricist psychology, while seeming to separate mental conceptions from external reality, only fictionalized both.[96] At birth, the mind was a blank sheet, void of any inscription and awaiting the uncontrollable influx of contaminated impressions or confused sensory perceptions. The problem with sensuous data was its jumble, its unformulated and unmethodical intricacy that darkly impinged on the passions without our comprehending why. Much of empiricist philosophy, therefore, was about carving out distinctions from the phenomenal noise. Muddled complex ideas had to be dissected or broken into their simple and irreducible components. Significantly, *aisthetica*, or things seen, were not

378

noetica, or things known, until they had undergone this anatomizing enumeration. Hobbes in the *Leviathan* (1651) commenced the analysis by attempting to divide properties inherent in an object from qualities belonging only to sense perception. He believed it absurd that mental images should be taken as accidents of the percipient. Rather, they belonged to external bodies that initiated motions within the receiver's animal spirits. The resulting impressions then pushed themselves toward the consciousness of the observer.

This argument sounded cut and dried. Ambiguity, however, entered in the form of the voyaging fancy, ranging from phantasm to phantasm. While "mental discourse" was frequently regulated by some design or wish, it could also wander unguided as impertinently as figures in a dream. Hobbes spoke of such licentious and farfetched fiction in terms of a *"Feign'd or Artificiall Person."* Persona, in Latin, designated "the *disguise,* or *outward appearance* of a man, counterfeited on the Stage; and sometimes more particularly that part of it which disguiseth the Face, as a Mask or Visard."[97] To impersonate or to act, then, lay at the root of the imagination's unauthorized images. Unreal representations pretended realistically to be the actual people or events deployed in nature. Hypostasis expressed sham entities so fully that, like strong evidence, they seemed to set material objects incontrovertibly before the eyes.[98]

But is was Hume, more than Locke, who spelled out the skepticism inherent in the problematic "way of ideas." He reduced all faculties to conception, or to the apprehension of what was present to the mind. Far from severing the phantasm from physical things, as the materialistic Hobbes had tried to do, he declared that "the very image which is present to the senses is with us the real body." A potentially even more disturbing conclusion—later arousing the aniconism of Immanuel Kant (1724–1804)—was that since perceptions differed from each other and from all other things in the universe, they were distinct and separable. Like the preformationist's encased germs, they had no need of anything else to support their existence.[99] This declaration prompted the German iconoclast to erect his language-based rationalist philosophy not on deceiving images, but on abstract schemata. Without their synthesizing mediation, no mere idol or appearance could ever attain the universality of a concept in the understanding.[100]

Hume's assertion that ideas and perceptions were identical, and identically visual, had repercussions for imagining. Conventionally taken to be only one form of conceiving, the imagination—even in Hume's early writings—came close to being identified with the entirety of the mind. Thus the associating and attracting fancy, in "the course of thinking," runs "easily from one idea to another that resembles it." Moreover, this magical faculty of the soul operated not only in nature but in the arts. When aspects of a scene or parts of a painted or a poetic composition were lacking, it obligingly supplied fictions, or "ideal presences," to make up for and supplement what was absent in the imitation.[101] Thus the powerful fantasy, roaming around in space collecting and joining ideas, seemed to come perilously close to providing extension to incorporeal and corporeal things alike. Andrew Michael Ramsay's *Travels of Cyrus* (1727) addressed this aspect of empiricist idolatry. "The imagination destitute of principles seeks to supply its indigence by creating a new world; it transforms all objects in order to embellish them, it exalts men into Gods, it debases Gods into men, it gives body to spirits and spirits to bodies . . . and its *marvellous* degrades the divine Nature, the agreeable and the gay take the place of the true sublime."[102]

The difficulty of telling the real from the chimerical, the actual from the mere perception or thought of it, goes a long way toward explaining the centrality of the metaphor of legibility to the Enlightenment. To discover what was legible, one needed to determine what was illegible. Recall how Lichtenberg, for example, claimed that inner being was unreadable. Lavater's physiognomic method, in contradistinction, was predicated on the model of the sacred text. The archive of the soul was capturable in the writing on the face. Its external characters could not "escape the eyes of the quick-sighted."[103] These two poles, in a nutshell, embodied a much greater empiricist and rationalist double bind. One could see shallow and unimportant things directly and enjoyably, without knowing them. Or one could see only for the purpose of deciphering and translating a profound script composed in an important but alien language. In either case, there was no guarantee that the world's plural significations corresponded to any subjective optical impression.

To my mind, the key figure to tackle this dilemma and to transmit it as a central issue for English, German, and French aesthetics was George Berkeley (1685–1753). His Neoplatonizing doctrine of immaterialism was antiempiricist and closer to the Cartesian tradition of Malebranche. Berkeley's focus on unmediated perception was meant to be a unique pictorial antidote to deceptive language. His thesis that a patchwork of light and color formed the immediate objects of vision, rather than solid bodies, remarkably anticipated

much Neoimpressionist theory concerning pure optical mixtures. A phenomenal world that was wholly the product of the mind of the thinking subject
also foreshadowed the Impressionist's representation of the sensation of light
itself rather than any objective reality. But it was especially Seurat who
seemed to benefit from the immaterialist notion that the perceiver married
nonphysical tints and tones in the very act of retinal apprehension. Berkeley
also adumbrated Gibson's distinction between visual field and visual world.
The former was the activity of getting intangible abstract information from
the ambient chromatic ray. The latter consisted of perambulating on and
around familiar surfaces and objects. We come to learn their edges and
boundaries only by feeling them over time.[104]

Both in the *New Theory of Vision* (1709) and in the *Principles of Human Knowledge*
(1710), Berkeley radically etherealized and internalized experience. These
works form a milestone in the history of visualization. He contended that we
do not see solids but only a diversity of colors subsisting in a visual, not a
geometrical, space. Space itself was spectral and participated in the mental
world. It was not prior to or outside the mind. Thus the immediate objects
of vision corresponded to the luminous and gravity-defying pictures painted
on the mirror of the retina. Ideas, for Berkeley, were scintillant chimeras,
the kaleidoscopic manifold of prismatic shapes perceived simultaneously.
Hence the misinterpretation of immaterialism, often taken in the eighteenth
century and beyond to say that no reality existed apart from the perceiving
mind. Recent interpreters have battled this skewing of Berkeley's argument.[105]
Nonetheless, it has to be admitted that the Dean of Derry and eventual
Bishop of Cloyne provided ammunition to the very skeptics and freethinkers
he was combating. To say "that what I see, hear, and feel *doth exist*, that is
to say, is perceived by me," and to maintain that fantasies are "ideas of our
own framing," seemed to suggest that all bodies were unextended and mental.
He exacerbated such misconstrual by claiming that "we eat and drink ideas,
and are clothed with ideas." He admitted that this statement sounded strange
because, in ordinary language, "idea" did not commonly signify "the several
combinations of sensible qualities which are called things."[106] The whole
world of visible objects became transmuted into phantasmagoria hovering in
the camera obscura brain. Blake—a similar exponent of inbred notions—in
his *Annotations to Berkeley's Siris* (ca. 1810) understood the British philosopher
in this light. Natural phenomena were only natural appearances. "They and
the phantomes that result from those appearances [are] *the children of imagination* grafted upon sense." Or, again, there is "according to Plato properly

no knowledge but only opinion concerning things sensible and perishing, not because they are naturally abstruse and involved in darkness: but because their nature and existence is uncertain, ever fleeting and changing."[107] Blake's slanted reception responded specifically to the visionary component of Berkeley's thought, its apparent downgrading of the senses. They do not inform us "that things exist without the mind." The illuminator-poet also found attractive the major role assigned to the imagination. Speculating that trees in a park or books in a closet existed with no one to perceive them only showed "you have the power of imagining or forming ideas in your mind.[108]

Berkeley's denial of the material world of the corpuscularians, then, resulted in his philosophy being misapprehended, from the early eighteenth century forward to Voltaire, Diderot, and Blake, as turning ideas into things. That is, conceptions were not the commonsense objects of our experience, as Hume and Berkeley had claimed, but a whole new class of ideal and, indeed, Romantic spectral objects in addition to the ordinary ones. Berkeley's emphasis on mind-dependedness, then, succeeded in arousing skepticism both toward things in themselves and toward their images. The anonymous *Enquiry into the Nature of the Human Soul* must stand for a whole class of criticism claiming that immaterialism went too far. The Anglican churchman was afraid Berkeley left no distinction between matter and mind, body and psyche. How could the passive and insubstantial spirit function like the physical and deluding senses? "A million or any number of nothings will never make something: nor will any number of *negations* of an idea ever make a real idea . . . therefore a real, solid, figured substance has to exist outside the mind."[109]

Berkeley was responsible for inventing what I term a new "imagistic." The perceptual mosaic, accessible to all, was the ungraspable, but everywhere present, speech of God. Not accidentally, his iconic system was composed at the time of a groundswell in universal grammars and "characteristics." The Royal Society launched the craze with John Wilkins's *Essay Towards a Real Character* (1668). As we already noted, Leibniz pursued his *ars characteristica* until the end of his days. Significantly, these and other philosophical or mathematical logics focused on simple, primary notions stripped of their "accidental" effects or secondary coloring properties.[110] As in Hooke's *Micrographia*, these schemes held that true nature was rock bottom essence separated from artful surface. Into this linguistic and taxonomic orthodoxy stepped the unorthodox Berkeley. Instead of being neatly analyzable into a set of decontextualized and combinable primitive words, roots, or syllables, nature was disorderly apparition and blinding or confusing spectacle. It was immediately and qualitatively present, yes, but quantitatively and semantically unrecuperable.

In the late dialogue *Alciphron: or the Minute Philosopher* (1732), Berkeley revealed that intangible magnifications had shaped his theological view of vision as a general language speaking to the gaze alone. The artificial contemplation of distant wonders made things appear to be both here and not here, floating somewhere outside or inside another, untouchable realm. Microscopy was a kind of oneirocriticism. The deceptive maximization of insignificant minima was like the specious heightening of imagery occurring in dreams. The multitudinousness of microorganisms, the ungraspable activity of densely patterned no-bodies, their manifest unlikeness to material objects available to the touch, made them the positive model for both fantastic and existential phantasmagoria.

Unlike national idioms or regional dialects, vision was practiced from birth. It transcended frontiers, did not differ capriciously from country to country, and was acquired "with so little pains." The meaning of visual language was plain because God himself "speaks every day and in every place to the eyes of all men."[111] Alluding to Berkeley's dictum that light and colors were only ideas in the mind, Addison similarly reified an imperial optics, or unconstrained sight, wandering passportless "up and down without containment." Analogously, Richardson noted that language was "very imperfect," whereas the painter can convey his ideas "of these things clearly and without ambiguity; and what he says everyone understands in the sense he [the artist] intends it." Men of all nations hear him because "the painter speaks to them in their mother tongue."[112] Might we not now also suppose that Lessing's praise of the poet and demotion of the painter were partly an irate response to Berkeley's imagism? Thus the fundamental and nonsensory thesis of the *Laocoön* was that "that which we find beautiful in a work of art is beautiful not to our eyes but to our imagination through our eyes." Lessing characterized the compulsory simultaneity of artistic expression as a form of imitation that should not be detailed or descriptive. Like Berkeley's vivid and coexisting optical sensations, Lessing's definition of pictorial representation severed it from the haptic or tangible flow of reasoned narrative. The difference between the two men, however, consisted in a fundamental shift in attitude. What was a superior mode of communication for one was inferior for the other.

Hence the German theorist's injunction that the artist must wait for the poet "in order to show us complete [that is, unfolded] what we have seen the poet making." This declaration attacked Berkeley's assertion that it was in the very nature of conceiving to behold the assembling and fitting together of perceptions.[113] Moreover, as both Campbell and Beattie picked up, Berkeley's visible alphabet devolved upon signs or signals that did not necessarily correspond to namable external entities.[114] Thus imagery further evaded Lessing's attempt to subsume it under the control of linguistics. The British philosopher fought the cheat of words by denying they were things. Unlike pictures, they bore no natural connection to our ideas.

Microscopy and its metaphors, however, also left a negative wake in Berkeley's thought. The arch-observer, or experimentalist, was "the minute philosopher." Like the pirate, he left mankind naked and desolate on a bleak beach. In this guise, the all-powerful seer was none other than the sophist, the libertine wit, or the modern freethinker, good for performing in the drawing room, the coffee or chocolate house, and the tavern. This empiricist belonged to that sect "which diminish all the most valuable things, the thoughts, views, and hopes of men . . . they reduce to sense, human nature they contract and degrade to the low standard of animal life." Alciphron, a modern member of this ancient coterie, claimed its members were no more to blame for the defects they discovered "than a faithful glass for making the wrinkles which it only shews." Perspicacity, or the best eyes, were necessary "to discern the minutest objects."[115]

Berkeley's stress on the subjective consciousness was not unlike Descartes's optical epistemology, feigning the world at pleasure.[116] Paradoxically, the Cartesian theory of vision also resembled the empiricist relativization of sensory judgment. Thus the three major and dominating schools of eighteenth-century philosophy illusionized, fantasized, or otherwise desubstantialized the universe and its contents. Visual effigies, species, specters—not words—were central in these systems to the fabrication of hallucinations. Descartes's single rational method for all of learning insisted upon the superiority of the pure data of clear and distinct ideas conceived after a mathematical model. The nub of the problem, however, was the same as that for the empiricists. More perfect or simpler ideas had to be abstracted from lesser, compounded elements. In the end, only visionary insight could inform us about such irreducible objects of intuition or propositions *per se*.[117]

We cannot pursue further the intertwisting of these separate strands, fully deserving a study to itself. What I hope I have demonstrated, however, is the extreme "Neoplatonizing" dissolution of sensory experience into ghostly counterlikenesses. Descartes, Hume, and Berkeley variously cast serious doubt and damaging suspicion on material solids, and on anything related to self-sufficient bodies. Simultaneously, they unmoored the corporeal imagination from reason and reduced it to manufacturing misperception and error. Having internalized and cognized space, Berkeley, in particular, left sensuous bodies open to the attack of being merely ideational or imaginary, the fanciful constructs of the mind (fig. 17). The implication of shadow play for the visual arts was both staggering and crippling. Already by the early eighteenth century it was the essence of a thing seen to be a specter. The steady transformation of appearance into apparition culminated in the antagonistic Neoclassical critique to which we shall turn at the end of this chapter.

For the moment, I want to draw together the threads we have been examining by looking at a concrete case. There is evidence for the impact of Berkeley's thought on Diderot's famous description of Jean-Honoré Fragonards' (1732–1806) smoky "Platonic dream." The *Coresus and Callirhoe* was exhibited to great acclaim at the Salon of 1765 (fig. 223). Although both the spectral painting and the *philosophe's* critique of falsehood have been interpreted many times, no one has tied them to immaterialism, or to the sophistic creation of deliberate fraud.[118] Nor has the picture itself been linked to the tradition of simulations meant to be seen in the dark or, more specifically, to an instrumentalized art of optical games. I believe Diderot's exposé was the locus classicus for the Enlightenment's skepticism concerning the delusory visual arts. It articulated the longstanding doubt about the perceptual and intellectual deceit inherent in the production of gossamer and light-containing colored appearances. His journalistic debunking was also a memorable, if biased, analysis of Fragonard's artificial persons. These tricking simulacra were brilliant and crisply defined, but not rationally clear. Unlike contemporaneous theatrical spectacles, Fragonard's picture—appropriately exhibited in the gloomy Grande Gallerie of the Louvre—was a wholly visual, bodiless enactment without a trace of the volumetric world. This lack of tangibility indicates its connection to more insubstantial modes of representation.[119]

Diderot began his account of the French artist's *morceau d'agrément* by informing his literary correspondent, Baron Melchior Grimm (1723–1807), of a vision he experienced the night before the opening of the Salon. This sudden

223. Jean-Honoré Fragonard, *Coresus and Callirhoe,* Salon of 1765. Oil on canvas, 186 × 309 cm. Musée du Louvre. (Photo: Réunion des Musées Nationaux.)

insight was precipitated by the reading of "certain Platonic dialogues."[120] His augmenting exposition consisted of four sequences, or *tableaux*, culminating in a fifth corresponding to Fragonard's actual work. The story of the unrequited love that Coresus, a priest of Dionysius at the Calydonian sanctuary, bore for the virgin Callirhoe was a history drawn from Pausanius (fl. 100 AD). Significantly, however, Diderot converted it into an allegory of falsehood. Fragonard's central tragic spectacle of simulations focused on the rescued but unconscious beloved and the self-immolating priest. The latter's death, intended to appease the despotic and irrational god, was observed by peripheral spectators and temple attendants. Sunlight streamed into the scene as if from the mouth of a cave. It struck the backs of the participants, and traced huge hemispherical reflections on the columns of the tenebrous interior. These incongruously sharp projections looked as if they were cast by a solar microscope (figs. 215, 217).

According to Diderot, the perfume-suffused and *enfumé* dusky cavern was the site of effeminate sensory pleasures and illicit love. Thus it microscopically mirrored the Platonic universe's macroscopic division into transitory phenomena and an unseizable eternal essence.[121] The tyrannical denizens of this cosmic camera obscura ranged from kings above to base "charlatans, artisans of illusion, and that entire troop of merchants of hope and fear" wandering below. Significantly, each illusionist possessed a provision of small, colored simulations appropriate to his rank and station. These "puppets" were so well wrought and so diverse that, Diderot claimed, they could stock the tragic, comic, and burlesque performances of life.[122] The *philosophe* situated these sleight-of-hand artisans out of sight, behind the gullible crowd and beyond the entrance of the cave. As with apparitions cast by optical apparatus, light originated from behind the operator. Literally bringing these sham wraiths into being, luminosity *appeared*, however, to emanate from within the image itself. Diderot speculated that the gigantic shadows and the dwarfed, glowing figures left black smudges and tinctured stains on a cloth— the actual canvas—stretched across the bottom of the cavern. Fragonard's "real" painting of fantastic fictions was thus the *denouement* to four hypothetical scenes. Diderot stressed that the picture appeared lifelike because it was located in the hallucinatory and dim quarters of the Salon. Delusory art was possible only in a compressed and obscure setting and from a contrived vantage. In a manipulated ambient, the public could be fooled into mistaking insubstantial and spotlit simulacra for the full-blooded reality lying outside in the sun. Grimm, for whose benefit this tale was spun, was made to conclude the account by paraphrasing the modern Plato, Bishop Berkeley. When Fragonard's painting was "lost" from the viewer's sight, the danger loomed that his sublime specters would vanish from the extended world like ghosts.[123]

Voltaire (1694–1778), in his *Eléments de Newton* (1726), had been the first French thinker to mention the British philosopher. Immaterialism also formed the subject of a later diatribe in the *Dictionnaire philosophique portatif* (1764). Yet the sober Grimm parroted the fallacy that ideas, or images in the mind, were things, the only things.[124] Supposed external bodies dwelled in the head. When they were no longer perceived, they no longer existed. Ironically, French materialism thus reached the same impasse as British immaterialism. As La Mettrie, D'Holbach, Le Camus, and Diderot himself indicated, the imagination, or the fantastic portion of the intellect, "alone perceives that it represents all objects to itself." Since there was no spiritual substance apart from the body, the supposed soul was nothing but the corporeal imagination, a property of matter, dedicated to conjuring phantasms. Diderot, both in the *Rêve de D'Alembert* (1769) and in the *Eléments de physiologie*, argued that dream *tableaux* appeared to exist externally while we were asleep. But in the end, we discover that "we see these imaginary *tableaux* precisely the way we see real *tableaux*, with our eyes."[125] According to this physiology of revery, life in the street or on the surface of the work of art was created by the material brain. Hence both were deceptive and visionary.

While much could be said about Diderot's ekphrastic exercise, I wish to underscore four points. They illuminate and connect his skepticism concerning aesthetic illusion with his attack on superstition in the *Encyclopédie*. The art critic's condemnation of counterfeiters in the *Salons* was linked to the *philosophe*'s excoriation of sophistic wonder-workers and their "nocturnal operations" in the *Dictionnaire raisonné*. This "minute philosophy" was practiced by Neoplatonic theurgists such as Iamblichus, Porphyry, and Proclus and in modern times by Bacon, Hobbes, Malebranche, Leibniz, and the rhapsodic Quietists. Fanatical idolatry came in for severe censure in the lengthy article devoted to "Ecclecticisme." Here, Diderot drew the important distinction between a legitimate eclecticism (selecting the best ideas from others) in religious, philosophical, and aesthetic matters, and an illegitimate syncretism. The latter's extravagant operators ceaselessly and improperly combined marvels and prodigies from the ruins of failed systems. Both crafters of sham beauties and "scientific" enthusiasts encouraged image worship by their spellbinding manual execution. They appealed emotionally to ignorant lovers of looking by performing prestidigitations in murky surroundings.[126] Diderot termed the false combiner, or syncretic experimentalist, an *idéaliste*. Such magician-fabricators of a *trompe l'oeil* art, or of a nonintellectual mathematics, relied on an extravagant ritual of deluding exorcisms and incantatory invocations. Unknowing, not knowing, was their aim.

Diderot, I suggest, specifically identified such artisanal irrationalism with the totalitarian frenzy of Fragonard's theme: an unjust "Asiatic" god unleashed an undeserved plague of drunkenness among the innocent Calydonians and demanded a barbaric blood sacrifice. Religious and political subjugation was synonymous with a concealing, infatuating, and falsifying technique. This hypnotic style bludgeoned citizens into submission just as much as if it were a truncheon wielded by an authoritarian dictator. The image of such partisan fanatics and their brutal tactics vividly emerged from Nicolas-Antoine Boulanger's (1722–1759) posthumously published *Recherches sur l'origine du despotisme oriental* (1761), the multivolume *L'Antiquité devoilée* (1766), and, indeed, from his articles for the *Encyclopédie*.[127] That Diderot wished to establish a correspondence between theological and aesthetic zealotry was evident from the swindling artistic procedures he highlighted during the course of his analysis. First and foremost among them was the mystifying and artificially produced *clair-obscur*, responsible for blinding critical reflection through glare. Second, the confusing and synesthetic sensory milieu was redolent of "monstrous mixtures" deceptively evoked in subterranean caverns. According to Diderot, Fragonard created a steamy hothouse filled with fiery braziers, dark mists, opaque smoke, and piano-forte light "echoes," rebounding ever more faintly from body to body. Third, the painter invented ambiguous, or visually similar, female and male figures. These languid "in-between" and sexually equivocal creatures were equally foggy, that is, neither straightforward nor rationally seizable. The *philosophe* likened them to insinuating "hermaphrodites" who have the air of, or play at being, real while in actuality they were merely *idéale* or chimerical. Fourth, the intervention of marvelous optical instrumentation was required to control the crowd. It endowed trivia with an unnatural magnitude acceptable to the inexperienced or undiscriminating masses. This ungenuine pictorial creation gave birth to false likenesses or propaganda. Carefully wrought but flimsy simulations could not resemble the substantial interior of things they seemed to replicate.

Thus Fragonard's high-tech *faux* painting, like idolatry or bigotry, claimed to be everything it was not. The aesthetic illusionist and the scientific technologist resembled the Eastern potentate or unreasonable god. They all dabbled in the diverting manufacture of controlling and controlled appearances that fed superstition. Significantly, Eugène Delacroix (1798–1863) in the *Death of Sardanapolus* (Paris, Musée du Louvre, 1827) Byronically recast Fragonard's picture, largely using the same means. His interpretive reception, colored by the Greek uprising against the Turks, made explicit the earlier artist's allusion to an "Oriental despotism." Delacroix created a cavernous harem, or chaotic and sensual *chambre obscure* with no exit. Masses of billowing smoke and glowing jewellike colors fitfully engulfed a coldly indifferent tyrant. The torrid atmosphere of King Solomon's mines illuminated helpless victimization by fiat. Delacroix thus deliberately alluded to the well-known panoply of artistic signs that conventionally designated sophistry. Not only in the eighteenth century, then, were optical snares unethical and to be mistrusted. For the Romantics, too, they were gawdy baubles convincing only to the unlettered crowd seated in the dark.

Yet the pessimistic Diderot, even while spurning painting on smoke, seemed to recognize that all important events in the real world were spearheaded by imagery. This awareness looks ahead to the late twentieth-century spectacle of electronically generated phantoms hovering in the windowless and highrise Platonic Cave. The new Faustian icon is a radiant and man-made deed. Atemporal in its total presentness, it reminds us of Berkeley's purely optical array. It can swiftly draw a complex community of millions of unique, individual human beings together in a just cause. Phosphorescently charged, it glows from within and enlightens and enlivens all disciplines (fig. 224). The British philosopher presciently and optimistically declared that, without touch, the spectator was left with liquid symbols. The freedom movement in Eastern Europe has shown just how contagious are those digitalized idols flowing across repressive borders. They are powerful enough to tear down even the most obdurate walls. No more convincing demonstration exists that colored beams of light do not merely oppress and beguile but, when handled responsibly, illuminate the night in a way that words cannot.

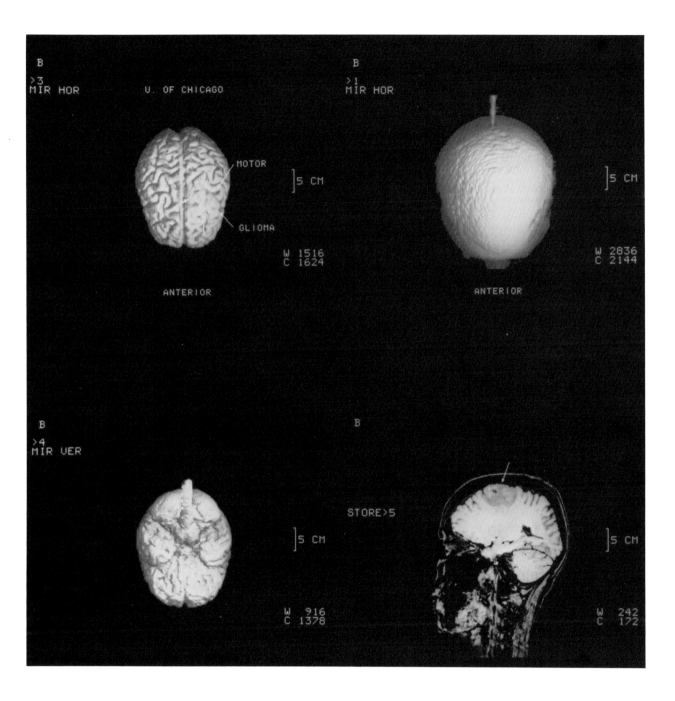

224. David N. Levin, *Facial and Cortical 3D Models Derived from MR Images.*
(Photo: Courtesy Maurice Goldblatt Magnetic Resonance Imaging Center, Department of Radiology, University of Chicago.)

Art _____

noun, *The power of doing something not taught by nature and instinct; as, to walk is normal, to dance is an art; a science; as, the liberal arts; a trade; artfulness; skill; dexterity; cunning; speculation.*

Dr. Johnson, *Dictionary*

Art _____

noun, *Abstract and metaphysical term. One commenced by making observations of nature, the function, use, qualities of beings and their symbols; then one conferred the name of the science, or the art, or the discipline in general, to the center or point of unification to which the observations led us.*

Diderot and D'Alembert, *Encyclopédie*

Even today, much eighteenth-century art is customarily dismissed by alluding to its ersatz visual pleasures.[128] Magical finishes, replications of rare wood grains, restorations of aged and worn patinas speak of fashion and the pursuit of looks rather than substance. Disguising decorative patterns and cunning paper marbling are used to sum up the period's supposed *faux* atmosphere. They stand for artful application without human touch. The key to good-looking effects made by the brush was that they did not appear false. With the panache of convincing surface treatment, fake was no longer fake but prestigious, opulent, expensive. The degenerate observer willingly succumbed to glamorized objects and scenery embedded in the cosmetic skin of paint.

The advance of the experimental sciences and optical technology raised an insuperable stumbling block for the Enlightenment. The progress of method and reason was impeded by an illusion-loving human nature. The childish taste for the marvelous, so it was believed, impelled mankind toward the fraudulent. The eye and the imagination were in collusion, encouraging an innate predilection for seeing patterns too readily, for falling for ideology, for swallowing the creations of our own prejudices and passions.[129] This troubling snag, interrupting an optimistic linear progression from the dark to the luminous, was nowhere better in evidence than in painting. Truthful messages had to be agreeably disguised as verisimilitude since, it seemed, only erroneous appearances easily slipped into the mind. Painting's other option was even more unattractive. It could improperly declare its falseness openly by creating worlds patently unlike our own. From Batteux to Laugier, imagery was increasingly denied the ability to exert tangible, temporal influence on actual life and was consigned to fabricating backstage simulations. Even David's abrupt and scratchy revolutionary style transferred historical processes and topical events onto a purified and visionary plateau (fig. 2).[130]

Sculpture, in principle, appeared to escape this opprobrium. It represented reality through an ingenious combination of elements derived from nature's media. Painting had no such direct contact. Moreover, it was bereft of the solidity and corporeality of objects. These could be feigned only in perspective and artfully distributed over a plane. This flatland, however, was wholly of our making and itself artificially bestrewn with points, lines, and colors whose duplicitous aim was to conceal their contrivance, or signs of labored manufacture. Hence the favoring of sculpture in Neoclassical art. Human bodies were consistently transformed into painted statuary because of the latter's perceived lack of pretense. Three-dimensional figures, as long as they did not behave uncharacteristically, i.e., pictorially, did not dupe the beholder. Straightforward imitations in the round did not ask him to believe what turned out not to be so.

Diderot revived this *paragone* in the *Salon of 1765*. It was there that Baudelaire later encountered and inverted it in his demolition of plastic boredom masquerading as sincerity. The distinction between the two arts, like Diderot's exposure of Fragonard's craftiness in the *Coresus and Callirhoe*, was part of a greater anti-Rococo campaign. It coincided with the *philosophe's* simultaneous attacks against François Boucher (1703–1770) as a painter *artifex*, and his call for a return to nature and truth. Relying on a major *topos* of the eighteenth century—the blind person who regained vision—Diderot declared that tactile sculpture was both for the sighted and the sightless. Conversely, impalpable painting, unlike that "severe, grave, and chaste art," addressed the eyes alone. Although restricted to fewer objects and themes, sculpture "suffered neither buffoonery, nor burlesque, nor the droll, rarely even the comical. Marble does not laugh. . . . It is voluptuous but never lewd." The toiling and enduring chisel, unlike the "libertine brush," was not permitted to "attach to the canvas a frivolous idea that could be created in an instant and effaced by a breath."[131]

Dubos's Lockean and rhetoric-based *Réflexions critiques* was an early and rare instance of the praise for "the dexterity of the artisan" and of a persuasive execution that did not need to conceal itself. There was no art criticism like it until Baudelaire's reviews of mid-nineteenth-century Salons and other Parisian exhibitions. Actually, the aesthetic assessments of this diplomat and royalist historian were in many ways superior to those of the Romantic poet because he did not permit the work of art to be swallowed by the interpretive text. As a sympathetic partisan of the pictorial over the discursive, Dubos maintained that "a painting could please independently of the object it represented." The defender of color over line, he admired the purely chromatic "counterfeiter" who knew how to delight, although he did not emotionally move us. He drew an important distinction between two types of poetics resulting in two sorts of eloquent, but nonlinguistic, figures. A "poetry of style" consisted in the selection of words considered as imitative signs of ideas. A "mechanics of poetry" chose and composed syllables according to their physical sounds to which no preformed meaning had been attached.

Thus, like verbal or polyphonic medleys, tints and tones could engender more or less harmonious effects depending on pigment combinations. The former produced phrases of sense that spoke to the imagination, while the latter gave birth to mellifluous verses attuned to the eyes. Dubos—like Berkeley in the area of perception and epistemology—thereby vindicated prismatic imagism and onomatopoeic *tableaux* composed of optical mixtures. For a brief moment, he also uncoupled spellbinding imagery from chicanery, or sharp practice. As a purely demonstrative form of expression, painting exerted even greater power over mankind than poetry. The deployment of natural, not artificial, signs meant that visual expression needed only to be seen, not read, in order to act on the emotions. Significantly, the superiority of the *coup d'oeil* over the lengthy discourse did *not* reside in the production of degrading illusions of reality, but in the disclosing presence of personal touch. Both pictures and drama proved that the greatest pleasure stemmed from a second viewing, or performance, when no mere stratagem or subterfuge could remain. Just as theater posters advertised only a "copy" of *Chimène* or *Phèdre*, so painting, like musical rhythms, announced its frank construction through individualized lines, colors, and *clair-obscur*.[132]

Honest figural signs or the manifest "pittoresque," guilelessly embedded in materials, found few eighteenth-century apologists.[133] Fuseli thought even Reynolds's subordination of physical colors to a lowly "ornamental" status vis-à-vis intellectual forms to be inadequate. Raising "a medium to a representative" debased art "to a mere vehicle of sensual pleasure." "Lumpy pulp" was manacled to "deformity," "meanness," and "vulgarity." A "slave of fashion," such disabusing painting was no more than "a mannered medium of play-ful tints."[134] But it was the Newtonian Abbé Batteux, in his ominously entitled *Les beaux-arts reduits à un même principe* (1747), who efficiently reduced painting to the eternal production of counterfeited images (*contrefaire*) and factitious sentiments. Moreover, for this zealot of a strict theology of the pure word, trumpery and jugglery were the very essence of the visual arts. They fabricated scamped simulations that were not natural but merely seemed to be so. Untrue imagery was verisimilar, by which he meant virtual or incantatory. Professor of literature and member of the Académie des Inscriptions et Belles-Lettres, this iconoclast took the Académie Royale de Peinture's Aristotelian doctrine of imitation, or noble *vraisemblance*, and turned it into hoodwinking. The section of his treatise devoted to painting was short, but telling. Nevertheless, painting fared better than music, epitomized in a scant three pages. Once the exemplary literary principle had been deduced, so the argument ran, it could easily be transposed. Painting, music, and dance were interchangeable and abstractable sign systems. Unlike nature, the fine arts created nothing but merely regulated usage and assigned conventional meaning. Without rules, visual forms of expression would be like "a prism which displays the most lovely hues, & does not make a picture. It would resemble a type of chromatic clavecin that proffers colors & passages in order to amuse the eyes, & surely bores the mind."

Reduced to simulation, painting was likened to indefinable poetry, not solid prose, in feeding on fiction. Such hypnotic substitutes, or "artificial portraits," were "perpetual lies" that acted as if they possessed the properties of truth. Batteux unleashed a tirade against figments steeped in the vocabulary of the wily and tactile forger. A string of Latin expletives: *facere, fingere, imitare,* summed up his disdain for the solely disingenuous power of images. The cozening and pettifogging arts were nothing but "imaginary things, feigned beings, copied & imitated after the real things."[135] He conveyed the impression that it was better to emulate the blind man of Puiseaux or the eyeless British mathematician Saunderson—unique in their reliance on unconfigured abstractions—than to be like the "vile populace" enslaved by mesmerizing and electrifying sights. Blindness, similar to those *acheiropoeita* about whose making human beings were left in the dark, revoked the hated epistemological primacy of the visual.[136] Similarly art, for Batteux, did not mean evident, or publicly available, handling. Rather, it was a nonoptical, backstairs compendium of rules practiced by the proud, the few, the philosophical in order to pauperize painting. The latter's diminished and diminishing task was totally summed up in *trompe l'oeil.* Its function was "to deceive the eyes by replication, to make us believe that the object is real, while it is merely an image." His monochromatic system adumbrated both Baumgarten's and Kant's aesthetics in shifting attention away from perception to logic, i.e., to the workings of a small number of a priori axioms universally applicable.[137] The lofty and hegemonic understanding forged laws to guarantee conformity to good taste and to model an order lying beyond the paltry power of the senses. "Art in general" became a sort of theoretical physics in which theorems shared the same fundamental principle irrespective of the medium. This body of propositions was necessary precisely because the erroneous easily infiltrated a vision bereft of mathematical or geometrical criteria. A perfect intelligence, like a *bon goût,* saw and experienced the simple, the natural, and the true distinctly, or "without cloud," thanks to a calculating method.[138]

Batteux was not unique in transforming art into a nonpresence, that is, either into bamboozling appearances or into a rational corpus of disembodied regulations. Lessing, of course, developed the dangerous antinomian implications inherent in the Frenchman's theory. By confining the visual arts to an inferior physical space—a space that had been progressively internalized, phantasmagorized, or metamorphosed into a bubble by empiricists and rationalists alike—he further denigrated pictorial expression to a beautiful but hollow window dressing. His debunking method was primitively circular, but effective. Once he had reduced the plastic arts to the production of mirage, they tautologically fulfilled their tendency to reproduce *phantasiae*. These waking dreams—to whose manufacture they had been conveniently relegated—were then deemed to require "close supervision by law." Lessing's segregation of iconic from verbal signs, to the detriment of the former, deliberately excluded them from the temporal sphere in which meaningful social activity unfurled and left an impact.[139] Images were no longer mysterious, ambiguous, magical, compelling, even insidious or perfidious. They were no longer the shining instrument of revelation or of nefarious incantation or, maddeningly, even of both at once. Turned into cold and calculated idols, they were denuded of their prophetic power to nurture the spirit and to inspire change in patterns of living. Merely untouchably mesmerizing, they were transformed by supercilious literary critics and contemptuous philosophers into tools for mystification. Lessing divided the lesser visual arts from higher narrative or drama on the pretext that they inhabited some homogeneous ether remote from unrolling history. Yet, ironically, like Batteux, he treated them as if they were fundamentally comparable. On two major fronts, then, imagery lost its special demonstrative characteristics, its complex untranslatability, to become the stepdaughter of texts.

From another angle, painting was allowed to revel in its bad faith. Free to be false, it came to embody unimportant play or irresponsible diversion. I suggest that the evasiveness and equivocation associated with grotesques and arabesques—traditionally allotted spots on peripheral pilasters or friezes and borders or frames—stood for the new and totally "decorative" role of art as unabashed prevarication. The task of visualization was summed up by the capricious formation and externalization of mental images whose existence was hypothetical. Félibien's description of Giovanni da Udine's (1487–1564) embellishments of the Vatican loggias stressed the pleasantness attendant on making unreal things appear real. "Nature does not produce fish, marine monsters, flowers, fruits, & a thousand other kinds of things one sees so perfectly painted that they seem true." The theme of "beautiful imaginings," "lovely fictions," and "feigned architecture" continued in his admiring account of Giulio Romano's *trompe l'oeil Room of the Giants* at Mantua. This brilliant painted joke—compounded of *faux* rusticated stones, deliberately misassembled doors, windows, and fireplace, all on the verge of tumbling down—hinged on the creation of a total illusion. By the force of his fantasy, Giulio invented "that which, indeed, was not, & supplemented with colors the deficiencies of real things in the very places where they ought to be."[140] In the preface to Dufresnoy's *Art of Painting*, Dryden defined its colluding task by citing Philostratus. The eyes and minds of beholders must be made to fasten "on Objects which have no real Being; as if they were truly Existent." "Fiction" was the substance of painting and poetry. These ornamental falsifiers were predicated on making resemblances "of Human Bodies, Things, and Actions, which are not Real."[141]

Remond de Sainte-Albine similarly underscored the separation of delusory spectacle, or mummery, from workaday life. His *Le Comédien* offered an unusual twist to the contrast between a theatrical and a pictorial performance. While the power of painting was extensive, its works "are only simple appearances, & quickly we recognize that it presents only phantoms in lieu of real objects. In vain, painting prides itself on making the canvas breathe. From its hands escape only inanimate productions." Dramatic poetry, on the other hand, furnished "ideas & feelings to the beings it engendered." This apologist for dramaturgy came to the same conclusion at which Lessing eventually arrived. Only vision was seduced by the deceptive sparkle and borrowed plumes of a picture, whereas the prestidigitations of the theater touched, in addition, the ears, the intellect, and the heart.[142] Painting's obvious tinsel and paste, as Laugier declared, was fabricated "only for the eyes" and intimately tied to the manufacture of "magical illusions." "Perfect" or "complete" simulacra were thus removed from the sphere of the everyday.[143] To be "painterlike" was to be sophistic, to craft with one art the semblance of all things, to make virtual presences that had no real support.[144] Unlike the stage, where a play was enacted to be witnessed from a particular perspective and worked only from that point of view, painting was obliged to reproduce a universal and self-sufficient dream for the waking.[145] When touch dropped out of visive experience, the material world vanished into impotent sights. Belonging no place, the liberated but socially powerless imagination could escape into the autonomous domain of the pictorial. In a utopian nowhere, all realms coexisted and were compossible.

Richard Hurd presciently foretold the coming of the Romantic *poietes*-maker. This artificer employed his tricks of the trade not to simulate actuality, but to create another, aesthetic dimension. The mysterious *novus mundus* was peopled with nonrealistic yet logical fictions, whole and entire in themselves. In praising the "Faery way of writing" found in medieval romances, Hurd spoke of the reader's willingness to give himself up to the imposture in spite of seeing through the falsehood. In this marvelous confected realm, what counted was not imitation of external experience, but "consistant imagination."[146] Playfulness became a viable option when meaning was uncoupled from tangible actions, when the spectator could no longer "feel" information in order to tell whether it had been deceptively enlarged or reduced (fig. 214). Thus Fuseli urged painters of "Fancy-Pictures" to mix their specters with recognizable creatures (figs. 139, 140, 160, 171). Without the collateral touchstone of physicality and an outside point of reference, these pure inventions resembled fantastic virtuosity in the playing of a musical composition. The beholder or auditor remained stupefied "by this superior kind of *legerdemain*, an exertion of ingenuity to no adequate end" (fig. 126).[147]

Fuseli's admonition went unheeded. Congeries of possible phenomena were the staple of Romanticism. Grandville's aptly entitled *Un autre monde* was Leibnizian in its vivid exhibition of a collection of potentially existing, spoofing abstractions systematized into being.[148] In playing with suppositious variables, the French lithographer uncovered a new fate for the erstwhile art of reproduction. He demonstrated how visual ideas might, indeed, become things. Thus in a miraculous turnabout, the artist's mighty pencil was made to announce to the writer's feeble pen: "You shall not in any way hinder my flight to the new spheres I wish to explore. Beyond infinity, there is a world awaiting its Christopher Columbus; in taking possession of that fantastic continent at the cost of a thousand dangers, I do not want another to rob me of the glory attached to my name." In tongue-in-cheek retribution for having been hemmed in by prescriptive authority, the controlling tool of language was obliged to stay home and patiently long for the rebellious pencil's return! The soaring artist, however, roamed beyond the horizon of the linguistic. Freed from the duty to copy, he voyaged in a visionary universe that was prior to the regulating Word.[149]

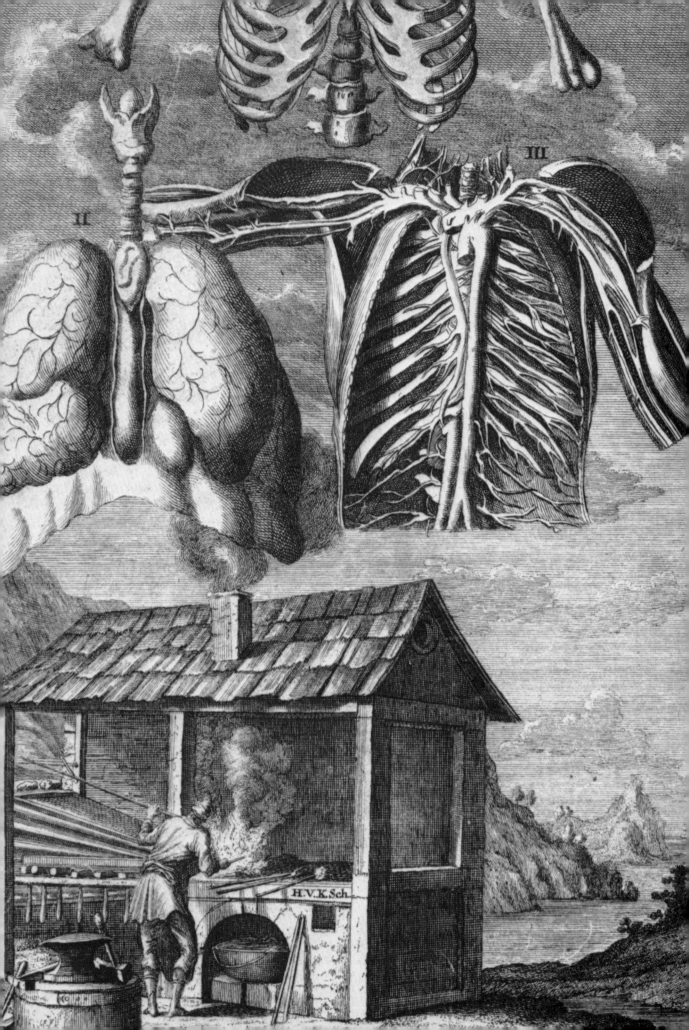

II

III

H.V.K.Sch.

6 SENSING

A Finer Touch

Consider the biological and aesthetic implications of a world where people existed solely as two-dimensional projections, as all surface and no depth. Tapping into intuitions was an attempt to turn flat appearances into three-dimensionality. Impalpable sights desubstantialized a tactile and external universe. Simultaneously, the medical study of invisible sensations pursued ways of looking inside what were formerly considered to be solid organs. The hunt after evanescent physiological functions increasingly transformed firm flesh and bone into an elastic and psychic atmosphere. Concepts, memories, fantasies, and feelings—the unseen and vanishing contents of the brain—deposited faint traces on the epidermis. Such ephemera could be experienced, if not exactly seen, by the able detector. Entry into the camera obscura of the somatic interior was achieved by searching for elusive signs and passing symptoms emitted by the nervous system coursing just under the skin (fig. 225). Unlike the anatomical slashes and dissecting probes examined in chapter 1, this finer visionary contact was as diluent as the fleeting emotions it elicited. Lying beyond the reach of the harrowing knife or the convulsive grip was a subtle sea of living processes. A quicksilver montage of telegraphic bursts, fast jump-cuts of pleasure and pain, and marbled footage comprised the kaleidoscopic collage of private identity. A refined medical and aesthetic phenomenology was required to examine the ductile point where existence and consciousness met.

Sign

noun, A token of anything; that by which any thing is shown; a wonder; a miracle; a prodigy; a picture hung at a door to give notice to what is sold within. . . . Note or token given without words; mark of distinction; cognizance; typical representation; symbol. . . . Also a symptom.

Dr. Johnson, *Dictionary*

Signe

noun, Everything destined to represent a thing. The sign comprises two ideas, one of the thing that represents, the other of the thing represented; and its nature consists in exciting the second by means of the first. . . . In medicine, symptôme *is ordinarily confounded with* signe, *and one defines a sign, or an assemblage of signs in a disease, as that which indicates its* [the disease's] *nature or quality.*

Diderot and D'Alembert, *Encyclopédie*

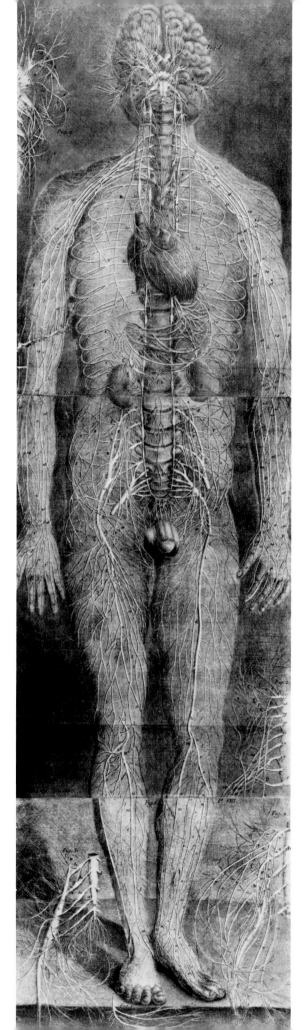

225. Jacques Gautier Dagoty, *Nervous
System,* from *Exposition anatomique des
organes des sens,* 1775, pl. 6. (Photo:
Courtesy National Library of Medicine,
Bethesda, Md.)

Liquefaction of corporeal and spiritual existence led to a haunting meteorology of hovering apparitions, misty spirits, volatile gases, and spectral airs. A simultaneously noetic and sensual pneumatology was connected to the rise of personalized climates of the soul. The lifting of constraining pressure, associated with intractable reason, was part of a new twilight zone of irrationalism. This late eighteenth-century dusk of unreality glimmered with ambiguous faculties and unseizable states of mind. Fluvial conception was exteriorized in drifting dreams, meandering somnambulism, and currents of animal magnetism. Flowing mental processes further metamorphosed the contoured body and its inaccessible recesses into an infinite source of kinetic spectacle. Not only morphology, but neurology, became solvent. Mental hydraulics, or the Romantic science of the brain's life in motion, studied a stream of soft and touching images that barely left an impact.

Berkeley, by removing sight from tactility, opened the door to both a scientific and a mystical simulation of thought itself. As we observed, the nature of ephemeral ideas, or of mental offspring, was fundamentally altered with the massive introduction of magical glasses. Through a new optical technology, instruments transmitted to their users the false feeling of existing in a completely different location, or even of being nowhere at all. As in contemporary artificial intelligence systems or robotics, the spectator's awareness of his weightless notions was progressively tied to his experience of synthetic surroundings. This fabricated sensory milieu, in which the viewer could roam through insight alone, corresponded to the fictitious character of the conceptual landscape. Although, no doubt, he would have been horrified at the comparison, Berkeley forecast the evolution of the preformationist "child in the mind" into a cleverly conjuring machine-controlled apparatus.[1] Moreover, the British immaterialist also predicted our modern culture of stealth. The more objects and events could be optically faked, the finer and more furtive the detecting devices required to separate false show from genuine reality. Hence the remaining four senses were summoned to unmask optical imposture. Hearing, smell, taste, and touch promised to expose the camouflage confounding conventional sight. Impinging directly on the nervous system, they seemed to offer new, nonvisual ways for ferreting out, or sensing, the secrets of the invisible. They lifted the superficial disguises fooling the eyes, and thereby forced the real or unseen actors to manifest themselves.

Berkeley realized that an immaterial consciousness, spun from colored light, posed the problem of just what was a subsisting person or a nonfictitious entity.[2] Because of its transience, the floating personality seemed incoherent and nonconstitutive, removed from the rootedness of historical development, the recorded continuation of heredity, or the physicality of sexual reproduction. Was there a single, intact observer beneath the Epicurean flux of constantly exfoliating perceptions? Was there even a stable character or abiding inner realm below the incessant unfurling of chromatic appearances? It was, I believe, in order to get at the prevailing substance—if it existed—under the blur that so much mid to late eighteenth-century medical and aesthetic theory was devoted to the exploits of the nervous system. George Cheyne (1671–1743), a Scot, was one of the most foremost physicians of the Augustan age and famous for promoting the medicinal properties of the hot springs at Bath. An early specialist in psychological ailments, he treated delicate, communicating "fibers" susceptible to becoming frayed, overstretched, or lax. His celebrated regimen was intended to ease struggling functions, to overcome the wretched sense of helplessness, and to restore the depressed and crumbling self. He labored to refine those debilitating secretions and sharp, viscous "juices" accompanying infirm and no longer toned nerves. This reforming advocate for "plain diet" and the "purity and simplicity of uncorrupted Nature, and unconquer'd Reason" also introduced precision into the chaotic nomenclature of splenetic, melancholic, hypochondriacal, hysterical, and vaporous symptoms conventionally associated with the "English malady." Seeking alternatives to Newtonian science and to mathematics as the sole way of interpreting reality, Cheyne converted to Berkeley's Idealism.[3] This spiritualized understanding of nature was embodied in his focus on the living filaments weaving together the animal organism. Hollow, in order to conduct the humors and spirits to the command center of the imagination, nerves were the intricate web and the animated biological hairlines of beauty (fig. 200, no. 123). The task of such almost invisible tiny cords was to draw together the far-flung continents floating within the submerged ocean of the psyche.[4] This new, cerebro-physiology was an internal medicine at the antipodes from crucifying anatomy. Whereas the latter was predicated on deep scrutiny and the agony of manually taking apart (figs. 3, 25), the former was a divination of physical, psychic, and ethical tendencies. It meant surreptitiously watching for intermittent vital signs indicative of concealed performances. Looking back on the accomplishments of the past century, Hippolyte Cloquet, in the preface to the anatomy volumes of the *Encyclopédie méthodique* (1819), summarized the importance of this new discipline. He predicted that neurology would eventually usurp the epistemological tasks and the high status previously accorded to philosophy. Although anatomy was inseparable

404

SENSING

from physiology, he had no doubt about the latter's superiority. As the science of "knowing oneself as well as possible," it linked all objects of experience by investigating the foundations of perceptual and intellectual operations. Its imposing goal was to reveal no less than the history of sensations, passions, and other moral phenomena.[5] For this *Idéologue*—following in the footsteps of Vicq d'Azyr, François-Xavier Bichat (1771–1802), and Pierre-Jean Cabanis (1757–1808)—physiology embraced the entirety of the body's motions, ideas, and sentiments.

Thomas Willis, who coined the term "neurologie," had already propounded during the late seventeenth century a doctrine of weak or unhealthy nerves. The "Proteus" of the sensitive soul could be "diversely disturbed and altered." Consequently, patients found themselves excessively stretched or expanded by profuse pleasure. Conversely, they might become exaggeratedly contracted by wracking grief. In either case, they tended to erect "an Idea in the Brain." The sick fantasy subsequently fixed on this "monstrous and very deformed Image; then stirs up all the Spirits, implanted both in the Brain and the Nervous Appendix, into a Detestation of this Imaginary Spectre."[6] Willis's metaphoric language indicated the dangerous metaphysical and theological terrain that the nervous system colonized. It flirted with invisible entitites, with structureless functions for which there were no corresponding visible organs.[7] As we have seen, anatomical procedures evoked their own problematic host of separating and analyzing critical tropes. But the dim and complex processes of physiology risked collapsing the rational soul into a changeable, vigorous or lethargic, cerebral cortex. Material convolutions (fig. 224) could thus be held responsible for the shape of a particular psychology and the idiosyncratic cast of a temperament.

More than Willis or Cheyne, the Göttingen naturalist Albrecht von Haller (1708–1777) and the Scottish physician Robert Whytt (1714–1766) elevated the nervous system to the lead role in the body. Through their writings, it attained the dominant position found in Cloquet's bird's-eye overview of the genesis and evolution of modern pathological studies. It was anticipated that the nuanced examination of biological systems would provide answers to the mysteries of the phantasmatic spirit and to the evanescent activity of the senses. Physiology was to illuminate vigorous conception and nervy feeling, acute or listless sensibility. It was to shed light on the very difference—if any—obtaining between man and other sentient creatures. Its purpose was to make visible the ontological modalities of thinking, to permit the perceiver to witness how data drizzled, cascaded, or rushed into the understanding and flooded the *corpus*. Haller's *Dissertation on the Sensible and Irritable Parts of Animals* (1755) recorded his struggles to devise experiments that might answer the contention of Descartes and other Neoplatonists that the soul was situated within the middle of the gray matter (fig. 71). The French philosopher set in motion the desperate search, extending throughout the eighteenth century, for ever more minimally scaled structures through which the spirit might act. The tiny pineal gland (fig. 47, C), invisibly embedded in the medulla, was the most famous of many quasi-incorporeal organs. These supposedly demonstrated the existence of a numinous principle in human beings that was also—although just barely—concretely evident.[8] The immaterialist Dagoty, in *Des organes des sens* (1775), still found it necessary to dispute with the Cartesians. Quite typically, his dissections convinced him that the soul must have a real location, even if it were only a hollow or negative space. He believed the *anima* resided in a void from which all traces of matter were expunged. It was in this vacancy that the nerves converged (fig. 225).[9]

Like Descartes, Willis, and Cheyne, Dagoty argued that, since the metaphysical soul was the form or activity of the body, its powers must have a corporeal habitation. More importantly, it must perform a corresponding somatic function.[10] At issue, then, for most eighteenth-century natural historians was the key question of where, exactly, this seat of sensation was. Where did that finer apprehension, capable of perceiving the secondary qualities of objects without their substance, actually reside? The strategies for capturing this evasive *sensus communis* became more intricate as more and more regions had to be abandoned. The inspection of the microscope and the probes of the surgeon's scalpel led to further physical attenuation. Inaccessible to the assisted eye or to the knife, the size of the spirit either shrank or became dispersed in a delicate network. Nevertheless, as had been true in Descartes's epistemology, the head tended to retain its superior status as the home of "the rational soul" (fig. 48).[11] The message conveyed by the *Organes des sens*, for example, was the preeminent role it played in receiving sensory impressions. From an elevated vantage, the mind "commands the whole machine with the aid of the nerves, utilizing the animal spirits concocted by the brain & which it distributes into those [channels] carrying it to different parts of the body; the admirable structure of these organs allows us to recognize the hand of the Creator." Dagoty praised this most reactive and expressive portion of the anatomy as "a compendium [*recueil*] of marvels."[12] This "masterpiece of nature" was so splendid largely because of the dense concentration of veins and vessels underlying the responsive dermis. The facial map of inextricable and excitable filaments exposed the fundamental sensitivity of human nature. Gamelin, in the *Ostéologie*, similarly praised those minuscule chains of vertical, transverse, and oblique threads from which the impressionable membranes were spun. On their tight or loose weave depended the total organism's muscular and mental tone.[13]

The notion that the head and the countenance were, in some way, the locus of neurology formed the topic of a lengthy and exhaustive tract in the *Mémoires de l'Académie royale de prusse*. The thesis of the *Dissertation anatomique sur les nerfs de la face* (1751) was that no other segment of the human body contained so many complex branchings. This abundance of "prodigiously multiplied" nerves was interpreted as nature's signal that the mien was a malleable mirror reflecting transitory passions and mutable sensations. The tract's author, the German physician Johann Friedrich Meckel (1781–1833), imputed to the webwork of the visage, in particular, a keen power of manifesting mental affects and corporeal afflictions. Because of their intimate correspondence and ties with other sections of the physiology, facial nerves possessed "an exquisite sensibility." He gave the vivid and erotic example of acutely susceptible lips (fig. 63). The friction caused by a kiss instantaneously transmitted a tingle to the ends of the limbs and members.[14] Significantly, what interested Meckel were precisely those tender, cutaneous titillations. He was fascinated by the normally secret succession of deep but fugitive gratifications superficially and momentarily registered on a cushiony bed of tissue. His treatise thus raised the fundamental issue of involuntary (kissing, blushing, pallor) and voluntary (walking, eating) muscular motions. During certain moving moments, the intractable anatomy became plastic, melted by a twinge or thrill profoundly or shallowly conveyed by the nerves. Lavater's hermeneutic enterprise, we recall, had been directed at somehow getting around those impermanent and undeliberate sentiments that were "felt rather than perceived." In the chapter of the *Essay* outlining the difficulties inherent in physiognomic analysis, he confessed his bafflement over automatic symptoms. The tenuous and flimsy signs most revealing of character were "almost beyond the grasp of the imagination itself." And, certainly, these physiological betrayals lay beyond the capability of description or draftsmanship.[15] Lichtenberg spurned Lavater's violation of the sanctuary of the breast through the useless piercing of the fixed anatomy. He maintained, on the contrary, that the infinitely flexible soul continued to be in unique "possession of its hidden treasures, and that the road which leads to them remains as inaccessible as it has been for ages past."[16]

C. Eisen del.   P. F. Tardieu sc.

The pathognomic finesse required to distinguish unconscious from conscious drives, unintentional from intentional expressions, was daunting. It returns us to a consideration of Haller's dissertation, first published in a Latin edition in 1752, on the much-debated difference between irritability and sensibility. He attacked the vitalist position of Théophile Bordeu (1722–1776), one of the major figures at the medical school of Montpellier. This friend of Diderot's and a key protagonist of the *Rêve de D'Alembert*, argued that the two activities constituted a single, sentient force.[17] Contrarily, Haller claimed that irritability was a special form of automatism. It represented an unperceived and consequently lesser, inhuman reaction to a sharp and dolorous stimulus. He credited the English scientist Francis Glisson for having first attributed such an innate power to solids. But for Haller it signified, in particular, the property of organized bodies to respond thoughtlessly without experiencing pleasure or pain. This obscure, almost insensible degree of feeling that was not quite a feeling was held to be essential for animal and possibly even plant life.[18]

It remains one of the dark paradoxes of the New Science and its aftermath, however, that in order to demonstrate physical perceptivity Haller dispassionately carried out barbaric operations on living dogs (fig. 6). Poisons,

408

caustics, abrasives, and an arsenal of stabbing knives induced cramps and pangs in burned and gouged flesh. Vivisection had been a routine practice for seventeenth-century English virtuosos. Harvey gutted gravid does. Hooke, as curator of experiments for the Royal Society, sacrificed hundreds of whimpering or howling brutes in his investigations of respiration that nauseated Newton. Even more were lost in the fruitless attempt to perform successful blood transfusions.[19] But it was the search for the origins of feeling, amid obvious visible torment, that made Haller's researches especially ironic. It is revealing that *sensible* readers found nothing incongruous in Charles-Dominique-Joseph Eisen's (1720–1778) sprightly engraved vignette after Antoine-François Tardieu's (1757–1822) Rococo design for the title page to the *Elementa Physiolgiae Corporis Humani* (1757–1766). Winged putti give lessons in physiology amid assorted knives, splayed dog, excised heart, and drawings of chicken embryos (fig. 226)![20] La Mettrie provided a by no means unusual anesthetized account of the Enlightenment experimental rack. The probing exposure and stinging of nerves was meant to offer an up-to-date testing of the Cartesian hypothesis that animals possessed no souls and thus were benumbed during high-minded torture. In *L'Homme machine*, he cited a series of gruesome trials conducted by Steno, Bacon, Boyle, and the then still unpublished demonstrations of irritability by Haller. Hearts were ripped out while still beating, bowels eviscerated, tracheas sliced open to stifle the yelping of frightened and suffering animals as they twitched or writhed. La Mettrie concluded from the evidence of these dreadful martyrdoms that Bordeu was right after all. A special principle of life resided in the tissues, but it was distinct from the conscious mind or higher soul. Each decentralized organ contained its own resources, thus explaining why beasts responded only "mechanically" to terror.[21]

But Robert Whytt, Haller's great contemporary and adversary, urged caution in leaping to the materialist judgment that groaning and wincing animals were "altogether insensible." In the *Physiological Essays* (1754), he remarked that such a conclusion would condemn "the uniform opinion of physicians in all ages concerning the parts which are affected in many diseases." If this doctrine of insentience were adopted by medical practitioners, he feared it would lead to fatal consequences. For Whytt, irritability was not a "muscular glue," or innate property, inhering in matter after the manner of lifeless gravity, electricity, or magnetism. Rather, it was a contractile reaction to an externally applied stimulus that aroused an uneasy feeling in the nerves. This active force was due to some immaterial cause since feeling could not be a

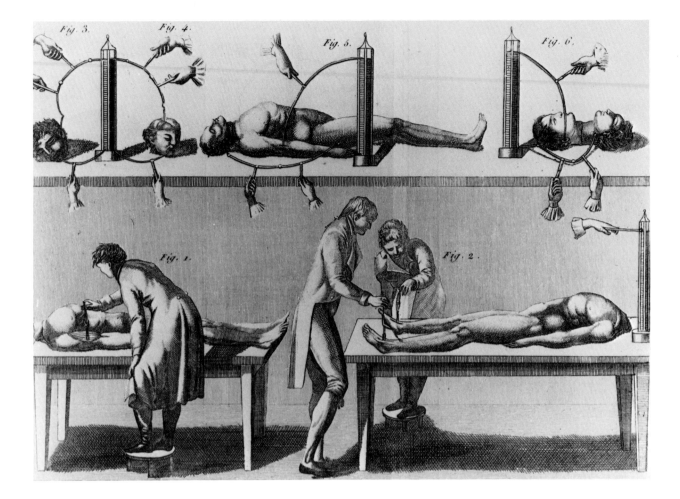

227. Giovanni Aldini, *Galvanic Experiments*, from *Essai théorique et expérimentale sur le galvanisme*, 1834, I, pl. 4. Engraving. (Photo: Courtesy National Library of Medicine, Bethesda, Md.)

proper activity of passive and inert substance. "And as *gravity* must finally be resolved into the power of that Being who upholds universal nature; so it is highly probable that the irritability of the muscles of animals is owing to that living sentient principle [the soul] which animates and enlivens their whole frame."[22]

Haller's breaking of beasts on the wheel of physiology unleashed a frenzy of research into the nervous system, especially into the functions of the viscera, the cerebrum, and the sensory organs. In Italy, Antonio Scarpa (1752–1832), professor at the Medical School of Pavia, and Caldani performed minute researches into this impossibly difficult area of the anatomy[23] (figs. 30, 68). The Bolognese Luigi Galvani (1737–1798) further introduced the battery, copper and zinc pile, and a laboratory of acids to put the Hallerian hypothesis to a rigorous test. But it was his protégé, Giovanni Aldini (1762–1834), who performed a long series of ghoulish experiments on *human*, not just animal, subjects with the permission of Napoleon—then engaged in his Italian campaign. He used corpses in order to determine precisely the responsiveness of different organ clusters (fig. 227). Aldini focused his attention on the meninges, brain, and heart. Using a Voltaic pile, he connected the electrodes to

SENSING

corporeal fragments. By running a current through the ears and mouths of the dead, he hoped to arrive at the exact quantity of vitality persisting within different segments of the body. His fundamental thesis derived from Galvani, namely, that muscular contractions were excited by the accumulation of fluids within portions of the animal fabric. These vital liquids were then conducted throughout the biological machine via the nerves, which, in turn, activated the muscles. Using the cadavers of two healthy criminals decapitated in Bologna in 1802, he subjected their crania to Galvanic shock. The result was an extreme contraction of the features. The traits "were so irregularly contorted, that they imitated the most hideous grimaces." Like Fontana's disemboweled anatomical waxes (fig. 33) or Buffon's monstrous white Negro (fig. 196), Aldini's grotesquely miming thieves illuminated the eighteenth-century taste for the macabre. A certain perversion marked the coupling of two heads neck to neck in order to observe them twisting and screwing up their faces at one another. Aldini described in gory detail how he stationed himself at the foot of the scaffold in order to receive the fresh and bloody bodies the moment the axe descended. Overcoming his repugnance, he abandoned the peaceful sort of experimentation customary to the tranquil *cabinet de physique* to haunt the gallows. This Galvinist confessed that he embarked upon a sort scientific Terror. The normal habit of using corpses of men who died because of disease meant that their fibers were already destroyed and their humors infected. He thus determined to snatch those cadavers still conserving the highest level of vital forces.[24]

The ironies attendant upon the sadistic nightmare of verifying the deep seat of enjoyment or anguish did not diminish with the search for the source of sensibility, or for an elevated principle of sentience. From Haller to Aldini, irritability had been the mere material capacity of prodded parts to respond by an unaware contraction, or an automatic tonic shortening and lengthening motion. Sensibility, on the other hand, was the tendency of the slightest sore or strongest ache to make the afflicted part throb with a corresponding commotion of which the sufferer was keenly aware.[25] The testing for both physiological capabilities belonged to the eighteenth-century interest in microscopic and minimal signs of life or death. Pursuing the elusive evidence of instinctive behavior formed part of the larger experimental enterprise of that observational age. Again, it was Whytt who pointed out the difficulty of tearing apart these transitory phenomena. Each involved the subtleties of arousal. "We never talk of irritating a stone, a piece of wood, a tree, or indeed anything that is destitute of feeling. Irritability, therefore, in the common

228. Jean-Baptiste Greuze, *The Dead
Bird,* 1792. Oil on canvas, 68 × 55 cm.
Musée du Louvre. (Photo: Réunion des
Musées Nationaux.)

229. Bernard Picart, *Different Agitations
of Convulsionaries,* from *Cérémonies et
coutumes religieuses de tous les peuples
du monde,* 1728–1743, IV. Engraving.
(Photo: Courtesy National Library of
Medicine, Bethesda, Md.)

SENSING

acceptation of the word among mankind, implies some kind of sensibility." Importantly, the Scottish physician also identified categories of people prone to this physical introspection and quasi-metaphysical susceptibility. Young children, in particular, were more impressionable because they were equipped with "tender nerves and fibers" that could be easily hurt or damaged (figs. 48, 228). Their pliant constitution, or femininely malleable temperament, was "more exquisite." The moist membranes of infants were open to being bruised or grazed by phantasmatic impressions. Youthful filaments thus possessed a greater degree of springiness and suppleness than those common to hardened adults. Whytt's image of the responsive and transformative growing mind had been adumbrated in Chardin's numerous paintings from the 1730s and 1740s devoted to childhood education through the medium of the senses. The French master's empirical scenes of pleasurable instruction through engrossing games—card tricks, top spinning, toying with knucklebones, blowing soap bubbles, registering optical ephemera—seemed to affirm the tenderness of undeveloped fibers. These fine cords were especially sensitive to the delights of a perceptually presented learning. Yet one could also discover among grown persons certain soft types endowed with "delicate nerves and very quick feelings," readily subject to spasms of enthusiasm or convulsions of desire (fig. 229).[26]

Significantly, the researches into irritability, or contractability, and into sensibility, or excitability, were part of a greater movement within the history of perception that sent vision inward bound. They demonstrated incontrovertibly the touching and pleasure-enhancing power of afflicting images. As the Winckelmann-Lessing polemic revealed, this propulsion into the somatic interior was accomplished primarily through the analysis of the sight of pain. Think, too, of how Jean-Baptiste Greuze (1762–1812), also from the 1760s forward, invented a whole class of *sensible* pubescent girls and provoked young women for whom the distresses of the world aroused pleasing aches (fig. 228).[27] Even the sight of an un-Hallerian intact dead bird could activate sensations of pity. In the manner of pricking needles or gnawing vitriol, these stirring visions plucked the sympathetic ganglia. The mechanism of sensibility thus displayed throbbing human emotions—ranging from the most intense throes of electroshock to the most sensual thrills that smart. At bottom, this physiological function was predicated on aesthetics, that is, on the eroticism of perception and the hedonistic observation of discomfort. Vibrating agitations and dainty rufflings of the soul, at the antipodes from lethargy or torpor, permitted the spectator to see irrational instincts that remained unseen under ordinary conditions.

The superficial registration of deep pangs or chafes finally managed to place the Glass of Momus in front of the heart. Gripping effusions and languid dilations made visible a subcutaneous psychological realm that was otherwise invisible.[28] They revealed a mysterious world of willed and unwilled actions and reactions that pulsed with a rhyme and reason of their own. Thus Alibert praised the autonomic nervous system for possessing the unexpected power of suddenly stimulating behavior demanding conscious attention. His language was appropriately epiphanic. "It unveils the astonishing connection of the physical faculties with the cognitive faculties, and drives these functions by the agency of the nerves." These "marvelous organs" received diverse blows from whence our movements derived. They contained within themselves, and distributed to the corporeal solids, the vivifying sap of life popularized by Johann Friedrich Blumenbach (1725–1840) as the *Lebenskraft*. In short, the nerves took on a spiritual aura. "They were the center and the means for all communications and sympathetic corresponences." On their harmonious or disturbed performance depended well-being or illness. These material structures of sensation were responsible for inner life, for imagination, reason, volition, appetite, passion, and "the wonders of thought."[29]

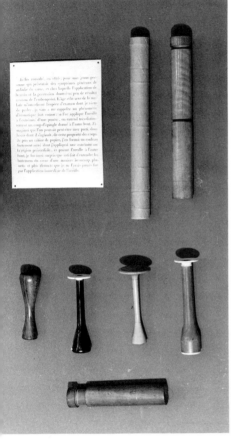

230. Théophile Laennec, *Stethoscopes,* 1819–1826. (Photo: Courtesy Université René Descartes, Musée d'Histoire de la Médecine.)

Like Théophile Laennec's (1781–1826) stethoscope, allowing the physician to listen to the murmurs of the distant heart, nervous sensibility was a form of visual auscultation (fig. 230).[30] Tight rolls of paper and slender cylinders of wood facilitated the profound study of inarticulate chest and pulmonary sounds. Analogously, impressionability as a rarefied type of visual touching provided access to a remote, obscure, and imprecise cardiac region. Paradoxically, then, from wrenching and all too tactile vivesectory butchery arose an aesthetics of projective empathy. Apprehension was the recording of an ineffable *feeling* of presence. Sensation was an immaterial and gentle percussion of worldly effects by the inner eye. Such perceptual acoustics resembled divination, the palpating of an apparitional consciousness or thin-skinned awareness.

Indeed, sensibility was none other than the ancient *fantasia* or *ingegno* brought scientifically up to date.[31] It was the almost supernatural gift of knowing objects from the inside out. It meant disembodiedly seizing their innermost nature. Since Chrysippus and the Middle Stoa, this "appearing" or "becoming

414

apparent" was tantamount to an *experience* of being affected. Pathos occurred in the command center or *hegemonikon* where physiological events flowed together. Chromatic specters from the outside "fell against," "stamped," "impressed," or otherwise subtly and uncontrollably "imprinted" the colored shape of a galling or fretting sensation upon the pneumatic vehicle of the soul.[32] Feeling-laden images were thus a sort of mute and impalpable gesture. As a matterless and transparent contact, they simultaneously brushed against the surface of the mind and the skin.[33] Thus Addison asserted that vision "may be considered a more delicate and diffusive kind of touch." The physiological pleasures of the imagination depended on the fact that ungraspable perception "spreads itself over an infinite multitude of bodies." The leitmotif of the *Spectator Papers*, "the freedom of sight," hinged upon the gaze's liberty to make immaterial contact with "unbounded views" and the "spacious horizon." These "wide and undetermined prospects" could later be refelt or represented in the fancy.[34]

Following in Addison's wake, Cozens's *Principles of Beauty* should be seen as a prime document teaching how sentiment can almost bypass the eye. The British artist created "tenderly marked" and noninsistent compound characters demanding an analogous keen perceptivity from the viewer (fig. 91). His sixteen rarefied types were redolent of the prevailing finer optic associated with the nerves. Significantly, he was most interested in that superior "tender," "feeling mind, or sensibility" accompanying a modest, languid "delicacy of constitution."[35] The more robust Algarotti also drew upon the same trope that made of the glance a *frisson*. Aptly, in the section devoted to the expression of the passions in the *Essai sur la peinture*, he claimed that "the eye seems not only able to touch and comprehend, but is susceptible to becoming enflamed."[36]

But it was Winckelmann's entire aesthetics, as we know, that revolved around the *Empfindung des Schönen* (1763). He distinguished between a merely external, or blunted and insensible, inspection and an almost imperceptible, "internal, feeling insight." The latter derived from a nonoptical sensitivity to the beautiful. In a moment of grace, the beholder was receptive to everything "sensible and delicate," to all that lay beyond the merely empirical.[37] Sulzer offered a reprise of the theme that faint outward signs aroused and made visible an invisible impact or immaterial effect.[38]

Le Camus, in the *Médecine de l'esprit*, presciently made of this simultaneously tangible and intangible capacity a Proustian "*sensible* memory." The visionary and impressionable faculty of remembrance was able to conjure up a total past or lost world when struck by a solitary note of music or the flash of an appearance. Just as the immaterialist Winckelmann spoke on behalf of the innate power of configured and moving conceptions, Le Camus cogently presented the materialist and, indeed, the empiricist, position. The latter was grounded in the belief that physical objects collided with the soul through the avenue of the senses.[39] For D'Holbach, sentiment arose when certain organs were agitated in the presence of a material thing. The transmission of feeling occurred "only by means of the nerves branching throughout the body, which itself is merely one large nerve." In the materialist scheme of existence, intrinsically shapeless and mobile atomistic human beings were themselves composed and combined from the strong or feeble hits inflicted on their idiosyncratically receptive fibers. Thus the individual was diversely modified depending on the ambient air, typical nourishment, but, above all, on "the objects with which his senses are continually bombarded and which, consequently, produce perpetual internal alterations."[40]

Watelet translated this sensationalist stance into aesthetic terms. For the painter, nature was a repository of abundant permanent and evanescent impressions. The artist's chief themes, light, color, and passion, possessed neither stability nor order. "The well-conformed organs of sight, directed to this subject, & mobilized by a *sensible* intelligence, were not only impinged upon by enduring events, but were struck by those effects which made only a momentary appearance."[41] Diderot's biological materialism, however, best summarized the physiological credo, "to feel is to live." The *Eléments de physiologie*, in particular, were dedicated to proving that the energetic mind was nothing without the vital and impulse-ridden body. A sensitivity to the optical bruises and strokes administered by the environment literally had the metamorphic power of transforming human beings into other species, or even into nonanthropocentric creatures. Reactive and responsive persons internalized the contents of an alien world. Thus they empathetically experienced every kind of existence. They became what they saw because they felt. Nothing was foreign to them, whether "inertia, sensibility, plant life, polyp life, animal life, human life." The *philosophe* claimed that this was because "man was always in the sensation," provocatively reacting to irritation or excitation. He was only an eye when he looked, a nose when he flared his nostrils, a fingertip when he tapped.

As an atheist, Diderot discredited the theological and metaphysical tradition that compounded humanity out of two antogonistic substances. If there was a soul, what was its anatomy? Where was its physical location? No, the conscious and nervy spirit did not differ from matter. Mobile, extended, sensible, and composite, it tired and rested with the body. Mankind was in thrall to its involuntary movements, to its automatic sensations recoiling or advancing from the touch of heat, cold, pain, or pleasure.[42] The living human being was no longer the Cartesian inflexible machine, manufactured from clockwork cogs and wheels, nor was it Condillac's inert marble statue. Rather, the organism was a *sensible* fluidity, shaped by the equally mutable environment. Both morphology and psychology existed only from moment to moment. The midcentury revelation of a pneumatological nervous system helped to unseat the model of a hard-core character persisting through time. Fixed identity was increasingly dissolved into a succession of airy phantoms.

Mental Meteorology

The great Enlightenment problem of the nature of thought led, as we have seen, to a doctrine of ideas corresponding to the lowest, or most phantasmal images of objects. When the nervous system—with its capacity to register touch in a way that was not quite touch—entered the epistemological lists, perception was further spectralized. Feelings were like simulacra. Resembling the fragile or intense dreams of things, they delicately or violently impressed the mind by a filmy caressing or striking of the fibers. An equivocal third entity, however, was needed to convey the interior to the exterior. The corporeal "principle of life" was first identified, in 1774, by Friedrich Casimir Medicus (1736–1806) with the *Lebenskraft*. This penetrating, intermediary and moist substance was believed to bind matter and spirit into a harmonious equilibrium. Haller's positing of irritability and, more notably, of sensibility, had already appeared to be a step in the direction of rendering concrete this elusive vitality at the root of organic existence.[43]

The eighteenth-century discovery of the nerves rekindled a Stoic physiology based on a *pneuma* theory. The human soul, according to this doctrine, was naturally populated with *pneumata*. Delusory and nonexistent fears, anxieties, hopes, pleasures, and pains descended like a fog over the unwatched and uncultivated landscape of the interior.[44] This theory of the misty passions was grounded in a conviction of the fundamental perceptual inadequacy of the senses. Not only were the things perceived through their clouded agency always in a state of flux, but they represented the world deficiently. Moreover,

Pneumatical/Pneumatick/
Pneumatology _____

adj., noun, *Moved by the wind; relative to the wind; consisting of spirit or wind. A branch of mechanicks, which considers the doctrine of the air, or laws according to which that fluid is condensed, or gravities. In the schools, the doctrine of spiritual substances, Gods, angels, and the souls of men. The doctrine of spiritual existence* [Reid].

Dr. Johnson, *Dictionary*

Pneumatique _____

noun, *The science occupied with spirits and spiritual substances. The science of the properties of the air and the laws obeyed by fluids in condensation, rarefaction, gravitation. Also: a technical explanation of the pneumatic machine, invented ca. 1654 by Otto de Guericke, Consul at Magdeburg.*

Diderot and D'Alembert, Encyclopédie

the befuddled perceiver had a tendency to yield to the persuasiveness of these unclear or false presentations. He succumbed to smoky *phantasmata*, that is, "to no presented objects." On one hand, then, aerial *pneumata* were connected to a host of deviant subjective conditions arising from the imagining of nonexistent things: dreams, ecstasies, deliria, and insanity. On the other hand, the material *pneuma* was also the *Archeus* or the ghostly principle of life. Consequently, metaphors of wind, breath, air, fire, and light designated the psychic weather within (fig. 231). Ideational and affective processes were envisaged as being at once material and spiritual, substantial and subtle, but, above all, as watery and ephemeral. The theological soul was increasingly dissolved in medical and aesthetic theory into a secular and mobile consciousness. This sensitive, humid medium momentarily registered and imparted a wavy configuration to mutable experiences that had none.

Novalis, in *Das Allgemeine Brouillon*, gave voice to the notion that a vaporous electromagnetical *spiritus*, *esprit*, *Geist*, or excitable wit—not clear and distinct reason—embodied the life of the mind as unseizable motion. "Our thinking is only a Galvanization, stimulating the earthly spirit [*Geist*] through a spiritual atmosphere. . . . Logic corresponds to *meteorology*. Atmospherology is meteorology."[45] The new elemental noetics, deriving from a study of the elastic and responsive nerves, was founded on a psychodynamics of vision. The "hard," sculptural and abstracted *Logos* was challenged by neurology. Only a "soft," imaginative, and distracted awareness could be congruent with the subtler phantasmatic aspects of conceiving. Furthermore, the psyche as flitting idea plus sensation was part of a nontextual and nontactile Epicurean domain. It, too, was involved with film making, with radiant effigies and exfoliating species. Such a fluent and biological construing of mental activity was a harbinger of today's digital ontology. The computer's accelerated time and the liquidity of electronic word processing similarly decongeals reality.[46] The fluctuating components of both past and present cognitive systems were equally removed from the manual carving procedures of the old-fashioned scribal, or contouring, graphic arts and the drudgery of anatomizing typesetting.

231. Jean-Jacques Scheuchzer, *Respiration*, from *Physique sacrée*, 1732– 1737 VI, pl. 521. Engraving by I. A. Fridrich. (Photo: Courtesy Resource Collections of the Getty Center for the History of Art and the Humanities.)

During the second half of the eighteenth century, there were many emerging hypotheses that invoked a medium or "ethers" to explain the transmission of forces within internal and external space. Newton's *Opticks* had accelerated the pace of converting gross bodies into light-shot porous atoms. These material motes were as refined as the nervous system required to apprehend

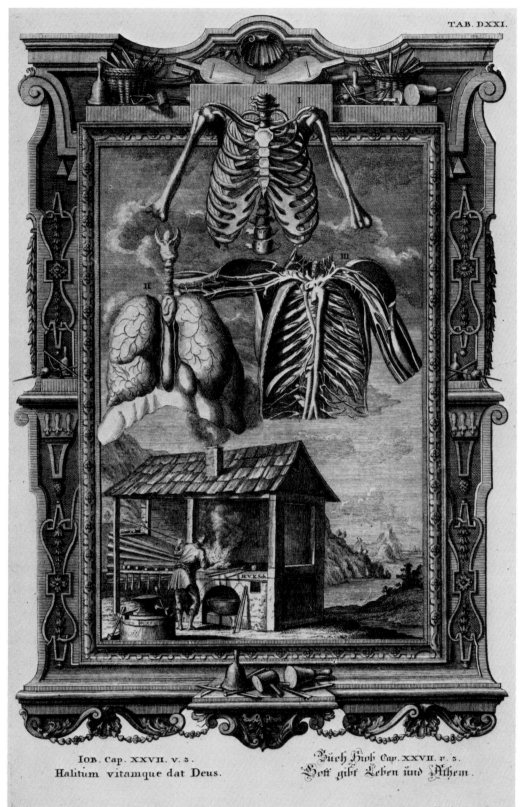

I. A. Fridrich sculps.

IOB. Cap. XXVII. v. 3.
Halitum vitamque dat Deus.

Buch Hiob Cap. XXVII. v. 3.
Gott gibt Leben und Athem.

them.[47] Sensation, or the ability to feel alterations occurring in the emotional atmosphere, was a form of smoky inner vision. It stood at the antipodes both from the perspicuity of the bare understanding and from a merely empirical looking. An intractable and absolute emptiness was essential to Newton's divinization and geometrization of the void. Conversely, an environmental fluidity was requisite for the rise of a personal ambient or changeable identity without durable support.[48] We need to expose the underpinnings beneath Newton's concept of that rare, elastic, and subtle spirit filling up the universe. Only then will we be able to comprehend the distinction between this sacred vacuum and a profane gassy milieu.

The mathematician's commitment to the reality of an invisible realm was determined by Henry More's notion of a contracting and dilating immaterial "Spirit of Nature."[49] In the *Immortality of the Soul*, More radically divided matter from spirit. He imparted a new and important twist—later reworked in Newton's concept of gravity—to an extreme antinomy. A universe "thick-set" with stuff was counterpointed to an "amphibion" self-actuating soul whose "tenuity" permitted it to pass through substance. More revived with a vengeance the Neoplatonic concept of a separable terrestrial vehicle, peeling off from the higher *animus* and forming a company of aerial genii, apparitions, specters, and noctambuli. Significantly, he made such emanations dependent upon "the wonderful force of the imagination" and its ability "to create this aiery spectrum."[50] Newton's *Opticks* (1706) and the second edition of the *Principia* (1729) reformulated More's theistic and necessitarian dualism into the model of the nutshell cosmos. This almost vacuous entity was operated on by phenomenal, yet incorporeal, forces.[51]

The English scientist's enormous intellectual influence throughout the eighteenth century reinforced the Neoplatonic view of the low degree of reality belonging to matter and, by analogy, to physical or sensory impressions. Not coincidentally, he transubstantiated the hard and atomy fabric of the world into spongy interstices. Importantly, what was true for the universe also held for bodily substance. There was a widespread belief, and not only among English natural historians, that material and somatic stuff constituted the least and most inconsiderable portion of the macrocosm and the microcosm. In Newton's mystical physics, the inward frame of things was therefore mentalized and ontologized into diffusive forces exerting their power over massy particles. He and his immaterialist followers of the 1730s engaged in a battle to break up Spinoza's and Leibniz's "atheistic" plenum.[52]

The occult tropes, praising the sacredness of emptiness, were offset by an antithetical group of gaseous metaphors. Subterranean exhalations, mine damps, mineral fumes, and metallic steams poisoned and congealed the clean spirit into mere air. Plutarch (?50–120? AD), in the *Obsolescence of Oracles*, drew the well-known Stoic distinction between a dry and ethereal "prophetic current" and moist winds and vapors dulling sight and hearing. Divine and holy breath, or inspiration, was the opposite of befouling respiration. "Moreover, the earth sends forth for men streams of many potencies; some of them produce derangements, diseases, or deaths; others are helpful, benignant, and beneficial." In this important essay from the *Moralia*, Plutarch forecast what would, in fact, happen in the early modern period. He worried that the transparent and running waters of prophecy, or the uncontaminated verbal art of impersonally transmitting and foretelling the future, would be resolved "into winds and vapours and exhalations." That is, rational and unambiguous oracles—emanating from on high—would become metamorphosed into an irrational and muddied pictorial medium distorted by subjective impressions and presentiments.[53]

Scheuchzer in the *Physique sacrée* similarly reminded his readers of the long Judeo-Christian pneumatic tradition summarized in Job 27:3. The Holy Ghost exhaled a vital spirit into the nostrils and lungs of Adam (fig. 231). This numinous breath of communication had to be kept unsullied so that it could serve as a conduit for lofty spiritual messages. Otherwise, it would become merely the source of idiosyncratic and infected sensory experience.[54] At issue was the realization that a clouded corporeal medium altered the way one sensed reality. Instead of hearing and imitating a foreign truth emitted from afar, the percipient created another, self-expressive world out of his native steamy atmosphere located near at hand. A perspicuous acoustic and linguistic metaphor was thus replaced by an obfuscating visual metaphor indicative of improper materializations or phantasmagoric sights.

This ancient atmospheric terminology of purity versus pollution infused late eighteenth-century English and French debates concerning the nature of the air. The polemic was complex and my purpose is not to provide a comprehensive history. I do, however, want to deal with notable links joining aesthetic with chemical thought. In 1767, Joseph Priestley (1733–1804) embarked on his systematic investigation of airs, eventually leading to the phlogiston-oxygen controversy with Lavoisier in the 1780s. The British chemist's various landmark disquisitions revealed just how profoundly eighteenth-

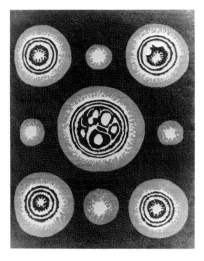

232. Ebenezer Sibly, *Electrical Stars,* from *A Key to Physic and the Occult Sciences,* 1804, p. 246. Engraving by Pass after Dodd. (Photo: Courtesy National Library of Medicine, Bethesda, Md.)

century scientific discussions of space were tied to the metaphysical and theological problems of matter and spirit. Significantly, the necessitarian Priestley rejected what he termed the vulgar or popular view of substance. Instead, he endowed it, following the lead of Roger Boscovich (1711–1787), with the propensities of attraction and repulsion.[55] Rather than creating separate, quickening spiritual forces—like Newton—he immaterialized matter into light and airy effects as surely as Berkeley had done. In *A Free Discussion* (1778), Priestley conjured up the vision of an impalpably interconnected universe. This model would be embraced by Mesmerists and other sophistic wheelers and dealers in the occult (fig. 232). He claimed there was no "such thing as real contact in nature" since there was no such thing as solidity. God, when he formed both the human body and the cosmos, "only fixed certain centers of various attractions and repulsions extending indefinitely in all directions, the whole effect of them to be upon each other; approaching or receding from each other and therefore carrying their peculiar spheres of attraction and repulsion with them. All effects in which bodies are concerned and of which we can be sensible by our eyes, touch, etc, may be resolved into attraction and repulsion."[56] The reason physical objects seemed hard and palpable was because when such indivisible points were placed within each other's circle of influence they appeared "compact." A wall-like resistance to the outsider's approach meant that one object was prevented from occupying the place of another. Consequently, to us, attracted and repelled entities looked as if they possessed demarcating edges and tangible contours.

Importantly, Priestley's chemical and electrical theory was filled with images of invisible powers acting on things "without actually impinging on them."[57] The model of springy physical air not only fueled his spiritual monism but undergirded the real topic of his treatise, the demolition of the soul. "The uniform composition of man or that what we call mind, or the principle of perception and thought, is not a substance distinct from the body, but the result of corporeal organization. The human mind is nothing more than a modification of matter (whatever it may be)."[58] He prominently mentioned Hartley's mechanical "vibrations," occurring in the ether of the brain and the nervous system, and the empiricist association of ideas. Both revealed the material manner whereby hidden somatic urges or furrowing trains of mental motions produced visible effects. Indeed, what was conventionally termed the unseen intelligible soul was transformed by Priestley into gray cells and elastic fibers, or into the neurological medium itself. "I do not see why the soul should be confined to the size of the brain only, exclusive of the nerves;

and then as the nerves are in every part of the body, the soul would, in fact be of the same form and size with the body to which it belongs, though with more interstices."[59] Thus Priestley did for biology what Berkeley had done for epistemology. For the latter, retinal ideas present to mind were congruent with actuality. For the former, the power of thinking belonged inseparably to the brain of man, "just as walking to his feet." "Man, who is *one being*, is composed of *one kind of substance*, made of *the dust of the earth*; that when he dies, he, of course, ceases to think; but when his *sleeping dust* shall be reanimated at the resurrection, his power of thinking, and his consciousness, will be restored to him."[60] Consequently, human beings were *eidola*, the transient and perishable emblems of corporeal movements or physiological functions. Priestley, in the words of Coleridge, stripped matter of its material properties and substituted airy or ideal powers. Where we expected to find a body, we discovered "nothing but a ghost, the *apparition* of a defunct substance."[61] The atmospheric medium had truly become the message.

The fundamental problem of overcoming a persistent dualism within the biological domain also underlay the critique launched by the Montpellier vitalists. They attacked both the Cartesian string and pulley crowd as well as the animists' belief in the possibility of transposing matter into spirit. The physician Paul-Joseph Barthez (1734–1806), unlike Priestley, drew on the Neoplatonic and Stoic precept of a third, intervening veil or vehicle. He cited Jean-Baptiste von Helmont's (1577–1646) "gas," or wild spirit, and the Cambridge Platonist Ralph Cudworth's (1617–1688) "plastic" active virtue. These media heralded a modern scientific principle of life distinct both from the body and the soul. Irritability and sensibility, in his system, were identified with the pneumatic *Archeus*. This medium literally was the mean substance floating between the rational faculties and mechanical operations.[62] If Priestley's hypothesis represented the reductive tendency of eighteenth-century thought, its penchant to collapse complex somatic behavior into a single material or spiritual force, Barthez's impulse was to pluralize the occult powers of the ancients. Air was no longer an abstraction, the finest and subtlest of elements, the quintessential covering or fiery dress of the soul, but the result of chemical combinations. Mixtures produced gaseous intermediaries, those chemical substances intuited by the Hebrews in their physical and metaphysical concept of *Rouach*, *Nepesch*, and *Neschamah*, or animating breath.[63] For Barthez and the vitalists, then, every organ of the living body not only possessed its own autonomous energy but was bathed by its own atmosphere. It was surrounded by its idiosyncratic exhalations and sympathetic currents out of which the total individual milieu was compounded.[64]

This effluvial language and the concept of organs awash in their own intentions and sensations derived, I believe, from Epicurus's (341–270 BC) model of tenuous idols exerting a subliminal effect on the perceiver.[65] The epiphanic propagation of a suffusing stream of *phantasiae*—including not only color, shape, texture, but pathos and character—comprised precisely those flimsy films that made up the body's internal emanations. Lucretius's (95–55 BC) *De rerum natura* was the single most important source for the eighteenth century of this Epicurean phenomenology of flying phantoms and airy specters.[66] His material yet immaterial metaphor of membranes exfoliating from the outer surfaces of things was singularly apt to the mirror or water paradigm of organic tissues throwing off *imagines, effigiae,* and *figurae.* Furthermore, when these cast-off simulacra lightly impinged on the eyes and the imagination, they induced empathetic thoughts or reveries, depending on whether the beholder was awake or asleep.[67] Lucretius's visionary physiology of surpassingly fine-textured semblances, scents, sounds, smoke, and heat was at the root of all those powerful and ontologized "thin" images that penetrated the pores of the body, thus exciting the analogously refined substance of the mind and arousing the subtle senses.

233. Ephraim Chambers, *Pneumaticks,* from *Cyclopaedia,* 1738, II. Engraving. (Photo: author.)

This mental landscape, drenched in mists and vapors, became incorporated into the fashion for studying the dreamy or nonlogical aspects of the psychic terrain. Pneumatics (also called pneumatology or pneumatosophy), according to Chambers, was the "doctrine and contemplation of spirits and spirtual substances." It was specifically associated with the mind's inquiry into its chimerical and foggy nature (fig. 233). This study of the weather within signified research into the innate and hazy principle of life, or what Barthez had termed "the intimate genius of all my being."[68] In scholasticism, the word had been commonly used to refer to the dogma of spirits. But in an enlightened and experimental age, the rubric covered the art of measuring the air and the laws whereby fluids were condensed. As "aerometry," it was also related to the atmosphere, elasticity, gravity, compression, condensation, rarefaction, and expansion.[69] Significantly, Robert Boyle's (1627–1689) monumental air pump dominated the plate devoted to *Pneumaticks* in the *Cyclopaedia.* It dwarfed those other instruments for feeling or sensing the variability of the air, such as Torricelli's barometer or Fahrenheit's improved thermometer and hygrometer. It was, however, the Scottish authors of the *Encyclopaedia Britannica*—accustomed to roaming in the dank gloaming—who specifically

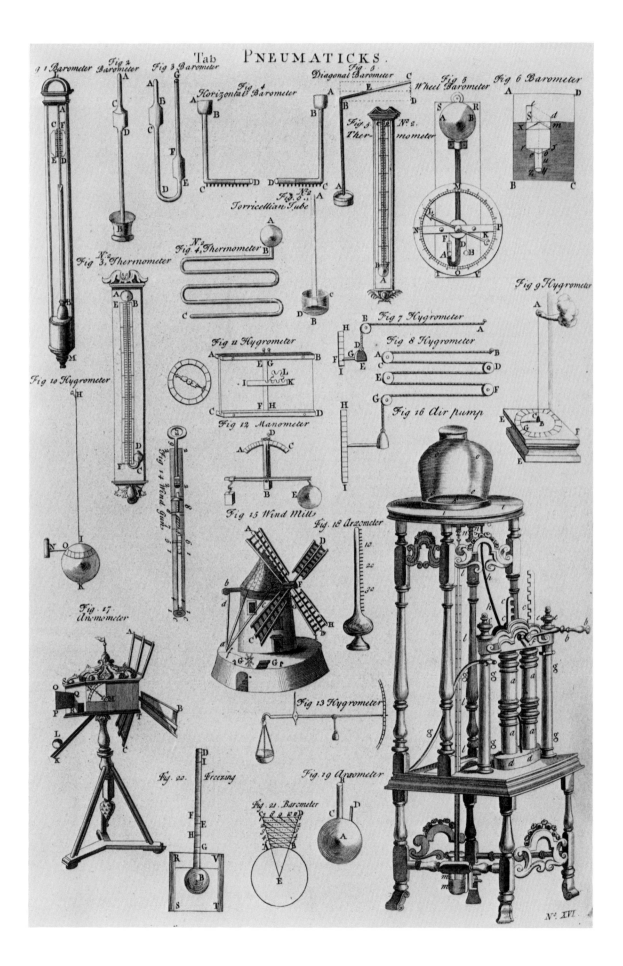

Tab PNEUMATICKS.

connected the total "metaphysical" knowledge of the nature and properties of thinking beings with their fluid physiology and damp psychology. Pneumatology swept together this panoply of moist and cloudy hosts, evading logic or reasoning. It pursued "the knowledge of the soul in general, and of man in particular."[70] This "recently invented term" designated both a sort of aerial chemistry and a phantasmic inner reflection simultaneously registering fumatory changes occurring inside itself and within the shifting environment. Pneumatology, or scientific metaphysics, imparted information concerning "all spirits and angels." Moreover, the *Encyclopaedia* article sarcastically recorded that it required an "infinite art to give an account of what we do not absolutely know and of which we can never know anything."[71]

The powers of the air—whether incarnated as the elastic aura radiating from the subjective consciousness or the putrid miasmas arising from chemical stench (fig. 234)—were part of a new physiological culture betrayed only by an appearance that had no fixed contours. Pneumatical presence was manifested by a passing aroma that could be sensed but was difficult to behold or pin down. Gillray satirized not only phantasmic *Pneumaticks* (1802), but the Baconian experimentalism of the Royal Institution, chartered in 1800. His burlesque spoof ably tied together the dual material and immaterial connotations of a physical substance with mystifying efficacy. Sir Humphrey Davy's (1778–1829) invention of "laughing gas" became part of a spate of fashionable lectures hosted by that organization. Their purpose was to initiate the stylish "higher ranks of society" into the functions of a new and complicated apparatus for trapping the invisible. Significantly, a ghostly fume induced both a mental distemper and a physiological reaction in its hapless subject. The operator, Professor Thomas Young, was shown administering nitrous oxide to Sir J. C. Hippisley, the manager of the Royal Institution, with explosive results.[72] The ideal substance of visions or inhaled *pabulum vitae*, constituting the energy of the soul, was thus also capable of provoking a corporeal "concert performed with vapors!" Both Grandville and Cruikshank, in different ways, poked fun at the continuing craze for hunting down the nonexistent, for seeking the negative or normally unseen features of the created world. Grandville's pneumatological sophist, Dr. Puff, invented a "steam orchestra" playing "the divine composition, the Self and the Non-Self, Symphony in C Major." The caricaturist reported, tongue-in-cheek, that the review of the concert, published in *The Literary and Musical Flageolet*, noted that the evening ended with an explosion. Grandville wittily evoked a bad case of the musical vapors. An ophicleide, overcharged with harmony,

234.   James Gillray, *Scientific Researches! New Discoveries in Pneumaticks!*, 1802. Colored etching. (Photo: Courtesy National Library of Medicine, Bethesda, Md.)

suddenly burst. "The blanks, the *grupetti* of sharps, of quavers, of semi-quavers, of clouds of tonal smoke and flames of melody diffused into the atmosphere."[73] Cruikshank, in turn, connected pneumatology with the rage for grasping an invisible inward flux through phrenology. The "organ of ideality," "remarkably conspicuous in poets," was believed to seize those demonic apparitions generated by an all-potent "mysterizing" imagination (fig. 235).[74]

Jests aside, the case of a colorless gas detected, or of an evanescent manifestation disclosed, revealed the serious role played by senses other than sight in the activity of perception. Investigations into the concealed operations of the nervous system had demonstrated the significance of a touchlike vision. Chemical researches into the nature of the air divulged gases as much through smell as through sight. Moreover, external and internal pneumatology were bound up with the long tradition associated with uncreated spirits unveiling themselves to the human heart through fragrance. Proclus asserted that not only the invisible gods but godlike innate notions, dreams, and other portions of our essential being exhaled "the scent of their knowledge." We could "not possess them by actual realization."[75] The *Encyclopédie* article "Parfum" similarly alluded to the sweet effluvium surrounding deities as betokening the sure sign of their ambrosial presence. The heavy musk, cloying civet, and pungent amber—popular in the preceding century—were replaced during the Enlightenment with soft and light fragrances congruent "with nerves that had become more delicate."[76] The penetrability of perfume was thus a means for relating fleeting and imprecise desires with an equally vaporous external milieu.

Le Camus's *Médecine de l'esprit* contained a lengthy section on aromatherapy. Thurification procured "artificial transports." He recalled how during the last century myrrh, chypre, and bergamot were worshiped to the point of superstition. People "perfumed their bodies, their clothes, their houses, in order to dispose themselves to study & to maintain their minds alert to the attractions of pleasure."[77] Again one is reminded of Proust's eighteenth-century mentality, his reliance on the notion that an acute sense of smell can generate emotions and collapse time. Le Camus vividly conjured up the suffusing power of balms and their ability to create a persisting individual atmosphere or a fleeting identity. "An astonishing quantity of particles so delicate & so subtle, escape from all odoriferous bodies. They can continue to emanate for many years without the body perceptibly diminishing in weight."[78] Further-

235. George Cruikshank, *Organ of Ideality,* from *Phrenological Illustrations,* 1826, pl. 5. Colored etching. (Photo: Courtesy National Library of Medicine, Bethesda, Md.)

more, by their freshness or foulness they could preserve health or provoke illness. Collapsing physiology into pneumatics, he maintained that the warm and dry quality of the brain itself favored a subtle sense of smell. That is, the air-inhaling nose possessed the same refined sensing properties as the susceptible ethereal imagination. Like Proust, Le Camus, too, evoked a vanishing aristocratic breed prone to inducing "sweet ecstasies." Hedonistic users of floral waters existed at the opposite end of the social scale from the rank and reeking multitude associated with the spread of urban contagion. The noisome fetidness of the hospital or the rancid prison were congruent with "thick" and deadened sensory organs incapable of the gentle sentiments awakened by suave aromatics.

For Le Camus, scents, sights, sounds, flavors, and touch were part of a general "science of taste," dedicated to procuring distracting sensations for the discriminating soul. D'Alembert's important article "Goût" (1757) in the *Encyclopédie* had made the case that the physiology of taste involved the motion of an organ in savoring a physical substance. Just as vision was frequently described as being a finer touch, taste was defined as a more subtle tact, and was deemed superior to it. Its objects were not tangible solids, but the diffusive liquors and saps imbuing delicacies and requiring extraction in order to be enjoyed. D'Alembert provided a minute analysis of the tongue's function in this alchemical process of transubstantiation and delectation. Covered with microscopic "mushrooms," or fleshy cones and pyramids, this dainty organ required an "attenuated" matter diluted enough to enter its minuscule pores. Palatable tidbits were relished precisely because of the unique arrangement of the ultraresponsive nerves crisscrossing its pulpy and sensitive surface. Well before Brillat-Savarin, D'Alembert not only noted the close affinities joining taste to smell but connected the entire science of savoring to a zest for the fine arts. For both the activities of eating and appreciating, it was not enough to see beauty, one also had to feel it. Nor was it sufficient to be touched by appetizing experiences in a confused and uncomprehending manner. "One must be able to distinguish nuances." According to the mathematician, there was a fundamental bond between the *gourmet*, who could detect the surreptitious mixing of two liqueurs, and the *connoisseur*, who could feel at a glance the mingling of two styles. Gustatory flaws added up to poor taste in both disciplines, and in others like physics as well. Overly spicy or piquant seasoning, and an excessively studied or mannered preparation, prevented the consumer from experiencing beautiful nature. Moreover, nauseating depravity was a sort of sickness and signified the selection of food that would disgust other men. It thus resembled that perversion found in the visual arts whereby pleasure was gained from revolting, repulsive, ridiculous, fantastic, and affected images (figs. 119, 120, 121). Ill-flavored meats and unsavory topics revealed "a malady of the spirit." Finally, and speaking proleptically, there were those Baudelairean "cold souls" or Manet-like "false wits," with their eccentric and skewed appetites, whose icy intellects amounted to having "no taste" at all.[79]

D'Alembert's and Le Camus's subtle analysis of *gusto*—going well beyond either lip-smacking gluttony or gall and wormwood dissection—represented a major and comprehensive attempt to introduce precision into the *purée* of the *je ne sais quoi*. This invisible "secret knot," toothsomely blending body and soul, had always been identified with an elusive, graceful, and even feminine internal motion. Relying on its connection to sapidity, Félibien termed it "an extremely subtle and hidden intermediary."[80] Sticotti continued to think of it as a sort of nectar or "an imperceptible charm, a natural grace in persons or things," leaving an agreeable aftertaste.[81] Enlightenment biology had demonstrated that women were different from men, down to their hysterical nerves. Similarly, the new cutaneous study of tasteful sensations or of the overall *sensible* sensory "system," in Alibert's words, increasingly became the aestheticized province of the female.[82] In the atmosphere of rational methodization characterizing the second half of the eighteenth century, it was easy to forget D'Alembert's injunction that one must also understand—during the moment of sensual gratification—the physical and intellectual ingredients of the delicious. The ability to discern the fine, the fragrant, or the flavorful—without thinking it—became an unmasculine aptitude removed from tougher cognitive skills.

Samuel-Auguste-André-David Tissot (1728–1797), in his *Essai sur les maladies des gens du monde* (1781), was inspired by Bernardino Ramazzini's (1633–1714) study of professional diseases. The groundbreaking *De Morbis Artificium Diatriba* (1700) had been translated, in 1713, into French, Italian, Dutch, and English. The Parisian physician, rather than discussing Ramazzini's cloistered nuns, spoke of sequestered society ladies and their effeminate hothouse counterparts, or "men of the world." These creatures of artifice were plagued by a hypersensibility, or an excessive awareness bereft of reason. Whereas the latter allowed their imagination to be misled by irritated nerves "creating chimeras at every instant," the former lived in continual agitation. In exposing the languid evils of sedentary life—also embraced by the indolent *savant* and the enfeebled poet—Tissot remarked how their sensibilities became exacerbated, their fibers high-strung to the point of delirium. Women, in particular, had their sleep troubled by "a thousand small social events, that a man absorbed in his work never perceives." And when awake, they suffered from the condition ridiculously termed "the vapors." Nonetheless, this designation aptly indicated how their volition and taste were subject to the same instability as their physiology. Tissot painted a lasting picture of the weak aesthete, or of the infinitely *sensible* womanly person of taste. This irrational and useless being was indiscriminately buffeted by every insubstantial impression. She was the image of distraction, swollen by fictions, and liable to more illusions than either the robust peasant or the virile man of affairs.[83]

Gynecoid fluff, of course, was the substance of the ghostly imagination. That "deceptive faculty" was mindlessly transfixed, according to Alibert, by the play of light and colors or with what "does not really exist." Females "see what they do not see; they feel what they do not feel."[84] For Sticotti, the feminine *forte* was illusion, falseness, or that "marvelous which ordinarily arrests us only for several moments." Members of the fair sex were governed by the imagination "since they are not occupied with anything solid." This fantastic and feminine portion of the brain was the "medullary screen" from which objects painted on the eye were "cast as if emitted by a magic lantern."[85] Consequently, an effeminate, distraught sensibility and a soft, artistic style were supposedly equally driven by excessive, personal, disorganized, and unduly ornamental feelings. Simultaneously loose and tumescent, womanly thought was pneumatic, irrational, and self-disclosing. Stimulated by, it also mimicked the Epicurean flux of the milieu. The image of distaff gray matter, like that of an unformed infant's, was one of an unhierarchical synoptic fusion of instantaneous sights, sounds, tastes, and smells. Alibert could have been describing the feminality of the present-day television monitor when he outlined his view of pliant organs receptive to, and hungry for, sensuous encounters. In this dermatology of the specular emotions, or of the flying passions touching the skin, errant impressions left no permanent mark. "They only grazed surfaces."[86]

We have been skirting the issue of the momentous relocation of the soul from the rigid, rear to the soft, frontal portion of the brain. Recall that Descartes had placed it in the *glandula pinealis*, Willis in the *corpus striatum*, Bonnet in the *corpus callosum*, and Haller in the *pons*. Increasingly, however, everything grossly material was excised from the *sensorum communis* and the *phantasia* to leave only melting motion. The nerves primarily were considered to cause this spiritual "watering" of the body. According to the Abbé Richard, their "subtle liquor" constituted the very "laboratory of the brain."[87] Alibert's investigations into the physiology of the passions also opened his eyes to the uniquely human reflective capacity to watch "the flux and reflux of thoughts like the waves of the sea." When the eyes were closed and the ears stopped up in meditation, then *sensible* man "unveils himself to physical impressions; he abandons himself entirely to the inspirations of his consciousness; he analyzes his perceptions; he associates ideas and images, in recognizing these interconnections; he retains what he has learned; he decomposes what he has experienced." Within this inner sensitive menstruum, the mobile, sublimating imagination and the echoing, illusionizing memory were the alkahest. They flowed like a watercolor "tinting everything at will; magnifying all points of view; substituting an enchanted world for the real world," and dissolving it into ideal "magic panoramas."[88]

But it was Theodore von Soemmering's (1755–1830) *Über das Organ der Seele* (1796) that gave voice to the Romantic view that the *Geist*, the nervous force of our individuality, or the wet substance of our most intimate "I," existed from the initial embryonic gobbet. This fetal liquidity contained the secret of animation and was related to other crystalline humors. The Göttingen naturalist asked what was the human being in the first hours after conception but "a tiny, from the outside insubstantial looking, transparent droplet of a homogeneous-seeming humidity, with a trace of organization but not yet any true physiology." The proof of this "ductility of spirit" was evident from a perusal of the animal kingdom. In youth, all creatures were moist. And how much stiffer and unyielding were those powers of fixed and directed attention stemming from the phrenologically obdurate adult brain. Von Soemmering compared the fluency of the *Lebenskraft* to the watery polyp (fig. 202) and to the translucent jelly of the aquatic *Doris Laevis*—as glaucous as the sea in which it drifted. If the "animated slime" of lower organisms possessed structure and vitality, why should the cranial juices not contain an uncongealed "inner sensibility" indicative of the flowing soul?[89]

Franz Baader (1765–1841), a key link in the transmission of Jakob Boehme's (1575–1624) mysticism into German Romantic thought, connected von Soemmering's genetic deliquescence to the schematizing Kantian symbol. The fundamental tenet of his philosophy was encapsulated in François Hemsterhuis's (1720–1790) Neoplatonic claim that the body "was a running soul" and the material universe "was a running God."[90] Citing John Hunter's opinion that the male semen decocted a "compositional principle" into the reproductive process, Baader further developed the physical and metaphysical antithesis between durity and dilution. He claimed that the chemistry of solvents, not rigid mechanics, was closely tied to the genesis of ideas and "to the physiology of internal sensations." Conception was a liquid and symbolizing process. Operating chemically, thought arose when representations held in mixed solution were condensed or precipitated. Both in the *Beyträge zur Elementar-Phisiologie* (1797) and the *Über das Pythagoraïsche Quadrat* (1798), then, he praised the borderless unification of mental and corporeal substances. The origin of these psychic and somatic streams emulated the initial birth of all organisms from the depths of the primal ocean.[91] Coleridge's theory of correspondences, or doctrine that "all organs of spirit are framed for a correspondent world of spirit," employed the identical infusory metaphors. The "common consciousness" was "connected to master-currents below the surface." The "Ante-Goshen" land of the spiritual, or of that obscurity "on the other side of our natural consciousness," was accessible only through a new or thawing medium. An efferent and fusive freedom was the "common ethereal element" of all beings.[92]

The prevailing trope of a feeling and misty thought-flow was vigorously challenged by Blake in the *Annotations to Reynolds*. "The man who asserts that there is no Such Thing as Softness in Art, and that everything in Art is Definite and Determinate, has not been told this by Practise, but by Inspiration & Vision, because Vision is Determinate & Perfect . . . Softness is produced alone by comparative Strength & Weakness in the marking out of Forms."[93] Mollification was not only a threat to a hard-edged abstraction and to a cartilaginous or tactile outline style (figs. 13, 53, 55, 57, 66, 72, 73, 74). Blake's abhorrence of lathering and flaccid oil paint betokened the greater fear of a medullary plasticity lubricated to the point of madness. Extreme mental liquefaction led to a river of pathological distractions, to a torrent of ghostly delusions and smoky hallucinations (figs. 95, 96).[94] As is true for modern sufferers from Tourette syndrome, the overexcited subcortex could become ominously uncongealed. The impulsive *ticqueur* leaches out his vital spirits in vaporizing phantoms, in chaotic sallies, jerks, noises, and other involuntary motions, or a "teratoma of the mind."[95] If dumpish torpor and sullen mopishness were a sort of insensibility or melancholic ossification (fig. 125), fissile mania was a hypersensibility and automatic ductility (figs. 122, 123, 124, 127). Aubry's "Sultan," "modern Leonidas," and "aristocrat,"

on display at Charenton, were subject to this hyperkinesis. Uncontrollable fluency manifested the brain's abandonment "to an ocean of conjectures" washed in and out by the uncontrollable tide of the five senses (fig. 236).[96]

According to Alibert, certain forms of alienation were characterized by an excessive limberness. The onrush of too many violent emotions prevented the insane not only from focusing on outer objects but from maintaining any stable sense of self. Victims of hallucination were the prey of a diseased sensibility. They were perpetually plunged into a flood "of incoherent ideas" welling up from the internal gush. Citing the pathological studies of Jean-Etienne-Dominique Esquirol (1772–1840), Alibert connected the dissolving "divagation of attention" to a "raging mania" (fig. 237).[97] How different this physiological and internal sense of too-muchness was from Lavater's anatomical, and merely externally derived, physiognomic storm (fig. 78).[98] Whether

236.   Charles Aubry, *Madness*, from *Album comique de pathologie pittoresque,* 1823. Lithograph by Langlumé. (Photo: Courtesy National Library of Medicine, Bethesda, Md.)

237. Jean-Etienne-Dominique Esquirol,
Maniac during Attack, from *Des maladies
mentales,* 1838, II, pl. 7. Engraving by
Ambroise Tardieu. (Photo: Courtesy
National Library of Medicine, Bethesda, Md.)

238. Jean-Etienne-Dominique Esquirol,
Maniac after Cure, from *Des maladies
mentales,* 1838, II, pl. 9. Engraving by
Ambroise Tardieu. (Photo: Courtesy
National Library of Medicine, Bethesda, Md.)

taking the form of vehement enthusiasm or of obsessive depression (fig. 238), monomania, for the Stoic-trained *Idéologues*, was characterized by chronic sensory illusions. These false passions or misleading perturbations occurred in an unstable physiology acutely susceptible to fluctuating imaginal activity.[99] Géricault's radically empirical portraits of the insane, painted between 1821 and 1824, were commissioned by Dr. Etienne-Jean Georget (1795–1828), one of Esquirol's disciples at the Salpêtrière. They captured, in a coldly diagnostic way, the fleeting expressions of a nervous condition difficult to describe verbally. Compulsive gamblers (fig. 46) and kleptomaniacs were shown non-symbolically as persevering in another world, that of the incoherent waking dream. Such nonfeverish "irresistible penchants" bubbled up when the fibers were too greatly tensed or declenched. This resulted either in autistically sealing off a patient or in breaking the sluice gate and inundating the public space with private delusions.[100] Manias thus disfigured not a face but thought. The soul was immersed in a deluge of specious apparitions and perverse impulses from which it was almost impossible to resurface.

Dreams have been explained as divine revelations, as otherworldly prophecies, and as fluid pneumatic vehicles washing out of the body to wander abroad at night. Investigations into the function of the nervous system suggested that the brain commanded involuntary corporeal movements in sleep as well as voluntary actions while awake. Nocturnal specters were tied to the growing eighteenth-century research into the physiological and psychological origin of an inner mental vision. Superior to mere physical sight, this power was closely intertwined with the ascendancy of the imagination over the imagistic fancy. The empiricist's "despotism of the eyes" seemed to be belied by the existence of intrinsically inchoate and metamorphic impulses. A welter of fantastic hallucinations, distorted remembrances, and other delusional experiences were imbued with a nonoptical intensity. Anxiety, fear, elation, or repressed wishes and unfulfilled desires had no visible objective correlative. Moreover, the bizarre grotesques of a creative dream style—distorting time or place, disguising persons, and patching instincts incongruously together—seemed not to be based on external cues or imitation. Nightmares, clairvoyancy, and somnambulism provided evidence that the brain stem generated its own energy. It shaped apparitional plots that were more lucid and rich, yet less substantial, than the epics of life. Whether woven of filmy residues of decaying memories or new and cryptic conceptions, the dream work and its trail of unruly phantoms further rendered questionable a tactile reality.

The Enlightenment opened a window onto the brain. Throughout history, visions, or the ghostly idols of the mind, figured strongly in myth, art, and literature. But during the eighteenth century they became refracted by the urgent need to distinguish true from false semblances. Automatic, phantasmagoric, and illogical, the vivid and haphazard imaginal flow raised the special question of whether one knew what one sensed or not. For Plato, *eikasia* was the basest form of knowing, a mere apparition or pseudo-knowledge at the antipodes from *dianoia, episteme,* and *noesis.* We have already observed how the major thrust of eighteenth-century philosophy was to turn these false simulacra into low-grade ideas. Such watery or mirrored reflections were reluctantly retained at all because it was realized that thought could not exist without images.[101] These, in turn, were generated by the camera obscura imagination suspended dubiously somewhere in the middle of the brain. It was the thick air of the body, not the light and immaterial spirit, that produced rotten imaginings or contaminated figural messages. Thus Baader—

Fantasm _____

noun, A thing not real, but appearing to the imagination. Fantastical/Fantastick, adj., Irrational; bred only in the imagination; unreal; apparent only; having the nature of phantoms which only assume visible forms occasionally. . . . Uncertain; unsteady; irregular; whimsical; fanciful; capricious; humourous; indulgent of one's own imagination.

Dr. Johnson, *Dictionary*

Phantase _____

noun, Deceptive divinity, who enchants the senses of those who are awake or asleep. Evil deity, surrounded by an innumerable host of winged lies flying around him, spreading obscurity and applying a subtle liquor to the eyes of those whom he wishes to deceive. . . . Fantôme, *noun, We apply the name of* phantom *to all those images that make us imagine corporeal beings outside of us that do not exist. . . .* Phantôme, *noun, Frightening specter. The same source from whence emanated oracles gave rise to the phantom. One fabricated Gods who inspired terror and fear of the very evil one believed them capable of creating: playing a greater role in the religion of various peoples than conscientiousness and the love of justice, minds became preoccupied with ideas of these redoutable divinities . . .*

Diderot and D'Alembert, *Encyclopédie*

an intellectual descendant of Lessing's—commented that space, or the realm of flitting images, was the domain of seduction. He contrasted this extended "glitter" to the force-filled and unseen inner dimension of unfurling time.[102]

Good visions had nothing in common with such foul shades or filthy vapors. They symbolically shed a divine luminosity around the blessed without palpably touching them. Plutarch described this moist and dreamy substance of the soul, deposited on the moon during the course of its descent, and composed of "the gentlest part of the air."[103] Our interest, however, rests with those likenesses emanating from material objects and identified by a host of negative imagistic terms: species, idol, and apparition. The substance of dreams during the eighteenth century was usually identified with the deluding phantasm. Spence cited the Roman poet Statius's (45–96 AD) description in the *Thebaid* of the staining denizens of the Castle of Sleep. Somnus, Morpheus, Phobaetor, and Phantasos inspired a vast number of dreams in men, animals, and even in inanimate objects. Legions of ghostly shapes were "sticking against the columns, and walls, in the Palace of Somnus; not unlike the bats, to which Homer compares the spirits in [H]Ades" (figs. 17, 142).[104] Statius was alluding to the fact that there were innumerable old, new, and interwoven images tied to a particular feeling. Lucian (120–180? AD), in *A True Story*, also regaled his readers with the manifold emotional forms and figural combinations populating "the Isle of Dreams." Although faint and uncertain to the eyes, he discerned that these specters differed from one another both in essence and in looks. "Some were tall, handsome and well-proportioned, while others were small and ugly; and some were rich, I thought, while others were humble and beggarly." As in sleep, so in life. "There were winged and portentous dreams among them, and there were others dressed up as if for carnival, being clothed to represent kings and gods and different characters of the sort we actually recognize, many of them whom we had seen long ago at home."[105] Fuseli prominently discussed the assigning of ectoplasmic shape to affective material by Quintilian, Cicero, and Ovid. The former, in particular, applied the term *visions* to what the Greeks called *phantasies*. The British academician related these fumatory appearances to "unpremeditated conceptions" pursuing the seer when his brain was in a state of rest or lost in a waking dream (fig. 111). He urged the aspiring painter to make use of this "vice of the mind" to prompt invention as the ancients had done. "Their Scylla and the Portress of Hell, their daemons and our spectres, the shade of Patroclus and the ghost of Hamlet, their niads [sic], nymphs, and oreads, and our sylphs, gnomes, and fairies, their furies and our witches, differ less in essence, than in local, temporary, social modifications: their common origin was fancy operating on the materials of nature, assisted by legendary tradition, and the curiosity implanted in us of diving into the invisible."[106] Fuseli's praise of Shakespeare's "spontaneous ebullitions" was based on that Macrobian poet's ability to make "Banquo see the weird sisters bubble up from the earth, and in their own air vanish."[107] His admiration for the imaginative and the imaginary was part of the late eighteenth-century taste for out-of-the-way thoughts and for a shadowy, ghostlike manner. Similarly, in Boudard's *Iconologie*, the winged imagination (fig. 138) was the emblem precisely of that inventive faculty. It enabled sensible things to be re-presented chimerically to the eye of the mind. Ideal objects could be shaped during sleep from prior traces and wispy impressions.[108]

The many passionate investigations into the nature of this baffling activity by renowned and obscure polemicists alike represented a new physiognomics of the unseen.[109] Oneirocriticism was a knifeless anatomical method for solving some of the most intractable problems with which the Enlightenment wrestled. Chief among them was the body-mind conundrum. Seeing deeply into the mechanism of the imagination, seeing inside the hidden and automatic workings of the nervous system, were attempts to uncover the ultimate concealed terrain. Divination, or spectral research, was a form of neurological microscopy putting the unconscious under the lens. The extreme spiritualist view of dreams was propounded early on by the anonymous author of the *Enquiry into the Nature of the Human Soul* (1730). Paradoxically, such treatises, along with those by the celebrated Hartley and Boscovich, had inspired Priestley to promote the immateriality of matter.[110] But the author of the *Enquiry* used dreams in order to prove the opposite thesis, namely, the complete difference of the soul. The advocacy of an exaggerated dualism in the 1730s and 1740s significantly followed in the wake of the much publicized Clarke-Leibniz debates on the merits and demerits of materialism and immaterialism. According to the author of the *Enquiry*—probably an Anglican clergyman—the homogeneous and uncompounded soul, for theological reasons, had to act willingly. It was repugnant to think that it voluntarily presented scenes to deceive itself. Thus foreign, material impressions, in a sort of mental violation or rape, had to thrust themselves upon its immaterial innocence. To say otherwise would be tantamount to claiming that "matter could give rise to thought," "that such an instance of life, action, and design is effected by the *temerarious*, surd jumble of dead atoms."[111] Dreams, in his view, were prompted by separate incorporeal beings. Otherwise, it "may not be me that thinks," and the "Cartesian *cogito* would no longer be true." The *Enquiry* derided Lucretius and his modern skeptical followers, especially Locke, who argued that the accidents of the body were also those of the soul. If one was disturbed or delirious, so the empiricists claimed, then so was the other. The urgency of his defense of the unconscious soul during sleep thus hinged on his religious fear that to accept self-reproductive *simulacra, membrana, effigiae*, or "monstrous compounds" would destroy its independence. The spirit would behave like a nonimitating echo, multiplying stimuli it had not received. Resembling Lucretius's carved piece of wood, it would idolatrously bring to life "a mere heap of substances."[112]

This by no means unique argument supported the power of the mind to receive ideas without consciously knowing them. In this bizarre state, it "felt sensations, without external objects seeming to make any impression on it; imagined entities; transported itself to places . . . & exercised no dominion over those phantoms which appeared or disappeared, affecting it in an agreeable or disagreeable manner without influencing it in what it was."[113] Obviously, this ecclesiastic was operating within the Neoplatonic paradigm of exfoliating conceptions, mentally passed down through physical generations without touching them, without mingling with their mortal substance. Further, such a view represented an exaggerated extension of Boethius's definition of human cognition as abstraction, or the immaterialization of the material world, the reverse of God's creation or materialization of being in space.

A more moderate immaterialist position was put forward by the Abbé Richard in *La théorie des songes*. As a natural historian, his aim differed from the purely theological polemic but was not free of it. He wished additionally as an enlightener to expunge from the subject every trace associated with the marvelous, the superstitious, and the terrible. The topic still beguiled "the common people," who took such visions seriously instead of heeding solid reasoning. Richard also criticized Locke. He was appalled by the British philosopher's claim that we know whether we think sometimes but not all the time. At issue was the perpetuation of identity, the awareness of a persisting me-ness despite the daily buffeting undergone by the senses. The scientist was outraged, as many were, that Locke could, in un-Cartesian fashion, doubt whether he had thought during the previous night. He attacked his supposed materialism, encapsulated in the argument that the soul had no more power over the body than the pendulum over the clock. This seemed to say there was no built-in continuity in the psyche. Dreaming, moreover, merely became an additional demonstration of the fragility and instability of consciousness. Richard, too, connected empiricism with Epicureanism. To adopt the notion that we do not know if the mind thought continually was to fall into the error of those who regarded it as "an assemblage of the most subtle parts of matter and always discovered the same person in Socrates whether sleeping, waking, or dreaming."[114] In this dangerous system, there was no rectifying internal gyroscope keeping the personality on a steady course. Nothing informed it whether it was slipping from the real into the unreal, from a voluntary revery into an involuntary delusion.

Richard also made explicit the threat posed by a self-activating imagination to a seamless hierarchy of being. It was unthinkable that this "purely material force, completely dependent on sensory organs, could conceive and arrange a consecutive series of events or reasonings necessarily dependent on a spiritual agency." He concluded one must therefore "admit the action of the soul in all dreams." Outlandish and disconnected imagery was not a denial of its immateriality. Jumble merely indicated there were no constraints imposed on the imagination obliging it to follow, in the reliving, an original chain of ideas. Cryptic and fragmentary dreams were compared to archaeological ruins and to epigraphic runes. Memory gaps and lacunae resembled eroded inscriptions on dilapidated buildings. "One part is still visible and could be read, the other is effaced and indecipherable: A person needs to know the history of the era to which it refers & its date to reconstruct it in its entirety" (fig. 107).[115] He approvingly alluded to the famous Italian historian Muratori and his natural, not supernatural, explanation of the imagination's erasures and couplings. Neither a form of augury nor of prophecy, the sleeping fancy merely threw disparate things extravagantly together. Incoherent dreams functioned like arabesques. In the manner of these illogical decorations, they stitched together a putto holding a festoon, attached to an eagle, joined to a horse, and all wrenched from their original contexts (fig. 239).[116]

The materialists also attempted to solve the riddle of the crazy-quilt dream work. Espousing an extramissionist theory, they looked upon such creative activity as biological, driving the organism from inside out. The vivid and autonomous imagination was responsible not only for producing the dreamer's patched other world but for his sense of a mood-drenched and patterned

239. Pierre Camper, *Grotesques from Frieze of Golden House of Nero* (after Winckelmann's *Monumenti antichi inediti* [*1767*]), from *Discours sur le moyen de représenter les passions*, 1792, III, p. 9. Engraving (Photo: Courtesy National Library of Medicine, Bethesda, Md.)

reality as well. Le Camus, somewhat disingenuously, protested against those who accused him of materialism. He readily granted that the soul was neither a Spinozistic modification of divine substance, nor an Epicurean modification of the body, nor a mere Hobbesian clump of earth. Yet, in the end, this physician agreed it had to be "a simple modification of matter." Medicine, he claimed, united metaphysics with physics, the study of spirits with that of morphologies. Tongue-in-cheek, he described his tactile profession as dealing with "the abstract combinations" of an unextended, immaterial, invisible soul, capable of reasoning, feeling, and judging. This incorporeal entity was then somehow to be felicitously melded with an extended, material, visible body—incapable of all the other could do! His explanation of the onset of dreams was appropriately neurophysiological. Sleep was the "restorative death that gives life." During its energizing passage, the fibers received a renewed stimulus from the memory, permitting them to vibrate again and thus to relive an event already experienced. Le Camus presciently credited reminiscence with the power for working through troubling material and for contributing to a persistent or disjunctive sense of self. It was responsible for feeding images to the cortex and then weaving them into a "story." Remembering allowed us to re-view at night friends with whom we had walked and talked during the day. Although the constitutive imagination depended on what the sensory apparatus provided, new information could mingle with random old snatches. Such compounding accounted for the frequently strange, personal, and nonimitative appearance of dreams.[117]

In addition, Le Camus was an enlightened reformer. He believed in medicine's therapeutic ability not only to preserve health and cure disease but to alter miserable or inadequate self-images through autosuggestion. By the modification of sensory organs and their subsequent education, one could engineer a subtle and productive *homme d'esprit* from a depressed and nonproductive person. Significantly, he spoke of the role played in this retooling process by the provocation of "artificial ecstasies" (fig. 229). He approvingly cited the example of inspired "Yaquis," Scythian tightrope walkers, and Hindu saints, "who induced visions by twirling around & compressing their eyes in a terrible manner." These deliberate methods for "lighting the fires of one's imagination" were praiseworthy. Such voluntary "enthusiasms" did not derive from heaven but from the earthly conceptual force of the mind, able "to paint not just ideas but feeling itself."[118]

442

But it was Diderot who offered the most penetrating materialist analysis of conscious and unconscious revery. The *Eléments de physiologie* identified the jumpy look of a ghost story recounted exclusively in the present tense. During dreaming, narrative continuity was fractured and the dramatic thread of one's life passed before the inner eye in chopped-up snippets and jolting atomized bits. Acting and reacting fibers make it seem "as if different people are speaking at the same time on different topics," and in "the pure tones of an unknown language." Diderot perceived a fundamental affinity between dream, frenzy, and madness. To persist in any one of these altered states signified insanity. Even in their milder, discontinuous forms they could shock the nervous system. "The passage from waking to sleeping is always a little delirium."[119]

At its most tormented extreme, prolonged dreaming was not a sign of health but of illness. Dr. Johnson spoke of it both as a play representing "something which does not really happen," and as "a groundless suspicion."[120] The nightmare stood for the ultimate threat posed by the subliminal and unguided imagination (fig. 240). The victims of this "sleep of horror" were masochistically in thrall to wild phantasms. An intense feeling of impotence flooded the tortured sleeper. Immobilized, the pathological dreamer was riveted to a bed with feet unable to stir or fingers to grip. This depressive disorder was bodied forth in what the Romans called the "incubus," or the overwhelming oppressor. Eighteenth-century authors routinely noted that the unfortunate sufferer tended to personify his awful experiences in "frightful, ghastly apparitions." For the radical immaterialist, these "ugly phantoms" arose not from a malfunctioning physiological mechanism but from external spirits. Conversely, according to the more modulated opinion of Richard, they were the corporeal signs of a serious malady. Healthy sleep meant perfect abstraction, or the suspension of mental operations. But since the body and soul remained joined, even in a condition of unconsciousness, it sometimes happened that the mind imagined "a new order of things." Distracted "composite dreaming" found the sleeper slipping "into an abyss of imaginary woes." Importantly Richard, like the *Encyclopédie*, drew a distinction in a way English writers could not between *rêves* and *songes*. The former were connected to a feverish delirium in which one beheld "only specters, monsters, precipices, and frightening or disquieting subjects." The overwrought sensory organs projected magnified impressions onto the screen of the imagination or the memory, causing vehement "idealities" to arise.[121] The *songe*, on the other hand, was

240.   Colin, *The Nightmare,* from *Album comique de pathologie pittoresque,* 1823. Lithograph by Langlumé. (Photo: Courtesy National Library of Medicine, Bethesda, Md.)

that seemingly bizarre but not malignant condition, commemorated in Goya's *sueño*, in which the mind experienced notions without being aware of them (fig. 17). The precious extract of the nerves, flowing through the body, guaranteed "the essential function of the soul: to have a series of conceptions uninterruptedly representing the universe to it." On occasion, however, this subtle liquor ran amok in the "laboratory of the brain." Furrows, leading to external entities that had most affected the spirit while awake, were thus violently reopened. When these ordinary events became abnormally reprogrammed, they appeared "unstitched and without order, without truth vis-à-vis reality."[122]

Eighteenth-century sleep researchers made headway in answering the ancient puzzle of what caused the nightmare or grotesque *rêve*. Robert Burton transmitted the folkloric tradition of "witch-ridden" sleepers who, when they lay on their backs, supposed an old woman sat so hard on them that they were almost stifled.[123] But it was John Bond's systematic scientific study, published in 1753, that gave a physiological account of the stagnation of the blood occurring when one was supine. The animistic and fairy-tale terminology of "hag-riding, wizard-pressing, mare-riding, witch-dancing" incarnated those frightful dreams. As a sufferer, he knew well those sensations of difficult breathing and of an unendurable weight on the breast. The alternation of dreadful torpor with uneasy palpitations arose, he thought, from a real affliction producing a "fit." While the body lay prone, the blood flowed abundantly to the head. Relying both on Newton's theory of gravity and on hydraulics, the physician postulated that there was less resistance to this pounding influx streaming from the carotid and vertebral arteries than when one was standing erect. Moreover, in a horizontal position, liquids tended to puddle in the cerebral vessels, causing vertigo.[124]

Tissot, in the *De la santé des gens de lettres* (1767), used the image of a torrent of sensations pressing on the brain and engendering delirium. The stale air of the bedroom, coupled with the unhealthy habit of placing pillows under the legs, prompted feminine nerves in particular to become unstrung.[125] Colin's *Le Cauchemar* (fig. 240), one of the several aberrations composing a picturesque pathology, not only spoofed Fuseli's convulsive painting (Detroit, Detroit Institute of Art, 1781), but summarized the complex medical and popular tradition surrounding nocturnal derangement. The letterpress reported the existence of two types of nightmare, both diseases. In the first, or fixed, condition the nervous system was constitutionally and chronically affected. In the second, or accidental, state some external excess of food or drink was the culprit. Colin's lithograph captured the latter, temporary condition. It also alluded to the common belief that weak and impressionable women were susceptible to having their nerves strongly "engraved" during sleep. Desires, fears, hopes, persons, and even entire scenes "cut trenchantly" into their soft and pliable filaments. He conjured up a comic teratological hell, populated with reified painful feelings. Deposited on the dressing table was a well-thumbed copy of Lord Byron's (1788–1824) *Vampire*. Its ghoulish subject matter materialized before the captive dreamer's inner vision in the guise of a bat-winged and bull-horned devil. Charles Nodier's (1780–1844) fantastic novels were flung on the floor along with a "bonnet à folle," or madcap night hat. A snoozing King Charles's spaniel pressed on the sufferer's bare chest to the amazement of her perplexed husband. This innocent, coiffed in the cuckold's monstrous headgear, had foolishly ventured into the fiend-ridden chamber.[126] Colin humorously, yet accurately, pictured the magical changes of shape and the calamitous sensations of obstruction and inflamation associated with internal commotion.

The nightmare was the unguided Romantic voyage within the mind, juxtaposing fragmentary opposites in vignette fashion (figs. 10, 201). It externalized exaggerated mental wandering from phantasm to phantasm. Tony Johannot's (1803–1852) and Grandville's imaginary adventures "to where one pleased" transposed the emotion-laden dream of life into a new, subterranean region organized by the nervous system. The cartography of this intermediate beyond, or scientific "purgatory," was scotch-plaided with unreal and real mutating images.[127] Metaphor constituted the Romantic hyperbolic dream style. Hieroglyphics bestrewed the light or somber subliminal geography. In the *Metamorphosis of a Dream* (fig. 241), Grandville's protagonist Hahblle was inundated by the elixir of love. When this potent juice finally touched the heart and brain, or the "seat of the affections and of ideas or instinct," his hallucinations resembled those of the opium-smoker and hashish-eater. A succession of disconnected yet fluent phantoms unrolled. Although Hahblle's unfaithful beloved, Gertrude, was lost to physical sight because of the intervening "mists of ecstasy," he seized her through "the eyes of the mind" as she underwent multiple transformations. Grandville brilliantly captured the underlying sense of frustration accompanying an elusive and vaporous object of desire. The airy semblance of the fickle Gertrude turned into a train of simulacra: a bird, a flying long-bow dragging a quiver behind it, a cup-and-ball, a baluster, and a ghost of her former self. But, alas, he held in his arms only a vase in which soaked a wilted blossom. When he threw himself on

446

SENSING

241. Grandville, *Metamorphosis of a Dream,* from *Un autre monde,* 1844, p. 243. Wood engraving. (Photo: Courtesy the Library of Congress.)

this evanescent apparition, "the form disappeared, he was lost in a cloud of flowers, in interlaced garlands, terminating in the rampant serpent, the undying and menacing emblem of woman."[128] Metastasis by no means ended the metamorphosis of the eternal feminine. Beyond this specific incident, however, *Un autre monde* was stocked with the mobile and magical imagery of pursuit (fig. 160). Grandville's art incarnated the vanishing *ars combinatoria* of the unconscious. In a deserted and "limitless space," he suddenly perceived

that which was not exactly a horse, nor absolutely a rider. Insofar as I could judge, considering the rapidity of his gait, the animal I witnessed egging on his mount in the chase after a green bear (which I saw become a bear-boa) possessed a great deal that was human, although his feet were those of a quadruped and its head was not entirely anthropomorphic. I heard the barking of a dog, but I beheld only the round back of a tortoise who seemed ardently to follow the track of this game.[129]

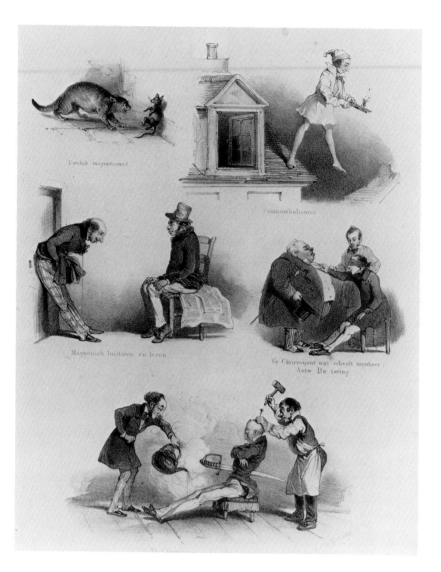

Grandville's dream totems pictorialized a formidable intuitive life unattached to the external world. In this vast extent down under, the sun of the imagination shone on the symbolizing processes of thought and feeling. But beyond even dreams or nightmares, somnambulism appeared to offer proof of a third, or inward, sense (fig. 242). Sleepwalking seemed to demonstrate the correctness of an extramissionist theory arguing that inner rays existed. A seductive force, residing in sight alone, had intrigued Leonardo, who studied the ability of certain animals to brighten the night. The nocturnal basilisk, wolf, ostrich, spider, snake, but above all the cat (fig. 17) saw in the dark. Their acknowledged powers were taken to indicate the emission of an ocular beam wafted on the wind like perfume.[130] The physical and phosphorescent eye, piercing a recipient, was metamorphosed in the late eighteenth century into an interior radiance shining with an intrinsic light.

The discovery of the nerves newly empowered the senses. But energized vision, according to a modern extramissionist physiology, was the most forceful organ of all. Insight extended its pneumatic substance over great areas.[131] Action at a distance—carrying the essential properties of a person—was central to that Mesmeric fascination that will occupy us in the final section of this chapter. For the moment, I want to focus on the belief that the mental eye has its own brightness that can issue forth in the absence of external illumination. Richard asserted that somnambulism incontrovertibly showed the strength of the imagination's contents. He contrasted the hesitancy and confusion of the blind man, bereft of mere physical light and walking in a threatening obscurity, with the deliberate, quick, and sure footing of the inwardly guided sleepwalker. This night traveler descended stairs without falling, traversed streets with impunity, and turned corners safely. Such clairvoyance was credited to the vividness of the imagination, whose objects were "very present" to the mind. Richard proclaimed the superiority of this inner eye over mere optics. "In these different operations, it [the imagination] provides all the little details that one could have through its means, & it guides the somnambulist in the various places where he dreams he must go."[132] Or, as Muratori pithily put it, outside "the cabinet [of the mind] there was no light." *Nottamboli* beheld the objects of their visions because they glittered as if they were in daylight. Unlike Richard, however, Muratori claimed that the memory of the solar beam impressed itself on the nerves and was transmitted to the brain to be reawakened when needed during dreaming. Nevertheless, both men agreed that the imaginal illumination could not help its dexterous and fearless adepts while awake, even if the objects of their deliria stood in front of them. As was the case for the total abstraction of ecstasy, mania, and dementia, the wide- or shut-eyed witnessing of an ideal cortege did not depend on the evidence of the senses. Contemplation was distinct from the observation of the real world and was the property of the creative fantasy.[133]

According to Franz Anton Mesmer (1734–1815), when the somnambulist said he beheld scenes, it was not his physical eyes that viewed them. Rather, he brought forms, figures, motions, colors, and places to sight through "a sort of translation in order to express his ideas in the language formulated for the inner sense." This involuntary apprehension again resided in the nervous system. A mysterious watching directed our paces through "an internal atmosphere," the way the glow-worm found its way through a tenebrous marsh.[134] For Mesmer, sleep was not a negative condition, but far surpassed mundane wakefulness. It was the clairvoyant and nervy state in which our intellectual faculties were not dormant but most keenly alert.[135] The somnambulist was thus the paradigm of the automaton, of Heinrich von Kleist's (1780–1811) technological marionette, able to perform perfectly, mechanically, and without reflection. Simultaneously, he was the Romantic subjective visionary, marching to no light but his own.

Communicable Feelings

Enthusiasm _____

noun, A vain belief of private revelation; a vain confidence of Divine favour or communication; heat or imagination; violence of passion; confidence of opinion; elevation of fancy; exaltation of ideas.

Dr. Johnson, *Dictionary*

Enthousiasme _____

noun, There is no perfectly satisfactory definition. . . . A sort of fury which spreads over the mind and takes hold of it, which inflames the imagination, raises it, and renders it fertile . . . but fury is only a violent attack of madness, and madness is an absence or a straying of reason; thus, when one defines enthusiasm, ecstasy, transport, it is as if one said it was a redoubled madness, and consequently forever incompatible with reason. It is reason alone that gives it birth; it is a fire it lights during the moments of its greatest superiority . . .

D'Alembert and Diderot, *Encyclopédie*

When everything could be optically simulated, it was of paramount importance to discover stealthier methods of detection immune from duping razzle-dazzle. Once ocular testimony became permanently allied with falsification, it fell to other, supposedly finer senses to sniff out automatic from controlled responses. In addition, attention was increasingly displaced from replicable spatial objects to an intervening, intellectualized, and force-filled medium. The ungraspable "middle" atmosphere through which psychic currents flowed constituted a new and subtle temporal milieu for direct and unadulterated private and mass communication (fig. 243). This chapter has been examining the concerted effort toward finding nonvisual ways for gauging what lies under paint or appearance. If dissection and abstraction revealed the dangers of an overly intellectual method, then distracting sensationalism showed the perils accompanying a heightened emotionalism. Both extremes signified a loss of balance. The attempt to discern the real and abiding substance under the ephemeral phantom led to the emergence of the charismatic and evangelizing sophist. Paradoxically, the main task of the telepathic and telecasting Mesmerist was to divine elusive feelings. The spiritual demagogue brought to the surface, or made manifest, a deep, supposedly authentic, and quasi-divine enthusiasm ordinarily invisible to the naked eye.

The Viennese physician Mesmer, active at the courts of Joseph II and Louis XVI, profited from the Enlightenment's sense of wonder for a tide of unseen phenomena.[136] A specialist in the psychosomatic physiology of the nerves, he singlehandedly turned the hypnotic trance, autosuggestion, touching rays, and the extramissionist stare into a flourishing medical industry. Magnetic effluvia and sympathetic or antipathetic emanations were the components of modern consciousness, with its intimations of liquidity. Violently controversial in his own day, this scientific seer attracted passionate partisans like the Puységur brothers, and equally indomitable enemies, including most members of Europe's medical schools. Mesmerism arrestingly exposes the late

243. Ebenezer Sibly, *Mesmerism: The Operator Inducing a Hypnotic Trance*, 1794, p. 260. Engraving after Dodd. (Photo: Courtesy National Library of Medicine, Bethesda, Md.)

244.   Jean-Jacques Paulet, *Satire on
Animal Magnetism,* from *L'Anti-
magnetisme,* 1784, frontispiece. Etching.
(Photo: Courtesy National Library of
Medicine, Bethesda, Md.)

eighteenth-century determination to break down barriers between the unconscious and the conscious faculties, between the senses and the intellect, or the body and the soul. Yet as critics complained, public convulsions and hysterical prestidigitations were merely a hyperbolic extension of the greater *fin-de-siècle* craze for charlantism (fig. 244). Mesmer was accused by the physician Paulet of preying on the depraved Parisian taste for concealed powers in nature, demonic spirits, and mystical or allegorical meanings (fig. 218). Amid secret schools of initiates, seditious clubs, Rosicrucian, Masonic, or "Harmonian" societies, and a torrent of cabalistic literature, animal magnetism simply represented the biggest aristocratic toy of all. Paulet connected the histrionic faith healer, equipped with a magnet, to a string of Neoplatonic mountebank-metaphysicians, to Gilbert, Paracelsus, Fludd, Kircher (figs. 220, 221), and von Helmont. Massaging, in order to remove painful symptoms, also did not strike this skeptic as being unique. There was the famous case of the seventeenth-century Irish "stroker," Valentine Greatraks, who applied light or heavy friction to various parts of the anatomy in order to draw off everything from scrofula to migraine.[137] A tribe of *toucheurs* continued to ply their trade in the eighteenth-century urban street. These quacks also claimed to possess uncanny gifts and the occult means for tapping into cosmic emissions.[138]

Armand-Marie-Jacques de Chastenet, the Marquis de Puységur (1751–1825), the premier eighteenth-century student of somnambulism, offered a rather different perspective on animal magnetism. This enlightened *amateur* of science reminded physicians of the continuing eruption of mental illness despite their laudable efforts. Specifically, he cited the "phantasmagoriques" of Alessandro Giuseppi Balsamo, or the infamous "Count" Cagliostro (1745–1795). That "thousands of participants" could be conned seemed indicative of the pervasiveness of mass mania. Then there were Emanuel Swedenborg's (1688–1772) deranged Prussians, who "believed in his visions, in his voyages into the second, third, and fourth heaven, in his habitual commerce with angels." He asked skeptical doctors to remember the Illuminati of Lyons and Avignon, the clandestine lodges of Germany, stocked with enthusiasts, the Anabaptists, Camisards, and holy rollers disporting themselves on the tomb of Saint Médard (fig. 229). With such evidence for the group "alienation of an interior sense," could they possibly doubt that insanity was as real and "contagious" as any bodily sickness?[139]

The frontispiece to Paulet's *L'Antimagnetisme* (1784) conveyed the excitement, hoopla, and mystification accompanying such outdoor demonstrations. They drew upon the crowd's infatuation with energy, machinery, technology, an inspirational personality, and the magic of long distance communication. The satire presented a comic synopsis of the crisis, trance, and seance induced by the master and his huckstering sorcerer-apprentices, or "turners of cranks."[140] Dominating this superstitious mayhem was the ubiquitous operator, or medium between the invisible and visible realms, worshipfully surrounded by gapers. According to Mesmer, he was the living conductor of the subtle material current in which all bodies floated. But for Paulet, this sophist's pneumatic and idolatrous talents were as unstable and explosive as a hydrogen-filled *Charlière*, and as inflated as the balloon on which he precariously balanced. The eroticism of a finer, masculine touch was embodied in telepathic rays searching out intimate emotions lodged within the tender female bosom. Nothing could be more explicit than the attractive *déshabillé* and vulnerable swoon of the young patient. The seductiveness of the conjurer was tied up with a nonphysical yet sensual contact made under the intense scrutiny of male *voyeurs*.

Although Mesmer insisted that hypnotic control was mutual and reciprocal, the numinous and benedictory gesture of the alert and erect manipulator clearly manifested who was in charge (fig. 243). The procedure went as follows. Because of the sympathy existing between the magnet and the insensible perspiration of the body, an ether could be passed and repassed through the pores of the cutis. The circulation of the global effluvium depended on "two beings acting on one another." This magnetic nuptial required that the participants be stationed in polar positions and that their "atmospheres" blended "to form one whole acting in a harmonic manner." Mesmer's matrimonial language was linear. The extension of sight or, rather, of "an interior sense," during this condition of half-wakefulness was propagated through "straight" "curved," and "diagonal" rays. By their means the couple became wedded to the universe.[141] The smoky and incense-laden scene also included the notorious vat, or "magnetic reservoir," with its iron wands and compass marking the poles of attraction and repulsion. There was even an allusion to Priestley's fashionable phlogiston and to Jan Ingenhousz's (1730–1799) chemistry of airs. In the "magneto-vegetable" variant of the treatment, the sick were gathered around a tree (located in the left background of the print) to inhale the vivifying streams pouring from the transpiration of leaves exposed to sunlight.[142]

The body was also an infinite source of spectacle at the domestic laboratory, or dim crisis clinic, run by Mesmer at the Hôtel Bullion in the 1780s. In this elegant and claustrophobic setting, dozens of high-strung and fainting aristocrats anxiously waited to be touched, stroked, or merely have the potent baton pointed in their direction (fig. 245). Nervous disorders were thus theatricalized into an overacted *Tale of the Tub*, performed within a Bedlamic interior. Emotional contagion was easier to arouse in a dark and oppressive environment conducive to the propagation of an infectious vision. Mesmer suggested that the extension of optics by microscopes, telescopes, and glasses had already augmented the power exerted by the "interior" of things on the sensitive beholder. He specifically compared his exposure and plumbing of the diseased nervous system to a deepening perspective, affecting not only sight but the other senses as well. The living "chain" of ailing bodies seated in close quarters, the iron bars that they clasped or attached to sore limbs, and the magnetized water precipitated a physical crisis. But it was the contagious and extramissionist gaze of the beguiler, as much as the circulation of animal electricity, that touched the participants and moved them to seizure and frenzy. Puységur described that catching moment when "the *empire* that

245. Anonymous, *Crisis Rooms at Mesmer's Hôtel Bullion* (?), 1780s. Engraving. (Photo: Courtesy National Library of Medicine, Bethesda, Md.)

one acquires over susceptible individuals [causes] them to enter into the magnetized state." He insisted that the hypnotized person could not be forced to do anything that went against the grain. Yet it was precisely the "powerful volition" of the Mephistophelian operator that became palpable in the closed room. To magnetize signified constraining someone to act "because you absolutely wish it."[143] Consequently, Mesmerism was an ambitious project to harness cosmic energy. Further, its intent was to transmit a corresponding human force, the inner strength of a personal will, through the eyes. Both entertainment and emotional release, this early form of group psychotherapy was also an attempt to find new bonds and linkages in a fragmented and disintegrating society. The imposition of the hypersensibility or *genius* of a superior being onto a passively receptive vessel involved the sharing of a universal fluid. Thus it was a means for discovering otherwise invisible commonalities of mind among different people. Alienated patients, as well as citizens of the world, could experience jointly that rare epidemic instant of unity when they all felt alike.

The mass appeal of touching vision, its ability to exteriorize hidden desires and to compel enthusiasm, was both the culmination of the old and the beginning of a new culture of affect. On one hand, seductive communication represented the zenith of the ancient tradition of "fascination." Bacon, in the *Sylva Sylvarum*, spoke picturesquely of that "infection" moving from spirit to spirit, and sending forth love, fear, or shame from the eyes. This magical and talismanic medicine was grounded in a nature spun from immaterial correspondences invisibly shaping the material world.[144] Significantly, the emitted force was not shallowly optical but derived from a subcutaneously watching intermediary substance. More's *Enthusiasmus Triumphatus* devoted a lengthy section to that incarnated power "in the witch's eye and imagination, by which for the most part she acts upon tender bodies." The Cambridge Platonist made plain that darting pestilential or beneficial spirits emanated from deep within, or from the "Eye of the Soul." The "fatal invasion" or enthralling "contagion" took the form of tenuous or "subtle streams and aporrhea's of minute particles, which pass from one body to another."[145] In the *Immortality of the Soul*, these extramissionist "reeks and vapours" of the fancy were related to the function of matter at large. The "Atmosphere (as I may so call it) of generation" diffused ethereal rays through the circles of the firmament in order to "allure" the soul in its descent (fig. 246). Thus an "Inmost Spirit," situated in the fourth ventricle of the brain and also existing as the *anima mundi*, emitted a plastic virtue. This internal power illuminated

246. Ebenezer Sibly, *System of the
Interior, or Empyrean Heaven, Shewing the
Fall of Lucifer*, from *A Key to Physic and
the Occult Sciences*, 1804, pl. 2. Engraving
by Prattent after Dodd. (Photo: Courtesy
National Library of Medicine, Bethesda, Md.)

both the "duskish aire" of the atmospheric psyche and the cloudy medium bathing the earth.[146] The pervasiveness of this view had been challenged by Blondel. Recall that he scoffed at the myth perpetrated by Turner that men could influence distant persons, or women could imprint their embryos, solely through the impact of the imagination. The British physician remarked that such injudicious comparisons were based on likening that faculty to a magnet with an extensive force field. The mental lodestone was believed analogously to attract, repel, detour, and turn upside down the animate and inanimate phenomena falling within its circumference.[147]

This Neoplatonic imagery of positive and negative impulses was retained not only in animal magnetism but, more generally, in Enlightenment physiology. Blazing spheres, particulate mists, and subtle fluids, however, were removed from the immaterial spatial system in which they had been initially inscribed and were relocated within an intensely physical milieu. For the materialists, the "instinct of imitation" or "irresistible desire" to model oneself on the actions of others was rooted in the sensory network of expanding sensibility and contracting irritability. Alibert commented that the substantial bond linking sentient beings and impelling them to fashion themselves after one another even governed the submerged nervous system. "Sympathies" were common among various organs, causing them automatically to copy pains, sufferings, and lesser responses such as yawning. Le Camus described how external pressures—the scratching of a head, the biting of nails, the drinking of alcohol, or smoking—could activate the flow of thought when ideas refused to come. The stimulation of psychic functions or behavioral changes was accomplished wholly through material means. A flux and reflux of animal spirits jostled the brain and shocked it into similar motion. This translation of abstract centripetal and centrifugal forces into tangible urges was revisionism with a vengence. It actualized the mysterious Newtonian "attraction" exerted on two bodies separated by an empty space. The general principle of gravity posited the existence both of a Pythagorean law of harmony and a hidden impalpable spirit pervading objects. By contrast, the ebb and flow of organic processes was a palpable tide. Somatic antitheses could not just be seamlessly elided, like mathematical points. At best, they had to be spasmodically joined through the external intervention of electricity and magnetism.[148]

What I wish to term the Enlightenment's "Epicureanization" of Newtonianism was brought about largely by the chemist Georges-Louis Le Sage (1724–

458

1803). It was this "Newtonian Lucretius" who filled the British physicist's empty pores of matter with "a subtle fluid agitated in every direction." Remember how Mesmer's river or torrent of corpuscles moved in rectilinear paths and impregnated the interstices of solids. The Viennese physician's substantialized spiritualism was modeled, I believe, on Le Sage's physicalization and exteriorization of unseen energies.[149] Consequently, animal magnetism was iconoclastic in more ways than one. It shifted attention from spirit to matter, from optics to the imagination, or to insightful and infectious feeling. It was at once practical and mystical, technological and fabulous, entrepreneurially engaged and aristocratically aloof. For the first time, Newton's invisible forces were harnessed to the business of telecommunication. Thus Mesmerism must be seen as a fundamental attempt to cope with the new informational abundance broadcast by the body. A seemingly endless and confusing stream of nervous emissions, requiring interpretation, continued to well up from a formerly concealed sensory and instinctual domain. Moreover, its pseudoscientific apparatus belonged to the eighteenth century's childlike delight in charming games and appealing goods created and manufactured in order to make the invisible visible (fig. 244).[150]

Talk of universal "currents," human "conductors," and friction or rubbing therapy also allied Mesmer to a new class of medical "electricians" flourishing in the 1770s and 1780s. Louis Jallabert (1712–1768), Nollet, Priestley, and Galvani had demonstrated that a flow of sparks induced convulsions. Dagoty maintained that animate bodies were "electrified" by the lungs.[151] Since the presence or absence of these vivifying particles in the arterial blood determined life or death, electricity's key curative role was not surprising. The Abbé Sans's *Guérison de la paralysie* (1772) recorded that radiant fluid's stunning impact, its magical ability to reanimate numbed and senseless limbs (fig. 247). The optimistic expectations held of the omnipotent "electrifying physician" were correspondingly boundless. In short, this thaumaturge was believed capable of affecting "a new resurrection of man." The frontispiece to Sans's important early study of paralysis and the collapse of the nervous system predictably apotheosized the Leyden jar. The claims made for it by this professor of experimental physics at the University of Perpignon were nothing short of miraculous. Disseminating a healing light, this wondrous phial reawakened a destroyed memory, reestablished a wandering reason, endowed a failing eyesight with renewed vigor, and imparted speech to a mute tongue.[152]

247.   Abbé Sans, *Electrical Cure of
Paralysis,* from *Guérison de la paralysie,*
1772, frontispiece. Engraving by Le Gouac
after J. B. Chevalier. (Photo: Courtesy
National Library of Medicine, Bethesda, Md.)

The electrician Aldini—reminiscent of the phantasmagorist Robertson who survived the Terror—went one step further. He nurtured the illusion of bringing the dead back to life. Moreover, like Madame Tussaud's blood-stained death masks of French aristocrats, Aldini's attempted revivifactions belonged to the late Enlightenment's physiognomic desire for accurate information and the recording of "true" features. The fabricating of facsimiles, as well as the probing for indisputable evidence of sensibility, mounted an attack on the age of visual sham. Instead, however, of projecting glass slides or producing wax casts simulating such famous victims of the guillotine as Lavoisier or Marat, Aldini attempted actual resuscitation. Going beyond the manufacture of simulacra, his galvanizations sought really to return the departed. Aldini's ghoulish experiments involved drowning innumerable dogs and cats and then exciting or electrifying them. Unfortunately, the process worked only if the current was immediately applied. If the animals remained submerged until all vital signs had disappeared, no jolt could stimulate them back into existence.[153]

The obvious danger inherent in such brutal partial or total reanimations elicited the demand for a "gentler" procedure. It was the Marquis de Puységur who specifically suggested that electricity provided the sole, "almost palpable" analogue for the magnetic stream continually circulating in the atmosphere. "All bodies are thus *saturated*, in their own manner, with the fluid we term electrical." Human physiology, too, was drenched in this energized liquid. Man, therefore, should be considered a living Voltaic pile, "an *electrical* animal machine, the most perfect that exists, because his thought, which governs all his actions, can conduct him to infinity."[154] For those, then, like the Abbé Sans or Leopoldo Cavallo Volta (1751–1823), who disapproved of administering violent shocks, magnetism offered a nonviolent alternative. A corporeal semiotics of gasps, blinks, tremors, and twitches could be provoked at a distance without the patient being plugged into an instrument (fig. 227). Indeed, just being in the presence of the quasi-divine substance might be sufficient. The English physician Ebenezer Sibly (1751–1800), in his *Key to Physic* (1794), described a visionary form of treatment surely inspired by Mesmerism. The sick were not subjected to an actual dose, but merely exposed "to *the electrical aura*," that is, to a soft and temperate air discharged from a wooden or iron pointer. This benevolent atmosphere assumed "the figure of stars and other beautiful ramifications" visualizing an internal and healing principle of order (fig. 232).[155]

Again, it was Puységur who reflected most deeply on the revolutionary significance of the new magnetic medicine. His meditations took the form of an open letter addressed to the hostile Paris Faculty of Medicine. "Inner man no doubt had already been intimated . . . but it was surely not until we ventured onto the route opened by M. Mesmer that we finally acquired physical certitude of this fact."[156] Significantly, he linked the discovery that interior sensations were a property of organized matter to the demise of an outmoded mathematical method. Mesmerism revealed the insufficiency of the Cartesian and Newtonian axiomatic model in the biological sphere. Externally directed quantification, he declared, would never lead to a knowledge of the source or principle of motion operating *within* the somatic and the material universe. He launched a powerful critique against Descartes and the modern proponents of a geometrical system. "The universe was not an abstraction: all the globes strewn in space were real and clearly visible objects: in order to demonstrate their function it was thus necessary to establish their study on a foundation that was equally real and truly palpable." Points, lines, and circles were "the image of a perfection one could never attain." Puységur empathized with the bitter irony undergirding Descartes's quest.

The infinite presented itself ceaselessly to him, it obsessed, so to speak, all his faculties, and became the goal of his work. But what satisfaction could he experience when, in advancing in his researches, he arrived, by means of the ellipse and the parabola, at the final result of the profundity of geometry, at hyperbole, which presents infinity to us in the guise of two lines that approach eternally and prolong themselves indefinitely without ever being able to join! What a revelation for a person who, like Descartes, searched so sincerely for truth! [Yet] he only needed to feel and to apprehend infinity![157]

Casting his glance back over the past century, the French aristocrat held the Cartesian and Newtonian "sectarians" ultimately responsible for the political discord and intellectual rupture of the Revolution. The "scandalous divisiveness" these philosophers sowed severed body from soul, matter from spirit, visible from invisible. Their antinomian tactics eventually caused "the destruction of all social bonds." Puységur shed new light on the reformationist and utopian significance not only of magnetism but of electricity, elasticity, and a host of mediating attracting and repelling currents. These subtle scientific fluids were no longer conceived as occult powers emanating from the remote One. As liquid properties inherent in material reality they facilitated communication among warring opposites. In the aftermath of cataclysm and upheaval, this naturalized milieu was clearly understood to constitute a new social lubricant. A force-filled atmosphere insinuated itself between antagonistic and antithetical entities, easing their frictions. Optimistically, Puységur argued that individuals, because of their ability to sense, could similarly transmit mollifying and mediating feelings. The persuasive and permeating message of a common humanity could be suffused by means of personal "actions and words," and thus influence the corresponding vital principle in others.[158] The luminous imagination, that venerable middle term of the mind, became the automating and informing Romantic medium. It mesmerized the interior world, not with massaging fingers nor with the outer gaze, but with metamorphic electrical symbols. Watery inwardness or the charged and mobile consciousness, it was hoped, would draw distant and diverse neurological networks together.

CHICAGO / RADIATION ON

CONCLUSION:

The Aesthetics of Almost

Metaphors embody and configure both the abiding and the changing preoccupations of an age. Having examined its basic human struggle for power and certainty in the midst of momentous change, we are now in a position to understand the eighteenth century in the full richness of its concerns. Looked at from the perspective of the information revolution of the 1980s and the visionary computer developments of the 1990s, this fertile and complex pictorial era will now, at last, come into its own. The Enlightenment paved the way for the advent of synthetic realism, disembodied information, animated automata, created environments, and clairvoyant visualization devices. Its chief thinkers—among them artists, natural historians, and physicians—pondered long and hard about the quality of magnified or diminished artificial life. They reflected on the rise of virtual imagery, simulated events, and an entire apparitional aesthetics of almost. They wrestled with the problem of connecting phantasmic entertainment with mass education as the culture shifted from text to image. They admirably, if not always successfully, attempted to integrate the latest scientific technology into all aspects of learning. The enabling and widely disseminated advances of color printing, the first manned balloon flights, the explorations of the nervous system, and the voyages into internal and external space, vastly increased the flow and visualization of knowledge. With refined lenses, they penetrated the inner sanctum of the material and immaterial realm in order to regain contact with the primal powers of body and mind. Only at the Romantic end of this epoch was there a full-scale retreat from the street into invented worlds, into an intensely private and contrived inwardness immune from social change.

I do not think it overstated to propose that every major aesthetic, critical, biological, or broadly humanistic issue now facing us would be illuminated by being refracted through the prism of the early modern period. It is easy to forget, if we ever knew it, that the original, or eighteenth-century, communications revolution was the source of our own. My central thesis has been that it was from the Enlightenment's multifaceted projects that many of our contemporary wonders and woes, controversies and dilemmas, arose. The constructs of dissecting and abstracting introduced us to a tenacious dualistic philosophy whose fundamentalist premises needed analysis. What continues inadequately to be termed Neoclassicism, was, in fact, the onset of the *rigor mortis* of an anemic "methodism." A "hard," prestigious method, deemed intellectually superior to the "soft," loose, irregular, or geometrically shapeless material it was supposed to regularize, was imposed from on high and from the outside. Its moral task—whether in anatomy, physiognomics, phrenology, literary criticism, or rationalist art theory—was to even out the odd.[1] When uncontrollable leakage occurred around the edges of organization, i.e., when certain kinds of "Rococo" data evaded such standardization, epitomization, and categorization, these formless entities were judged unimportant, lax, or merely phenomenal.

Analogously, the current breakdown in doctor-patient relationships points to the persistence of an identical adversarial mode. Polarization occurs around the two intractable positions of the administrating overseer and the shackled overseen. Furthermore, the growth of impersonal prepaid medical plans and of the "business" of healing encourages people to look upon physicians as merely interchangeable and greedy sophistic operators manipulating their clients.[2] Conversely, the unrealistic expectation of genetic flawlessness and the exaggerated demand for perfect and unerring diagnosis—fed by body imaging breakthroughs—exceed the bounds of what medicine can actually do. Hostile and litigious consumers represent a denial of mortality rampant in our society. The blind faith in the limitless ability of a God-like magician to cure the ailments associated with the inevitability of aging, sickness, pain, and loss of memory, or merely of looks, constitutes a belief in an immortal ideal. Erasure of the signs of humanity is predicated on the same negative method and inhuman example of morphological perfection Winckelmann thought he discerned in the immaculate sculpture of Greek heroes and divinities.

466

The antinomian construction of reality and its accompanying regulatory procedures lop off too much irregular experience. Yet this is not to say that those of us toiling with the messy and equivocal materials of existence can prove nothing. The pernicious legacy of dualism is also a radical and irresponsible relativism. Either everything is explainable and interpretable by a single, absolutist hermeneutics, or nothing is. To accept that only what is numerically and textually managed and manageable is worthwhile is also to give in to a paralyzing skepticism and to *laissez-faire*. We saw how the major epistemological trends of the eighteenth century removed unruly sensory experiences—especially those originating in sight—from the sphere of intellectual and public importance. In addition, these individual modes of judging the flux of ordinary life were relocated to a false, inferior, and subjective domain. Monitoring human performance on the basis of a simple, reductive criterion is a perverse denial of fallibility and a masculine delusion of divine potency. Ironically, conceptual schemes are neat and tidy at the expense of the mostly complex, eccentric, affective, or "feminine" aspects of life. From the domineering vantage of isolating and narrowing systems, chromatics, pathos, and difference either become irrelevant, or, worse, are barbarically cut out. In the unified world we now hope is emerging, this oppression and rupture will not endure. Noninvasive and freely traveling electronic imagery is the appropriate and pacific medium for the decentralized and nonhierarchical universe of the twenty-first century. For, as Puységur so admirably put it, violence was intrinsic to the old totalitarian animosities and warring divisions. These aggressive and splitting philosophies were based on conquest and victimization, on a dualistic system of master and slave, on the oppression of the weak by the strong. For the first time, the opportunity exists not only to free the image from patriarchal rule, but to liberate other, supposedly lesser orders of being from domination and a false sense of superiority. These "inferior" forms of nature include any sex other than male, races other than white, creatures other than man, and environments other than industrial or corporative.

The Epicurean and experimental strain of the eighteenth-century mentality began, instead, from the indubitable fact that human beings successfully interact with their surroundings. Looking, listening, touching, and moving guided them in the pursuit of mobile appearances flitting across colored surfaces. This pathognomic hunt was grounded in exploratory perception, in a total somatic awareness, not just the cerebral analysis, of shifting surroundings. But the extreme distinction between a visible and an invisible, a corporeal and a spiritual dimension was endemic to an overly empirical as well as to an overly theoretical tradition. The fundamental impulse toward both homogeneity and the segregation of opposites emerged from the opprobrium attached to unclassifiable mixtures. From a regulatory standpoint, heterogeneity was dangerous because it nakedly coupled, and thereby undermined, dichotomies. Thus biological barbarisms and artistic allegories were looked upon as providing visible testimony for wrongful mental and physical joinings. Intrinsically exhibitionist monsters and nonimitative hybrids sinned against grammatic and genetic purity. They provided tangible evidence of obstetric malpractice, of something that incorrectly came to be. Deformity and infirmity scrambled the clear channels of otherworldly transmission and defiled the nonmanual flow of symbolic revelation.

Neoplatonic and Manichean metaphors of blotless health or wholeness and of contaminating shadowy marks flourished in this supposedly secular age. The pointillist pathology and uncontaminated aesthetics of the Enlightenment rested on the venerable theology of original sin, fulminating against the perils of multiplication. Reproductive sex, like infectious illness, introduced a wound, blemish, or divisive fracture into the originally seamless, white, and spotless integument of being. After the Fall, animality, carnality, and disfiguring disease fragmented and stained the once-intact skin and soul of prelapsarian Adam. Only the abstracted ideal, the unearthly fiction, the artificial person calculatingly fabricated by means of a geometrical art, could escape discoloring by this hereditary vice. Conversely, the Romantic grotesque was born when, in weighing the likelihood of success in the production of such superhuman automata, the artist stopped to estimate his chances of failure. The distracted collage, or misfitted *ars combinatoria*, resulted from the despair arising when he reckoned the incongruity of his aspiration and gauged the infinite distance separating the one from the many.

Aesthetic and biological formalism, whether bare or prismatic, represented a shift in expectation from approximate knowledge, or probability, to mathematical necessity. New and larger areas of common life had become regular and reliable during the Enlightenment.[3] Dictionaries and encyclopedias specifically encouraged the application of calculative reasoning to more and often inappropriate disciplines, urging them to maximize certainty within their own uncertain situations. The quantification of common sense and the partitioning of the associational flow of ideas into a rule-bound sequence or logic was enhanced also by the period's infatuation with optical instruments.

Microscopes, telescopes, and amplifying glasses were believed to provide computable increments of insight into unseen and unknown terrain. Magnification, it had been hoped, would yield deep and precise information about deceptive superficial signs. The perceptual activity of enlargement became confused with an ethical and rational compulsion to attain intellectual exactitude. The failure of such scrutinizing probes to exhibit the bedrock of changeless substance, to distinguish infallibly between matter and spirit, subjective and objective experience, dreaming and wakefulness, contributed to the large-scale illusionizing of life. Vision and visual disciplines suffered then, as they do now in our electronic civilization, from the stigma of idolatrous charlatanism. In the new iconoclasm characterizing the second half of the eighteenth century, optic-based media were reduced to being didactic tools of discourse or thoughtlessly replicating toys. Bereft of philosophical control and textual guidance, they were demoted to fictions casting abroad deceptions. These eye-catchers pleased the illiterate, or those undemanding women and half-conscious children satisfied with gaping at fantasies unfurling in the dark.

Not surprisingly, as greater areas of inner and outer life became visible or visualizable, a renewed and intensified premium was placed on things invisible. Layers of corporeal mysteries, concealed cognitive structures, and instinctive reactions—hidden beneath the phenomenal tide—were to be exposed by nonoptical and keener means of detection. The assumption that the other senses could penetrate strategically where vision failed further shored up the broader conceptual prejudice against the lure of supposedly nonintellectual images and hallucinatory emotions. Eighteenth-century concerns over simulation were rephrased and retooled in nineteenth-century debates surrounding photographic imitation. Thus the unequal dialectic between variable perception and invariant reason protracted and maintained the old metaphysics of doubt. Positivists and idealists, "realists" or "symbolists," continued to be obsessed with the mathematization either of empirica or of noetica. Consequently, they perpetuated the same hierarchical divisions. Each, in his own way, persisted in underestimating the complexity and subtlety of the information processing occurring during the sensory and affective apprehension of the milieu. They forgot that perceiving, feeling, and understanding are so mixed and intermingled that we cannot straightly do one without involving the others.

Having visited and revisited this cluster of powerful and pervasive imagery, the viewer-reader will have discerned that this book was patterned pictorially, not sequentially. Each chapter with its ruling metaphor, like an entry in an Enlightenment encyclopedia, constantly made cross-references to conceptions that preceded or followed it. The deliberately fragmentary or incomplete nature of this study—only six, albeit major, metaphors observed laterally and in depth—also implied process with an eye to the future. To be, in this sense, unfinished acknowledges the dynamics of rapidly changing information. By inviting my audience actively to compare and contrast ideas, I, too, hope to inspire additional and fresh juxtapositions. For, it seems to me, only through novel and mutually refracting analogies can we begin to alter stereotypical ways of thinking about the eighteenth century and its aftermath. To that end, as in a painting, my intention is to keep complex material complexly, continually, and simultaneously present to sight without reducing it to a false simplicity. Thus, inside the pliant frame, or between the initial parenthesis of aggressive dissection and its permeable closure in the delicate tactility of sensation, there surges a back and forth flow of interconnected and sensualized concepts. These mobile configurations, as well as the book's kinetic organization, are meant to demonstrate how intricately and visually the Enlightenment shaped knowledge.

Now, too, is the appropriate moment to reiterate that my distinctly lowercase and prismatic method is devised to avoid those twin incarnations of the ancient and imprisoning negative way. Still haunting the late twentieth century, they were a hyperbolic Cartesian or empiricist skepticism and an absolute, universal, and rational—not reasoned—criticism. The latter's systematic or extravagant doubt and mistrust produced a tyrannical metaphysics. Kant's triadic aspiration to break the recurring dyad of dogmatism and skepticism by the insertion of the concept of the critical, paradoxically, has led to the dogmatization of an independent and transcendent Method.[4]

Is there, then, a third road, exploratory and free, that is neither the narrowly "correct" right nor the "deviant" left way but a humane, modest, and reconciliatory path running somewhere in between the desperate yearning for order and its radical denial? I believe so. In abandoning divisive antinomies and arrogant intellectual supra-structures, vast portions of denigrated experience could be reclaimed from non-being for being. Like medical ethics, a healthy aesthetical ethics would help to alleviate the suffering of exclusion.[5] Unlike a remote and lofty skeptical criticism, this flexible, helpful, and caring judgment of individual existential matters could allay that desperate sense—held by so many—of belonging nowhere. As we have witnessed, this diseased state of disinheritance afflicted those ambiguous phenomena—epitomized by the optical—judged to be subordinate, outside, or unreal. In short, this new praxis would visibilize the intellectually, culturally, and socially invisible, thus making it possible for the unseen to participate tangibly at last.

As we approach our own *fin-de-siècle*, how can we remedy the immemorial rift between knowing and seeing, internal cause and external effect? More importantly, how can we overcome the unproductive attitude that places a wedge between the "substantial" sciences and the "insubstantial" humanities, or divorces "high" ratiocination from "merely manual" and miracle—mongering technology?[6] How can we regain the lost honor of our craft? We have seen where we have been. But, to paraphrase Gauguin, who are we imagists and, more to the point, where are we going? Consider a different, cross- and pluridisciplinary viewpoint, one in which there is a profound interplay between observation and theory. More necessary than interaction, however, is a fundamental reorientation. In Gibson's words, attention needs to be understood as an achievement, not just as a triggered impression or as a mindless reflex.[7] Surely in some enlightened and not too distant future, the Platonic bias against image fabrication will no longer be viable or sustainable. The marvels of noninvasive medical body scans are but one small instance in our culture of an undeniable pictorial power for the good. Images, no more and no less than any other form of human expression, require understanding and knowledgeable use. This timely shift toward organic cooperation among the representing arts and the experimental sciences will have a salutary impact on the interpretation of experience as a whole. Now is the time to formulate a new and nonreductive model of knowing that escapes the old, imprisoning, and binary gridlock of either-or. In the face of an amplifying and diluting pan-"Image-World"[8]—polluted by the proliferation of electric signs, flashing billboards, video, high definition television, and doctored rephotographs—manipulated by cynical advertisers, the visually skilled and trained person has a special, advocating role. Who else will demonstrate that one does not necessarily become dumb watching? Who else will show the need for visual aptitude, not just reading literacy? Who else will teach the difference between empty merchandizing or narcotic, plasmic propaganda and the constitutive imaging arts, encouraging and persuading the actively engaged beholder to think?

A paradox of our supposedly uneducated media culture is that it remains an heir to the overestimation of written language. From the Neoclassical diagram, or universal, stripped-down "characteristic," to the Romantic grammar of chemical elements, to the Cubists' punning words and elaborate letters, to Conceptual Art's decontextualized inscriptions, to Jenny Holzer's terse captions—texts, charts, definitions, and documentation increasingly turned graphics into linguistics. The dual seduction of bombarding and numbing consumer clichés, or of clean and laconic explanations, deprives visual expression of being the complex result of its own imperatives. Analogously, contemporary art historical research and criticism too often perpetuate the long tradition of borrowing their methodology from the outdated model of the discursive printed word. Why not, instead, look to the advanced study of pattern recognition, to the total bodily and histrionic rhetoric of soliciting and convincing, and to the development and evolution of perception? But more of this at the end. This is not to deny that all disciplines must be drawn upon in the interpretation of complex and multisensory effects. Yet, as imagists coming together from many areas, we possess special proficiencies and have particular responsibilities for our profession. Indeed, as seems to have gone unrecognized, we are eminently useful and have much to give to other fields. Our contribution lies not in the imposition of yet another hegemonic method onto inappropriate material, but in the asking of thought-provoking questions. Our strength consists precisely in the knowledge of visual rhetoric and its history. From that informed vantage, we can inquire of our medical colleagues, for example, whether they have sufficiently considered the hidden aesthetic biases underlying some of their clinical judgments and decisions. In that sense, the humanistic study of art can and ought to make a deep social and even anthropological impact. From a combined investigative strength—composed of different talents focusing on the same perceptual problem—should finally arise a properly visual hermeneutics, the imaging art-science of tomorrow.

The difficulty of distinguishing fact from fiction has been intrinsic to historical studies since their inception.[9] Uncritically to ally ourselves with those who treat actions and pictures merely as decodable texts or as some ignoble form of knowing will not reduce uncertainty nor guarantee the production of more rigorous research. The moment has surely come to forge theoretical models congruent with the showing and demonstrative nature of the fleeting appearances under investigation. We might take our therapeutic cue from those eighteenth-century physicians who remained alert to probable or improbable symptoms, who compared and judged psychosomatic signs that they saw and heard in order to conjecture about what was unseen or unheard.[10] These doctors were engaged in a fundamentally *aesthetic* activity. The dialogue between diagnosing practitioner and a responsive individual surface was based on being sensitive to a vanishing variety of effects beheld. Similarly, the inferential reconstruction of a shared and embodied "reality" must depend on coming to grips with what can be viewed, or can be made commonly accessible. The study of the changing structure and function of seeing within a specific case or culture is also the epiphanic discipline of our visual future.

For an egalitarian theory of the image—not just another hierarchical theory of the concept masquerading as aesthetics—we need a decentralized, process-oriented, and interlocking social structure. Figures must cease being taken for *parerga*. Rather than disposable accessories hovering on the intellectual margins, they must become integrated into, and shape, the mainstream of civic life. The outcry currently being raised against television's crassness has obliterated the recognition that picture-making and perception allow us to establish contact with the common somatic existence of the human race.[11] Beneath the articulation of texts lies an unspeakable and shared utterance not requiring translation into another, written mode. When not suppressed but permitted democratically to surface, this Vichean performative and primal *lingua mentale commune* flourishes in directly transmitable and understandable sights, sounds, passions, gestures, and corporeal movements.[12] Rather than a segregating and minimalist body criticism, this approach uncovers a total body expressiveness possessing its own complex and densely physical ideas. My hope is that in the subtle sensory milieu of the future, imagery will no longer function as worthless supports for "more important" information or as disposable and emaciated beasts of burden for political posturing and commodity-driven commercials.[13] Art as graphical excellence will again become synonymous with the well-designed creation and presentation of interesting and engaging data that would otherwise remain unseen. The actualization of such intricate and multivariate perception depends on over-coming the trivializing notion that graphics are only for the crudely unso-phisticated reader for whom words are too difficult.[14]

Support for the view that art—thus broadly defined—will eventually per-meate everywhere and, indeed, constitutes a new form of global communi-cation is growing. Whether this is viewed as a welcome occurrence or not, the image has become a formidable instrument of power. Modern visualization technology is predicated on the fact that half of our neurological machinery is devoted to vision. Optically, the eye is an organ that throws a two-dimensional image of the world onto the retina. Multiple sensory messages, complexly overlaid or superimposed on one another, are projected onto the cortex where external representations are reconstituted. The task lying before those of us attempting to interpret continuously varying flat patterns is to explain how one comes to see ideas, or to discover analogies. For it is mental and physical pictures that best convey this original, holistic, emotional, and nonverbal nature of thinking. Imagery corresponds to that intuitive ability of the mind to perceive the truth of some proposition that cannot be settled according to a formal system. Moreover, certain types of pictures, for example the caricatures and grotesques discussed earlier, visualize the jumpy discontinuities that accompany a perspicuous consciousness of the world. They externalize and configure discrete and often painful states without the use of narrative intermediaries. Breaking up phenomenal fluency into individual quanta also facilitates the transmission of information without degrading or altering the directness and intactness of the experience conveyed. The converging fields of computer graphics, image processing and storage, animation, and user-interface prototypes have based themselves on this growing awareness of the significant role played by perception in cognition. Novel knowledge-representation schemes accessible to a broad range of users in geology, meterology, astronomy, paleontology, archaeology, medicine, and biology continue to be invented. In these forward-looking disciplines, visuals are called upon when words or numbers are misleading, insufficiently descriptive, or confusing. Significantly, "research artists" have become an intrinsic part of supercomputer teams. They shape models enabling scientists to see relationships invisible in our space and time. Moreover, with the aid of graphic tablets and digitizers they produce the processes that generate or make it possible for a work to appear and to evolve before one's eyes.[15] Further, the ubiquity of word processing itself constitutes an educational and an epistemological revolution. Representing a dramatic extension of the Enlightenment's visual encyclopedism, infinitely combinable texts and dynamic images are now freed from the fixity of the old paper-print technology. Manipulable and locationless energized elements not only flit across a monitor, but are generally available in an oceanic data base flowing immediately below the screen.[16]

474

The aesthetics of almost, then, continues to evolve in the world of digitized animations and of information machines engendering virtual images. Neither real nor imaginery, ghostly simulations swim somewhere in between. They exist without existing. More gravity-defying and intangible than even Berkeley's sights, etherealized re-creations testify to the unbearable lightness of being, to its immaterial fluidity. "Heavy" oil painting, solid sculpture, and linear sentences no longer seem consonant with an era of insubstantial and endlessly variable transformations. The new visibles have erased Plato's divided line. The continuous electrification of images has turned them into swiftly flowing shadows (*skiai*) or unseizable appearances (*phantasmata, phainesthai*) "showing themselves" in watery mirrors and on other shiny planes.[17] Moreover, the venerable Cartesian dualism of mind and body, or of separate internal and external systems, has become outmoded. Nothing impedes us from beholding the "inside" and "outside" of things cast simultaneously on an artificial surface. Consequently, only in the late twentieth century has art, like the mythic Narcissus, totally embraced the phenomenal pool. Only now do computerized *trompe l'oeil* techniques generate, transmit, and receive effects without apparent support.[18] Holography, with its incantatory spiritual aura, comes closest to providing complete optical information about a given entity. In this apparitional and silent medium, Lessing's limiting and divisive strictures concerning the necessary separation of spatial and temporal activities are finally undone. An object's existence depends solely on the play of light, frozen in a moment, yet requiring lengthy contemplation by the viewer in order to absorb the entirety of its signals. Transparent, nontactile, whole, interactive, absorbing, holography epitomizes virtual presence.[19] Resulting from refraction rather than focalization, it behaves prismatically like Newton's luminous and substanceless specter castigated by Goethe. Eternal, believeable, and touchless illusions give credence to the German poet's and, even earlier, to Castel's fears. That is, light and colors thus conceived were not *Urphänomene* but merely incorporeal or mental visions made from a succession of photonic points and, consequently, lacking in interiority. These images that are nowhere and everywhere become actualized only in the presence of variable perceiving subjects.[20] In this contemporary optical alchemy, an unresisting and no longer opaque matter is transmuted into chromatic phantoms. Concealed structure is diaphanously revealed through a softened and permeable physiognomy. Laser beams render objects specular. Everything, therefore, is connected to everything else coming into being within a mediating field generated by meta-tools.

The exciting challenges posed by our postindustrial and postmanual society are intertwined with the positive acceptance of a new reality. Today, the visual has become the most efficient and effective form of communication; it is not the lowest common denominator. This realization calls for a new pedagogy. The public has to be educated to tackle multisensory problems. Inventiveness and flexibility in the automated workplace depend on a familiarity with many interconnected and different types of operations. From this perspective, reading simply becomes another form of visual perception and not *the* semiotic paradigm for *the* correct type of semantic literacy.[21] This latitudinarian attitude, as well as so much more, was foreshadowed in the deeply humanistic and encompassing theory of information pickup put forward by Gibson. Keeping in touch with the world meant the full and well-rounded experiencing of things, not merely the passive having of experiences. Awareness-of (eighteenth-century psychologists and physiologists termed it *sensibility*) was not just awareness, or reflexive irritability. Neither an exclusively mental nor an entirely bodily act, it hinged upon the continual psychosomatic interlocking of the observer with the plastic, limitless, and heterogeneous flux of the environment. Looking around, not looking at, and staying in motion, also meant that things hidden from one point of view could later come into sight. Misperceptions could eventually be rectified. Learning to perceive got acuter, finer, and wider with time. Gibson's optimistic insight was that, during the course of living, human beings will have traveled similar routes and have seen the same persisting layout, but at different moments.[22]

This common ground of common sense, made up of individual and group perceptions, is the ample domain of the visual arts. It suggests that art history, or the history of perception as I would prefer to call it, embraces a crucial segment of a broader and fuller pictology. Because of the very nature of the images under investigation, this generously defined discipline needs to continue having informed eye contact with objects, not merely an intellectual knowledge of texts or mediated access through photographs. Moreover, future makers and students of images, I think, will have to learn some very hard neurobiology, genetics, optical processing, and even artificial intelligence. Conversely, physicists, sociobiologists, philosophers, and psychologists will have to learn some equally difficult art history. Without it, they can neither understand nor respect how synthetic representations functioned in the past and behave in the present. Perhaps most importantly, however, those historians from other fields who still cavalierly use illustrations to embroider their discourse will have to come around to recognizing that figures and monuments possess records and chronicles of their own.[23] The many experiences of art make visible the countless ways that have existed for apprehending, feeling, and reconstructing the three-dimensional world. A picture is a historical record of what its creator noticed and considered worth noticing within a given culture at a particular moment. The artist might choose to abstract, i.e., to pick up a simple, limited, and reduced number of structural invariants as Lavater, Camper, and Cozens had done. Or, like Piranesi, he might include a high level of distracting and conflicting "noise" in his Romantically intricate rendition of the world.[24] Neither view nor the information it contains, however, can claim to be complete and dogmatically superior to other perspectives. Thus picture-making and its study form an important and integral component of visual experience as a whole.

Finally, since a paradigm shift of Copernican proportions seems called for to convert Western culture to a configured wisdom, it is appropriate to inquire what are the chances for the new imagistic's success. It takes labor and determination to overcome strongly etched biases and convenient habits of mind. A significant number of people have to acquire new patterns of thought or alter their preconceptions. They also have to be convinced that the work this metamorphosis entails is worth the considerable psychic expenditure.[25] Visual education must in some way be about persuading this crucial and forefront audience that such a currently unfashionable view is consonant with other, socially respectable findings. Indeed, it is being corroborated daily both by scientific discoveries and by technological imaging innovations. More importantly, the general population, as well as our language-based academic colleagues, would have to be trained to see that a perceptual and affective model of knowing actually corresponds to our understanding of how the brain functions. Rather than feeling threatened by the loss of an unjustifiable power, they should rejoice at the mind's poetic manner of informally patterning thought, its way of clustering disparate bundles of information. A coherent and concerted rhetorical effort on the part of imagists, that is, by artists, historians, and experimentalists of all stripes, would get us beyond the initial hurdle of age-old prejudice, dismissal, and facile disbelief. Then would follow the turning point and, at last, would come the irresistible contagion of coming to see the fundamental intellectual value and dignity of seeing.

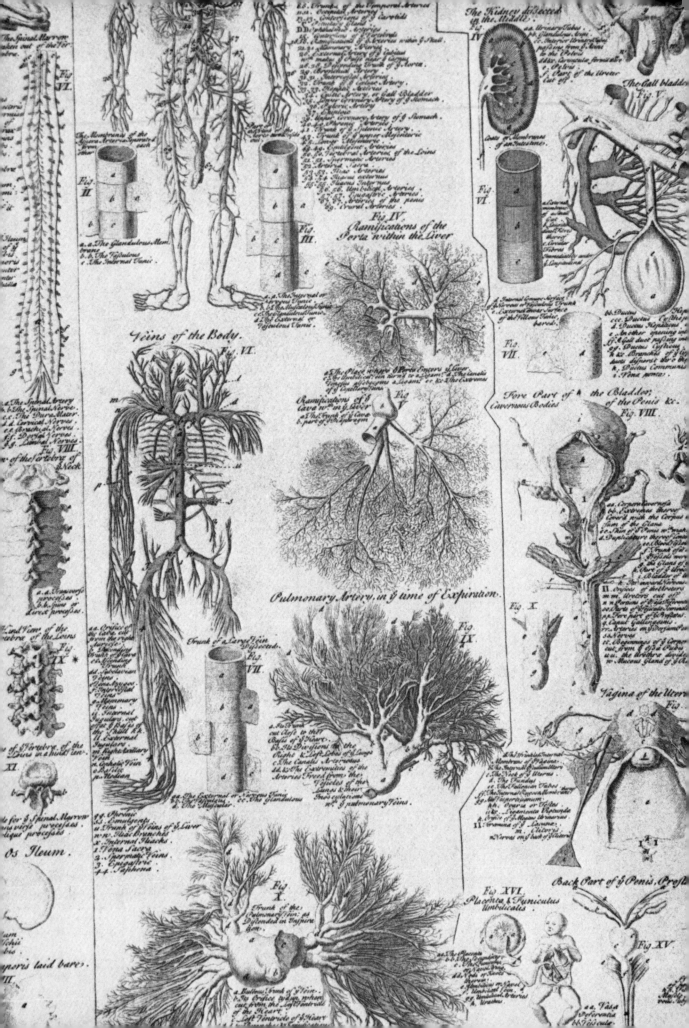

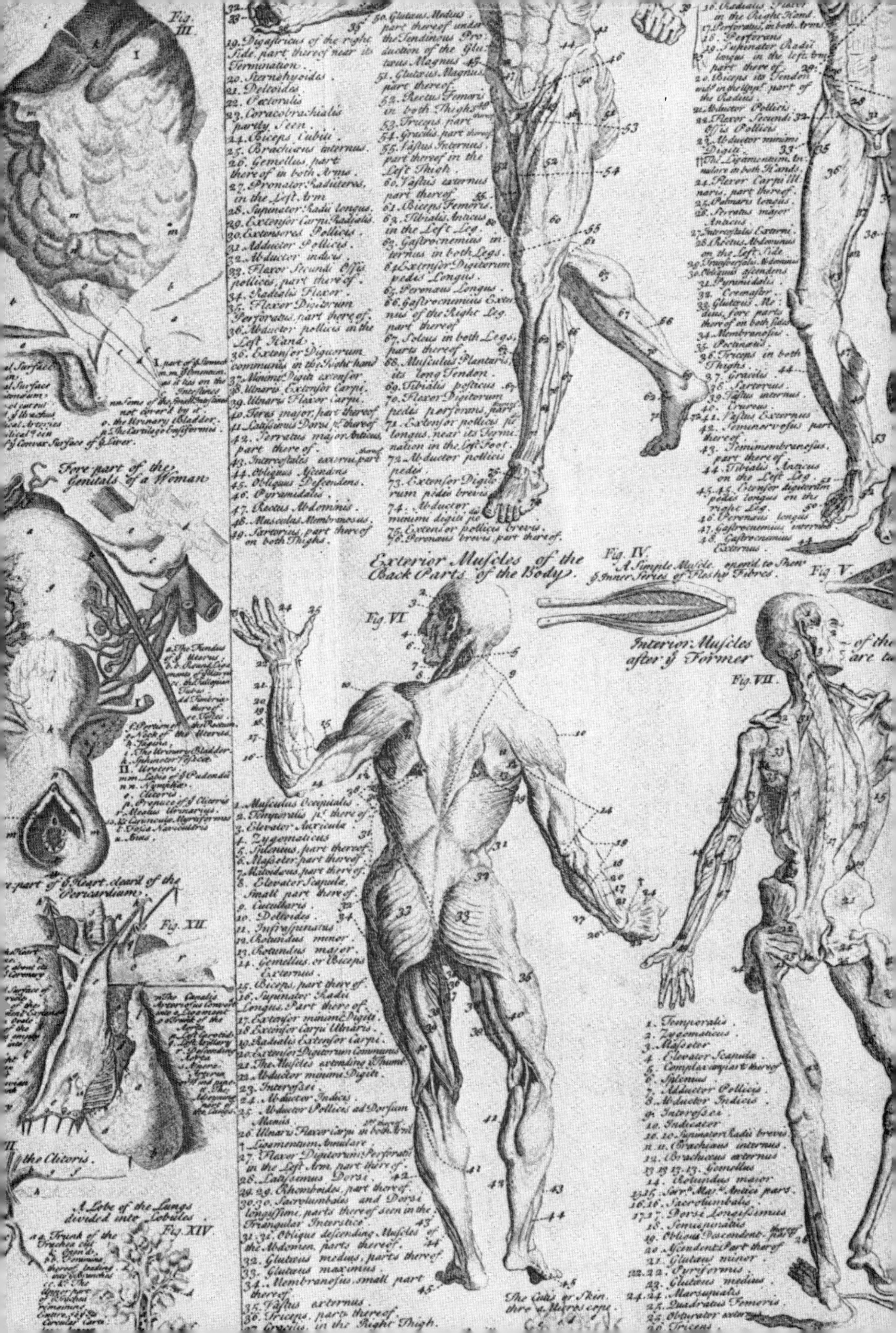

Fig. III.

Fore part of the Genitals of a Woman

Fig. XII.

A Lobe of the Lungs divided into Lobules
Fig. XIV.

19. Digastricus of the right side, part thereof near its Termination.
20. Sternohyoides.
21. Deltoides.
22. Pectoralis.
23. Coracobrachialis partly seen.
24. Biceps Cubiti.
25. Brachiæus internus.
26. Gemellus, part thereof in both Arms.
27. Pronator Radii teres, in the Left Arm.
28. Supinator Radii longus.
29. Extensor Carpi Radialis.
30. Extensores Pollicis.
31. Adductor Pollicis.
32. Abductor indicis.
33. Flexor Secundi Ossis pollicis, part thereof.
34. Radialis Flexor.
35. Flexor Digitorum Perforatus, part thereof.
36. Abductor pollicis in the Left Hand.
36. Extensor Digitorum communis in the Right hand.
37. Minimi Digiti extensor.
38. Ulnaris Extensor Carpi.
39. Ulnaris Flexor Carpi.
40. Teres major, part thereof.
41. Latissimus Dorsi, part thereof.
42. Serratus major Anticus, part thereof.
43. Intercostales externi, part
44. Obliquus Ascendens.
45. Obliquus Descendens.
46. Pyramidalis.
47. Rectus Abdominis.
48. Musculus Membranosus.
49. Sartorius, part thereof on both Thighs.

50. Glutæus Medius, part thereof under the Tendinous Production of the Glutæus Magnus.
51. Glutæus Magnus, part thereof.
52. Rectus Femoris in both Thighs.
53. Triceps, part
54. Gracilis, part thereof
55. Vastus Internus, part thereof in the Left Thigh.
60. Vastus externus, part thereof.
61. Biceps Femoris.
62. Tibialis Anticus in the Left Leg.
63. Gastrocnemius internus in both Legs.
64. Extensor Digitorum pedis longus.
65. Peronæus Longus.
66. Gastrocnemius Externus of the Right Leg, part thereof.
67. Soleus in both Legs, part thereof.
68. Musculus Plantaris, its long Tendon.
69. Tibialis posticus.
70. Flexor Digitorum pedis perforans, part
71. Extensor pollicis pedis longus, near its Termination in the Left Foot.
72. Abductor pollicis pedis.
73. Extensor Digitorum pedis.
74. Abductor minimi digiti pedis.
75. Extensor pollicis brevis.
76. Peronæus brevis part thereof.

Exterior Muscles of the Back Parts of the Body.

Fig. IV.
A Simple Muscle opened to Shew
g Inner Series of Fleshy Fibres

Fig. V.

Interior Muscles after y Former.

Fig. VI.

Fig. VII.

1. Musculus Occipitalis.
2. Temporalis, part thereof.
3. Elevator Auriculæ.
4. Zygomaticus.
5. Splenius, part thereof.
6. Masseter, part thereof.
7. Mastoideus, part thereof.
8. Elevator Scapulæ, small part thereof.
9. Cucullaris.
10. Deltoides.
11. Infraspinatus.
12. Rotundus minor.
13. Rotundus major.
14. Gemellus, or Biceps Externus.
15. Biceps, part thereof.
16. Supinator Radii Longus, Part thereof.
17. Extensor minimi Digiti.
18. Extensor Carpi Ulnaris.
19. Radialis Extensor Carpi.
20. Extensor Digitorum Communis.
21. The Muscles extending y Thumb.
22. Abductor minimi Digiti.
23. Interossei.
24. Abductor Indicis.
25. Abductor Pollicis ad Dorsum Manûs.
26. Ulnaris Flexor Carpi in both Arms.
26. Ligamentum Annulare.
27. Flexor Digitorum Perforati in the Left Arm, part thereof.
28. Latissimus Dorsi.
29. Rhomboides, part thereof.
30. Sacrolumbalis and Dorsi longissimi, parts thereof seen in the Triangular Interstice.
31. Obliquus descending Muscles of the Abdomen, parts thereof.
32. Glutæus medius, parts thereof.
33. Glutæus maximus.
34. Membranosus, small part thereof.
35. Vastus externus.
36. Triceps, part thereof.
37. Gracilis, in the Right Thigh.

1. Temporalis.
2. Zygomaticus.
3. Masseter.
4. Elevator Scapulæ.
5. Complexus, part thereof.
6. Splenius.
7. Adductor Pollicis.
8. Abductor Indicis.
9. Interossei.
10. Indicator.
10. Supinator Radii brevis.
11. Brachiæus internus.
12. Brachiæus externus.
13. 13. 13. Gemellus.
14. Rotundus major.
14. 15. Serr. Maj. Antica pars.
16. 16. Dorsi longissimus.
17. 17. Dorsi Longissimus.
18. Semispinatus.
19. Obliquus Descendens.
20. Ascendens, part thereof.
21. Glutæus minor.
22. 22. Pyriformis.
23. Glutæus medius.
24. 24. Marsupialis.
25. Quadratus Femoris.
26. Obturator externus.

INTRODUCTION:
The Visualization of Knowledge

1. On dualism as a fair price for certainty and on the perceived need for an authoritarian system of management from Descartes to Carnap, see Manfred Sommer, *Husserl und der frühe Positivismus* (Frankfurt am Main: Vittorio Klostermann, 1985), pp. 9–11.

2. Hans Blumenberg, "Paradigmen zu einer Metapherologie," *Archiv für Begriffsgeschichte,* 4 (1960), 83.

3. Ibid., pp. 10–11.

4. Hans Blumenberg, "Ausblick auf eine Theorie der Unbegrifflichkeit," in *Schiffbruch mit Zuschauer. Paradigma einer Daseinsmetapher* (Frankfurt am Main: Suhrkamp Verlag, 1979), p. 77.

5. Alexander Gottlieb Baumgarten, *Texte zur Grundlegung der Ästhetik* (1750), trans. and ed. Hans Rudolf Schweizer (Hamburg: Felix Meiner Verlag, 1983), p. 79. Baumgarten defined the *science* of aesthetics as a *gnoselogia inferior.*

6. On "lived concepts," see Ferdinand Fellmann, *Phänomenologie als ästhetische Theorie* (Munich and Freiburg: Verlag Alber, 1989), p. 211.

7. Plato, *Republic* VII. 514A–517A.

8. Michael J. Morgan, *Molyneux's Question: Vision, Touch and the Philosophy of Perception* (Cambridge: Cambridge University Press, 1977), p. 6.

9. Hans Blumenberg, *Lebenzeit und Weltzeit* (Frankfurt am Main: Suhrkamp Verlag, 1986), p. 210.

10. Hans Blumenberg, *Höhlenausgänge* (Frankfurt am Main: Suhrkamp Verlag, 1989), pp. 147–153.

11. Ibid., pp. 142–143.

12. Hans Blumenberg, *Arbeit am Mythos* (Frankfurt am Main: Suhrkamp Verlag, 1979), p. 36.

13. See the important connection of astronomy (Tobias Mayr's librations of the moon) with the early development of statistics, in Stephen M. Stigler, *The History of Statistics: The Measurement of Uncertainty before 1900* (Cambridge, Mass.: The Belknap Press of Harvard University Press, 1986), pp. 25–30.

14. For the importance of encyclopedism both as a style and a method to the Enlightenment mentality, see my "The Eighteenth Century: Towards an Interdisciplinary Model," *Art Bulletin,* 70 (March 1988), 12–14.

15. See, especially Peter Brown, *The Body and Society: Men, Women and Sexual Renunciation in Early Christianity* (New York: Columbia University Press, 1988), pp. 223ff, for how the Desert Fathers in the third and fourth centuries remade their yielding, material bodies into calibrated instruments for Christian decorum. For Christian ascetic ethics, in contrast to the fleshiness of paganism, also see Brown's "Late Antiquity," in *A History of Private Life: From Pagan Rome to Byzantium,* ed. Paul Veyne (Cambridge, Mass.: Belknap Press of Harvard University Press, 1987), I, 235–312.

16. Blumenberg, *Arbeit am Mythos,* p. 135.

17. Antoine Schnapper, ed., *Jacques-Louis David, 1748–1825,* exh. cat. (Paris: Editions de la Réunion des Musées Nationaux, 1989), p. 209.

18. For an overview see the recent compendium of essays, *Fragments for a History of the Body,* ed. Michel Feher with Ramona Naddaff and Nadia Tazi (Cambridge, Mass.: MIT Press Zone Books, 1989), 3 vols.

19. Roland Mortier, "'Lumière' et 'Lumières': histoire d'une image et d'une idée," in *Clartés et ombres du siècle des Lumières: Etudes sur le XVIIIe siècle littéraire* (Geneva: Librairie Droz, 1969), pp. 13–59.

20. Richard Brilliant, *Gesture and Rank in Roman Art: The Use of Gestures to Denote Status in Roman Sculpture and Coinage* (New

Haven: Connecticut Academy of Arts & Sciences, 1963), pp. 9–10. For the prevalence of illiteracy in classical antiquity and the dominant role of rhetoric among the educated and uneducated classes, also see his *Visual Narratives: Storytelling in Etruscan and Roman Art* (Ithaca: Cornell University Press, 1984), p. 15.

21. For important eighteenth-century shifts in biology, see especially Jean Ehrard, *L'Idée de la nature dans la première moitié du XVIIIe siècle* (Paris: Ecole Pratique des Hautes Etudes, VI Section), vol. I; Jacques Roger, *Les Sciences de la vie dans la pensée française du XVIIIe siècle: la géneration des animaux de Descartes à l'Encyclopédie* (Paris: Armand Colin, 1963); and Philip C. Ritterbush, *Overtures to Biology* (New Haven: Yale University Press, 1964).

22. Thomas Puttfarken, *Roger de Piles' Theory of Art* (New Haven: Yale University Press, 1985), pp. 75–79.

23. For an entire class of alternative, nonacademic and burlesque Salon criticism that spoke for the *bas peuple*, see the excellent article by Bernadette Fort, "Voice of the Public: The Carnivalization of Salon Art in Prerevolutionary France," *Eighteenth-Century Studies*, 20 (Spring 1989), 368–394.

24. Thomas E. Crow, in *Painters and Public Life in Eighteenth-Century Paris* (New Haven: Yale University Press, 1985), pp. 217–237, has noted that both the positive and negative critical response to the *Horatii* and the *Death of Socrates* was to speak of their dissonant awkwardness and inattention to the fine points of the painter's craft.

25. For the gymnastic aspects of the Neoclassical nude, see Karl Simon, "Körperlichkeit und Stil im Wandel von Rokoko zum Klassizismus," *Jahrbuch des freien deutschen Hochstifts Frankfurt am Main* (Halle, 1931), p. 137; and Colin Eisler, "The Athlete of Virtue: The Iconography of Asceticism," in *De Artibus Opuscula, XL, Essays in Honor of Erwin Panofsky*, ed. Mil-

lard Meiss (Zurich, 1960), pp. 82–84. Also see my "Arena of Virtue and Temple of Immortality: An Early Nineteenth-Century Museum Project," *Journal of the Society of Architectural Historians*, 35 (March 1976), 21–34. This lengthy tradition is not mentioned in Dorothy Johnson, "Corporeality and Communication: The Gestural Revolution of Diderot, David, and *The Oath of the Horatii*," *Art Bulletin*, 71 (March 1989), 92–113.

26. See especially Edgar Munhall, *Jean-Baptiste Greuze, 1705–1805*, exh. cat. (Hartford, Conn.: The Wadsworth Atheneum, 1976).

27. Contrast this pliancy with the increasing professional self-assertiveness found in the self-portraits by women artists. See, for example, Joseph Baillio, *Elisabeth Louise Vigée Le Brun, 1755–1842*, exh. cat. (Fort Worth: Kimbell Art Museum, 1982).

28. Carolyn Williams, "The Changing Face of Change: Fe/Male In/Constancy," *British Journal for Eighteenth-Century Studies*, 12 (Spring 1989), 13–28. Also see Virgil, *Aeneid*, 4.569–570.

29. Gerhard Charles Rump, *George Romney (1734–1802): zur Bildform der bürgerlichen Mitte in der englischen Neoklassik* (Hildesheim: Georg Olms Verlag, 1974).

30. Peter K. Knoefel, "Florentine Anatomical Models in Wax and Wood," *Medicine nei Secoli*, 15 (1978), 329–340.

31. Anthony Turner, *Early Scientific Instruments: Europe 1400–1800* (London: Sotheby's Publications, 1987), p. 120.

32. Virginia P. Dawson, *Nature's Enigma: The Problem of the Polyp in the Letters of Bonnet, Trembley and Réaumur* (Philadelphia: American Philosophical Society, 1987), pp. 5–10. Also see Shirley A. Roe, "John Turberville Needham and the Generation of Living Organisms," *Isis*, 74 (1983), 159–184; and Aram Vartanian, "Trembley's Polyp, La Mettrie, and Eighteenth-Century French Materialism,"

Journal of the History of Ideas, 11 (1950), 259–286.

33. Anesthesia was unknown to the eighteenth century either for animal or human subjects. There is no comprehensive study of rampant eighteenth-century vivisectionist practices. For a useful beginning, see MacDonald Daly, "Vivisection in Eighteenth-Century Britain," in *British Journal for Eighteenth-Century Studies*, 12 (Spring 1989), 57–68.

34. See Shirley A. Roe, *Matter, Life and Generation: 18th Century Embryology and the Haller-Wolff Debate* (Cambridge: Cambridge University Press, 1981), for the post-1740 move toward vitalism in natural historical explanations.

35. See my "'Peculiar Marks': Lavater and the Countenance of Blemished Thought," *Art Journal* 46 (Fall 1987), 185–192.

36. See Shoshana Zuboff, *In the Age of the Smart Machine: The Future of Work and Power* (New York: Basic Books, 1988), p. 23, on the abstraction of computer-generated work and the redefinition of labor from toil to the manipulation of visual symbols.

37. Bruce H. McCormick, Thomas A. DeFanti, and Maxine Brown, eds., "Visualization in Scientific Computing," *Computer Graphics*, 21 (November 1987).

38. See my "Presuming Images and Consuming Words: On the Visualization of Knowledge from the Enlightenment to Post-Modernism," in *Culture and Consumption: The World of Goods*, ed. John Brewer and Roy Porter (London: Routledge, forthcoming).

39. Jean DHombres, "Books: Reshaping Science," in *Revolution in Print: The Press in France 1775–1800*, ed. Robert Darnton and Daniel Roche, exh. cat. (New York: New York Public Library, 1989), pp. 177–202.

40. Edward R. Tufte, *The Visual Display of Quantitative Information* (Cheshire, Conn.: Graphics Press, 1983), has persuasively argued for the need to reintroduce such excellence into contemporary graphics. He has also called for the return of detail, discrimination, and refinement in communication devices because they are part of the process of *clarification*. See his "Attention to Detail or Less Is a Bore," in *PC Computing*, 1 (November 1988), 110–115.

41. See Eleanor A. Sayre, "Introduction to the Prints and Drawings Series," in *Goya and the Spirit of Enlightenment*, exh. cat. (Boston: Museum of Fine Arts, 1989), pp. xcv–cxxvii.

42. See especially John W. Ittmann, "The Triumph of Color: Technical Innovations in Printmaking," in John W. Ittmann, et al., *Regency to Empire: French Print-Making 1715–1814*, exh. cat. (Minneapolis: The Minneapolis Institute of Arts, 1985), pp. 23ff. For a thorough discussion of Piranesi's techniques, see Andrew Robison, *Piranesi: Early Architectural Fantasies: A Catalogue Raisonné of the Etchings* (Chicago: University of Chicago Press, 1985).

43. From Lucretius to Leibniz to Novalis (and, indeed, to Borges), the comparison obtained: as with mathematics, so with language. Through the play of wit and the manipulation of alphabetical or numerical symbols, the mathematician-writer/artist can grammatically or logically construct a world. See John Neubauer, *Symbolismus und symbolische Logik. Die Idee der Ars Combinatoria in der Entwicklung der modernen Dichtung* (Munich: Wilhelm Fink Verlag, 1978), p. 12. On the Romantic symbol, more generally, see Tzvetan Todorov, *Theories of the Symbol*, trans. C. Porter (Ithaca: Cornell University Press, 1982), pp. 147–221.

44. Morselized television advertisements and anonymous, ghost-written messages tend to foster a free-floating "ready-made" expression. See Kathleen Hall Jamieson,

Eloquence in an Electronic Age: The Transformation of Public Speechmaking (Oxford: Oxford University Press, 1988), pp. 221–243.

45. Hans Blumenberg, *Die Lesbarkeit der Welt* (Munich: Suhrkamptaschenbuch Wissenschaft, 1986), p. 380.

46. The historical and cultural concept of disease does not appear to have engaged American medical ethicists. There is, however, an interesting German literature on the topic. See. for example, the views discussed in Michael N. Magin, *Ethos und Logos in der Medizin. Das anthropologische Verhältnis von Krankheitsbegriff und medizinischer Ethik* (Freiburg and Munich: Verlag Karl Alber, 1981), pp. 236–238.

47. For the idea that television has now become our native language, see Mark Crispin Miller, *Boxed-In: The Culture of TV* (Evanston, Ill.: Northwestern University Press, 1988), p. 10.

48. On this point, see Christopher C. McConnell and Daryl T. Lawton, "IU Software Environments," in *Image Understanding Workshop. Proceedings of a Workshop Held at Cambridge, Massachusetts April 6–8, 1988* (San Mateo, Calif.: Morgan Kaufmann Publishers, 1988), II, 666–677.

49. John R. Kender, Peter K. Allen, Terrance E. Boult, and Hussein A.H. Ibrahim, "Image Understanding and Robotics Research at Columbia University," in *Image Understanding Workshop*, I, 79, 85.

50. On the imaginary voyage, and on *Gulliver's Travels* (1726) specifically, see Percy G. Adams, *Travel Literature and the Evolution of the Novel* (Lexingon, Ky.: The University Press of Kentucky, 1983), pp. 142–145.

51. These new worlds of scientific visualization and visual communication are available to scholarly visitors at the Supercomputing Center (directed by Larry Smarr), Beckman Institute, University of Illinois at Champaign-Urbana.

52. Joshua Smith, *The Photography of Invention*, exh. cat. (Washington, D.C.: National Museum of American Art, 1989).

53. For my initial outline of the problem see "From 'Brilliant Ideas' to 'Fitful Thoughts': Conjecturing the Unseen in Late-Eighteenth-Century Art," *Zeitschrift für Kunstgeschichte*, 48 (no. 1, 1985), 329–335.

54. The inability to conceive of wholes was, perhaps, most poignantly embodied in Novalis's encyclopedia of fragments. Standing in complete antithesis to the multivolume, folio *Encyclopédie*, it was not even a book. This slim compilation of loose pages was composed of disjointed rubrics, incomplete sentences, and a stammering *mise-en-page*: all visualizing the breakup of knowledge. See Novalis, *Das Allgemeine Brouillon (Materialen zur Enzyklopädistik) 1798/99*, in *Das philosophische-theoretische Werk*, ed. Hans-Joachim Mahl (Munich and Vienna: Carl Hauser Verlag, 1978), II, 474ff.

55. Frank Paul Bowman, "Illuminism, Utopia, Mythology," in *The French Romantics*, ed. D. G. Charlton (Cambridge: Cambridge University Press, 1984), I, 82–83. Also see Karl Kroeber, *British Romantic Art* (Berkeley and Los Angeles: University of California Press, 1986), pp. 26–27.

56. For the role of an ontologized chemistry in the Romantic impulse to sublimate and purify earthly dross, see Donald C. Goellnicht, *The Poet-Physician: Keats and Medical Science* (Pittsburgh: University of Pittsburgh Press, 1984), pp. 50–72.

57. See especially the excellent study by Marianne Roland Michel, *Lajoüe et l'art rocaille* (Paris: ARTHENA, 1984), pp. 153–155. For Germany, see Karsten Harries, *The Bavarian Rococo Church: Between Faith and Aestheticism* (New Haven: Yale University Press, 1983), p. 192.

58. This polemic against the bizarre, grotesque, virtuoso, and capricious belongs to a larger tradition hostile to the unbridled imagination. See Lucrezia Hartmann, *"Capriccio"—Bild und Begriff* (Nuremberg: Drucksnelldienst, 1973), pp. 7–19. For the connection of this comic art to the *ridiculosa, ludere, burla, gioco, facetiae*, see Paul Barolsky, *Infinite Jest: Wit and Humor in Italian Renaissance Art* (Columbia: University of Missouri Press, 1978), pp. 6–7.

59. See my "Beauty of the Invisible: Winckelmann and the Aesthetics of Imperceptibility," in *Zeitschrift für Kunstgeschichte*, 43 (special issue, 1980), 65–78.

60. On the impropriety of ostentatiously characterized or assertively specialized sexual forms—in contradistinction to the *concept*, not the monstrous reality, of androgyny as a pure vision of spirit—see Marie Delcourt, *Hermaphrodite: Myths and Rites of the Bisexual Figure in Classical Antiquity*, trans. Jennifer Nicholson (London: Studio Books, 1961), p. 45.

61. Robert S. Brumbaugh, *Plato's Mathematical Imagination: The Mathematical Passages in the Dialogues and Their Interpretation* (Bloomington: Indiana University Press, 1954), pp. 264–271. Appendix B, "Symbolism: The Significance of the Specific Figures Chosen as Illustrations from Pure Mathematics," notes how Leibniz's and other modern philosophers' appreciation of Plato's schemata for logic led them to denote moral (and, I will argue, virile aesthetic) qualities by distinctive geometrical figures.

62. Recent feminist critiques have explored ways in which thinking about the body has gone awry within a male-dominated European philosophical tradition. See, for example, Jane Gallop, *Thinking through the Body* (New York: Columbia University Press, 1988), p. 72.

63. A few contemporary historians of philosophy are bravely arguing that thought grows out of bodily experience, that embodiment is central to our highest imaginative processes. See Mark Johnson, *The Body in the Mind: The Bodily Basis of Meaning, Imagination, and Reason* (Chicago: University of Chicago Press, 1987), especially his astute critique of Kant's theory of the imagination that left a gap between the intellectual and the sensuous, pp. 166–170.

64. On the post-Newtonian process of axiomization, see E. J. Dijksterhuis, *The Mechanization of the World Picture*, trans. C. Dikshoorn (Oxford: Clarendon Press, 1961), pp. 464–477.

65. Hans Belting has recently reflected on this impasse. See his *Das Ende der Kunstgeschichte? Überlegung zur heutigen Kunsterfahrung und historischen Kunstforschung* (Munich: Deutscher Kunst-Verlag, 1983), pp. 11–62. Also see John M. Ellis, *Against Deconstruction* (Princeton, N.J.: Princeton University Press, 1989).

66. Walter Cahn, *Masterpieces: Chapters on the History of an Idea* (Princeton, N.J.: Princeton University Press, 1978), pp. 3–22, 104–130.

67. Philippe Desan, *Naissance de la méthode. (Machiavel, La Ramée, Bodin, Montaigne, Descartes)* (Paris: Librairie A.-G. Nizet, 1987), pp. 148–149.

68. Peter A. Schouls, *The Imposition of Method: A Study of Descartes and Locke* (Oxford: Clarendon Press, 1980), p. 147.

69. Paul Feyerabend, *Against Method* (London: New Left, 1975).

70. See my "'Fantastic Images': From Unenlightening to Enlightening 'Appearances' Meant to Be Seen in the Dark," in *Aesthetic Illusion*, ed. Frederick Burwick and Walter Pape (Berlin: De Gruyter Verlag, 1990), pp. 158–179.

71. Benson Mates, *The Philosophy of Leibniz: Metaphysics and Language* (New York and Oxford: Oxford University Press, 1986), p. 188.

72. Maria Vitale, "Lo Specchio e l'Immaginario," in *Lo Specchio e il Doppio. Dallo Stagno di Narciso allo Schermo televiso*, exh. cat. (Turin: Mole Antonelliana, 1987), p. 128.

73. Philip D. Cummins, "On the Status of Visuals in Berkeley's *New Theory of Vision*," in *Essays on the Philosophy of George Berkeley,* ed. Ernest Sosa (Dordrecht: D. Reidel Publishing Company, 1987), pp. 165–194.

74. Wesley Trimpi, *Muses of One Mind: The Literary Analysis of Experience and Its Continuity* (Princeton, N.J.: Princeton University Press, 1983).

75. Albert R. Jonsen and Stephen Toulmin, *The Abuse of Casuistry: A History of Moral Reasoning* (Berkeley and Los Angeles: University of California Press, 1988).

76. Allan Franklin, *The Neglect of Experiment* (Cambridge: Cambridge University Press, 1986).

77. Stephen Jay Gould, "Mighty Manchester," *The New York Review of Books,* 35 (October 27, 1988), pp. 32–35.

78. Howard Margolis, *Patterns, Thinking, and Cognition: A Theory of Judgment* (Chicago: University of Chicago Press, 1987).

79. Bryan G. Norton, *Why Preserve Natural Variety?* (Princeton, N.J.: Princeton University Press, 1987).

80. David Summers, *The Judgment of Sense: Renaissance Naturalism and the Rise of Aesthetics* (Cambridge: Cambridge University Press, 1987).

81. Barbara Maria Stafford, *Symbol and Myth: Humbert de Superville's Essay on Absolute Signs in Art* (Cranbury, N.J.: Associated University Presses, 1979).

82. For the importance of both these thinkers, see Milton Singer, "Emblems of Identity: A Semiotic Exploration," in *Symbols in Anthropology,* ed. J. Maquet (Malibu, Cal.: Undena Publications, 1982), pp. 72–132.

83. Barbara Maria Stafford, *Voyage into Substance: Art, Science, Nature, and the Illustrated Travel Account, 1760–1840* (Cambridge, Mass.: MIT Press, 1984).

1 DISSECTING

1. Galen, *On the Natural Faculties* 2:3.

2. Philip Merlan, "Abstraction and Metaphysics in Saint Thomas' *Summa,*" *Journal of the History of Ideas,* 14 (April 1983), 284–291.

3. Devon L. Hodges, *Renaissance Fictions* (Amherst: University of Massachusetts Press, 1985), p. 38.

4. Zuboff, *Age of the Smart Machine,* pp. 206, 320–332.

5. Jon Darius, *Beyond Vision* (Oxford and New York: Oxford University Press, 1984), pp. 14–15.

6. Ephraim Chambers, *Cyclopaedia: or an Universal Dictionary of Arts and Sciences; Containing the Definitions of the Terms and Accounts of the Things signif'd thereby in the Several Arts both Liberal and Mechanical,* 2 vols. (1728; 2d ed., London: Printed for James and John Knapton, 1738), I, n.p.

7. Ibid., p. 209. Also see Renatus James Croissant [de] Garengeot, *A Treatise of Chirurgical Operations; according to the Mechanism of the Parts of the Humane Body, and the Theory and Practice of the Most Learned and Experienced Surgeons in Paris with the Bandages for Each Apparatus and a Description of the Instruments proper for Chirurgical Operations,* trans. M. André (London: Printed for Tho. Woodward, 1723), p. 2.

8. Marie-José Imbault-Huart, "Les Chirurgiens et l'esprit chirurgical en France au XVIIIe siècle," *Clio Medica,* 15 (April 1981), p. 146.

9. Toby Gelfand, *Professionalizing Modern Medicine: Paris Surgeons and Medical Science and Institutions in the Eighteenth Century* (Westport, Conn.: Greenwood Press, 1980), p. 90.

10. Ambroise Paré, *Les Oeuvres de . . . , conseiler et premier chirurgien du roy. Corigées et augmentées par luy-mesme, peu au paravant son decés* (7th ed., Paris: Chez Nicolas Buon, 1614), *préface.*

11. William Schupbach, *The Paradox of Rembrandt's 'Anatomy of Dr. Tulp'*, *Medical History*, supplement No. 2 (London: Wellcome Institute for the History of Medicine, 1982), pp. 8, 17–19.

12. Imbault-Huard, "Chirurgiens au XVIIIe siècle," pp. 146–148.

13. Garengeot, *Chirurgical Operations*, pp. 5–6.

14. See Jean-Jacques Scheuchzer, *Physique sacrée, ou histoire naturelle de la Bible*, 8 vols. (Amsterdam: Chez Pierre Schenk et Pierre Mortier, 1732–1737), II, 21–23.

15. René Croissant de Garengeot, *Splanchnologie, ou l'anatomie des viscères; avec des figures originales tirées d'après les cadavres, suivie d'une dissertation sur l'origine de la chirurgie*, 2 vols. (2d rev. ed., Paris: Chez Charles Osmont, 1742), II, 323–325, 346.

16. Ibid., p. 357.

17. Ibid., pp. 367–369.

18. Ibid., pp. 370–371.

19. Imbault-Huard, "Chirurgiens au XVIIIe siècle," p. 151.

20. Summers, *Judgment of Sense*, p. 17.

21. Dio Chrysostom [of Prusa], *The Twelfth, or Olympic, Discourse: On Man's First Conception of God*, 5 vols., trans. J.W. Cohoon (Cambridge, Mass.: Harvard University Press, 1960), II, 73.

22. H. P. L'Orange, *Studies on the Iconography of Cosmic Kingship* (Oslo: H. Aschehoug & Co., 1953), p. 184.

23. Thomas R. Forbes, "'To Be Dissected and Anatomized,'" *Journal of the History of Medicine and Applied Sciences*, 36 (October 1981), 490–491.

24. William Schupbach, "Some Cabinets of Curiosities in European Academic Institutions," in *The Origins of Museums: The Cabinet of Curiosities in Sixteenth- and Seventeenth-Century Europe*, ed. Oliver Impey and Arthur MacGregor (Oxford: Clarendon Press, 1985), p. 170. Also see Lunsingh Scheurleer, "Un amphithéâtre d'anatomie moralisée," in *Leiden University in the Seventeenth Century: An Exchange of Learning*, ed. Th. H. Scheurleer and G. H. M. Posthumus Meyjes (Leiden: E.J. Brill, 1975), pp. 220–222.

25. Jaap Bolten, *Method and Practice: Dutch and Flemish Drawing Books 1600–1750* (Stuttgart: Edition PVA, 1985), p. 233.

26. P.N. Gerdy, *Anatomie des formes extérieures du corps humains, appliquée à la peinture, à la sculpture et à la chirurgie* (Paris: Chez Béchet Jeune, Libraire, and Brussels: au Dépôt de Librairie médicale française, 1829), pp. xii–xiii.

27. Jonathan Richardson, *The Works: I. The Theory of Painting. II. Essay on the Art of Criticism, (So Far as It Relates to Painting). III. The Science of a Connoisseur; with an Essay on the Knowledge of Prints, and Cautions to Collectors* (London: T. and J. Egerton, 1792), p. 113 (italics mine). On the difference between Richardson as painter and critic, see Richard Wendorf, "Jonathan Richardson: The Painter as Biographer," *New Literary History*, 15 (1983–1984), 541–542.

28. Jean-Martin Papillon, *Traité historique et pratique de la gravure en bois*, 2 vols. (Paris: Chez Pierre Guillaume Simon, 1766), pp. 10–11. Also see Henry Fuseli, *Lectures on Painting delivered at the Royal Academy. With Additional Observations and Notes* (London: Henry Colburn and Richard Bentley, 1830), p. 11.

29. William Hogarth, *The Analysis of Beauty* (London: The Scolar Press, 1969), pp. 7–8. Also see Joseph Burke, *Hogarth and Reynolds: A Contrast in English Art Theory* (London and Oxford: Oxford University Press, 1943), pp. 8–12.

30. Hogarth, *Analysis of Beauty*, pp. 54–55, 57.

31. William Blake, *Public Address* (ca. 1810), in *The Complete Writings*, ed. Geoffrey Keynes (London: Oxford University Press, 1966), p. 602. Also see Nelson Hilton, *Literal Imagination: Blake's Vision of Words* (Berkeley and Los Angeles: University of California Press, 1983), p. 22; and

Raymond Lister, *Infernal Methods: A Study of William Blake's Art Techniques* (London: G. Bell & Sons, 1975), p. 30.

32. Graham Reynolds, "The Elegance of George Stubbs," *Apollo* (January 1985), pp. 22–23. On his "typically English reticence," see Judy Egerton, introduction to *George Stubbs, 1724–1806*, exh. cat. (London: Salem House, 1985), p. 19.

33. Alexander Potts, "Winckelmann's Interpretation of Ancient Art in Its Eighteenth-Century Context" (Ph.D. dissertation, Warburg Institute, n.d.), p. 109.

34. Laurent Natter, *Traité de la méthode antique de graver en pierres fines, comparée avec la méthode moderne* (London: J. Haberkorn, 1754), pp. 4–6, 39–41.

35. Michel Huber, *Handbuch für Kunstliebhaber und Sammler über die vornehmsten Kupferstecher und ihre Werke. Vom Anfange dieser Kunst bis auf gegenwärtige Zeit. Chronologisch und in Schulen geordnet* (Zurich: Bey Orell, Gessner, Füssli und Compagnie, 1796), p. 1. Also see George Levitine, "French Eighteenth-Century Printmaking," in Ittmann et al., *Regency to Empire*, pp. 14–19.

36. David Bindman, *Blake as Artist* (Oxford: Phaidon, 1977), pp. 38–39; and Lister, *Infernal Methods*, p. 69.

37. Charles Singer, *The Evolution of Anatomy: A Short History of Anatomical and Physiological Discovery to Harvey* (New York: Alfred A. Knopf, 1925), pp. 111–135. Also see William Cowper, *Anatomia Corporum Humanorum* (Ultrajecti: Nicolaum Muntendam, 1750), pl. 20. For Cowper, see André Hahn, Paule Dumaitre, and Janine Samion-Contet, *Histoire de la médecine et du livre médicale* (Paris: Olivier Perrin Editeur, 1962), p. 284.

38. Sofia Ameisenowa, *The Problem of the écorché and the Three Anatomical Models in the Jagiellonia Library*, trans. Andrzej Potocki (Warsaw: Wydewnictwo Polskiej Akademii Nauk, 1963), pp. 44–46. On Vesalius, also see Carsten-Peter Warncke, *Sprechende Bilder-Sichtbare Worte. Das Bilderverständnis in der frühen Neuzeit*, Wolfenbütteler Forschungen, Bd. 33 (Wiesbaden: Otto Harrassowitz, 1987), p. 225; and Glenn Harcourt, "Andreas Vesalius and the Anatomy of Antique Sculpture," *Representations*, 17 (Winter 1987), 30–36.

39. Piranesi's connection to medical books remains unexplored. Marguerite Yourcenar, *The Dark Brain of Piranesi and Other Essays*, trans. Richard Howard (New York: Farrar, Straus, Giroux, 1984), p. 99, has suggested that antiquarian research was for him what the dissection of cadavers is for the painter of the nude. One would like to know, however, what impact Giovanni Maria Lancisi's 1714 edition of the lost plates of Eustachius (1550–1574), or Albinus's 1744 *Explicatio Tabularum Anatomicorum Bartholomei Eustachii*, made. On their history and importance, see Howard B. Adelmann, *Marcello Malpighi and the Evolution of Embryology* (Ithaca: Cornell University Press, 1966), I, 634–636. Concerning this unexplored connection between anatomy and archaeology in Piranesi's work, it is significant that Robin Middleton, "G.-B. Piranesi (1720–1778). Review of Recent Literature," *Journal of the Society of Architectural Historians*, 40 (1982), 333–344, concluded that no fully convincing analysis of his work and its content has yet been made.

40. Mary A. B. Brazier, *A History of Neurophysiology in the Seventeenth and Eighteenth Centuries: From Concept to Experiment* (New York: Raven Press, 1984), pp. 138–143.

41. For Piranesi's pictorial metaphors of dissection, see especially William L. MacDonald, *Piranesi's "Carceri": Sources of Invention* (Northampton: Smith College, 1979), pp. 92–93; and John Wilton-Ely, *The Mind and Art of Giovanni Battista Piranesi* (London: Thames and Hudson, 1978), pp. 55–57. On the afterlife of the archaeological metaphor of ruin in nineteenth-century Italy, see Carolyn Sprin-

ger, *The Marble Wilderness: Ruins and Representation in Italian Romanticism, 1775–1850* (Cambridge: Cambridge University Press, 1987), pp. 2–3.

42. For Fontana's silent sanctuary of colored anatomical waxes, see Mario Bucci, *Anatomia come arte* (Florence: Edizione d'Arte Il Fiorino, 1969), pp. 189–191. Also see, Francesco Algarotti, *Oeuvres*, 7 vols. (Berlin: Chez D. J. Decker, 1772), II, 137. On Algarotti, see Francis Haskell, *Patrons and Painters: A Study in the Relations between Italian Art and Society in the Age of the Baroque* (rev. ed., New Haven: Yale University Press, 1983), pp. 347–360. More recently, his scientific and intellectual circle is discussed in Martin Kemp, *The Science of Art* (New Haven: Yale University Press, 1990), pp. 142–143.

43. Mary Wollstonecraft Shelley, *Frankenstein or the Modern Prometheus* (New York: Harrison Smith and Robert Haas, 1934).

44. Philippe Sorel et al., *Palais-Royal*, exh. cat. (Paris: Musée du Carnavelet, 1988), pp. 179–180. Also see Jean Adhémar, "Les musées de cire en France. Curtius, le 'banquet royal,' les têtes coupées," *Gazette des Beaux-Arts*, 92 (no. 2, 1978), 206–207.

45. Jacques Gamelin, *Nouveau recueil d'ostéologie et de myologie, dessiné d'après nature par . . . de Carcasonne, professeur de peinture, de l'Académie de Saint Luc . . . : pour l'utilité des sciences et des arts*, 2 vols. (Toulouse: De l'Imprimerie de J. F. Desclassan, 1779), II, n.p.

46. Ibid.

47. On Géricault's portraits of the insane, see John M. MacGregor, *The Discovery of the Art of the Insane* (Princeton, N.J.: Princeton University Press, 1989), pp. 42–43.

48. J. C. Le Blon, *L'Art d'imprimer les tableaux. Traité d'après les écrits, les opérations & les instructions verbales* (Paris: Ches P. G.

Le Mercier, Jean Luc Nyon, Michel Lambert, 1756), p. 30.

49. Algarotti, *Lettres sur la peinture*, in *Oeuvres*, VI, 52.

50. Jacques Gautier Dagoty, *Chroa-Genésie ou génération des couleurs, contre le systême de Newton*, 2 vols. (Paris: Chez Antoine Boudet, 1751), II, ix–xi.

51. Hahn, Dumaitre, and Samion-Contet, *Histoire de la médecine*, pp. 305–306.

52. Jacques Gautier Dagoty, *Essai d'anatomie en tableaux imprimés, de la face, du col, de la tête, de la langue & du larinx, d'après les parties disséquées & préparées, par Monsieur Duverney, maître en chirurgie à Paris, membre de l'Académie de chirurgie & demonstrateur en anatomie au Jardin du roy* (Paris: Chez le Sieur Gautier, 1745), p. 52.

53. Jacques Gautier Dagoty, *Anatomie de la tête, en tableaux imprimés qui représentent au naturel le cerveau sous différentes coupes, la distribution des vaisseaux dans toutes les parties de la tête, les organes des sens, & une partie de la névrologie d'après les pièces disséquées & préparées par Mr. Duverney* (Paris: Chez le Sieur Gautier, M. Duverney, 1748), n.p.

54. Dagoty, *Chroa-Genésie*, II, xxi. On the Italian and French modelers in wax, see Michel Lemire, *Les Modèles anatomiques en cire colorée du XVIIIe siècle et du XIXe siècle* (Paris: Musée National d'Histoire Naturelle, Laboratoire d'Anatomie Comparée, 1987); and *Les Siècles d'or de la médecine. Padoue XV–XVIII*, exh. cat. (Milan: Electa, 1989), pp. 152–166.

55. Huber, *Handbuch*, p. 29.

56. Denis Diderot, *Salons*, ed. Jean Seznec and Jean Adhémar, 4 vols. (Oxford: Clarendon Press, 1957–1967), II, p. 58. For the praise of *le tact* in painting, see also Michel-François Dandré-Bardon, *Traité de peinture, suivi d'un essai sur la sculpture* (1765; Geneva: Minkoff Reprint, 1972), p. 126.

57. Charles - Marguerite - Jean - Baptiste - Mercier Dupaty, *Lettres sur l'Italie en 1785*

(2d ed., Paris: Desenne, 1792), pp. 116–120.

58. Chambers, *Cyclopaedia*, I, n.p.

59. Crow, *Painters and Public Life*, pp. 25–28.

60. J. G. Sulzer, "A New Critical Examination of the Word *Thought* as applied to the Fine Arts, with Rules for Judging of the Beauties of Painting, Music, and Poetry," *Annual Register*, 17 (1774), 167. On rules and health, see also Gérard Hoet, *Les principaux fondements du dessein, pour l'usage des curieux, mise en l'umière par le trés fameux peintre . . .* (Leiden: Jean Arnold, 1723), introduction; Anton Raphael Mengs, *Sämmtliche hinterlassene Schriften*, 2 vols. in 1, ed. Dr. G. Schilling (Bonn: H. B. König, 1843), II, 143; Dominique Bouhours, *La manière de bien penser dans les ouvrages d'esprit, Dialogues* (Paris: Chez les Libraires Associés, 1771), p. 9.

61. André Félibien, *Entretiens sur les vies et sur les ouvrages des plus excellens peintres anciens et modernes; avec la vie des architectes* (Farnborough, Harts.: Gregg Press, 1967), p. 68.

62. Algarotti, *Essai sur la peinture*, in *Oeuvres*, II, 57.

63. Daniel Webb, *An Inquiry into the Beauties of Painting; and into the Merits of the Most Celebrated Painters, Ancient and Modern* (2d ed. London: Printed for R. and J. Dodsley, 1761), pp. x–xii.

64. Anthony Ashley Cooper, Earl of Shaftesbury, *Characteristics*, 2 vols. (London: n.p., 1738), II, 189. On Shaftesbury, see Morris Eaves, *William Blake's Theory of Art* (Princeton, N.J.: Princeton University Press, 1982), p. 169. On the ancient notion that the ability of the artist to execute could not exceed his mastery of the use of rules, see Bernhard Schweitzer, "Der bildende Künstler und der Begriff des künstlerischen in der Antike," *Neue Heidelberger Jahr-Bücher*, n.s. (1925), p. 66.

65. Betty Jo Teeter Dobbs, *The Foundations of Newton's Alchemy, or "The Hunting of the Greene Lyon"* (Cambridge: Cambridge University Press, 1975), pp. 134–135.

66. Jean-Baptiste Dubos, *Réflexions critiques sur la poésie et sur la peinture. Ut Pictura Poesis*, 2 vols. (Paris: Chez Jean Mariette, 1719), II, 6.

67. Richardson, *Art of Criticism*, pp. 140–164, 178.

68. Edwyn Bevan, *Holy Images: An Inquiry into Idolatry and Image-Worship in Ancient Paganism and Christianity* (London: George Allen & Unwin, 1933), p. 146. On *acheiropoieta*, see also Hans Belting, *Bild und Kult. Eine Geschichte des Bildes vor dem Zeitalter der Kunst* (Munich: Verlag C. H. Beck, 1990), pp. 60–61, 66–69.

69. Johann Joachim Winckelmann, *Abhandlung von der Fähigkeit der Empfindung des Schönen in der Kunst, und dem Unterrichte in derselben* (Dresden: In der Walterischen Buchhandlung, 1763), p. 31. For Reynolds's analogous disdain, see John Barrell, *The Political Theory of Painting from Reynolds to Hazlitt: "The Body of the Public"* (New Haven and London: Yale University Press, 1986), p. 12.

70. Roland Mortier, *Clartés et ombres*, pp. 21–25. Also see Harriett Ann Watts, *Chance: A Perspective on Dada* (Ann Arbor: UMI Research Press, 1980), pp. 39–43.

71. *Encyclopaedia Britannica, or, A Dictionary of Arts and Sciences, Compiled upon a New Plan. In Which the Different Sciences and Arts Are Digested into Distinct Treatises or Systems . . .*, 3 vols. (London: Printed for Edward and Charles Dilly, 1773), I, 292; John Oldmixon, *An Essay on Criticism as It Regards Design, Thought, and Expression, in Prose and Verse* (London: Printed for J. Pemberton, 1728), p. 4; Richardson, *Science of a Connoisseur*, p. 187; and Sulzer, "Thought," p. 166.

72. Webb, *Inquiry into Painting*, p. 18; Richardson, *Art of Criticism*, pp. 122–123; Marc-Antoine Laugier, *Manière de bien juger des ouvrages de peinture* (Paris: Chez Claude-Antoine Jombert, 1771), pp. 26–

41, 50–56; Dubos, *Réflexions*, II, 303. For an analysis of Dubos's attitude toward the public, see Thomas E. Kaiser, "Rhetoric in the Service of the King: The Abbé Dubos and the Concept of Public Judgment," *Eighteenth-Century Studies*, 23 (Winter 1989–1990), 182–199.

73. Johann Caspar Lavater, *Essays on Physiognomy. Designed to promote the Knowledge and the Love of Mankind . . .* , trans. Henry Hunter, 3 vols. in 5 (London: John Murray and T. Holloway, 1792), I, I, 31–32; Richardson, *Theory of Painting* and *Art of Criticism*, pp. 40, 167–168.

74. Johann Georg Sulzer, *Allgemeine Theorie der Schönen Künste . . .* , 2 vols. in 4 (Biel: In der Heilmannischer Buchhandlung, 1777), I, I, 259.

75. Marin Cureau de La Chambre, *L'Art de connoistre les hommes* (Amsterdam: Chez Jacques Le Jeune, 1660), pp. 1–2, 15, 143–144. On *médiocrité*, see A. F. Sticotti, *Dictionnaire des gens du monde, historique, littéraire, critique, moral, physique, militaire, politique, caractéristique & social*, 3 vols. (Paris: Chez J. P. Costard, 1771), II, 382.

76. Hiram Caton, *The Origin of Subjectivity: An Essay on Descartes* (New Haven: Yale University Press, 1973), pp. 43–50.

77. Cureau de La Chambre, *L'Art de connoistre*, pp. 192–193.

78. Antoine-Joseph Pernety, *Dictionnaire mytho-hermétique, dans lequel on trouve les allégories fabuleuses des poètes, les métaphores, les enigmes et les termes barbares des philosophes hermétiques expliqués* (Paris: Chez Delalain l'aîné, 1787), pp. 17–19, 109–115, 501.

79. Antoine-Joseph Pernety, *Discours sur la physionomie, et les avantages de connoissances physionomiques* (Berlin: Chez Samuel Pitra, 1769), pp. 12–18, 30, 63.

80. Denis Diderot, *Interprétation de la nature*, in *Oeuvres philosophiques*, 10 vols. (Paris: Editions Garnier Frères, 1964), II, 46–47.

81. Pernety, *Discours*, pp. 16–25, 39–47. Also see Jacques Proust, "Diderot et la physiognomie," in *Cahiers de l'Association des études françaises*, 13 (June 1961), 328.

82. Antoine-Joseph Pernety, *Observations sur les maladies de l'âme pour servir de suite au traité de la connoissance de l'homme moral par celle de l'homme physique* (Berlin: Chez G. J. Decker, 1777), pp. 64–65, 80–82, 91–95, 140–144, 167–177. Also see the entry "grotesque," in his *Dictionnaire portatif de peinture, sculpture et gravure; avec un traité pratique des différentes manières de peindre* (Berlin: Chez Bauche, 1758), pp. 354–355. On the dominance of fashion, see Roy Porter, "Making Faces: Physiognomy and Fashion in Eighteenth-Century England," *Etudes Anglaises Grande-Bretagne; Etats-Unis*, 38 (October–December 1985), 385–396; and Crow, *Painters and Public Life*, p. 68.

83. Pernety, *Discours*, pp. 84–90. Also see Diadochus Proclus, *Über die Existenz des Bösen*, trans. and ed. Michael Erler (Meisenheim am Glan: Verlag Anton Hain, 1978), pp. 188–190.

84. Scheuchzer, *Physique sacrée*, I, 46–47.

85. Antoine-Joseph Pernety, *La Connoissance de l'homme moral par celle de l'homme physique*, 2 vols. (Berlin: Chez G. J. Decker, 1776), I, 111–113, 174. Also see Diadochus Proclus, *Alcibiades I: A Translation and Commentary* (The Hague: Martinus Nijhoff, 1971), p. 58.

86. Carol Louise Hall, *Blake and Fuseli: A Study in the Transmission of Ideas* (New York: Garland, 1985), pp. 14–16, 51–52. Also see Jean Turner, "Fuseli and Lavater: The Personification of Character," *Athanor*, 4 (1985), 34. For the publication history of the *Essays* see John Graham, "Lavater's *Physiognomy* in England," *Journal of the History of Ideas*, 22 (December 1961), 561–572.

87. Lavater, *Essays*, I, II, 49–57. Also see Gottfried W. Locher, *Zwingli's Thought: New Perspectives* (Leiden: E. J. Brill, 1981), p. 67.

88. Origen, *The Song of Songs: Commentary and Homilies*, trans. R. P. Lawson (Westminster, Md., and London: Newman Press and Longmans, Green and Co., 1957), pp. 234, 237–238; and *Homilies on Genesis and Exodus*, trans. Ronald E. Heine (Washington, D.C.: Catholic University of America Press, 1981), p. 173.

89. Lavater, *Essays*, I, II, 59, 67–68. On the supposed Pauline devaluation of the body, see J. Murphy-O'Connor, "'Being at Home in the Body We Are in Exile from the Lord' (II Cor. 5:6b)," *Revue Biblique*, 93 (April 1986), 219.

90. Lavater, *Essays*, II,II, 409. For the representation of Christ, see also Leonid Ouspensky and Vladimir Lossky, *The Meaning of Icons* (Boston: Boston Book and Art Shop, 1952), pp. 21–22, 35; and Fuseli, *Lectures on Painting*, pp. 15–17.

91. Lavater, *Essays*, I,I, 24–25. Also see Proclus, *Alcibiades*, p. 91.

92. Lavater, *Essays*, I,I, 29–30; I, II, 21–25.

93. Lavater, *Essays*, I, I, 87.

94. Lavater, *Essays*, III,II, 260. On character-writing, see also J. W. Smeed, *The Theophrastan "Character": The History of a Literary Genre* (Oxford: Clarendon Press, 1985), p. 294.

95. Lavater, *Essays*, I,I, 20; II,II, 394–399.

96. Lavater, *Essays*, I,II, 122, 133. Also see Martin Frobène Ledermüller, *Troisième cinquantaine des amusemens microscopiques* (Nuremberg: Adam Wolfgang Winter-Schmidt graveur et marchand en tailles douces, 1768), pp. 58–60; A. J. Rössel von Rosenhof, *Die Näturliche Historie der Frösche hiesigen Landes* (Nuremberg: Johann Joseph Fleischmann, 1758), pl. XI. On the importance of silhouettes, see Jean-Claude Lemagny and André Rouillé, eds., *A History of Photography: Social and Cultural Perspectives* (Cambridge: Cambridge University Press, 1986), p. 15; and Graeme Tytler, *Physiognomy in the European Novel: Faces and Fortunes* (Princeton, N.J.: Princeton University Press, 1982), p. 57.

97. Lavater, *Essays*, II,II, 177, 407.

98. Ibid., pp. 91, 227–228.

99. Ibid., p. 168. Also see Antoine Louis, *Lettres sur la certitude des signes de la mort. Où l'on rassure les citoyens de la crainte d'être enterrés vivans. Avec des observations & des expériences sur les noyés* (Paris: Chez Michel Lambert, 1772), p. 133.

100. Lavater, *Essays*, III,II, 405. Also see Anne-Claude-Philippe, Comte de Caylus, *Recueil d'antiquités égyptiennes, étrusques, grecques et romaines*, 7 vols. (Paris: Chez Desaint & Saillant, 1752–1767), II, 153–155. On aphoristic "miniatures," see Susan Stewart, *On Longing: Narratives of the Miniature, the Gigantic, the Souvenir, the Collection* (Baltimore: The Johns Hopkins University Press, 1984), p. 53; James Obelkevich, "Proverbs and Social History," in *The Social History of Language*, ed. Peter Burke and Roy Porter (Cambridge: Cambridge University Press, 1987), pp. 43–72; and Hall, *Blake*, pp. 132–135.

101. Lavater, *Essays*, II,II, 416. Also see his *Von der Physiognomik*, 2 vols. in 1 (Leipzig: Bey Weidmanns Erben und Reich, 1772), II, 49.

102. Karl Heinrich Baumgärtner, *Krankenphysiognomik* (2d rev. ed. Stuttgart: Druck und Verlag von L. F. Rieger & Comp., 1842), pp. 4–20. On Baumgärtner, see Helmut Vogt, *Das Bilden des Kranken. Die Darstellung äusserer Veränderungen durch innere Leiden und ihrer Heilmassnahmen von der Renaissance bis in unsere Zeit* (Munich: J. F. Lehmanns Verlag, 1969), p. 268.

103. Lavater, *Essays*, I,I, 106. Also see, Robert K. Merton, David L. Sills, and Stephen M. Stigler, "The Kelvin Dictum and Social Science: An Excursion into the History of an Idea," *Journal of the History of the Behavioral Sciences*, 20 (October 1984), 319–331.

104. Douglas Lane Patey, *Probability and Literary Form: Philosophical Theory and Lit-*

erary Practice in the Augustan Age (Cambridge: Cambridge University Press, 1984), pp. 10–12; and Jonsen and Toulmin, *Casuistry*, pp. 171–175.

105. Martha C. Nussbaum, *The Fragility of Goodness: Luck and Ethics in Greek Tragedy and Philosophy* (Cambridge: Cambridge University Press, 1986), pp. 90–98, 106–112. Also see Granville C. Henry, Jr., *Logos: Mathematics and Christian Theology* (Lewisburg: Bucknell University Press, 1976), pp. 84–88.

106. Brumbaugh, *Plato's Mathematical Imagination*, pp. 5–7. Also see A. C. Lloyd, "Procession and Division in Proclus," in *Soul and the Structure of Being in Late Neoplatonism: Syrianus, Proclus and Simplicius*, ed. H. J. Blumenthal and A. C. Lloyd (Liverpool: Liverpool University Press, 1982), p. 32.

107. Diadochus Proclus, *A Commentary on the First Book of Euclid's Elements*, trans. Glenn R. Morrow (Princeton, N.J.: Princeton University Press, 1970), p. 21. On linguistic standardization, see Louis T. Milic, "Singularity and Style in Eighteenth-Century English Prose," *Poetica*, 14 (1982), 94.

108. Proclus, *Euclid*, pp. 17–24, 106–107, 117–123; and *Das Böse (De Malorum Subsistentia)*, pp. 104–107.

109. Stigler, *History of Statistics*, pp. 63–70, 88–98.

110. William H. Kruskal, "Miracles and Statistics: The Casual Assumption of Independence," *Journal of the American Statistical Association*, 83 (December 1988), 929–940.

111. Georges Canguilhem, *La Connaissance de la vie* (Paris: Librairie Philosophique J. Vrin, 1965), p. 155.

112. William H. Kruskal and William Mosteller, "Representative Sampling, I: Non-Scientific Literature," *International Statistical Review*, XLVII (1979), 13–24. On the transmission of a theory of ideal beauty from Italy, to France, and then to England, see, Burke, *Hogarth and Reynolds*, p. 3.

113. Harcourt, "Vesalius," pp. 28, 39, 50.

114. Pietro Corsi, "Models and Analogies for the Reform of Natural History: Features of the French Debate, 1790–1800," in *Lazzaro Spallanzani e la biologia del Settecento. Teorie, esperimenti, istituzioni scientifiche*, ed. Walter Bernardi and Antonello La Vergata (Florence: Leo S. Olschki, 1982), pp. 383–394.

115. For the major French crystallographers, see my *Voyage into Substance*, pp. 299–305.

116. Félix Vicq d'Azyr and Hippolyte Cloquet, *Encyclopédie méthodique. Système anatomique. Dictionnaire raisonné des termes d'anatomie et de physiologie*, 4 vols. (Paris: Chez Mme. Veuve Agasse, 1792–1823), II, i–v. Also see Russell C. Maulitz, *Morbid Appearances: The Anatomy of Pathology in the Early Nineteenth Century* (Cambridge: Cambridge University Press, 1987), p. 227.

117. J. Schuller tot Persum-Meijer, *Petrus Camper (1722–1789). Onderzoeker van Nature*, exh. cat. (Groningen: Universiteits Museum, 1989), pp. 65–68. For Vicq d'Azyr's funeral *éloge* of Camper, delivered before Marie-Antoinette, see *Tentoonstelling ter Herdenking van den 150sten Sterbdag van Petrus Camper* (Groningen: J. B. Wolters, 1939), pp. 10–14.

118. Petrus Camper, *Oratio de mundo optimo. En Prolegomena in Philosophiam (1751)*, ed. Jacob van Sluis (Ljouwert: Fryske Akademy, 1988), pp. 11–13.

119. Hendrik Punt, *Bernard Siegfried Albinus (1697–1770). On "Human Nature." Anatomical and Physiological Ideas in Eighteenth-Century Leiden* (Amsterdam: B. M. Israël B. V., 1983), pp. 14–17.

120. Béatrice Didier, "Ledoux écrivain," in *Soufflot et l'architecture des Lumières*, Les Cahiers de la recherche architecturale, Supplément (October 1980), p. 258. Also see Anthony Vidler, *The Writing of the*

Walls: Architectural Theory in the Late Enlightenment (Princeton, N.J.: Princeton Architectural Press, 1987), p. 121, and my "Science as Fine Art: Another Look at Boullée's *Cenotaph for Newton*," *Studies in Eighteenth-Century Culture*, 11, ed. Harry C. Payne (Madison: University of Wisconsin Press, 1982), 241–278.

121. Michael Baxandall, "The Bearing of the Scientific Study of Vision on Painting in the Eighteenth Century: Pieter Camper's *De Visu* (1746)," in *The Natural Sciences and the Arts. Aspects of Interaction from the Renaissance to the Twentieth Century. An International Symposium* (Uppsala: Almquist & Wiksell International, 1985), p. 127.

122. Londa Schiebinger, "Skeletons in the Closet: The First Illustrations of the Female Skeleton in Eighteenth-Century Anatomy," *Representations*, 14 (Spring 1986), 54, 60; and James Elkins, "Two Conceptions of the Human Form: Bernard Siegfried Albinus and Andreas Vesalius," *Artibus et Historiae*, 14 (1986), 94.

123. Adrien Camper, *Description succincte du musée de Pierre Camper par son fils* (Amsterdam and The Hague: Chez Les Frères Van Cleef, 1811), pp. iii–vi. Camper's museum was established first in Kleinhankum, then moved to Franker, and finally, in 1820, was transposed to Groningen.

124. For Camper, see John L. Thornton, *Jan van Rymsdyk: Medical Artist of the Eighteenth Century* (Cambridge and New York: Oleander Press, 1982), p. 16; Hahn, Dumaitre, and Samion-Contet, *Histoire de la médecine*, pp. 287–288. For Quetelet's concept of the average man as both epitome and assemblage—formulated between 1827 and 1835—see Stigler, *Statistics*, pp. 162–169.

125. Robert Paul Willem Visser, *The Zoological Work of Petrus Camper (1722–1789)* (Amsterdam: Rodopi, 1985), pp. 96–97. On aesthetics and early-nineteenth-century racial theories, see also Hugh Honour, *The Image of the Black in Western Art. IV. From the American Revolution to World War I. 2. Black Models and White Myths* (Cambridge, Mass.: Harvard University Press, 1989), pp. 15–18.

126. Petrus Camper, *The Works of the Late Professor . . . on the Connexion between the Science of Anatomy and the Arts of Drawing, Painting, Statuary, in Two Books [in 1]* (2d ed., London: C. Dilly, 1794), trans. T. Cogan, M. D., pp. vii–xi, 2–4, 14–20. Also see Bernard Lens, *Bowles's New Preceptor in Drawing . . .* (London: Printed for Carrington Bowles, 1787), p. 5.

127. Camper, *Works*, pp. 100, 105, 114, 128–129.

128. Ibid., pp. 79–80, 95.

129. Sergio Moravia, "The Capture of the Invisible: For a (Pre)History of Psychology in Eighteenth-Century France," *Journal of the History of Behavioral Sciences*, 19 (October 1983), 372; and William F. Bynum, "The Anatomical Method: Natural Theology and the Functions of the Brain," *Isis*, 64 (September 1973), 466–468.

130. Jean-Joseph Sue, *Essai sur la physiognomie des corps vivans, considerée depuis l'homme jusqu'à la plante. Ouvrage où l'on traite principalement de la nécessité de cette étude dans les arts d'imitation, des véritables règles de la béauté et des graces, des proportions du corps humains, de l'expression, des passions, etc.* (Paris: Chez l'Auteur, 1797), pp. vii, 4–5, 52–53.

131. Ibid., pp. 17–19, 25, 182–183. Also see Proclus, *Alcibiades*, pp. 213–214, and *Euclid*, pp. 6, 14.

132. Thomas Willis, *Practice of Physick, Being the Whole Works of That Renowned and Famous Physician: Containing These Eleven Several Treatises*, trans. S. P. (London: Printed for T. Dring, C. Harper, and J. Leigh, 1684), p. 210. Also see Johann Georg Spurzheim, *The Physiognomical System of Drs. Gall and . . . , founded on Ana-*

tomical and Physiological Examination of the Nervous System in General, and of the Brain in Particular; and indicating the Dispositions and Manifestations of the Mind (2d ed., London: Baldwin, Cradock, & Joy, 1815).

133. George Cruikshank, *Phrenological Illustrations, or An Artist's View of the Craniological System of Doctor's Gall and Spurzheim* (1826; London: Republished for the Artist by Frederick Arnold, 1873), n.p. Also see Albert M. Cohn, *George Cruikshank. A Catalogue Raisonné of the Works executed during the Years 1806–1877. With Collations, Notes, Approximate Values, Facsimiles, and Illustrations* (London: From the Office of "The Bookman's Journal," 1924), p. 258.

134. John Varley, *A Treatise on Zodiacal Physiognomy; Illustrated by Engravings of Heads and Features; and accompanied by Tables of the Time of Rising of the Twelve Signs of the Zodiac; and containing also New and Astrological Explanations of Some Remarkable Portions of Ancient Mythological History* (London: author, 1828), pp. 56–57. For Blake, Varley, and the "Visionary Heads," see Corlette Rossiter Walker, *William Blake in the Art of His Time*, exh. cat. (Santa Barbara: University of California, 1976), pp. 70–73.

135. Baumgärtner, *Krankenphysiognomik*, pp. 19–21.

136. Manfred Stanley, *The Technological Conscience: Survival and Dignity in an Age of Expertise* (New York: The Free Press, London: Collier Macmillan Publishers, 1978), pp. 10–14, 141–142.

137. Gallop, *Thinking through the Body*, pp. 141–145.

138. Gary Schwarz, "Connoisseurship: The Penalty of Ahistoricism," *Artibus et Historiae*, 18 (1988), 203.

139. Rosanna Cioffi Martinelli, *La Ragione dell'arte. Teoria e critica nel Anton Raphael Mengs e Johann Joachim Winckelmann* (Naples: Liguori Editore, 1981), pp. 96–101.

140. Philip J. Pauly, *Controlling Life: Jacques Loeb and the Engineering Ideal in Biology* (New York: Oxford University Press, 1987), pp. 199–200.

141. Jane Simon, "Surgeon Sculpts New Image," *Midway*, 4 (December 1989), 59.

142. "Plastic Surgery," *Art News* (February 1989), pp. 15–16.

143. Thomas Pruzinsky, "Collaboration of Plastic Surgeon and Medical Psychotherapist: Elective Cosmetic Surgery," *Medical Psychotherapy*, 1 (1988), 9.

144. Hogarth, *Analysis of Beauty*, pp. 24–25. Also see N. Katherine Hayles, *The Cosmic Web: Scientific Field Models and Literary Strategies in the Twentieth Century* (Ithaca: Cornell University Press, 1984), pp. 70–71.

145. James L. Gibson, *The Ecological Approach to Visual Perception* (Boston: Houghton Mifflin Company, 1979), pp. 2–8, 16–17.

146. Georg Christoph Lichtenberg, *Aphorismen Auswahl*, ed. Friedrich Sengle (Stuttgart: Philipp Reclam Jun., 1966), p. 114.

147. Lavater, *Essays*, I, II, 235. On the centrality of pattern recognition to thinking, see Margolis, *Patterns*, pp. 3, 33–36.

148. Proclus, *Euclid*, p. 141. For the *flâneur* and Impressionism, see Robert L. Herbert, *Impressionism: Leisure and Parisian Society* (New Haven: Yale University Press, 1988), pp. 35–40.

149. Desan, *Naissance de la méthode*, p. 65. Also see Oscar Kenshur, *Open Form and the Shape of Ideas: Literary Structures as Representations of Philosophical Concepts in the Seventeenth and Eighteenth Centuries* (Lewisburg: Bucknell University Press, 1986), pp. 33–34.

150. Warncke, *Sprechende Bilder*, p. 225.

151. Ferdinand Dölte, "Die historische Entwicklung des Jagdrechtes in Österreich," in *Jagd Einst und Jetzt*, exh. cat. (Schloss Marchegg: Niederösterreichische Landesausstellung, 1978), pp. 43–44.

152. Ortwin Gamber, "Die Jagdwaffe vom Mittelalter bis zum Biedermeier," and Karl Michael Kisler, "Die Jagd in der Literatur," in *Jagd Einst und Jetzt*, pp. 24, 62.

153. "Chasse," in *Encyclopédie, ou Dictionnaire raisonné des sciences, des arts, et des métiers, par une société de gens de lettres mis en ordre et publié par M. Diderot; et quant à la partie mathématique, par M. D'Alembert*, 17 vols. (Paris: Chez Briasson, David l'aîné, Le Breton, Durand, 1751–1780), III, 225.

154. Ibid., pp. 224–227.

155. M. Leroi, "Vénerie," *Encyclopédie*, XVI, 916, 920–922.

156. Ibid., p. 924.

157. Plato, *Sophist* 218d–223c; *Theatetus* 222b–223b.

158. James Parsons, *Human Physiognomy Explain'd: In the Crounian Lectures on Muscular Motion. For the Year MDCCXLVI. Read before the Royal Society. Being a Supplement to the Philosophical Transactions for That Year* (London: printed for C. Davis, 1747), pp. 1–11, 32–37, 43. On Parsons see Shearer West, "Polemic and the Passions: Dr. James Parsons' *Human Physiognomy Explained* and Hogarth's Aspirations for British History Painting," *British Journal for Eighteenth-Century Studies*, 13 (Spring 1990), 73–90.

159. Parsons, *Human Physiognomy*, pp. 46–47, 73–74. Also see Oliver Sacks, *The Man Who Mistook His Wife for a Hat and Other Clinical Tales*, pp. 77–78.

160. Georg Christoph Lichtenberg, *Über Physiognomik, wider die Physiognomen. Zu Beförderung der Menschenliebe und Menschenkenntniss* (Steinbach: Anabas Verlag Günter Kämpf, 1970), pp. 20–22. Also see *Tag und Dämmerung. Aphorismen, Schriften, Briefe, Tagebücher* (Leipzig: In der Dieterich'schen Verlagsbuchhandlung, 1941), p. 273.

161. Gibson, *Ecological Perception*, pp. 23–28.

162. Lavater, *Essays*, II,I, 44.

163. Lichtenberg, *Über Physiognomik*, pp. 23–25, 29–30.

164. Ibid., pp. 22–23.

165. Ibid., pp. 58–63.

166. Claude-Henri Watelet, *L'Art de peindre. Poëme avec des réflexions sur les différentes parties de la peinture* (Amsterdam: Aux dépens de la Compagnie, 1761), pp. 40, 161. Also see the censure of the Epicureans (Zeno, late 2nd–early 1st century BC) for their discrediting of geometry in Proclus, *Euclid*, p. 156.

167. Jean-René Gaborit, *Jean-Baptiste Pigalle (1714–1785). Sculptures au Musée du Louvre* (Paris: Editions de la Réunion des Musées Nationaux, 1985), pp. 72–74.

168. Lichtenberg, *Über Physiognomik*, pp. 33–35, 37–40.

169. Lichtenberg, *Tag und Dämmerung*, p. 269. Also see James Caulfield, *Portraits. Memoirs and Characters of Remarkable Persons, from the Revolution in 1688 to the End of the Reign of George II. Collected from the Most Authentic Accounts Extant*, 4 vols. (London: H. R. Young and T. H. Whitely, 1819), I, 121–123. On Hogarth's humorous account of life in the urban world, see Sean Shesgreen, *Hogarth and the Times-of-the-Day Tradition* (Ithaca: Cornell University Press, 1983), pp. 133–134.

170. David Kunzle, "Goethe and Caricature: From Hogarth to Töpffer," *Journal of the Warburg and Courtauld Institutes*, 48 (1985), 166–167.

171. Georg Christoph Lichtenberg, *Hogarth on High Life: The Marriage à la Mode Series from . . . Commentaries*, trans. and ed. Arthur S. Wensinger with W. B. Coley (Middletown, Conn.: Wesleyan University Press, 1970), pp. 10–11, 46.

2 ABSTRACTING

1. Raymond D. Havens, "Simplicity, a Changing Concept," *Journal of the History of Ideas*, 14 (January 1953), 4.

2. Vladimir Lossky, *The Mythical Theology of the Eastern Church* (Crestwood, N.Y.: St. Vladimir's Seminary Press, 1976), pp. 28–30. Also see Giancarlo Maiorino, "The Legend of Geometry Fulfilled: Abstraction and the Denaturalization of Matter in the Paintings of Piero della Francesca and Piet Mondrian," *Gazette des Beaux-Arts*, 107 (March 1986), 111–117. For the importance of the diagrammatic to computer graphics, see Aaron Marcus, "Diagrammatic Visible Language: An Investigation of Visual Logic," *Leonardo*, 20, no. 1 (1987), 9–16.

3. John E. Bowlt, "H_2SO_4: Dada in Russia," in *Dada/Dimensions*, ed. Stephen C. Foster (Ann Arbor: UMI Research Press, 1986), pp. 234–236; and Yve-Alain Bois, "Malevitch, le carré, le dégré zéro," *Macula*, 1 (1976), 28–40. For a theological analysis of the dualism that divides man into soul and body, see Paul Ricoeur, *The Symbolism of Evil* (New York: Harper & Row Publishers, 1967), pp. 279–285.

4. On rhetoric, see Ernesto Grassi, *Die Macht der Phantasie. Zur Geschichte abendländische Denkens* (Königstein/ TS: Athenäum, 1979), p. 164. For the need to supplant philosophy with it, see Larry R. Churchill, "Bioethical Reductionism and Our Sense of the Human," *Man and Medicine*, 5, no. 4 (1980), 230.

5. Henry, *Mathematics*, pp. 90–92, 98–100, 154–159.

6. René Descartes, *Discourse on Method* (1637), trans. John Veitch (Chicago: Open Court Press, 1962), pp. 3,7; Chambers, *Cyclopaedia*, II, "method/methodus." On the importance of method see A. I. Sabra, *Theories of Light from Descartes to Newton* (Cambridge: Cambridge University Press, 1981), p. 25; Peter A. Schouls, *The Imposition of Method: A Study of Descartes and Locke* (Oxford: Clarendon Press, 1980), pp. 5–6; and Caton, *Origin of Subjectivity*, p. 35.

7. Chambers, *Cyclopaedia*, I, "abstract, abstraction"; and Thomas Corneille, *Le Dictionnaire des arts et des sciences*, 2 vols. (Paris: Chez Rollin père, 1732), I, 5. On abstraction as radical reduction, see Hilary Gatti, "Minimum and Maximum, Finite and Infinite: Bruno and the Northumberland Circle," *Journal of the History of Ideas*, 48 (1985), 152–153; and Nelson Goodman, *Problems and Projects* (Indianapolis: Bobbs-Merrill, 1972), pp. 279–281.

8. Thomas Whittaker, *Neo-Platonists* (Hildesheim: Olm, 1970), p. 266; and Julius Weinberg, "Abstraction in the Formation of Concepts," *Dictionary of the History of Ideas*, 5 vols. (New York: Scribners, 1973–1974), I, 1–9.

9. Boethius, *The Theological Tractates*, trans. H. F. Stewart and E. K. Rand (London: William Heinemann, 1936), pp. 11–19, 34–35, 43–51.

10. Gottfried Wilhelm Freiherr von Leibniz, *New Essays (1765)*, trans. Alfred Langley (LaSalle, Ill.: Open Court Publishing Company, 1949), pp. 27, 277–278, 498, 728.

11. George Campbell, *Of the Philosophy of Rhetoric*, 2 vols. (London: W. Strahan and T. Cadell; Edinburgh: W. Creech, 1776), II, 105–107, 119–120. Campbell cites Locke's *Essay*, 2.11,10, and 4.7,9.

12. Carl Friedrich Flögels, *Einleitung in die Erfindungskunst* (Breslau and Leipzig: Bey Johann Ernst Meyer, 1760), pp. 363–365, 370–381.

13. William Wotton, *Reflections upon Ancient and Modern Learning* (London: Printed by J. Leake, 1694), pp. 300–301; and Shafestbury, *Characteristics*, II, 211–213, 313–314.

14. John Dennis, *The Grounds of Criticism in Poetry, Contain'd in Some New Discoveries never made before requisite for the Writing and*

Judging of Poems Surely (London: George Straham, 1704), p. 5; and Jean-Pierre de Crousaz, *Traité du beau, où l'on montre en quoi consiste ce que l'on nomme ainsi, par des exemples tirez de la plûpart des arts & des sciences* (Amsterdam: Chez François l'Honoré, 1715), pp. 99–101, 162–164. Also see his *Commentaire sur l'analyse des infiniment petits* (Paris: Chez Montalembert, 1721), pp. 1–4, 15.

15. Richardson, *Theory of Painting*, pp. 12–15, 31, 35, 49.

16. Fuseli, *Lectures*, pp. 7, 18. For the Neoclassical identification of painting with writing and a universal grammar, see my *Symbol and Myth*, pp. 133–153.

17. R. M. Pariset, *Nouveau livre des principes de dessein recueilli des études des meilleures maîtres tant anciens que modernes, & dirigé par . . .* (Paris: Chez L. Surugue, n.d.), n.p.; William Austin, *A Specimen of sketching Landscapes, In a Free and Masterly Manner, with a Pen or Pencil; Exemplified in Thirty Etchings, done from Original Drawings of Lucatelli, after the Life, in and about Rome* (London: Author, n.d.), pp. 3–4; and Hoet, *Principaux du dessein*, n.p.

18. James Beattie, *Dissertations Moral and Critical* (London: Printed for W. Strahan and T. Cadell, 1783), pp. 26–27, 103. George Bickham Senior was prolific. See his *The British Youth's Instructor; or, the Useful Penman. A New Copybook, Containing Alphabets and Sentences in Round Text, Large and Small, Round Hand, and Running Hand; An Abstract of the Theory of Writing, Initial Letters, Struck Capitals, and Other Curious Decorations. Written by Several of the Best Masters and Engraved by . . . Designed for the Use of Schools and Families* (London: Robert Sayer, 1754), pp. 4–6; *The Universal Penman; or the Art of Writing made useful to the Gentleman and Scholar, as well as the Man of Business* (London: Printed for the Author, 1741), pp. 13, 81–82, 112; and *The Art of Writing, In Its Theory and Practice by Charles Snell Writing Master at the Free Writing School in Forster-Lane, London, and Engraved by . . .* (London: Henry Overton, 1772), pp. 6–7, 11.

19. Beattie, *Dissertations*, pp. 8, 46.

20. See, for example, such manuals as: *The Proportions of the Human Body, Measured from the Most Beautiful Antique Statues; by Monsieur Audran, Engraver to the Late King of France. Done from the Originals, Engraved at Paris* (12th ed., London: Printed for Bowles and Carver, n.d.), preface; Saint-Igny, *Elémens de pourtraiture, ou la méthode de représenter toutes les parties du corps humain* (Paris: Chez François l'Anglois, n.d.), pls. pp. 3, 4, 17; and Gabriel Smith, *The School of Art; or the Most Complete Drawing-Book extant: Consisting of an Extensive Series of Well-Chosen Examples, selected from the Designs of Those Eminent Masters Watteau, Boucher, Bouchardon, Le Brun, Eisen, etc. Engraved on Sixty Folio Copper Plates in the Chalk Manner* (London: Printed for John Bowles 1765), pp. 1–2.

21. Richardson, *Art of Criticism*, p. 157; Reynolds, *Discourses*, p. 170; Mengs, *Hinterlassene Schriften*, pp. 145, 202, 210, and *Réflexions sur la beauté*, in *Oeuvres complètes d'Antoine-Raphaël Mengs*, trans. from the Italian, 2 vols. (Paris: à l'Hôtel de Thou, 1786), I, 82. On *idea*, see also Anne D. R. Sheppard, *Studies on the 5th and 6th Essays of Proclus' Commentary on the Republic* (Göttingen: Vandenhoeck and Ruprecht, 1980), pp. 129–130.

22. Chambers, *Cyclopaedia*, I, "criticism"; *Encyclopaedia Britannica*, I, 292. Also see Gerard de Lairesse, *The Art of Painting in All Its Branches, Methodically demonstrated by Discourses and Plates, and Exemplified by Remarks on the Painting of the Best Master*, trans. Frederick Fritsch (London: Printed for S. Vandenbergh; Messrs. Payne, White, Robson and Co., Walter, and Sewell, 1778), pp. 102–104; Laugier, *Manière de bien juger*, pp. 10, 16; and *The Works in Architecture of Robert and James Adam* (1773), ed. Robert Oresko, 3 vols. (London: Academy Editions; New York: St. Martin's Press, 1975), I, 46. On Goya's critique of corrective criticism, see Hubert Damisch, "L'Art de Goya et les contradictions de l'esprit de Lumières," in *Utopie et institutions au XVIIIe siècle, le pragmatisme des Lumières*, ed. Pierre Francastel (Paris and the Hague: Mouton, 1963), pp. 248–257.

23. Richardson, *Science of a Connoisseur*, p. 219. On the importance of manuals of instruction, see Dominique Julia, "Livres de classe et usages pédagogiques," and Alain-Marie Bassy, "Le texte et l'image," in *Histoire de l'édition française*, ed. Roger Chartier and Henri-Jean Martin (Paris: Promodis, 1984), II, 148–153, 468–497.

24. Bruno Jammes, "Le livre de science," in *L'Edition française*, pp. 211–215; and Bassy, "Le texte et l'image," p. 149. On the collision between strongly iconic and strongly iconoclastic impulses, see Ernest B. Gilman, *Iconoclasm and Poetry in the English Reformation* (Chicago: University of Chicago Press, 1986), p. 27.

25. Ulrich Dierse, *Enzyklopädie. Zur Geschichte eines philosophischen und wissenschaftstheoretischen Begriffs* (Bonn: Bourvier Verlag Herbert Grundmann, 1977), pp. 22–26, 53–56.

26. John Harris, *Lexicon Technicum: or an Universal English Dictionary of Arts and Sciences: Explaining not only the Terms of Art, but the Arts Themselves*, 2 vols. (London: D. Brown, 1704), I, preface.

27. See especially Carol Shammas, "Changes in Consumer Demand in Early Modern England and America"; John Styles, "Implementing Visual Design in Eighteenth-Century English Manufactures"; and Lorna Weatherill, "Patterns of Consumption in Britain, c. 1660–1760," in *Culture and Consumption: The World of Goods*, ed. Roy Porter and John Brewer (London: Routledge, 1990).

28. Chambers, *Cyclopaedia*, I, preface; "anatomy." On the increasingly divergent pictorial and geometrical strands in per- spective science, see Martin Kemp, "Simon Stevin and Pieter Saenredam: A Study of Mathematics and Vision in Dutch Science and Art," *Art Bulletin*, 68 (June 1986), 238–239.

29. *The Commentaries of Proclus on the Timaeus of Plato: Containing a Treasury of Pythagoric and Platonic Physiology, Translated from the Greek, by Thomas Taylor*, 2 vols. in 1 (London: printed for and sold by the author, 1820), II, 332. Also see Proclus, *Commentary on Euclid*, 37, 43. On the influence of Proclus's theory of geometrical figuration on eighteenth-century philosophers such as Berkeley and Leibniz, see Evanghélos Moutsopoulos, *Les structures de l'imaginaire dans la philosophie de Proclus* (Paris: Société d'Edition "Les Belles Lettres," 1985), p. 59.

30. Proclus, *Commentary on Euclid*, p. 71. Also see Aristotle, *Poetics* 1450a35–1450b.

31. Proclus, *Alcibiades*, pp. 36, 40, 55–57; *Timaeus*, p. 287.

32. Kim Sloan, *Alexander and John Robert Cozens: The Poetry of Landscape* (New Haven: Yale University Press, 1986), pp. 31, 40, 66–68; and "A New Chronology for Alexander Cozens. Part I: 1717–1759," *Burlington*, 127 (February 1985), 70–75.

33. Alexander Cozens, *Principles of Beauty Relative to the Human Head* (London: Printed by James Dixwell, 1778), pp. 1–3, 7–10. On cartographic methods as forms of spatial summarization, see Mark Monmonier and George A. Schnell, *Map Appreciation* (Englewood Cliffs, N.J.: Prentice Hall, 1988), pp. 3–4, 73, 109; and David J. Cuff and Mark T. Mattson, *Thematic Maps: Their Design and Production* (New York and London: Methuen, 1982), pp. 3, 10–14.

34. Cozens, *Principles of Beauty*, p. 9. Also see Jean-Michel Maulpoix, "Eloge de la ponctuation," and Louis Marin, "Ponctuation," in *Traverses*, 43 (February 1988), 105, 19–21.

35. Cozens, *Principles of Beauty*, p. 9; Fuseli, *Lectures on Painting*, pp. 41, 75–76; and Franciscus Junius, *The Painting of the Ancients in Three Books: Declaring by Historical Observations and Examples, the Beginning, Progresse, and Consummation of That Most Noble Art, And How Those Ancient Artificers attained to Their still so much admired Excellencie*, trans. from the Latin (London: Printed by Richard Hodgkinsonne, 1638), pp. 7, 280–281. The recent exhibition *The Spiritual in Art: Abstract Painting 1890–1985*, curated by Maurice Tuchman, reminded the viewer of the persistence of the diagram in past and present occult art (exh. cat., Los Angeles County Museum, 1987, pp. 89–91).

36. Lavater, *Règles physiognomiques, ou observations sur quelques traits caractéristiques* (The Hague and Paris: Chez I. van Cleef et A. A. Renouard, 1803), pp. 61, 73. On the logocentric illusion, see Hubert Damisch, *Ruptures cultures* (Paris: Les Editions de Minuit, 1976), pp. 134–135.

37. Gibson, *Ecological Approach*, pp. 79, 198–199.

38. Reynolds, *Discourses*, pp. 151–152; and Richardson, *Science of a Connoisseur*, p. 190.

39. Oldmixon, *Essay on Criticism*, pp. 36–38; Bouhours, *La manière de bien penser*, pp. 166–167, 325; and Bernard Le Bovier de Fontenelle, *Nouveaux dialogues des morts* (1683), ed. Jean Dagen (Paris: Librairie Marcel Didier, 1971), pp. 122–125.

40. Sander L. Gilman, *Seeing the Insane: A Cultural History of Madness and Art in the Western World* (New York: John Wiley & Sons and Brunner/Mazel Publishers, 1982), pp. 41–42. On Gillray, see the catalogue of the exhibition *James Gillray (1756–1815): Drawings and Caricatures* (London: Arts Council of Great Britain, 1967); and especially *The Satirical Etchings of James Gillray*, ed. Draper Hill (New York: Dover Publications, 1976).

41. Antoine Le Camus, *Médecine de l'esprit: où l'on traite des dispositions & des causes physiques qui en conséque l'union de l'âme avec le corps, influent sur les opérations de l'esprit; & des moyens de maintenir ces opérations dans un bon état, ou de les corriger lorsqu'elles sont viciées*, 2 vols. (Paris: Chez Ganeau, 1753), p. 51; Jérôme Richard, *La Théorie des songes* (Paris: Chez les Frères Estienne, 1766), pp. 230–235; and Lodovigo Antonio Muratori, *Della forza della fantasia umana trattato* (Venice: Presso Giambattista Pasquali, 1745), pp. 172–173, 241.

42. Beattie, *Dissertations*, p. 18; and Sticotti, *Dictionnaire*, III, 419.

43. Cozens, *Principles of Beauty*, pp. 7–8; Bouhours, *Manière de bien penser*, pp. 167, 197–198. On the artist's personal accent imprinting his work, see Dandré-Bardon, *Traité de peinture*, pp. 23–24.

44. Bevan, *Holy Images*, p. 145.

45. Bouhours, *Manière de bien penser*, pp. 156, 230–233; Watelet, *Réflexions sur la peinture*, p. 95; and Dandré-Bardon, *Traité de peinture*, p. 105. For Winckelmann's critique of false sentiments or affectations, see Johann Joachim Winckelmann, *On the Imitation of the Painting and Sculpture of the Greeks* (1755), in *Winckelmann: Writings on Art*, ed. David Irwin (London: Phaidon, 1972), pp. 72–73.

46. Winckelmann, *Empfindung des Schönen*, pp. 5–6, 12–15. On Winckelmann's watery metaphors, see my "Beauty of the Invisible, Winckelmann and the Aesthetics of Imperceptibility," *Zeitschrift für Kunstgeschichte*, 43 (1980), 65–77.

47. On the medical characteristics of water drinkers, see Le Camus, *Médecine de l'esprit*, I, 332. Dubos, *Réflexions critiques*, II, 264–267, spoke at length of the unhealthiness of modern Rome. For the foulness of eighteenth-century water supplies, see Guy Williams, *The Age of Agony: The Art of Healing c. 1700–1800* (London: Constable, 1975), pp. 139–141. For William Heath's (1795–1846) satire on the contamination of the Thames's water supply, see Carl Zigrosser, *Medicine and the Artist: One Hundred and Thirty Seven Great Prints selected with Commentary* (New York: Dover, 1969), pp. 156–157.

48. Delcourt, *Hermaphrodite*, pp. 50, 53–54. On the rebellious psychology associated with ideological nudity (i.e., the desire to be free to wear only the thinnest and lightest kinds of clothes), see also J. C. Flugel, *The Psychology of Clothes* (London: The Hogarth Press Ltd. and the Institute of Psycho-Analysis, 1950), pp. 87, 91–93.

49. On real hermaphrodites, see l'Abbé de La Chau and l'Abbé Le Blond, *Description des principales pierres gravées du Cabinet de S.A.S. Monsieur le Duc d'Orléans, Premier Prince du Sang*, 2 vols. (Paris: Chez Chau et Le Blond, 1780), I, 107–110. On the look and role of the castrato in Roman society, see Franca Trinchier Camiz, "The *Castrato* Singer: From Informal to Formal Portraiture," *Artibus et Asiae*, 18 (1988), 183.

50. Garengeot, *Traité des opérations*, I, 5–8.

51. Chambers, *Cyclopaedia*, II, "suture."

52. Jean-Jacques Paulet, *Histoire de la petite vérole, avec les moyens d'en préserver les enfans et d'en arrêter la contagion en France*, 2 vols. (Paris: Chez Ganeau, 1768), I, 209; Lichtenberg, *Tag und Dämmerung*, p. 279; Anthony Ashley Cooper, Lord Shaftesbury, *The life, Unpublished Letters, and Philosophical Regimen*, ed. Benjamin Rand (Folcroft, Pa.: Folcroft Library Editions, 1977), p. 165; Joseph Trapp, *Lectures on Poetry Read in the Schools of Natural Philosophy at Oxford*, trans. from the Latin (London: Printed for C. Hitch and C. Davis, 1742), pp. 261–262; and Mengs, *Hinterlassene Schiften*, II, 161.

53. I. B. Cohen, *The Newtonian Revolution, with Illustrations of the Transformation of Scientific Ideas* (Cambridge: Cambridge University Press, 1980), pp. 40–41.

54. Locher, *Zwingli's Thought*, p. 207; and Ricoeur, *Symbolism of Evil*, p. 70. Also see Paul Ricoeur on original sin in *The Conflict of Interpretations: Essays in Hermeneutics* (Evanston: Northwestern University Press, 1974), pp. 269–286.

55. Diderot, *Interprétation de la nature*, pp. 6, 18–19, 23–24, 42–43.

56. Note the nonalphabetical and pell-mell treatment of material in Francis Bacon, *Sylva Sylvarum: or A Natural History. In Ten Centuries. Whereunto is newly added the History naturall and Experimentall of Life and Death, or of the Prolongation of Life* (6th ed., London: Printed by J. F. for William Lee, 1651). On rhetoric and the empirical, see Michael Mooney, *Vico in the Tradition of Rhetoric* (Princeton: Princeton University Press, 1985), p. 10.

57. Chambers, *Cyclopaedia*, I, "empiric," "experience."

58. Joseph M. Levine, *Humanism and History: Origins of Modern English Historiography* (Ithaca and London: Cornell University Press, 1987), pp. 100–105, 184–185.

59. Pierre Bayle, *Dictionnaire historique et critique*, 4 vols. (3d rev. and aug. ed., Rotterdam: Chez Michel Bohm, 1720), I, ii. This edition was dedicated to the Duc d'Orléans.

60. Bayle, *Dictionnaire*, I, vi; and Chambers, *Cyclopaedia*, I, "criterium/criterion," "criticism." Also see Giuseppi Bartoli (1717–1788), "Dictionnaire des arts et des sciences" (ca. 1746; manuscript, Resource Collections of the Getty Center for the History of Art and the Humanities), "critique."

61. Chambers, *Cyclopaedia*, II, "polymathy"; and Caylus, *Recueil d'antiquités*, I, iii–viii. Also see Joseph Spence, *Polymetis: or, an Enquiry concerning the Agreement between the Works of the Roman Poets, and the Remains of the Ancient Artists. Being an Attempt to illustrate Them Mutually from One Another* (2d rev. ed., London: Printed for R. and J. Dodsley, 1755), p. 287.

62. Bayle, *Dictionnaire*, IV, 3011–3016.

63. Diderot and D'Alembert, *Encyclopédie*, V, 271; and Chambers, *Cyclopaedia*, I, "eclectic." On the connection between syncretism and polytheism, see Erik Hornung, *Conceptions of God in Ancient Egypt: The One and the Many* (Ithaca: Cornell University Press, 1982), pp. 91–99.

64. Chambers, *Cyclopaedia*, I, "compendium."

65. Chambers, *Cyclopaedia*, I, "encyclopaedia"; and *Encyclopaedia Britannica*, I, preface.

66. Harris, *Lexicon Technicum*, II, introduction. On the problems inherent in alphabetical ordering, see Kenshur, *Open Form*, pp. 107–108, 122–123; and Wilda C. Anderson, *Between the Library and the Laboratory: The Language of Chemistry in Eighteenth-Century France* (Baltimore: Johns Hopkins University Press, 1984), pp. 43–45.

67. Giovanni Battista Piranesi, *Lapides Capitolini sive fasti Consulares Triumphales Q Romanorum ab Urbe condita usque ad Tiberium Caesarem* (Rome: author, 1761). The dedication was to Clement XIII. Piranesi appears to have been aware of Etruscan cinerary urns that deliberately detached narrative bits from mythic cycles, and of the Roman practice of breaking up the narrative line in post-Trajanic friezes. See Brilliant, *Visual Narratives*, pp. 20–22, 37–41. For the literary habit of stealing fragments and piecing together compositions, see Thomas M. Greene, *The Light in Troy: Imitation and Discovery in Renaissance Poetry* (New Haven: Yale University Press, 1982), pp. 174–177, 297.

68. Giovanni Battista Piranesi, *The Polemical Works. Rome 1757, 1761, 1765, 1769*, ed. John Wilton-Ely (Westmead: Gregg International Publishers, 1972), pp. 5–12, 33–35. Also see Trapp, *Lectures on Poetry*, pp. 220–221. Significantly, Piranesi's compatriot Giambattista Vico conceived of the *ingenium* as a similar "satiric" faculty for collecting and grasping as opposed to deducing. See Ernesto Grassi, *Rhetoric as Philosophy: The Humanist Tradition* (University Park: Pennsylvania State University Press, 1980), p. 45.

69. On eighteenth-century restoration practices, see Seymour Howard, *Bartolomeo Cavaceppi, Eighteenth-Century Restorer* (New York and London: Garland Publishers, 1982), pp. 147, 215, 244. On Piranesi's method of taking unprepossessing fragments and arranging them in aesthetically pleasing compositions, without sacrificing scholarly information, see John Wilton-Ely, "Piranesi and the Role of the Archaeological Illustration," in *Piranesi e la cultura antiquaria. Gli antecedenti e il contesto*, Atti di Convegno 14–17 novembre 1979 (Rome: Multigrafica Editrice, 1983), p. 318.

70. Piranesi's etchings are a form of social interaction and operate in the manner of open-ended interviews. See Seymour Sudiman and Norman Bradburn, *Asking Questions* (San Francisco: Jossey-Bass Publishers, 1983), pp. 7–9.

71. Robert G. Colodny, *Logic, Laws & Life: Some Philosophical Complications* (Pittsburgh, Pa.: University of Pittsburgh Press, 1977), pp. 107–109. Also see Julia Kristeva, *Histoires d'amour* (Paris: Denöel, 1983), pp. 278–279.

72. Pernety, *Maladies de l'âme*, pp. 10–12. For the connection between *sangfroid* and geometry, see Crousaz, *Traité du beau*, pp. 11–14.

73. Origen, *Homilies on Exodus*, pp. 367–369; and Proclus, *Über das Böse*, p. 109.

74. Proclus, *Alcibiades*, p. 100; and Pernety, *Maladies de l'âme*, p. 13. On the chromatic language of Democritus, see Eva Keuls, *Plato and Greek Painting* (Leiden: E. J. Brill, 1978), pp. 82–83. On intarsia and *pietre dure*, see Celestine Dars, *Images of Deception: The Art of Trompe-l'Oeil* (Oxford: Phaidon, 1979), pp. 16–17, 46.

75. Victor Anthony Rudowski, "Lessing *contra* Winckelmann," *Journal of Aesthetics and Art Criticism*, 44 (Spring 1986), 235–237; and Martinelli, *Mengs e Winckelmann*, pp. 139–141.

76. Gotthold Ephraim Lessing, *Laocoön: An Essay on the Limits of Painting and Poetry*, trans. Edward Allen McCormick (Baltimore: Johns Hopkins University Press, 1984), pp. 8–10, 17–20, 128.

77. Ibid., pp. 24–26, 95, 130–135. Also see Dandré-Bardon, *Traité de peinture*, p. 156.

78. Regine Reynolds Cornell, "Silence as a Rhetorical Device in Marguerite de Navarre's *Theatre profane*," *The Sixteenth Century Journal*, 17 (Spring 1986), 30. On Job, see Paul Ricoeur, *Essays on Biblical Interpretation*, ed. Lewis S. Mudge (Philadelphia, Pa.: Fortress Press, 1980), pp. 86–87.

79. Christian Ludwig von Hagedorn, *Réflexions sur la peinture*, trans. M. Huber, 2 vols. (Leipzig: Chez Gaspar Fritsch, 1775), I, 105–108, 111–117. Also see Charles Batteux, *Principes de la littérature. I: Traité. Les beaux-arts réduits en général, ou les beaux-arts réduits d'un même principe* (1747; Paris: Chez Desaint & Saillant, 1764), p. 90.

80. Barolsky, *Infinite Jest*, p. 9.

81. Oliver Sacks, *A Leg to Stand On* (New York: Summit Books, 1984), pp. 210–211.

82. Gibson, *Ecological Approach*, p. 184.

83. Lessing, *Laocoön*, pp. 13–14; Hagedorn, *Réflexions*, p. 93; Sulzer, *Allgemeine Theorie*, I, I, 414–415. On the eucharistic metaphor of imperial, incorruptible substance versus corruptible flesh, see Louis Marin, *La Parole mangée et autres essais théologico-politiques* (Paris: Méridiens Klincksieck, 1986), p. 227; and Redondi, *Galileo Heretic*, pp. 207–212. On the medieval diagramming of disease, see *Medieval Medical Miniatures* (Austin: University of Texas Press, 1984), p. 52.

84. On the development of caricature in Britain, see *James Gillray*, p. 5; and Ronald Paulson, "The Severed Head: The Impact of French Revolutionary Caricatures on England," in *French Caricature and the French Revolution, 1789–1799*, ed. James Cuno, exh. cat. (Los Angeles: UCLA, 1988), pp. 56–58. On the literary process of reification, see Stephen A. Barney, *Allegories of History, Allegories of Love* (Hamden, Conn.: Archon Books, 1979), pp. 34–37.

85. David Hume, *A Treatise of Human Nature, Reprinted from the Original Edition in Three Volumes*, ed. L. A. Selby-Bigge (1739; Oxford: Clarendon Press, 1967), pp. 287, 276, 319. Also see Beattie, *Dissertations*, p. 125, on the unpleasant ideas occasioned by the sight of a person crippled with gout, old age, labor, corpulency.

86. Gian Biagio Conte, *The Rhetoric of Imitation: Genre and Poetic Memory in Virgil and Other Latin Poets*, trans. Charles Segal (Ithaca: Cornell University Press, 1986), pp. 23, 47, 150. Also see A. MacC. Armstrong, "The Idea of the Comic," *British Journal of Aesthetics*, 25 (Summer 1985), 5–6.

87. James Beattie, *Essays. On the Nature and Immutability of Truth, in Opposition to Sophistry. On Poetry and Music, as They affect the Mind, on Laughter, and Ludicrous Compositions. On the Utility of Learning* (Edinburgh: Printed for William Creech, 1776), p. 262.

88. Paul-Henry Thomas, Baron D'Holbach, *Système de la nature ou des lois du monde physique et du monde moral* (1769), ed. and rev. by Diderot, 2 vols. (Hildesheim: Georg Olms Verlag, 1966), I, 115, 132–133; and Albrecht von Haller, *A Dissertation on the Sensible and Irritable Parts of Animals*, trans. M. Tissot (London: J. Nourse, 1755), p. 4. Also see Le Camus, *Médecine de l'esprit*, II, 111–112, 203.

89. Denis Diderot, *Eléments de physiologie* (1778), ed. Jean Mayer (Paris: Librairie Marcel Didier, 1964), p. 230.

90. On the techniques of allegory, see Barney, *Allegories of History*, pp. 40, 48; Smeed, *Theophrastan "Character,"* pp. 5, 10; and Jean-Pierre Mileur, *Vision and Revision: Coleridge's Art of Immanence* (Berkeley and Los Angeles: University of California Press, 1982), p. 20. On fetishes and theurgy, see Bernard Frischer, *The Sculpted Word: Epicureanism and Philosophical Recruitment in Ancient Greece* (Berkeley and Los Angeles: University of California Press, 1982), pp. 17–111. On Dubuffet, see Hubert Damisch, *Fenêtre jaune cadmium. Ou les dessous de la peinture* (Paris: Editions du Seuil, 1984), pp. 108–111.

91. Louis Poinsinet de Sivry, *Traité des causes physiques et morales du rire relativement à l'art de l'exciter* (Amsterdam: Marc-Michel Rey, 1768), pp. 19, 75.

92. George Young, *A Treatise on Opium, Founded upon Practical Observations* (London: Printed for A. Millar, 1753), pp. 19, 25, 132; Haller, *Sensible and Irritable Parts*, p. xiv; and Pernety, *Maladies de l'âme*, pp. 157, 185. Also see Aletha Hayter, *Opium and the Romantic Imagination* (Berkeley and Los Angeles: University of California Press, 1970), pp. 27–28.

93. Le Camus, *Medécine de l'esprit*, pp. 66–67. Also see Willis, *Practice of Physick*, pp. 153, 180–181.

94. Robert Burton, *The Anatomy of Melancholy. What It is, with All the Kinds, Causes, Symptoms, Prognostickes, & Severall Cures of It. In Three Partitions with Their Severall Sections, Members & Subsections* (7th ed., London: Printed for John Garway, 1660), pp. 11–12, 166, 187.

95. On seventeenth-century definitions of insanity, see, Michael MacDonald, *Mystical Bedlam. Madness, Anxiety, and Healing in Seventeenth-Century England* (Cambridge: Cambridge University Press, 1981), pp. 23–25.

96. Laurentius Bellini, *A Mechanical Account of Fevers*, trans. into English (London: Printed for A. Bell, J. Senex, W. Taylor, J. Osborn, 1720), pp. 21, 32–33.

97. Vogt, *Das Bild des Kranken*, p. 331. On the troops of spirits unleashed by dreams, see also Willis, *Practice of Physick*, pp. 94, 148.

98. Chambers, *Cyclopaedia*, II, "marbled paper." Also see C. W. Woolnough, *The Art of Marbling, as applied to Book Edges and Paper. Containing Full Instructions for Executing British, French, Spanish, Italian, Nonpareil, etc. Illustrated with Specimens. With a Brief Notice of Its Recent Application to Textile Fabrics, and Particularly to the Cloths so Extensively used by Book Binders* (London: Alexander Heylin, 1853), pp. 9–10.

99. Peter J. de Voogd, "Laurence Sterne, the Marbled Page, and 'the Use of Accidents,'" *Word & Image*, 1 (July-September 1985), 280.

100. Roger Chartier, ed., *A History of Private Life*, III: *Passions of the Renaissance*, trans. Arthur Goldhammer (Cambridge, Mass.: Harvard University, Belknap Press, 1989).

101. Mark C. Taylor, *Erring: A Postmodern A/Theology* (Chicago: University of Chicago Press, 1985), pp. 11–12.

102. Ricoeur, *Symbolism of Evil*, pp. 72–73, 313. Also see Moutsoupoulos, *L'Imaginaire dans Proclus*, pp. 142–143, 146–147.

103. Henri-Charles Puech, *Sur le manichéisme et autres essais* (Paris: Flammarion, 1979), pp. 64, 120–121, 286.

104. Tertullian, *Treatises on Marriage and Remarriage. To His Wife (Ad Uxorum). An Exhortation to Chastity (De Exhortatione Castitatis). Monogamy (De Monogamia)* (212/213 AD), trans. and annotated by William P. Le Saint (Westminster, Md.: The Newman Press, 1951), p. 10. On the additive method, see Umberto Eco, "Un art d'oublier. Est-il concevable?" *Traverses*, 40 (April 1987), 133–134.

105. Françoise Teynac, Pierre Nolot, and Jean-Denis Vivien, *Wallpaper: A History* (New York: Rizzoli, 1982), pp. 21–22; and

Albert Haemmerle and Olga Hirsch, *Buntpapier, Herkommen, Geschichte, Techniken, Beziehungen zur Kunst* (Munich: Verlag Georg D. W. Callwey, 1961), pp. 13–16. Also see Adam, *Works*, I, 47; and Damie Stillman, *The Decorative Work of Robert Adam* (London: Academy Editions; New York: St. Martin's Press, 1973), p. 16.

106. John Trusler, *Principles of Politeness and of Knowing the World, by the Late Lord Chesterfield. Methodised and Digested under Distinct Heads, with Additions by the Rev. Dr. . . . : Containing Every Instruction Necessary to complete the Gentleman and Man of Fashion: to teach him a Knowledge of Life, and make him well-received in All Countries* (Portsmouth, N.H.: Printed by Melcher and Osborn, 1786). I am deeply grateful to Dr. M. Mirjam Foot of the British Library, who not only showed me that institution's unparalleled collection of decorated papers but located this example of overprinting for me. Such examples are rare not because they were atypical, but because it was in the very nature of books to be rebound. See her "The Olga Hirsch Collection of Decorated Paper," *British Library Journal*, 7 (Spring 1981), 12–38.

107. Alan Hausman, "Innate Ideas," in *Studies in Perception: Interrelations in the History of Philosophy and Science*, ed. Peter K. Machamer and Robert G. Turnbull (Columbus: Ohio State University Press, 1978), pp. 215–216.

108. Charles M. Briquet, *Les Filigranes* (New York: Hacker Art Books, 1985).

109. Gerhard Schneider, *Der Libertin. Zur Geistes- und Sozialgeschichte des Bürgertums im 16. und 17. Jahrhundert* (Stuttgart: J. B. Metzler, 1970), pp. 216–220, 238–240.

110. Robert J. Ellrich, "Modes of Discourse and the Language of Sexual Reference in Eighteenth-Century French Fiction"; and G. S. Rousseau, "The Pursuit of Homosexuality in the Eighteenth Century: 'Utterly Confused Category' and/or Rich Depository," in *'Tis Nature's Fault: Unauthorized Sexuality during the Enlightenment*, ed. Robert Purk Maccubbin (Cambridge: Cambridge University Press, 1987), pp. 217, 148.

111. Gretchen Finney, "'Organical Musick' and Ecstasy," *Journal of the History of Ideas*, 8 (June 1947), 291–292; John Neubauer, *The Emancipation of Music from Language: Departure from Mimesis in Eighteenth-Century Aesthetics* (New Haven: Yale University Press, 1986), p. 2; and Simon Schama, *The Embarrassment of Riches: An Interpretation of Dutch Culture in the Golden Age* (New York: Alfred A. Knopf, 1987), pp. 165, 351.

112. René Taveneaux, *La Vie quotidienne des jansénistes aux XVIIe et XVIIIe siècles* (Paris: Hachette Littérature, 1985), pp. 126–128, 158–159, 175–176.

113. David Savan, "Spinoza: Scientist and Theorist of Scientific Method," in *Spinoza and the Sciences*, ed. Marjorie Grene and Deborah Nails (Dordrecht: D. Reidel Publishing Company, 1986), pp. 107–108; and Gilman, *Disease and Representation*, p. 3.

114. Peter J. Burt, "Algorithms and Architecture for Smart Sensing," in *Image Understanding Workshop, Proceedings of Workshop held at Cambridge, Mass. April 6–8, 1988*, 2 vols. (San Mateo, Calif.: Morgan Kaufmann Publishers, 1988), I, 145.

115. On dyers and the color/sound analogy, see R. P. Bertrand Castel, *L'Optique des couleurs, fondée sur les simples observations, & tournée sur-tout à la pratique de la peinture, de la teinture & des autres arts coloristes* (Paris: Chez Briasson, 1740), pp. 5, 14. Also see MacDonald, *Mystical Bedlam*, p. 143.

116. Terence Cave, *The Cornucopian Text: Problems of Writing in the French Renaissance* (Oxford: Clarendon Press, 1979), pp. 5, 145.

117. Molly Myerowitz, *Ovid's Game of Love* (Detroit: Wayne State University Press, 1985), pp. 132–133. Also see Georges Canguilhem, *On the Normal and the Patho-*

logical, trans. Carolyn R. Fawcett, ed. Robert S. Cohen (Dordrecht: D. Reidel Publishing Co., 1978), p. xix.

118. Martin Battersby, *Trompe-L'Oeil: The Eye Deceived* (London: Academy Editions, 1974), pp. 10, 21. Also see John Onians, "Abstraction and Imagination in Late Antiquity," *Art History*, 3 (March 1980), 9–11.

119. Novalis, *Das allgemeine Brouillon*, p. 544. Also see Neubauer, *Symbolismus*, pp. 14, 51, 137–139. On Mannerism, see Gustav René Hocke, *Die Welt als Labyrinth. Manierismus in der Europäischer Kunst und Literatur* (rev. ed., Reinbeck bei Hamburg: Rowohlt, 1987), p. 105. See also chapter 5, below.

120. Geoffrey Galt Harpham, *On the Grotesque: Strategies of Contradiction in Art and Literature* (Princeton, N.J.: Princeton University Press, 1982), p. 180.

121. Haemmerle, *Buntpapier*, pp. 16–18, 41, 54; and Teynac, Nolot, and Vivien *Wallpaper*, p. 216.

122. Papillon, *Gravure en bois*, I, 20–21, 380–386; and "Domino," *Encyclopédie*, V, 35. On the change occurring in eighteenth-century domino papers, also see Haemmerle, *Buntpapier*, pp. 131–133; and Teynac, Nolot, and Vivien, *Wallpaper*, p. 19.

123. Rae Beth Gordon, "Aboli bibelot? The Influence of the Decorative Arts on Stéphane Mallarmé and Gustave Moreau," *Art Journal*, 45 (Summer 1985), 105–112. Pierre Schneider discussed the spiritual "wallpapers" designed by Matisse after 1945, in which the human element no longer broke the unity of the vegetal texture. See *Matisse* (New York: Rizzoli, 1984), p. 176.

124. See, especially, Elizabeth Wynne Easton, ed., *The Intimate Interiors of Edouard Vuillard*, exh. cat. (Houston: Museum of Fine Arts, 1990).

125. Edward N. Lee, "Epicurus on Seeing and Hearing," in Machamer and Turnbull, *Studies in Perception*, pp. 44–45.

3 CONCEIVING

1. Daniel Callahan, "How Technology Is Reframing the Abortion Debate," *Hastings Center Report* (February 1986), pp. 33–42. Also see the comprehensive analysis of why discussions of the abortion issue often go nowhere: Laurence H. Tribe, *The Clash of Absolutes* (New York: W. W. Norton & Company, 1990).

2. Arnaldo Momigliano, "The Disadvantages of Monotheism for a Universal State," *Classical Philogy*, 18 (October 1986), 285–291.

3. Spence, *Polymetis*, p. 4; and Beattie, *Dissertations*, p. 330.

4. Dio Chrysostom, *Twelfth, or Olympic Discourse*, pp. 63–65.

5. Richard Merz, *Die numinose Mischgestalt. Methodenkritische Untersuchungen zu* Lanckorońska and Richard Oehler, *Die Buchillustration des XVIII Jahrhunderts in Deutschland, Osterreich und der Schweiz. Erster Teil: Die Deutsche Buchillustration des Spätbarock und Rokoko* (Leipzig: Im Insel-Verlag, 1932), pp. 32–35.

6. Hornung, *Conceptions of God in Egypt*, pp. 110–113, 117–118.

7. Proclus, *Commentary on the Timaeus*, pp. vi, xii; *Commentary on Euclid*, pp. 77, 111–113, 136; and *Alcibiades*, p. 122. Also see Sheppard, *Proclus on the Republic*, pp. 197–200.

8. Puech, *Sur le manichéisme*, pp. 26–28, 35–36, 4; and Brown, *Body and Society*, pp. 47–50. Also see Sofia Ameisenowa, "Animal-Headed Gods: Evangelists, Saints and Righteous Men," *Journal of the Warburg and Courtauld Institutes*, 12 (1949), 23–24, 38–40.

9. Peter Brown, "Late Antiquity," in *A History of Private Life. From Pagan Rome to Byzantium*. I, ed. Paul Veyne, trans. Arthur Goldhammer (Cambridge, Mass.: Belknap Press of Harvard University Press, 1987), 306–308. Also see Friedrich Billicsich, *Das Probleme des Übels in der Phi-*

losophie des Abendlandes, 2 vols. (2d rev. ed., Vienna: Verlag A. Sexl, 1955), I, 254–257.

10. Tertullian, *Treatises on Marriage and Remarriage*, p. 28.

11. Margaret Camden Jacob, "John Toland and the Newtonian Ideology," *Journal of the Warburg and Courtauld Institutes*, 32 (1969), 308–311, 318.

12. Bayle, *Dictionnaire critique*, III, 2631, "Spinoza"; Corneille, *Dictionnaire*, I, 649, "Libertin"; and Chambers, *Cyclopaedia*, II, "Libertines."

13. Chambers, *Cyclopaedia*, "Sophism"; and *Encyclopaedia Britannica*, III, 618, "Sophism," "Sophist," "Sophistication." On sophistry, or being on the level with the multitude, see also Proclus, *Alcibiades*, p. 165.

14. Louis-Emile Edmond Duranty, "Promenades au Louvre. Remarques à propos de l'art égyptien," *Gazette des Beaux-Arts*, 29 (October–March 1878–1879), 209–213, 323–325.

15. Piranesi, *Chimneys*, in *Polemical Works*, pp. 5, 9–12, 18–19.

16. Hogarth, *Analysis of Beauty*, pp. 31–32; and Lavater, *Essays*, II, II, 297, 300.

17. Charles-Antoine Dufresnoy, *The Art of Painting. Translated into English, with an Original Preface, Containing a Parallel between Painting and Poetry by Mr. Dryden. As Also a Short Account of the Most Eminent Painters, Both Ancient and Modern by Richard Graham, Esq.*, 2 vols. (London: Printed for Henry Lintot, 1750), I, xxviii. On Horace and deformed or overloaded compositions, see the art manuals by George Bickham, *An Introductive Essay on Drawing, With the Nature and Beauty of Lights and Shadows, and Cuts suitable for the Young Practioner, in the Manner of the Greatest Masters* (London: Printed for the Author, 1747), pp. 11–12; Audran, *Proportions of the Human Body*, preface; and Lens, *Bowles's New Preceptor*, p. 3.

18. Beattie, *Essays*, pp. 586–600, 601–603, 608–611.

19. Francis Grose, *Rules for drawing Caricaturas: With An Essay on Comic Painting, Illustrated with Twenty-One Copper Plates, Seventeen of Which were etched by Himself* (2d ed., London: Printed for Hooper & Wigstead, 1796), pp. 4–6, 8.

20. Nicolas Andry, *L'Orthopédie, ou l'art de prevenir et de corriger dans les enfans les difformités du corps. Le Tout par des moyens à la portée des pères et des mères, & de toutes les personnes qui ont des enfans à élever*, 2 vols. (Paris: Chez la Veuve Alix, & Lambert & Durand, 1741), I, lxxvi–lxxvii.

21. Bouhours, *Manière de bien penser*, p. 410; Origen, *Homilies on Exodus*, p. 323; and Campbell, *Philosophy of Rhetoric*, II, 67.

22. Marcus Fabius Quintilianus, *Institutes of Oratory or, Education of an Orator. In Twelve Books*, 2 vols., trans. John Selby Watson (London: George Bell and Sons, 1875), II, 83–85, 97–99.

23. Joseph Addison, *Critical Essays from The Spectator, With Four Essays by Richard Steele*, ed. by Donald F. Bond (Oxford: Clarendon Press, 1970), p. 9.

24. Addison, *Critical Essays*, p. 12. Also see Galileo Galilei, *Considerazioni al Tasso di . . . e Discorso di Giuseppe Iseo sopra il poema di M. Torquato Tasso* (Rome: Nella Stamperia Pagliarini, 1793), pp. 1–4, 8. Also see Erwin Panofsky, *Galileo as a Critic of the Arts* (The Hague: Martinus Nijhoff, 1954), pp. 17–20. On poetic labyrinths, see Ulrich Ernst, "The Figured Poem: Towards a Definition of Genre," *Visible Language*, 20 (Winter 1986), 11–13, 15–16.

25. Emmanuele Tesauro, *Il Canocchiale aristotelico, o sia Idea delle argutezza heroiche vulgaremente chiamate Imprese. E di tutta l'arte simbolica, et lapidaria* (Venice: Presso Paolo Baglioni, 1655), p. 470.

26. Campbell, *Philosophy of Rhetoric*, II, 65–66, 412–413, 456, 531. Also see Beattie, *Essays*, p. 619.

27. Spence, *Polymetis*, pp. 291–292; and Trapp, *Lectures on Poetry*, p. 52. Also see Samuel Johnson, *Lives of the English Poets, Cowley-Dryden* (1783), 3 vols, ed. George Birbeck Hill (New York: Octagon Books, 1967), I, 21.

28. Richardson, *Science of a Connoisseur*, p. 180; Algarotti, *Oeuvres*, II, 318, 333–334. Also see Pierre Remond de Sainte-Albine, *Le Comédien. Ouvrage divisé en deux parties* (new rev. ed., Paris: Chez Vincent, 1749), p. 217.

29. Dufresnoy, *Art of Painting*, pp. xxxix, 57–59; Diderot, *Salon of 1765*, II, 211; and Lavater, *Essays*, I, I, advertisement; II,II, 299, 302, 364.

30. Lessing, *Laocoön*, p. 13.

31. Spence, *Polymetis*, pp. 28, 300–302.

32. Potts, "Winckelmann's Interpretation of Ancient Art," p. 154. Also see Johann Joachim Winckelmann, *Versuch einer Allegorie, besonders für die Kunst* (Dresden: In der Walterischen Hof-Buchhandlung, 1766), p. 121.

33. Lairesse, *Art of Painting*, p. 97.

34. Félibien, *Entretiens*, II, 184; Dubos, *Réflexions critiques*, I, 184, 190–191; Bouhours, *Manière de bien penser*, p. 391; and Dandré-Bardon, *Traité de peinture*, p. 91.

35. Jean-Baptiste Boudard, *Iconologie tirée de divers auteurs. Ouvrage utile aux gens de lettres, aux poëtes, aux artistes, & généralement à tous les amateurs des beaux-arts*, 3 vols. (Vienna: Chez Jean-Thomas de Trattnern, Imprimeur et Libraire de la Cour, 1766), I, 2, 8–9.

36. Campbell, *Philosophy of Rhetoric*, II, 5–9, 17–23.

37. Shaftesbury, *Characteristics*, II, 200, 204, 209.

38. Richard Hurd, *Letters on Chivalry and Romance* (London: Printed for A. Miller, W. Thurlbourn and J. Woodyer, 1762), pp. 3, 31, 67–69, 89, 106.

39. Dufresnoy, *Art of Painting*, p. 35; Richardson, *Science of a Connoisseur*, p. 204; and Fuseli, *Lectures on Painting*, p. 58.

40. Oldmixon, *Essay on Criticism*, pp. 18–19.

41. Bouhours, *Manière de bien penser*, p. 399.

42. Félibien, *Entretiens*, II, 75.

43. Louis-Sébastien Mercier, *Du Théâtre ou nouvel essai sur l'art dramatique* (Amsterdam: Chez E. van Harrevelt 1773), pp. 297–300.

44. Trapp, *Lectures on Poetry*, p. 260; and Adam, *Works*, I, fn. A. For the growing body of criticism against the indecorous, see David Cast, "Seeing Vanbrugh and Hawksmoor," *Journal of the Society of Architectural Historians*, 43 (December 1984), 310–327.

45. Lessing, *Laocoön*, pp. 9–10.

46. Samel Taylor Coleridge, *Biographia Literaria, or Biographical Sketches of My Literary Life and Opinions*, ed. George Watson (London: J. M. Dent & Sons, Ltd; New York: E. P. Dutton & Co., 1975), pp. 89–90, 97.

47. Fuseli, *Lectures on Painting*, p. 8. Also see Sulzer, *Allgemeine Theorie*, II, 40–41.

48. Robert G. Turnbull, "Zeno's Stricture and Predication in Plato, Aristotle, and Plotinus," in *How Things Are: Studies in Predication and the History of Philosophy and Science*, ed. James Bogen and James E. McGuire (Dordrecht: D. Reidel Publishing Company, 1985), pp. 42–43.

49. Lossky, *Mystical Theology*, pp. 114–115. Also see S. E. Gersh, *KINESIS AKINHOS: A Study of Spiritual Motion in the Philosophy of Proclus* (Leiden: E. J. Brill, 1973), pp. 100–104.

50. Diadochus Proclus, *Théologie platonicienne, Livre III*, ed. and trans. H. D. Saffrey and L. G. Westerink (Paris: Société d'Edition "Les Belles Lettres," 1978), pp. 13, 22–23. On the divine henads and intelligible gods, see also Turnbull, "Zeno's Strictures," in Bogen and McGuire, *Studies in Predication*, pp. 44–45; Lloyd, "Procession in Proclus," pp. 23–24; and Gersh, *Spiritual Motion*, pp. 37, 46.

51. Proclus, *Commentary on Euclid*, pp. 88, 105, 227. Also see Peter Crome, *Symbol und Unzulänglichkeit der Sprache. Jamblichos, Plotin, Porphyrios, Proklos* (Munich: Wilhelm Fink Verlag, 1970), p. 203.

52. Donald Verene, *Vico's Science of Imagination* (Ithaca: Cornell University Press, 1987), p. 114.

53. Coleridge, *Biographia Literia*, p. 202. Also see Moutsopoulos, *L'Imaginaire chez Proclus*, pp. 221–224.

54. H. J. Sheppard, "The Redemption Theme and Hellenistic Alchemy," *Ambix*, 7 (February 1959), 45–46. Also see Josef Stiglmayr, "Der NeuPlatoniker Proclus als Vorlage des sogenannten Dionysius Areopagita in der Lehre vom Uebel," *Historisches Jahrbuch*, 16 (1895), 263.

55. Proclus, *Théologie platonicienne*, pp. 40–41; *Commentary on the Timaeus*, p. 113; and *Commentary on Euclid*, pp. 64, 275.

56. Scheuchzer, *Physique sacrée*, I, 2, 8, 12. Also see Roland Mortier, "Un dieu-araignée?", *Enlightenment Essays in Memory of Robert Shackleton*, ed. Gilles Barber and C. P. Courtney (Oxford: Voltaire Foundation, 1988), pp. 223–229.

57. Scheuchzer, *Physique sacrée*, I, xxxv, 29–32; and William Cowper, *The Anatomy of the Human Body with Figures drawn after the life by Some of the Best Masters in Europe, and Curiously Engraven in One Hundred and Fourteen Copper Plates. Illustrated with Large Explications, Containing Many New Anatomical Discoveries, and Chirurgical Observations: To Which is added an Introduction explaining the Animal Oeconomy* (Oxford: Printed at The Theater, for Sam Smith and Benjamin Walford, Printers to the Royal Society, 1698), letterpress for pl. 100. For Ruysch, see Th. H. Lunsingh Scheurleer, "Early Dutch Cabinets of Curiosities," in Impey and MacGregor, *Origin of Museums*, pp. 119–120. On Scheuchzer, see Maria Lanckorońska and Richard Oehler, *Die Buchillustration des XVIII Jahrhunderts in Deutschland, Osterreich und der Schweiz. Erster Teil: Die Deutsche Buchillustration des Spätbarock und Rokoko* (Leipzig: Im Insel-Verlag, 1932), pp. 32–35.

58. Claude E. Dolman, "Spallanzani in the English-Speaking World," in Bernardi and La Vergata, *Lazzaro Spallanzani*, pp. 244–245. Also see Thomas L. Hankins, *Science and the Enlightenment* (Cambridge: Cambridge University Press, 1985), p. 153.

59. Scheuchzer, *Physique sacrée*, I, 24. Also see Eric Charles White, *Kaironomia: On the Will-to-Invent* (Ithaca: Cornell University Press, 1987), p. 98.

60. William Harvey, *Anatomical Exercitations concerning the Generation of Living Creatures: To Which are added Particular Discourses of Births, and of Conceptions, etc.* (London: Printed by James Young, 1653), pp. 539–555 passim. On the dominating role of Aristotle's biological doctrines, see George K. Plochmann, "Nature and the Living Thing in Aristotle's Biology," *Journal of the History of Ideas*, 14 (April 1953), 167, 187–188; and Anne-Liese Thomasen, "Historia Animalium' contra 'Gynaecia' in der Literatur des Mittelalters," *Clio Medica*, 15 (December 1980), 9.

61. Junius, *Painting of the Ancients*, pp. 6–7.

62. Henry More, *Immortality of the Soul*, in *A Collection of Several Philosophical Writings* (London: Printed by James Flesher, 1662), pp. 167–168. Also see J. E. McGuire, "Force, Active Principles, and Newton's Invisible Realm," *Ambix*, 15 (1968), 191–193.

63. On Shaftesbury's connection to the Cambridge Platonists, see Martinelli, *La Ragione dell'arte*, pp. 70–71.

64. Shaftesbury, *Characteristics*, II, 402–405, 411–413.

65. Richardson, *Theory of Painting*, pp. 72, 77–78; *Science of a Connoisseur*, p. 238; and Félibien, *Entretiens*, pp. 307–309.

66. For a discussion of Berkeley and Malebranche, see Le Camus, *Médecine de*

l'esprit, pp. 167–168. Also see Mortier, *Clartés et ombres*, p. 61.

67. Martinelli, *La ragione dell'arte*, pp. 158, 163.

68. Winckelmann, *Imitation of the Greeks*, pp. 62, 65. Also see Proclus, *Commentary on the Timaeus*, p. xi.

69. Ibid., pp. 83–84.

70. Winckelmann speaks of a similar chemical transmutation in *Imitation of the Greeks*, p. 68. Also see Plutarch, *The Obsolescence of Oracles*, in *Moralia*, 15 vos., trans. Frank Cole Babbitt (Cambridge, Mass.: Harvard University Press; London: William Heineman, 1962), V, 379.

71. Richard Chapon, "L'Humour: Origine et analyse," in *Actes de l'Académie nationale des sciences, belles-lettres et arts de Bordeaux*, 5th ser., 8 (1983 [1984]), 251–260.

72. Winckelmann, *Imitation of the Greeks*, pp. 63–64. Also see Myerowitz, *Ovid's Game of Love*, p. 174.

73. On interior molds, see Paul Lawrence Farber, "Buffon and Daubenton: Divergent Traditions within the *Histoire naturelle*," *Isis*, 66 (March 1975), 69. On Winckelmann's empty outline see also Michael Fried, "Painting Memories—On the Containment of the Past in Baudelaire and Manet," *Critical Inquiry*, 10 (1984), 510–542.

74. Winckelmann, *Imitation of the Greeks*, p. 76. Also see Albert E. Elsen, ed., *Rodin Rediscovered*, exh. cat. (Washington, D.C.: National Gallery of Art, 1981), pp. 137–140.

75. Winckelmann, *Imitation of the Greeks*, pp. 78–80.

76. Bevan, *Holy Images*, p. 158.

77. Potts, in his study "Winckelmann's Interpretation of Ancient Art," p. 101, has not, however, connected this artistic progression to the Neoplatonic "plan." Charles Bonnet, the most famous exponent of *emboîtement*, gathered together his earlier thoughts on "pre-organization," "preordination," and "preformation" in the *Contemplation de la nature* [*1764*] (2d ed., Amsterdam: Chez Marc-Michel Rey, 1769), I, xii–xxii. It was published in the same year as Winckelmann's *Geschichte der Kunst*.

78. Mengs, *Hinterlassene Schriften*, I, 215; and Mengs, *Réflexions sur la beauté*, in *Oeuvres*, I, 92. On the relationship between Mengs and Winckelmann while they were in Italy, see Martinelli, *La ragione dell'arte*, pp. 163–165.

79. Pernety, *Connoissance de l'homme*, I, 93–95. Also see "Ideal in Philosophy from the Renaissance to 1780," in *Dictionary of the History of Ideas*, II, 551.

80. Johann Caspar Lavater, *Physiognomische Fragmente. Zur Berförderung der Menschenkenntniss und Menschenliebe* (Leipzig and Winterthur: Bey Weidmanns Erben und Reich, 1775–1778), IV, 65.

81. Coleridge, *Biographia Literaria*, pp. 168–169, 173; and Blake, *Annotations to Reynolds*, in *Complete Writings*, p. 459. On *Witz*, see Sulzer, *Allgemeine Theorie*, II,II, 930.

82. Julien Offray de La Mettrie, *L'Homme machine*, ed. Paul-Laurent Assoun (Paris: Denoël/Gonthier, 1981), pp. 115, 131; Diderot, *Elémens de physiologie*, p. 266; D'Holbach, *Système de la nature*, I, 40–41, 104–105. Also see Aram Vartanian, "Erotisme et philosophie chez Diderot," *Cahiers de l'association internationale des études françaises*, 13 (May 1961), 382–385, 388–89.

83. Scott Altran, *Fondements de l'histoire naturelle. Pour une anthropologie de la science* (Brussels: Editions Complexe, 1986), pp. 25, 34–40. Also see Gilbert Lascault, *Le monstre dans l'art occidental. Un problème esthétique* (Paris: Klincksieck, 1973), pp. 19–22.

84. Edmé Guyot, *Nouvelles récréations physiques et mathématiques, contenant ce qui à été imaginé de plus curieux dans ce genre & ce qui se découvre journellement, auxquelles on a*

joint leurs causes, leurs effets, la manière de les construire, & l'amusement qu'on en peut tirer pour étonner & surprendre agréablement, 8 vols. (2d ed., Paris: Chez l'Auteur et Chez Gueffier, 1772), VI, 85, 93–94. Also see Georges Bataille, *Documents*, ed. Bernard Noël (Paris: Mercure de France, 1968), p. 178; and Henri-Claude Cousseau, "Origins and Deviations: A Short History of *Art Brut*," *Art and Text*, 27 (December–February 1988), 7, 26–28.

85. Pernety, *Connoissance de l'homme*, I, 98.

86. Canguilhem, *Connaissance de la vie*, p. 178.

87. John Block Friedman, *The Monstrous Races in Medieval Art and Thought* (Cambridge, Mass.: Harvard University Press, 1981), p. 187.

88. Giovanni Paolo Lomazzo, *Idea del Tempio della Pittura*, 2 vols., ed. and trans. Robert Klein (Florence: Nella Sede dell' Istituto Palazzo Strozzi, 1974), I, 80; and Tomaso Garzoni, *Il seraglio degli stupori del mondo . . . Cioè de mostri, prodigi, prestigi, sorti, oracoli, sibille, sogni, curiosità, miracoli, maraviglie* (Venice: n.p., 1613), p. 67. Also see Hocke, *Welt als Labyrinth*, p. 49.

89. Fortunius Licetus, *De Monstris, Ex Recensione Gerardi Blasii, M.D. & P.P. Qui Monstra quaedam nova & Rariora ex Recentiorum Scriptis Addidit* (Amsterdam: Andreae Frisii, 1665). Also see Hahn, *Histoire de la médecine*, p. 249.

90. Jean-Ignace Isidore Gérard, called Grandville, *Un autre monde: Transformations, visions, incarnations, ascensions, locomotions, explorations, pérégrinations, excursions, stations, cosmogonies, fantasmagories, rêveries, folâtreries, facéties, lubies, métamorphoses, zoomorphoses, lithomorphoses, métempsychoses, apothéoses, et autres choses* (Paris: H. Fournier, 1844), pp. 115–116. Also see Philippe Kaenel, "Le Buffon de l'humanité. La zoologie politique de J. I. Grandville (1803–1807)," *La Revue de l'art*, 76 (1986), 22–26. On the Saint-Hilaires,

see Laurent Goulven, "La cheminement d'Etienne Geoffroy Saint-Hilaire (1772–1844) vers un transformisme scientifique," *Revue d'histoire des sciences*, 30 (January 1977), 60–63; and Toby A. Appel, *The Cuvier-Geoffroy Debate: French Biology in the Decades before Darwin* (New York and Oxford: Oxford University Press, 1987), pp. 126–128.

91. Chambers, *Cyclopaedia*, II, "monster." Also see Katherine Park and Lorraine J. Daston, "Unnatural Conceptions: The Study of Monsters in Sixteenth- and Seventeenth-Century France and England," *Past and Present*, 92 (August 1981), 25; and Elizabeth Scheicher, "The Collection of Archduke Ferdinand II at Schloss Ambras: Its Purpose, Composition and Evolution," in Impey and MacGregor, *Museums*, p. 38.

92. Theodore Eller, "Description d'un monstre cyclope, mis au monde à Berlin, le 19 de févier de l'année MDCCLV," *Mémoires de l'académie royale de Prusse*, 10 vols. (Avignon: Chez Jean-Joseph Niel, Imprimeur, 1768), IV, 167–173. Also see Pierre-Louis Moreau de Maupertuis, *The Earthly Venus* [*Vénus physique*], trans. Simone Brangier Boas (New York and London: Johnson Reprint Corporation, 1966), pp. 45–47; and "Génération," *Encyclopédie*, VII, 563–573.

93. Lanckorońska and Oehler, *Buchillustration*, pp. 30–31. Also see Hal Opperman, *J. B. Oudry (1686–1755)*, exh. cat. (Fort Worth: Kimbell Art Museum, 1983), pp. 204–206.

94. Caulfield, *Remarkable Characters*, I, 134–135. Also see Viktor Hamburger, "Monsters in Nature," *Ciba Symposia*, 9 (August–September 1947), 671–674.

95. Maupertuis, *Earthly Venus*, pp. 54–58.

96. Hahn, Dumaitre, and Samion-Contet, *Histoire de la médecine*, p. 250.

97. M. Gleditsch, "Sur une excrescence monstrueuse trouvée sur un sapin," *Mé-*

moires de l'académie royale de Prusse, V, 19–34. Also see Paulet, *Histoire de la petite vérole*, II, 105–107.

98. Nicholas Russell, *Like Engend'ring Like: Heredity and Animal Breeding in Early Modern England* (Cambridge: Cambridge University Press, 1986), pp. 66–71. Also see Stephen Jay Gould, *The Mismeasure of Man* (New York: W. W. Norton, 1981), p. 41; and Canguilhem, *Connaissance de la vie*, p. 175.

99. John Hunter, *Observations on Certain Parts of the Animal Oeconomy* (London: Sold at Castle-Street, 1786), pp. 46–49, 64–65. Also see Russell, *Like Engend'ring Like*, p. 2.

100. Delcourt, *Hermaphrodite*, pp. 5, 43–45. Also see Heinz Mode, *Fabulous Beasts and Demons* (London: Phaidon, 1975), p. 7.

101. Jacques Gautier Dagoty, *Observations sur l'histoire naturelle sur la physique et sur la peinture* (Paris: Chez Delaguette, 1752), p. 17.

102. Beattie, *Dissertations*, p. 328; La Chau and Le Blond, *Pierres gravées*, I, 105–106. Also see Charles-Louis de Montesquieu, "Essai sur le goût dans les choses de la nature & de l'art," *Encyclopédie*, VII, 765.

103. Galen, *De usu Partium* 3.1.

104. Ameisenowa, "Animal-Headed Gods," p. 25.

105. Spence, *Polymetis*, pp. 5–9, 258–261, 267.

106. *Le gemme antiche figurate de Michelangelo Causeo de La Chausse, Parigino, consagrate al Eminentissimo e Reverendissimo Principe il Signor Cardinale Cesare d'Estrées* (Rome: Giacomo Komarek Boemo, 1700), pp. 74–75.

107. Antonia Mulas, *Eros in Antiquity* (Milan: Arnoldo Mondadori Editore, 1978), pp. 12–13. Also see Philippe Morel, "Priape à la Renaissance. Les guirlandes de Giovanni da Udine à la Farnésine," *Revue de l'art*, 69 (1985), 18–22; David Freedburg, "Johannes Molanus on Provocative Paintings: *De Historia Sanctarum Ima-*

ginum et Picturarum, Book II, Chapter 42," *Journal of the Warburg and Courtauld Institutes*, 34 (1971), 241–243; and Eduard Fuchs, *Geschichte der Erotischen Kunst* (Munich: Albert Langen, 1908), p. 129.

108. Antonio Francisco Gori, *Thesaurus Gemmarum Antiquarium Astriferarium*, 3 vols. (Florence: Ex Officina Typogr. Albiziniana, 1750), II, 171; and La Chau and Le Blond, *Pierres gravées*, II, 173.

109. For the ancient view of *grylli* and a splendid modern typological analysis, see Duncan G. N. Barker, "*Grylli, Verstand und Unsinn* in Classical Glyptics" (M. A. thesis, University of Chicago, 1989). It should be a consolation to eighteenth-century interpreters that their twentieth-century colleagues are equally perplexed.

110. Caylus, *Recueil d'antiquités*, III, 280; VI, 133–134, 290–291.

111. Trapp, *Lectures on Poetry*, pp. 223–226, 230, 259.

112. Antoine Schnapper, *Le Géant, la licorne, et la tulipe. Collections et collectionneurs dans la France du XVIIe siècle, I: Histoire et histoire naturelle* (Paris: Flammarion, 1988), 84–86. Also see Wolfgang Born, "Monsters in Art," *Ciba Symposia*, p. 684; and Park, "Unnatural Conceptions," p. 37.

113. Louis Marin, *Le Portrait du roi* (Paris: Les Editions de Minuit, 1981), pp. 111–114.

114. Lascault, *Le Monstre dans l'art*, pp. 32–33. Also see *Der Schlaf der Vernunft gebiert Ungeheuer. Francisco de Goya (1746–1828). Die "Caprichos,"* exh. cat. (Karlsruhe: Kunsthalle, 1976–1977), p. 24.

115. Christiane Andersson, "Polemical Prints in Reformation Nuremberg," *New Perspectives on the Art of Renaissance Nuremberg: Five Essays*, ed. Jeffrey Chipps Smith (Austin: The Archer M. Huntington Art Library of the University of Texas, 1985), p. 51.

116. Jean Céard and Jean-Claude Margolin, *Rébus de la Renaissance. Des images qui* *parlent*, 2 vols. (Paris: Maisonneuve et La Rose, 1986), I, 71–73, 76; and Max Hasse, "Spott mit dem Spott treiben. Bildzitate in der Karikature des ausgehenden 18. Jahrhunderts," *Zeitschrift für Kunstgeschichte*, 47 (1984), 528. Also see E. H. Gombrich, *Icones Symbolicae: Philosphies of Symbolism and Their Bearing on Art*, in *Symbolical Images: Studies in the Art of the Renaissance*, II (Chicago: University of Chicago Press, 1972), 144.

117. Jackson I. Cope, *Dramaturgy of the Daemonic: Studies in Antigeneric Theater from Ruzante to Grimaldi* (Baltimore: Johns Hopkins University Press, 1984), pp. xi, 107–11. Also see A. Graeme Mitchell, *Medical Caricature, Proceedings of the California Academy of Medicine*, reprint (1939–1940), n.p.

118. Poinsinet de Sivry, *Traité de rire*, p. 105; and Sticotti, *Dictionnaire*, II, 42.

119. Mengs, *Réflexions sur la beauté*, in *Oeuvres*, I, 107–109. Also see Paul Mus, "The Iconography of an Aniconic Art," *Res*, 14 (Autumn 1987), 7.

120. Caulfield, *Remarkable Persons*, I, 22–23, 108–110, 114–115; and Horace Walpole, *Anecdotes of Painting in England, with Some Account of the Principal Artists; and Incidental Notes on Other Arts*, 5 vols., ed Frederick W. Hilles and Philip B. Daghlian (New Haven and London: Yale University Press and Oxford University Press, 1937), V, 35. Also see Sander L. Gilman, *Disease and Representation: Images of Illness from Madness to AIDS* (Ithaca: Cornell University Press, 1988), pp. 231–241.

121. Schama, *Embarrassment of Riches*, pp. 580–581. Also see Ricky Jay, *Learned Pigs and Fire Proof Women* (New York: Villard Books, 1986), pp. 60–63.

122. Lessing, *Laocoön*, p. 153. Also see Smeed, *Theophrastan "Character,"* pp. 151, 186–187. On madness as evilly composed and divided in appearance, see Willis, *Practice of Physick*, p. 179; and MacDonald, *Mystical Bedlam*, pp. 112–113, 130–131.

123. Lessing, *Laocoön*, pp. 121–122; and Sulzer, *Allgemeine Theorie*, II, I, 309.

124. Origen, *Commentary on the Song of Songs*, p. 152; Quintilian, *Institutes*, II, 122; Junius, *Painting of the Ancients*, p. 156; and Spence, *Polymetis*, p. 21. On masquerade, see Chambers, *Cyclopaedia*, II, "masque," "masquerade"; and also Aileen Ribeiro, *A Visual History of Costume: The Eighteenth Century* (New York and London: B. T. Batsford, 1983), pp. 23–27, 35.

125. Crousaz, *Traité du beau*, pp. 22–26.

126. Batteux, *Les Beaux-arts réduits*, pp. 168, 239.

127. Dennis, *Grounds of Criticism*, p. 63; and Oldmixon, *Essay on Criticism*, p. 21.

128. Hogarth, *Analysis of Beauty*, p. 72; and Lichtenberg, *Hogarth on High Life*, pp. 77–80.

4 MARKING

1. For a history of dermatology, see Gérard Tilles, *La Naissance de la dermatologie (1776–1880)* (Paris: Les Editions Roger Dacosta, 1989), especially pp. 31–45.

2. Georges Solente, "Le Musée de l'Hôpital Saint-Louis," *American Journal of Dermatology*, 5 (October 1983), 483–489.

3. *Cipriani's Rudiments of Drawing engraved by G. Bartolozzi* (London: n.p., 1790), p. 1.

4. Bickham, *Essay on Drawing*, p. 11.

5. Algarotti, *Essai sur la peinture*, in *Oeuvres*, II, 129.

6. Diderot, *Eléments de physiologie*, pp. 296, 307.

7. Diderot, *Salons*, III, 57–60, 62. On portraiture, also see Richardson, *Theory of Painting*, pp. 13–14; Félibien, *Entretiens*, p. 92; and Lavater, *Essays*, I, I, 271–272.

8. Laugier, *Manière de bien juger*, p. 58. Also see Dufresnoy, *Art of Painting*, pp. v–vi.

9.   Lavater, *Essays*, II, II, 365, 370; III, I, 74, 80, 85, 139–140.

10.   Mengs, *Hinterlassene Schriften*, I, 199–200. Also see Origen, *Song of Songs*, p. 251.

11.   Robert G. Turnbull, "The Role of the 'Special Sensibles' in the Perception Theories of Plato and Aristotle," in Machamer and Turnbull, eds., *Studies in Perception*, p. 12.

12.   Quintilian, *Institutes*, II, 147; and Junius, *Painting of the Ancients,* pp. 288, 315. Also see Warren Dotz, "Albrecht Dürer: Depictions of Facies as Expressions of Personality," *American Journal of Dermapathology*, 3 (Spring 1981), 61–63.

13.   Algarotti, *Dialogues sur l'optique* and *Essai sur la peinture*, in *Ouevres*, I, 272; II, 172–173, 180.

14.   Père Cherubim D'Orléans, *La Dioptrique oculaire* (Paris: n.p., 1671), p. 298. On solar and lunar spots, also see Scheuchzer, *Physique sacrée*, I, 21.

15.   Cowper, *Anatomy of the Human Body*, letterpress of pl. IV.

16.   Antoine Fueldez, *Observations curieuses touchant la petite vérole, vraye peste des petits enfans: Et le bézahar son antidote* (Lyons: Chez Jean-Antoine Huguetan, 1645), 149. This work is full of recipes to remove pots, pits, and scars.

17.   Andry, *L'Orthopédie*, II, 208–210. Also see Elizabeth Wilson, *Adorned in Dreams: Fashion and Modernity* (London: Virago Press, 1985), p. 118.

18.   Algarotti, *Essai sur la nécessité d'écrire en sa propre langue*, in *Oeuvres*, III, 13, 15, 25–26.

19.   Myerowitz, *Ovid's Game of Love*, pp. 138–140.

20.   Charles Baudelaire, "In Praise of Make-Up," in *Strangeness and Beauty: An Anthology of Aesthetic Criticism 1840–1910*, ed. Eric Warner and Graham Hough, 2 vols. (Cambridge: Cambridge University Press, 1983), I, 219.

21.   Ibid., p. 220.

22.   Quintilian, *Institutes*, II, 101; Bouhours, *La Manière de bien penser*, pp. 334, 353–357.

23.   Reinhold R. Grimm, *Paradisus Coelestis, Paradisus Terrestris* (Munich: Wilhelm Fink Verlag, 1977), p. 41.

24.   Proclus, *Alcibiades*, pp. 38, 160–161. Also see Brown, "Late Antiquity," in *A History of Private Life*, I, 253–254, 283.

25.   Richard A. Etlin, *The Architecture of Death* (Cambridge, Mass.: MIT Press, 1984), pp. 12–17.

26.   Jackie Pigeaud, *La Maladie de l'âme. Etude sur la relation de l'âme et du corps dans la tradition médico-philosophique antique* (Paris: Société d'Edition "Les Belles Lettres," 1981), pp. 239–242.

27.   Joseph Adams, *An Inquiry into the Laws of Different Epidemic Diseases, with the View to determine the Means of preserving Individuals and Communities from Each, and also to ascertain the Probability of Exterminating the Small-Pox* (London: J. Johnson, J. Callow, and W. Grace, 1809), pp. 11–12, 19–21.

28.   Bellini, *Account of Fevers*, pp. 34–35.

29.   James Carmichael Smyth, *The Effect of the Nitrous Vapour, in preventing and destroying Contagion; ascertained, from a Variety of Trials, made chiefly by Surgeon's of His Majesty's Navy, in Prisons, Hospitals, and on Board of Ships: With An Introduction respecting the Nature of the Contagion which gives Rise to the Jail or Hospital Fever; and the Various Methods formerly employed to prevent or destroy This* (London: J. Johnson, 1799), pp. 2–3, 5–9, 11–17.

30.   Ibid., pp. 41–42.

31.   Othmar Kell, "The Politics of Health and the Institutionalization of Clinical Practice in Europe in the Second Half of the Eighteenth Century," in *William Hunter and the Eighteenth-Century Medical World*, ed. W. F. Bynum and Roy Porter (Cambridge: Cambridge University Press, 1985), pp. 208, 230.

32. N. Sainte Fare Garnot, *La Révolution française et les hôpitaux parisiens*, exh. cat. (Paris: Musée de l'Assistance Publique, 1989), pp. 33, 41, 49.

33. Ibid., pp. 17, 23, 72–73.

34. William B. Ober, "Can the Leper Change His Spots? The Iconography of Leprosy, Part I," *American Journal of Dermapathology*, 5 (February 1983), 48–49, 52–53.

35. John Gage, "Colour in History: Relative and Absolute," *Art History*, 1 (March 1978), 119–120.

36. Saul Nathaniel Brody, *The Disease of the Soul: Leprosy in Medieval Literature* (Ithaca: Cornell University Press, 1974), pp. 34, 51–52, 108, 125.

37. Proclus, *Alcibiades*, p. 198.

38. Peter-Klaus Schuster, "Abstraktion, Agitation und Einfühlung. Formen Protestantischer Kunst im 16. Jahrhundert," in *Luther und die Folgen für die Kunst*, ed. Werner Hofmann, exh. cat. (Hamburg: Hamburger Kunsthalle, 1983), pp. 292–293.

39. Charles Aubry et al. [Chazal, Colin, Bellangé, Pigal], *Album comique de pathologie pittoresque. Recueil de vingt caricatures médicales dessinées par* . . . (Paris: Chez Ambroise Tardieu, Editeur, 1823), letterpress to *La petite vérole*.

40. Edward Jenner, *An Inquiry into the Causes and Effects of the Variolae Vaccinae, A Disease discovered in some of the Western Counties of England, particularly Gloucestershire, and Known by the Name of the Cow Pox* (London: Printed for the Author, 1798), pl. I. This treatise was accompanied by four illustrations of the dairymaid Sarah Nelme's hand and arm, designed by Edward Pearce and engraved by William Skelton. The plates to the second edition of 1801 were hand-colored by William Cuff. Also see W. R. Le Fanu, *A Bio-Bibliography of Edward Jenner (1749–1823)* (London: Harvey and Blythe, 1951), p. 55.

41. Joel N. Shurkin, *The Invisible Fire: The Story of Mankind's Victory over the Ancient Scourge of Small Pox* (New York: G. P. Putnam's Sons, 1979), p. 42.

42. Paulet, *Histoire de la petite vérole*, I, 84–86, 88–89, 113.

43. Jacques Gautier Dagoty, *Exposition anatomique des maux vénériens, sur les parties de l'homme & de la femme et les remèdes les plus usites dans ces sortes de maladies* (Paris: Chez J. B. Brunet & Demonville, 1773), p. 1.

44. René Graziani, "Fracastoro's 'Syphilis' and Priapus," *Clio Medica*, 16 (December 1981), 93–95. Also see Thomas P. Gariepy, "Hyacum; et *Lues Venerea*," *Journal of the History of Medicine*, 36 (July 1981), 325.

45. Paulet, *Histoire de la petite vérole*, I, 115. Also see Paré, *Oeuvres*, p. 691.

46. John Hunter, *A Treatise on the Venereal Disease* (London: sold at Castle-Street, Leicester Square, 1786), pp. 10–11, 14–15, 23–26.

47. Pierre Fabre, *Traité des maladies vénériennes* (Paris: Chez P. Fr. Didot Le Jeune, 1773), p. 2. Also see Hunter, *Venereal Disease*, pp. 293–296.

48. John Gregory, *A Comparative View of the State and Faculties of Man with Those of the Animal World* (7th ed., London: Printed for J. Dodsley, 1774), p. 22.

49. John Wall, *Plain Directions, etc. for The Cure of the Venereal Disease. Together with Efficacious and Approved Remedies, adapted to Every Symptom of the Disorder. Sufficient to enable Persons to cure Themselves . . . Designed Chiefly to rescue the Poor, and People of Small Fortunes from the Destructive Hands of Unskillful Apothecaries and Quack Doctors* (London: W. Griffin, G. Kearsley; York: E. Etherington, 1764), pp. 26, 29, 36–37.

50. Lichtenberg, *Hogarth on High Life*, pp. 36, 49, 56–57.

51. Jean-Louis Alibert, *Physiologie des passions, ou nouvelle doctrine des sentiments moraux*, 2 vols. (Paris: Chez Béchet Jeune, Libraire, 1825), I, 274–276.

52. Vogt, *Das Bilden des Kranken*, p. 51.

53. Jean-Louis Alibert, *Clinique de l'Hôpital Saint-Louis, ou traité complet des maladies de la peau, contenant la description de ces maladies et leurs meilleurs modes de traitement*, 2 vols. in 1 (Paris: Chez B. Cormon et Blanc, Libraries; Lyon: S. P. Imprimerie de Casimir, 1833), p. xxiii. There was, in addition, an Italian edition published in Venice in 1835. Also see Hahn, Dumaitre, and Samion-Contet, *Histoire de la médecine*, pp. 345–346.

54. Robert Willan, *Description and Treatment of Cutaneous Diseases. Order I. Papulous Eruptions on the Skin* (London: Printed for J. Johnson, 1798), introduction. Also see Thomas Bateman, *Delineations of Cutaneous Diseases exhibiting the Characteristic Appearances of the Principal Genera and Species* (London: Longmans, 1817).

55. Alibert, *Clinique de l'Hôpital Saint-Louis*, pp. xxii–xxiii. Also see Gérard Tilles and Daniel Wallach, "Histoire de la nosologie en dermatologie," *Annales Dermatologiques Vénéréologiques*, 106 (1989), p. 19.

56. Aubry et al., *Album comique*, letterpress for *Les loupes* [Pigal]. Also see M. Gleditsch, "Sur une excrescence monstrueuse trouvée sur un sapin," *Memoires de l'Académie Royale de Prusse*, 5 (1755), 6, 14–15, 18.

57. Alibert, *Clinique de l'Hôpital Saint-Louis*, pp. 215–216.

58. Ibid., pp. 70–71, 152, 185, 195, 253, 341. Also see Jenner, *Inquiry*, p. 1.

59. Alibert, *Clinique de l'Hôpital Saint-Louis*, p. 258.

60. Aubry et al., *Album comique*, letterpress to *Les envies de femmes grosses*.

61. Roger B. Dworkin, "The New Genetics," in *Biolaw*, ed. James F. Childress et al. (New York: University Publications of America, 1986), pp. 89–90, 96–98; and Roger B. Dworkin and Gilbert S. Omenn, "Legal Aspects of Human Genetics," *Annual Review of Public Health*, 5 (1985), 113–115.

62. Barbara M. Stafford, John La Puma, M.D., and David Schiedermayer, M.D., "One Face of Beauty, One Picture of Health: The Hidden Aesthetic of Medical Practice," *Journal of Medicine and Philosophy*, 14 (1989), 225–226.

63. Nicolas Malebranche, *De la recherche de la vérité, où l'on traite de la nature de l'esprit de l'homme, & de l'usage qu'il en doit faire pour éviter l'erreur dans les sciences*, 4 vols. (Paris: Chez Michel David, 1712), I, 468–469.

64. Jean-Louis Fischer, "Defense et critiques de la thèse 'imaginationiste' à l'époque de Spallanzani," in Bernardi and La Vergata, eds., *Lazzaro Spallanzani*, p. 427. Also see Canguilhem, *La Connaissance de la vie*, p. 175.

65. Ricoeur, *Conflict of Interpretations*, pp. 276–279.

66. James Augustus Blondel, *The Power of the Mother's Imagination over the Foetus examin'd in Answer to Dr. Daniel Turner's Book Intitled A Defence of the XIIth Chapter of the First Part of a Treatise, De Morbis Cutaneis* (London: John Brotherton, 1729), p. 86. Also see Russell, *Like Engend'ring Like*, pp. 34–36.

67. Egerton, *Stubbs*, p. 142.

68. Ibid., pp. 12, 184. Also see Lorenz E. A. Eitner, *Géricault: His Life and Work* (London: Orbis Publishing, 1983), p. 65.

69. Paré, *Oeuvres*, p. 1021.

70. Junius, *Painting of the Ancients*, pp. 95–96.

71. Ibid., p. 138.

72. Harvey, *Anatomical Exercitations*, p. 550.

73. Henry More, *Enthusiasmus Triumphatus, or, a Discourse of the Nature, Causes, Kinds, and Cure of Enthusiasme* (London: Printed by J. Flesher, 1656), pp. 15, 28; and *Immortality of the Soul*, pp. 169–170.

74. Fischer, "La Thèse 'imaginationiste,'" pp. 413–414.

75. Malebranche, *Recherche de la vérité*, I, 310.

76. Ibid., 317.

77. Ibid., pp. 323–326.

78. Ibid., pp. 329–330.

79. Philip K. Wilson, "'Out of Sight, Out of Mind?' The Daniel Turner–James Blondel Debate over Maternal Impressions" (M.A. thesis, The Johns Hopkins University, 1987), pp. 5–25.

80. Blondel, *Power of Mother's Imagination*, pp. xi–xiii.

81. Ibid., p. 111.

82. La Mettrie, *L'Homme machine*, p. 135; Le Camus, *Médecine de l'esprit*, II, 156; and Muratori, *Forza della fantasia*, pp. 26, 155–156.

83. Pierre-Louis Moreau de Maupertuis, *Dissertation physique à l'occasion du nègre blanc* (Leiden: n. p., 1744), p. 40; and *Earthly Venus*, pp. 49–50.

84. Maupertuis, *Le Nègre blanc*, p. 100.

85. Theodore Eller, "Recherches sur la force de l'imagination des femmes enceintes; sur le foetus, à l'occasion d'un chien monstrueux," *Mémoires de l'Académie Royale de Prusse*, 5 (1756), 166–198.

86. See, for example, M. Roussel, *Système physique et moral de la femme, suivi du système physique et moral de l'homme, et d'un fragment sur la sensibilité, précédé de l'éloge historique de l'auteur par J. L. Alibert* (Paris: Chez Crapart, Caille et Ravier, 1805), pp. 144–150; and Gabriel Jouard, *Des monstruosités et bizarreries de la nature, principalement de celles qui ont rapport à la génération; de leurs causes; de la manière dont elles s'opèrent, etc., avec des réflexions philosophiques sur le monstrueux et dangereux empiètemens des sciences accessoires, telles que la chimie, la droguerie, etc. sur la vraie médecine; ouvrage très-propre à mettre les mères à l'abri des effets des affections de l'âme, de l'imagination, des envies, des frayeurs, des maléfices, etc. . . . , 2 vols. in 1 (Paris: Chez Allut, Impr.-Libr., et Propriétaire du Journal de la Vraie Théorie Médicale, 1806).*

87. Lessing, *Laocoön*, p. 14.

88. Mengs, *Hinterlassene Schriften*, I, 206.

89. Lavater, *Essays*, III, I, 185–188.

90. Augustine, *Against Julian*, trans. Matthew A. Schumacher, C.S.C. (New York: The Fathers of the Church, Inc., 1957), XVI, 8; 10–11, 16, 21, 57, 63–64. On Augustine, see John Bowden and Alan Richardson, *Westminster Dictionary of Christian Theology* (Philadelphia: Westminster Press, 1983), pp. 539–540; and Billicsich, *Das Probleme des Übels*, I, 253.

91. Augustine, *Against Julian*, p. 329.

92. Malebranche, *Recherche de la vérité*, I, 334–336; IV, 96.

93. On original sin, see John McClintock and James Strong, *Cyclopedia of Biblical Literature* (New York: Arno Press, 1969), IX–X, 763–767; R. J. Werblowsky and Zwi and Wigoder Geiffrey, eds., *The Encyclopedia of the Jewish Religion* (New York: Holt, Rinehart and Winston, 1966), pp. 136–141; J. C. J. Metford, *Dictionary of Christian Lore and Legend* (London: Thames and Hudson, 1983), p. 96; and *Dictionary of the History of Ideas*, IV, 224–233.

94. Blondel, *Power of Mother's Imagination*, p. 9. On original sin, see also Ricoeur, *Conflict of Interpretations*, pp. 272–273.

95. Shaftesbury, *Philosophical Regimen*, p. 164.

96. Blake, *Complete Writings*, p. 471. Also see Reynolds, *Discourses*, p. 44.

97. Jay Macpherson, *The Spirit of Solitude: Conventions and Continuities in Late Romance* (New Haven: Yale University Press, 1982), p. 194.

98. Licetus, *De Monstris*, pp. 149–150. On domino, see Aileen Ribeiro, *The Dress Worn at Masquerade in England, 1730–1790, and Its Relation to Fancy Dress in Portraiture* (New York: Garland, 1984), pp. 30–31, 33–34.

99. Alibert, *Clinique de l'Hôpital Saint-Louis*, pp. 338–339. Also see John H. Dirckx, "Dermatologic Terms in the *De Medicina* of Celsus," *American Journal of*

Dermapathology, 5 (August 1983), 368–369.

100. R. Blanchard, "Sur un cas inédit de négresse-pie au XVIIIe siècle," *Zoologische Annalen*, 1 (1904), 45.

101. On the contents of Curtius's *cabinet*, see Sorel, *Palais-Royal*, p. 180.

102. Blanchard, "Sur un cas inédit," pp. 43–44.

103. Maupertuis, *Le Nègre blanc*, pp. 93–95. Also see Jacques Roger, *Les Sciences de la vie dans la pensée française du XVIIIe siècle* (2d rev. ed., Paris: Armand Colin, 1971), pp. 477–478.

104. Maupertuis, *Earthly Venus*, pp. 75–76.

105. Ibid., pp. 66–67.

106. Jacques Roger, "Histoire naturelle et biologie chez Buffon," in Bernardi and La Vergata, eds., *Lazzaro Spallanzani*, pp. 354–355; and R. Mauzi and S. Menant, *Littérature française. Le XVIIIe siècle, 1750–1778* (Paris: Arthaud, 1977), II, 152–156.

107. Georges-Louis Le Clerc, Comte de Buffon, *Histoire naturelle, générale et particulière, avec la description du cabinet du roi*, 44 vols. (Paris: De l'Imprimerie Royale, 1749–1803), I, 250–253, 257–259.

108. There was a whole series of essays on the topic. See especially the exchange between the two Berlin physicians Meckel and Le Cat: "Nouvelles observations sur l'épiderme & le cerveau des nègres," *Mémoires de l'Académie Royale de Prusse*, 6 (1757), 8–9, 60–79.

109. Jean-Anthelme Brillat-Savarin, *The Physiology of Taste, or Meditations on Transcendental Gastronomy* [*1825*], intro. by Arthur Machen (New York: Dover Publishing, Inc., 1960), see, especially, Chapter II, "Of Taste," pp. 21–33.

110. Bouhours, *La Manière de bien penser*, p. 156.

111. Ibid., p. 366.

112. Blake, *Complete Writings*, p. 599.

113. Richardson, *Theory of Painting*, p. 67.

114. Dufresnoy, *Art of Painting*, pp. xliv, l, lvi–lviii, 197–198.

115. Lairesse, *Art of Painting*, pp. 160–161, 169; Jean Dubreuil, *The Practice of Perspective: Or, An Easy Method of representing Natural Objects according to the Rules of Art*, trans. Ephraim Chambers (London: Printed for Tho. Bowles and John Bowles, 1726), p. 143. On figural elongation and distension, see Edward J. Olszewski, "Distortions, Shadows, and Conventions, in Sixteenth-Century Italian Art," *Artibus et Historiae*, 6 (1985), 111–112.

116. Hagedorn, *Réflexions sur la peinture*, p. 126.

117. Abraham Bosse, *Le Peintre converty aux précises et universelles règles de son art. Sentiments sur la distinction des diverses manières de peinture, dessin et gravure* (1667), ed. R. A. Wigert (Paris: Hermann, 1964), pp. 164–166.

118. Le Blon, *L'Art d'imprimer*, pp. 64–68.

119. Hogarth, *Analysis of Beauty*, pp. 116–119.

120. Ibid., pp. 95–97, 105, 111–112.

121. Lichtenberg, *Hogarth on High Life*, pp. 85–89, 107. Also see Huber, *Handbuch für Kunstliebhaber*, p. 17.

122. Georges Stubbs, *An Illustrated Lecture on Sketching from Nature in Pencil and Water Colour: With Hints on Light and Shadow, on a Method of Study, etc. To be a Series of Lessons Out of Doors* (London: Day and Son, n.d.), p. 11.

123. Richardson, *Essay on Prints*, pp. 270–271. Also see Margaret Deutsch Caroll, "Rembrandt as Meditational Printmaker," *Art Bulletin*, 63 (December 1981), 604.

124. Ludwig Munz, *A Critical Catalogue of Rembrandt's Etchings and the Etchings of His School Formerly attributed to the Master with an Essay on Rembrandt's Technique and Documentary Sources*, 2 vols. (London: Phaidon Press, 1952), II, 212.

125. Jean-Baptiste Descamps, *La Vie des peintres flamands, allemands, et hollandais*, 2 vols. (Paris: Chez Charles-Antoine Jombert, 1754), II, 92. Also see Stephanie S.

Rickey, "'Judicious Negligence': Rembrandt Transforms an Emblematic Convention," *Art Bulletin*, 68 (June 1986), 253.

126. Antoine-Nicolas Dézallier d'Argenville, *Abrégé de la vie des plus fameux peintres*, 3 vols. (Paris: De Bure l'Aîné, 1745–1752), pp. 116, 118; and Pernety, *Dictionnaire*, p. 244.

127. Fuseli, *Lectures on Painting*, pp. 92–93. For Ruskin's criticism, see David Park Curry, *James McNeill Whistler at the Freer Gallery of Art*, exh. cat. (Washington, D.C.: Freer Gallery of Art, Smithsonian Institution, 1984), p. 75.

128. Fuseli, *Lectures on Painting*, p. 97.

129. Blake, *Complete Writings*, pp. 447, 450, 477, 595. On Reynolds's emulation of Rembrandt, see Nicholas Penny, ed., *Reynolds*, exh. cat. (London: Royal Academy of Arts, 1986), pp. 175–176, 206.

130. Sulzer, *Allgemeine Theorie*, I, II, 745, 746.

131. Eleanor A. Sayre, *The Changing Image: Prints by Francisco Goya*, exh. cat. (Boston: Museum of Fine Arts, 1974), pp. 55–56; and *Schlaf der Vernunft*, p. 25. On the *Carceri*, see Andrew Robison, *Piranesi: Early Architectural Fantasies* (Chicago: University of Chicago Press, 1985), p. 165.

132. Wotton, *Ancient and Modern Learning*, p. 76.

133. Joshua Gilder, "I Think about Death Every Day," *Flash Art*, 112 (May 1983), 17–20. Also see Lawrence Gowing et al., *Francis Bacon Retrospective*, exh. cat. (Washington, D.C.: Hirshhorn Museum & Sculpture Garden, Smithsonian Institution, 1989).

134. Marjorie Hope Nicolson, *The Breaking of the Circle: Studies in the Effect of the "New Science" upon Seventeenth-Century Poetry* (New York: Columbia University Press, 1960), p. 123.

135. Moravia, "Capture of the Invisible," pp. 374–375. Also see Mauzi and Menant, *Littérature française*, II, 192.

136. Lossky, *Mystical Theology*, pp. 121–122.

137. Eaves, *Blake's Theory of Art*, pp. 63, 161; and Hilton, *Literal Imagination*, p. 13.

138. Anna Sigridur Arnar, *Encyclopedism from Pliny to Borges*, exh. cat. (Chicago: University of Chicago Library, 1990), p. 28.

139. Novalis, *Das Philosophische-Theoretische Werk*, II, 474, 491. Also see Dierse, *Enzyklopädie*, pp. 70–71, 125–131.

140. Novalis, *Das Philosophische-Theoretische Werk*, II, 483, 488. Also see Neubauer, *Symbolismus*, pp. 80–81, 91.

141. Sacks, *Man Who Mistook His Wife for a Hat*, pp. 12–16, 29, 104–107. Also see Grassi, *Macht der Phantasie*, pp. 182–184.

142. Goellnicht, *Keats*, pp. 99–101.

143. See, for example, Juliet Wilson Bareau, "The Hidden Face of Manet: An Investigation of the Artist's Working Process," *Burlington*, 127 (April 1986), 6–8, 12–15.

144. Coleridge, *Biographia Literaria*, pp. 11, 20. Also see Thomas McFarland, *Originality & Imagination* (Baltimore: Johns Hopkins University Press, 1985), pp. 103–106, 155; and Trevor H. Levere, *Poetry Realized in Nature: Samuel Taylor Coleridge and Early Nineteenth-Century Science* (Cambridge: Cambridge University Press, 1981), pp. 95–96.

145. Hessel Miedema, "On Mannerism and *Maniera*," *Simiolus*, 10 (1978–1979), 22. Also see Hugo Friedrich, "Über die *Silvae* des Statius (inbesondere V, 4, *Somnus*) und die Frage des Literarischen Manierismus," *Wort und Text. Festschrift für Fritz Schalk*, ed. Harri Meier and Hans Sikommodau (Frankfurt am Main: Vittorio Klostermann, 1963), pp. 38–40.

146. Winckelmann, *Versuch einer Allegorie*, p. 2.

147. Hocke, *Die Welt als Labyrinth*, pp. 486–490. Also see Jonsen and Toulmin, *Abuse of Casuistry*, pp. 143–145.

148. Miedema, "On Mannerism," pp. 24–25; and Conte, *Rhetoric of Imitation*, pp. 82–83, 87–88.

149. Marc Fumaroli, *L'Age d'éloquence. Rhétorique et "res literaria" de la Renaissance au seuil de l'époque classique* (Geneva: Librairie Droz, 1980), p. 4.

150. Willi Hirdt, "Zu *Milieu* und Sprache im Französichen Roman des 19. Jahrhunderts," *Archiv*, 215, no. 2 (1978), 337.

151. Eitner, *Géricault*, pp. 43–44.

152. Kenshur, *Open Form*, pp. 19–20; and Barney, *Allegories of History*, pp. 147–148.

153. Crome, *Symbol und Unzulänglichkeit*, pp. 209–211.

154. Coleridge, *Biographia Literaria*, p. 179.

155. Brilliant, *Visual Narratives*, pp. 51–52, 104.

156. Winckelmann, *Versuch einer Allegorie*, pp. 5–6.

157. Warncke, *Sprechende Bilder*, pp. 191–198.

158. Winckelmann, *Versuch einer Allegorie*, pp. 2–3.

159. Stigler, *History of Statistics*, pp. 171–172.

160. Barbara C. Bowen, "Two Literary Genres: The Emblem and the Joke," *Journal of Medieval and Renaissance Studies*, 15 (Spring 1985), special issue, 34–35. Also see Gerta Calmann, "The Picture of Nobody," *Journal of the Warburg and Courtauld Institutes*, 23 (1960), 60.

161. Céard and Margolin, *Rébus de la Renaissance*, I, 37–38, 63–64.

162. Benjamin Buchloh, "Figures of Authority, Ciphers of Regression: Notes on the Return of Representation in European Painting," *October*, no. 16 (Spring 1981), 42–45, 54.

163. Gordon, "Aboli Bibelot?," pp. 106–17.

164. Giuseppi Biorci and Vincenzo Tagliasco, "Tecnologia e rappresentazione del corpo," in *Lo Specchio e il doppio. Della stagno di Narciso allo schermo televisio*, exh. cat. (Turin: Mole Antonelliana, 1987), p. 100.

165. For the common view that memorable words are being replaced by unmemorable visual moments, see Jamieson, *Eloquence in an Electronic Age*, pp. x, 9–10.

166. Edward Tufte, "Envisioning Information," *Personal Computing Forum*, 1 (1988), 78, 79; "The Power of Graphics: Escaping the Flatland of Chartjunk to the Multivariate World of Hyperspace," *PC Computing*, 1 (August 1988), 88–90; and "Attention to Detail," p. 112.

5 MAGNIFYING

1. Philip and Phylis Morrison, *Powers of Ten: A Book about the Relative Size of Things in the Universe and the Effect of Adding Another Zero* (New York: Scientific American Library, 1982).

2. Rémy G. Saisselin, *The Bourgeois and the Bibelot* (New Brunswick, N.J.: Rutgers University Press, 1984), pp. 205–207.

3. Barbara Maria Stafford, "'Magnifications': The Eighteenth-Century Fortunes of a Primitive and Universal 'Imagistic,'" *Prospettiva*, 57–60 (April 1989–October 1990), pp. 308–315.

4. Algarotti, *Dialogues sur l'optique*, *Oeuvres*, I, 109–110.

5. Le Camus, *Médecine de l'esprit*, II, 100. On the same point, see Johann Franz Griendel von Ach, *Micrographia Nova: oder Neu-Curieuse Beschreibung Verschiedener Kleiner Körper welche vermittelst einer absonderlichen von dem Authore Neuerfunden Vergrösser-Glasses verwünderlich Gross vorgestellet werden* (Nürnberg: In Verlegung Johann Ziegers Buchhändlers, 1687), introduction.

6. Edward S. Casey, *Imagining: A Phenomenological Study* (Bloomington: Indiana University Press, 1976), pp. 232–233.

7. Donat de Chapeaurouge, *"Das Auge ist ein Herr, das Ohr ein Knecht." Der Weg von der Mittelalterlichen zur Abstrakten Malerei* (Wiesbaden: Franz Steiner Verlag, 1983), pp. 86–119.

8. Turner, *Early Scientific Instruments*, pp. 94–96.

9. Scheuchzer, *Physique sacrée*, II, 45.

10. Robert Hooke, *Micrographia: or Some Physiological Descriptions of Minute Bodies made by Magnifying Glasses with Observations and Inquiries Thereupon* (London: Printed for James Allestry, 1665), preface. On Hooke, see Sabra, *Theories of Light*, pp. 191–192, 321.

11. Henry Powers, *Experimental Philosophy in Three Books: Containing New Experiments Microscopical, Mercurial, Magnetical* (London: Printed by T. Roycroft for John Martin and James Allestry, 1664), preface.

12. Addison, *Critical Essays*, p. 203.

13. George Adams, *Micrographia Illustrata, or, The Knowledge of the Microscope explain'd: Together with an Account of A New Invented Universal Single or Double Microscope. Either of Which is capable of being applied to An Improv'd Solar Apparatus* (London: Printed and Sold by the Author, 1747), pp. 110–111.

14. On Buffon's views, see Fabre, *Recherches sur la nature de l'homme*, pp. 102–103. On spontaneous generation, see Thomas S. Hall, "Spallanzani on Matter and Life: With Notes on the Influence of Descartes," and Richard Toellner, "Lazzaro Spallanzani, the 'Generatio Spontanea' and the Conception of the World," in Bernardi and La Vergata, eds., *Lazzaro Spallanzani*, pp. 71, 111, 119. Also see Hankins, *Science and the Enlightenment*, pp. 130–131.

15. Toellner, "The 'Generatio Spontanea,'" pp. 115–117.

16. Rössel von Rosenhof, *Historia Naturalis Ranarum*, especially pls. X, XI, XVII.

17. *Encyclopaedia Britannica*, III, 503.

18. Hooke, *Micrographia*, preface.

19. Ibid.

20. Ibid.

21. Proclus, *Commentary on the Timaeus*, p. 296. Also see Catherine Wilson, "Visual Surface and Visual Symbol: The Microscope and the Occult in Early Modern Science," *Journal of the History of Ideas*, 49 (January–March 1988), 100–101.

22. Hooke, *Micrographia*, preface.

23. More, *Immortality of the Soul*, pp. 23, 27, 62.

24. Oldmixon, *Essay on Criticism*, p. 45.

25. Hooke, *Micrographia*, p. 8.

26. Brian Vickers, ed., *English Science: Bacon to Newton* (Cambridge: Cambridge University Press, 1984), pp. 16–20.

27. Schama, *Embarrassment of Riches*, pp. 263–265.

28. Lairesse, *Art of Painting*, p. 259. Also see Mengs, *Hinterlassene Schriften*, II, 154, 217.

29. Hooke, *Micrographia*, pp. 113, 123–126.

30. Ibid., pp. 2–3.

31. Power, *Experimental Philosophy*, p. 53.

32. Hooke, *Micrographia*, p. 8.

33. Joscelyn Godwin, *Athanasius Kircher: A Renaissance Man and the Quest for Lost Knowledge* (London: Thames and Hudson, 1979), p. 13.

34. Athanasius Kircher, *Ars Magna Lucis et Umbrae. In Decem Libros digesta*, 2 vols. (Rome: Sumptibus Hermanni Scheus, 1646), II, 812. Also see Roland Barthes, *Arcimboldo* (Milan: Franco Maria Riccia, 1980), pp. 34–36.

35. Hooke, *Micrographia*, p. 82.

36. Jacques Ozanam, *Récréations mathématiques et physiques, qui contiennent plusieurs problêmes d'arthmétiques . . . & de physique*, 4 vols. (rev. ed., Paris: Chez C. A. Jombert, 1735), IV, 140.

37. Harris, *Lexicon Technicum*, II, "Micrography," "Microscope"; Chambers, *Cyclopaedia*, II, "Microscopy," "Reflec-

tion"; *Encyclopaedia Britannica*, III, "Of Microscopes," 420–421.

38. Turner, *Early Scientific Instruments*, pp. 120–122.

39. Ibid., p. 173.

40. Adams, *Micrographia Illustrata*, pp. 5–6, 8–10, 11.

41. Caroline Walker Bynum, *Docere Verbo et Exemplo: An Aspect of Twelfth-Century Spirituality* (Missoula, Montana: Scholars Press, 1979), pp. 79–80.

42. Jean-Antoine Nollet, *Leçons de physique expérimentale* (2d ed., Paris: Chez Hippolyte-Louis Guérin & Louis-François Delatour, 1758), 572, 575.

43. Martin Frobène Ledermüller, *Troisieme-cinquantaine des amusemens microscopiques* (Nuremberg: Adams Wolfgang Winter-Schmidt graveur et marchand en tailles douces, 1768), pp. 8–10.

44. Isaac Newton, *Opticks or A Treatise of the Reflections, Refractions, Inflections & Colours of Light* (reprinted from the 4th ed., 1730); New York: Dover Publications, 1952), p. 16.

45. Algarotti, *Dialogues sur l'optique*, in *Ouevres*, I, 328. Also see Newton, *Opticks*, p. 26.

46. Castel, *L'Optique des couleurs*, pp. 382, 393, 458. Also see Julia L. Epstein and Mark L. Greenberg, "Decomposing Newton's Rainbow," *Journal of the History of Ideas*, 45 (March 1984), 117, 121.

47. Castel, *L'Optique des couleurs*, pp. 47, 376. Also see Algarotti, *Dialogues sur l'optique*, in *Oeuvres*, I, 152.

48. Herbert Grabes, *The Mutable Glass: Mirror-Imagery in Titles and Texts of the Middle Ages and the English Renaissance*, trans. Gordon Collier (Cambridge: Cambridge University Press, 1982), p. 131. Also see Marco Bussagli, "Lo Specchio e l'artista," pp. 194, 216–217.

49. Porter, "The Language of Quackery," pp. 75–78, 84; Ribeiro, *Masquerade*, pp. 8–9.

50. Serge Soupel, "Science and Medicine and the Mid-Eighteenth Century Novel: Literature and the Language of Science," in *Literature and Science and Medicine*, ed. Serge Soupel and Roger A. Hambridge (Los Angeles: University of California Press, 1982), pp. 48–52.

51. Chambers, *Cyclopaedia*, I, "Empiric," "Charlatan/Charletan."

52. Calmann, "The Picture of No-Body," p. 66.

53. On French and English illiteracy, see Lynn Hunt, "The Political Psychology of Revolutionary Caricature," in Cuno, ed., *French Caricature*, pp. 33–35; and Barrell, *Political Theory of Painting*, pp. 77–82.

54. Webb, *Inquiry into Painting*, p. 9.

55. Gilman, *Iconoclasm and Poetry*, pp. 41–44; Marin, *Etudes semiologiques*, pp. 205–206; and Trimpi, *Muses of One Mind*, p. 115.

56. Monique Canto, "Acts of Fake: The Icon in Platonic Thought," *Representations*, 10 (Spring 1985), 125–126.

57. Ozanam, *Récréations mathématiques*, I, introduction.

58. Moréri, *Grand Dictionnaire*, IV, 407.

59. Corneille, *Dictionnaire*, II, 436.

60. Bartoli, *Dictionnaire*, "critique."

61. Chambers, *Cyclopaedia*, II, "Magic/Magia."

62. Coleridge, *Biographia Literaria*, p. 68. On the Romantic rebellion against the visual gimmicks of stagecraft, see Frederick Burwick, "Stage Illusion and the Stage Designs of Goethe and Hugo," *Word & Image*, 4 (July–December 1988), 692–718.

63. Coleridge, *Biographia Literaria*, p. 75.

64. William Pietz, "The Problem of the Fetish, II: The Origin of the Fetish," *Res*, 13 (Spring 1987), 26, 35. Also see Bevan, *Holy Images*, p. 37.

65. Sheppard, *Proclus on the Republic*, pp. 145–146.

66. Corneille, *Dictionnaire*, I, "gnostiques," 517. Also see Brown, *Body and*

Society, p. 107; Rudolf Bultmann, "Zur Geschichte der Licht-Symbolik im Althertum," *Philogus*, 97 (1948), 32–36; and Horst Rüdiger, "*Curiositas* und *Magie*— Apuleius und Lucius des Literarische Archetypen der Faust-Gestalt," in Meier and Sikommodau, eds., *Wort und Text*, p. 234.

67. Jeffrey Burton Russell, *Satan: The Early Christian Tradition* (Ithaca: Cornell University Press, 1981), pp. 94–101. Also see L'Orange, *Cosmic Kingship*, p. 123.

68. Laurent Bordelon, *L'Histoire des imaginations extravagantes de Monsieur Oufle causées par la lecture des livres, qui traitent de la magie, du grimoire, des démoniaques, sorciers, loups-garoux, incubes, succubes & du sabbat: des fées, ogres, esprits folets, génies, phantômes & d'autres revenans; des songes . . . enfin de toutes les sortes d'apparitions, de divinations, de sortilèges, d'enchantemens, & d'autres superstitions pratiqués*, 2 vols. (Amsterdam: Chez Estienne Roger, Pierre Humbert, Pierre de Coup, et les Frères Chatelain, 1710), II, 50, 70–72. The debate over good and evil apparitions was alive and well during the eighteenth century. Also see Carré de Montgeron, *La Vérité des miracles operés par l'intercession de M. de Pâris et autres appellans, demontrée contre M. l'archevêque de Sens*, 3 vols. (2d ed., Cologne: Chez Les Libraries de la Compagnie, 1745), II, 213–214, 219–223.

69. Philippe Ariès, *Centuries of Childhood: A Social History of Family Life*, trans. Robert Baldick (New York: Alfred A. Knopf, 1962), pp. 68–69.

70. Constance King, *The Encyclopedia of Toys* (New York: Crown Publishers, 1978), pp. 244–247.

71. Jamnes, "Le Livre de science," in Chartier, ed., *Histoire de l'edition française*, pp. 210–211.

72. Edmé Guyot, I, introduction.

73. Barolsky, *Infinite Jest*, p. 9.

74. *Encyclopaedia Britannica*, III, "Of the Multiplying Glass," 425. Also see David C. Lindberg, *Theories of Vision from Al-Kindi to Kepler* (Chicago: University of Chicago Press, 1976), pp. 188–189; and Lemagny, *Photography*, p. 12.

75. Scheuchzer, *Physique sacrée*, VII, 40–41.

76. P. Conor Reilly, *Athanasius Kircher, Master of A Hundred Arts, 1602–1680* (Wiesbaden and Rome: Edizioni del Mondo, 1974), p. 76.

77. Algarotti, *Essai sur la peinture*, in *Oeuvres*, II, 183, 186.

78. Alfredo Corno, "Le Scattole ottiche e il loro uso," in Giorgio Strehler, ed., *La Camera dei sortilegi. Autoritratto di una società nei diorami teatrali del '700*, exh. cat. (Milan: Museo Teatrale alla Scala, 1987), pp. 27–30.

79. David Robinson, "Augsburg Peepshows," *Print Quarterly*, 5 (June 1988), 180–189.

80. Guyot, *Nouvelles récréations*, I, 64. On de Loutherbourg, who was scene-master for Garrick at Drury Lane, see Ellis Waterhouse, *Gainsborough* (London: Spring Books, 1958), p. 25.

81. Corno, "Le Scattole ottiche," in Strehler, ed., *La Camera dei sortilegi*, p. 26.

82. Thomas Rees, *Theatre Lighting in the Age of Gas* (London: Society for Theater Research, 1978), pp. 81–82.

83. Ozanam, *Récréations mathématiques*, I, 429, 437–439; III, 275–276.

84. Ralph Hyde, *Panoramania! The Art and Entertainment of the "All-Embracing" View*, exh. cat. (London: Barbican Art Gallery, 1988), pp. 17, 109–111. On Sir David Brewster, see also Darius, *Beyond Vision*, p. 28; and Emmanuel Pernoud, "Baudelaire, Guys et le kaléidoscope," *Gazette des Beaux-Arts*, 104 (September 1984), 73.

85. Tesauro, *Il Cannocchiale aristotelico*, p. 30. Also see James Elkins, "Linear Perspective in Renaissance Practice and in Modern Scholarship" (Ph.D dissertation, University of Chicago, 1988), pp. 279–

281; and Hocke, *Die Welt als Labyrinth*, p. 152.

86. Edward Orme, *An Essay on Transparent Prints and on Transparencies in General* (London: Printed for, and Sold by, the Author, 1807), p. 9.

87. Ibid., p. iv.

88. Helmut von Erffa and Allen Staley, *The Painting of Benjamin West* (New Haven: Yale University Press, 1986), p. 90.

89. Orme, *Transparencies*, p. 17.

90. Quintilian, *Institutes*, II, 143–144; Junius, *Painting of the Ancients*, pp. 300, 304. Also see Eva Keuls, "Rhetoric and Visual Aids in Greece and Rome," in *Communication Arts in the Ancient World*, ed. Eric A. Havelock and Jackson P. Hershkell (New York: Hastings House Publishers, 1978), p. 124.

91. John Hayes and Lindsay Stainton, *Gainsborough Drawings*, exh. cat. (Washington, D.C.: International Exhibitions Foundation, 1983), p. 136.

92. Barbara Maria Stafford, "Endymion's Moonbath: Art and Science in Girodet's Early Masterpiece," *Leonardo*, 15, no. 3 (1982), 193–198. For Girodet's deliberate seeking out of nocturnal effects, see also my "Les *météores* de Girodet," *La Revue de l'Art*, 46 (1979), 46–51.

93. Priscella E. Miller, *Goya's "Black" Paintings: Truth and Reason—Light and Liberty* (New York: Hispanic Society of America, 1984), pp. 28–29.

94. *Images animées, Lumière et magie. Les Fantasmagories de Robertson*, exh. cat. (Paris: Musée National des Techniques, 1990), n.p.

95. Richard, *Théorie des songes*, p. 116. On vivid interior vision, see Quintilian, *Institutes*, I, 427; Origen, *Homilies on Genesis and Exodus*, p. 106, and *Commentary on the Song of Songs*, p. 80; and Junius, *Painting of the Ancients*, p. 60. On mental contents becoming autonomous, see Grassi, *Rhetoric as Philosophy*, p. 65.

96. Ludwig Pfeiffer, "Fiction: On the Fate of a Concept between Philosophy and Literary Theory," in *Aesthetic Illusion*, ed. Frederick Burwick and Walter Pape (Berlin: De Gruyter Verlag, 1990), pp. 92–105.

97. Thomas Hobbes, *Leviathan* (1651; New York: E. P. Dutton and Co.; London: J. M. Dent and Sons, 1950), pp. 133–134. Also see Elizabeth J. Cook, "Thomas Hobbes and the 'Far-Fetched,'" *Journal of the Warburg and Courtauld Institutes*, 44 (1981), 230.

98. Quintilian, *Institutes*, II, 162–164.

99. Hume, *Treatise of Human Nature*, I, IV, II, pp. 205–207.

100. Immanuel Kant, *Critique of Pure Reason*, trans. Norman Kemp Smith (London: Macmillan, 1963), B 178–182, pp. 181–183. For a rare historian of philosophy who notes Kant's deleterious effect on aesthetic theory, see Johnson, *The Body in the Mind*, especially pp. 166–170.

101. Hume, *Treatise of Human Nature*, I, I, IV, pp. 11–13. Also see John Yolton, *Perceptual Acquaintance from Descartes to Reid* (Minneapolis: University of Minnesota Press, 1984), pp. 167–168.

102. Chevalier [Andrew Michael] Ramsay, *The Travels of Cyrus, To Which is annexed, A Discourse upon the Theology and Mythology of the Pagans* (London: Printed by James Bettenham, 1752), p. xxiii.

103. Lavater, *Essays*, II, II, 364. Also see Blumenberg, *Die Lesbarkeit der Welt*, p. 199.

104. On Idealism, Neoplatonism, and the purity of optical mixtures, see Paul Smith, "Paul Adam, *Soi* et les 'peintres impressionistes': la génèse d'un discours moderniste," *Revue de l'Art*, 82 (1988), 41, 43–44. Also see Gibson, *Ecological Approach to Perception*, pp. 206–207.

105. See especially Yolton, *Perceptual Acquaintance*, pp. 135–136; and Alan Donagan, "Berkeley's Theory of the Immediate Objects of Vision," in Machamer and Turnbull, eds., *Studies in Perception*, pp.

319–320, 330–331. Also see Edward Grant, *Much Ado about Nothing: Theories of Space and Vacuum from the Middle Ages to the Scientific Revolution* (Cambridge: Cambridge University Press, 1981), pp. 195–196, 226.

106. George Berkeley, *A Treatise Concerning the Principles of Human Knowledge*, in *A New Theory of Vision* (London: J. M. Dent & Sons; New York: E. P. Dutton, 1919), sects. XXXIII, XL, pp. 129, 132.

107. Blake, *Complete Writings*, pp. 773–774.

108. Berkeley, *Principles*, sect. XXIII, p. 124.

109. Anonymous, *An Enquiry into the Nature of the Human Soul: Wherein the Immateriality of the Soul is Evinced from the Principles of Reason and Philosophy*, 2 vols. (3d ed., London: A. Millar, 1745), II, 239–240, 279.

110. M. M. Slaughter, *Universal Languages and Scientific Taxonomy in the Seventeenth Century* (Cambridge: Cambridge University Press, 1982), pp. 128, 153–154. Also see Atran, *Fondements de l'histoire naturelle*, p. 89; and Dierse, *Enzyklopädie*, pp. 31–35.

111. George Berkeley, *Alciphron: or the Minute Philosopher*, in *The Works*, 2 vols. (Dublin: John Exshaw, 1784), II, sects. IV, X–XV, pp. 457–463. On the primacy of a visual divine language in Berkeley's system and its connection to his Christian, anti-Deistic stance, see A. David Kline, "Berkeley's Divine Language Argument," in *Essays on the Philosophy of George Berkeley*, ed. Ernest Sosa (Dordrecht: D. Reidel Publishing Company, 1987), pp. 129–142.

112. Addison, *Pleasures of the Imagination*, pp. 183–185; Richardson, *Theory of Painting*, p. 6.

113. Lessing, *Laocoön*, pp. 41, 80, 89.

114. Campbell, *Philosophy of Rhetoric*, II, 93–94; and Beattie, *Dissertations*, p. 243.

115. Berkeley, *Alciphron*, sects. XX–XXII, pp. 345, 347.

116. Caton, *Origin of Subjectivity*, pp. 84–86.

117. Descartes, *Discourse on Method*, pp. 38–40. Also see Schouls, *Imposition of Method*, p. 37.

118. Recent interpreters include: Marc Eli Blanchard, "The Pleasures of Description," *Diacritics* (June 1977), pp. 22–34; and Blanchard, "Writing the Museum: Diderot's Bodies in the Salons," in *Diderot Digression and Dispersion: A Bicentennial Tribute*, ed. Jack Undank and Herbert Josephs (Lexington, Ky.: French Forum Publishers, 1984), pp. 21–35. Also see Norman Bryson, *Wora and Image: French Painting of the Ancien Régime* (Cambridge: Cambridge University Press, 1981), p. 185; and Marian Hobson, *The Object of Art: The Theory of Illusion in Eighteenth-Century France* (Cambridge: Cambridge University Press, 1982), p. 205. The best total reading is provided by Mary D. Sheriff, *Fragonard: Art and Eroticism* (Chicago: University of Chicago Press, 1990), pp. 30–46. Also see my "'Fantastic Images': From Unenlightening to Enlightening 'Appearances' Meant to Be Seen in the Dark," in Burwick and Pape, eds., *Aesthetic Illusion*.

119. For the idea that Fragonard's spectacle owed its inspiration to contemporary plays, ballets, and illustrations in *livrets*, see Beth S. Wright, "New (Stage) Light on Fragonard's *Coresus*," *Arts Magazine*, 60 (June 1986), 54–59.

120. Diderot, *Salons*, II; see especially the section entitled, "L'Antre de Platon," pp. 189–198.

121. Note that this is not proper *sfumato*. Throughout the eighteenth century, *enfumé* had a negative connotation. See René Verbraeken, *Clair-Obscur, histoire d'un mot* (Nogent-le-Roi: Librarie des Arts et Métiers-Editions, 1979), p. 58.

122. Diderot is paraphrasing Plato, *Republic* X, 521C, and the *Sophist* 235D–236C.

123. Phillip D. Cummins, "On the Status of Visuals in Berkeley's *New Theory of*

Vision"; and George S. Pappas, "Berkeley and Immediate Perception," in Sosa, ed., *Essays on the Philosophy of Berkeley*, pp. 165–194, 195–213. Also see Lester Crocker, "The Problem of Truth and Falsehood in the Enlightenment," *Journal of the History of Ideas*, 14 (October 1953), 575–603.

124. François-Marie Arouet de Voltaire, *Dictionnaire philosophique comprenant les 118 articles parus sous ce titre du vivant de Voltaire avec leurs suppléments parus dans les Questions sur l'Encyclopédie* (1764), ed. Raymond Nzaves and Julien Benda (rev. ed., Paris: Editions Garnier Frères, 1967), "Corps," pp. 149–151. On Berkeley's reception in France, see Otis Fellows, "George Berkeley, His Door, and the *Philosophes*," in *Studies in Eighteenth-Century Literature Presented to Robert Niklaus*, ed. J. H. Fox, M. H. Waddicor, and D. A. Watts (Exeter: University of Exeter, 1975), pp. 57–59.

125. La Mettrie, *L'Homme machine*, p. 113; D'Holbach, *Système de la nature*, I, 110; Le Camus, *Médecine de l'esprit*, II, 152; and Diderot, *Eléments de physiologie*, p. 253.

126. I am grateful to Wesley Trimpi for having drawn my attention to this article. See Diderot, "Ecclecticisme," *Encyclopédie*, V, 251–292.

127. Paul Sadrin, *Nicolas-Antoine Boulanger (1722–1759), ou avant nous le déluge* (Oxford: Voltaire Foundation, 1986), pp. 55ff. Beth Wilson suggested a connection between the contemporary Calas affair and the subject of religious fanaticism. See her "*Coresus*," p. 57. I believe the issues are deeper than just one instantiation.

128. See my state-of-the-field essay, "The Eighteenth Century: Towards an Interdisciplinary Model," *Art Bulletin*, 70 (March 1988), 7–24.

129. Mortier, *Clartés et ombres*, pp. 65–68. On the need for distinguishing message from propaganda, see also William H. Kruskal, "Criteria for Judging Statistical Graphics," *Utilitas Mathematica*, 21 B (May 1982), 283–285.

130. Klaus Herding, "Visual Codes in the Graphic Art of the French Revolution," in Cuno, *French Caricature*, pp. 96–97.

131. Diderot, *Salons*, II, 209. Also see Charles Baudelaire, *Art in Paris: Reviews of Salons and Other Exhibitions* (London: Phaidon, 1965), pp. 204–205.

132. Dubos, *Réflexions critiques*, I, 284, 375–376, 621–624.

133. Watelet, *L'Art de peindre*, p. 163.

134. Fuseli, *Lectures on Painting*, pp. 29–31.

135. Batteux, *Principes de la littérature*, pp. 19–26. Also see Bouhours, *Manière de bien penser*, p. 11.

136. William R. Paulson, *Enlightenment, Romanticism, and the Blind in France* (Princeton, N.J.: Princeton University Press, 1987), p. 57.

137. Batteux, *Principes de la littérature*, pp. 6–12, 29–32, 63. Also see M. H. Abrams, "From Addison to Kant: Modern Aesthetics and the Exemplary Art," in *Studies in Eighteenth-Century British Art and Aesthetics*, ed. Ralph Cohen (Berkeley and Los Angeles: University of California Press, 1985), pp. 34–35.

138. Batteux, *Principes de la littérature*, pp. xvii–xix.

139. Lessing, *Laocoön*, pp. 15, 218, 78.

140. Félibien, *Entretiens*, II, 173–185, 229, 239.

141. Dufresnoy, *Art of Painting*, I, xv, xxii.

142. Remond de Sainte-Albine, *Le Comédien*, pp. 14–15.

143. Laugier, *Manière de bien juger*, pp. 105, 148, 157.

144. Lairesse, *Art of Painting*, p. 258.

145. Mercier, *Du théâtre*, p. 294.

146. Hurd, *Letters on Chivalry*, pp. 91–92.

147. Fuseli, *Lectures on Painting*, pp. 6, 110. Also see Sulzer, *Allgemeine Theorie*, II, 491, "Fantasieren, Fantasie."

148. Mates, *Philosophy of Leibniz*, pp. 70–73, 184.

149. Grandville, *Un autre monde*, pp. 5, 8.

6 SENSING

1. Hans Moravec, *Mind Children: The Future of Robot and Human Intelligence* (Cambridge, Mass.: Harvard University Press, 1989).

2. Berkeley, *New Theory of Vision*, sect. XLIX, p. 34. On the flux of self, see the excellent study by Christopher Fox, *Locke and the Scriblerians: Identity and Consciousness in Early Modern Britain* (Berkeley and Los Angeles: University of California Press, 1988), pp. 46, 94, 193.

3. George Cheyne, *The English Malady: or, A Treatise of Nervous Diseases of All Kinds, as Spleen, Vapours, Lowness of Spirits, Hypochondriacal, and Hysterical Distempers, etc. In Three Parts* (London: Printed for G. Strahan, 1733), pp. 65–66; 192–194. Also see G. S. Rousseau, "Nerves, Spirits, and Fibres: Towards Defining the Origins of Sensibility," in *Studies in the Eighteenth Century*, III, ed. R. F. Brissenden and J. C. Earde (Toronto: University of Toronto Press, 1976), III, 137–157; and Rousseau, "Mysticism and Millenarianism: 'Immortal Dr. Cheyne,'" in *Millenarianism and Messianism in English Literature and Thought, 1650–1800* ed. Richard Popkin (Leiden: Brill, 1988). For a different view of Cheyne, see Anita Guerrini, "Medical Practice and the Birth of the Consumer Society," *Clark Library Seminar*, 3 February 1989, typescript.

4. For Cheyne and the eighteenth-century conception of nerves, see Hilton, *Literal Imagination*, p. 91; and W. F. Bynum, "The Nervous Patient in Eighteenth- and Nineteenth-Century Britain: The Psychiatric Origins of British Neurology," in *The Anatomy of Madness: Essays in the History of Psychiatry*, ed. W. F. Bynum, Roy Porter, and Michael Shepherd, 2 vols. (London and New York: Tavistock Publications, 1985), I, 91.

5. Cloquet, *Encyclopédie méthodique*, III, ii–111. Also see John E. Lesch, *Science and Medicine in France: The Emergence of Experimental Physiology, 1799–1855* (Cambridge, Mass.: Harvard University Press, 1984), p. 35.

6. Willis, *Practice of Physick*, p. 51.

7. Bynum, "Anatomical Method," pp. 448–450.

8. Jacques Gautier Dagoty, *Exposition anatomique des organes des sens, jointe à la nevrologie entières du corps humain, et conjectures sur l'éléctricité animale et le siège de l'âme* (Paris: Chez Demonville Imprimeur-Librairie, 1775), letterpress for pl. 5.

9. Ibid., pp. 20–21, 34–42, and pl. 6.

10. Ibid., pp. 24ff.

11. Caton, *Origin of Subjectivity*, pp. 79–80.

12. Dagoty, *Des organes des sens*, letterpress to pl. 1.

13. Gamelin, *Ostéologie*, II, 81.

14. Johann Friedrich Meckel, "Dissertation anatomique sur les nerfs de la face," *Mémoires de l'académie royale de Prusse*, III (1751), 14, 178.

15. Lavater, *Essays*, I, I, 99.

16. Ibid., p. 231. (Lavater cites Lichtenberg on this point.)

17. For the Montpellier vitalists, see Sergio Moravia, "From *Homme Machine* to *Homme Sensible*: Changing Eighteenth-Century Models of Man's Image," *Journal of the History of Ideas*, 39 (1978), 45–60.

18. Haller, *Dissertation on Sensible and Irritable Parts*, pp. iv–vi.

19. On vivisection, see G. A. Lindeboom, "Dog and Frog—Physiological Experiments," in Scheurleer, et al., *Leiden University*, pp. 279–280; and Gale E. Christianson, *In the Presence of the Creator: Isaac Newton and His Time* (New York: The Free Press; London: Collier Macmillan Publishers, 1984), pp. 154–160.

20. Albrecht von Haller, *Elementa Physiologiae Corporis Humani*, 8 vols. (Lausanne: Sumptibus M. M. Busquet, 1757–1766), I, title page.

21. La Mettrie, *L'Homme machine*, pp. 132–133. On the connection between La Mettrie and Haller, see Jacques Roger, "The Mechanistic Conception of Life," in *God and Nature: Historical Essays on the Encounter between Christianity and Science*, ed. David C. Lindberg and Ronald Numbers (Berkeley and Los Angeles: University of California Press, 1986), p. 288.

22. Robert Whytt, *Physiological Essays containing an Inquiry into the Causes Which promote the Circulation of Fluids in the Very Small Vessels of Animals: Observations on the Sensibility and Irritability of the Parts of Men and Other Animals: Occasioned by Dr. Haller's Late Treatise on These Subjects* (Edinburgh: Hamilton, Balfour, and Neill, 1754), pp. 136–137, 186–188.

23. Brazier, *History of Neurophysiology*, pp. 156, 169, 192. Also see Hahn, Dumaitre, and Samion-Contet, *Histoire de la médecine*, p. 289.

24. Jean Aldini, *Essai théorique et expérimental sur le galvinisme avec une série d'expériences faites en présence des commissaires de l'Institute National de France et en divers amphithéâtres de Londres*, 2 vols. (Paris: De l'Imprimerie de Fournier Fils, 1834), I, ii–ix, 121–128.

25. Haller, *Sensible and Irritable Parts*, pp. xv–xvi.

26. Whytt, *Physiological Essays*, pp. 189–190. On certain types of people being more susceptible to pain than others, also see the section on "Des signes diagnostiques" in Antoine Louis, *Traité des maladies des os, dans lequel on a représenté les appareils & les machines qui conviennent a leur guérison* (2d rev. ed., Paris: Chez P. G. Cavelier, 1772), p. 25.

27. Much has been written on Greuze. See, most recently, Régis Michel, *Le Beau idéale*, exh. cat. (Paris: Editions de la Réunion des musées nationaux, 1989), pp. 30–35. Anita Brookner, however, was the first to connect *sensibilité* with Greuze's effort. See her *Greuze: The Rise and Fall of an Eighteenth-Century Phenomenon* (Greenwich, Conn.: New York Graphic Society, 1972). I do not believe that the "Greuze phenomenon" has been set within the broader cultural perspective I am developing here.

28. On this naturalizing and sentimentalizing movement, see L. J. Jordanova, "Naturalizing the Family: Literature and the Biomedical Sciences in the Late Eighteenth Century," and James Rogers, "Sensibility, Sympathy, Benevolence: Physiology and Moral Philosophy in *Tristram Shandy*," in Jordanova, ed., *Languages of Nature: Critical Essays on Science and Literature* (New Brunswick, N.J.: Rutgers University Press, 1986), pp. 94, 123–128.

29. Jean-Louis Alibert, *Nosologie naturelle, ou les maladies du corps humain distribuées par familles* (Paris: De l'Imprimerie de Crapelet, 1817), pp. lxv–lxvi.

30. Théophile Laennec, *Traité de l'auscultation médiate, peut-elle servir au progrès de la médecine pratique?*, 2 vols. (Paris: J.-A. Brosson et J.-S., Naudé, 1819).

31. Bernard Schweitzer, "Mimesis und Phantasia," *Philologus*, n.s. 89, no. 3 (1934), 297–298.

32. See David E. Hahn, "Early Hellenistic Theories of Vision and the Perception of Color," and Heinrich von Staden, "The Stoic Theory of Perception and its 'Platonic' Critics," in Machamer and Turnbull, *Studies in Perception*, pp. 84–85, 97–110.

33. Verene, *Vico's Science of Imagination*, pp. 86–88.

34. Addison, *Critical Essays*, pp. 175–179.

35. Cozens, *Principles of Beauty*, p. 4.

36. Algarotti, *Essai sur la peinture*, p. 155.

37. Winckelmann, *Empfindung des Schönen*, p. 10. Also see Edouard Pommier, "Le Concepte de la grâce chez Winckelmann," in *Winckelmann*, ed. Edouard Pommier (Paris: Musée du Louvre, forthcoming).

38. Sulzer, *Allgemeine Theorie*, I, I, 140.

39. Le Camus, *Médecine de l'esprit*, II, 97–101, 175–176.

40. D'Holbach, *Système de la nature*, pp. 86–87, 125–127, 141–149.

41. Watelet, *L'Art de peindre*, pp. 124, 130.

42. Diderot, *Eléments de physiologie*, pp. 53–60, 263–265. On the connection between mid-eighteenth-century materialist biological theories and atheism, see Shirley A. Roe, "Voltaire versus Needham: Atheism, Materialism, and the Generation of Life," *Journal of the History of Ideas*, 46 (January–March 1985), 65.

43. Marielene Putscher, *Pneuma, Spiritus, Geist. Vorstellungen vom Lebensantrieb in ihren Geschichtlichen Wandlungen* (Wiesbaden: Franz Steiner Verlag, 1973), pp. 13, 31–33, 41–43. Also see Brigitte Lohft, "Zur Geschichte der Lehre von der Lebenskraft," *Clio Medica*, 16 (December 1981), 103–106.

44. Brown, *Body and Society*, pp. 117, 129–130.

45. Novalis, *Das Allgemeine Brouillon*, p. 496.

46. Michael Heim, *Electric Language: A Philosophical Study of Word Processing* (New Haven and London: Yale University Press, 1987), p. 114.

47. Newton, *Opticks*, pp. xxv, 280. Larry Laudan, "The Medium and Its Message: A Study of Some Philosophical Controversies about the Ether," in *Conceptions of Ether: Studies in the History of Ether Theories, 1740–1900*, ed. G. N. Cantor and M. J. S. Hodge (Cambridge: Cambridge University Press, 1984), p. 159. On the metaphysical nature of the last Queries to the *Opticks*, see David Castillejo, *The Expanding Force in Newton's Cosmos as shown in His Unpublished Papers* (Madrid: Ediciones de Arte y Bibliofilia, 1981), pp. 108–115.

48. Grant, *Much Ado about Nothing*, p. 142. Also see Canguilhem, *La Connaissance de la vie*, pp. 130–134.

49. McGuire, "Newton's Invisible Realm," p. 185.

50. More, *Immortality of the Soul*, pp. 32, 122–124, 168.

51. Isaac Newton, *Mathematical Principles of Natural Philosophy and His System of the World*, trans. Andrew Motte, revised by Florian Cajori (Berkeley: University of California Press, 1934); see especially Roger Cotes's preface to the second edition, and the General Scholium to Book III, pp. 545–547.

52. Arnold Thackray, "'Matter in a Nutshell': Newton's *Opticks* and Eighteenth-Century Chemistry," *Ambix*, 15 (February 1968), 33–44.

53. Plutarch, *Moralia*, V, 471, 483, 495.

54. Scheuchzer, *Physique sacrée*, VI, 98–99.

55. Joseph Priestley, *A Free Discussion of the Doctrines of Materialism, and Philosophical Necessity. In a Correspondence between Dr. Price, and Dr. Priestley* (London: Printed for J. Johnson and T. Cadell, 1778), pp. 231–233, 244–246. For the influence of Boscovich, also see Priestley's *The History and Present State of Discoveries relating to Vision, Light, and Colours* (London: Printed for J. Johnson, 1772), p. 392.

56. Ibid., pp. 248–252. On Priestley, see Mikulás Teich, "Circulation, Transformation, Conservation of Matter and the Balancing of the Biological World in the Eighteenth Century," in Bernardi and La Vergata, *Lazzaro Spallanzani*, pp. 369–372.

57. Joseph Priestley, *The History and Present State of Electricity, With Original Experiments* (2d rev. ed., London: Printed for J. Dodsley, J. Johnson, J. Payne, and T. Cadell, 1769), pp. x–xii, 566–567.

58. Priestley, *A Free Discussion*, p. 240.

59. Ibid., p. 272.

60. Ibid., p. 279.

61. Coleridge, *Biographia Literaria*, p. 83.

62. Paul-Joseph Barthez, *Nouveaux elémens de la science de l'homme*, 2 vols. (1778; 3d rev. ed., Paris: Chez Goujon, Libraire,

1806), 78–80, 87. On Barthez, see Roselyne Rey, "L'Approche de la folie chez quelques médecins vitalistes du XVIIIe siècle," in *La Folie et le corps*, ed. Jean Céard (Paris: Presses de l'Ecole Normale Supérieure, 1985), pp. 112–113.

63. Barthez, *Nouveaux élémens*, I, 55, 66–67.

64. Alain Corbin, *Le Miasme et la jonquille. L'Odorat et l'imaginaire social, XVIIIe–XIXe siècles* (Paris: Editions Aubier Montaigne, 1982), p. 41.

65. Frischer, *The Sculpted Word*, pp. 119–121. Also see Brilliant, *Visual Narratives*, pp. 77–78.

66. Lucretius, *De Rerum Natura*, trans. W. H. D. Rouse (Cambridge, Mass.: Harvard University Press, and London: William Heinemann, 1975), IV, 26–44, p. 279. The anonymous 1768 French translation of the *De Rerum Natura* reawakened Voltaire's attacks against Newtonianism and what he perceived to be the dangerously atheistic tendencies in contemporary biological views. See Roe, "Voltaire versus Needham," p. 77. For the coupling of Epicureanism, Newtonianism, and atheism, also see Blake, *Complete Writings*, p. 475.

67. Already by the early eighteenth century, Epicureanism was linked to the production of specters and phantoms. See Bordelon, *Histoire des imaginations*, I, 93–94, 125–126.

68. Barthez, *Nouveaux élémens*, I, 75.

69. Chambers, *Cyclopaedia*, II, "pneumatics."

70. Charles Stewart-Robertson, "The Pneumatics and Georgics of the Eighteenth-Century Mind," *Eighteenth-Century Studies*, 20 (Spring 1987), 300–303, 310. Also see Terry Castle, "The Female Thermometer," *Representations*, no. 17 (Winter 1987), 2.

71. *Encyclopaedia Britannica*, III, 175.

72. Gillray, *Drawings and Caricatures*, p. 39.

73. Grandville, *Un autre monde*, pp. 17–23.

74. Cruikshank, *Phrenological Illustrations*, letterpress to pl. 5.

75. Proclus, *Alcibiades*, p. 127. On Egyptian deities betrayed by their aroma, see Hornung, *Conceptions of God in Egypt*, p. 134.

76. "Parfum," *Encyclopédie*, XI (1765), 940–941. Also see Corbin, *Le Miasme*, pp. 87–88.

77. Le Camus, *Médecine de l'esprit*, II, 90.

78. Ibid., p. 88.

79. Jean Le Rond D'Alembert, "Goût," *Encyclopédie*, VII, 761.

80. Félibien, *Entretiens*, I, 85.

81. Sticotti, *Dictionnaire*, II, 257–258.

82. Alibert, *Physiologie des passions*, l, ix.

83. Samuel-Auguste-André-David Tissot, *Essai sur les maladies des gens du monde* (Lausanne: Chez François Grasset & Comp., 1781), pp. viii–ix, 42–43. On Ramazzini, see John F. Moffitt, "Painters 'Born under Saturn': The Physiological Explanation," *Art History*, II (June 1988), 209.

84. Alibert, *Physiologie des passions*, I, lvii. Also see Thomas Laqueur, "Orgasm, Generation, and the Politics of Reproductive Biology," *Representations*, no. 14 (Spring 1986), 18.

85. Sticotti, *Dictionnaire*, II, 194.

86. Alibert, *Physiologie des passions*, I, xv–xvi. Also see Jamieson, *Eloquence in An Electronic Age*, pp. 76–84.

87. Richard, *La Théorie des songes*, p. 67.

88. Alibert, *Physiologie des passions*, I, iii, xxxiii–xxxiv, lv–l.

89. G. Theodore von Soemmering, *Über das Organ der Seele* (Königsberg: Bey Friedrich Nicolovius, 1796), pp. 33–43, 44. Significantly, the volume was dedicated to "our Kant."

90. Franz Baader, *Über das Pythagoräische Quadrat in der Natur oder die Vier Weltgegenden* (n.p.: n.p., 1798), p. 40.

91. Franz Baader, *Beyträge zur Elementar-*

Phisiologie (Hamburg: Bei Carl Ernst Bohn, 1797), pp. 36–37, 47, 68–72, and *Pythagoraïsche Quadrat*, pp. 45–51.

92. Coleridge, *Biographia Literaria*, pp. 145–146.

93. Blake, *Complete Writings*, p. 457.

94. Eric Klinger, "Therapy and the Flow of Thought," in *Imagery: Its Many Dimensions and Applications*, ed. Joseph E. Shorr, Gail E. Sobel, Pennee Robin, and Jack A. Connella (New York and London: Plenum Press, 1980), pp. 8–14.

95. Sacks, *Man Who Mistook His Wife for a Hat*, pp. 82–93.

96. Burton, *Anatomy of Melancholy*, p. 9. Also see, Aubry, et al., *Album comique*, letterpress for *La folie*.

97. Alibert, *Physiologie des passions*, I, xxii. Also see Chambers, *Cyclopaedia*, II, "mania." On types of insanity, from raving to moping, see MacDonald, *Mystical Bedlam*, pp. 120, 149–162.

98. Lavater, *Essays*, II, I, 68.

99. On the importance of Stoicism to the *Idéologue*'s medical and psychological theory, see Pigeaud, *La maladie de l'âme*, pp. 245–251. Also see L. J. Jordanova, *Lamarck* (Oxford and New York: Oxford University Press, 1984), p. 78.

100. Eitner, *Géricault*, pp. 245–248. On Georget, see Gilman, *Disease and Representation*, pp. 35–36. On Esquirol, see Pigeaud, *La Maladie de l'âme*, pp. 122, 133–135, and Janet Browne, "Darwin and the Face of Madness," in Bynum, *Anatomy of Madness*, p. 155.

101. Henry George Liddell and Robert Scott, *A Greek-English Lexicon With a Supplement* (Oxford: Clarendon Press, 1968), p. 483.

102. Baader, *Elementar-Phisiologie*, p. 35.

103. Plutarch, *Moralia*, XII, 215. Also see Crome, *Symbol und Unzulänglichkeit*, pp. 40–41.

104. Spence, *Polymetis*, p. 266.

105. Lucian, *A True Story (Verae Historiae)*, 8 vols., trans. A. M. Harmon (Cambridge, Mass.: Harvard University Press, and London: William Heinemann, 1913), I, 341.

106. Fuseli, *Lectures on Painting*, pp. 109, 112. Fuseli was surely also inspired by Cicero's *Dream of Scipio*. See Pierre Boyancé, *Etudes sur le songe de Scipion* [with a translation] (Limoges: Imprimerie A. Bontemps, 1936), p. 33.

107. Fuseli, *Lectures on Painting*, p. 114.

108. Boudard, *Iconologie*, II, 103.

109. On the connection between divination and oneirocriticism in seventeenth-century dream literature, see Lise Andries, "L'Interprétation populaire des songes," *Revue des Sciences Humaines*, 211, no. 3 (1988), 53–54.

110. Priestley, *Discoveries Relating to Vision*, pp. 391–392.

111. Anonymous, *Nature of the Human Soul*, I, 218–219; II, 9–24. On the thinking matter controversy, see the excellent study by John W. Yolton, *Thinking Matter: Materialism in Eighteenth-Century Britain* (Minneapolis: University of Minnesota Press, 1983), p. 138.

112. Anonymous, *Nature of the Human Soul*, I, 364, 367; II, 54.

113. M. de Formey, "Essai sur les songes," in *Mémoires de l'académie royale de Prusse*, I, 246.

114. Richard, *Théorie des songes*, pp. 121, 136.

115. Ibid., pp. 61, 143.

116. Ibid., p. xxii. Also see Muratori, *Forza della fantasia*, pp. 48–50.

117. Le Camus, *Médecine de l'esprit*, I, xvii–xix, 3, 104–105, 366.

118. Ibid., II, 54, 150.

119. Diderot, *Eléments de physiologie*, pp. 246, 259–261.

120. Samuel Johnson, *A Dictionary of the English Language: In Which the Words are deduced from Their Originals, and Illustrated in Their Different Significations by Examples from the Best Authors* (1755; London: Joseph Ogle Robinson, 1828), p. 369.

121. Anonymous, *Nature of the Human Soul*, II, 141; and Richard, *Théorie des songes*, pp. 56, 78–80.

122. Ibid., pp. 57, 64, 145.

123. Burton, *Anatomy of Melancholy*, p. 93.

124. John Bond, *An Essay on the Incubus, or Night-Mare* (London: Printed for D. Wilson, 1753), preface, and pp. 3–8, 11–16. Bond comments that this is the first essay ever written on the subject.

125. Samuel-Auguste-André-David Tissot, *De la santé des gens de lettres* (2d ed., Lausanne: J. F. Bassompierre, Fils, 1772), pp. 67–69.

126. Aubry, et al., *Album comique*, letterpress to *Le Cauchemar*. For a study of Fuseli's painting, see Nicolas Powell, *Fuseli: The Nightmare, Art in Context*, ed. John Fleming and Hugh Honour (London: Penguin Press, 1973).

127. Tony Johannot, Alfred de Musset, and P.-J. Stahl, *Voyage où il vous plaira* (Paris: J. Hetzel, 1843), pp. 14–15, 161. Also see Jacques Le Goff, *La Naissance du purgatoire* (Paris: Editions Gallimard, 1981), pp. 15, 149.

128. Grandville, *Un autre monde*, pp. 242–247.

129. Ibid., p. 106.

130. Lindberg, *Theories of Vision*, p. 160.

131. [Le Meltier], *Lettre adressée à Monsieur le Marquis de Puiségur, sur une observation faite à la lune, précédée d'un système nouveau sur le méchanisme de la vue* (Amsterdam: n.p., 1787), p. 64. Here it is specifically stated that the "new" Mesmerist optics is extramissionist.

132. Richard, *Théorie des songes*, pp. 222–223.

133. Muratori, *Forza della fantasia*, pp. 64–75, 104–105.

134. Franz Anton Mesmer, *Mémoire sur ses découvertes* (Paris: Chez Fuchs Libraire, [1798-9]), pp. 96–97. Also see Ebenezer Sibly, *A Key to Physic, and the Occult Sciences. Opening to Mental View, The System and Order of the Interior and Exterior Heavens.*

The Analogy betwixt Angels, and Spirits of Men, and the Sympathy between Celestial and Terrestrial Bodies (1794; London: Printed for the Author, 1804), p. 275.

135. Mesmer, *Mémoire*, p. 59.

136. For an excellent general biography of Mesmer, see Vincent Buranelli, *The Wizard from Vienna* (New York: Coward, McCann, & Geoghegan, 1975), pp. 17–26. On the fashion for Mesmerism see Robert Darnton, *Mesmerism and the End of the Enlightenment in France* (Cambridge, Mass.: Harvard University Press, 1968).

137. [Jean-Jacques Paulet], *Anti-Magnetismus oder Ursprung, Fortgang, Verfall, Erneuerung und Widerlegung des Thierischen Magnetismus*, trans. from the French edition (Gera: Bey Heinrich Gottlieb Rothe, 1788), pp. 15–26.

138. Theodosius Purland, "For the History of Mesmerism, Clairvoyance, Animal Magnetism, etc." (4 vols. of pamphlets, tracts, clippings, autograph letters, original drawings, in the National Library of Medicine, Bethesda, Md.; produced in London, 1848–1854), IV, "Valentine Greatarick."

139. Armand-Marie-Jacques Chastenet de Puységur, *Recherches, expériences et observations physiologiques sur l'homme dans l'état de somnambulisme provoqué par l'acte magnétique* (Paris: J. G. Dentu, Imprimeur-Libraire, 1811), pp. 235–238.

140. Note Puységur's similar disdain for Mesmer's followers, in Armand-Marie-Jacques Chastenet de Puységur, *Mémoires pour servir à l'histoire et à l'établissement du magnétisme animal* (Paris: n.p., 1784), p. 14.

141. Caulet de Vaumorel, *Aphorismes de M. Mesmer* (Paris: Chez Gastelier, Libraire, 1785), p. 18; and Mesmer, *Mémoire*, pp. 57–58.

142. On the magneto-vegetable cure, see Puységur, *Mémoires*, pp. 22–24.

143. Ibid., pp. 182–185. Also see Pierre Saint-Amand, *Séduire, ou la passion des*

Lumières (Paris: Méridiens Klincksiek, 1987), p. 14.

144. Bacon, *Sylva Sylvarum*, p. 210. Also see Katherine Park, "Bacon's 'Enchanted Glass,'" *Isis*, 75 (June 1984), 292–293.

145. More, *Enthusiasmus Triumphatus*, pp. 20–24.

146. More, *Immortality of the Soul*, pp. 25–26, 121–122.

147. Blondel, *Power of the Mother's Imagination*, pp. 11–13.

148. Alibert, *Physiologie des passions*, I, 269–274; and Le Camus, *Médecine de l'esprit*, II, 149–151.

149. Georges-Louis Le Sage, "The Le Sage Theory of Gravitation [1782]," trans. C. G. Abbott, in *Annual Report of the Board of Regents of the Smithsonian Institution* (Washington, D.C.: Government Printing Office, 1899), pp. 139–160. Puységur mentions Le Sage. See his *Mémoires*, p. 12.

150. For Newton's "magnetical" language, see *Mathematical Principles*, p. 5. Also see Dijksterhuis, *The Mechanization of the World Picture*, pp. 479–484. For magnetic games, see Guyot, *Nouvelles récréations*, II, pls. 5, 20.

151. Dagoty, *Des organes des sens*, pp. 9–10.

152. Abbé Sans, *Guérison de la paralysie par l'électricité ou cette expérience physique* (Paris: Chez Cailleau, 1772), pp. ix–xi.

153. Aldini, *Essai sur le galvinisme*, I, 207–215. On the search for signs of death, also see Louis, *Lettres*, p. 9. For the guillotined death heads modeled by Marie Gresholtz, see Pauline Chapman, *The French Revolution as seen by Madame Tussaud Witness Extraordinary* (London: Quiller Press, 1989), pl. 20.

154. Puységur, *Mémoires*, pp. 10–12.

155. Sans, *Guérison*, p. 129. Also see Sibly, *Key to Physic*, p. 247. For Mesmer's electrical language, see Vaumorel, *Aphorismes*, pp. 35–40.

156. Puységur, *Recherches sur somnambulisme*, p. v.

157. Armand-Marie-Jacques Chastenet de Puységur, *Du magnétisme animal, considéré dans ses rapports avec diverses branches de la physique générale* (Paris: De l'Imprimerie de Cellot, 1807), pp. 89–90.

158. Ibid., pp. 103–105.

CONCLUSION:
The Aesthetics of Almost

1. For the problems attendant on such mathematical formalism, see Wesley Trimpi, "Mimesis as Appropriate Representation," *Renascence: Essays on Values in Literature*, 37 (Spring 1985), 203–207.

2. Lisa Belkin, "Many in Profession are Calling Rules a Professional Malaise," *New York Times* (February 19, 1990), pp. A1, A9, and Gina Kolata, "Wariness is Replacing the Trust between Physician and Patient," *New York Times* (February 20, 1990), pp. A1, A10.

3. Lorraine Daston, *Classical Probability in the Enlightenment* (Princeton, N.J.: Princeton University Press, 1988), p. 197. Also see the review by Jeffrey Barnouw, *Eighteenth-Century Studies*, 23 (Winter 1989–1990), 200–204.

4. Werner Schneiders, "Vernünftiger Zweifel und wahre Eklektik. Zur Entstehung des modernen Kritikbegriffes," *Studia Leibnitiana*, 17, no. 2 (1985), 160–161.

5. On the need for aesthetic ethicists—in light of the recent controversy surrounding the reauthorization of the NEA—see my "Voyeur or Observer? Enlightenment Thoughts on the Dilemmas of Display," in *Issues & Debates* (Los Angeles: Getty Center for the History of Art and the Humanities, forthcoming).

6. On the bias of scientists against the current visual culture and against techologists, see Thomas A. DeFanti, "Cultural Roadblocks to Visualization," *Computers in Science* (January–February 1988), guest editorial.

7. Gibson, *Ecological Perception*, p. 239.

8. See Marvin Heiferman et al., *Image-World* (exh. cat. (New York: Whitney Museum of Art, 1990).

9. Arnaldo Momigliano, "History between Medicine and Rhetoric" (typescript of unpublished paper, 1985).

10. Rhys Isaac, *The Transformation of Virginia, 1740–1790* (Chapel Hill: University of North Carolina Press, 1982), pp. 48–49.

11. Miller, *Boxed-In*, pp. 32, 45, 96.

12. Verene, *Vico's Science of the Imagination*, pp. 68–72, 86, 178.

13. Vilèm Flusser, "The Photograph as Post-Industrial Object: An Essay on the Ontological Standing of Objects," *Leonardo*, 19, no. 4 (1986), 331.

14. Tufte, *Visual Display*, pp. 30, 51, 80–86.

15. Donna J. Cox, "Using the Supercomputer to Visualize Higher Dimensions: An Artist's Contribution to Scientific Visualization," *Leonardo*, 20, no. 3 (1988), 234–238. Also see DeFanti, "Cultural Roadblocks," pp. 4–6.

16. Heim, *Electric Language*, p. 11.

17. Ernesto Grassi, "Die Metapher, Die auflösende und schaffende Macht der Kunst," *Argo. Festschrift für Kurt Badt*, ed. Martin Gosebruch and Lorenz Dittmann (Cologne: Verlag M. DuMont Schauberg, 1970), p. 49. Also see Edmond Couchot, "L'Odyssée, mille fois où les machines à langage," *Traverses*, 44–45 (September 1988), 90–93, and Turnbull, "Role of 'Special Sensibles,'" in Machamer and Turnbull, *Studies in Perception*, pp. 16–18.

18. Castillejo, *Newton*, p. 108. Also see Alberti, *On Painting*, p. 63. For the contemporary liquidity of information, see Fred I. Dretske, *Knowledge and the Flow of Information* (Cambridge, Mass.: MIT Press, 1981), p. vii.

19. For a survey of these developments, see Jürgen Claus, *Chipppkunst: Computer, Holographie, Kybernetik, Laser* (Frankfurt am Main: Ullstein, 1985). Also see the articles by Daniel de Kerckhove, "Le virtuel," *Traverses*, 44–45 (September 1988), 82, and Michael Bret, "Procedural Art with Computer Graphics," *Leonardo*, 21, no. 1 (1988), 3–10.

20. Johann Wolfgang von Goethe, *Farbenlehre (1790–1808)*, intro. by Hans Wohlbold (Tübingen: Wissenschaftliche Buchgemeinschaft E.V., 1953), pp. 15–18, 27–32.

21. Lawrence E. Murr and James B. Williams, "Half-Brained Ideas about Education: Thinking and Learning with Both the Left Brain and the Right Brain in a Visual Culture," *Leonardo*, 21, no. 4 (1988), 413–420.

22. Gibson, *Ecological Perception*, pp. 203–206, 239–240, 255.

23. On this point, see also Jean-René Gaborit, "Péchés véniels," *Revue de l'Art*, 58 (1989), 5–7.

24. Gibson, *Ecological Perception*, p. 274. Art historians are now beginning to discover Gibson. See, for example, John Steer, "Art History and Direct Perception: A General View," *Art History*, 12 (March 1989), 98–104. On the need to keep in touch with the sensuous substances of art, see Ebitz, "Connoisseurship as Practice," p. 208.

25. Margolis, *Pattern-Recognition*, pp. 77, 183–184.

SELECTED BIBLIOGRAPHY

1 PRIMARY SOURCES

Adams, Joseph. *An Inquiry into the Laws of Different Epidemic Diseases, with the View to determine the Means of preserving Individuals and Communities from Each, and also to ascertain the Probability of Exterminating the Small-Pox.* London: J. Johnson, J. Callow, and W. Grace, 1809.

Adams, Robert, and James Adams. *The Works in Architecture of Robert and James Adams* (1773). Ed. Robert Oresko. London: Academy Editions; New York: St. Martin's Press, 1975.

Addison, Joseph. *Critical Essays from The Spectator, with Four Essays by Richard Steele.* Ed. Donald F. Bond. Oxford: Clarendon Press, 1970.

Aldini, Jean. *Essai théorique et expérimental sur le galvinisme avec une série d'expériences faites en présence des commissaires de l'Institute National de France et en divers ampithéâtres de Londres.* 2 vols. Paris: De l'Imprimerie de Fournier Fils, 1834.

Algarotti, Francesco. *Oeuvres.* 7 vols. Berlin: Chez D. J. Decker, 1772.

Alibert, Jean-Louis. *Clinique de l'Hôpital Saint-Louis, ou traité complet des maladies de la peau, contenant la description de ces maladies et leurs meilleurs modes de traitement.* 2 vols. in 1. Paris: Chez B. Cormon et Blanc, Libraires; Lyons: S. P. Imprimerie de Casimir, 1833.

Alibert, Jean-Louis. *Nosologie naturelle, ou les maladies du corps humain distribuées par familles.* Paris: De l'Imprimerie de Crapelet, 1817.

Alibert, Jean-Louis. *Physiologie des passions, ou nouvelle doctrine des sentiments moraux.* 2 vols. Paris: Chez Béchet Jeune, Libraire, 1825.

Andry, Nicolas. *L'Orthopédie, ou l'art de prevenir et de corriger dans les enfans les difformités du corps. Le Tout par des moyens à la portée des pères et des mères, & de toutes les personnes qui ont des enfans à élever,* 2 vols. Paris: Chez la Veuve Alix, & Lambert & Durand, 1741.

Aubry, Charles, et al. [Chazal, Colin, Bellangé, Pigal]. *Album comique de pathologie pittoresque. Recueil de vingt caricatures médicales dessinées par . . .* Paris: Chez Ambroise Tardieu, Editeur, 1823.

Audran, [Claude]. *The Proportions of the Human Body, Measured from the Most Beautiful Antique Statues; by . . . , Engraver to the Late King of France. Done from the Originals, Engraved at Paris.* 12th ed., London: Printed for Bowles and Carver, n.d.

Augustine. *Against Julian.* Trans. Matthew A. Schumacher, C.S.C. New York: The Fathers of the Church, Inc., 1957.

Austin, William. *A Specimen of sketching Landscapes. In a Free and Masterly Manner, with a Pen or Pencil; Exemplified in Thirty Etchings, done from Original Drawings of Lucatelli, after the Life, in and about Rome.* London: Author, n.d.

Baader, Franz. *Beyträge zur Elementar-Phisiologie.* Hamburg: Bei Carl Ernst Bohn, 1797.

Baader, Franz. *Über das Pythagoraïsche Quadrat in der Natur oder die Vier Weltgegenden.* N.p.: n.p., 1798.

Bacon, Francis. *Sylva Sylvarum: or A Natural History. In Ten Centuries. Whereunto is newly added the History naturall and Experimentall of Life and Death, or of the Prolongation of Life.* 6th ed., London: Printed by J. F. for William Lee, 1651.

Barthez, Paul-Joseph. *Nouveaux élémens de la science de l'homme* (1778). 2 vols. 3rd rev. ed., Paris: Chez Goujon, Libraire, 1806.

Bartoli, Giuseppi. "Dictonnaire des arts et des sciences" (ca. 1746). Manuscript in the resource collections of the Getty Center for the History of Art and the Humanities.

Bateman, Thomas. *Delineations of Cutaneous Diseases exhibiting the Characteristic Appearances of the Principal Genera and Species.* London: Longmans, 1817.

Batteux, Charles. *Principes de la littérature. I: Traité. Les beaux-arts réduits en général, ou les beaux-arts réduits d'un même principe* (1747). Paris: Chez Desaint & Saillant, 1764.

Baudelaire, Charles. "In Praise of Make-Up." *Strangeness and Beauty: An Anthology of Aesthetic Criticism 1840–1910.* Ed. Eric Warner and Graham Hough. 2 vol. Cambridge: Cambridge University Press, 1983.

Baumgarten, Alexander Gottlieb. *Texte zur Grundlegung der Ästhetik* (1750). Trans and ed. Hans Rudolf Schweizer. Hamburg: Felix Meiner Verlag, 1983.

Baumgärtner, Karl Heinrich. *Krankenphysiognomik.* 2d rev. ed., Stuttgart: Druck und Verlag von L. F. Rieger & Comp., 1842.

Bayle, Pierre. *Dictionnaire historique et critique.* 4 vols. 3d rev. and aug. ed., Rotterdam: Chez Michel Bohm, 1720.

Beattie, James. *Dissertations Moral and Critical.* London: Printed for W. Strahan and T. Cadell, 1783.

Beattie, James. *Essays On the Nature and Immutability of Truth, in Opposition to Sophistry. On Poetry and Music, as They affect the Mind, on Laughter, and Ludicrous Compositions. On the Utility of Learning.* Edinburgh: Printed for William Creech, 1776.

Bellini, Laurentius. *A Mechanical Account of Fevers.* Trans. into English. London: Printed for A. Bell, J. Senex, W. Taylor, J. Osborn, 1720.

Bickham, George, Sr. *The Art of Writing. In Its Theory and Practice by Charles Snell Writing Master at the Free Writing School in Forster-Lane, London, and Engraved by . . .* London: Henry Overton, 1772.

Bickham, George, Sr. *The British Youth's Instructor: or, the Useful Penman. A New Copybook. Containing Alphabets and Sentences in Round Text, Large and Small. Round Hand, and Running Hand: An Abstract of the Theory of Writing, Initial Letters, Struck Capitals, and Other Curious Decorations. Written by Several of the Best Masters and Engraved by . . . Designed for the Use of Schools and Families.* London: Robert Sayer, 1754.

Bickham, George, Sr. *An Introductive Essay on Drawing. With the Nature and Beauty of Lights and Shadows, and Cuts suitable for the Young Practitioner, in the Manner of the Greatest Masters.* London: Printed for the Author, 1747.

Bickham, George, Sr. *The Universal Penman; or the Art of Writing made useful to the Gentleman and Scholar, as well as the Man of Business.* London: Printed for the Author, 1741.

Blake, William. *The Complete Writings.* Ed. Geoffrey Keynes. London: Oxford University Press, 1966.

Blondel, James Augustus. *The Power of the Mother's Imagination over the Foetus examin'd in Answer to Dr. Daniel Turner's Book Intitled A Defence of the XIIth Chapter of the First Part of a Treatise, De Morbis Cutaneis.* London: John Brotherton, 1729.

Boethius, Anicius Manlius Severinus. *The Theological Tractates*. Trans. H. F. Stewart and E. K. Rand. London: William Heinemann, Ltd., 1936.

Bond, John. *An Essay on the Incubus, or Night-Mare*. London: Printed for D. Wilson, 1753.

Bonnet, Charles. *Contemplation de la nature* (1764). 2d ed., Amsterdam: Chez Marc-Michel Rey, 1769.

Bonnet, Charles. *La Palingénésie philosophique, ou idées sur l'état passé et sur l'état futur des êtres vivans. Ouvrage destiné à servir de supplément aux derniers écrits de l'auteur*. 2 vols. Geneva: Chez Claude Philibert et Barthelmi Chirol, 1769.

Bordelon, Laurent. *L'Histoire des imaginations extravagantes de Monsieur Oufle causées par la lecture des livres, qui traitent de la magie, du grimoire, des démoniaques, sorciers, loups-garoux, incubes, succubes & du sabbat; des fées, ogres, esprits folets, génies, phantômes & d'autres superstitions pratiques*. 2 vols. Amsterdam: Chez Estienne Roger, Pierre Humbert, Pierre de Coup, & Les Frères Chatelain, 1710.

Bosse, Abraham. *Le Peintre converty aux précises et universelles règles de son art. Sentiments sur la distinction des diverses manières de peinture, dessin et gravure* (1667). Ed. R. A. Wigert. Paris: Hermann, 1964.

Boudard, Jean-Baptiste. *Iconologie tirée de divers auteurs. Ouvrage utile aux gens de lettres, aux poëtes, aux artistes, & généralement à tous les amateurs des beaux-arts*. 3 vols. Vienna: Chez Jean-Thomas de Trattnern, Imprimeur et Libraire de la Cour, 1766.

Bouhours, Dominique. *La Manière de bien penser dans les ouvrages d'esprit, Dialogues*. Paris: Chez les Libraires Associés, 1771.

Boyancé, Pierre. *Etudes sur le songe de Scipion* [with a translation]. Limoges: Imprimerie A. Bontemps, 1936.

Brillat-Savarin, Jean-Anthelme. *The Physiology of Taste, or Meditations on Transcendental Gastronomy* (1825). Intro. Arthur Machen. New York: Dover Publishing, Inc., 1960.

Buffon, Georges-Louis Le Clerc, Comte de. *Histoire naturelle, générale et particulière, avec la description du cabinet du roi*. 44 vols. Paris: De l'Imprimerie Royale, 1749–1803.

Burton, Robert. *The Anatomy of Melancholy. What It is, With All the Kinds, Causes, Symptoms, Prognostickes, & Severall Cures of It, In Three Partitions with Their Severall Sections, Members & Subsections*. 7th ed., London: Printed for John Garway, 1660.

Campbell, George. *Of the Philosophy of Rhetoric*. 2 vols. London: W. Strahan and T. Cadell; Edinburgh: W. Creech, 1776.

Camper, Petrus. *Oratoria de Mundo Optimo. En Prolegomenon in Philosophiam*. Ed. Jacob van Sluis. Ljouwert: Fryske Akademy, 1988.

Camper, Petrus. *The Works of the Late Professor . . . on the Connexion between the Science of Anatomy and the Arts of Drawing, Painting, Statuary, in Two Books* [in 1]. Trans. T. Cogan, M.D. 2d ed., London: C. Dilly, 1794.

Castel, R. P. Bertrand. *L'Optique des couleurs, fondée sur les simples observations, & tournée surtout à la pratique de la peinture, de la teinture & des autres arts coloristes*. Paris: Chez Briasson, 1740.

Caulfield, James. *Portraits. Memoirs and Characters of Remarkable Persons, from the Revolution in 1688 to the End of the Reign of George II. Collected from the Most Authentic Accounts extant.* 4 vols. London: H. R. Young and T. H. Whitely, 1819.

Caylus, Anne-Claude-Philippe, Comte de. *Recueil d'antiquités égyptiennes, étrusques, grecques et romaines.* 7 vols. Paris: Chez Desaint & Saillant, 1752–1767.

Chambers, Ephraim. *Cyclopaedia: or an Universal Dictionary of Arts and Sciences; Containing the Definitions of the Terms and Accounts of the Things signif'd thereby in the Several Arts both Liberal and Mechanical* (1728). 2 vols. 2d ed., London: Printed for James and John Knapton, 1738.

Chrystostom, Dio [of Prusa]. *The Twelfth, or Olympic, Discourse: On Man's First Conception of God.* 5 vols. trans. J. W. Cohoon. Cambridge, Mass.: Harvard University Press, 1960.

Cipriani's Rudiments of Drawing engraved by G. Bartolozzi. London: n.p., 1790.

Coleridge, Samuel Taylor. *Biographia Literaria, or Biographical Sketches of My Literary Life and Opinions.* Ed. George Watson. London: J. M. Dent & Sons, Ltd; New York: E. P. Dutton & Co., 1975.

Corneille, Thomas. *Le Dictionnaire des arts et des sciences.* 2 vols. Paris: Chez Rollin père, 1732.

Cowper, William. *Anatomia Corporum Humanorum.* Ultrajecti: Nicolaum Muntendam, 1750.

Cowper, William. *The Anatomy of the Human Body with Figures drawn after the life by Some of the Best Masters in Europe, and Curiously Engraven in One Hundred and Fourteen Copper Plates, Illustrated with Large Explications, Containing Many New Anatomical Discoveries, and Chirurgical Observations: To Which is added an Introduction explaining the Animal Oeconomy.* Oxford: Printed at The Theater, for Sam Smith and Benjamin Walford, Printers to the Royal Society, 1698.

Cozens, Alexander. *Principles of Beauty, Relative to the Human Head.* London: Printed by James Dixwell, 1778.

Crousaz, Jean-Pierre de. *Commentaire sur l'analyse des infiniment petits.* Paris: Chez Montalembert, 1721.

Crousaz, Jean-Pierre de. *Traité du beau, où l'on montre en quoi consiste ce que l'on nomme ainsi, par des exemples tirez de la plûpart des arts & des sciences.* Amsterdam: Chez François l'Honoré, 1715.

Cruikshank, George. *Phrenological Illustrations, or An Artist's View of the Craniological System of Doctor's Gall and Spurzheim* (1826). London: Republished for the Artist by Frederick Arnold, 1873.

Cureau de La Chambre, Marin. *L'Art de connoistre les hommes.* Amsterdam: Chez Jacques Le Jeune, 1660.

Dagoty, Jacques Gautier. *Anatomie de la tête, en tableaux imprimés qui représentent au naturel le cerveau sous différentes coupes, la distribution des vaisseaux dans toutes les parties de la tête, les organes des sens, & une partie de la névrologie d'après les pièces disséquées & préparées par Mr. Duverney.* Paris: Chez le Sieur Gautier, M. Duverney, 1748.

Dagoty, Jacques Gautier. *Chroa-Genésie ou génération des couleurs, contre le système de Newton.* 2 vols. Paris: Chez Antoine Boudet, 1751.

Dagoty, Jacques Gautier. *Essai d'anatomie en tableaux imprimés, de la face, du col, de la tête, de la langue & du larinx, d'après les parties disséquées & préparées, par Monsieur Duverney, maître en chirurgie à Paris, membre de l'Académie de chirurgie & demonstrateur en anatomie au Jardin du roy.* Paris: Chez le Sieur Gautier, 1745.

Dagoty, Jacques Gautier. *Exposition anatomique des maux vénériens, sur les parties de l'homme & de la femme et les rémèdes les plus usites dans ces sortes de maladies.* Paris: Chez J. B. Brunet & Demonville, 1773.

Dagoty, Jacques Gautier. *Exposition anatomique des organes des sens, jointe à la nevrologie entières du corps humain, et conjectures sur l'éléctricité animale et le siège de l'âme.* Paris: Chez Demonville Imprimeur-Librairie, 1775.

Dagoty, Jacques Gautier. *Observations sur l'histoire naturelle sur la physique et sur la peinture.* Paris: Chez Delaguette, 1752.

Dandré-Bardon, Michel-François. *Traité de peinture, suivi d'un essai sur la sculpture* (1765). Geneva: Minkoff Reprint, 1772.

Dennis, John. *The Grounds of Criticism in Poetry, Contain'd in Some New Discoveries never made before requisite for the Writing and Judging of Poems Surely.* London: George Straham, 1704.

Descamps, Jean-Baptiste. *La Vie des peintres flamands, allemands, et hollandais.* 2 vols. Paris: Chez Charles-Antoine Jombert, 1754.

Descartes, René. *Discourse on Method* (1637). Trans. John Veitch. Chicago: Open Court Press, 1962.

Dézallier d'Argenville, Antoine-Nicholas. *Abrégé de la vie des plus fameux peintres.* 3 vols. Paris: De Bure l'aîné, 1745–1752.

D'Holbach, Paul-Henry Thomas, Baron. *Système de la nature ou des lois du monde physique et du monde moral* (1769). Ed. and rev. Diderot. 2 vols. Hildesheim: Georg Olms Verlag, 1966.

Diderot, Denis. *Eléments de physiologie* (1778). Ed. Jean Mayer. Paris: Librairie Marcel Didier, 1964.

Diderot, Denis. *Interprétation de la nature. Oeuvres philosophiques.* 10 vols. Paris: Editions Garnier Frères, 1964.

Diderot, Denis. *Salons.* Ed. Jean Seznec and Jean Adhémar. 4 vols. Oxford: Clarendon Press, 1957–1967.

D'Orléans, Père Chérubim. *La Dioptrique oculaire.* Paris: n.p., 1671.

Dubos, Jean-Baptiste. *Réflexions critiques sur la poésie et sur la peinture. Ut Pictura Poesis.* 2 vols. Paris: Chez Jean Mariette, 1719.

Dubreuil, Jean. *The Practice of Perspective: Or, An Easy Method of representing Natural Objects according to the Rules of Art.* Trans. Ephraim Chambers. London: Printed for Tho. Bowles and John Bowles, 1726.

Dufresnoy, Charles-Antoine. *The Art of Painting. Translated into English, with an Original Preface, Containing a Parallel between Painting and Poetry by Mr. Dryden. As Also a Short Account of the Most Eminent Painters, Both Ancient and Modern by Richard Graham, Esq.* 2 vols. London: Printed for Henry Lintot, 1750.

Dupaty, Charles-Marguerite-Jean-Baptiste-Mercier. *Lettres sur l'Italie en 1785.* 2d. ed., Paris: Desenne, 1792.

Duranty, Louis-Emile Edmond. "Promenades au Louvre. Remarques à propos de l'art égyptien." *Gazette des Beaux-Arts*, 29 (October-March 1878–1879), 209–224, 320–336.

Encyclopaedia Britannica, or, A Dictionary of Arts and Sciences, Compiled upon a New Plan. In Which the Different Sciences and Arts Are Digested into Distinct Treatises or Systems . . . 3 vols. London: Printed for Edward and Charles Dilly, 1773.

Encyclopédie, ou Dictionnaire raisonné des sciences, des arts, et des métiers, par une société de gens de lettres mis en ordre et publié par M. Diderot; et quant à la partie mathématique, par M. D'Alembert. 17 vols. Paris: Chez Briasson, David l'aîné, Le Breton, Durand, 1751–1780.

An Enquiry into the Nature of the Human Soul: Wherein the Immateriality of the Soul is Evinced From the Principles of Reason and Philosophy, 2 vols. 3d rev. ed., London: A. Millar, 1745.

Fabre, Pierre. *Traité des maladies vénériennes.* Paris: Chez P. Fr. Didot Le Jeune, 1773.

Félibien, André. *Entretiens sur les vies et sur les ouvrages de plus excellens peintres anciens et modernes; avec la vie des architectes.* Farnborough, Harts.: Gregg Press, Ltd., 1967.

Flögels, Carl Friedrich. *Einleitung in die Erfindungskunst.* Breslau and Leipzig: Bey Johann Ernst Meyer, 1760.

Fontenelle, Bernard le Bouvier de. *Nouveaux dialogues des morts* (1683). Ed. Jean Dagen. Paris: Librairie Marcel Didier, 1971.

Fueldez, Antoine. *Observations curieuses touchant la petite vérole. vraye peste des petits enfans: Et le bézahar son antidote.* Lyons: Chez Jean-Antoine Huguetan, 1645.

Fuseli, Henry. *Lectures on Painting delivered at the Royal Academy. With Additional Observations and Notes.* London: Henry Colburn and Richard Bentley, 1830.

Galilei, Galileo. *Considerazioni al Tasso di* . . . *e Discorso di Giuseppe Iseo sopra il poema di M. Torquato Tasso.* Rome: Nella Stamperia Pagliarini, 1793.

Gamelin, Jacques. *Nouveau recueil d'ostéologie et de myologie, dessiné d'aprés nature par* . . . *de Carcassonne, professeur de peinture, de l'Académie de Saint Luc* . . . *pour l'utilité des sciences et des arts.* 2 vols. Toulouse: De l'Imprimerie de J. F. Desclassan, 1779.

Garengeot, René Croissant de. *Splanchnologie, ou l'anatomie des viscères; avec des figures originales tirées d'après les cadavres, suivie d'une dissertation sur l'origine de la chirurgie.* 2 vols. 2d rev. ed., Paris: Chez Charles Osmont, 1742.

Garengeot, René Croissant de. *A Treatise of Chirurgical Operations; according to the Mechanism of the Parts of the Humane Body, and the Theory and Practice of the Most Learned and Experienced Surgeons in Paris with the Bandages for Each Apparatus and a Description of the Instruments proper for Chirurgical Operations.* Trans. M. André. London: Printed for Tho. Woodward, 1723.

Garzoni, Tomaso. *Il Seraglio degli stupori del mondo* . . . *Cioè de mostri, prodigi, prestigi, sorti, oracoli, sibille, sogni, curiosità, miracoli, maraviglie.* Venice: n.p., 1613.

Le Gemme antiche figurate de Michelangelo Causeo de La Chausse, Parigino, consagrate al Eminentissimo e Reverendissimo Principe il Signor Cardinale Cesare d'Estrées. Rome: Giacomo Komarek Boemo, 1700.

Gerdy, P. N. *Anatomie des formes extérieures du corps humains, appliquée à la peinture, à la sculpture et à la chirurgie.* Paris: Chez Béchet Jeune, Libraire; Brussels: au Dépot de Librairie médicale française, 1829.

Goethe, Johann Wolfgang von. *Farbenlehre* (1790–1808). Intro. Hans Wohlbold. Tübingen: Wissenschaftliche Buchgemeinschaft E.V., 1953.

Gori, Antonio Francisco. *Thesaurus Gemmarum Antiquarium Astriferarium.* 3 vols. Florence: Ex Officina Typogr. Albiziniana, 1750.

Grandville (Jean-Ignace Isidore Gérard). *Un autre monde: Transformations, visions, incarnations, ascensions, locomotions, explorations, pérégrinations, excursions, stations, cosmogonies, fantasmagories, rêveries, folâtreries, facéties, lubies, métamorphoses, zoomorphoses, lithomorphoses, métempsychoses, apothéoses, et autres choses.* Paris: H. Fournier, 1844.

Gregory, John. *A Comparative View of the State and Faculties of Man with Those of the Animal World.* 7th ed., London: Printed for J. Dodsley, 1774.

Grose, Francis. *Rules for drawing Caricaturas: With An Essay on Comic Painting. Illustrated with Twenty-One Copper Plates. Seventeen of Which were etched by Himself.* 2d ed., London: Printed for Hooper & Wigstead, 1796.

Guyot, Edmé. *Nouvelles récréations physiques et mathématiques, contenant ce qui à été imaginé de plus curieux dans ce genre, & ce qui se découvre journellement, auxquelles on a joint leurs causes, leurs effets, la manière de les construire, & l'amusement qu'on en peut tirer pour étonner & surprendre agréablement.* 8 vols. 2d ed., Paris: Chez l'Auteur et Chez Gueffier, 1772.

Hagedorn, Christian Ludwig von. *Réflexions sur la peinture.* Trans. M. Huber. 2 vols. Leipzig: Chez Gasper Fritsch, 1775.

Haller, Albrecht von. *A Dissertation on the Sensible and Irritable Parts of Animals.* Trans. M. Tissot. London: J. Nourse, 1755.

Haller, Albrecht von. *Elementa Physiologiae Corporis Humani.* 8 vols. Lausanne: Sumptibus M. M. Busquet, 1757–1766.

Harris, John. *Lexicon Technicum: or an Universal English Dictionary of Arts and Sciences: Explaining not only the Terms of Art, but the Arts Themselves.* 2 vols. London: D. Brown, 1704.

Harvey, William. *Anatomical Exercitations concerning the Generation of Living Creatures: To Which are added Particular Discourses of Births, and of Conceptions, etc.* London: Printed by James Young, 1653.

Hoet, Gérard. *Les Principaux fondements du dessein, pour l'usage des curieux, mise en l'umière par le très fameux peintre . . .* Leiden: Jean Arnold, 1723.

Hogarth, William. *The Analysis of Beauty* (1753). London: The Scolar Press, 1969.

Huber, Michel. *Handbuch für Kunstliebhaber und Sammler über die vornehmsten Kupferstecher und ihre Werke. Vom Anfange dieser Kunst bis auf gegenwärtige Zeit. Chronologisch und in Schulen geordnet.* Zurich: Bey Orell, Gessner, Füssli und Compagnie, 1796.

Hume, David. *A Treatise of Human Nature* [1739]. *Reprinted from the Original Edition in Three Volumes.* Ed. L. A. Selby-Bigge. Oxford: Clarendon Press, 1967.

Hunter, John. *Observations on Certain Parts of the Animal Oeconomy.* London: Sold at Castle-Street, Leicester Square, 1786.

Hunter, John. *A Treatise on the Veneral Disease*. London: Sold at Castle-Street, Leicester Square, 1786.

Hurd, Richard. *Letters on Chivalry and Romance*. London: Printed for A. Miller, W. Thurlbourn and J. Woodyer, 1762.

Jenner, Edward. *An Inquiry into the Causes and Effects of the Variolae Vaccinae, A Disease discovered in some of the Western Counties of England, particularly Gloucestershire, and Known by the Name of the Cow Pox*. London: Printed for the Author, 1798.

Johannot, Tony, Alfred de Musset, and P.-J. Stahl. *Voyage où il vous plaira*. Paris: J. Hetzel, 1843.

Johnson, Samuel. *A Dictionary of the English Language: In Which the Words are deduced from Their Originals, and Illustrated in Their Different Significations by Examples from the Best Authors* (1755). London: Joseph Ogle Robinson, 1828.

Johnson, Samuel. *Lives of the English Poets. Cowley-Dryden* (1783). 3 vols. Ed. George Birbeck Hill. New York: Octagon Books, 1967.

Jouard, Gabriel. *Des monstruosités et bizarreries de la nature, principalement de celles qui ont rapport à la génération; de leurs causes; de la manière dont elles s'opèrent, etc., avec des réflexions philosophiques sur le monstrueux et dangereux empiètemens des sciences accessoires, telles que la chimie, la droguerie, etc. sur la vraie médecine; ouvrage très-propre à mettre les mères à l'abri des effets des affections de l'âme, de l'imagination, des envies, des frayeurs, des maléfices, etc. . . .* 2 vols. in 1. Paris: Chez Allut, Impr.-Libr., et Propriétaire du Journal de la Vraie Théorie Médicale, 1806.

Junius, Franciscus. *The Painting of the Ancients in Three Books: Declaring by Historical Observations and Examples, the Beginning, Progresse, and Consummation of That Most Noble Art. And How Those Ancient Artificers attained to Their still so much admired Excellencie*. Trans. from the Latin. London: Printed by Richard Hodgkinsonne, 1638.

La Chau, l'Abbé de, and l'Abbé Le Blond. *Description des principales pierres gravées du Cabinet de S.A.S. Monsieur le Duc d'Orléans, Premier Prince du Sang*. 2 vols. Paris: Chez Chau et Le Blond, 1780.

Laennec, Théophile. *Traité de l'auscultation médiate, peut-elle servir au progrès de la médecine pratique?* 2 vols. Paris: J.-A. Brosson et J.-S. Naudé, 1819.

Lairesse, Gerard de. *The Art of Painting in All Its Branches, Methodically demonstrated by Discourses and Plates, and Exemplified by Remarks on the Painting of the Best Master*. Trans. Frederick Fritsch. London: Printed for S. Vandenbergh; Messers. Payne, White, Robson and Co., Walter and Sewell, 1778.

La Mettrie, Julien Offray de. *L'Homme machine*. Ed. Paul-Laurent Assoun. Paris: Denoël/Gonthier, 1981.

Laugier, Marc-Antoine [Abbé]. *Manière de bien juger des ouvrages de peinture*. Paris: Chez Claude-Antoine Jombert, 1771.

Lavater, Johann Caspar. *Essays on Physiognomy. Designed to promote the Knowledge and the Love of Mankind . . .* Trans. Henry Hunter. 3 vols. in 5. London: John Murray and T. Holloway, 1792.

Lavater, Johann Caspar. *Physiognomische Fragmente. Zur Beförderung der Menschenkenntniss und Menschenliebe*. Leipzig and Winterthur: Bey Weidmanns Erben und Reich, 1775–1778.

Lavater, Johann Caspar. *Règles physiognomiques, ou observations sur quelques traits caractéristiques*. The Hague and Paris: Chez I. van Cleef et A. A. Renouard, 1803.

Lavater, Johann Caspar. *Von der Physiognomik*. 2 vols. in 1. Leipzig: Bey Weidmanns Erben und Reich, 1772.

Le Blon, J. C. *L'Art d'imprimer les tableaux. Traité d'après les écrits, les opérations & les instructions verbales*. Paris: Ches P. G. Le Mercier, Jean Luc Nyon, Michel Lambert, 1756.

Le Camus, Antoine. *Médecine de l'esprit; où l'on traite des dispositions & des causes physiques qui en conséque l'union de l'âme avec le corps, influent sur les opérations de l'esprit; & des moyens de maintenir ces opérations dans un bon état, ou de les corriger lorsqu'elles sont viciées*. 2 vols. Paris: Chez Ganeau, 1753.

Ledermüller, Martin Frobène. *Troisième cinquantaine des amusemens microscopiques*. Nuremberg: Adam Wolfgang Winter-Schmidt graveur et marchand en tailles douces, 1768.

Leibniz, Gottfried Wilhelm Freiherr von. *New Essays* (1765). trans. Alfred Langley. LaSalle, Ill.: The Open Court Publishing Company. 1949.

[Le Meltier]. *Lettre adressée à Monsieur le Marquis de Puiségur, sur une observation faite à la lune, précédée d'un système nouveau sur le méchanisme de la vue*. Amsterdam: n.p., 1787.

Lens, Bernard. *Bowles's New Preceptor in Drawing* . . . London: Printed for Carrington Bowles, 1787.

Le Sage, Georges-Louis. "The Le Sage Theory of Gravitation" (1782). Trans. C. G. Abbott. *Annual Report of the Board of Regents of the Smithsonian Institution*. Washington, D.C.: Government Printing Office, 1899.

Lessing, Gotthold Ephraim. *Laocoön. An Essay on the Limits of Painting and Poetry*. Trans. Edward Allen McCormick. Baltimore: Johns Hopkins University Press, 1984.

Licetus, Fortunius. *De Monstris. Ex Recensione Gerardi Blasii, M.D. & P.P. Qui Monstra quaedam nova & Rariora ex Recentiorum Scriptis Addidit*. Amsterdam: Andreae Frisii, 1665.

Lichtenberg, Georg Christoph. *Aphorismen Auswahl*. Ed. Friedrich Sengle. Stuttgart: Philipp Reclam Jun., 1966.

Lichtenberg, Georg Christoph. *Hogarth on High Life: The Marriage à la Mode Series from* . . . *Commentaries*. Trans. and ed. Arthur S. Wensinger with W. B. Coley. Middletown, Conn.: Wesleyan University Press, 1970.

Lichtenberg, Georg Christoph. *Tag und Dämmerung. Aphorismen, Schriften, Briefe, Tagebücher*. Leipzig: In der Dieterich'schen Verlagsbuchhandlung, 1941.

Lichtenberg, Georg Christoph. *Über Physiognomik, wider die Physiognomen. Zu Beförderung der Menschenliebe und Menschenkenntniss*. Steinbach: Anabas Verlag Günter Kämpf, 1970.

Lomazzo, Giovanni Paolo. *Idea del Tempio della Pittura*. 2 vols. Ed. and trans. Robert Klein. Florence: Nella Sede dell' Istituto Palazzo Strozzi, 1974.

Louis, Antoine. *Lettres sur la certitude des signes de la mort. Où l'on rassure les citoyens de la crainte d'être enterrés vivans. Avec des observations & des expériences sur les noyés*. Paris: Chez Michel Lambert, 1772.

Louis, Antoine. *Traité des maladies des os, dans lequel on a représenté les appareils & les machines qui conviennent a leur guérison.* 2d rev. ed., Paris: Chez P. G. Cavelier, 1772.

Lucian. *A True Story [Verae Historiae].* 8 vols. Trans. A. M. Harmon. Cambridge, Mass.: Harvard University Press; London: William Heinemann, Ltd., 1913.

Lucretius (Titus Lucretius Carus). *De Rerum Natura.* Trans. W. H. D. Rouse. Cambridge, Mass.: Harvard University Press; London: William Heinemann Ltd., 1975.

Malebranche, Nicolas. *De la recherche de la vérité, où l'on traite de la nature de l'esprit de l'homme, & de l'usage qu'il en doit faire pour éviter l'erreur dans les sciences.* 4 vols. Paris: Chez Michel David, 1712.

Maupertuis, Pierre-Louis Moreau de. *Dissertation physique à l'occasion du nègre blanc.* Leiden: n.p., 1744.

Maupertuis, Pierre-Louis Moreau de. *The Earthly Venus [Vénus physique].* Trans. Simone Brangier Boas. New York and London: Johnson Reprint Corporation, 1966.

Mémoires de l'académie royale de Prusse. 10 vols. Avignon: Chez Jean-Joseph Niel, Imprimeur, 1768.

Mengs, Antoine-Raphael. *Oeuvres complètes d'Antoine-Raphaël Mengs.* Trans. from the Italian. 2 vols. Paris: à l'Hôtel de Thou, 1786.

Mengs, Antoine-Raphael. *Sämmtliche hinterlassene Schriften.* 2 vols. in 1. Ed. Dr. G. Schilling. Bonn: H. B. König, 1843.

Mercier, Louis-Sébastien. *Du Théâtre ou nouvel essai sur l'art dramatique.* Amsterdam: Chez E. van Harrevelt, 1773.

Mesmer, Franz Anton. *Mémoire sur ses découvertes.* Paris: Chez Fuchs Libraire, 1798–9.

Montesquieu, Charles-Louis de. "Essai sur le goût dans les choses de la nature & de l'art." *Encyclopédie,* VII, pp. 762–763.

More, Henry. *Enthusiasmus Triumphatus, or, a Discourse of the Nature, Causes, Kinds, and Cure of Enthusiasme.* London: Printed by J. Flesher, 1656.

More, Henry. *Immortality of the Soul.* In *A Collection of Several Philosophical Writings.* London: Printed by James Flesher, 1662.

Muratori, Lodovigo Antonio. *Della forza della fantasia umana trattato.* Venice: Presso Giambattista Pasquali, 1745.

Natter, Laurent. *Traité de la méthode antique de graver en pierres fines, comparée avec la méthode moderne.* London: J. Haberkorn, 1754.

Newton, Isaac. *Mathematical Principles of Natural Philosophy and His System of the World.* Trans. Andrew Motte, rev. Florian Cajori. Berkeley: University of California Press, 1934.

Novalis (Baron Friedrich von Hardenberg). *Das allgemeine Brouillon (Materialen zur Enzyklopädistik)* (1798/99). In *Das philosophische-theoretische Werk.* Ed. Hans-Joachim Mahl. Munich and Vienna: Carl Hauser Verlag, 1978.

Oldmixon, John. *An Essay on Criticism as It regards Design, Thought, and Expression, in Prose and Verse.* London: Printed for J. Pemberton, 1728.

Origen. *Homilies on Genesis and Exodus.* Trans. Ronald E. Heine. Washington, D.C.: The Catholic University of America Press, 1981.

Origen. *The Song of Songs: Commentary and Homilies.* Trans. R. P. Lawson. Westminster, Md., and London: The Newman Press and Longmans, Green and Co., 1957.

Papillon, Jean-Martin. *Traité historique et pratique de la gravure en bois.* 2 vols. Paris: Chez Pierre Guillaume Simon, 1766.

Paré, Ambroise. *Les Oeuvres de . . . , conseiler et premier chirurgien du roy. Corigées et augmentées par luy-mesme, peu au paravant son decés.* 7th ed., Paris: Chez Nicolas Buon, 1614.

Pariset, R. M. *Nouveau livre des principes de dessein recueilli des études des meilleures maîtres tant anciens que modernes, & dirigé par . . .* Paris: Chez L. Surugue, n.d.

Parsons, James. *Human Physiognomy explain'd : In the Crounian Lectures on Muscular Motion. For the Year MDCCXLVI. Read before the Royal Society. Being a Supplement to the Philosophical Transactions for That Year.* London: Printed for C. Davis, 1747.

[Paulet, Jean-Jacques]. *Anti-Magnetismus oder Ursprung, Fortgang, Verfall, Erneuerung und Widerlegung des thierischen Magnetismus.* Trans. from the French edition. Gera: Bey Heinrich Gottlieb Rothe, 1788.

Paulet, Jean-Jacques. *Histoire de la petite vérole, avec les moyens d'en préserver les enfans et d'en arrêter la contagion en France.* 2 vols. Paris: Chez Ganeau, 1768.

Pernety, Antoine-Joseph. *La Connoissance de l'homme moral par celle de l'homme physique.* 2 vols. Berlin: Chez G. J. Decker, 1776.

Pernety, Antoine-Joseph. *Dictionnaire mytho-hermétique, dans lequel on trouve les allégories fabuleuses des poètes, les métaphores, les enigmes et les termes barbares des philosophes hermétiques expliqués.* Paris: Chez Delalain l'aîné, 1787.

Pernety, Antoine-Joseph. *Dictionnaire portatif de peinture, sculpture et gravure; avec un traité pratique des différentes manières de peindre.* Berlin: Chez Bauche, 1758.

Pernety, Antoine-Joseph. *Discours sur la physionomie, et les avantages de connoissances physionomiques.* Berlin: Chez Samuel Pitra, 1769.

Pernety, Antoine-Joseph. *Observations sur les maladies de l'âme pour servir de suite au traité de la connoissance de l'homme moral par celle de l'homme physique.* Berlin: Chez G. J. Decker, 1777.

Piranesi, Giovanni Battista. *Lapides Capitolini sive fasti Consulares Triumphales Q Romanorum ab Urbe condita usque ad Tiberium Caesarem.* Rome: Author, 1761.

Piranesi, Giovanni Battista. *The Polemical Works. Rome 1757, 1761, 1765, 1769.* Ed. John Wilton-Ely. Westmead: Gregg International Publishers Ltd., 1972.

Plutarch. *The Obsolescence of Oracles.* In *Moralia.* 15 vols. Trans. Frank Cole Babbitt. Cambridge, Mass.: Harvard University Press and London: William Heineman Ltd., 1962.

Priestley, Joseph. *A Free Discussion of the Doctrines of Materialism, and Philosophical Necessity,*

In a Correspondence between Dr. Price, and Dr. Priestley. London: Printed for J. Johnson and T. Cadell, 1778.

Priestley, Joseph. *The History and Present State of Discoveries relating to Vision, Light, and Colours.* London: Printed for J. Johnson, 1772.

Priestley, Joseph. *The History and Present State of Electricity, With Original Experiments.* 2d rev. ed., London: Printed for J. Dodsley, J. Johnson, J. Payne, and T. Cadell, 1769.

Proclus, Diadochus. *Alcibiades I. A Translation and Commentary.* 2d ed. Trans. William O'Neill. The Hague: Martinus Nijhoff, 1971.

Proclus, Diadochus. *A Commentary on the First Book of Euclid's Elements.* Trans. Glenn R. Morrow. Princeton, N.J.: Princeton University Press, 1970.

Proclus, Diadochus. *Théologie platonicienne, Livre III.* Ed. and trans. H. D. Saffrey and L. G. Westerink. Paris: Société d'Edition "Les Belles Lettres," 1978.

Proclus, Diadochus. *Über die Existenz des Bösen.* Trans. and ed. Michael Erler. Meisenheim am Glan: Verlag Anton Hain, 1978.

Purland, Theodosius. "For the History of Mesmerism, Clairvoyance, Animal Magnetism, etc." 4 vols. of pamphlets, tracts, clippings, autograph letters, original drawings, in the National Library of Medicine, Bethesda, Md.; produced in London, 1848–1854.

Puységur, Armand-Marie-Jacques Chastenet, Marquis de. *Du magnétisme animal, considéré dans ses rapports avec diverses branches de la physique générale.* Paris: De l'Imprimerie de Cellot. 1807.

Puységur, Armand-Marie-Jacques Chastenet, Marquis de. *Mémoires pour servir à l'histoire et à l'établissement du magnétisme animal.* Paris: n.p., 1784.

Puységur, Armand-Marie-Jacques Chastenet, Marquis de. *Recherches, expériences et observations physiologiques sur l'homme dans l'état de somnambulisme provoqué par l'acte magnétique.* Paris: J. G. Dentu, Imprimeur-Libraire, 1811.

Quintilianus, Marcus Fabius. *Institutes of Oratory or, Education of an Orator. In Twelve Books.* 2 vols. Trans. John Selby Watson. London: George Bell and Sons, 1875.

Reynolds, Joshua. *Discourses on Art.* ed. Robert R. Wark. San Marino: Huntington Library, 1959.

Richard, Jérôme [Abbé]. *La Théorie des songes.* Paris: Chez les Frères Estienne, 1766.

Richardson, Jonathan. *The Works: I. The Theory of Painting. II. Essay on the Art of Criticism. (So Far as it relates to Painting). III. The Science of a Connoisseur; With an Essay on the Knowledge of Prints, and Cautions to Collectors.* London: T. and J. Egerton, 1792.

Rosenhof, A. J. Rösel von. *Die näturliche Historie der Frösche hiesigen Landes.* Nuremberg: Johann Joseph Fleischmann, 1758.

Roussel, M. *Système physique et moral de la femme, suivi du système physique et moral de l'homme, et d'un fragment sur la sensibilité, précédé de l'éloge historique de l'auteur par J. L. Alibert.* Paris: Chez Crapart, Caille et Ravier, 1805.

Sainte-Albine, Pierre Remond de. *Le Comédien, Ouvrage divisé en deux parties.* New rev. ed., Paris: Chez Vincent, 1749.

Saint-Igny. *Elémens de pourtraiture, ou la méthode de représenter toutes les parties du corps humain.* Paris: Chez François l'Anglois, n.d. [17th century].

Sans, Abbé. *Guérison de la paralysie par l'éléctricité ou cette expérience physique.* Paris: Chez Cailleau, 1772.

Scheuchzer, Jean-Jacques. *Physique sacrée, ou histoire naturelle de la Bible.* 8 vols. Amsterdam: Chez Pierre Schenk et Pierre Mortier, 1732–1737.

Shaftesbury, Anthony Ashley Cooper, Earl of. *Characteristics.* 2 vols. London: n.p., 1738.

Shaftesbury, Anthony Ashley Cooper, Earl of. *The Life, Unpublished Letters, and Philosophical Regimen.* Ed. Benjamin Rand. Folcroft, Pa.: Folcroft Library Editions, 1977.

Shelley, Mary Wollstonecraft. *Frankenstein or the Modern Prometheus.* New York: Harrison Smith and Robert Haas, 1934.

Sibly, Ebenezer. *A Key to Physic, and the Occult Sciences. Opening to Mental View, The System and Order of the Interior and Exterior Heavens. The Analogy betwixt Angels, and Spirits of Men, and the Sympathy between Celestial and Terrestrial Bodies* (1794). London: Printed for the Author, 1804.

Sivry, Louis Poinsinet de. *Traité des causes physiques et morales du rire relativement à l'art de l'exciter.* Amsterdam: Marc-Michel Rey, 1768.

Smith, Gabriel. *The School of Art; or the Most Complete Drawing-Book extant: Consisting of an Extensive Series of Well-Chosen Examples, selected from the Designs of Those Eminent Masters Watteau, Boucher, Bouchardon, Le Brun, Eisen, etc. Engraved on Sixty Folio Copper Plates in the Chalk Manner.* London: Printed for John Bowles, 1765.

Smyth, James Carmichael. *The Effect of the Nitrous Vapour, in preventing and destroying Contagion; ascertained, from a Variety of Trials, made chiefly by Surgeon's of His Majesty's Navy, in Prisons, Hospitals, and on Board of Ships: With An Introduction respecting the Nature of the Contagion which gives Rise to the Jail or Hospital Fever; and the Various Methods formerly employed to prevent or destroy This.* London: J. Johnson, 1799.

Soemmering, G. Theodore von. *Über das Organ der Seele.* Königsberg: Bey Friedrich Nicolovius, 1796.

Spence, Joseph. *Polymetis: or, an Enquiry concerning the Agreement between the Works of the Roman Poets, and the Remains of the Ancient Artists. Being An Attempt to illustrate Them Mutually from One Another.* 2d rev. ed., London: Printed for R. and J. Dodsley, 1755.

Spurzheim, Johann Georg. *The Physiognomical System of Drs. Gall and . . . , founded on Anatomical and Physiological Examination of the Nervous System in General, and of the Brain in Particular; and indicating the Dispositions and Manifestations of the Mind.* 2d ed., London: Baldwin, Cradock, & Joy, 1815.

Sticotti, A. F. *Dictionnaire des gens du monde, historique, littéraire, critique, moral, physique, militaire, politique, caractéristique & social.* 3 vols. Paris: Chez J. P. Costard, 1771.

Stubbs, Georges. *An Illustrated Lecture on Sketching from Nature in Pencil and Water Colour: With Hints on Light and Shadow, on a Method of Study, etc. To be a Series of Lessons Out of Doors.* London: Day and Son, n.d.

Sue, Jean-Joseph. *Essai sur la physiognomie des corps vivans, considerée depuis l'homme jusqu'à la plante. Ouvrage où l'on traite principalement de la nécessité de cette étude dans les arts d'imitation, des véritables règles de la béauté et des graces, des proportions du corps humains, de l'expression, des passions, etc.* Paris: Chez l'Auteur, 1797.

Sulzer, Johann Georg. *Allgemeine Theorie der schönen Künste* . . . 2 vols. in 4. Biel: In der Heilmannischer Buchhandlung, 1777.

Sulzer, Johann Georg. "A New Critical Examination of the Word *Thought* as applied to the Fine Arts, with Rules for Judging of the Beauties of Painting, Music, and Poetry." *Annual Register*, XVII (1774).

Taylor, Thomas, ed. *The Commentaries of Proclus on the Timaeus of Plato; Containing a Treasury of Pythagoric and Platonic Physiology. Translated from the Greek.* 2 vols. in 1. London: Printed for and sold by the Author, 1820.

Tertullian (Quintus Septimius Florens Tertullianus). *Treatises on Marriage and, Remarriage. To His Wife (Ad Uxorum), An Exhortation to Chastity (De Exhortatione Castitatis), Monogamy (De Monogamia)* (212/213 AD). Trans. and annotated by William P. Le Saint. Westminster, Md.: The Newman Press, 1951.

Tesauro, Emmanuele. *Il Canocchiale aristotelico, o sia Idea delle argutezza heroiche vulgaremente chiamate Imprese. E di tutta l'arte simbolica, et Lapidaria.* Venice: Presso Paolo Baglioni, 1655.

Tissot, Samuel-Auguste-André-David. *De la santé des gens de lettres.* 2d ed., Lausanne: J. F. Bassompierre, Fils, 1772.

Tissot, Samuel-Auguste-André-David. *Essai sur les maladies des gens du monde.* Lausanne: Chez François Grasset & Comp., 1781.

Trapp, Joseph. *Lectures on Poetry Read in the Schools of Natural Philosophy at Oxford.* Trans. from the Latin. London: Printed for C. Hitch and C. Davis, 1742.

Trusler, John. *Principles of Politeness and of Knowing the World, by the late Lord Chesterfield. Methodised and Digested under Distinct Heads, with Additions by the Rev. Dr. . . . : Containing Every Instruction Necessary to complete the Gentleman and Man of Fashion: to teach him a Knowledge of Life, and make him well-received in All Countries.* Portsmouth, N.H.: Printed by Melcher and Osborn, 1786.

Varley, John. *A Treatise on Zodiacal Physiognomy; Illustrated by Engravings of Heads and Features; and accompanied by Tables of the Time of Rising of the Twelve Signs of the Zodiac; and containing also New and Astrological Explanations of Some Remarkable Portions of Ancient Mythological History.* London: Author, 1828.

Vaumorel, Caulet de. *Aphorismes de M. Mesmer.* Paris: Chez Gastelier, Libraire, 1785.

Vicq d'Azyr, Félix, and Hippolyte Cloquet. *Encyclopédie méthodique. Système anatomique. Dictionnaire raisonné des termes d'anatomie et de physiologie.* 4 vols. Paris: Chez Mme. Veuve Agasse, 1792–1823.

Wall, John. *Plain Directions, etc. for The Cure of the Venereal Disease. Together with Efficacious and Approved Remedies, adapted to Every Symptom of the Disorder. Sufficient to enable Persons to cure Themselves . . . Designed Chiefly to rescue the Poor, and People of Small Fortunes from the Destructive Hands of Unskillful Apothecaries and Quack Doctors.* London: W. Griffin, G. Kearsley; York: E. Etherington, 1764.

Walpole, Horace. *Anecdotes of Painting in England, with Some Account of the Principal Artists; and Incidental Notes on Other Arts.* 5 vols. Ed. Frederick W. Hilles and Philip B. Daghlian. New Haven and London: Yale University Press and Oxford University Press, 1937.

Watelet, Claude-Henri. *L'Art de peindre. Poëme avec des réflexions sur les différentes parties de la peinture.* Amsterdam: Aux dépens de la Compagnie, 1761.

Webb, Daniel. *An Inquiry into the Beauties of Painting; and into the Merits of the Most Celebrated Painters, Ancient and Modern.* 2d ed., London: Printed for R. and J. Dodsley, 1761.

Whytt, Robert. *Physiological Essays containing an Inquiry into the Causes Which promote the Circulation of Fluids in the Very Small Vessels of Animals; Observations on the Sensibility and Irritability of the Parts of Men and Other Animals; Occasioned by Dr. Haller's Late Treatise on These Subjects.* Edinburgh: Hamilton, Balfour, and Neill, 1754.

Willan, Robert. *Description and Treatment of Cutaneous Diseases. Order I. Papulous Eruptions on the Skin.* London: Printed for J. Johnson, 1798.

Willis, Thomas. *Practice of Physick, Being the Whole Works of That Renowned and Famous Physician: Containing These Eleven Several Treatises.* Trans. S. P. London: Printed for T. Dring, C. Harper, and J. Leigh, 1684.

Winckelmann, Johann Joachim. *Abhandlung von der Fahigkeit der Empfindung des Schönen in der Kunst, und dem Unterrichte in derselben.* Dresden: In der Walterischen Buchhandlung, 1763.

Winckelmann, Johann Joachim. *On the Imitation of the Painting and Sculpture of the Greeks* (1755). In *Winckelmann: Writings on Art.* Ed. David Irwin. London: Phaidon, 1972.

Winckelmann, Johann Joachim. *Versuch einer Allegorie, besonders für die Kunst.* Dresden: In der Walterischen Hof-Buchhandlung, 1766.

Woolnough, C. W. *The Art of Marbling, as applied to Book Edges and Paper, Containing Full Instructions for Executing British, French, Spanish, Italian, Nonpareil, etc. Illustrated with Specimens. With a Brief Notice of Its Recent Application to Textile Fabrics, and Particularly to the Cloths so Extensively used by Book Binders.* London: Alexander Heylin, 1853.

Wotton, William. *Reflections upon Ancient and Modern Learning.* London: Printed by J. Leake, 1694.

Young, George. *A Treatise on Opium, Founded upon Practical Observations.* London: Printed for A. Millar, 1753.

2 SECONDARY SOURCES

Adams, Percy G. *Travel Literature and the Evolution of the Novel*. Lexingon, Ky.: The University Press of Kentucky, 1983.

Adelmann, Howard B. *Marcello Malpighi and the Evolution of Embryology*. Ithaca: Cornell University Press, 1966.

Adhémar, Jean. "Les Musées de cire en France. Curtius, le 'banquet royal,' les têtes coupées." *Gazette des Beaux-Arts*, 92, no. 2 (1978), 206–207.

Altran, Scott. *Fondements de l'histoire naturelle. Pour une anthropologie de la science*. Brussels: Editions Complexe, 1986.

Ameisenowa, Sofia. "Animal-Headed Gods: Evangelists, Saints and Righteous Men." *Journal of the Warburg and Courtauld Institutes*, 12 (1949), 21–45.

Ameisenowa, Sofia. *The Problem of the Écorché and the Three Anatomical Models in the Jagiellonia Library*. Trans. Andrzej Potocki. Warsaw: Wydewnictwo Polskiej Akademii Nauk, 1963.

Anderson, Wilda C. *Between the Library and the Laboratory: The Language of Chemistry in Eighteenth-Century France*. Baltimore: Johns Hopkins University Press, 1984.

Andries, Lise. "L'Interprétation populaire des songes." *Revue des Sciences Humaines*, 211, no. 3 (1988), 49–64.

Appel, Toby A. *The Cuvier-Geoffroy Debate: French Biology in the Decades before Darwin*. New York and Oxford: Oxford University Press, 1987.

Ariès, Philippe. *Centuries of Childhood: A Social History of Family Life*. Trans. Robert Baldick. New York: Alfred A. Knopf, 1962.

Armstrong, A. MacC. "The Idea of the Comic." *British Journal of Aesthetics*, 25 (Summer 1985), 232–238.

Arnar, Anna Sigridur. *Encyclopedism from Pliny to Borges*. Exh. cat. Chicago: The University of Chicago Library, 1990.

Baillio, Joseph. *Elisabeth Louise Vigée Le Brun, 1755–1842*. Exh. Cat. Fort Worth: Kimbell Art Museum, 1982.

Barker, Duncan G. N. "*Grylli, Verstand und Unsinn* in Classical Glyptics." M.A. thesis, University of Chicago, 1989.

Barney, Stephen A. *Allegories of History, Allegories of Love*. Hamden, Conn.: Archon Books, 1979.

Barolsky, Paul. *Infinite Jest: Wit and Humor in Italian Renaissance Art*. Columbia and London: University of Missouri Press, 1978.

Barrell, John. *The Political Theory of Painting from Reynolds to Hazlitt: "The Body of the Public."* New Haven: Yale University Press, 1986.

Barthes, Roland. *Arcimboldo*. Milan: Franco Maria Riccia, 1980.

Bataille, George. *Documents*. Ed. Bernard Noël. Paris: Mercure de France. 1968.

Battersby, Martin. *Trompe-l'Oeil: The Eye Deceived*. London: Academy Editions, 1974.

Beierwaltes, Werner. *Platonismus und Idealismus*. Frankfurt am Main: Vittorio Klostermann, 1972.

Belting, Hans. *Bild und Kult, eine Geschichte des Bildes vor dem Zeitalter der Kunst*. Munich: Verlag C. H. Beck, 1990.

Belting, Hans. *Das Ende der Kunstgeschichte? Überlegung zur heutigen Kunsterfahrung und historischen Kunstforschung*. Munich: Deutscher Kunst-Verlag, 1983.

Bernardi, Walter, and Antonello La Vergata, eds. *Lazzaro Spallanzani e la biologia del Settecento. Teorie, esperimenti, istituzioni scientifiche*. Florence: Leo S. Olschki, 1982.

Bevan, Edwyn. *Holy Images: An Inquiry into Idolatry and Image-Worship in Ancient Paganism and Christianity*. London: George Allen & Unwin Ltd., 1933.

Billicsich, Friedrich. *Das Probleme des Übels in der Philosophie des Abendlandes*. 2 vols. 2d rev. ed., Vienna: Verlag A. Sexl, 1955.

Bindman, David. *Blake as Artist*. Oxford: Phaidon, 1977.

Blanchard, Marc Eli. "The Pleasures of Description." *Diacritics* (June 1977), 22–34.

Blanchard, Marc Eli. "Writing the Museum: Diderot's Bodies in the Salons." *Diderot Digression and Dispersion: A Bicentennial Tribute*. Ed. Jack Undank and Herbert Josephs. Lexington, Ky.: French Forum Publishers, 1984.

Blumenberg, Hans. *Arbeit am Mythos*. Frankfurt am Main: Suhrkamp, 1979.

Blumenberg, Hans. *Ausblick auf eine Theorie der Unbegrifflichkeit. Schiffbruch mit Zuschauer. Paradigma einer Daseinsmetapher*. Frankfurt am Main: Suhrkamp, 1979.

Blumenberg, Hans. *Höhlenausgänge*. Frankfurt am Main: Suhrkamp, 1989.

Blumenberg, Hans. *Lebenzeit und Weltzeit*. Frankfurt am Main: Suhrkamp, 1986.

Blumenberg, Hans. *Die Lesbarkeit der Welt*. Munich: Suhrkamptaschenbuch Wissenschaft, 1986.

Blumenberg, Hans. "Paradigmen zu einer Metapherologie." *Archiv für Begriffsgeschichte*, 4 (1960).

Blumenthal, H. J., and A. C. Lloyd. *Soul and the Structure of Being in Late Neoplatonism: Syrianus, Proclus and Simplicius*. Liverpool: Liverpool University Press, 1982.

Bogen, James, and James E. McGuire, eds. *How Things Are: Studies in Predication and the History of Philosophy and Science*. Dordrecht: D. Reidel Publishing Company, 1985.

Bolten, Jaap. *Method and Practice: Dutch and Flemish Drawing Books 1600–1750*. Stuttgart: Edition PVA, 1985.

Born, Wolfgang. "Monsters in Art." *Ciba Symposia*, 9 (August–September 1947), 684–696.

Bowden, John, and Alan Richardson. *Westminster Dictionary of Christian Theology*. Philadelphia: Westminster Press, 1983.

Bowen, Barbara C. "Two Literary Genres: The Emblem and the Joke." *Journal of Medieval and Renaissance Studies*, 15 (Spring 1985), 29–36.

Brazier, Mary A. B. *A History of Neurophysiology in the Seventeenth and Eighteenth Centuries: From Concept to Experiment.* New York: Raven Press, 1984.

Bret, Michael. "Procedural Art with Computer Graphics." *Leonardo.* 21, no. 1 (1988), 3–10.

Brilliant, Richard. *Gesture and Rank in Roman Art: The Use of Gestures to Denote Status in Roman Sculpture and Coinage.* New Haven: Connecticut Academy of Arts & Sciences, 1963.

Brilliant, Richard. *Visual Narratives: Storytelling in Etruscan and Roman Art.* Ithaca: Cornell University Press, 1984.

Briquet, Charles M. *Les Filigranes.* New York: Hacker Art Books, 1985.

Brody, Saul Nathaniel. *The Disease of the Soul: Leprosy in Medieval Literature.* Ithaca: Cornell University Press, 1974.

Brookner, Anita. *Greuze: The Rise and Fall of an Eighteenth-Century Phenomenon.* Greenwich, Conn.: New York Graphic Society, 1972.

Brown, Peter. *The Body and Society: Men, Women and Sexual Renunciation in Early Christianity.* New York: Columbia University Press, 1988.

Brumbaugh, Robert S. *Plato's Mathematical Imagination: The Mathematical Passages in the Dialogues and Their Interpretation.* Bloomington: Indiana University Press, 1954.

Bryson, Norman. *Word and Image: French Painting of the Ancien Régime.* Cambridge: Cambridge University Press, 1981.

Bucci, Mario. *Anatomia come arte.* Florence: Edizione d'Arte Il Fiorino, 1969.

Buchloh, Benjamin. "Figures of Authority, Ciphers of Regression: Notes on the Return of Representation in European Painting." *October,* no. 16 (Spring 1981), 38–68.

Bultmann, Rudolf. "Zur Geschichte der Licht-Symbolik im Althertum." *Philologus,* 97 (1948), 1–36.

Buranelli, Vincent. *The Wizard from Vienna.* New York: Coward, McCann, & Geoghegan, Inc., 1975.

Burke, Joseph. *Hogarth and Reynolds: A Contrast in English Art Theory.* London and Oxford: Oxford University Press, 1943.

Burke, Peter, and Roy Porter, eds. *The Social History of Language.* Cambridge: Cambridge University Press, 1987.

Burwick, Frederick. "The Hermeneutic of Lichtenberg's Interpretation of Hogarth." *Lessing Yearbook,* 19 (1987), 167–191.

Burwick, Frederick. "Stage Illusion and the Stage Designs of Goethe and Hugo." *Word & Image,* 4 (July–December 1988), 692–718.

Bynum, Caroline Walker. *Docere Verbo et Exemplo: An Aspect of Twelfth-Century Spirituality.* Missoula, Montana: Scholars Press, 1979.

Bynum, W. F. "The Anatomical Method: Natural Theology and the Functions of the Brain." *Isis,* 64 (September 1973), 445–468.

Bynum, W. F., and Roy Porter. *William Hunter and the Eighteenth-Century Medical World.* Cambridge: Cambridge University Press. 1985.

Bynum, W. F., Roy Porter, and Michael Shephard, eds. *The Anatomy of Madness: Essays in the History of Psychiatry*. 2 vols. London and New York: Tavistock Publications, 1985.

Cahn, Walter. *Masterpieces: Chapters on the History of an Idea*. Princeton, N.J.: Princeton University Press, 1978.

Callahan, Daniel. "How Technology is Reframing the Abortion Debate." *Hastings Center Report*. February 1986.

Calmann, Gerta. "The Picture of No-Body." *Journal of the Warburg and Courtauld Institutes*, 23 (1960), 60–104.

Campbell, Eila M. T. "An English Philosophico-Chronographical Chart." *Imago Mundi* 4 (1950), 79–84.

Camiz, Franca Trinchier. "The *Castrato* Singer: From Informal to Formal Portraiture." *Artibus et Asiae*, 18 (1988), 171–186.

Canguilhem, Georges. *La Connaissance de la vie*. Paris: Librairie Philosophique J. Vrin, 1965.

Canguilhem, Georges. *On the Normal and the Pathological*. Trans. Carolyn R. Fawcett, ed. Robert S. Cohen. Dordrecht: D. Reidel Publishing Co., 1978.

Canto, Monique. "Acts of Fake: The Icon in Platonic Thought." *Representations*, no. 10 (Spring 1985), 124–144.

Cantor, G. N., and M. J. S. Hodge, eds. *Conceptions of Ether: Studies in the History of Ether Theories, 1740–1900*. Cambridge: Cambridge University Press, 1984.

Caroll, Margaret Deutsch. "Rembrandt as Meditational Printmaker." *Art Bulletin*, 63 (December 1981), 585–610.

Casey, Edward S. *Imagining: A Phenomenological Study*. Bloomington: Indiana University Press, 1976.

Cast, David. "Seeing Vanbrugh and Hawksmoor." *Journal of the Society of Architectural Historians*, 43 (December 1984), 310–327.

Castillejo, David. *The Expanding Force in Newton's Cosmos as Shown in His Unpublished Papers*. Madrid: Ediciones de Arte y Bibliofilia, 1981.

Castle, Terry. "The Female Thermometer." *Representations*, no. 17 (Winter 1987), 1–27.

Caton, Hiram. *The Origin of Subjectivity: An Essay on Descartes*. New Haven: Yale University Press: 1973.

Cave Terence. *The Cornucopian Text: Problems of Writing in the French Renaissance*. Oxford: Clarendon Press, 1979.

Céard, Jean, ed. *La Folie et le corps*. Paris: Presses de l'Ecole Normale Supérieure, 1985.

Céard, Jean, and Jean-Claude Margolin. *Rébus de la Renaissance. Des images qui parlent*. 2 vols. Paris: Maisonneuve et La Rose, 1986.

Chapeaurouge, Donat de. *"Das Auge ist ein Herr, das Ohr ein Knecht." Der Weg von der Mittelalterlichen zur Abstrakten Malerei*. Wiesbaden: Franz Steiner Verlag, 1983.

Chapon, Richard. "L'Humour: Origine et analyse." *Actes de l'Académie nationale des sciences, belles-lettres et arts de Bordeaux*. 5th ser., 8 (1984), 251–260.

Charlton, D. G., ed. *The French Romantics*. Cambridge: Cambridge University Press, 1984.

Chartier, Roger, ed. *A History of Private Life*. III: *Passions of the Renaissance*. Trans. Arthur Goldhammer. Cambridge, Mass.: Harvard University, Belknap Press, 1989.

Chartier, Roger, and Henri-Jean Martin, eds. *Histoire de l'édition française*. Paris: Promodis, 1984.

Christianson, Gale E. *In the Presence of the Creator: Isaac Newton and His Time*. New York: The Free Press; London: Collier Macmillan Publishers, 1984.

Churchill, Larry R. "Bioethical Reductionism and Our Sense of the Human." *Man and Medicine*, 5, no. 4 (1980), 229–249.

Claus, Jürgen. *Chipppkunst: Computer, Holographie, Kybernetik, Laser*. Frankfurt am Main: Ullstein, 1985.

Cohen, I. B. *The Newtonian Revolution. With Illustrations of the Transformation of Scientific Ideas*. Cambridge: Cambridge University Press, 1980.

Cohen, Ralph, ed. *Studies in Eighteenth-Century British Art and Aesthetics*. Berkeley and Los Angeles: University of California Press, 1985.

Cohn, Albert M. *George Cruikshank: A Catalogue Raisonné of the Works Executed during the Years 1806–1877. With Collations, Notes, Approximate Values, Facsimiles, and Illustrations*. London: From the Office of "The Bookman's Journal," 1924.

Colodny, Robert G. *Logic, Laws & Life: Some Philosophical Complications*. Pittsburgh, Pa.: University of Pittsburgh Press, 1977.

Conte, Gian Biagio. *The Rhetoric of Imitation: Genre and Poetic Memory in Virgil and Other Latin Poets*. Trans. Charles Segal. Ithaca: Cornell University Press, 1986.

Cook, Elizabeth J. "Thomas Hobbes and the 'Far-Fetched.'" *Journal of the Warburg and Courtauld Institutes*, 44 (1981), 222–232.

Cope, Jackson I. *Dramaturgy of the Daemonic: Studies in Antigeneric Theater from Ruzante to Grimaldi*. Baltimore: Johns Hopkins University Press, 1984.

Corbin, Alain. *Le Miasme et la jonquille. L'Odorat et l'imaginaire social, XVIIIe–XIXe siècles*. Paris: Editions Aubier Montaigne, 1982.

Cornell, Regine Reynolds. "Silence as a Rhetorical Device in Marguerite de Navarre's *Theatre profane*." *The Sixteenth Century Journal*, 17 (Spring 1986), 17–32.

Couchot, Edmond. "L'Odysée, mille fois ou les machines à langage." *Traverses*, 44–45 (September 1988), 86–95.

Cousseau, Henri-Claude. "Origins and Deviations: A Short History of *Art Brut*." *Art and Text*, 27 (December–February 1988), 16–29.

Cox, Donna J. "Using the Supercomputer to Visualize Higher Dimensions: An Artist's Contribution to Scientific Visualization." *Leonardo*, 20, no. 4 (1986), 234–238.

Crocker, Lester. "The Problem of Truth and Falsehood in the Enlightenment." *Journal of the History of Ideas*, 14 (October 1953), 573–603.

Crome, Peter. *Symbol und Unzulänglichkeit der Sprache, Jamblichos, Plotin, Porphyrios, Proklos*. Munich: Wilhelm Fink Verlag, 1970.

Crow, Thomas E. *Painters and Public Life in Eighteenth-Century Paris*. New Haven: Yale University Press, 1985.

Cuff, David J., and Mark T. Mattson. *Thematic Maps: Their Design and Production*. New York and London: Methuen, 1982.

Cuno, James, ed. *French Caricature and the French Revolution, 1789–1799*. Exh. cat. Grunwald Center for the Graphic Arts, Wright Art Gallery, UCLA. Los Angeles: University of California Press, 1988.

Curry, David Park. *James McNeill Whistler at the Freer Gallery of Art*. Exh. cat. Washington, D.C.: Freer Gallery of Art, Smithsonian Institution, 1984.

Daly, MacDonald. "Vivisection in Eighteenth-Century Britain." *British Journal for Eighteenth-Century Studies*, 12 (Spring 1989), 57–68.

Damisch, Hubert. "L'Art de Goya et les contradictions de l'esprit de Lumières." In *Utopie et institutions au XVIIIe siècle, le pragmatisme des Lumières*. Ed. Pierre Francastel. Paris and The Hague: Mouton, 1963.

Damisch, Hubert. *Fenêtre jaune cadmium. Ou les dessous de la peinture*. Paris: Editions du Seuil, 1984.

Damisch, Hubert. *Ruptures cultures*. Paris: Les Editions de Minuit, 1976.

Darius, Jon. *Beyond Vision*. Oxford and New York: Oxford University Press, 1984.

Darnton, Robert. *Mesmerism and the End of the Enlightenment in France*. Cambridge, Mass.: Harvard University Press, 1968.

Darnton, Robert, and Daniel Roche, eds. *Revolution in Print: The Press in France 1775–1800*. Exh. cat. New York: New York Public Library, 1989.

Dars, Celestine. *Images of Deception: The Art of Trompe-l'Oeil*. Oxford: Phaidon, 1979.

Daston, Lorraine. *Classical Probability in the Enlightenment*. Princeton, N.J.: Princeton University Press, 1988.

Dawson, Virginia P. *Nature's Enigma: The Problem of the Polyp in the Letters of Bonnet, Trembley and Réaumur*. Philadelphia: American Philosophical Society, 1987.

DeFanti, Thomas A. "Cultural Roadblocks to Visualization." *Computers in Science* (January–February 1988), 4–6.

Delcourt, Marie. *Hermaphrodite: Myths and Rites of the Bisexual Figure in Classical Antiquity*. Trans. Jennifer Nicholson. London: Studio Books, 1961.

Desan, Philippe. *Naissance de la méthode. (Machiavel, La Ramée, Bodin, Montaigne, Descartes)*. Paris: Librairie A.-G. Nizet, 1987.

Dierse, Ulrich. *Enzyklopädie. Zur Geschichte eines philosophischen und wissenschaftstheoretischen Begriffs*. Bonn: Bourvier Verlag Herbert Grundmann, 1977.

Dijksterhuis, E. J. *The Mechanization of the World Picture*. Trans. C. Dikshoorn. Oxford: Clarendon Press, 1961.

Dirckx, John H. "Dermatologic Terms in the *De Medicina* of Celsus." *American Journal of Dermapathology*, 5 (August 1983), 363–370.

Dobbs, Betty Jo Teeter. *The Foundations of Newton's Alchemy, or "The Hunting of the Greene Lyon."* Cambridge: Cambridge University Press, 1975.

Dölte, Ferdinand. "Die historische Entwicklung des Jagdrechtes in Österreich." *Jagd Einst und Jetzt.* Exh. cat. Schloss Marchegg: Niederösterreichische Landesausstellung, 1978.

Dotz, Warren. "Albrecht Dürer: Depictions of Facies as Expressions of Personality." *American Journal of Dermapathology*, 3 (Spring 1981), 59–66.

Dretske, Fred I. *Knowledge and the Flow of Information.* Cambridge, Mass.: MIT Press, 1981.

Dworkin, Roger B. "The New Genetics." In *Biolaw.* Ed. James F. Childress et al. New York: University Publications of America, 1986.

Dworkin, Roger B., and Gilbert S. Omenn. "Legal Aspects of Human Genetics." *Annual Review of Public Health*, 5 (1985), 107–130.

Eaves, Morris. *William Blake's Theory of Art.* Princeton, N.J.: Princeton University Press, 1982.

Eco, Umberto. "Un art d'oublier. Est-il concevable?" *Traverses*, 40 (April 1987), 125–135.

Egerton, Judy. *George Stubbs, 1724–1806.* Exh. cat. London: Salem House, 1985.

Ehrard, Jean. *L'Idée de la nature dans la première moitié du XVIIIe siècle.* Paris: Ecole Pratique des Hautes Etudes, 1963.

Eitner, Lorenz E. A. *Géricault: His Life and Work.* London: Orbis Publishing, 1983.

Elkins, James. "Linear Perspective in Renaissance Practice and in Modern Scholarship." Ph.D. dissertation, University of Chicago, 1988.

Elkins, James. "Two Conceptions of the Human Form: Bernard Siegfried Albinus and Andreas Vesalius." *Artibus et Historiae*, 14 (1986), 91–106.

Elsen, Albert E., ed. *Rodin Rediscovered.* Exh. cat. Washington, D.C.: National Gallery of Art, 1981.

Epstein, Julia L., and Mark L. Greenberg. "Decomposing Newton's Rainbow." *Journal of the History of Ideas*, 45 (March 1984), 115–140.

Erffa, Helmut von, and Allen Staley. *The Painting of Benjamin West.* New Haven: Yale University Press, 1986.

Ernst, Ulrich. "The Figured Poem: Towards a Definition of Genre." *Visible Language*, 20 (Winter 1986), 8–27.

Etlin, Richard A. *The Architecture of Death.* Cambridge, Mass.: MIT Press, 1984.

Farber, Paul Lawrence. "Buffon and Daubenton: Divergent Traditions within the *Histoire naturelle.*" *Isis*, 66 (March 1975), 63–74.

Feher, Michael, ed., with Ramona Naddaff and Nadia Tazi. *Fragments for a History of the Body.* 3 vols. Cambridge, Mass.: MIT Press Zone Books, 1989.

Fellman, Ferdinand. *Phänomenologie als ästhetische Theorie.* Munich and Freiburg: Verlag Alber, 1989.

Fellows, Otis. "George Berkeley, His Door, and the *Philosophes*." *Studies in Eighteenth-Century Literature Presented to Robert Niklaus*. Ed. J. H. Fox, M. H. Waddicor, and D. A. Watts. Exeter: University of Exeter, 1975.

Feyerabend, Paul. *Against Method*. London: New Left, 1975.

Finney, Gretchen. "'Organical Musick' and Ecstasy." *Journal of the History of Ideas*, 8 (June 1947), 273–292.

Flugel, J. C. *The Psychology of Clothes*. London: The Hogarth Press Ltd. and the Institute of Psycho-Analysis, 1950.

Flusser, Vilèm. "The Photograph as Post-Industrial Object: An Essay on the Ontological Standing of Objects." *Leonardo*, 19, no. 4 (1986), 329–332.

Foot, Mirjam. "The Olga Hirsch Collection of Decorated Paper." *British Library Journal*, 7 (Spring 1981), 12–38.

Forbes, Thomas R. "'To Be Dissected and Anatomized.'" *Journal of the History of Medicine and Applied Sciences*, 36 (October 1981), 490–492.

Fort, Bernadette. "Voice of the Public: The Carnivalization of Salon Art in Prerevolutionary France." *Eighteenth-Century Studies*, 20 (Spring 1989), 368–394.

Foster, Stephen C., ed. *Dada/Dimensions*. Ann Arbor: UMI Research Press, 1986.

Fox, Christopher. *Locke and the Scriblerians: Identity and Consciousness in Early Modern Britain*. Berkeley and Los Angeles: University of California Press, 1988.

Franklin, Allan. *The Neglect of Experiment*. Cambridge: Cambridge University Press, 1986.

Freedburg, David. "Johannes Molanus on Provocative Paintings. *De Historia Sanctarum Imaginum et Picturarum, Book II, Chapter 42*." *Journal of the Warburg and Courtauld Institutes*, 34 (1971), 229–245.

Fried, Michael. "Painting Memories—On the Containment of the Past in Baudelaire and Manet." *Critical Inquiry*, 10, no. 3 (1984), 510–542.

Friedman, John Block. *The Monstrous Races in Medieval Art and Thought*. Cambridge, Mass.: Harvard University Press, 1981.

Frischer, Bernard. *The Sculpted Word: Epicureanism and Philosophical Recruitment in Ancient Greece*. Berkeley and Los Angeles: University of California Press, 1982.

Fuchs, Eduard. *Geschichte der erotischen Kunst*. Munich: Albert Langen, 1908.

Fumaroli, Marc. *L'Age d'éloquence. Rhétorique et "res literaria" de la Renaissance au seuil de l'époque classique*. Geneva: Librairie Droz, 1980.

Gaborit, Jean-René. *Jean-Baptiste Pigalle (1714–1785). Sculptures au Musée du Louvre*. Paris: Editions de la Réunion des Musées Nationaux, 1985.

Gage, John. "Colour in History: Relative and Absolute." *Art History*, 1 (March 1978), 104–130.

Gallop, Jane. *Thinking through the Body*. New York: Columbia University Press, 1988.

Garnot, N. Sainte Fare. *La Révolution française et les hôpitaux parisiens*. Exh. cat. Paris: Musée de l'Assistance Publique, 1989.

Gatti, Hilary. "Minimum and Maximum, Finite and Infinite: Bruno and the Northumberland Circle." *Journal of the History of Ideas*, 48 (1985), 144–163.

Gelfand, Toby. *Professionalizing Modern Medicine: Paris Surgeons and Medical Science and Institutions in the Eighteenth Century*. Westport, Conn.: Greenwood Press, 1980.

Gersh, S. E. *KINESIS AKINHOS: A Study of Spiritual Motion in the Philosophy of Proclus*. Leiden: E. J. Brill, 1973.

Gibson, James L. *The Ecological Approach to Visual Perception*. Boston: Houghton Mifflin Company, 1979.

Gilman, Ernest B. *Iconoclasm and Poetry in the English Reformation*. Chicago: University of Chicago Press, 1986.

Gilman, Sander L. *Disease and Representation: Images of Illness from Madness to AIDS*. Ithaca: Cornell University Press, 1988.

Gilman, Sander L. *Seeing the Insane: A Cultural History of Madness and Art in the Western World*. New York: John Wiley & Sons and Brunner/Mazel Publishers, 1982.

Godwin, Joscelyn. *Athanasius Kircher: A Renaissance Man and the Quest for Lost Knowledge*. London: Thames and Hudson, 1979.

Goellnicht, Donald C. *The Poet-Physician: Keats and Medical Science*. Pittsburgh: University of Pittsburgh Press, 1984.

Gombrich, E. H. "*Icones Symbolicae*: Philosophies of Symbolism and Their Bearing on Art." In *Symbolical Images: Studies in the Art of the Renaissance*, vol. II. Chicago: University of Chicago Press, 1972.

Goodman, Nelson. *Problems and Projects*. Indianapolis: Bobbs-Merrill, 1972.

Gordon, Rae Beth. "Aboli bibelot? The Influence of the Decorative Arts on Stéphane Mallarmé and Gustave Moreau." *Art Journal*, 45 (Summer 1985), 105–112.

Gould, Stephen Jay. *The Mismeasure of Man*. New York: W.W. Norton & Co., 1981.

Goulven, Laurent. "La Cheminement d'Etienne Geoffroy Saint-Hilaire (1772–1844) vers un transformisme scientifique." *Revue d'histoire des sciences*, 30 (January 1977), 42–70.

Gowing, Lawrence, et al. *Francis Bacon Retrospective*. Exh. cat. Washington, D.C.: Hirshhorn Museum & Sculpture Garden, Smithsonian Institution, 1989.

Grabes, Herbert. *The Mutable Glass: Mirror-Imagery in Titles and Texts of the Middle Ages and the English Renaissance*. Trans. Gordon Collier. Cambridge: Cambridge University Press, 1982.

Grant, Edward. *Much Ado about Nothing: Theories of Space and Vacuum from the Middle Ages to the Scientific Revolution*. Cambridge: Cambridge University Press, 1981.

Grassi, Ernesto. *Die Macht der Phantasie. Zur Geschichte abendländische Denkens*. Königstein/TS: Athenäum, 1979.

Grassi, Ernesto. "Die Metapher. Die auflösende und schaffende Machte der Kunst." In *Argo. Festschrift für Kurt Badt*. Ed. Martin Gosebruch and Lorenz Dittmann. Cologne: Verlag M. DuMont Schauberg, 1970.

Graziani, René. "Fracastoro's 'Syphilis' and Priapus." *Clio Medica*, 16 (December 1981), 93–99.

Greene, Thomas M. *The Light in Troy: Imitation and Discovery in Renaissance Poetry*. New Haven: Yale University Press, 1982.

Grene, Marjorie, and Deborah Nails, eds. *Spinoza and the Sciences*. Dordrecht: D. Reidel Publishing Company, 1986.

Grimm, Reinhold R. *Paradisus Coelestis, Paradisus Terrestris*. Munich: Wilhelm Fink Verlag, 1977.

Guerrini, Anita. "Medical Practice and the Birth of the Consumer Society." *Clark Library Seminar*, 3 February 1989 (typescript).

Haemmerle, Albert, and Olga, Hirsch. *Buntpapier. Herkommen, Geschichte, Techniken, Beziehungen zur Kunst*. Munich: Verlag Georg D. W. Callwey, 1961.

Hahn, André, Paule Dumaitre, and Janine Samion-Contet. *Histoire de la médecine et du livre médicale*. Paris: Olivier Perrin Editeur, 1962.

Hall, Carol Louise. *Blake and Fuseli: A Study in the Transmission of Ideas*. New York: Garland, 1985.

Hamburger, Viktor. "Monsters in Nature." *Ciba Symposia*, 9 (August–September 1947), 666–683.

Hankins, Thomas L. *Science and the Enlightenment*. Cambridge: Cambridge University Press, 1985.

Harcourt, Glenn. "Andreas Vesalius and the Anatomy of Antique Sculpture." *Representations*, no. 17 (Winter 1987), 128–161.

Harpham, Geoffrey Galt. *On the Grotesque: Strategies of Contradiction in Art and Literature*. Princeton, N.J.: Princeton University Press, 1982.

Harries, Karsten. *The Bavarian Rococo Church: Between Faith and Aestheticism*. New Haven: Yale University Press, 1983.

Hartman, Lucrezia. *"Capriccio"—Bild und Begriff*. Nuremberg: Drucksnelldienst, 1972.

Haskell, Francis. *Patrons and Painters: A Study in the Relations between Italian Art and Society in the Age of the Baroque*. Rev. ed., New Haven: Yale University Press, 1983.

Hasse, Max. "Spott mit dem Spott treiben. Bildzitate in der Karikature des ausgehenden 18. Jahrhunderts." *Zeitschrift für Kunstgeschichte*, 47 (1984), 523–534.

Havelock, Eric A., and Jackson P. Hershkell, eds. *Communication Arts in the Ancient World*. New York: Hastings House Publishers, 1978.

Havens, Raymond D. "Simplicity, a Changing Concept." *Journal of the History of Ideas*, 14 (January 1953), 3–32.

Hayes, John, and Lindsay Stainton. *Gainsborough Drawings*. Exh. cat. Washington, D.C.: International Exhibitions Foundation, 1983.

Hayles, N. Katherine. *The Cosmic Web: Scientific Field Models and Literary Strategies in the Twentieth Century*. Ithaca: Cornell University Press, 1984.

Hayter, Aletha. *Opium and the Romantic Imagination*. Berkeley and Los Angeles: University of California Press, 1970.

Heiferman, Marvin, and Lisa Phillips, with John G. Hanhardt, eds. *Image-World*. Exh. cat. New York: Whitney Museum of Art, 1990.

Heim, Michael. *Electric Language: A Philosophical Study of Word Processing*. New Haven: Yale University Press, 1987.

Henry, Granville C., Jr. *Logos: Mathematics and Christian Theology*. Lewisburg: Bucknell University Press, 1976.

Herbert, Robert L. *Impressionism: Leisure and Parisian Society*. New Haven: Yale University Press, 1988.

Hill, Draper, ed. *The Satirical Etchings of James Gillray*. New York: Dover Publications, Inc., 1976.

Hilton, Nelson. *Literal Imagination: Blake's Vision of Words*. Berkeley and Los Angeles: University of California Press, 1983.

Hirdt, Willi. "Zu *Milieu* und Sprache im franzöischen Roman des 19. Jahrhunderts." *Archiv*, 215, no. 2 (1978), 337–346.

Hobson, Marian. *The Object of Art: The Theory of Illusion in Eighteenth-Century France*. Cambridge: Cambridge University Press, 1982.

Hocke, Gustav René. *Die Welt als Labyrinth. Manier und Manie in der europäischen Kunst von 1520 bis 1650 und in der Gegenwart*. Rev. ed., Hamburg: Rowohlt, 1987.

Hodges, Devon L. *Renaissance Fictions*. Amherst: University of Massachusetts Press, 1985.

Hofmann, Werner, ed. *Luther und die Folgen für die Kunst*. Exh. cat. Hamburg: Hamburger Kunsthalle, 1983.

Honour, Hugh. *The Image of the Black in Western Art*. IV. *From the American Revolution to World War I*. 2. *Black Models and White Myths*. Cambridge, Mass.: Harvard University Press, 1989.

Hornung, Erik. *Conceptions of God in Ancient Egypt: The One and the Many*. Ithaca: Cornell University Press, 1982.

Howard, Seymour. *Bartolomeo Cavaceppi, Eighteenth-Century Restorer*. New York: Garland Publishers, Inc., 1982.

Hyde, Ralph. *Panoramania! The Art and Entertainment of the "All-Embracing" View*. Exh. cat. London: Barbican Art Gallery, 1988.

Images animées. Lumière et magie. Les Fantasmagories de Robertson. Exh. cat. Paris: Musée National des Techniques, 1990.

Image Understanding Workshop. Proceedings of a Workshop held at Cambridge, Mass. April 6–8, 1988. 2 vols. San Mateo, Calif.: Morgan Kaufmann Publishers, 1988.

Imbault-Huart, Marie-José. "Les Chirurgiens et l'esprit chirurgical en France au XVIIIe siècle." *Clio Medica*, 15 (April 1981), 143–157.

Impey, Oliver, and Arthur MacGregor, eds. *The Origins of Museums: The Cabinet of Curiosities in Sixteenth- and Seventeenth-Century Europe*. Oxford: Clarendon Press, 1985.

Isaac, Rhys. *The Transformation of Virginia, 1740–1790*. Chapel Hill: University of North Carolina Press, 1982.

Ittman, John W., et al., eds. *Regency to Empire: French Print-Making 1715–1814*. Exh. cat. Minneapolis: The Minneapolis Institute of Arts, 1985.

Jacob, Margaret Camden. "John Toland and the Newtonian Ideology." *Journal of the Warburg and Courtauld Institutes*, 32 (1969), 307–331.

James Gillray. (1756–1815). Drawings and Caricatures. London: Arts Council of Great Britain, 1967.

Jamieson, Kathleen Hall. *Eloquence in an Electronic Age: The Transformation of Public Speechmaking*. Oxford: Oxford University Press, 1988.

Jay, Ricky. *Learned Pigs and Fire Proof Women*. New York: Villard Books, 1986.

Johnson, Dorothy. "Corporeality and Communication: The Gestural Revolution of Diderot, David, and *The Oath of the Horatii*." *Art Bulletin*, 71 (March 1989), 92–113.

Johnson, Mark. *The Body in the Mind: The Bodily Basis of Meaning, Imagination and Reason*. Chicago: University of Chicago Press, 1987.

Jonsen, Albert R., and Stephen Toulmin, *The Abuse of Casuistry: A History of Moral Reasoning*. Berkeley and Los Angeles: University of California Press, 1988.

Jordanova, L. J. *Lamarck*. Oxford and New York: Oxford University Press, 1984.

Jordanova, L. J., ed. *Languages of Nature: Critical Essays on Science and Literature*. New Brunswick, N.J.: Rutgers University Press, 1986.

Kaenel, Philippe. "Le Buffon de l'humanité. La zoologie politique de J. I. Grandville [1803–1807]." *Revue de l'art* 76 (1986), 21–28.

Kaiser, Thomas E. "Rhetoric in the Service of the King: The Abbé Dubos and the Concept of Public Judgment." *Eighteenth-Century Studies*, 23 (Winter 1989–1990), 182–199.

Kemp, Martin. *The Science of Art*. New Haven: Yale University Press, 1990.

Kemp, Martin. "Simon Stevin and Pieter Saenredam: A Study of Mathematics and Vision in Dutch Science and Art." *Art Bulletin*, 68 (June 1986), 237–252.

Kenshur, Oscar. *Open Form and the Shape of Ideas: Literary Structures as Representations of Philosophical Concepts in the Seventeenth and Eighteenth Centuries*. Lewisburg: Bucknell University Press, 1986.

Kerckhove, Daniel de. "Le Virtuel imaginaire technologique." *Traverses*, 44–45 (September 1988), 75–85.

Keuls, Eva. *Plato and Greek Painting*. Leiden: E. J. Brill, 1978.

King, Constance. *The Encyclopedia of Toys*. New York: Crown Publishers, Inc., 1978.

Knoefel, Peter K. "Florentine Anatomical Models in Wax and Wood." *Medicine nei Secoli*, 15 (1978), 329–340.

Kristeva, Julia. *Histoires d'amour*. Paris: Denöel, 1983.

Kroeber, Karl. *British Romantic Art.* Berkeley and Los Angeles: University of California Press, 1986.

Kruskal, William H. "Criteria for Judging Statistical Graphics." *Utilitas Mathematica*, 21 B (May 1982), 283–309.

Kruskal, William H. "Miracles and Statistics: The Casual Assumption of Independence." *Journal of the American Statistical Association*, 83 (December 1988), 929–940.

Kruskal, William H. "The *n* Cultures." *Proceedings of the Fourth Annual Research Conference, Bureau of the Census.* Washington, D.C.: U.S. Department of Commerce, 1988.

Kruskal, William H., and William Mosteller. "Representative Sampling, I: Non-Scientific Literature." *International Statistical Review*, 47 (1979), 13–24.

Kunzle, David. "Goethe and Caricature: From Hogarth to Töpffer." *Journal of the Warburg and Courtauld Institutes*, 48 (1985), 164–188.

Lanckorońska, Maria, and Richard Oehler. *Die Buchillustration des XVIII Jahrhunderts in Deutschland, Österreich und der Schweiz. Erster Teil: Die deutsche Buchillustration des Spätbarock und Rokoko.* Leipzig: Im Insel-Verlag, 1932.

Laqueur, Thomas. "Orgasm, Generation, and the Politics of Reproductive Biology." *Representations*, no. 14 (Spring 1986), 1–41.

Lascault, Gilbert. *Le Monstre dans l'art occidental. Un problème esthétique.* Paris: Klincksieck, 1973.

Le Fanu, W. R. *A Bio-Bibliography of Edward Jenner (1749–1823).* London: Harvey and Blythe, Ltd, 1951.

Le Goff, Jacques. *La Naissance du purgatoire.* Paris: Editions Gallimard, 1981.

Lemagny, Jean-Claude, and André Rouillé, eds. *A History of Photography: Social and Cultural Perspectives.* Cambridge: Cambridge University Press, 1986.

Lemire, Michel. *Les Modèles anatomiques en cire colorée du XVIIIe siècle et du XIXe siècle.* Paris: Musée National d'Histoire Naturelle, Laboratoire d'Anatomie Comparée, 1987.

Lesch, John E. *Science and Medicine in France: The Emergence of Experimental Physiology, 1799–1855.* Cambridge, Mass.: Harvard University Press, 1984.

Levere, Trevor H. *Poetry Realized in Nature: Samuel Taylor Coleridge and Early Nineteenth-Century Science.* Cambridge: Cambridge University Press, 1981.

Levine, Joseph M. *Humanism and History: Origins of Modern English Historiography.* Ithaca: Cornell University Press, 1987.

Liddell, Henry George, and Robert Scott. *A Greek-English Lexicon with a Supplement.* Oxford: Clarendon Press, 1968.

Lindberg, David C. *Theories of Vision from Al-Kindi to Kepler.* Chicago: University of Chicago Press, 1976.

Lindberg, David C., and Ronald Numbers, eds. *God and Nature: Historical Essays on the Encounter between Christianity and Science.* Berkeley and Los Angeles: University of California Press, 1986.

Lister, Raymond. *Infernal Methods: A Study of William Blake's Art Techniques.* London: G. Bell & Sons, Ltd., 1975.

Locher, Gottfried W. *Zwingli's Thought: New Perspectives.* Leiden: E. J. Brill, 1981.

Lohft, Brigitte. "Zur Geschichte der Lehre von der Lebenskraft." *Clio Medica*, 16 (December 1981), 101–112.

L'Orange, H. P. *Studies on the Iconography of Cosmic Kingship.* Oslo: H. Aschehoug & Co., 1953.

Lossky, Vladimir. *The Mythical Theology of the Eastern Church.* Crestwood, N.Y.: St. Vladimir's Seminary Press, 1976.

McClintock, John, and James Strong. *Cyclopedia of Biblical Literature.* New York: Arno Press, 1969.

McConnell, Christopher C., and Daryl T. Lawton. "IU Software Environments." In *Image Understanding Workshop. Proceedings of a Workshop Held at Cambridge, Massachusetts April 6–8, 1988.* San Mateo, Calif.: Morgan Kaufmann Publishers, 1988.

Maccubbin, Robert Purk, ed. *'Tis Nature's Fault: Unauthorized Sexuality during the Enlightenment.* Cambridge: Cambridge University Press, 1987.

MacDonald, Michael. *Mystical Bedlam: Madness, Anxiety, and Healing in Seventeenth-Century England.* Cambridge: Cambridge University Press, 1981.

MacDonald, William L. *Piranesi's 'Carceri': Sources of Invention.* Northampton: Smith College, 1979.

McFarland, Thomas. *Originality & Imagination.* Baltimore: Johns Hopkins University Press, 1985.

McGuire, J. E. "Force, Active Principles, and Newton's Invisible Realm." *Ambix*, 15 (1968), 154–208.

Machamer, Peter K., and Robert G. Turnbull, eds. *Studies in Perception: Interrelations in the History of Philosophy and Science.* Columbus: Ohio State University Press, 1978.

Macpherson, Jay. *The Spirit of Solitude: Conventions and Continuities in Late Romance.* New Haven: Yale University Press, 1982.

Maiorino, Giancarlo. "The Legend of Geometry Fulfilled: Abstraction and the Denaturalization of Matter in the Paintings of Piero della Francesca and Piet Mondrian." *Gazette des Beaux-Arts*, 107 (March 1986), 111–117.

Marcus, Aaron. "Diagrammatic Visible Language: An Investigation of Visual Logic." *Leonardo*, 20, no. 1 (1987), 9–15.

Margolis, Howard. *Patterns, Thinking, and Cognition: A Theory of Judgment.* Chicago: University of Chicago Press, 1987.

Marin, Louis. *Etudes sémiologiques. Ecritures, peintures.* Paris: Klinksieck, 1971.

Marin, Louis. *La Parole mangée et autres essais théologico-politiques.* Paris: Méridiens Klinksieck, 1986.

Marin, Louis. "Ponctuation." *Traverses*, 43 (February 1988), 103–105.

Marin, Louis. *Le Portrait du roi*. Paris: Les Editions de Minuit, 1981.

Martinelli, Rosanna Cioffi. *La Ragione dell'arte. Teoria e critica nel Anton Raphael Mengs e Johann Joachim Winckelmann*. Naples: Liguori Editore, 1981.

Mates, Benson. *The Philosophy of Leibniz: Metaphysics and Language*. New York and Oxford: Oxford University Press, 1986.

Maulitz, Russell C. *Morbid Appearances: The Anatomy of Pathology in the Early Nineteenth Century*. Cambridge: Cambridge University Press, 1987.

Maulpoix, Jean-Michel. "Eloge de la ponctuation." *Traverses*, 43 (February 1988), 19–28.

Mauzi, R., and S. Menant. *Littérature française. Le XVIIIe siècle, 1750–1778*. Paris: Arthaud, 1977.

Medieval Medical Miniatures. Austin: University of Texas Press, 1984.

Meier, Harri, and Hans Sikommodau, eds. *Wort und Text. Festschrift für Fritz Schalk*. Frankfurt am Main: Vittorio Klostermann, 1963.

Merlan, Philip. "Abstraction and Metaphysics in Saint Thomas' *Summa*." *Journal of the History of Ideas*, 14 (April 1983), 284–291.

Merton, Robert K., David L. Sills, and Stephen M. Stigler. "The Kelvin Dictum and Social Science: An Excursion into the History of an Idea." *Journal of the History of the Behavioral Sciences*, 20 (October 1984), 319–331.

Merz, Richard. *Die numinose Mischgestalt. Methodenkritische Untersuchungen zu tiermenschlichen Erscheinungen Altägyptens, der Eiszeit, und der Aranda in Australien, religionsgeschichtliche Vorsuche und Vorarbeiten*. XXXVI. Ed. Walter Burkert and Carsten Colpe. Berlin: Walter de Gruyter, 1978.

Metford, J. C. J. *Dictionary of Christian Lore and Legend*. London: Thames and Hudson, 1983.

Michel, Marianne Roland. *Lajoüe et l'art rocaille*. Paris: ARTHENA, 1984.

Michel, Régis. *Le Beau idéale*. Exh. cat. Paris: Editions de la Réunion des musées nationaux, 1989.

Middleton, Robin. "G.-B. Piranesi (1720–1778). Review of Recent Literature." *Journal of the Society of Architectural Historians*, 40 (1982), 333–344.

Miedema, Hessel. "On Mannerism and *Maniera*." *Simiolus*, 10 (1978–1979), 19–45.

Mileur, Jean-Pierre. *Vision and Revision: Coleridge's Art of Immanence*. Berkeley and Los Angeles: University of California Press, 1982.

Milic, Louis T. "Singularity and Style in Eighteenth-Century English Prose." *Poetica*, 14 (1982), 91–112.

Miller, Mark Crispin. *Boxed-In: The Culture of TV*. Evanston, Ill.: Northwestern University Press, 1988.

Miller, Priscella E. *Goya's "Black" Paintings: Truth and Reason—Light and Liberty*. New York: The Hispanic Society of America, 1984.

Mitchell, A. Graeme. *Medical Caricature, Proceedings of the California Academy of Medicine*. Reprinting, 1939–1940.

Mode, Heinz. *Fabulous Beasts and Demons.* London: Phaidon, 1975.

Moffitt, John F. "Painters 'Born under Saturn': The Physiological Explanation." *Art History,* 11 (June 1988), 195–216.

Momigliano, Arnaldo. "The Disadvantages of Monotheism for a Universal State." *Classical Philology,* 18 (October 1986), 285–297.

Momigliano, Arnaldo. "History between Medicine and Rhetoric." Unpublished paper, 1985.

Monmonier, Mark, and George A. Schnell. *Map Appreciation.* Englewood Cliffs, N.J.: Prentice Hall, 1988.

Mooney, Michael. *Vico in the Tradition of Rhetoric.* Princeton: Princeton University Press, 1985.

Moravec, Hans. *Mind Children: The Future of Robot and Human Intelligence.* Cambridge, Mass.: Harvard University Press, 1989.

Moravia, Sergio. "The Capture of the Invisible: For a (Pre)History of Psychology in Eighteenth-Century France." *Journal of the History of Behavioral Sciences,* 19 (October 1983), 370–378.

Moravia, Sergio. "From *Homme Machine* to *Homme Sensible:* Changing Eighteenth-Century Models of Man's Image." *Journal of the History of Ideas,* 39 (1978), 45–60.

Morel, Philippe. "Priape à la Renaissance. Les guirlandes de Giovanni da Udine à la Farnésine." *Revue de l'art,* 69 (1985), 13–28.

Morgan, Michael. *Molyneux's Question, Vision, Touch, and the Philosophy of Perception.* Cambridge: Cambridge University Press, 1977.

Morrison, Philip and Phylis. *Powers of Ten: A Book about the Relative Size of Things in the Universe and the Effect of Adding Another Zero.* New York: Scientific American Library, 1982.

Mortier, Roland. *Clartés et ombres du siècle des lumières. Etudes sur le XVIIIe siècle littéraire.* Geneva: Librairie Droz, 1969.

Mortier, Roland. "Un dieu-araignée?" In *Enlightenment Essays in Memory of Robert Shackleton.* Ed. Gilles Barber and C. P. Courtney. Oxford: Voltaire Foundation, 1988.

Moutsopoulos, Evanghélos. *Les Structures de l'imaginaire dans la philosophie de Proclus.* Paris: Société d'Edition "Les Belles Lettres," 1985.

Mulas, Antonia. *Eros in Antiquity.* Milan: Arnoldo Mondadori Editore, 1978.

Munhall, Edgar. *Jean-Baptiste Greuze, 1705–1805.* Exh. cat. Hartford, Conn.: The Wadsworth Atheneum, 1976.

Munz, Ludwig. *A Critical Catalogue of Rembrandt's Etchings and the Etchings of His School Formerly Attributed to the Master with an Essay on Rembrandt's Technique and Documentary Sources.* 2 vols. London: Phaidon Press, 1952.

Murphy-O'Connor, J. "'Being at Home in the Body We Are in Exile from the Lord' (II Cor. 5:6b)." *Revue Biblique,* 93 (April 1986), 214–222.

Murr, Lawrence E., and James B. Williams. "Half-brained Ideas about Education: Thinking and Learning with Both the Left Brain and the Right Brain in a Visual Culture." *Leonardo,* 21, no. 4 (1988), 413–419.

Mus, Paul. "The Iconography of an Aniconic Art." *Res*, 14 (Autumn 1987), 5–26.

Myerowitz, Molly. *Ovid's Game of Love*. Detroit: Wayne State University Press, 1985.

Neubauer, John. *The Emancipation of Music from Language: Departure from Mimesis in Eighteenth-Century Aesthetics*. New Haven: Yale University Press, 1986.

Neubauer, John. *Symbolismus und symbolische Logik. Die Idee der Ars Combinatoria in der Entwicklung der modernen Dichtung*. Munich: Wilhelm Fink Verlag, 1978.

Nicolson, Marjorie Hope. *The Breaking of the Circle: Studies in the Effect of the "New Science" upon Seventeenth-Century Poetry*. New York: Columbia University Press, 1960.

Norton, Bryan G. *Why Preserve Natural Variety?* Princeton, N.J.: Princeton University Press, 1987.

Nussbaum, Martha C. *The Fragility of Goodness: Luck and Ethics in Greek Tragedy and Philosophy*. Cambridge: Cambridge University Press, 1986.

Ober, William B. "Can the Leper Change His Spots? The Iconography of Leprosy, Part I." *The American Journal of Dermapathology*, 5 (February 1983), 43–58.

Olszewski, Edward J. "Distortions, Shadows, and Conventions in Sixteenth-Century Italian Art." *Artibus et Historiae*, 6 (1985), 102–124.

Onians, John. "Abstraction and Imagination in Late Antiquity." *Art History*, 3 (March 1980), 1–24.

Opperman, Hal. *J. B. Oudry, 1686–1755*. Exh. cat. Fort Worth: Kimbell Art Museum, 1983.

Ouspensky, Leonid, and Vladimir Lossky. *The Meaning of Icons*. Boston: Boston Book and Art Shop, 1952.

Panofsky, Erwin. *Galileo as a Critic of the Arts*. The Hague: Martinus Nijhoff, 1954.

Park, Katherine. "Bacon's 'Enchanted Glass.'" *Isis*, 75 (June 1984), 290–301.

Park, Katherine, and Lorraine J. Daston. "Unnatural Conceptions: The Study of Monsters in Sixteenth- and Seventeenth-Century France and England." *Past and Present*, 92 (August 1981), 20–54.

Patey, Douglas Lane. *Probability and Literary Form: Philosophical Theory and Literary Practice in the Augustan Age*. Cambridge: Cambridge University Press, 1984.

Paulson, William R. *Enlightenment, Romanticism, and the Blind in France*. Princeton, N.J.: Princeton University Press, 1987.

Pauly, Philip J. *Controlling Life: Jacques Loeb and the Engineering Ideal in Biology*. New York and Oxford: Oxford University Press, 1987.

Penny, Nicholas, ed. *Reynolds*. Exh. cat. London: Royal Academy of Arts, 1986.

Pernoud, Emmanuel. "Baudelaire, Guys et le kaléidoscope." *Gazette des Beaux-Arts*, 104 (September 1984), 73–77.

Persum-Meijer, J. Schullertot, and W. R. H. Koops. *Petrus Camper (1722–1789). Onderzoeker van nature*. Exh. cat. Groningen: Universiteits Museum, 1979.

Pfeiffer, Ludwig. "Fiction: On the Fate of a Concept between Philosophy and Literary Theory." In *Aesthetic Illusion* Ed. Frederick Burwick and Walter Pape. Berlin: De Gruyter Verlag, 1990.

Pietz, William. "The Problem of the Fetish. II: The Origin of the Fetish." *Res*, 13 (Spring 1987), 23–46.

Pigeaud, Jackie. *La Maladie de l'âme. Etude sur la relation de l'âme et du corps dans la tradition médico-philosophique antique*. Paris: Société d'Edition "Les Belles Lettres," 1981.

Piranesi e la cultura antiquaria. Gli antecedenti e il contesto. Atti di Convegno 14–17 novembre 1979. Rome: Multigrafica Editrice, 1983.

"Plastic Surgery." *Art News* (February 1989), 15–16.

Plochmann, George K. "Nature and the Living Thing in Aristotle's Biology." *Journal of the History of Ideas*, 14 (April 1953), 167–190.

Pommier, Edouard. "Le Concepte de la grâce chez Winckelmann." In *Winckelmann*, ed. Edouard Pommier. Paris: Editions de la Réunion des musées nationaux, forthcoming.

Popkin, Richard, ed. *Millenarianism and Messianism in English Literature and Thought, 1650–1800*. Leiden: Brill, 1988.

Porter, Roy. "Making Faces: Physiognomy and Fashion in Eighteenth-Century England." *Etudes Anglaises Grande-Bretagne; Etats-Unis*, 38 (October–December 1985), 385–396.

Porter, Roy, and John Brewer, eds. *Culture and Consumption: The World of Goods*. London: Routledge, 1990.

Potts, Alexander. "Winckelmann's Interpretation of Ancient Art in Its Eighteenth-Century Context." Ph.D. dissertation, Warburg Institute, n.d.

Powell, Nicolas. *Fuseli: The Nightmare, Art in Context*. ed. John Fleming and Hugh Honour. London: Penguin Press, 1973.

Proust, Jacques. "Diderot et la physiognomie." *Cahiers de l'Association des études françaises*, 13 (June 1961), 317–329.

Pruzinsky, Thomas. "Collaboration of Plastic Surgeon and Medical Psychotherapist: Elective Cosmetic Surgery." *Medical Psychotherapy*, 1 (1988), 1–13.

Puech, Henri-Charles. *Sur le manichéisme et autres essais*. Paris: Flammarion, 1979.

Punt, Hendrick. *Bernard Siegfried Albinus (1697–1770) On "Human Nature": Anatomical and Physiological Ideas in Eighteenth-Century Leiden*. Amsterdam: B. M. Israel B.V., 1983.

Putscher, Marielene. *Pneuma, Spiritus, Geist. Vorstellungen vom Lebensantrieb in ihren geschichtlichen Wandlungen*. Wiesbaden: Franz Steiner Verlag, 1973.

Puttfarken, Thomas. *Roger de Piles' Theory of Art*. New Haven: Yale University Press, 1985.

Redondi, Pietro. *Galileo Heresies*. Trans. Raymond Rosenthal. Princeton, N.J.: Princeton University Press, 1987.

Rees, Thomas. *Theatre Lighting in the Age of Gas*. London: Society for Theater Research, 1978.

Reilly, P. Conor. *Athanasius Kircher, Master of a Hundred Arts, 1602–1680*. Wiesbaden and Rome: Edizioni del Mondo, 1974.

Reynolds, Graham. "The Elegance of George Stubbs." *Apollo* (January 1985), 22–23.

Ribeiro, Aileen. *The Dress Worn at Masquerade in England, 1730–1790, and Its Relation to Fancy Dress in Portraiture*. New York: Garland, 1984.

Ribeiro, Aileen. *A Visual History of Costume: The Eighteenth Century*. New York and London: B.T. Batsford, Ltd., 1983.

Rickey, Stephanie S. "'Judicious Negligence': Rembrandt Transforms an Emblematic Convention." *Art Bulletin*, 68 (June 1986), 253–262.

Ricoeur, Paul. *The Conflict of Interpretations: Essays in Hermeneutics*. Evanston: Northwestern University Press, 1974.

Ricoeur, Paul. *Essays on Biblical Interpretation*. Ed. Lewis S. Mudge. Philadelphia, Pa.: Fortress Press, 1980.

Ricoeur, Paul. *The Symbolism of Evil*. New York: Harper & Row Publishers, 1967.

Ritterbush, Philip C. *Overtures to Biology*. New Haven: Yale University Press, 1964.

Robinson, David. "Augsburg Peepshows." *Print Quarterly*, 5 (June 1988), 188–190.

Robison, Andrew. *Piranesi: Early Architectural Fantasies. A Catalogue Raisonné of the Etchings*. Chicago: University of Chicago Press, 1985.

Roe, Shirley A. "John Turberville Needham and the Generation of Living Organisms." *Isis*, 74 (1983), 159–184.

Roe, Shirley A. *Matter, Life and Generation: 18th Century Embryology and the Haller-Wolff Debate*. Cambridge: Cambridge University Press, 1981.

Roe, Shirley A. "Voltaire versus Needham: Atheism, Materialism, and the Generation of Life." *Journal of the History of Ideas*, 46 (January–March 1985), 65–87.

Roger, Jacques. *Les Sciences de la vie dans la pensée française du XVIIIe siècle: la génération des animaux de Descartes à l'Encyclopédie*. Paris: Armand Colin, 1963.

Rousseau, G. S. "Nerves, Spirits, and Fibres: Towards defining the Origins of Sensibility." In *Studies in the Eighteenth Century*. Ed. R. F. Brissenden and J. C. Earde. Toronto: University of Toronto Press, 1976.

Rudowski, Victor Anthony. "Lessing *contra* Winckelmann." *Journal of Aesthetics and Art Criticism*, 44 (Spring 1986), 235–243.

Rump, Gerhard Charles. *George Romney (1734–1802): zur Bildform der bürgerlichen Mitte in der englischen Neoklassik*. Hildesheim: Georg Olms Verlag, 1974.

Russell, Jeffrey Burton. *Satan: The Early Christian Tradition*. Ithaca: Cornell University Press, 1981.

Russell, Nicholas. *Like Engend'ring Like: Heredity and Animal Breeding in Eary Modern England*. Cambridge: Cambridge University Press, 1986.

Sabra, A. I. *Theories of Light from Descartes to Newton.* Cambridge: Cambridge University Press, 1981.

Sacks, Oliver. *A Leg to Stand On.* New York: Summit Books, 1984.

Sacks, Oliver. *The Man Who Mistook His Wife for a Hat and Other Clinical Tales.* New York: Summit Books, 1985.

Sadrin, Paul. *Nicolas-Antoine Boulanger (1722–1759), ou avant nous le déluge.* Oxford: The Voltaire Foundation, 1986.

Saint-Amand, Pierre. *Séduire, ou la passion des Lumières.* Paris: Méridiens Klincksiek. 1987.

Saisselin, Rémy G. *The Bourgeois and the Bibelot.* New Brunswick, N.J.: Rutgers University Press, 1984.

Sayre, Eleanor A. *The Changing Image: Prints by Francisco Goya.* Exh. cat. Boston: Museum of Fine Arts, 1974.

Sayre, Eleanor A. *Goya and the Spirit of Enlightenment.* Exh. cat. Boston: Museum of Fine Arts, 1989.

Schama, Simon. *The Embarrassment of Riches: An Interpretation of Dutch Culture in the Golden Age.* New York: Alfred A. Knopf, 1987.

Scheurleer, Th. H., and G. H. M. Posthumus Meyjes, èds. *Leiden University in the Seventeenth Century: An Exchange of Learning.* Leiden: E. J. Brill, 1975.

Schiebinger, Londa. "Skeletons in the Closet: The First Illustrations of the Female Skeleton in Eighteenth-Century Anatomy." *Representations,* no. 14 (Spring 1986), 42–82.

Schlaf der Vernunft gebiert Ungeheuer. Francisco de Goya 1746–1828. Die "Caprichos." Exh. cat. Karlsruhe: Kunsthalle, 1976–1977.

Schnapper, Antoine. *Le Géant, la licorne, et la tulipe. Collections et collectionneurs dans la France du XVIIe siècle. I: Histoire et histoire naturelle.* Paris: Flammarion, 1988.

Schneider, Gerhard. *Der Libertin. Zur Geistes- und Sozialgeschichte des Bürgertums im 16. und 17. Jahrhundert.* Stuttgart: J. B. Metzler, 1970.

Schneider, Pierre. *Matisse.* New York: Rizzoli, 1984.

Schouls, Peter A. *The Imposition of Method: A Study of Descartes and Locke.* Oxford: Clarendon Press, 1980.

Schupbach, William. *The Paradox of Rembrandt's 'Anatomy of Dr. Tulp'. Medical History,* supplement no. 2. London: Wellcome Institute for the History of Medicine, 1982.

Schwarz, Gary. "Connoisseurship: The Penalty of Ahistoricism." *Artibus et Historiae,* 18 (1988), 201–206.

Schweitzer, Bernhard. "Der bildende Künstler und der Begriff des Künstlerischen in der Antike." *Neue Heidelberger Jahr-Bücher,* n.s. (1925), 28–132.

Schweitzer, Bernhard. "Mimesis und Phantasia." *Philologus,* n.s. 89, no. 3 (1934), 286–300.

Sheppard, Anne D. R. *Studies on the 5th and 6th Essays of Proclus' Commentary on the Republic.* Göttingen: Vandenhoeck and Ruprecht, 1980.

Sheppard, H. J. "The Redemption Theme and Hellenistic Alchemy." *Ambix,* 7 (February 1959), 42–62.

Shesgreen, Sean. *Hogarth and the Times-of-the-Day Tradition.* Ithaca: Cornell University Press, 1983.

Shorr, Joseph E., Gail E. Sobel, Pennee Robin, and Jack A. Connella, eds. *Imagery: Its Many Dimensions and Applications.* New York: Plenum Press, 1980.

Shurkin, Joel N. *The Invisible Fire: The Story of Mankind's Victory over the Ancient Scourge of Small Pox.* New York: G. P. Putnam's Sons, 1979.

Les Siècles d'or de la médecine. Padoue XV–XVIII. Exh. cat. Milan: Electa, 1989.

Singer, Charles. *The Evolution of Anatomy: A Short History of Anatomical and Physiological Discovery to Harvey.* New York: Alfred A. Knopf, 1925.

Singer, Milton. "Emblems of Identity: A Semiotic Exploration." In *Symbols in Anthropology.* Ed. J. Maquet. Malibu, Cal.: Undena Publications, 1982.

Slaughter, M. M. *Universal Languages and Scientific Taxonomy in the Seventeenth Century.* Cambridge: Cambridge University Press, 1982.

Sloan, Kim. *Alexander and John Robert Cozens: The Poetry of Landscape.* New Haven: Yale University Press, 1986.

Sloan, Kim. "A New Chronology for Alexander Cozens. Part I: 1717–1759." *Burlington,* 127 (February 1985), 70–75.

Smeed, J. W. *The Theophrastan "Character": The History of a Literary Genre.* Oxford: Clarendon Press, 1985.

Smith, Jeffrey Chipps, ed. *New Perspectives on the Art of Renaissance Nuremberg: Five Essays.* Austin: The Archer M. Huntington Art Library of the University of Texas, 1985.

Smith, Joshua. *The Photography of Invention.* Exh. cat. Washington, D.C.: National Museum of American Art, 1989.

Smith, Paul. "Paul Adam, *Soi* et les 'peintres impressionistes': la génèse d'un discours moderniste." *Revue de l'Art,* 82 (1988), 39–50.

Solente, Georges. "Le Musée de l'Hôpital Saint-Louis." *American Journal of Dermatology,* 5 (October 1983), 453–489.

Somer, Manfred. *Husserl und der frühe Positivismus.* Frankfurt am Main: Vittorio Klostermann, 1985.

Sorel, Philippe, et al. *Palais-Royal.* Exh. cat. Paris: Musée du Carnavalet, 1988.

Sosa, Ernest, ed. *Essays on the Philosophy of George Berkeley.* Dordrecht: D. Reidel Publishing Company, 1987.

Soufflot et l'architecture des Lumières. Les Cahiers de la recherche architecturale. Supplément (October 1980).

Soupel, Serge, and Roger A. Hambridge, eds. *Literature and Science and Medicine.* Los Angeles: University of California Press, 1982.

Lo Specchio e il doppio. Della stagno di Narciso allo schermo televisio. Exh. cat. Turin: Mole Antonelliana, 1987.

Springer, Carolyn. *The Marble Wilderness: Ruins and Representation in Italian Romanticism, 1775–1850.* Cambridge: Cambridge University Press, 1987.

Stafford, Barbara Maria. "Arena of Virtue and Temple of Immortality: An Early Nineteenth-Century Museum Project." *Journal of the Society of Architectural Historians*, 35 (March 1976), 21–34.

Stafford, Barbara Maria. "Beauty of the Invisible: Winckelmann and the Aesthetics of Imperceptibility." *Zeitschrift für Kunstgeschichte*, 43 (1980), 65–78.

Stafford, Barbara Maria. "The Eighteenth Century: Towards an Interdisciplinary Model." *Art Bulletin*, 70 (March 1988), 7–24.

Stafford, Barbara Maria. "Endymion's Moonbath: Art and Science in Girodet's Early Masterpiece." *Leonardo*, 15, no. 3 (1982), 193–198.

Stafford, Barbara Maria. "'Fantastic Images': From Unenlightening to Enlightening 'Appearances' Meant to Be Seen in the Dark." In *Aesthetic Illusion*. Ed. Frederick Burwick and Walter Pape. Berlin: De Gruyter Verlag, 1990.

Stafford, Barbara Maria. "From 'Brilliant Ideas' to 'Fitful Thoughts': Conjecturing the Unseen in Late-Eighteenth-Century Art." *Zeitschrift für Kunstgeschichte*, 48, no. 1 (1985), 329–363.

Stafford, Barbara Maria. "'Magnifications': The Eighteenth-Century Fortunes of a Primitive and Universal 'Imagistic.'" *Prospettiva*, 57–60 (April 1989–October 1990), 308–315.

Stafford, Barbara Maria. "Les *météores* de Girodet." *Revue de l'Art*, 46 (1979), 46–51.

Stafford, Barbara Maria. "'Peculiar Marks': Lavater and the Countenance of Blemished Thought." *Art Journal*, 46 (Fall 1987), 185–192.

Stafford, Barbara Maria. "Presuming Images and Consuming Words: On the Visualization of Knowledge from the Enlightenment to Post-Modernism." In *Culture and Consumption, The World of Goods*. Ed. John Brewer and Roy Porter. London: Routledge University Press, 1990.

Stafford, Barbara Maria. "Science as Fine Art: Another Look at Boullée's *Cenotaph for Newton*." *Studies in Eighteenth-Century Culture*, 11. Ed. Harry C. Payne. Madison: University of Wisconsin Press, 1982.

Stafford, Barbara Maria. *Symbol and Myth: Humbert de Superville's Essay on Absolute Signs in Art*. Cranbury, N.J.: Associated University Presses, 1979.

Stafford, Barbara Maria. *Voyage into Substance: Art, Science, Nature, and the Illustrated Travel Account (1760–1840)*. Cambridge, Mass.: MIT Press, 1984.

Stafford, Barbara M., John La Puma, M.D., and David Schiedermayer, M.D. "One Face of Beauty, One Picture of Health: The Hidden Aesthetic of Medical Practice." *Journal of Medicine and Philosophy*, 14 (1989), 213–230.

Stanley, Manfred. *The Technological Conscience: Survival and Dignity in an Age of Expertise*. New York: The Free Press; London: Collier Macmillan Publishers, 1978.

Steer, John. "Art History and Direct Perception: A General View." *Art History*, 17 (March 1989), 92–106.

Stewart, Susan. *On Longing: Narratives of the Miniature, the Gigantic, the Souvenir, the Collection*. Baltimore: Johns Hopkins University Press, 1984.

Stewart-Robertson, Charles. "The Pneumatics and Georgics of the Eighteenth-Century Mind." *Eighteenth-Century Studies*, 20 (Spring 1987), 296–312.

Stigler, Stephen M. *The History of Statistics: The Measurement of Uncertainty before 1900.* Cambridge: The Belknap Press of Harvard University Press, 1986.

Stiglmayr, Josef. "Der NeuPlatoniker Proclus als Vorlage des sogennanten Dionysius Areopagita in der Lehre vom Uebel." *Historisches Jahrbuch*, 16 (1895), 253–273, 721–748.

Stillman, Damie. *The Decorative Work of Robert Adam.* London: Academy Editions; New York: St. Martin's Press, 1973.

Strehler, Giorgio, ed. *La Camera dei sortilegi. Autoritratto di una società nei diorami teatrali del '700.* Exh. cat. Milan: Museo Teatrale alla Scala, 1987.

Sudiman, Seymour, and Norman Bradburn. *Asking Questions.* San Francisco: Jossey-Bass Publishers, 1983.

Summers, David. *The Judgment of Sense: Renaissance Naturalism and the Rise of Aesthetics.* Cambridge: Cambridge University Press, 1987.

Taveneaux, René. *La Vie quotidienne des jansénistes aux XVIIe et XVIIIe siècles.* Paris: Hachette Littérature, 1985.

Taylor, Mark C. *Erring: A Postmodern A/Theology.* Chicago: University of Chicago Press, 1985.

Teynac, Françoise, Pierre Nolot, and Jean-Denis Vivien. *Wallpaper: A History.* New York: Rizzoli, 1982.

Thackray, Arnold. "'Matter in a Nutshell': Newton's *Opticks* and Eighteenth-Century Chemistry." *Ambix*, 15 (February 1968), 29–53.

Thomasen, Anne-Liese. "'Historia Animalicum' contra 'Gynaecia' in der Literatur des Mittelalters." *Clio Medica*, 15 (December 1980), 5–24.

Thornton, John L. *Jan van Rymsdyk: Medical Artist of the Eighteenth Century.* Cambridge and New York: Oleander Press, 1982.

Tilles, Gérard. *La Naissance de la dermatologie (1776–1880).* Paris: Les Editions Roger Dacosta, 1989.

Tilles, Gérard, and Daniel Wallach. "Histoire de la nosologie en dermatologie." *Annales Dermatologiques Vénéréologiques*, 106 (1989), 9–26.

Todorov, Tzvetan. *Theories of the Symbol.* Trans. C. Porter. Ithaca, N.Y.: Cornell University Press, 1982.

Trimpi, Wesley. "Mimesis as Appropriate Representation." *Renascence: Essays on Values in Literature*, 37 (Spring 1985): 203–207.

Trimpi, Wesley. *Muses of One Mind: The Literary Analysis of Experience and Its Continuity.* Princeton, N.J.: Princeton University Press, 1983.

Tuchman, Maurice, ed. *The Spiritual in Art: Abstract Painting 1890–1985.* Los Angeles: Los Angeles County Museum, 1987.

Tufte, Edward R. "Attention to Detail or Less Is a Bore." *PC Computing*, 1 (November 1988): 110–115.

Tufte, Edward R. "Envisioning Information." *Personal Computing Forum*, 1 (1988): 77–92.

Tufte, Edward R. "The Power of Graphics: Escaping the Flatland of Chartjunk to the Multivariate World of Hyperspace." *PC Computing,* 1 (August 1988): 88–92.

Tufte, Edward R. *The Visual Display of Quantitative Information.* Cheshire, Conn.: Graphics Press, 1983.

Turner, Anthony. *Early Scientific Instruments: Europe 1400–1800.* London: Sotheby's Publications, 1987.

Turner, Jean. "Fuseli and Lavater: The Personification of Character." *Athanor,* 4 (1985): 33–41.

Tytler, Graeme. *Physiognomy in the European Novel: Faces and Fortunes.* Princeton, N.J.: Princeton University Press, 1982.

Vartanian, Aram. "Erotisme et philosophie chez Diderot." *Cahiers de l'association internationale des études françaises,* 13 (May 1961): 367–390.

Vartanian, Aram. "Trembley's Polyp, La Mettrie, and Eighteenth-Century French Materialism." *Journal of the History of Ideas,* 11 (1950): 259–286.

Verbraeken, René. *Clair-Obscur, histoire d'un mot.* Nogent-le-Roi: Librairie des Arts et Métiers-Editions, 1979.

Verene, Donald. *Vico's Science of Imagination.* Ithaca: Cornell University Press, 1987.

Veyne, Paul, ed. *A History of Private Life: From Pagan Rome to Byzantium.* Cambridge, Mass.: Belknap Press of Harvard University Press, 1987.

Vickers, Brian, ed. *English Science, Bacon to Newton.* Cambridge: Cambridge University Press, 1984.

Vidler, Anthony. *The Writing of the Walls: Architectural Theory in the Late Enlightenment.* Princeton, N.J.: Princeton Architectural Press, 1987.

Vogt, Helmut. *Das Bilden des Kranken. Die Darstellung äusserer Veränderungen durch innere Leiden und ihrer Heilmassnahmen von der Renaissance bis in unsere Zeit.* Munich: J. F. Lehmanns Verlag, 1969.

Walker, Corlette Rossiter. *William Blake in the Art of His Time.* Exh. cat. Santa Barbara: University of California, 1976.

Warncke, Carsten-Peter. *Sprechende Bilder—Sichtbare Worte. Das Bilderverständnis in der frühen Neuzeit.* Wolfenbütteler Forschungen, vol. 33. Wiesbaden: Otto Harrassowitz, 1987.

Waterhouse, Ellis. *Gainsborough.* London: Spring Books, 1958.

Watts, Harriett Ann. *Chance: A Perspective on Dada.* Ann Arbor: UMI Research Press, 1980.

Weiner, Philip Paul, ed. *Dictionary of the History of Ideas: Studies of Selected Pivotal Ideas.* 5 vols. New York: Scribner, 1973–1974.

Wendorf, Richard. "Jonathan Richardson: The Painter as Biographer." *New Literary History,* 15 (1983–1984): 539–557.

Werblowsky, R. J., and Zwi and Wigoder Geiffrey, eds. *The Encyclopedia of the Jewish Religion.* New York: Holt, Rinehart and Winston, Inc., 1966.

SELECTED BIBLIOGRAPHY

White, Eric Charles. *Kaironomia: On the Will-to-Invent*. Ithaca: Cornell University Press, 1987.

Whittaker, Thomas. *Neo-Platonists*. Hildesheim: Olm, 1970.

Williams, Carolyn. "The Changing Face of Change: Fe/Male In/Constancy." *British Journal for Eighteenth-Century Studies*, 12 (Spring 1989): 13–28.

Williams, Guy. *The Age of Agony: The Art of Healing c. 1700–1800*. London: Constable, 1975.

Wilson, Catherine. "Visual Surface and Visual Symbol: The Microscope and the Occult in Early Modern Science." *Journal of the History of Ideas*, 49 (January–March 1988): 85–108.

Wilson, Elizabeth. *Adorned in Dreams: Fashion and Modernity*. London: Virago Press, 1985.

Wilson, Philip K. "'Out of Sight, Out of Mind?' The Daniel Turner–James Blondel Debate over Maternal Impressions." M. A. thesis, Johns Hopkins University, 1987.

Wilton-Ely, John. *The Mind and Art of Giovanni Battista Piranesi*. London: Thames and Hudson, 1978.

Wright, Beth S. "New (Stage) Light on Fragonard's *Coresus*." *Arts Magazine*, 60 (June 1986): 54–59.

Yolton, John W. *Perceptual Acquaintance from Descartes to Reid*. Minneapolis: University of Minnesota Press, 1984.

Yolton, John W. *Thinking Matter: Materialism in Eighteenth-Century Britain*. Minneapolis: University of Minnesota Press, 1983.

Yourcenar, Marguerite. *The Dark Brain of Piranesi and Other Essays*. Trans. Richard Howard. New York: Farrar, Straus, Giroux, 1984.

Zigrosser, Carl. *Medicine and the Artist: One Hundred and Thirty Seven Great Prints selected with Commentary*. New York: Dover, 1969.

Zuboff, Shoshana. *In the Age of the Smart Machine: The Future of Work and Power*. New York: Basic Books, 1988.

Abortion controversy, 211–212

Académie Royale de Chirurgie, 53

Adam, Robert, 142, 232

Adams, George, 349, 358–360

Adams, Joseph, 291–292

Addison, Joseph, 222, 349, 383, 415

Adulteration, 81, 216

AIDS, 283

Alberti, Leon Battista, 28, 36

Albinism, 319–323

Albinus, Bernard, 59, 110

Alcibiades, 214

Aldini, Giovanni
    Galvanic Experiments, 410–411 (fig. 227), 461

Algarotti, Francesco
    on beauty, 80, 284, 288
    on camera obscura, 371
    on color, 64–66, 76
    on opera, 225–226
    on sensing, 415

Alibert, Jean-Louis, 300–304, 329
    Freckles, 23 (fig. 8), 285, 302, 304, 319
    and Hôpital Saint-Louis, 293, 300
    Lepra Nigricans, 304 (fig. 190), 338
    Pustulant Smallpox, 295 (fig. 182), 300, 338
    Tree of Dermatological Diseases, 302 (fig. 188)
    Tumor, 302 (fig. 185), 304, 338
    Vitiligo, 319 (fig. 198), 338

Allegory, 188, 197, 336–337

Amusements, 368–375

Anagrams, 222–223

Anamorphic perspective, 354–356

Anatomy, 54

Andry, Nicolas, 289

Animal magnetism, 450–462

Apollo Belvedere, 157, 250

Appian, 309

Aquatinting, 24

Aquinas, Saint Thomas, 134–135

Archaeology, 64

Architecture, 59, 110–111, 172–176, 232

Ariosto, Ludovico, 223

Aromatherapy, 428–430

Asian peoples, 322

Astruc, Jean, 23, 281

Aubry, Charles, 295, 434–435
    Madness, 435 (fig. 236)

Augustine, Saint, 215, 308, 317

Austin, William, 138

Baader, Franz, 433–434, 437–438

Bacon, Francis, 188, 207, 388
    Sylva Sylvarum, 164, 456

Bacon, Francis (painter), 329

Baker, Robert, 373

Baldinucci, Filippo, 327

Balsamo, Alessandro Giuseppi, 453

Barbarisms, 211–233

Baretta, Jules-Pierre-François, 281
    Wax and Resin Casts of Cutaneous Diseases, 281 (fig. 178)

Barthez, Paul-Joseph, 423

Bartoli, Giuseppi, 168

Bateman, Thomas, 302

Batteux, Charles, 29, 184, 279, 394–395

Baudelaire, Charles, 29
    on abstracting, 178
    on dissecting, 104
    on magnifying, 393
    on marking, 284, 289–290

Baumgarten, Alexander Gottlieb, 34, 248, 395

Baumgärtner, Karl Heinrich, 102–103

Bayes, Thomas, 107

Bayle, Pierre, 163–170, 204
    Alexander ab Alexandro, 166 (fig. 102), 227, 350

Beattie, James, 138, 140, 217, 266, 384

Beauty, 15, 114–115, 179–180

Bentham, Jeremy, 48

Berkeley, George, 36, 380–384, 385, 403

Bernini, Giovanni Lorenzo, 157

Bernoulli family, 107, 345

Bichat, François-Xavier, 405

Bickham, George, 140

Bidloo, Govert, 59

Birth defects. *See* Fetal abnormalities

Birthmarks, 314, 318

Blacks, 113–114, 128, 322–323

Blake, William
  on conceiving, 252–253
  on dissecting, 58
  on magnifying, 381–382
  on marking, 318, 324, 328, 332
  on sensing, 55, 434
  With Dreams upon My Bed, 181 (fig. 111), 438
Blenheim Palace, 232
Blondel, James Augustus, 314–315
Blumenbach, Johann Friedrich, 414
Boby, John, 311
Body politic, 12, 162
Boehme, Jakob, 433
Boethius, Anicius Manlius Severinus, 134
Bond, John, 443
Bonnard, Pierre, 208
Bonnet, Charles, 349, 432
Bordelon, Laurent
  Diabolic Visions, 366 (fig. 218), 453
Bordeu, Théophile, 408
Borges, Jorge Luis, 24
Boscovich, Roger, 422, 439
Bosse, Abraham, 324
Boucher, François, 88, 393
Boudard, Jean-Baptiste
  Iconologie, 229
  Imagination, 220 (fig. 138), 224, 337, 439
  Obscurity, 229 (fig. 142), 337, 438
Bougainville, Louis Antoine de, 298
Bouhours, Dominique
  on abstracting, 154, 156
  on conceiving, 220, 229, 231–232
  on dissecting, 80
  on marking, 290
Boulanger, Nicolas-Antoine, 389
Boullée, Etienne-Louis, 110
Bouquet
  Combed Marbled Paper, 207 (fig. 132), 230
Boyle, Robert, 424
Brewster, David, 373
Bronzino, Angelo, 77
Buffon, Georges-Louis Le Clerc, Comte de, 114, 322–323

A Black Albino Child, 316 (fig. 196), 319, 321, 323, 326–327, 411
Bunbury, Henry William
  Origin of the Gout, 188 (fig. 117), 227
Burton, Robert
  Types of Melancholy, 195 (fig. 125), 434
Byron, George Gordon, Lord, 446

Cabanis, Pierre-Jean, 293, 405
Cabinets of curiosities, 29–31, 223, 262, 270, 299, 360–361, 368
Cagliostro, Count Alessandro, 453
Caldani, Leopoldo Marco Antonio
  Fetus in Utero, 247 (fig. 154), 315
  Gravid Uterus, 246 (fig. 153)
  Venous and Arterial Systems, 63 (figs. 28, 30), 343, 410
Callot, Jacques, 232
Camera obscura, 358, 369–372
Campbell, George, 220, 384
  Philosophy of Rhetoric, 135, 223
Camper, Adriaan Gilles, 112
Camper, Petrus (Pierre), 48, 103
  Comparative Morphology, 152 (fig. 92), 311
  From Ape to Apollo, 110 (fig. 72), 114, 128, 204, 277, 434
  Grotesques from Frieze of Golden House of Nero, 441 (fig. 239)
  Various Measurements of Facial Angles, 110 (fig. 73), 114, 204, 227, 323, 434
  Youth to Age, 113 (fig. 74), 204, 227, 434
Caricature of Magnetism, Somnambulism, and Clairvoyancy, 448 (fig. 242)
Caricatures, 150, 184, 191–195, 217–220, 474
Carracci, Annibale, 137
Cassini family, 345
Castel, Louis Bertrand, 361, 362
Castle Howard, 232
Caylus, Anne-Claude-Philippe, Comte de, 55, 169, 266
  Body Fragments Resulting from Surgery, 47 (fig. 18), 101

A Collection of Antiquities, 169 (fig.
104), 223, 368
Grylli, 269 (fig. 167), 350
Gryllus, 176 (fig. 110), 205, 227, 269
Roman Ithyphallic Grotesque, 217 (fig.
133), 267, 274
Satire or "Critique," 184 (fig. 114), 205,
213, 264, 265, 267, 269
Chambers, Ephraim, 49, 134, 147–148,
161, 164, 168–172, 363
Anatomy, 148 (fig. 89), 227
Miscellany, 168 (fig. 103), 224, 227
Organization of Knowledge, 147 (fig. 88),
148, 150, 170
Pneumaticks, 424 (fig. 233)
A Visual Summa, 170 (fig. 105), 227,
371
Chambers, William, 176
Chardin, Jean-Baptiste-Siméon, 164, 413
The Ray, 78 (fig. 50)
Cheyne, George, 404
Cholera Prevention, 276 (fig. 177), 338,
362
Christ, 92–93
Cicero, Marcus Tullius, 87, 438
Clarke, Samuel, 439
Clavareau, Nicolas-Marie, 293
Cloquet, Hippolyte, 108, 404
Cochin, Charles-Nicolas, 266
Cogan, Thomas, 311
Coins, 56
Coleridge, Samuel Taylor, 29
on conceiving, 233, 236, 252
on dissecting, 104
on magnifying, 365
on marking, 334–335
Colin
The Nightmare, 443 (fig. 240), 445–446
Collage, 95, 339
Color mezzotints, 76
Color printing, 24, 64, 78
Computer graphics, 132
Computers, 24, 48, 474
Conceptualism, 132
Connoisseurship, 81–82, 84–85, 118–
119, 251
Contagion, 281–304, 311, 421

Contamination, 306
Cook, James, 27, 128, 298
Corneille, Thomas
The Arts and Sciences, 145 (fig. 86), 166,
170
Dictionnaire, 134, 170, 364
Corruption, 285–286
Cosmetics, 289
Cosmetic surgery, 119
Cowper, William, 59
External Muscles and Diverse Parts of the
Human Body, 61 (fig. 25), 112, 404
Fetal Development, 240 (fig. 147), 343
Skeleton Stepping into Tomb, 69 (fig. 36),
73, 112
Various Portions of the Cuticula, 288 (fig.
180)
Cozens, Alexander, 156
The Artful, 151 (fig. 91), 204, 415
Principles of Beauty, 150, 415
Simple Beauty, 33 (fig. 13), 148, 150,
154, 434
Creation, 233–234, 235
Criminals, 54, 411
Crisis Rooms at Mesmer's Hôtel Bullion, 455
(fig. 245)
Criticism, 34–35, 82–83, 140–142, 168,
364
Crousaz, Jean-Pierre de, 104, 279
Traité du beau, 136–137
Cruikshank, George, 188, 193, 426
The Blue Devils, 195 (fig. 123), 227,
331, 338, 434
Bumpology, 117 (fig. 77)
The Cholic, 191 (fig. 120), 227, 331, 431
Hallucinations, 195 (fig. 124), 197, 227,
331, 338, 434
The Indigestion, 191 (fig. 119), 227, 331,
431
Organ of Ideality, 428 (fig. 235)
Cudworth, Ralph, 423
Cuff, John, 358
Cureau de La Chambre, Marin, 48, 85–
86
Curtius, Philippe-Guillaume Mathé, 67,
321
Cyclops, 256, 260, 261

Dagoty, Jacques Gautier, 76–78, 459
  Assemblages of Legs and Feet, 69 (fig. 34)
  Back Muscles, 77 (fig. 49), 112
  Human Embryo, 241 (fig. 148), 343
  Nervous System, 401 (fig. 225)
  Two Dissected Male Heads, 77 (fig. 47), 406
  The Vessels of the Skin, 77 (fig. 48), 406, 413
Dagoty, Jean-Fabien Gautier
  Quartzose and Cellular "Sports," 108 (fig. 69)
Daguerre, Louis-Jacques-Mandé, 373
D'Alembert, Jean Le Rond, 431. *See also Encyclopédie*
Dandré-Bardon, Michel-François, 156, 181, 222
Daumier, Honoré, 193
  Colic, 191 (fig. 121), 227, 431
  Misanthropy, 199 (fig. 127), 227, 338, 434
David, Jacques-Louis
  Brutus, 17–18
  Dead Marat, 18, 162
  Death of Socrates, 12–17 (fig. 2), 303, 392
  Oath of the Horatii, 18
Davy, Humphrey, 426
Deception, 85, 122
Deformity, 308
Delacroix, Eugène, 390
Delusion, 396–398
Democritus, 178
Dennis, John, 136, 279
Dent, William
  The Cutter Cut Up, 219 (fig. 135), 220, 222, 227, 276, 338
Dermatology, 283
Derôme, Nicolas-Denis
  "Stone" marbled papers, 205 (fig. 130), 207, 230
Descamps, Jean-Baptiste, 327
Descartes, René, 35, 85, 133, 384, 432
Desnoues, Guillaume, 78
Dézallier d'Argenville, Antoine-Nicolas, 328

D'Holbach, Paul-Henry Thomas, Baron, 191, 215, 388, 416
Diagrams, 148–150, 152, 178
Dictionaries, 5, 142–144, 226–227
Diderot, Denis. *See also Encyclopédie*
  on abstracting, 162–164, 170
  on conceiving, 215, 226, 253
  on dissecting, 78, 87, 104
  on magnifying, 385–390, 393
  on marking, 284–285, 322
  on sensing, 416, 443
Dio Chrysostom, 53, 214
Disease, 80, 281–283
Divination, 439
DNA, 235
Donne, John, 334
D'Orléans, Chérubim
  Lunar Spots, 288 (fig. 179)
Drawing, 96
Drawing manuals, 5, 24, 56–58, 80, 112–115, 138, 142, 226–227, 284
Dreams, 11, 378, 437–450
Dryden, John, 216, 397
Dubos, Jean-Baptiste, 81, 83, 229, 393–394
Dubreuil, Jean, 324
  Cast Shadows in Artificial Light, 324 (fig. 199), 369
Dubuffet, Jean, 193
Duchamp, Marcel, 82
Dufresnoy, Charles-Antoine, 216, 226, 231, 324, 397
Dupaty, Jean-Baptiste, 78–80
Duranty, Louis-Emile Edmond, 216
Durkheim, Emile, 41
Duverney, Joseph Guichard, 76

Ecole de Chirurgie (Paris), 49
Ecole Pratique de la Dissection, 53
Egyptian art, 176, 184
Egyptian hieroglyphs, 54, 214, 216, 336
Eisen, Charles-Dominique-Joseph, 409
Electricity, 459–461
Eller, Theodore, 316, 323
Elsheimer, Adam, 184
Embryology, 244

Empiricism, 335, 363, 378–379

Encaustic painting, 55

Encyclopaedia Britannica, 82, 172, 350, 424–426

   Optics, 142 (fig. 84), 166, 204, 227, 357, 366, 369

Encyclopedias, 164–176, 226–227

Encyclopédie, 144, 208, 260, 428, 443

   Bandages and Surgical Instruments, 158 (fig. 99), 172, 227

   Ecorché, 19 (fig. 3), 404

   "Goût," 430

Encyclopedists, 35

Engraving, 325–326

Enquiry into the Nature of the Human Soul (anonymous, 1730), 382, 439

Entertainment, 356–361, 368

Epicurus, 424

Epitomes, 144

Esquirol, Jean-Etienne-Dominique

   Maniac after Cure, 436 (fig. 238)

   Maniac during Attack, 435 (fig. 237)

Etching, 24, 58–59

Euclid, 214

Experimental sciences, 51, 87, 121, 163–164, 392, 467

Fabre, Pierre, 299

Fahrenheit, Gabriel, 358, 424

Fallopius, Gabriel, 297

Félibien, André, 80, 229, 248, 396

Fetal abnormalities, 180, 219–220, 264, 283, 308

Fludd, Robert, 453

   The Mystery of the Human Mind, 110 (fig. 71), 406

Flugel, Carl Friedrich, 135–136

Fontana, Felice Gaspar Ferdinand, 21, 63

   Anatomical Wax Figure, 64 (fig. 33), 411

Fontenelle, Bernard Le Bouvier de, 154

Fourcroy, Antoine-François, 303

Fragonard, Jean-Honoré

   Coresus and Callirhoe, 385–390 (fig. 223)

Franklin, Allan, 40

Freckles, 23 (fig. 8), 285, 302, 319

Frederick II of Prussia, 100 (fig. 61)

Freud, Sigmund, 103, 118

Friedrich, Caspar David, 29

Furetière and Moréri

   Grand Dictionnaire, 144–145

Fuseli, Johann Heinrich

   on abstracting, 151

   on conceiving, 231

   on dissecting, 55, 91, 92, 107

   on magnifying, 377, 394, 398

   on marking, 328

   on sensing, 438, 439, 443, 445

Füssli, Johann Melchior, 240

Gainsborough, Thomas, 377

Galilei, Galileo, 222–223

Gall, Franz Josef, 103, 116

Galvani, Luigi, 410, 459

Gamelin, Jacques, 70–74, 407

   Anatomy Theater, 54 (fig. 20)

   Artists Studying Anatomy, 74 (fig. 44)

   Death Holding Sheet of Drawings, 73 (fig. 39), 112

   The Entrance of Death, 74 (fig. 43)

   The Rape of Death, 73 (fig. 42)

   Skeleton, 73 (fig. 40), 112

   Study of Male Musculature, 74 (fig. 45), 112

   Triumph of Death, 73 (fig. 41)

Garengeot, René Croissant de, 51–53, 83

Garzoni, Tommaso, 256

Generation, 233–254

Gene therapy, 26

Genetic testing, 118, 308

Genome project, 212

Geoffroy de Saint-Hilaire, Etienne and Isidore, 259

Georget, Etienne-Jean, 436

Gérard, François-Pascal, 78

Gerdy, P. N., 54

Géricault, Théodore, 335–336

   The Madwoman: Monomania of Gambling, 75 (fig. 46), 300, 436

   Wounded Cuirassier, 309–311

Germany, reunification of, 7

Gibson, James L., 120, 381

Gilbert, William, 453

Gillray, James, 193

The Cow-Pock, 295 (fig. 181)

The Dissolution, 154 (fig. 96), 192, 227, 246, 434

Doublûres of Characters, 262 (fig. 166)

French Generals Retiring on Account of Their Health, 186 (fig. 115), 227, 262, 331

The Gout, 188 (fig. 116), 227

Scientific Researches! New Discoveries in Pneumaticks, 426 (fig. 234)

Girodet-Trioson, Anne-Louis, 302

Sleep of Endymion, 377

Glass of Momus, 87, 414

Glisson, Francis, 408

Rickets, 219 (fig. 137), 264

Gnosticism, 215

Gondouin, Jacques

Amphitheater, 49 (fig. 19)

Gori, Francesco, 266

Gothic romances, 230, 334, 375

Gould, Stephen Jay, 40

Gout, 188–189

Goya, Francisco de, 270–274, 377

All Will Fall, 270 (fig. 171), 272, 276, 329, 398

Correction, 24 (fig. 9), 142

Here Comes the Bogey-Man, 272 (fig. 172), 324, 329

The Sleep of Reason Produces Monsters, 36 (fig. 17), 199, 329, 333–334, 385, 438, 445, 448

They Spruce Themselves Up, 199 (fig. 126), 227, 338, 398

Those Specks of Dust, 272 (fig. 173), 324, 329

To Rise and to Fall, 225 (fig. 140), 276, 337, 398

Until Death, 183 (fig. 112)

When Day Breaks We Will Be Off, 276 (fig. 176), 324, 329

Will No One Unbind Us?, 225 (fig. 139), 262, 276, 337

Grandville (Jean-Ignace-Isidore Gérard), 426, 446

The Great and the Small, 357 (fig. 214), 366, 398

Metamorphosis of a Dream, 446 (fig. 241)

Misery, Hypocrisy, Covetousness, 269 (fig. 168), 338

The Pursuit, 259 (fig. 160), 276, 338, 398, 447

Greatraks, Valentine, 453

Greece, ancient, 249, 285–286

Gregory, John, 299

Gregory of Tours, 295

Greuter, Matthaus, 154

Physician Curing Fantasy, 154 (fig. 95), 198, 246, 434

Greuze, Jean-Baptiste

The Dead Bird, 413 (fig. 228)

Village Betrothal, 18

Grimm, Melchior, 385–388

Gros, Antoine-Jean

The Pesthouse at Jaffa, 302 (fig. 186)

Grose, Francis

Profile Heads, 151 (fig. 90), 217

Rules for Drawing Caricaturas, 217

Grotesques, 184, 216–217, 229, 266–279, 396, 411, 437, 474

Guérin, Pierre-Narcisse, 302

Guyot, Edmé

Anamorphoses, 256 (fig. 157), 269, 319, 336, 366, 372

Conical Mirror and "Misshapen" Reflections, 366 (fig. 219), 369, 372

Nouvelles récréations, 368–369

Hagedorn, Christian Ludwig von, 181, 186, 324

Haller, Albrecht von, 23, 405–406, 410, 417, 432

Demonstrations of Physiology, 409 (fig. 226)

Vivisection, 23 (fig. 6), 262, 368, 408–409

Handwriting manuals, 138–140

Harris, John

Arteries and Veins, 147 (fig. 87), 227, 341

John Marshall's Double Microscope, 144
(fig. 85), 147, 166, 204, 227, 345,
346, 371
Lexicon Technicum, 144–146
Mr. Wilson's Microscope, 21 (fig. 4), 341
Hartley, David, 365, 422, 439
Harvey, William, 248, 313, 322
Anatomical Exercises, 244–246
Zeus Opening the Cosmic Egg, 246 (fig.
152), 343
Hawthorne, Nathaniel, 318
Heath, William
Monster Soup, 158 (fig. 97), 223, 227,
246, 357
Hebra, Ferdinand
Leucoderma, 302 (fig. 187), 304, 319
Helmont, Jean-Baptiste von, 423, 453
Hemsterhuis, François, 110, 433
Hermaphrodites, 33, 158, 265–266
Hesiod, 181–183
Hess, David
Cranioscopic Examinations, 117 (fig. 76)
Hippocrates, 308
Hoadley, Benjamin, 55
Hobbes, Thomas, 215, 378–379, 388
Hoet, Gérard, 138
Hogarth, William, 55, 128, 216, 279
The Country Dance, 325–326 (fig. 200),
330–331, 338, 404
Visit to the Quack Doctor, 299 (fig. 184),
368
Holzer, Jenny, 472
Hooke, Robert, 346–348, 350–356, 363–
364, 382, 409
"Diamants" or Sparks in Flints, 351 (fig.
210), 353, 356
The Point of a Sharp Needle, 353 (fig.
211)
Hôpital Saint-Louis, 281, 293, 300, 304
Horace, 184, 216
Hospice de Bicêtre, 293
Hospitals, 292–293
Hôtel-Dieu (Paris), 293
Huber, Michel, 78
Humbert de Superville, David Pierre
Giottin, 41

Colossus of Memnon, 106 (fig. 65)
Platonic Solids, 105 (fig. 64), 113
Hume, David, 188, 191, 379–380, 384
Hunter, John, 110, 265, 297, 434
Hunting, 120–123
Hurd, Richard, 230–231, 398
Huysmans, J. K., 24
Hybrids, 29, 184, 237–238, 264–265,
295, 468

Iamblichus, 42, 388
Idols, 184, 365, 424
Imperfection, 353–354
Incompleteness, 330–333
Infirmerie de la Charité, 293
Ingenhousz, Jan, 454
Ingres, Jean-Auguste-Dominique, 29, 78,
377
Inoculation, 295
Insanity, 74, 436
Intaglio, 54, 56, 61–63
Intarsia, 24, 178, 191, 223
Irritability, 411–413

Jallabert, Louis, 459
Jansenism, 204
Jenner, Edward
*Cowpox Pustules on the Hand of Sarah
Nelmes*, 23 (fig. 7), 285, 295
Johannot, Tony
Introduction, Voyage où il vous plaira, 27
(fig. 10), 227, 338, 446
What Courageous and Bold Travelers, 336
(fig. 201), 446
Johnson, Samuel, 225, 443
Josephinium (Vienna), 21
Junius, Franciscus, 246, 248, 311–312

Kaleidoscopes, 373
Kant, Immanuel, 34, 379, 395
Kaplan, Mark, 119
Kauffmann, Angelica, 18
Keats, John, 333
Kent, William, 231
Kepler, Johannes, 345

Kircher, Athanasius, 208, 369–370
  Catoptric Theater, 373 (fig. 221), 453
  Kaleidoscope, 369 (fig. 220), 373, 453
  *Natural Impressions: Anamorphic Land-
    scape*, 356 (fig. 213), 358, 369
Kleist, Heinrich von, 333, 450
Kruger, Barbara, 28

La Chau, l'Abbé de, and l'Abbé Le
    Blond
  Assemblage of Eight Heads, 269 (fig. 169),
    350
  Hermaphrodite, 33 (fig. 15), 158, 265
  Pierres gravées, 266
Laennec, Théophile
  Stethoscopes, 414 (fig. 230)
Lagrange, Joseph-Louis, 133
Lairesse, Gerard de, 59, 142, 229, 324
Lambert, Johann Heinrich, 107
La Mettrie, Julien Offray de, 253, 315,
    388, 409
Laocoön Group, 179, 383
La Pérouse, Jean-François de Galaup de,
    27
Laplace, Pierre-Antoine de, 107
Lasers, 24
Laughter, 191
Laugier, Marc-Antoine, 83, 142, 397
Lavater, Johann Caspar
  on abstracting, 138
  Calculating Facial Disproportion, 33
    (fig. 14), 103
  Cipher of Madness, 152 (fig. 93)
  on conceiving, 215, 226, 234, 252
  on dissecting, 48, 84, 89–93, 96, 103,
    104, 107
  Frederick II, 101 (fig. 61), 127
  The Georgian and the Bashkir, 108
    (fig. 66), 434
  Girl with Birthmarks, 316 (fig. 195), 319
  Hair Growing from a Mole, 152 (fig. 94),
    325
  Head of Christ, 92 (fig. 54)
  Human Variety, 126 (fig. 80)
  Lips, 101 (fig. 63), 407

  Machine for Drawing Silhouettes, 96
    (fig. 57), 127
  on marking, 285–286, 308, 317–318,
    323
  Physiognomische Fragmente, 91
  Rage, 123 (fig. 78), 435
  Régles physiognomiques, 152
  Seeing Darkly, 91–92 (fig. 52)
  Silhouettes of Christ, 92 (fig. 53), 103,
    434
  Silhouettes of Clerics, 95 (fig. 55), 434
  *Silhouettes of Mendelssohn, Spalding,
    Rochow, and Nicolai*, 95 (fig. 56), 127
  Voltaire, 101 (fig. 62)
  Wrinkled Countenance, 113 (fig. 75),
    126, 183
Lavoisier, Antoine-Laurent, 303
Le Blon, Jacques-Christophe, 76, 324–
    325
Le Camus, Antoine
  on abstracting, 154–155, 195
  on magnifying, 345, 388
  on marking, 315
  on sensing, 416, 428–431, 442, 458
Ledermüller, Martin Frobène, 360–361
  Coral Salt "Aureole," 343 (fig. 203)
  Dissected Frog, 98 (fig. 59), 341, 358
  "Eels" in Vinegar, 349 (fig. 209)
  Flint Sparks, 343 (fig. 206)
  Fresh Water Polyp and Magnifying Glass,
    341 (fig. 202)
  Lace and Spider's Web, 354 (fig. 212)
  Magnifying Glasses and Hand Microscope,
    36 (fig. 16), 345
  *Reproduction and Multiplication of Fresh
    Water Polyps*, 21 (fig. 5), 242, 345,
    349
  Solar Microscope and Optical Cabinet, 358
    (fig. 215), 361, 387
  *Solar Miscroscope and Prismatic Projec-
    tions*, 361 (fig. 217), 387
  Wilson Hand Microscope and Slides, 346
    (fig. 207), 358, 366
Ledoux, Claude-Nicolas, 112
Leeuwenhoek, Anton van, 21, 345, 353

Leibniz, Gottfried Wilhelm, Freiherr
    von, 439
  on abstracting, 135
  on conceiving, 235, 248, 252
  on magnifying, 345, 382, 388
  on marking, 331
Le Masurier (artist), 321
Lemery, Louis, 260
Leonardo da Vinci, 186
Leprosy, 294
Le Sage, Georges-Louis, 458–459
Lessing, Gotthold Ephraim, 29
  on abstracting, 179–181, 186
  on conceiving, 222, 226, 233
  on magnifying, 383–384, 396
  on marking, 316
Levin, David N.
  3D Models Derived from MR Images, 108
    (fig. 70), 390 (fig. 224)
Levine, Sherrie, 28
Lévi-Strauss, Claude, 41
Libertinage, 204
Licetus, Fortunius, 256
  Amorphous Monster, 219 (figs. 134, 136),
    260, 266, 398
  Faceless and Limbless Monsters, 256
    (fig. 158), 260
  Medusa Head Found in an Egg, 184
    (fig. 113), 264
  Nature and Her Monsters, 158 (fig. 98),
    220, 337
Lichtenberg, Georg Christoph
  on abstracting, 132, 201
  on conceiving, 234, 279
  on dissecting, 48, 120, 125–129
  on magnifying, 380
  on marking, 284, 323, 326
  on sensing, 407
Lieberkühn, Johann, 358
Lips, 101–102
Locke, John, 133, 148, 378
  Essay concerning Human Understanding,
    35, 135
Lomazzo, Giovanni Paolo, 256
Longhi, Pietro, 371
Lorrain, Claude, 327

Lorry, Charles, 281
Loutherbourg, Philippe Jacques de, 372
Lucian, 266, 438
Lucretius (Titus Lucretius Carus), 424

Macé-Ruette
  Fine-Combed Paper, 207 (fig. 131), 230
McLean, T.
  The Body Politic, 12 (fig. 1), 219, 227,
    338
Magic, 364
Magnasco, Alexandro, 371
Malebranche, Nicolas
  on conceiving, 248
  on magnifying, 388
  on marking, 308, 313–314, 317–318
Malevich, Kasimir, 132
Mallarmé, Stéphane, 82
Malpighi, Marcello, 345
Manet, Edouard, 333
Mania, 436
Manicheanism, 215
Mannerism, 334–336
Manual skills, 39, 52–53, 131, 350, 393
Maratta, Carlo, 76
Marbling, 199–209, 230–231, 313, 392
Margolis, Howard, 40
Mariette, Jean, 170
Marius, Bishop of Avranches, 295
Marshall, John, 345
Masons, 453
Maternal impressions, 306–309, 313–314,
    319–322
Mathematical recreations, 372
Mathematics, 104–106, 133, 364
Maupertuis, Pierre-Louis Moreau de,
    114, 259–261, 264, 322
  Earthly Venus, 315
  Le Nègre blanc, 321
Measurement, 48
Meckel, Johann Friedrich, 113, 407
Medical imaging, 8–9, 26, 48, 212, 471
Medicine, 466
Medicus, Friedrich Casimir, 417
Melancholy, 195–196
Mendelsohn, Moses, 181

Mengs, Anton Raphael, 17, 18
  on abstracting, 142
  on conceiving, 251–252
  on dissecting, 80, 119
  on magnifying, 286
Menippus, 270
Mercier, Louis-Sébastien, 232
Mesmer, Franz Anton, 449–450, 450–456
Metaphor, 4–7
Microscopy, 21, 36, 54, 83, 330, 341–361, 384
Mies van der Rohe, Ludwig, 132
Mirabeau, Comte de (Honoré-Gabriel-Victor Riqueti), 297
Mirrors, 91, 362, 365
Misbirths. *See* Fetal abnormalities
Mixtures, 214–215, 323–329
Momigliano, Arnaldo, 213
Mondrian, Piet, 132
Monsters, 184, 254–266, 338–339, 366, 468
Montesquieu, Charles de Secondat de, 266, 322
Montfaucon, Bernard de, 266, 267
More, Henry, 247, 248, 251, 352, 420
  Enthusiasmus Triumphatus, 456
  Saducismus Triumphatus, 313
Moreau, Gustave, 339
Moréri, Louis, 166, 364
Morveau, Louis-Bernard Guyton de, 292
Mothers, 306–309, 314–315
Muratori, Lodovigo Antonio, 155–156, 449
Museum of Physics and Natural History (Florence), 21
Museums, 64, 112. *See also* Cabinets of curiosities

Natter, Johann Lorenz, 266
  Athlete, 56 (fig. 22), 158
  Chimera, 176 (fig. 109), 184, 204, 213, 227, 267
  Diverse Symbols, 176 (fig. 108), 205, 213, 227, 267
  Head of Jupiter Serapis, 56 (fig. 21), 213

Nattier, Jean-Marc
  Joseph Bonnier de La Mosson, 31 (fig. 12), 324, 360, 366
Natural history cabinets. *See* Cabinets of curiosities
Necker, Jacques, 293
Needham, John Tuberville, 349
Neoclassicism, 9, 137–138, 186, 204–205, 235–236, 329–330, 466
Neoplatonism, 11–12, 29, 53, 104, 151, 234–236, 252
Neurology, 403–413, 449
Newton, Isaac, 288, 345, 361, 362
  Opticks, 418–420
  Principia Mathematica, 133
Nightmares, 443–450
Nodier, Charles, 446
Nollet, Jean-Antoine, 360, 361, 459
Non-western peoples, 115–116, 128, 322
Normality, 15, 107–108, 112–113, 308, 466
Norton, Bryan G., 40
Novalis (Friedrich von Hardenberg), 418
  Das Allgemeine Brouillon, 331–332

Oldmixon, John, 82, 231, 279
Opera, 225–226
Optical boxes, 371
Optical instruments, 342, 345, 358, 362, 366–375, 392, 403, 468–469
Optical tricks, 354–356
Organ transplants, 295
Origen, 91, 178, 220
Original sin, 162, 170, 235, 308, 317–318, 468
Orme, Edward
  An Essay on Transparent Prints, 375
  Philosopher in His Study, 375–376 (fig. 222)
  Specimens of Windows, Lamps, Screens, 358 (fig. 216)
Ornament, 176, 204, 208, 215, 231
Oudry, Jean-Baptiste, 261
  Gout and the Spider, 188 (fig. 118)
Ovid (Publius Ovidius Naso), 438
Ozanam, Jacques, 364, 372–373

Pain, 178–179

Painting, 36, 180–181, 393–395, 416

Panathenaic festival, 236

Papillon, Jean-Martin, 54–55, 208

Paracelsus, Philippus Aureolus, 453

Paré, Ambroise, 295
  Pygmy, Hairy Woman, and the Man-Calf, 311 (fig. 194)

Pariset, R. M.
  Allegory of Painting, 138 (fig. 81)

Parsons, James, 123–124
  Sneering Woman, 124 (fig. 79)

Pascal, Blaise, 85

Passeri, Giuseppe, 266

Pathognomics, 120–129

Paul, Saint, 215

Paulet, Jean-Jacques, 295, 297, 453–454
  Satire on Animal Magnetism, 453 (fig. 244), 459

Pausanius, 387

Pauson, 186

Peirce, Charles Saunders, 41

Perception, 341–356

Pernety, Antoine-Joseph, 104, 204, 252
  Discours sur la physiognomie, 86–89
  on Rembrandt, 328
  on skin color, 323

Phantasms, 285, 333, 352, 361, 377–378, 379, 437, 475

Phidias, 214

Phrenology, 115–118

Physiognomics, 84–103

Picart, Bernard
  Different Agitations of Convulsionaries, 413 (fig. 229), 442, 453

Pigal
  The Desires of Pregnant Women, 306 (fig. 191)
  Neoplasms, 304 (fig. 189)

Pigalle, Jean-Baptiste, 128

Piles, Roger de, 83

Pinel, Philippe, 108, 293

Pinson (surgeon), 78

Piranesi, Giovanni Battista, 24, 58–70, 176, 216
  The Baths of Caracalla, 63 (fig. 29), 69 (fig. 35), 328

  Campo Vaccino, 70 (fig. 37)
  Hadrian's Villa, Tivoli, 64 (fig. 32)
  Lapides Capitolini, 172 (fig. 106)
  Piazza di S. Pietro, 70 (fig. 38)
  Roman Fragments, 172 (fig. 107), 227, 328, 331, 441
  So-Called Temple of Minerva Medica, 59 (fig. 24)
  Tempio delle Tosse near Tivoli, 59 (fig. 23)
  Temple of Cybele, 61 (fig. 26), 328
  Temple of the Sybil, Tivoli, 63 (fig. 27), 67, 328
  Temple of Vespasian, 64 (fig. 31), 69

Plato, 9, 10–11, 365
  allegory of the cave, 2, 6, 390

Pliny (Gaius Plinius Secundus), 313

Plutarch, 250, 312, 421, 438

Pneumatics, 417–436

Polygnotus, 137

Polytheism, 213–214, 215, 267

Poor people, 292–293

Porphyry, 42, 388

Porta, Giovanni Battista della, 369

Portraiture, 93

Power, Henry, 348, 353

Prenatal screening, 118

Priestley, Joseph, 421–422, 454, 459

Printing flaws, 354

Printing techniques, 54–55

Prisms, 361

Prisons, 292

Privacy, 201

Proclus, 42
  on abstracting, 134, 148, 178
  on conceiving, 214, 217, 235–236, 248–249
  on dissecting, 104–105
  on magnifying, 388
  on sensing, 428

Proust, Marcel, 428

Puns, 222, 388

Puységur, Armand-Marie-Jacques Chastenet, Marquis de, 453, 455, 461–462

Pyreicus, 186

Pythagoras, 365

Quetelet, L. Adolphe, 112
Quietists, 388
Quintilian (Marcus Fabius Quintilianus),
 220, 222, 286, 363, 438

Rabelais, François, 297
Ramazzini, Bernardino, 431
Ramsay, Andrew Michael, 380
Raphael (Raffaello Sanzio), 137
Regnault, Nicolas-François
 Cyclops Cat, 261 (fig. 163)
 Dog with Three Posteriors, 261 (fig. 164)
 Double Child, 260 (fig. 161), 276
 *Monstrous Child with Multiple Sensory
  Organs*, 260 (fig. 162)
 Monstrous Man (with "Parasite"), 254
  (fig. 156), 262, 276, 319, 366
Rembrandt van Rijn, 324, 327–328
 Anatomy Lesson of Dr. Tulp, 49
Reynolds, Joshua, 140–142, 152, 318,
 328, 394
Ricci, Marco, 327
Richard, Jérôme, 377, 432, 440–441,
 443, 449
 Théorie des songes, 155
Richardson, Jonathan
 on abstracting, 152
 on conceiving, 225, 231
 on dissecting, 54, 81–83, 84
 on magnifying, 383
 on marking, 284, 324
Riedinger, Johann Elias, 261
Riolan, Jean
 Cyclops, 256 (fig. 159), 337
Ripa, Cesare, 224
Rivati, G. F.
 Bacteria, 254 (fig. 155), 342
Robert, Etienne-Gaspard, 377
Rocha, Joaquim Leonardo, 321
Rodin, Auguste, 250
Roman empire, 229
Roman literature, 286, 334
Romano, Giulio, 186, 397
Romanticism, 329–332, 334–336
Romney, George, 21

Rosenhof, August Johann Rösel von
 Copulating Frogs and the Laying of Eggs,
  242 (fig. 149), 276
 Historia Naturalis Ranarum, 350
 Larval Development, 242 (fig. 150), 342,
  350
 Pinned Frog, 98 (fig. 58)
Rosicrucians, 453
Rosso, Medardo, 250
Rowlandson, Thomas, 188, 372
 The Bum Shop, 276 (fig. 175)
 The Hypochondriac, 192–193 (fig. 122),
  227, 331, 434
 A Magic Lantern, 274 (fig. 174), 358,
  372
 Napoleon, 270 (fig. 170), 276
Rubens, Peter Paul, 184, 229, 324, 328
Runes, 54
Ruskin, John, 328
Ruysch, Frederick, 240

Sacks, Oliver, 124, 186, 333
Saint-Aubin, Gabriel-Jacques de, 127
Sainte-Albine, Pierre Remond de, 226,
 397
Salpetrière, 293
Sans, Abbé, 461
 Electrical Cure of Paralysis, 459 (fig. 247)
Satire, 176, 426–427
Scarpa, Antonio, 410
Scars, 161–162
Scheuchzer, Jean-Jacques, 421
 Creation of the Universe, 238 (fig. 143),
  336
 Development of the Chicken Embryo, 244
  (fig. 151), 343
 First Day of Creation, 229 (fig. 141), 337
 The Human Eye as the Work of God, 345
  (fig. 205), 369
 Human Generation, 240 (fig. 146), 274,
  338, 343
 Magnified Louse, 346 (fig. 208)
 Physicians Embalming, 29 (fig. 11), 52,
  223
 Respiration, 418 (fig. 231)
 Second Day of Creation, 240 (fig. 144)

Third Day of Creation, 240 (fig. 145), 338

The Wrathful and Jealous Cain, 89 (fig. 51)

Scientific instruments, 24, 147

Scientific popularization, 144, 358–361, 368, 426, 453

Sculpture, 392–393

Sensation, 401–417

Seurat, Georges, 290, 381

Sexuality, 215, 267–268. *See also* Original sin

Shaftesbury, Anthony Ashley Cooper, Third Earl of, 29

    on abstracting, 136

    on conceiving, 230, 248, 251

    on dissecting, 81, 104

Shelley, Mary Wollstonecraft, 66

Sherman, Cindy, 28

Siamese Brothers, 262 (fig. 165), 276, 319, 366

Siamese twins, 260, 262

Sibly, Ebenezer

    Electrical Stars, 422 (fig. 232), 461

    Mesmerism: The Operator Inducing a Hypnotic Trance, 450 (fig. 243)

    System of the Interior, or Empyrean Heaven, Shewing the Fall of Lucifer, 456 (fig. 246)

Sick France Being Diagnosed, 162 (fig. 101)

Sighting of Jupiter and Saturn, 345 (fig. 204)

Silhouette, Etienne de, 96

Silhouettes, 92, 95–101

Simon Magus, 366

Sivry, Louis Poinsinet de, 195, 274

Skeletons, 69

Skin coloration, 319–323

Skin diseases, 283, 290

Smallpox, 23, 291, 294–296, 304

Smyth, James Carmichael, 292

Soemmering, G. Theodore von, 433

Somnambulism, 448–450

Sophists, 11, 89, 363–364

Soul, 432–433

Spallanzani, Lazzaro, 349

Spanish Marble Paper, 199 (fig. 128), 230

Spence, Joseph, 169, 224, 229, 267, 438

Spenser, Edmund, 230

Spinoza, Benedict, 215, 238

Spontaneous generation, 349–350

Spots, 23, 281–341

Sprat, Thomas, 352

Spurzheim, Johann Georg, 103, 116

Statistics, 107

Statius, Publius Papinius, 438

Sterne, Laurence, 199

Sticotti, A. F., 156, 274, 432

Stijl, De, 132

Stimpson, George William, 107

Stubbs, George, 55

Stubbs, Georges, 327

    Brown and White Norfolk or Water Spaniel, 309 (fig. 192)

    Formal Studies, 140 (fig. 82)

    Landscape Studies, 140 (fig. 83)

Sue, Jean-Joseph, 103, 115

Sulzer, Johann Georg, 82, 84

Summers, David, 40

Suprematism, 132

Surgery, 47, 49–53, 158

Susini, Clemente, 64

Swedenborg, Emanuel, 453

Synesius, 42

Syphilis, 23, 297–299, 304

Tardieu, Antoine-François, 409

Tasso, Torquato, 223, 230

Taste, 156, 430–431

Taxonomy, 254–266

Taylor, Thomas, 134, 214

Television, 254–256, 339

Tertullian (Quintus Septimius Florens Tertullianus), 215

Tesauro, Emmanuele, 373

Tessier

    Bust of Mirabeau, 297 (fig. 183), 331

Thucydides, 295

Tiepolo, Giandomenico, 371

Tissot, Samuel-Auguste-André-David, 431–432, 443

Torricelli, Evangelista, 424

Touch, 36

Traité des opérations de chirurgie, 51

Transparencies, 377–378

Trapp, Joseph, 162, 176, 232, 270

Trembley, Abraham, 21, 349

Tresca, Salvatore, 302

Trimpi, Wesley, 40

Trompe l'oeil, 397

Turner, Daniel, 314, 458

Udine, Giovanni da, 396

Ugliness, 179–182

Valvile (painter), 302

Vanbrugh, John, 232

Varley, John, 118

Varro, Marcus Terentius, 270, 309

Vasari, Giorgio, 250

Vico, Giambattista, 176, 235, 236

Vicq d'Azyr, Félix, 108, 293, 405
    Dissection of the Meninges, 108 (fig. 68),
        204, 246, 410
    Transverse View of Brain, 108 (fig. 67)

Virtual reality, 26–27, 394, 403, 465

Vision as touch, 414–415

Visual deception, 362–378. *See also*
    Phantasms

Visual information, 342–361

Vitiligo, 311, 319–321

Vivisection, 23, 349–350, 408–410

Volta, Leopoldo Cavallo, 461

Voltaire (François-Marie Arouet), 382
    Eléments de Newton, 101 (fig. 62), 388

Vuillard, Edouard, 208

Wall, John, 299

Wallis, George, 298

Wandelaar, Jan, 59, 110

Watelet, Claude-Henri, 156, 416

Water metaphor, 179, 249–250

Watteau, Antoine, 127

Wax casts, 461

Wax sculpture, 21, 64, 77, 250–251

Weaving, 201, 237

Webb, Daniel, 81, 83, 363

Whistler, James McNeill, 328

Whytt, Robert, 405, 409–410, 411

Wilkins, John, 382

Willan, Robert, 281, 302

Willis, Thomas, 117, 405–406, 432

Winckelmann, Johann Joachim, 29, 33
    on abstracting, 156–157, 179
    on conceiving, 215, 229, 234, 242–244,
        248, 249, 251, 276
    on dissecting, 82, 104, 119
    on marking, 284, 334–335
    on sensing, 415

Winslow, Jacques Bénigné, 260

Women, 18–19, 201, 306, 431–432

The Wonderful Spotted Indian John Boby,
    311 (fig. 193), 319, 366

Woodward, George Moutard
    A Doctor in Purgatory, 161 (fig. 100)

Wordsworth, William, 236

Wotton, William, 136

Wounds, 158–177

Wright, Joseph, of Derby, 358, 377
    The Corinthian Maid, 98 (fig. 60), 127,
        137

Young, Thomas, 426

Zoroaster, 364

Zumbo, Gaetano, 65, 77